D0515633

AA

ILLUSTRATED
GUIDE TO

Country Towns and Villages of Britain

AA ILLUSTRATED GUIDE TO COUNTRY TOWNS AND VILLAGES OF BRITAIN
was edited and designed by The Reader's Digest Association Limited
for Drive Publications Limited, Berkeley Square House, London W1X 5PD

First Edition Copyright © 1985
Drive Publications Limited

All rights reserved. No part of this book may be reproduced, stored in a retrieval system, or transmitted in any form or by any means, electronic, electrostatic, magnetic tape, mechanical, photocopying, recording or otherwise without permission in writing from the publishers

Printed in Great Britain
Text typeface 9pt and 10pt Spectrum roman

PICTURES *left to right* • Tithe barn at Thame, Oxfordshire; house at Leighton, Shropshire; Broughton, Borders; Beverley, Humberside.
ENDPAPERS • Church choir seat carvings at Ripple, Hereford and Worcester.
COVER • Okeford Fitzpaine, Dorset, by Eric Meacher.

AA

ILLUSTRATED GUIDE TO

Country Towns and Villages of Britain

PUBLISHED BY DRIVE PUBLICATIONS LIMITED FOR THE AUTOMOBILE ASSOCIATION
FANUM HOUSE, BASINGSTOKE, HAMPSHIRE RG21 2EA

Contributors

The publishers would like to thank
the following people for major contributions to this book:

Writers

Geoffrey Berry, John Burke, Anthony Burton, Russell Chamberlin, Ted Connolly, Ross Finlay, Ted Forrest, Ron Freethy, Bill Grundy, Belinda Hunt, Andrew Lawson, Philip Llewellin, Robin Hunter Neillands, Adam Nicolson, Jenni Rodger, Robert Sackville-West, Don Seaman, Colin Speakman, Roger Thomas, Rex Wailes, Tim Ware, Gerald Wilkinson.

Photographers

Nigel Cassidy, Robert Eames, Clive Friend, David Gallant, John Glover, Neil Holmes, Andrew Lawson, Susan Lund, Sheila and Oliver Mathews, Eric Meacher, Robin Miles, Colin Molyneux, Rich Newton, Ceri Norman, Jason Shenai, John Sims, Patrick Thurston, Titanic Photography, Pete Wilkie, Tim Woodcock, Jon Wyand, John Robert Young.

Artists

Malcolm McGregor, Andrew Vass.

PICTURES *left to right* • Doorway in Godshill, Isle of Wight; church at Swinbrook, Oxfordshire; pargeting at Saffron Walden, Essex; village green at Honington, Warwickshire.

Contents

FINDING YOUR WAY AROUND

The index map opposite shows 36 areas of Britain chosen for the outstanding beauty and interest of their country towns and villages. In the book there are also detailed maps of each area, showing the country towns, villages and places to visit described in the text. The index map gives the number of each of these area maps, and you will find them on the pages listed below. If, for example, you want to explore some of the towns and villages in the countryside near Exeter, you should look at area map 3, which is on page 26.

AREAS, MAP NUMBERS AND PAGE GUIDE

HOW TO USE THE MAPS

All towns and villages with entries in the text are shown in black – towns in block capitals. Other towns and cities are in red; and so are places described in the text, but with no entry of their own. The inset panel gives neighbouring areas, with the number of each and the page on which you will find its map. There are also references to the area maps at the beginning of each entry. Other symbols are explained in the key.

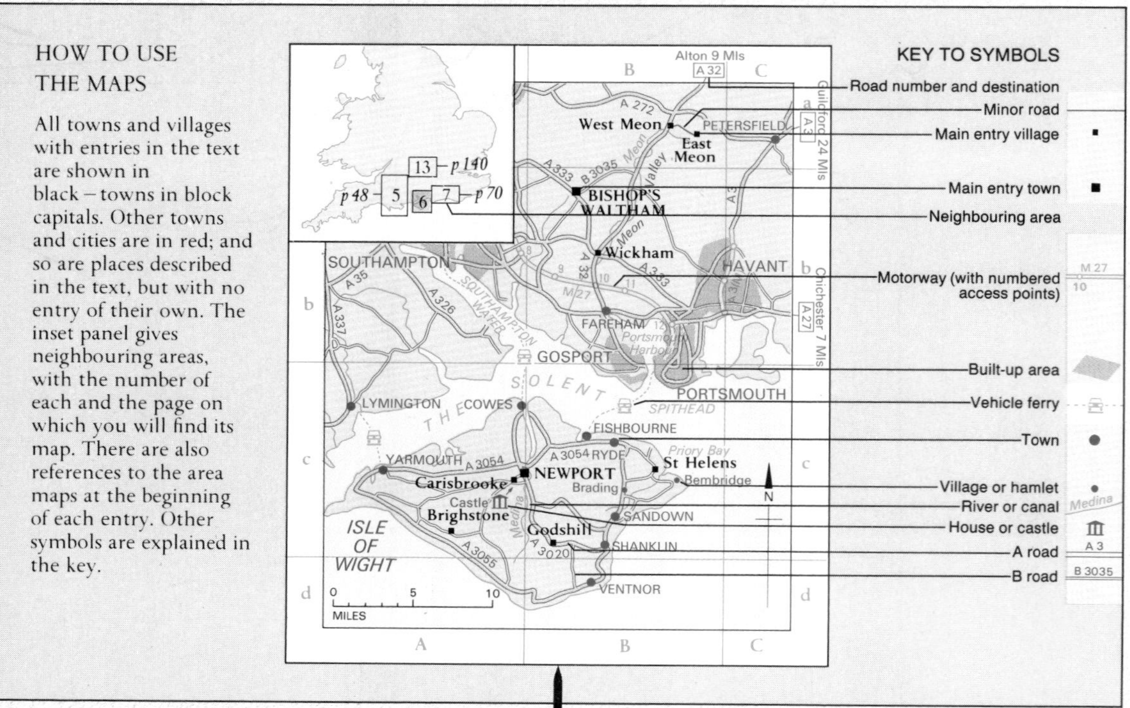

INDEX TO MAPS

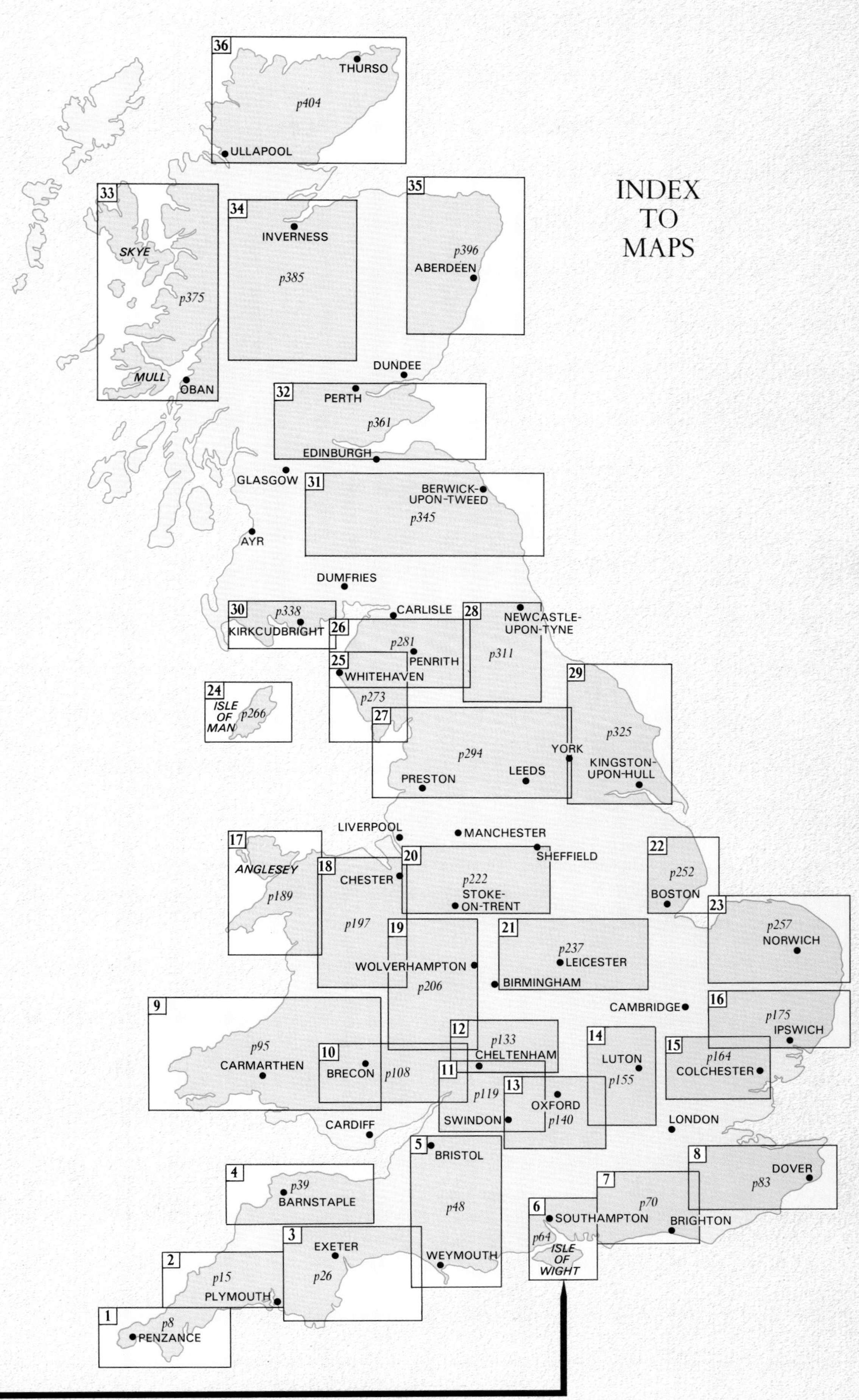

MAP 1

LAND'S END SPECTACULAR AND THE CORNISH RIVIERA

Spectacular cliffs and crashing surf mark where England's granite 'toe' kicks the Atlantic. The last mainland village before America is here; and the Lizard and Longships lights of home for sailors. Once the more sinister lights of wreckers lured ships to their doom; pirates and smugglers haunted secret inlets of the subtropical Cornish Riviera . . . all folklore now in quayside pubs, in friendly villages down switchback lanes, and in ancient towns.

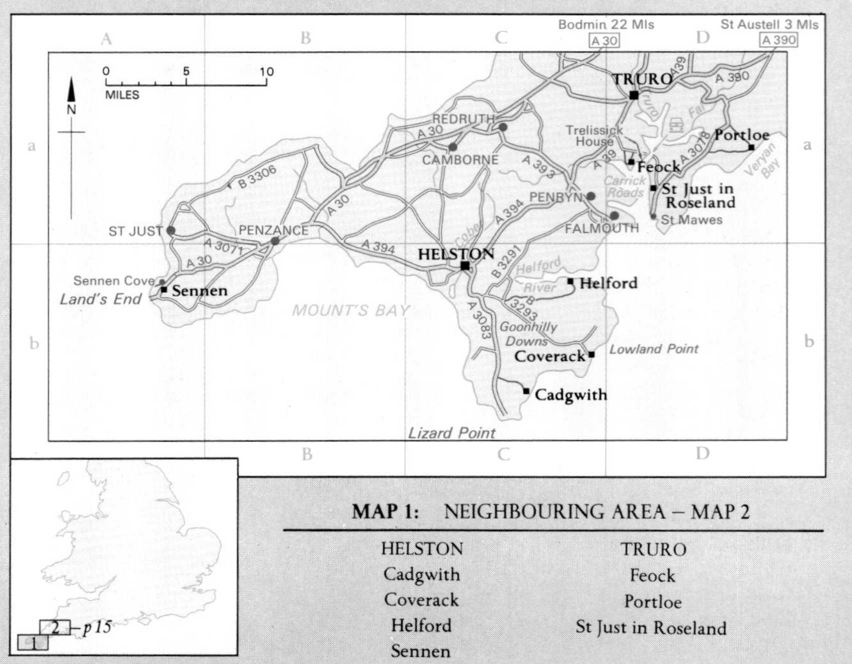

MAP 1: NEIGHBOURING AREA – MAP 2

HELSTON	TRURO
Cadgwith	Feock
Coverack	Portloe
Helford	St Just in Roseland
Sennen	

HELSTON

CORNWALL

18 miles south-west of Truro (PAGE 8 Cb)

At the beginning of every May, the age-old Furry dance weaves its way through the narrow, winding streets of this little market town. The dancers whirl in and out of shops, offices, banks and houses – entering by one door and leaving by another. Dancing around gardens left open for them, they sway past the thousands of spectators lining the gaily decorated streets, and eventually make a full circuit of the town – starting and ending at the Guildhall.

The Furry is thought to date from pre-Christian times, and to represent the triumph of spring over winter, of life over death. The traditional tune that accompanies it is a stirring affirmation of man's determination to survive. The word 'furry' probably derives from the Latin *feria*, a feast, or holy day, and the dance is also sometimes known as the Flora, after the Roman goddess of flowers.

Helston is set high on the Lizard peninsula. Its granite and slate buildings climb up from the River Cober. The town gathers around its main and broadest street, Coinagehall Street, named in the Middle Ages when a corner or 'coin' of tin was cut from each ingot mined in the area and tested for purity in Coinage Hall, long vanished.

Two open channels of water run swiftly along either side of the street, which curves steeply down towards the River Cober. The top of the street is dominated by the severely classical Guildhall, a granite building dating from 1838. Close by is the Angel Hotel, the former town house of the Earls of Godolphin and their families. Part of the building dates from the 16th century, including its elegant Assembly Room, complete with minstrels' gallery. At the foot of the street is a Gothic folly – a gateway built in 1834 in memory of a former mayor, Humphrey Millet Grylls.

A maze of streets, lanes and alleyways radiates from Coinagehall Street – and set among them are some charming old-world gardens. In Wendron Street the most prominent building is the Old Grammar School, built in 1610, whose most illustrious old boy was Charles Kingsley, author of *The Water Babies*. Near by is a trim, granite-built house that in 1862 was the birthplace of the boxer Bob Fitzsimmons – world heavyweight champion from 1897 – 9.

The patron saint of Helston is St Michael, whose parish church stands at the end of Church Street. Built by the Earl of Godolphin in 1751 – 61, it replaced an earlier building that was struck by lightning and burnt down. The churchyard contains the grave of Henry Trengrouse, inventor of a rocket-fired, life-saving device for sailors. The original invention is in the Helston Museum, in Church Street. It is open to the public on weekdays.

St Michael is said to have defeated a dragon which once threatened the town – and his victory made the townsfolk dance in the streets with joy. Appropriately, the church's east window, designed in 1938, depicts St Michael slaying the dragon and shows two angels sedately performing the Furry dance.

● **Parking** Trengrouse Way; Market, off Porthleven Road; Tyacke Road; St John's Road (all car parks) ● **Early closing** Wednesday ● **Market days** Monday, Saturday ● **Events** Furry dance (May); Harvest Fair (September) ● **AA 24 hour service** TEL. Truro 76455.

Cadgwith CORNWALL

11 miles south-east of Helston (PAGE 8 Cb)

Cadgwith lies in a cove of Lilliputian proportions, with a resident population of about 100 souls. Old stone-built cottages with roofs of thatch and slate line its lower slopes on either side of a rushing brook. Boats are hauled up above the tide on the tiny harbour's pebble beach. Lobster pots crowd every available space off The Todden, the central point of the village's steep, twisting street.

It is a fisherman's village, once renowned for its prodigious catches of pilchards; they still talk of the times when it took three days to empty a seine net. But apart from the memories, all that remains of that era is a hut on the clifftop, where the huer, or lookout, kept watch for the blood-red shoals of pilchards, invisible at sea level. As soon as he spotted a likely shoal, the huer would signal, with branches cut from the clifftop gorse bushes, to the waiting seine boats below.

Tallies of the daily catches are still marked on the beams of the old seine loft at the harbour. The record catch was 1,300,000 in a single day, which was sold at 19 shillings (95p) per 1000. Nothing was wasted from the pilchard catch in its brief, six-week season. The natural oils, squeezed from the tiny fish as they were packed into barrels, ran along grooves in the stone floors of the packing sheds, and into tanks where it was stored and later used to light the evening lamps.

Over-fishing, by power-driven boats from bigger ports using enormous drift nets, so depleted the pilchard shoals that they have vanished for good; seine fishing from Cadgwith ended in 1910.

Most of the village is built from a hard local stone, called serpentine because of its snake-like markings. It is found in red, green, black and a delicate 'cream and treacle'. Red serpentine, the hardest to cut and polish, is the most costly. All three churches in the parish of Ruan Minor, which includes Cadgwith, have towers built of serpentine and granite. Landewednack church, 2 miles from the village, has a red serpentine pulpit from which the last sermon preached in Cornish was delivered in 1678.

Like the pilchard fishing, the stone-cutting industry has died. Visitors to lonely, beautiful Carleon Cove, a mile north-east of Cadgwith, will find the water wheel which once powered the stone-cutting machinery standing still in a wood beside a tumbling trout stream. Below it, the serpentine factory is a ruin, and the cove where ships berthed to load the stone is filled with rocks and pebbles washed in by the sea. The National Trust manages the land, and along the coastal path you can walk or picnic in a setting that is old and unchanged Cornwall.

The most dramatic of Cadgwith's natural attractions is the Devil's Frying-pan, once an enormous cavern whose roof crashed in, probably early in the 19th century, though there are no authenticated records. It was known then as Hugga Driggee – *hugo* or *ogo* means 'cave' in Cornish. Today the sea rushes through its narrow entrance, the handle of the frying pan, beneath an arch of rock, and foams over a mass of stone and shingle in the pool beyond. At high tide in a strong wind, when the water boils menacingly in the basin, looking down into it can induce a strong feeling of vertigo.

ALL ASHORE *Fishing boats are drawn up stem to stern on the tiny pebbled beach of Cadgwith, before cottages built of a hard local stone called serpentine because it is marked like a snake.*

Coverack CORNWALL

12 miles south-east of Helston (PAGE 8 Cb)

The road to unspoilt Coverack runs across Goonhilly Downs, wild moorland where prehistoric burial mounds, known as bowl barrows, lie beside soaring, Space Age satellite-tracking saucers 100 ft in diameter. As you drop down the wooded hillside into this once remote village, it is easy to see why for 200 years many of Coverack's farmers and fishermen were also occupied in smuggling.

The white and thatched cottages, built of local stone and cob, a clay and straw mix, look east across the bay towards France, nearly 100 miles away. There are families here whose great-great-grandfathers used to row all the way there and back to pick up loads of silk, tobacco and spirits. One of them is said to have made the round trip in only 31 hours.

Tamarisk Cottage, on the pathway from Lowland Point to the village, dates from the early 18th century and is reputed to have been a lair for smugglers during the Napoleonic Wars. While restoring the cottage, the present owners uncovered a magnificent inglenook fireplace and a cavity, 4 ft square, in the wall of one bedroom – large enough to take two people. So far, they have not found the secret tunnel said to lead from the cottage to the beach 50 ft below.

UP THE GARDEN PATH *A steep pathway winds uphill from Coverack harbour, dividing cottages from their immaculate gardens.*

The pathway joins Coverack's single street that follows the curve of the bay. The only pub stands on the quay opposite what used to be a lifeboat house. The Coverack lifeboat was once the pride of the village, and every young man's ambition was to become a member of its volunteer crew. But today the rescue of anyone in peril on the sea off Coverack is the primary responsibility of the helicopter crews at the Royal Naval Air Station at Culdrose, 10 miles away, near Helston. The Royal National Lifeboat Institution at Falmouth and The Lizard also provide help.

They carry out this all-too-frequent task with the same brand of heroism that the fishermen showed. Wrecks litter the coast, many of them on the dreaded Manacles reef. This can be clearly seen from Lowland Point as the tide drops, scattered less than a mile offshore, right in the path of ships heading for Falmouth. The name, Manacles, has no connection with handcuffs, firmly though the rocks grip any ship unfortunate enough to fall on them. It may be derived from the old Cornish *meyn eglos*, meaning 'church stones'. A wall map on the bar of the pub lists 28 vessels trapped on the Manacles between 1787 and 1915 – and the pub itself is named after the 10,500 ton passenger ship *City of Paris*, which ran aground in 1899.

For all its timeless appearance, the way of life is slowly changing in Coverack. The number of men putting to sea for bass, pollack, whiting, mackerel, crab and lobster grows fewer and fewer year by year, as costs rise and catches decline. Until the late 1960s, two Coverack fishermen were the only lobster suppliers to the House of Commons. All they landed weighing between 1 lb and $1\frac{1}{4}$ lb – reckoned to be a proper portion for an MP – were sent to Westminster; the record was 50 in a day. The crabs are still about, but the lobsters have largely gone; however, there is still good rod-and-line fishing, especially for bass in the autumn.

In the height of summer, many visitors abandon holiday pursuits to join in the village's most spectacular annual event – a great August Sunday jamboree of old hymn singing down by the harbour. A brass band and massed choirs, organised by the Methodist Church in this good John Wesley country, make it a joyful and memorable occasion.

Helford CORNWALL

10 miles east of Helston (PAGE 8 Cb)

In Helford the Celts found tin, which they panned from the river rather like later gold prospectors; the Romans found oysters; and the monks of Ireland and Brittany discovered a restful place where they could be devout. But over the centuries most people have come to Helford for what its name says it is – the road or crossing at the estuary.

The village stands on the Helford River at a fordable point where it has an ancient ferry. Like the river it takes its name from the old Cornish *hayle*, meaning 'estuary'. Slate-roofed cottages fan out along tiny lanes on either side of a creek, spanned by a wooden footbridge.

Though Helford once bustled with travellers on the ancient road to the south and Lizard Point, all it allows now along its narrow byways in the crowded summer are pedestrians. The village is only just big enough to accommodate residents' cars. Visitors must park beside the picnic spot on the hill with its lovely views above the creek, and walk down to Helford where they are often followed by the Muscovy ducks which waddle up out of the creek.

They share the water with a handful of pleasure boats, riding at moorings once infested with smugglers and pirates. Carew, an Elizabethan historian, recorded that 'local pirates brought many a ship into the Helford Creek to plunder at their leisure'.

Captain William Bligh, victim of the mutiny on the *Bounty* and a skilled map-maker, was mistakenly arrested as a French spy while surveying the Helford River for the Admiralty – and was considerably annoyed about it. Half a mile upstream is Frenchman's Creek, the romantic setting for the best-selling novel of that name by Daphne du Maurier.

There have been oyster beds in the river since pre-Roman times, and there is an oyster farm owned by the Duchy of Cornwall, part of the Prince of Wales's estates, at Porth Navas, just across the river from

Helford. The delicacy has caused some bitterness between the oyster farmers and the locals, who often felt that the shellfish, like other fish in the river, are there for all to enjoy.

In Helford's only pub, the Shipwright's Arms, which looks out over the bobbing boats in the creek to the wooded slopes beyond, hangs a copy of a judgment delivered by Mr Justice Coleridge in 1839 when he sentenced three men for oyster stealing. It reads like a permanent warning to the covetous: 'The owner of a fishery must be as safe in the enjoyment and possession of his property as the owner of a house. He is paying a rent of £450 a year for the enjoyment of all this. How is he to pay the rent if all people are to go and take away the oysters, and if one can do so others may do it. You have no more right to do that than you have to go into a field and take a sheep.' All three were sentenced to six weeks' hard labour.

Helford lies on the edge of Goonhilly Downs, which became a magnet for monks in the early part of the Dark Ages. The parish, called Manaccan, was first mentioned in a charter of King Edgar in AD 976, when it was known as Desmanoc or the place of the monks.

Helford's small mission church has a granite door lintel, with a slate porch supported by two tree trunks that are pockmarked with woodworm. Its single bell comes from the wreck of *The Bay of Panama*, a sailing ship lost in a blizzard in 1891. Manaccan's church is part Norman, and has an unforgettable feature – a fig tree, believed to be more than 200 years old, growing out of its south-west wall.

Sennen CORNWALL

23 miles west of Helston (PAGE 8 Ab)

The final few steps on the way to Land's End are littered with the 'first and last' pub, church, cafe and so on. Below the granite cliffs to the north-east, facing the fury of the winter gales, lies the village of Sennen Cove, where it is easy to feel that this really is the first and last inhabited place in the land.

Here is England's most westerly mainland village; only the vast Atlantic lies between it and America. Sennen Cove, with its peerless lifeboat station but dwindling number of fishermen, is a cluster of stone and white-painted cottages at the foot of the hill.

A mile or so inland lies the separate village of Sennen. The tiny church was probably founded by the Irish saint, Senan, in the 6th century. Its granite tower, south aisle and font, date from the early 15th century, when the villagers successfully petitioned Pope Martin V in Rome for permission to bury their dead around the ancient chapel, rather than make a 3 mile journey to St Buryan. There was nothing lazy about their plea – they genuinely feared 'pirates and enemies' plundering the village in their absence.

According to legend, King Arthur marched from Tintagel to Sennen to defeat a horde of Danes at the Battle of Vellan-ducher. He and some fellow Celtic kings are said to have celebrated their victory by feasting at a great block of granite known as the Table-Men – *men* means 'stone' in Cornish. The stone, 8 ft long and 3 ft high, and believed to be one of Cornwall's holy altars, is half a mile from the church behind a local greengrocer's shop.

Another adventurer who chose to land at Sennen and came to a sorry end was Perkin Warbeck, a Flemish pretender to the English throne. His claim seems to have been as thin as the support he mustered on a march to Exeter, where he was soundly beaten by Henry VII's loyal troops in 1497. The people of Sennen were fined by the king for their part in the abortive rebellion, and Warbeck was executed two years later.

From Sennen Cove, with its little jetty pointing out into the waves, you can follow a path to the clifftop and a National Trust walk to Land's End, overlooking some of the most spectacular scenery in all Cornwall. The path rounds Maen Castle, an Iron Age hill-fort above the granite cliffs that plunge hundreds of feet into the surf. Jagged rocks stretch out to the Longships lighthouse, built in 1797, and 8 miles beyond to the Wolf lighthouse, both solid warnings of the treacherous coast.

Between Land's End and the Scilly Isles, 28 miles to the south-west, the lost land of Lyonesse is said to lie, drowned with its 146 churches, its people, villages and hedgerows in an awful natural catastrophe untold years ago.

TRURO

CORNWALL

15 miles south-west of St Austell (PAGE 8 Da)

One of Britain's most modern cathedrals towers over Truro, the unofficial capital of Cornwall. The see was founded in 1877 and the cathedral was completed in 1910, after 30 years' work. It has a 250 ft high spire, in Early English style, which makes it look much older than it is. The cathedral incorporates part of the 16th-century parish church of St Mary, and among its treasures is a superb 19th-century terracotta relief, on the wall of the north choir aisle, of Christ's journey to Calvary.

Around the cathedral the streets are in keeping with its venerable appearance. Lemon Street, with its array of Georgian houses, is particularly well preserved. Strangways Terrace, which branches from it, contains fine Regency houses, as does Walsingham Place, a handsome crescent built in the 1820s.

Situated at the head of the Fal estuary, the town exported locally mined tin in medieval times. From the Middle Ages until the 19th century the tin was weighed and taxed in Truro (one of Cornwall's four stannary towns). As if in warning to dishonest traders, a stone in the old Market Hall was inscribed: 'Who Seks To Find Eternal Tresure Must Use No Guile In Waight Or Measure – 1615.' The stone is now inside the entrance to the mid-19th-century City Hall.

Fashionable society gathered at High Cross, in the Assembly Rooms built in 1787 with a fine façade and now an estate agent's office. Many of the important Cornish families used to own houses in the town – as did some of the rich merchants living in the neighbourhood. Among Truro's most famous sons was Richard Lemon Lander, who explored the River Niger in West Africa in 1830. His statue stands on a column at the top of Lemon Street.

The administrative centre of Cornwall, Truro was created a city by Queen Victoria in 1877 – but in size and feeling it is very much a small and cosy market town. Even so, its impressive Victorian City Hall, in dark granite, would grace any city. And its museum and art gallery, in River Street, is the best in the county. Among its exhibits are three gold collars from

PINNACLES OF PERFECTION *Truro Cathedral looks like a rock of ages, but was completed as recently as 1910. It is, in fact, meant to look*

the Bronze Age, and a painting by Sir Godfrey Kneller (1646 – 1723) of the Cornish Giant who served under the Royalist commander Sir Bevil Grenville in the Civil War. The giant stood 7 ft 4 in. and weighed 532 lb.

• **Parking** Moorfield, off Calenick Street; Lemon Quay; St Clement Street; Lower Lemon Quay; Castle Street; Old Bridge (all car parks) • **Early closing** Thursday • **Market day** Wednesday • **Cinema** Plaza, Lemon Street • **Events** Three Spires Festival (June); Carnival (August) • **Information** TEL. Truro 74555 • **AA 24 hour service** TEL. Truro 76455.

Feock CORNWALL

5 miles south of Truro (PAGE 8 Da)

It is a 2 mile walk these days from Feock to the nearest pub, The Punchbowl and Ladle at Penelewey, which may well be an over-reaction to a bibulous past. Feock hugs the low shore overlooking Carrick Roads and, apart from a little boatbuilding, its basic industry has

ancient — it was designed in the style of the 13th century, and took 30 years to build. The main spire soars 250 ft above the pinnacled roof.

always been farming. But it had one vigorous, prosperous fling during the Industrial Revolution when its tin mines thrived and a smelting plant roared away at Penpol, a mile or so north-west. Ships moored offshore and trains on the Redruth and Chacewater Railway puffed in and out.

Free-spending miners, sailors and rail gangers filled the area, shops and businesses sprang up and traders bustled for business. Drinking there seems to have been fairly basic, with the thirsty workmen taking turns to dip their mugs into a single tin bath filled with booze, and reeling to their lodgings only when the bath was empty.

Feock itself had an inn then – The Red, White and Blue – which also did a roaring trade with the miners, many of whom dug out tin 40 ft beneath the bed of Restronguet Creek in considerable discomfort and danger.

By the late 19th century the mines were exhausted, so the smelting plant shut down, the ships stopped arriving in the early 1900s, and the railway closed in 1917 – and with them went the inn. Feock soon slipped back into its former agricultural ways.

A little hammering and planing went on down by the shore, where small boatbuilding yards thrived, producing schooners, smaller cutters and ketches for the estuary trade. They have gone too, and yachts, motor boats and dinghies float moored offshore. Only one yard, near Penpol, still flourishes.

The Church of St Feoca is 19th century, but has some old Flemish panels and a late Norman font. It stands some way from the west tower of a long-gone, 13th-century church. Until the 17th century, vicars administered the sacrament in Cornish.

Feock stands on a gentle promontory halfway between Truro and Falmouth, yet quite remote from both. It is a comfortable collection of stone and cob cottages, some thatched, with a feeling of cosy unity.

Farther up the Fal, overlooking Falmouth Harbour and Henry VIII's Pendennis Castle, is 18th-century Trelissick House, with a splendid garden maintained by the National Trust and open to visitors.

Portloe CORNWALL

13 miles south-east of Truro (PAGE 8 Da)

When the faithful parishioners of Portloe sing 'For those in peril on the sea . . .' they may well do so with added feeling. For the tiny church at the water's edge of this rocky little fishing village was once the old lifeboat station.

All Saints is small, spartan and as functional as it was when it served its original purpose. There are 18 open benches on a wooden parquet floor, a small pedal organ and one electric radiator plugged into the wall below the pedestal altar. The building was erected in 1870 to house the 33 ft long, self-righting lifeboat *Gorfenkle*, which was crewed by 13 men with ten oars. The boathouse cost £169 and the boat £269, paid for by a legacy of a Liverpudlian, Jacob Gorfenkle.

Sadly it was not a success – the boat was never once called out in an emergency. A history of the church records, matter-of-factly: 'Unfortunately, the crew had great difficulty in getting the vessel out of the house for launching in Portloe's cove. Once, during a launch, the lifeboat ran away out of control and smashed into a shop.'

So, in 1877, a new lifeboat station was built against the cliff next to The Lugger hotel, and the *Gorfenkle* was moved in there. With practical economy, the people of Portloe added a chancel, a sanctuary and a side aisle to the old station and it became All Saints. For ten more years the lifeboat waited in vain for a call to action but, in 1887, the station was finally shut down. Careful as ever, the villagers turned the second station into a school, and as such it served several generations of Portloe children.

Most, like their fathers, became fishermen. Their stone cottages follow the winding street down to the quay, where lobster pots are piled up beside the crabbers, hauled up on the pebbles in the little harbour.

Lying sheltered in Veryan Bay, which is overhung on one side by the towering Dodman Point, on the other by Nare Head, Portloe's craggy shore is a delight for the rod-and-line man.

There are magnificent views from the rambling coastal paths, meticulously maintained by the National Trust. The nearest beaches are at Portholland, $2\frac{1}{2}$ miles north-east, or Pendower, 3 miles west below Carne.

St Just in Roseland CORNWALL

9 miles south of Truro (via King Harry ferry) (PAGE 8 Da)

On their return to England, after the Battle of Trafalgar, several of Nelson's victorious ships were quarantined for a few months in St Just Pool, a lovely inlet off the Carrick Roads, around which are scattered the handful of stone cottage terraces that make up the village of St Just in Roseland. Few places could be more peaceful for a man-of-war.

Indeed, the last conflict of note in St Just was in 1396, when the rector, Sir Thomas Raulyn, had to flee to the sanctuary of his own chancel in the uproar that followed a funeral. As was the custom at the time, Sir Thomas claimed the best garment of the man he had interred. But the relatives refused to hand it over, the rector excommunicated them all, and one named Alan Bugules threatened to kill Sir Thomas. After hiding in the chancel, he fled to the rectory and for some time refused to leave for fear of his life. Eventually, however, the gentleness of St Just somehow brought the matter to an amicable end, and Sir Thomas stayed on as rector until 1431.

No rector today would take too kindly to being besieged in his home and so parted from the church, claimed by the villagers, with some justification, to be the most beautiful in all the land. Its setting certainly is not bettered. You reach it through a lych gate, down a pathway which winds along the hillside and through a garden alight with flowering shrubs and exotic plants. The church, with its castellated stone tower, stands on a pebbly shore of the creek, framed by trees.

Flourishing on the warm, sheltered cliffside are bamboos 20 ft high, palm trees, Chilean fire bushes, azaleas, a strawberry tree, rhododendrons, magnolias and broom. Beside a second lych gate, lower down the hill, is a spring sheltered by a moss-covered, tiled roof, from which water has been taken for centuries to baptise children in the church font.

There was a mild altercation here at the end of the Commonwealth in 1660. The Puritan rector appointed by Cromwell was replaced by a Royalist after the Restoration. But the sacked rector was so popular in the village that he stayed on, becoming a close friend of his successor.

Since 1733, every rector has received 10 shillings (50p) for preaching a funeral sermon on December 27, under a bequest from John Randall, a parishioner who was determined to be remembered for 1000 years. His bequest lasts until July 2733.

JUST CLAIM *Villagers aver that the 13th-century church at St Just is the most beautiful in the land. Its castellated tower rises amid subtropical shrubs and plants on the pebbly shore of a creek.*

MAP 2

BODMIN MOOR AND THE SEA-DOGS' LAIR

Raleigh, Grenville and Drake . . . the old sea-dogs' names ring around West Country harbours and villages like a call to arms and adventure. Here were bred the heroes and their doughty crews. And here, folk believe, a far older hero built his sea-girt Camelot at Tintagel. More heroes, more legends haunt Bodmin's moorlands.

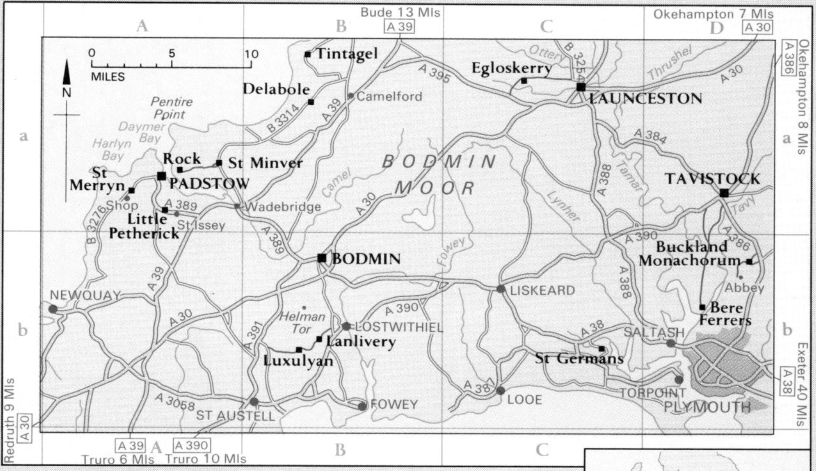

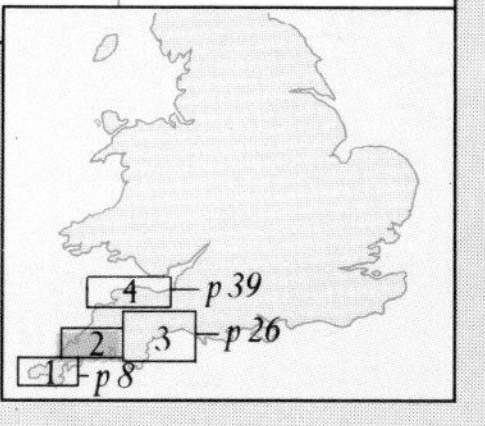

MAP 2: NEIGHBOURING AREAS – MAPS 1, 3, 4

BODMIN	LAUNCESTON	PADSTOW	TAVISTOCK
Lanlivery	Delabole	Little Petherick	Bere Ferrers
Luxulyan	Egloskerry	Rock	Buckland Monachorum
	Tintagel	St Merryn	St Germans
		St Minver	

BODMIN

CORNWALL

30 miles west of Plymouth (PAGE 15 Bb)

Set on the slope of a steep and beautiful valley, Bodmin lends its name to the wild, dramatic moor which stretches for miles to the north-east. The town developed around a priory, founded in the 11th century and dedicated to the Welsh-born St Petroc – who founded three monasteries in north Cornwall in the 6th century and lived a hermit's life on Bodmin Moor.

Petroc was first buried at Padstow, the centre of a cult which grew up about him. Then his remains were transferred to Bodmin. But in 1177 a discontented Bodmin monk named Martin stole the saint's bones and took them to France. However, after the intervention of Henry II, most of the bones were recovered; and though the remains themselves have disappeared over the centuries, the exquisite ivory casket in which they were kept is displayed on the south wall in St Petroc's Church.

The largest parish church in Cornwall, St Petroc's is 151 ft long and 65 ft wide. Built of light-coloured Cornish stone in the 15th century, the church once had a 150 ft high spire, which was destroyed by lightning in 1699 and not replaced. It contains several fine monuments, including a memorial slate to a former mayor, Richard Durant, who died in 1632. It shows him with his two wives and the 20 children which, between them, they bore him.

In the north aisle the battle honours of the Duke of Cornwall's Light Infantry hang in tattered glory. And there is a splendid free-standing monument to one of the last Priors of Bodmin, Thomas Vivyan, who died in 1533.

To the west of the church is Bodmin's narrow main street, Fore Street, which leads into the broader and steeper Bore Street. Many of the houses are of red and buff stone, which has weathered a warm, friendly brown colour.

An elegant granite-faced building, the Shire Hall, houses the Crown Courts for Cornwall. Set in Mount Folly Square, it faces Shire House, which was built in 1837 as the Judge's Lodgings and is now council offices. Near by is the old county jail, in which public hangings were held until 1862. The jail – now a restaurant – was where the Crown Jewels and the Domesday Book were hidden during the First World War. This was only fitting, as Bodmin is the sole Cornish town named in the book.

The square was the scene of a macabre hanging in 1549, when the Cornish-speaking townsfolk helped lead a revolt against the introduction of the Book of Common Prayer in English, instead of Latin. The rebels were put down by Edward VI, who sent his Provost-Marshal to Bodmin to deal with the troublemakers. The mayor, Nicholas Boyer, gave a banquet for the Provost, and during the meal the visitor asked that a gallows be erected outside Boyer's house. This was quickly done and, when the wining and dining was over, the two men went to inspect the gallows. 'Think you it be strong enough?' asked the Provost. The mayor assured him that it was, and was told: 'Well then, get you up. For you have been a busy rebel – and this is your reward!'

On The Beacon, a hill to the south-west of the town, a 144 ft high granite obelisk was built in 1856 as a memorial to Lieutenant-General Sir Walter Raleigh Gilbert, a distant descendant of the great English sea captain and courtier. The general was born in Bodmin and distinguished himself fighting against the Sikhs in India.

• **Parking** Mount Folly Square; Dennison Road (both car parks); Fore Street • **Early closing** Wednesday • **Market day** Saturday • **Cinema** Palace, Fore Street • **Event** Carnival (August) • **Information** TEL. Bodmin 4159 • **AA 24 hour service** TEL. Truro 76455.

Lanlivery CORNWALL

6 miles south of Bodmin (PAGE 15 Bb)

Lanlivery stands on a bare shoulder of land, swept by the south winds and overlooked by the brooding mass of Helman Tor, a granite outcrop 687 ft above sea level. Between the tor and the slate-roofed farmhouses that crowd around the village church lies a squelchy heathland known as Red Moor, as ancient as the rock itself and with a hint of mystery.

Unfenced lanes wander near by, passing tin workings not used since pre-Christian times and crowded over with willow, broom and gorse. Looming above the scene on the tor is a huge rocking stone, a precariously balanced boulder that sways in the wind.

For 500 years from medieval times, prospectors went 'streaming' for tin on Red Moor, sieving it from running streams, rather in the way that gold miners 'pan' for gold. Lanlivery is now a dairy-farming centre, fanning out around the pub and the church, which has a turreted tower reaching 97 ft into the sky. One side of the tower used to be painted white, to stand out as a landmark for sailors off Gribbin Head, 6 miles to the south-east.

No satisfactory explanation has ever been found for the name Lanlivery. *Lan*, or *nant* in Cornish, means 'churchyard'. The rest is obscure, although it is believed that 'livery' may have been a personal name. Even the dedication of the church is uncertain. It is named St Brevita, or Bryvyth, but parishioners believe that the true patron saint is St Dunstan, the 10th-century reforming Archbishop of Canterbury. Lanlivery holds its feast day in the month of St Dunstan's Day (May 19). The existing church dates from the 15th century, when an earlier building was restored, and has a font large enough for total immersion.

Outside the church entrance is a large, lidless stone coffin. There is no inscription, but the coffin is said to have once contained the body of a Cornish prince, carried from the chapel at Restormel Castle, a few miles to the north-east on the banks of the River Fowey, when the chapel was secularised.

A board on the church tower dated 1811 carries a bellringers' rhyme, recording that anyone who mars a peal shall 'pay sixpence for each single crime to make him cautious against another time'.

Luxulyan CORNWALL

8 miles south of Bodmin (PAGE 15 Bb)

The grey mass of Sir Joseph Treffry's huge viaduct rears out of the trees on the thickly wooded slopes of Luxulyan's valley and strides through the valley in ten magnificent arches about a mile south of the village.

GRACEFUL GIANT *Towering over the valley, the viaduct built by Sir Joseph Treffry provides a man-made contrast with the splendours of nature at Luxulyan.*

Here is a place where man and nature have combined to make a dramatic landscape.

Strewn across the wide valley and among the houses that make up Luxulyan are huge granite boulders rising out of the grassy fields like enormous mushrooms. Many weigh hundreds of tons and dwarf the stone cottages near by. Through the valley and past the village runs a swift stream known as the White River because it used to be coloured milky white from china clay workings, but it is now filtered.

Across this vigorous scene, Treffry flung his impressive viaduct, made of granite cut from the local quarries. It took three years to build (1839–42), is 93 ft high and 648 ft long and overlooks the two halves of the village, Luxulyan and Bridges, where most of the homes are still those of clay workers and quarrymen.

The viaduct was designed to carry a railway above a canal, so it is really a viaduct-aqueduct – a masterpiece of engineering. It linked Newquay on the north-west Cornish coast with Par in the south-east, and carried away granite from Luxulyan's quarries.

Treffry, born Austen, adopted his mother's name in 1838 and carved the Treffry arms in stone on the viaduct. He was both an industrialist and a visionary, and also built Par harbour to ship copper from the Fowey mines to South Wales for smelting. He died at Place House, Fowey, leaving to posterity a bold vision of harmony between landscape and engineering.

Luxulyan's two halves are linked today by a new estate. The older houses are built of granite, which has been quarried in the valley for 500 years. A rare variety found nowhere else – a black-based rock with pink felspar crystals called tourmaline – was used to make the Duke of Wellington's sarcophagus in the crypt at

St Paul's Cathedral. When the old Iron Duke died in 1852, all England was scoured to find a material suitable for a memorial to the nation's hero. The tourmaline was discovered at Luxulyan, in a field still known as Shabby Rock Field, and the block used cost the huge sum (for those days) of £100. Not until the nondescript-looking stone has been cut and polished is its sombre beauty revealed.

The village's church is dedicated to St Cyriac and his mother St Julitta, who were said to have lived in Asia Minor in the 3rd century and whose cult may have been brought to Europe by the Crusaders. In the granite wall of the chancel is a window memorial to Sylvanus Trevail, twice president of the Society of Architects, who designed Luxulyan's Board School along with 34 other schools in Cornwall. At the height of his fame, he shot himself dead on the train between Lostwithiel and Bodmin Road Station. It was said that business worries had unhinged his mind.

Methrose Farm, a medieval hall-house (having one large room) with 14th and 15th-century additions, stands just south of the village. Its name was originally Medros, Cornish for middle of the moor or heath. The Methodist preacher John Wesley stayed there a number of times, his last visit probably being in 1778. At the other end of the parish is Castilly Henge, an ancient place of worship. No standing stones remain.

LAUNCESTON

CORNWALL

23 miles north-west of Plymouth (PAGE 15 Ca)

Launceston is set on the side of a steep hill that is crowned by the stark ruins of a castle. Built in the 13th century on the site of an earlier wooden Norman fortification, this hilltop fortress once guarded the main route from Cornwall to Devon. It was later used as an Assize Court and prison. The Quaker leader George Fox was imprisoned there in 1656, in a room by the north gate. His crime was distributing 'dangerous' religious pamphlets in St Ives. Until 1821 public hangings were held on the castle green.

A wall was built around Launceston in the reign of Henry III. The imposing South Gate still stands and has one entrance for traffic and another for pedestrians. Near by in Southgate Street is the birthplace of Launceston's most famous son, Philip King. He was Governor of New South Wales, Australia, from 1800 to 1806 and named the town of Launceston, Tasmania, in

GHOST OF A FORTRESS

The circular stone keep of Launceston Castle broods over what was, until 1835, Cornwall's county town. Splendid Georgian houses are a reminder of Launceston's former status. So are churches like St Mary Magdalene, just below the castle.

St Mary Magdalene, Launceston parish church

Ruins of the castle

1805. Between the gate and the castle is Castle Street, which has a superb array of red-brick Georgian houses. These include Lawrence House, the former meeting-place of French officers who were paroled in the town after being captured during the Napoleonic Wars. The house is now the local museum.

The narrow streets are centred around The Square where there is an old coaching inn, the White Hart. The inn has a door taken from a former Augustinian priory that stood in the nearby hamlet of St Thomas until 1539. The town's Church of St Thomas lies north of the castle beside the River Kensey and has a Norman font. Most of the church was built in the 15th century, but it was substantially restored in the 1870s.

The parish church of St Mary Magdalene, just below the castle, dates largely from 1524 although it has a 14th-century tower. It is the only church in England made from carved Cornish granite. The carvings swarm all over the outside, and include the plants – such as nard and pomegranate – used to make the ointment with which Mary Magdalene anointed Christ's feet. Other carvings show a donkey taking sackloads of corn from a windmill to a mansion, a beggar waiting for a dole of bread, St Martin of Tours cutting his coat in two to give one half to a beggar, and St George fighting the dragon.

On the east wall is a large recumbent figure of Mary Magdalene. And farther along is a band of musicians playing a lute, bagpipes, hand-organ, clarions (medieval trumpets) and a rebec (a pear-shaped stringed instrument played with a bow). The church has a fine carved pulpit which dates from before the Reformation.

• **Parking** Race Hill; rear of Town Hall, off Westgate Street; The Walk (all car parks); The Square • **Early closing** Thursday • **Market days** Tuesday, Saturday • **Events** The Cuthbert Mayne Pilgrimage (June); Carnival (November) • **Information** TEL. Launceston 3693 • **AA 24 hour service** TEL. Plymouth 669989.

Delabole CORNWALL

22 miles west of Launceston (PAGE 15 Ba)

Delabole slate has been quarried for centuries, yet curiously the village, which stands on a vast bed of the stuff, was not called Delabole (after the quarry of that name) until the railway arrived in 1893. Before that it consisted of the slaters' hamlets of Pengelly, Medrose and Rockhead. All three are now linked by a mile-long High Street lined with terraced, stone-built houses roofed with the high-quality product of the great quarry.

The old Pengelly to Medrose road led through this enormous man-made hole in the ground, which covers just under 50 acres, is 500 ft deep in places, and measures nearly half a mile across. Some fine old one-up, one-down slaters' cottages can be found in West Lane, outside the quarry entrance in Pengelly. They still have their original walls and roofs, and form a small, cosy scene against the stark backcloth of the workings.

Newer properties were built by quarrymen at the turn of the last century – also of local stone and with the inevitable Delabole slate roofs. By tradition all the old terraced houses hereabouts kept a pig in their tiny back gardens, a practice which continued until the early 1920s.

Quarrying began here 450 years ago, when pack-saddle donkeys carried away the slate. The donkeys were succeeded by horses and carts – but all had to be loaded by hand. A Cornish antiquarian described the work in 1758: 'The slate is carried with no small danger on men's backs, which are guarded from the weight by a kind of leather apron or cushion.' Mechanically loaded dump trucks do it all today.

Production peaked at the turn of the century, when 500 to 600 local men and boys were employed, and the slate went to markets throughout Britain, Europe and North America. Competition from cheaper man-made tiles has now reduced the labour force to around 60, and even the railway station has closed. But the quarry is being redeveloped.

The village pub is called the Bettle and Chisel. A bettle is a wooden mallet, bound with iron and made at the quarry from old railway sleepers. It is used with a slender, wide-bladed chisel to split slates. The 12,000 tons quarried annually is first loosened by charges of gunpowder – still known here by its old name, black-powder – the 'gentlest' of explosives, used because slate must be quarried with little disturbance.

This fascinating place is open to the public. There is a quarry museum and you can buy slates and other souvenirs.

The village is staunch Methodist, and the chapel at Medrose has been superbly maintained. In the 19th-century Anglican Church of St John Evangelist the high altar is of Delabole slate, and so, too, are most of the headstones.

Egloskerry CORNWALL

5 miles west of Launceston (PAGE 15 Ca)

A neat little village, set in glorious green countryside on the old road between Launceston and Camelford, Egloskerry takes its name from the Cornish word *eglos* meaning 'church', and a Welsh saint, Keri, who preached here in the 6th century.

Little is known about the saint, not even his (or her) sex; he (or she) was one of the large family of the Welsh chieftain St Brychan, who came to Cornwall some 1400 years ago and had more than 20 children. St Keri is believed to have built a chapel between the River Kensey, which flows south of the village, and the Ottery river, to the north.

Cottages of local stone with slate roofs line the village street, along with some modern bungalows. The village pump stands in a flower garden by the roadside, its creaking voice stilled by a chain around the handle.

St Keri's Church is in the centre of the village, by the old market square, and its north and south doorways, north wall and transept are all Norman. Above the north door, now blocked, is a stone carving of a dragon snapping at its tail. The south aisle was added by Sir John Speccott, Lord of the Manor of Penheale, in 1622. He lies buried in the chancel, and his helmet and armour gauntlets rest on the window ledge at the east end of the south aisle.

In a wall cavity below lies a damaged alabaster effigy, believed to be that of Sir Guy de Blanchminster, which has suffered at the hands of a rather inexpert restorer. The rose-pink nose has been crudely stuck on and there are a couple of curious decorations on the breast. These, apparently, were the pompoms on his slippers, placed in their present position when the effigy's feet broke off.

Tintagel CORNWALL

23 miles west of Launceston (PAGE 15 Ba)

Nothing quite captures the imagination like the spectacle of an ancient castle standing high on a wave-pounded rock, its gaunt ruin silhouetted against a cloud-swept sky while the boom of the surf echoes among the surrounding cliffs. 'King Arthur's Castle' at Tintagel is such a spectacle, and has inspired writers and artists for centuries – all perpetuating the myth that this was the seat of the legendary king.

Historians believe that King Arthur was indeed a living legend – but he certainly did not live at Tintagel's castle, which was built by the Earl of Cornwall, son of Henry I, some 600 years after the time when Arthur is thought to have died. A later Earl of Cornwall extended it in the 13th century, and also built the Iron Gate and a sea wall. In the 14th century the castle belonged to Edward, the Black Prince; by the end of the century it was being used as a prison, and finally became derelict in the 16th century.

The castle was built originally on a headland, which is now virtually an island connected to the mainland by a narrow neck of rock. The earliest parts, dating from about 1145, are on the island; the later 14th and 15th-century parts are on the mainland. The whole site is under the care of the Department of the Environment and is open to the public daily.

Despite a lack of evidence, the village still clings to the legend that its castle was Arthur's Camelot. There is even a King Arthur's Castle Hotel, a massive Edwardian edifice on the cliff edge; and the extraordinary King Arthur's Hall. This was built between 1928 and 1933 to commemorate Arthur and his knights and to celebrate their ideals of chivalry. It has 73 stained-glass windows, some depicting Arthurian scenes and others representing chivalrous virtues such as love, purity, truth, humility and wisdom.

Apart from the castle and hall, Tintagel's most interesting building is the Old Post Office, originally a small, 14th-century manor house. It has a charming tumbledown look, its stone roof sagging like a half-erected marquee and its stone walls encrusted with moss and lichen. Towards the end of the 19th century it was the village post office, and was bought by the National Trust in 1900 for £100.

Inside it is surprisingly spacious, with a parlour, bedchamber and a hall which reaches the full height of the house to sooty rafters. The Post Room has been preserved as a Victorian post office.

Tintagel Castle from the air

Old Post Office

A DREAM OF CAMELOT

The people of Tintagel like to believe their castle was really the Camelot of Arthurian legend. Historians think King Arthur existed – but long before the castle was built. The Old Post Office has no regal pretensions, but was once a manor house.

PADSTOW

CORNWALL

45 miles north-west of Plymouth (PAGE 15 Aa)

The harbour of this small, cheerful fishing port is a fascinating jumble of stone houses, boat slips, studios, cafes, craft shops, quays – and a home-made fudge shop. Little of the town was planned – its slate-hung, colour-washed buildings simply grew and spread along the waterside and up the slope behind it over the generations. Despite this, Padstow is all of a piece, with its narrow, curving streets leading down to the crescent-shaped quayside.

On the corner of North Quay is a bench called the Long Lugger, the traditional meeting-place of the town's 'old boys'. They sit here swapping yarns and watching the fishing boats and pleasure craft.

On the South Quay is the 16th-century Court House, home of Sir Walter Raleigh (about 1554 – 1618) when he was Warden of the Cornish stannary towns – Helston, Liskeard, Lostwithiel and Truro – where the county's tin was assayed.

Set in a narrow gully on the estuary where the River Camel flows into the Atlantic, Padstow is well sheltered from the prevailing south-west winds. Its history goes back to the 6th century, when St Petroc of Wales sailed up the Camel and founded a monastery high on the west bank. The monastery has long since vanished, but the parish church, dating from the 13th to 15th centuries, is still dedicated to St Petroc.

Standing on a hill overlooking the town, the church has a sturdy, battlemented tower and fine ironwork gates in the churchyard dating from the 18th century. Inside are several monuments to the local Prideaux family, including an early 17th-century wall-monument to Sir Nicholas Prideaux and life-size figures of his four children.

Close by is the family's house, Prideaux Place, thought to stand on the site of St Petroc's old monastery. It is a splendid Elizabethan mansion, with battlements and mullioned windows.

On May Day, Padstow holds its annual 'Obby 'Oss (Hobby Horse) ceremony, an ancient pagan fertility rite. The 'Obby 'Oss is a grotesquely masked man in a black cape hanging from a round wooden frame. He wears a plume and a horsehair tail and prances around the flower-bedecked town while the citizens dance and sing a special May Song, which includes the lines:

Arise up Mr . . . and joy you betide,
For summer is acome unto day,
And bright is your bride that lies by your side,
In the merry morning of May.

The festivities end with the ritual death of the 'Obby 'Oss – which is born again the following year, symbolising nature's power of renewal.

• **Parking** Link Road; The Lawn, School Hill; The Old Railway, Station Road; The Harbour (all car parks) • **Early closing** Wednesday • **Cinema** Capitol, Lanadwell Street • **Events** 'Obby 'Oss Festival (May); Carnival and Regatta (July) • **Information** TEL. Padstow 532296 • **AA 24 hour service** TEL. Truro 76455.

Little Petherick CORNWALL

2 miles south of Padstow (PAGE 15 Aa)

Most people pass Little Petherick by: it gets no more than a glance from holidaymakers hurrying to the hotspots of the north Cornish coast. But those who choose to explore will find a village of charm on a delightful creek of the Camel river. Snugged down in a wooded valley at the head of the creek, Little Petherick's business is mainly farming – as it has been for centuries.

Known also as St Petroc Minor, the village takes its name from St Petroc. An older name for the place was Nansfounteyn, derived from the two Cornish words, *nans fenten*, meaning 'spring in the valley'.

There are a mere 160 or so inhabitants, and their houses are of stone. Mill House, minus its wheel, but with gardens a blaze of colour in spring and summer, once ground corn that arrived by barge. The Maltsters was the village pub, but now you must walk a mile for a pint, to the Ring o' Bells at St Issey. The old granary on the quay is now Quay House, a private home.

A path near here runs along the estuary shore to Padstow, 2 miles away, and from it you can watch the dinghy sailors in the creek, or the anglers casting for bass. The little humpbacked bridge crossing the stream at the head of the creek dates from 1805. Before then, carts on their way between Padstow and Wadebridge had to splash through a ford.

The creek, the quay, and most of all the church were the real reasons for Little Petherick's existence in those days. The church, like Padstow's, is dedicated to St Petroc, who probably had a small cell and preaching cross at the site where the church now stands. Mainly 14th century, it was much restored in the 19th century, and again early in the 20th century under the patronage of the traveller and leading Anglo-Catholic Athelstan Riley. A great slab of Delabole slate in the south aisle is engraved with the name of every rector since 1264. Among them is Richard Lyne (1812 – 34), who became so alarmed by imagined danger of renewed religious persecution in Britain, that he had copies of Foxe's *Book of Martyrs* chained in the church.

Little Petherick has a village hall designed and given to the village by Athelstan Riley, but it has no post office, no school, no shop (although you can get bread and groceries in the garden centre), no industry, and these days it shares a parson with St Issey, where the children also go to school. What Little Petherick does have is an abundance of natural beauty, a sense of remoteness and isolation from the traffic that rumbles past its front door.

SAINTLY STONES *A little church dedicated to St Petroc stands guard over delightful stone cottages at Little Petherick. Petroc spent 30 years in Cornwall in the 6th century.*

Rock CORNWALL

1 mile north-east of Padstow (via ferry) (PAGE 15 Aa)

There is so much sand about this village on the east bank of the Camel estuary that visitors must wonder why it was ever called Rock. The name comes from an outcrop of dark greenstone, known locally as Blacktor or Black Rock, which pushes its head up out of the sand near the village. Perhaps in the past it was the only permanent feature that remained uncovered by the wind-blown, shifting sand that has so often buried parts of this eroded coastline. Even the Church of St Enodoc, not far from Black Rock, was for many years almost completely lost in sand, quite out of use until it was dug out in 1863.

St Enodoc's, which stands near the site of a Roman camp, is mostly Norman but has a 13th-century spire. In its churchyard is buried the former Poet Laureate Sir John Betjeman (1906 – 84), who had a home at nearby Trebetherick. Adjoining the churchyard is a golf course.

Rock is a spreading village looking out across the Camel to Padstow. These days it is almost entirely devoted to summer pursuits, possessing a beach safe for swimming, a sheltered anchorage ideal for dinghy sailors and an area especially buoyed off for the use of water-skiers.

The thriving sailing club's headquarters, built of stone and granite in the 1850s, is just about the only relic of Rock's commercial past. It was once used by a Padstow trading company to store solid fuels and animal foodstuffs. Rock also dealt in corn, which was shipped from here in large quantities before the anchorage silted up a century ago. By then the other local industry, lead mining, had also died and, until the late Victorians began holidaymaking, Rock was a tiny community of farmers and a few cockle fishermen. Through good times and bad, and through six centuries, a ferryboat called the *Blacktor* has plied between Rock and Padstow. It started in 1337, using a rowing boat, which was later replaced by a sailboat, and now the *Blacktor* – all boats have had the same name – is a motor launch operated by Padstow Harbour commissioners. Its ancient charter requires it to run from sunrise to sunset seven days a week, and it still runs continuously every day from April to October – but in winter there is only a restricted service and none on Sundays.

The village has grown considerably in recent times and now has six hotels, two pubs, a bakery, a post office, three general stores and a butcher's – and a health club with a sauna.

Off the foreshore, beneath the high tides in Daymer Bay, lies a submerged forest. After a storm in 1857 it was exposed 12 ft below the high-water mark. Stumps and roots of oak and yew were found with hazelnuts and the horns and teeth of red deer which once roamed there. Old tree roots are still washed ashore in rough weather, while on calm days aqualung divers can explore the submerged glades.

St Merryn CORNWALL

3 miles south-west of Padstow (PAGE 15 Aa)

The houses of St Merryn hide behind a small rise in the Cornish landscape, as though keeping their heads down from the Atlantic winds which sweep in over Harlyn Bay, a mile to the north. This is an ancient place. A builder digging foundations for a new house by the bay in 1900 struck a stone slab with his spade some 15 ft down in the sand – and uncovered an Iron Age burial ground. More than 2000 tons of sand were shovelled away, revealing 130 slate coffins, arranged in lines – some laid on top of each other.

Inside the coffins some of the dead had their skulls crushed in, probably flattened by the collapse of the covering stone, and were buried in the crouched position commonly used at the time. But two, an adult and a child, had been buried near a boundary wall of slate and rock, and laid out flat. Finds from the graves include awls and slate needles for sewing skins or net-making, brooches, and slate knives for hunting. All the relics are in Truro museum.

Harlyn Bay is now a playground for the surfers, sun-lovers, walkers and fishermen who seek out this happy mix of countryside and seaside. The village of St Merryn, typically Cornish, is in two halves; the bigger and busier half, called Shop by the locals, is half a mile from the church.

Around the 15th-century Church of St Marina, which has an unusual three-stage tower, are the vicarage, the village inn, a farmhouse and a row of old cottages. Behind them is a small meadow known as The Green, bequeathed to the young men of the parish 'for their recreation' more than 450 years ago by Thomas de Tregew of Harlyn.

The Poundpark, behind the Cornish Arms, is so called because in medieval times stray animals were kept there until claimed. In the 19th century the Poundpark was famous throughout west Cornwall for its Cornish wrestling matches, especially the exploits of the legendary Chapman family – father, grandfather and two sons – who for years in late Victorian times dominated the duels fought here. They are still talked about in the local pubs today.

In the church itself is one of the county's most beautiful fonts, made in the late 14th century from catacleuse, a blue slate obtained from the local Cataclews quarry.

Down at Shop, the appropriately named part of the village, are the baker, the butcher, the post office, another pub, and a garage. Some distance away, beyond Trevithick, is a former Royal Naval Air Station, which has been turned into holiday chalets. Officers who once served there would now find visitors drinking in their old wardroom.

St Marina's Church

FONT IN BLUE

A beautiful font, made in the 14th century from a local blue slate, can be seen in the parish church at St Merryn. Around the deep bowl are superb carvings of the 12 apostles. Near by is an ancient burial ground, probably in use until about 300 BC.

Blue slate font

St Minver CORNWALL

4 miles east of Padstow (PAGE 15 Aa)

St Minver seems an honest enough place, standing four-square to the elements on the big green rump of land, bounded by the Atlantic and Pentire Point, to the north and east of the Camel estuary. Yet the old village stocks, made in the 1400s, are still on show in the church porch, as if warning any would-be miscreants. In fact, the stocks were in use less than 100 years ago. Two boys who had stolen apples from an orchard were locked in them for three hours, with the written consent of their fathers, to avoid facing a trial at the petty sessions.

The apples probably came from the squire's trees. St Minver is an old manorial village; its local stone and slate-roofed cottages, some with pretty bow windows, surround the church, the old manor and the village pub, The Four Ways Inn. Only a summer caravan park, part-hidden by trees beside the church, reveals that anything has changed in the past few centuries.

The church is dedicated to St Menefreda, one of the children of the legendary Welsh chieftain Brychan – he is reputed to have had more than 20 children, all of whom are said to have become saints or missionaries.

It has a spire which leans noticeably to one side. But despite the tilt – or perhaps because of it – the spire is a landmark for sailors. Standing 120 ft over the village and 330 ft above sea level, it is visible from miles out to sea.

Crude slate coffins found in the churchyard suggest that this was a place of pagan worship some centuries before early Christians set up a church in the 5th century. Parts of the present structure are Norman, but most of the church is 15th century. The spire is the most recent addition. When the old one was found to be unsafe, it was pulled down and replaced by the present, leaning, version in 1875.

St Menefreda's has a copy of the famous Vinegar Bible, published in 1717 and containing the misprint which gives it its name. The page heading for St Luke chapter 20 reads 'The Parable of the Vinegar' instead of 'The Parable of the Vineyard'. This is the most notorious of a number of misprints in the edition. As the printer was a man called John Baskett, his Bible has sometimes been called 'a baskettful of errors'.

An entry in the parish register dated October 10, 1666 reads: 'Collected in this parish towards the relief of the citizens of London whose great loss was occasioned by the late disastrous fire which destroyed the greater part of their city, the sum of one pound and one penny.'

TAVISTOCK

DEVON

15 miles north of Plymouth (PAGE 15 Da)

Though this is the western gateway to Dartmoor, what with Duke Street, Bedford Square, Russell Street, the Bedford Hotel and so on, one might well be in London's Bloomsbury. The reason is that the Russell Dukes of Bedford owned both places and scattered their names and titles about them. At the same time, they were able to complement their Devonshire possessions at least by taking the title of Marquis of Tavistock for their heirs.

The town began, long before dukes were thought of, in the prehistoric camp whose outlines can still be traced on the hill beside Kelly College. Much later, the Saxons built an abbey that the Danes burnt down, but it rose again from the ashes to become the largest and most important religious house in the South-West. Its wealth was based upon wool and cloth, and then upon tin, as was that of the market town that grew up around it.

As early as 1281, Tavistock was designated a stannary town – an official centre for assaying and stamping tin. At the Dissolution of the Monasteries in 1539, the abbey lands passed to the Russells and the building itself mouldered. Some idea of its size may be gained from the extent of its remains scattered through the town – a gate here and there, Betsy Grimbal's Tower (thought to be named after a girl murdered in it by a monk or a soldier), and the great Court Gate building in Bedford Square that now houses not only an antiques shop, but the Community College, police station, Mountain Rescue Service, and the tourist information centre.

The discovery of copper in the district in the late 18th century led to a huge mining boom. The Devon Great Consols was the richest copper mine in Europe; its by-product was enough arsenic, it is said, to slay every living thing on the planet, but it was put to no more lethal use than the destruction of the boll weevil in American cotton plantations.

Copper ore was transported down to the Tamar by a 4 mile canal, part of which still runs through a pretty public park, though it is only used nowadays by Muscovy ducks and boys catching minnows. On the other side of the park is the undisciplined River Tavy, bustling among rocks to remind visitors that, despite its urban surroundings, this is still a Dartmoor river.

Rich already, the Dukes of Bedford became very rich indeed upon the royalties from the mines. In gratitude the 7th Duke built 100 miners' cottages on the southern edge of the town in the 1860s, and entirely remodelled the town centre. His Gothic municipal buildings, using the local sea-green, volcanic stone, mingle well with the remains of the abbey. So, too, does his greenish, pensive statue in the foreground; quite rightly, it is a casting of bronze composed of Great Consols tin and copper.

Another bronze statue is that of Sir Francis Drake, whose father lived at Crowndale, a little to the south of the town. Nothing now remains of Sir Francis's birthplace, though Buckland Abbey, the house he purchased with Spanish gold in his later years, is not far away (see Buckland Monachorum, page 23).

The mainly 15th-century Church of St Eustachius reflects the wealth of the town's medieval cloth merchants – a lovely building, soaring high upon slim pillars, and containing some fine monuments. In the churchyard there is a descendant, by budding, of the Holy Thorn of Glastonbury that is said to have grown from the staff of Joseph of Arimathea. Like its famous ancestor it occasionally blooms on Christmas Day.

• **Parking** By Guildhall in Bedford Square; The Wharf, off Plymouth Road; Pixon Lane (all car parks) • **Early closing** Wednesday • **Market day** Tuesday (crafts), Friday, Pannier Market • **Event** Goose Fair (2nd Wednesday in October) • **Information** TEL. Tavistock 2938 (summer) • **AA 24 hour service** TEL. Plymouth 669989.

Tavistock, looking north

Drake statue

GOOD LOOKOUT FOR DRAKE

The houses, church and old railway viaduct at Tavistock together make a delightful vista, typical of a country town. Yet some of the street names are duplicated in Bloomsbury, London. The link is the Russell family – Dukes of Bedford and landowners in both areas. Sir Francis Drake was born near Tavistock, and his statue, made in 1883, appears to be surveying Plymouth Road.

Bere Ferrers DEVON

8 miles south of Tavistock (PAGE 15 Db)

The village is defended by a maze of lanes whose banks are thick in spring and early summer with ragged robin, primroses, celandines, bluebells and anemones – a glimpse of what many an English hedgerow looked like before the invention of herbicides. The lanes turn and twist and plunge over mossy bridges and up steep hills, coming at last to Bere Ferrers.

This is a little, white-painted, stone place often described as being strangely peaceful, though with the wind coming off the half-mile wide River Tavy, it can also be strangely exuberant. In the Middle Ages the village was famous for its silver mines and later for the production of lead. Little can be seen of these activities now, apart from the name of Silver Street and a few ruinous quays, kilns and mine workings along the banks of the river.

At the centre of the village, beside the War Memorial, there is a drinking fountain (now dry), apparently inspired by Stonehenge. It was given by Frances, Lady Shelley for the benefit of the poor in her son's parish in 1852; her son, Sir Frederick Shelley, was rector for some 30 years. His church, St Andrew's, is one of the oldest in south Devon, and the churchyard is crammed with slate and granite tombstones whose inscriptions seem never to wear away. One, inscribed in the 18th century, reads:

> *'To you dear wife i bid a diew*
> *I leave my children to God and you*
> *The children are yours as well as mine*
> *Bid them to serve the Lord be time.'*

Others are more concise and telling in their brevity: there is a scattering of black slate markers throughout the churchyard that simply declare 'Cholera 1849', with no further inscription.

St Andrew's is everyone's idea of a village church, with old, worn benches, knights and a lady in stone effigy, and some of the finest medieval glass in Devon. It was partly rebuilt in the 1330s by Sir William de Ferrers, who also converted the building into a collegiate church supporting an archpriest, a deacon and four priests; the rector carries the additional title of archpriest to this day. It is touching that Sir William is portrayed in the stained glass, armoured, and holding a model of the church he endowed; he appears again in effigy, lying beside his wife Matilda upon their tomb.

Fragments of Sir William's castle are incorporated in Bere Barton Farm, a magnificent stone manor house next door to the church. A secret passage supposedly connects farm and church – for what reason, nobody seems to know.

Buckland Monachorum

DEVON

6 miles south of Tavistock (PAGE 15 Db)

The name means Buckland of the Monks, the monks concerned being the Cistercians who established the abbey, about a mile away, in 1278. From then until the Reformation the village and much of the surrounding countryside was totally dependent upon the abbey for its livelihood.

Buckland Abbey was endowed by a grant of land by Amicia, Dowager Countess of Devon; her likeness, carved in granite, can still be seen above one of the

Buckland Monachorum, looking west

Buckland Abbey

Drake's Drum

WHERE ELIZABETH'S SEA DOGS HAD THEIR LAIR

Half submerged in an ocean of greenery, drowsy Buckland Monachorum dreams of the swashbuckling Elizabethan admirals who vied for possession of the lovely old mansion that was once an abbey. Sir Richard Grenville was the sea dog who transformed it into a gracious house; then his arch-rival Sir Francis Drake, awash with Spanish gold, bought it for a huge sum. It still holds its treasures from that stirring age, including Drake's Drum, to call him from the deep should another Elizabeth need him.

doorways. For centuries it was one of the important religious foundations in the West Country.

Then, at the Dissolution in 1539, the buildings and land were acquired by Sir Richard Grenville simply to extend his estates, and it was not until the days of his grandson, Admiral Sir Richard Grenville, of *Revenge* fame, that the abbey was given its present glorious metamorphosis as a country house.

Later it was bought by an even more famous sea dog, Sir Francis Drake, for what was then a staggering sum of £3400. Sir Francis had done well out of raids upon Spanish treasure ships during his circumnavigation of the globe – a project that Grenville had planned and wanted to carry out himself.

Drake died and was buried at sea in 1596 while on an expedition to the Spanish West Indies, and left his estates to his brother Thomas; it was Thomas's line which continued to live at Buckland until 1938.

During the Civil War the house was seized by another Sir Richard Grenville, grandson of the admiral and Royalist commander in the West. Known as 'Skellum' (something between devil and villain) Grenville, he was hated almost as much by his own side as by the forces of Parliament; in fact, in all the years since, he seems to have found only one defender, Daphne du Maurier, who based her novel *The King's General* upon him. At any rate, when the Royalists were defeated in 1646, the Drakes took great pleasure in expelling a Grenville from Buckland for the second time in its history.

Memories of all its stirring times are still writ plain upon the house, which belongs to the National Trust and is open daily from Good Friday to September. Monastic days are recalled by the austere little chapel where Amicia, the founder, and several abbots are buried, and by the enormous tithe barn that still carries its early 15th-century roof timbers. Grenville's Great Hall is much as he left it, and relics of Drake are everywhere – the banners flown by the *Golden Hind* when she returned from her voyage round the world, the Armada documents and, most famous of all, the admiral's drum whose summons Drake promised to answer if ever it was beaten at some hour of England's danger. The old stone house itself, with its square tower, lies deep in a grassy hollow, and in consequence seems always hushed and tranquil.

At the top of the village street at Buckland Monachorum, a notice tells visitors that the 16th-century Drake Manor Inn is a cable's length away, and so it is, complete with Drake's Haunt and Armada Bar. Understandably, there is a good deal of Drake about the village. The admiral himself was, of course, buried at sea, but members of his family lie in the Drake Chapel in St Andrew's Church, and with them is General George Augustus Eliott who married into the family and was later created Lord Heathfield for his epic defence of Gibraltar in 1779. His large and breathtaking monument features Britannia, a fierce cherub and reliefs of incidents during the Siege of Gibraltar.

Next to the church is the School House that was endowed in 1702. About it, and down the long slope of the village street, there is a pretty collection of stone cottages. Many show signs of Tudor origins.

St Germans CORNWALL

22 miles south-west of Tavistock (PAGE 15 Cb)

The village has a peninsula to itself in the bewildering tangle of estuaries west of Plymouth that drain into the Hamoaze. At the quay at the bottom of the hill, halyards rattle against masts belonging to the Quay Sailing Club. Where the yachts and dinghies lie now was once a busy little port, until the railway came and built the viaduct that makes gigantic stone strides through the muddy sands of the creek. A handsome stone warehouse is now the club's home.

The glory of the village is St Germans Church, embraced in its setting of steep lawns and sweet-scented shrubs. It is a building of great majesty and cathedral-like dimensions, with a vast twin-towered west front pierced by a Norman doorway of astonishing size. The church dates mainly from around 1200, but it stands on the site of the former cathedral church of the Saxon Bishopric of Cornwall.

For a century before the Conquest, bishops owing allegiance to Canterbury ruled the diocese of Cornwall from St Germans, until the diocese was amalgamated with that of Crediton to form the see of Exeter in early Norman times. The present building was once even larger – the north aisle was demolished early in the 19th century. The remaining south aisle and the nave are more or less the same size, giving a curious impression of a double church. The interior is of scraped, rough stone, filled with flowers and with soft, coloured light falling from Victorian stained-glass windows. The Great East Window, made in 1896, is by the Pre-Raphaelite artist Sir Edward Burne-Jones. There are memorials to the Eliot family who have been lords of the manor almost since the Reformation. In particular, there is an ornate one by the Flemish sculptor Rysbrack to Edward Eliot who died in 1722. Owing to a quirk of fashion of the time he is portrayed in Roman costume.

A medieval misericord (the back of a choir seat) is carved with the figures of a hunter and his hounds. This is Dando, a 14th-century monk at the priory who, for his habit of hunting on the Sabbath, was dragged by the Devil into the River Lynher. To the accompaniment of demoniac wails and a hiss of steam, Dando, hounds and all disappeared into a pool.

Next door to the church and lower down the slope is the house of Port Eliot. It stands on the site of the medieval priory and is a large, castellated building of dark, local stone with a huge portico. The house looks out upon a delicious prospect of distant wooded hills that was the creation of the great landscape gardener Humphry Repton in 1792.

There is a long village street with a high causewayed pavement and stone cottages, some pebble-dashed, some white-painted, but most left in their natural livery of brownish, uneven rock. The street sweeps through a graceful, descending 'S', and ends at the Sir Walter Moyle's Almshouses of 1583.

CHARMS OF CHURCH AND CHARITY

St Germans may be a village, but its church is as big as a cathedral. It stands on the site of a Saxon church from which the whole diocese of Cornwall was ruled. The present building, with its huge Norman doorway, has a striking garden setting; next door is the impressive house of Port Eliot. The Sir Walter Moyle's Almshouses, a delightful row of double-decker cottages, have a more homely charm.

Sir Walter Moyle's Almshouses

Church doorway with Port Eliot in background

MAP 3

DARTMOOR AND THE DEVON RIVIERA

Devon is not all cream and cider and seaside holidays. Inland from the county's Riviera lies Dartmoor, with its emptiness and silence. Between the carefree coast and the wild moorland are dozens of lovely villages of varied charm and history. The towns include carpet-making Axminster and Totnes with its reminders of Tudor wealth.

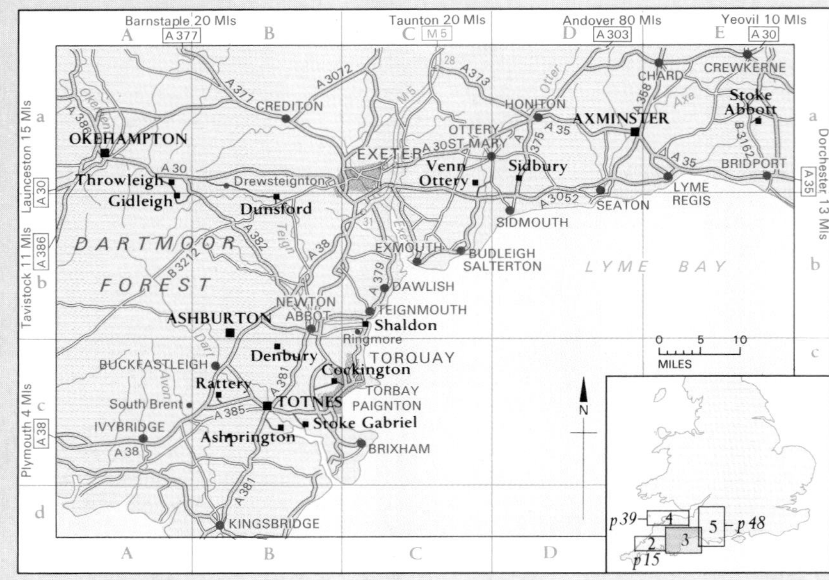

MAP 3:
NEIGHBOURING AREAS – MAPS 2, 4, 5

ASHBURTON
Denbury
Shaldon

AXMINSTER
Sidbury
Stoke Abbott
Venn Ottery

OKEHAMPTON
Dunsford
Gidleigh
Throwleigh

TOTNES
Ashprington
Cockington
Rattery
Stoke Gabriel

ASHBURTON

DEVON

20 miles south-west of Exeter (PAGE 26 Bb)

A lively market town in the valley of the River Ashburn, Ashburton is known as 'The Gateway to Dartmoor'. In the Middle Ages Ashburton was on the main road from Plymouth to Exeter, but today the road bypasses the town which retains much of its old-world atmosphere and appearance.

The town is divided by three long streets – East Street, West Street and North Street – all containing fine slate-hung buildings. In East Street, No. 31 has particularly attractive overlapping scallop-shaped slates. Farther along, the 18th-century Golden Lion Hotel faces the Conduit, a recently restored stone structure from which water taps used to project. It dates from the late 1790s and no longer supplies water. Next to the hotel is a group of three-storey Regency houses with delicate, wrought-iron balconies.

East Street continues into West Street, where, set back from the road, is the parish church of St Andrew. It dates from the 12th century, and has an elegant 15th-century tower, but was substantially rebuilt 300 years later and restored in 1883. It contains a late 15th-century oak chest complete with its original keys, and near the foot of the tower is the grave of a French prisoner of war who died in July 1815 – a month after the Battle of Waterloo. He was one of many French prisoners billeted on parole in the town during the Napoleonic Wars. The church overlooks Blogishay Lane, a narrow twisting footpath whose high limestone walls are clad with a variety of ferns and flowers.

The path emerges at St Lawrence Lane, leading to the Chapel of St Lawrence. All that remains of the original 14th-century chapel is the tower. Although this was roughcast in the 1930s, the present building dates from the 18th century. The name Chapel of St Lawrence is now used to describe the tower and the room to the east of it. The chapel was part of the ancient Grammar School until 1938, when it was taken over by the Primary School. The school stopped using the building in 1983 but wooden pews, bearing the graffiti of generations of schoolchildren, can still be seen in the former classrooms.

The town museum, once a brush factory, marks the division between East Street and West Street. Leading from it is North Street, where there is a 17th-century former gaming house called the Card House from the patterns on its slate-hung façade. It is now a grocery store.

Close by is the former Mermaid Inn – now an ironmonger's – that was the headquarters of the Roundhead general, Sir Thomas Fairfax (1612 – 71), for a short while during the Civil War.

Running between North Street and the town car park is the River Ashburn, spanned by the single arch of King's Bridge. The houses backing onto the river have overhanging slates which were quarried locally. The Ashburn flows westwards out of the town, where it passes St Gudula's Well – a small spring marked by an old granite cross. St Gudula is patroness of the blind, and the spring water was thought to be beneficial to the eyes.

In the Middle Ages Ashburton was one of Dartmoor's four stannary towns, to which locally mined tin was brought to be weighed and valued. But its history as a 'port' or market town goes back to Saxon times, when it held sales of cattle and property. The sales were witnessed and recorded by a 'portreeve', an official appointed by the Crown. The town's first portreeve began work in AD 820, and the office has been retained, although it is now just an honorary title. Each Carnival Week the portreeve asserts his official right to taste the quality of the ale of all public houses and hotels.

Ashburton still flourishes as a market town, and cattle and sheep sales are held periodically throughout the year. A sale of Dartmoor ponies also takes place each October and November.

• **Parking** Kingsbridge Lane (car park) • **Early closing** Wednesday • **Market days** Tuesday, Thursday • **Events** Ale-tasting ceremony during Carnival Week (June/July); Court and Law Day (November) • **Information** TEL. Newton Abbot 61101 • **AA 24 hour service** TEL. Torquay 25903.

Denbury DEVON

5 miles east of Ashburton (PAGE 26 Bc)

The approach to Denbury from Ashburton, and maybe an unfair proportion of the village itself, is overhung by a massive park wall that grows higher and higher as the village is entered. It shields the Manor House that long ago was a cell of the monks of Tavistock, but had a house built upon it in the 17th century.

The centre of the village is the church and a curious 18th-century water pump house given a new role as a war memorial. Round about are streets of stone cottages, many with massive outside chimneys indicating their 16th-century origin.

A roughcast wall dressing is the local fashion, and a pleasant one too, especially when colour has been added; then it looks as though the pastel-hued buildings have taken root and simply sprouted from the edges of the street.

St Mary's Church, consisting of little more than a barrel-roofed nave, probably looks much as it did when it was completed in the early 14th century. A brass plaque reads: 'In pious memory of Aeldred, a priest in Denbury who became Archbishop of York and crowned William the Conqueror' – that was in Westminster Abbey on Christmas Day, 1066.

There is a Norman font in pink sandstone and monuments to the Taylor family, soldiers and sailors all, who lived in the village's Manor House in the years between 1720 and 1820.

In the peaceful little churchyard, surrounded by low stone cottages, there is an unusual, half-size monument to a Boy Scout who died in 1932.

Over all stands a green, tree-topped hill whose summit has been carved into the causeways and ramparts of an Iron Age hill-fort. No one knows much about it, but it is thought to have been re-fortified during the Dark Ages, at the time of Saxon invasions. Then it was called Defnas Burh – the fortress of the men of Devon. The village itself gained its name from the same two words.

Shaldon DEVON

14 miles east of Ashburton (PAGE 26 Cb)

This pretty little seaside-resort village looks within itself as though it belongs to an older time, when seaside holidays were more stylish than they are now; the Victorian era, perhaps. However, its beaches of red sand face busy Teignmouth, across an estuary filled with anchored yachts and cabin cruisers. The town, with its docks and housing estates climbing the hills, is most certainly of our own time. As long ago as the 9th century, the two places were connected by a ferry; now they are more conveniently joined by a road bridge.

Shaldon, crowded between the coast and the wooded, landscaped hills behind, is constricted to a narrow maze of streets – little more than walkways – along the shore. Most of these are very attractive, with slate-roofed cottages colour-washed pink, primrose or cream, and here and there a dash of thatch, like the totally unexpected Wyche Cottage, a tiny black-and-white house, heavily clad in creeper, in Dagmar Street.

Occasionally the lanes open out to something more imposing like tiny, colour-washed Crown Square, or Fore Street, full of intriguing shops and where, with care, two cars might pass one another. At the street's beginning – and the village's too – is a restaurant called Hunter's Lodge that bears the date 1650 and a stone festoon of foxes' heads. Despite its declared date, its outer aspect at least is jolly, early Victorian Gothic.

Throughout Shaldon there are many small-scale Georgian-style houses, all delightful, including some that were built quite recently but conform to the surrounding mood. Everywhere, even down to the water's edge, there are gardens filled with the season's flowers. The culmination is The Green, a potpourri of pastel-hued Georgian cottages looking out over a square consisting of flowerbeds, a bowling green and a lawn to sit upon.

The village comes to its seaward end at The Ness Ho, a huge red-sandstone bluff pierced by Smugglers' Tunnel. This is a bluff too, since – although it may possibly have incorporated part of a smugglers' tunnel – it was actually cut by Lord Clifford in the early 1800s to provide access to his private beach.

Back along the coast from Hunter's Lodge is the near-adjoining village of Ringmore. It is considerably smaller than Shaldon, but Georgian too, with Victorian touches. Spare a glance especially for the red-stone, Gothic-style Ringmore Towers built in 1890, and more than a glance for the little 13th-century Chapel of St Nicholas, and its serene, plain interior.

AXMINSTER

DEVON

26 miles east of Exeter (PAGE 26 Da)

Just to the north of Trinity Square – the hub of this small and thriving market town – is the factory in which the first Axminster carpet was started on Midsummer's Day, 1755. It was made by a native of the town, the weaver Thomas Whitty, with the help of his

Whitty carpet at new factory

THE CARPET KING

Here is one of the first carpets that spread the name of Axminster throughout the world. Made by Thomas Whitty and his family in the 1750s, it can now be seen at the town's modern carpet factory. Whitty's early carpets were woven by a lengthy, painstaking hand-tufting technique – an operation, he said, best performed by the 'pliant fingers of little children', like the five young daughters who helped him. Among his surviving carpets, apart from the one shown above, is one in London's Victoria and Albert Museum. It was made for no less a person than the Prince Regent to go in the Throne Room of his palace, Carlton House in London. There is a fragment of another Whitty carpet in Axminster's Guildhall. The house where he lived still stands.

Whitty's factory and (right) his house

five young daughters and sister Elizabeth. Whitty was inspired by the quality of a large and beautiful Turkey carpet he had seen at Cheapside, in London, which measured 36 ft by 24 ft.

By 1835, however, machine-made carpets had put Whitty's factory out of business, and Axminster carpets were not made again until 1937. Today the new factory near the railway station produces a million square yards of top quality carpets each year. On weekdays visitors can, by appointment, watch the various weaving and finishing processes.

The town is set in the charming Axe valley, and from Trinity Hill – a 670 ft high expanse of woodland and common south of the town – the view stretches 5 miles to the English Channel. Most of the shops and houses are Georgian or early Victorian.

The intricate network of narrow streets is drawn together in Trinity Square, the site of St Mary's Church, which is said to enshrine the history of the town. It was endowed in AD 937 by the Saxon King Athelstan, but has been totally rebuilt over the centuries since. The south aisle has a Norman doorway and there is a 13th-century tower, which was damaged in the Civil War when some Cavaliers were besieged in the church by Roundheads. The carved Jacobean pulpit and reading-desk date, as does the altar, from the early 1600s.

Overlooking the square is one of Axminster's finest buildings, the George Hotel. The 18th-century hotel has a splendid first-floor assembly room built by Robert Adam (1728 – 92) with a handsome fireplace, a musicians' gallery, and Venetian windows. To the east of Chard Street is the Georgian Oak House, once an 'Academy for Young Gentlemen', but now converted into a number of flats.

Thursday is market day in Axminster – three times over. A cattle market, pannier market and street market attract buyers from Devon, Somerset and Dorset – and the pubs are open all day.

• **Parking** Chard Street; Coombe Lane; South Street; West Street (all car parks) • **Early closing** Wednesday • **Market day** Thursday • **Event** Carnival (September) • **Information** TEL. Axminster 34386 (summer only) • **AA 24 hour service** TEL. Exeter 32121.

SWEET BELLS OF SUCCESS

The bells of St Mary's Church, Axminster, used to peal out a salute to every new carpet produced at Thomas Whitty's factory. This was the signal for people to throng into the town centre and inspect the latest Whitty achievement. The church – totally rebuilt since it was founded in Saxon times – has notable features from various periods, including this handsome Jacobean carved reading-desk.

St Mary's Church belfry

Jacobean reading-desk

Sidbury DEVON

15 miles south-west of Axminster (PAGE 26 Da)

The Devon Riviera, with its high-powered appeal to holidaymakers, is not far from Sidbury, so the village's 20th-century course is more or less mapped out for it. It involves a fair number of shops selling cakes and clotted cream, Devonshire teas and honey, and a considerable amount of Gothic lettering on The Old Clock House and The Old Bakery. A modicum of restraint prevails, however, and the phrase 'Ye Olde' is nowhere to be seen.

The village is a pretty place of thatch and slate and whitewashed cob – a mixture of clay and straw. Many of the cottages belong to the 16th century, as do the stone, bow-windowed Court House and Court Hall, though they were considerably extended a couple of hundred years later. There are attractive groups of buildings everywhere – the cottages like stone dolls' houses at the bottom of Church Street, for example, and the cob and thatch cottages in Bridge Street; or the two pleasant pubs almost next door to each other, the Red Lion in red and white and the green-and-white Royal Oak, with its high arch – a relic of busy coaching days.

The Church of St Giles and St Peter is big and rugged and full of landmarks left along the 1300 years of its existence. There is a Saxon crypt, worn Norman effigies of patron saints on the tower, medieval wall paintings, a monument to a 17th-century freemason and a delicate 17th-century gallery.

The village stands about midway along the length of the River Sid before it flows on to Sidmouth, and in a deep bowl of hills that have sheep and big, thatched farmhouses on their lower slopes and a fleece of woodland on their summits. On one of these hills is the imposing, double-ramparted Iron Age hill-fort that gave the village its name – Sid-burh, 'the fort on the Sid'. The manor was ancient long before the Normans arrived in Normandy, let alone England, and there is still a Manor House, though the present version dates only from the 1870s. Its park stretches away behind Sidbury, helping to complete the serene picture that brought the accolade of 'Best Kept' to the village in 1982.

Stoke Abbott DORSET

13 miles east of Axminster (PAGE 26 Ea)

Ravine-like lanes, guarded by silvery-barked beech trees and fringed by hedgerows aglow in early summer with ragged robin and bluebells, lead the traveller to Stoke Abbott, lying in a fold of the Dorset hills.

In the middle of the village is the New Inn, which is not so new as all that, since parts of it date from the 16th century. As well as being an inn in the usual sense, it is a small and pleasant hotel whose dark mustard-coloured stone and golden thatch set the theme of the village.

Its sign depicts monks tending cows and reads: 'The former name of this village was Abbot Stock and is said to relate to the dairy farm of the manor of the abbots which no longer exists.' Dairy farming is still the major occupation. There is hardly a building in the place that is not a delight, from the cottages with absurd little thatched hats over their doors to the big stone farmhouses festooned with lilac and wisteria in summer. The village street curves serenely up a hillside. About halfway up the street, at the bottom of Norway Lane, is an oak, still fairly slim by local standards, yet it was planted to commemorate the beginning of Edward VII's reign in 1901. Beside it, a pair of springs gush forth, one into an ancient trough and the other from the mouth of a stone lion. A notice warns that the water is unfit for drinking.

About the crest of the hill there is a handsome group of 17th and 18th-century farms, the Old Rectory and the Village Hall, formerly the village school. Between them, well-trodden by cattle, a lane runs to a farmyard and to the Church of St Mary in its steep churchyard. Here brown and white sheep graze among the tombstones, several of which bear gaily painted carvings of weeping willows.

Many of the graves are sheltered by the branches of a yew of immense girth, dignity and age. In fact, it is probably a near-contemporary of the church, and that was remodelled in the 13th century. Inside is a beautifully carved Norman font and a memorial tablet in the porch to William Crowe, rector and poet, who died in 1829.

Crowe was a delightful old gentleman who liked to climb nearby Lewesdon Hill – one of a great ring of hills. Another, Waddon Hill, still bears the marks of a

JUST THE PARISH FOR A POET

This farmhouse, dating from 1751, and the Old Rectory are just two of the delights of Stoke Abbott, where nearly every building is a thing of charm. Fittingly, this village of both natural and man-made beauty once had a poet, William Crowe, as its parson.

Eighteenth-century farmhouse, Stoke Abbott

The Old Rectory

fort built about AD 43, nearly a century after the Roman invasion. Resting on Lewesdon Hill's high, wooded summit, Crowe 'garnered worthy thoughts, the fruit of frequent musings', according to his monument. One May morning, he composed a blank-verse poem upon its slopes. He found that:

'Above the noise and stir of yonder fields
Uplifted on this height I feel the mind
Expand itself in wider liberty . . .'

One can readily understand why so many liked him.

The good parson was also Public Orator to Oxford University, and had to go there regularly. But, having little of this world's goods, he used to walk the distance of over 100 miles, carrying his clothes over his arm and composing Latin speeches as he went.

Venn Ottery DEVON

18 miles south-west of Axminster (PAGE 26 Ca)

The country round about Venn Ottery is of quite incredible grandeur and symmetry. Fields and hedges and shapely woods form a gigantic counterpane that has been smoothed over the great billows of the hills, looking as though the whole thing has been composed by a celestial landscape gardener; Capability Brown, perhaps, in an after-life.

Venn Ottery is not to the same scale. It is a secret little place, reached by deep lanes and having a population of around 100, with quite a few engaged in farming. Population and occupation were probably much the same at the time of the Domesday Survey. Tiny though the village is, it has clung tenaciously to life for 1000 years and more. The name implies a fen, or marsh, by the River Otter, and even as late as 1630, a traveller reported 'Venn Ottery, alias Fen Ottery, a dirty place perchance, for fen and dirt is all one'. Perhaps the inhabitants took this laboured witticism to heart, for there is no sign of marshiness now.

The church is dedicated to St Gregory – Pope Gregory I (AD 590 – 604), who sent St Augustine to convert the English. It is reached by a narrow, green tunnel of a lane whose banks are a mass of ragged robin, bluebells and uncurling bracken. The old, worn tower of local stone was built about 1095, and contrasts with the remainder of the church, rebuilt following a fire that swept the village in the latter part of the 18th century. Some fine Tudor bench-end carvings also survived the blaze, and there is a window that commemorates the Reverend Augustus Toplady, vicar of Venn Ottery from 1766 to 1768. He was the composer of *Rock of Ages*, whose inspiration came to him, it is said, while taking shelter from a thunderstorm in a rocky cleft at Burrington Combe, in Avon.

The church apart, the oldest building in the village is Venn Ottery Barton. 'Barton' is a fairly common term in the West Country and means, more or less, an independent manor farm. The one at Venn Ottery was built by a yeoman during the reign of Henry VIII. The material is cob – a mud and straw mixture – on a sturdy boulder footing.

A little farther up the lane is Elliot's Farm, a pretty, pink-washed confection that also dates in part from the 16th century. It is approached by two imposing flights of steps running up its steep lawns and is fronted by immaculate topiary – five enormous goblets of yew – and two monkey puzzle trees. The windows seem small in relation to the big, square house, but the reason is simple. They were shrunk to reduce Window Tax in the late 18th century, and no one has yet got around to enlarging them.

OKEHAMPTON

DEVON

25 miles west of Exeter (PAGE 26 Aa)

Two rivers, the East and West Okement, join at Dartmoor's northern tip. People travelling along them would meet there, and later came roads. The roads brought the market, and the market brought the castle and church – though not, maybe, in that order. It is thought that a Saxon settlement was gathered about the site of All Saints' Church, above the present town. The castle was then built by the Normans.

But a market in the modern idiom – shopping centre – is still what Okehampton is all about. There is a large car park in Market Street, in front of which is the old Market Hall and the adjoining Charter Hall, a fine stone building, reconstructed in 1973 to commemorate the 300th anniversary of the town's Royal Charter. Beside this is the pedestrian precinct of Red Lion Yard, with shops, restaurants and cafes.

Red Lion Yard leads through a discreet arch to Fore Street, whose 200 yds or so between St James's Chapel and the West Okement Bridge is really the heart of the town.

St James's dates mostly from the 1860s but has a 14th-century tower. It was for many years the Corporation's chapel and the chaplain was also the master of the Old Grammar School near the West Bridge. Many people, it is said, mistake it for the parish church, though this is difficult to credit while the mighty tower of All Saints, on its high green hill, looms against the sky to the west of the town. The tower is 15th century but the remainder was rebuilt in 1842, after a disastrous fire.

Fore Street is a broad and lively thoroughfare with buildings of many periods, from the pretty, glass-roofed shopping arcade built in 1901 to the 17th-century Town Hall, which backs onto Charter Hall at the corner of Market Street. By the White Hart is the Old Mill, which contains the recently opened Museum of Dartmoor Life.

A castle, high on a knoll above the river, was built by Baldwin de Bryonis, Sheriff of Devon, shortly after the Norman Conquest. But of the surviving castle ruins, only the keep is Norman – the rest dates from the early 14th century. Nevertheless, the ruins make a picturesque group which has attracted several artists, including Turner. They are also haunted by a Lady Howard, who murdered at least two of her four husbands. She is said to expiate her crimes by travelling nightly between Tavistock and Okehampton in a coach made of her husbands' bones. The equipage stops at the castle mound, where she picks a single blade of grass before returning to Tavistock; not until the mound is bare will she be allowed to rest.

• **Parking** Market Street; Mill Road • **Early closing** Wednesday • **Market day** Saturday (Pannier) • **Cinema** Carlton, Fairplace Terrace • **Events** Ten Tors Expedition (May); Agricultural Show (early August); Carnival (October) • **Information** TEL. Okehampton 3020 (summer) • **AA 24 hour service** TEL. Exeter 32121.

Farmhouse and gardens, Dunsford

Dunsford cottages

Fulford monument in church

SO BRIGHT ON THE HEIGHTS

Luxuriant foliage, a smooth lawn, creeper-covered stone walls and neatly thatched roofs – a rich combination of nature and art – bring a special charm to this Dunsford farmhouse. The whitewashed cottages add brightness to the delightful hill village. And there is even a cheerful quality in the church monument to Sir Thomas and Lady Fulford with their seven children.

Dunsford DEVON

18 miles east of Okehampton (PAGE 26 Bb)

From the west, you come to Dunsford by way of a single-track road. The village stands among towering, timber-clad hills that look, from the bottom of the ravine cut by the River Teign, like the foothills of the Himalayas.

Dunsford is, indeed, the nearest thing to a mountain village that one might find in southern England. Cottages and houses along the steep streets are mostly stone overlaid with white or colour-washed roughcast and topped by thatch that, as it ages, grows a rich bloom of old-gold lichen. From the spaces between the stones in most of the garden walls, succulents and aubrietias grow.

St Mary's Church and its churchyard stand high on a bank that is prevented from sliding into the street by a stout wall. By the path to the church door there is a stone inscribed to the memory of poor Jonathan May 'who was murdered as he was returning from Moreton Fair about ten o'clock on the evening of 16 July 1835'. Nobody knows what happened to whoever killed him.

The church is bright and cheerful, and obviously much loved by the community. The north aisle monuments to the Fulford family include an exuberant Jacobean one that depicts Sir Thomas Fulford, his wife Ursula and their seven children in full colour.

Thomas's eldest son held Fulford House against the guns of the Parliamentarian General Fairfax for ten days in 1645, and his descendant lives there still. In fact, Fulfords have lived in a house on the same site – a couple of miles to the north-west of the village – since the days of Richard the Lionheart (1189 – 99). For 800 years the family have farmed their estate, and in all that time the inheritance has always passed through the direct male line.

Gidleigh DEVON

8 miles south-east of Okehampton (PAGE 26 Ab)

The way to Gidleigh from the east is by single-track leafy tunnels, rather than lanes, that leap up and down steep gradients. At the bottom of each plunge, stone bridges cross joyous little streams of the colour of sparkling pale ale.

There is very little of Gidleigh, but all of it is a delight. It stands, more or less, on the 900 ft contour on the borders of what is known locally as the Dartmoor in-country (steep meadows enclosed by thick hedgerows and coppices) and the dun wilderness of the open moor. The village consists of Holy Trinity Church and a few stone houses, a Youth Hostel, and a roofless, creeper-clad Norman keep.

Not much more than 20 ft across, the keep resembles a toy fort, and is girt about by a charming – and private – garden hummocked over buried ruins. On the other side of the road there is an animal pound and a well dating from the Middle Ages, but obviously Gidleigh is much older than these. It is thought that the manor was once held by Gydda, mother of King Harold, and from her the place may have gained its name.

The churchyard is filled with snowdrops in spring, and is bisected by a little stream that runs beneath a stone bridge. Gravestones dating from the 17th century, with their rough-cut inscriptions picked out in red, are set against the wall of the church, whose interior is bright and colourful, with a 16th-century screen in blue, gold and crimson.

Buildings have changed, but the basic layout of the parish – the roads, the big solid farms, the grouping of houses and church – is much the same as when the screen was made, and probably long before that. Old, too, is the Mariners' Way, which crosses the village. This path was probably made by sailors who, carousing at Dartmouth, had missed their ships and had to take the shortest route to Bideford to catch them up. Now the way makes a delightful path out into the stilled

sea of Dartmoor, with its rocky tors and the black water of its peat hags – places where peat has been dug out allowing small boggy pools of water to form. Also in the moor, within a mile or so of the village, there are marks of habitation – stone circles, hut foundations, standing stones – beside whose ancient origins, Gidleigh was born but yesterday.

Whether in so wild a place you find the signs of ancient humanity eerie or comforting, there is an odd feeling in the twilight sometimes that the old builders have not yet quite departed. Hence, it is said, the legends of the piskeys who, unless placated with a dish of cream, will bring down a mist and lead you to your destruction upon the moor. In such circumstances, victims are advised to turn their coats inside out; it confuses the pesky piskeys, apparently.

Throwleigh DEVON

6 miles south-west of Okehampton (PAGE 26 Aa)

Since it possesses a village store and a bed-and-breakfast, Throwleigh is more of a metropolis than not-so-far-off Gidleigh. But, like Gidleigh, this too is a village of the Dartmoor uplands, sharing the same air of remoteness and serenity. These virtues can be appreciated by taking the deep path that runs from the back of Throwleigh churchyard to a little iron gate – a grand thing to lean upon while contemplating the clear, sweeping curves of the moorland horizon. That is in fine weather; when the mists roll in, it is the remoteness alone that strikes the dominant note.

The centre of the village is a cross inscribed by the rector and parishioners in 1897 to commemorate Queen Victoria's Diamond Jubilee. Like the cross, most of the village is built of immortal granite, in cut blocks or in uneven stones mortared roughly together. Many houses and cottages are roofed in reed or longstraw that, when new, gleams as sleekly as the fur of a Siamese cat.

The most unusual of British thatching methods, longstraw is probably seen at its best in Devon, where its poured-on effect, flowing lightly over the tops of windows and doorways, provides a perfect foil to the heaviness of the stone. The more common reed thatch is laid on with the butt ends of the stalks all facing the outside; the butt ends are then patted into a sharply regimented surface with a tool called a leggett. But longstraw is laid on in bundles where the stalks face in both directions and are combed downwards with a side rake. It is a highly attractive technique that in Throwleigh can be seen on many of the older houses and

View from lych gate at Throwleigh

SUNLIT SPOT IN A SOMBRE SETTING

Sunshine and shadow bring out the beauty of Throwleigh, where the church lych gate opens onto the village street. But near this comfortable place of thatched roofs and old stone houses is an eerie prehistoric stone circle that measures 30 yds across – and grim Dartmoor stretches all around, giving the village a curious air of remoteness.

Shelstone farmhouse

Prehistoric stone circle

even on the church porch. Another fine thatched building is The Barton, an old farmhouse, long and low, with massive stone window surrounds.

Tucked into a corner beside the cross is a pretty, stone-backed pond surrounded by foliage of near-tropical luxuriance. From it, the village street curves up to the lych gate and to the handsome, four-square Church House. Both, of course, are deeply thatched, and beyond them is the ancient Church of St Mary. Its treasures include a celebrated Easter Sepulchre; a wooden carving of St George, in memory of a young man who was killed on a Malta convoy during the Second World War; and the figures of the Crucifixion on the rood screen that were brought from Oberammergau, in West Germany.

All about the churchyard are the airy distances of Dartmoor, with its curious and disturbing mixture of emptiness and the ancient and continuing presence of man. See especially the splendid—and still very active—medieval stone farmhouses scattered about this part of the moor, and compare them with the loneliness of the prehistoric stone circle 90 ft across that lies only a short distance from the village.

TOTNES

DEVON

9 miles west of Torquay (PAGE 26 Bc)

In 1523 Totnes was one of the 12 richest towns in England—and the wool and tin merchants' houses crammed together in the main street bear witness to this. The showpiece among them is a lovingly restored Elizabethan house, now the Totnes Museum. It contains displays of local trades, toys, costumes and the interior of a Victorian grocer's shop. There is also an exhibition of the history of computers, dedicated to Charles Babbage (1792–1871), the scientist who drew the first plans of an Analytical Engine, or calculator. Babbage was educated in the town at the King Edward VI Grammar School (now a comprehensive), and his theoretical invention was a forerunner of the computer. Fore Street climbs up from the River Dart, from which the merchants' products were exported. According to local legend, Brutus, last survivor of the

ECHOES OF A TUDOR BOOM TOWN

Houses huddle together in a town which was one of England's richest in the 16th century. Many of the Elizabethan homes of prosperous Totnes merchants were built on narrow sites in High Street and Fore Street, and were gradually extended at the back. For prestige, their owners gave them elaborately decorated fronts. One carefully restored house, now a museum, has charming carved figures on its outside timbers. In contrast, the theatre masks verge on the grotesque. Two town gates, the East and the North, survive, but the East Gate was given a facelift in 1837. The basket maker is just one of the old-style craftsmen to be found operating in Totnes.

Togetherness: the roofs of Totnes

East Gate

Elizabethan house turned museum—with guardian

Theatre mask

Willow basket maker's shop

besieged garrison of Troy, sailed up the Dart and landed near a stone on the shore. Standing on the stone, he proclaimed the foundation of the town of Totnes – from Dodonesse, 'the rocky place'. The Brutus Stone, now in Fore Street, is still used as a platform for making important announcements. But most scholars believe the town was founded by the Saxons, and that the name is derived from Totta's 'ness' or headland.

As Fore Street passes under the medieval East Gate, it becomes the High Street. The East Gate, one of the town's two surviving gates, was enlarged in 1837; the other is North Gate, higher up the hill on which Totnes stands. On the northern side of the High Street is the red-sandstone Church of St Mary. Built mainly in the 15th century, its battlemented tower is capped by four decorative pinnacles. Inside, a magnificent stone rood screen was added in 1460, along the lines of the screen in Exeter Cathedral.

Immediately behind the church is the Guildhall, built in 1553 on the site of a demolished Norman priory. The hall has its own local history collection, which includes displays of coins and paintings. The Guildhall's granite pillars date from 1616 and were taken from the old Merchants' Exchange which stood in front of St Mary's. It was demolished in 1878 to open up the view of the church.

The High Street continues past the Butterwalk and the Poultry Walk, to the remains of Totnes Castle. Built in the 12th century, the Norman castle is a classic example of the motte (mound) and bailey (outer wall) type of fortress.

Beyond the streets and houses is a graceful stone bridge across the River Dart, built in the late 1820s downstream from the sturdy foundations of the original 13th-century bridge. On the Totnes side of the river are quays and warehouses used by ships from Russia and Scandinavia, which regularly bring cargoes of timber. The Totnes Motor Museum, a fine collection of vintage sports and racing cars and motorcycles, now occupies an old warehouse on Steamer Quay.

Each Tuesday from June to September the town steps back 400 years to the first Elizabethan age. To aid charities, many residents walk the streets in Elizabethan costume, tend stalls in the Pannier Market, serve ale in the inns and wait at table in the restaurants.

• **Parking** North Street; South Street (2); Steamer Quay (2); Leechwell Street; Cistern Street; Industrial Estate; Warland (all car parks) • **Early closing** Thursday • **Market days** Tuesday (summer, Elizabethan charity market); Friday (Pannier) • **Events** Agricultural show (July); Carnival (August) • **Information** TEL. Totnes 863168 • **AA 24 hour service** TEL. Torquay 25903.

Ashprington church pulpit

OLD AND NEW TREASURES

The exquisitely carved pulpit of St David's Church, Ashprington, is modern. But the font, made of local stone, dates from Norman times. The church is dedicated to St David – unusual outside Wales – and is considered something of a beauty. Most of Ashprington's cottages are 19th century.

Norman font

Local cottages

Ashprington DEVON

3 miles south of Totnes (PAGE 26 Bc)

Hereabouts, the deep russet of the ploughland mingles with the green of the high, sloping meadows above the River Dart to produce – when the sun shines – an odd, highlighting effect upon the landscape, so that leaves and flowers seem almost to take on an inward glow. Perched high among the hills of this opulent countryside is Ashprington, a village largely composed of fairly uniform 19th-century cottages with little roofed doorways and lattice windows. The only true rebel is a black-and-white, timber-and-plaster cottage, built as a coach house also in the 19th century, with an overhung timbered upper storey, next door to the Durant Arms. With a couple of shops added, they make altogether a very attractive grouping on the

GHOST CREEK *Here at Tuckenhay, on a creek of the Dart near Ashprington, a Mr Tucker set up an industrial complex in 1806. It included a gasworks – a year before the first one in London.*

slope about the church. Steep slate steps lead from the street to the lych gate. Sheltered by its roof there is a considerately placed slate table, so that pall-bearers can rest their burden for a moment before proceeding into the churchyard. This, like most features round about, is a hill, with splendid views extending far out across country and, closer at hand, of a pond with sheep grazing about it.

The church is one of the few outside Wales to have been dedicated to St David. It boasts a tall, slim 14th-century tower and contains a fine modern pulpit and a massive Norman font. Its greatest treasure, however, is the silver-gilt chalice, from which the Sacrament has been received by parishioners since the first rector was appointed in 1267.

Above the village, the road swings around and comes to an end in a private park landscaped by Capability Brown in the 18th century, and still containing the fine specimen trees that he planted. The park is attached to Sharpham House, a Palladian mansion built on the site of an Elizabethan house by Captain Philemon Pownoll RN, in 1770, out of the considerable fortune he amassed in prize-money in the wars against France.

But Captain Pownoll did not enjoy his new home for long. As his monument in the church puts it, he preferred 'the perils of the ocean . . . to a life of ease and tranquillity which his affluence would have afforded', and was killed in action in June 1780.

At the bottom of the hill below the village there is a side creek of the Dart, and a sign pointing along it to Tuckenhay. Here, in 1806, a Mr Tucker built up a business of paper milling and exporting road stone. He also built a gas house to supply the district with gaslight at a time when it was a novelty in London.

The industries have faded, but the workers' cottages, quays and warehouses remain, gradually being translated to other uses, such as flats and boathouses, and a winery specialising in a wine produced from apples. Should the visitor wish to ponder on the

changeability of things, he could wander along the quay to the Maltsters' Arms, or sit in the garden of the pretty, stone Watermans' Arms and let the green waters of the Dart, and time, slip gently by.

Cockington DEVON

9 miles south-east of Ashburton (PAGE 26 Bc)

Delightful Cockington works for Torbay Corporation and does a very thorough job. Its profession is to attract visitors by being the most Devonish village in England, and never was soil redder, nor approach lanes deeper or banked with a greater profusion of flowers. Never was thatch more smoothly laid.

The centre of the village is the Old Forge – it really is a very old forge, dating from the 14th century, but nowadays it sells horse brasses and miniature hand-made horseshoes. Nearby cottages have other merchandise to offer the strolling customer.

There is the big, opulently thatched Drum Inn that was architect Sir Edwin Lutyens' idea of a country pub in 1934, and next to it is the Old Mill, now a cafe, where a huge iron water wheel still turns.

At the top of the hill is the incredibly rustic Higher Lodge, whose projecting upper storey is supported by tree trunks. This marks the entrance of Cockington Court park – now a public park – and in its midst is Cockington Court itself, a pleasant mixture of Georgian and Tudor.

Away from the centre of the village, Cockington's charm becomes rather more relaxed – though just as pretty. The square-towered Church of St George and St Mary grew up from a Norman chapel built in about 1075. Thatched and slated buildings are backed by banks of magnificent trees. To complete this picture, a diamond-clear stream runs down a rocky channel by the roadside; and to appreciate the ensemble you

Devon delight . . . a Cockington view

THIS BE DEAR OLD DEVON!

Delightful thatched houses ringed by trees . . . everyone's idea of the romantic British countryside. In some ways the show village of Cockington may seem almost too heavenly Devonly, even too commercial. Rose Cottage, for instance, sells Devon violet perfume and it has both Ye Olde Wishing Well and Ye Olde Stocks in the garden. The Old Mill has been made into a cafe, but its iron wheel still turns, and in spite of all, Cockington remains, perhaps surprisingly, a genuinely beautiful village.

The Old Mill, with real wheel

Rose Cottage

Stream and footbridge

do not even have to walk, since the village is constantly perambulated by a picturesque horse and carriage.

Cockington lies deep in a hollow which has protected it from the winds off the sea and from the sight of Torquay's steady advance inland. It really is a very pretty place, and is fairly light-hearted about it – even if cottages that do not sell anything have to put up notices to declare the fact.

Rattery DEVON

4 miles west of Totnes (PAGE 26 Bc)

Ale came to Rattery about 100 years before the parson, if the Church House Inn was indeed founded in the 11th century as its sign proclaims. There is no particular reason to doubt it. It is a long, low, stone-flagged, snug sort of place that would have been just as enticing to visitors 900 years ago as it is today.

Rattery is a little, helter-skelter village, whose lanes swirl down a hillside, opening up now and then to reveal groups of thatched, whitewashed cottages, pleasant, modernish houses, or old stone farms. On one side there is the great dun sweep of Dartmoor climbing up to Brent Hill; and on the other, the lower hills of green meadows marching off to Torbay.

At the peak of the village is St Mary's with its lofty churchyard, whose gravestones look down upon the roofs of the village. The first vicar was appointed in 1199, which is about the period of the nave, the chancel and the unusual red-sandstone font. The remainder is 13th and 15th century, though the Victorians added plasterwork in a sprightly pattern in an entirely successful attempt to enliven the dark stone interior. Sadly, it is subject to attack by damp, which is hardly surprising, since apparently the average rainfall is something like 60 in. a year.

A short distance off, by the Exeter to Plymouth road, is a large Georgian mansion that used to be called Marley House, but has been renamed Syon Abbey by the Bridgettine nuns who live there. It is named after their original foundation on the western outskirts of London, from which they were expelled at the Reformation. The community moved to the Continent and remained there until its resettlement in England in 1861. Four miles west of the village, near South Brent, is Lydia Bridge, where a couple of cottages overlook an ancient packhorse bridge and the River Avon – here a stream of rapids and waterfalls.

Stoke Gabriel DEVON

5 miles south-east of Totnes (PAGE 26 Bc)

Half a century or so ago, the reigning squire of Stoke Gabriel dammed the mouth of a creek of the Dart estuary, so that it no longer drains away at low tide, and the village rises tier upon tier from what is in effect a lake, with steep woods climbing up its far side. The situation is quite lovely, and a fair number of people have seized upon it and inserted modern houses among the old cottages and up the near-vertical buttercup-strewn meadows. One of the things that distinguish new from old are names like Hunter's Moon and Yvantide among the more traditional Hillside, Vine and Jasmine cottages.

On the whole, it is still the older Stoke Gabriel that commands. There is the mainly 15th-century Church of St Mary and St Gabriel which has an ancient, guardian yew; and near by there is a plunging, narrow lane labelled, imaginatively and accurately, Combe Shute. This is a breathtaking curve of whitewashed stone cottages with brightly painted woodwork. About halfway down there is the Victoria and Albert, a ruggedly handsome pub that looks considerably older than its namesakes. There are a couple of other fine inns in the village: the Church House, also built of massive, rough stones; and The Castle, looking for all the world like an 18th or 19th-century castellated stage set.

Perhaps Stoke Gabriel is just a little touristy, but it does very well by visitors and residents alike with its pretty shops and restaurants and, most memorably, with its flowers. Many of the houses are surrounded by high stone walls that in season are a riotous, delicious mass of wisteria, lilac and valerian.

Combe Shute cottages, Stoke Gabriel

FLOWER POWER IN THE SHUTE

The splendidly named Combe Shute is a lovely lane plunging down through Stoke Gabriel. It has fine whitewashed cottages – some with seashell patterns round the doorways – and in every nook and cranny flowers growing in profusion.

Doorway with seashells

MAP 4

DOONE COUNTRY AND THE BRENDON HILLS

Here are the high moors and green valleys where the fierce Doone family held sway in the 17th century – and were later immortalised by R. D. Blackmore in his romantic novel *Lorna Doone*. Rugged cliffs and tempting beaches are mixed on an equally romantic coast, where Bideford bred seamen who fought with Grenville. And the tree-clad Brendon Hills rise in the east.

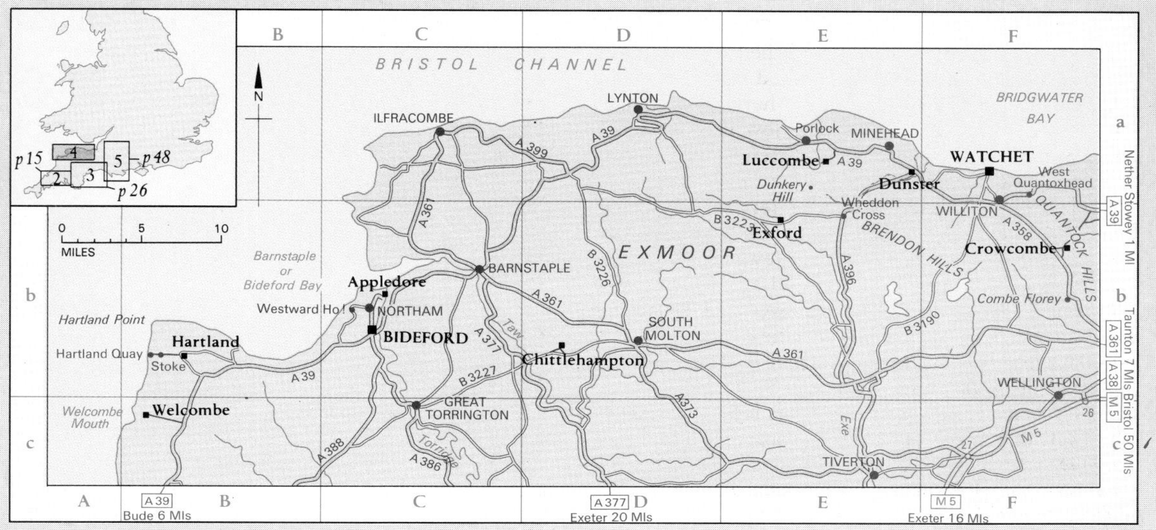

MAP 4: NEIGHBOURING AREAS – MAPS 2, 3, 5

BIDEFORD Appledore Chittlehampton Hartland Welcombe
WATCHET Crowcombe Dunster Exford Luccombe

BIDEFORD

DEVON

9 miles south-west of Barnstaple (PAGE 39 Cb)

Bideford rises in tiers of sedate, stone houses from The Quay – the town's mile-long tree-shaded main street. Here at the waterside, coasters dock and unload timber from the Continent – reminders of the time, 300 years ago, when Bideford was North Devon's chief port.

Just off The Quay is the town's most graceful thoroughfare, Bridgeland Street, climbing steeply up into the town proper. Laid out in the late 17th century, Bideford retains its period charm and appearance – especially as some of its former cloth and wool merchants' houses are still standing.

Bideford straddles the River Torridge, and its narrow, crooked streets look down on the 677 ft long bridge spanning the water. Originally built of timber in the 14th century, the bridge has 24 arches, each a different width. It was clad with stone in the 15th century, and has been strengthened and widened over the centuries since. The bridge links the main part of the town with the suburb dubbed 'East-the-Water'.

In 1854, the novelist Charles Kingsley (1819 – 75) wrote part of *Westward Ho!* in Bideford. He was renting Northdown House, still standing off The Strand. His exciting tale of Elizabethan seamen and their exploits was published the following year, and the opening scenes are set around Bideford.

Mariners from the town did, in fact, fight the Spanish Armada in July 1588, and enemy cannons captured from ships of the Armada are set around the former bandstand in Victoria Park. Bideford men also formed the crew of the *Revenge*, in which the flamboyant naval commander Sir Richard Grenville engaged a fleet of Spanish treasure ships off the Azores three years later. Sir Richard and many of his crew were killed in the one-sided encounter.

The Royal Hotel, built in the late 17th century around a merchant's house, represented Bideford at its most prosperous and elegant. It still has some magnificent plasterwork of the time – including a ceiling famed for its intricate foliage and flowers. Its main staircase is suitably broad and sweeping.

Before the bridge was built to 'East-the-Water', travellers had to ford the river at its most shallow point at the southern end of the town. This is marked by Old Ford House, which dates in part from medieval times. It is now a West Country arts and crafts gallery. The Torridge still plays an active role in the town's life, and each year, usually during the first week in September, the Bideford Regatta is held on it. On the west bank of the Torridge a riverside walk leads to the village of Appledore.

• **Parking** The Quay; The Pill; Bridge Street (all car parks) • **Early closing** Wednesday • **Market days** Tuesday, Saturday

Bideford – bridge and town

Bideford – The Quay

Rainhead in Bridgeland Street

WITH A VIEW TO THE PAST

Looking at Bideford is like going back in time, for most of the trim terraced houses rising in snug rows above the riverside date from Victorian days and earlier. At the quayside, yachts and working coasters wait for the tide. Back in town, an ornate black-and-gold rainhead neatly decorates the mellow brickwork of a 17th-century merchant's home.

• **Cinema** The Strand, Kingsley Road • **Events** Water festival (July or August); Regatta Week (September) • **Information** TEL. Bideford 77676 (summer) • **AA 24 hour service** TEL. Barnstaple 45691.

Appledore DEVON

4 miles north of Bideford (PAGE 39 Cb)

Sheltered from Atlantic storms by a hill, Appledore hugs the contour of the Torridge estuary as it curls around the promontory to meet its sister river, the Taw. The combined rivers reach the open sea about 2 miles to the north-west of Appledore. This is a perfect site for a fishing and shipbuilding village, and there is evidence of salmon fishing in the river here as far back as the 9th century.

Today, as in the past, the water is the focus of attention in Appledore – at every turn of the narrow streets above the Quay there are glimpses of the blue estuary, animated with white and red triangles of sails.

The brilliant colours of the waterside are echoed in the cheerful paintwork of the houses. The Georgian and Victorian ship-owners and master mariners built themselves sober and imposing residences in commanding positions above the village. Several of these can be seen in Odun Road and one of them, Odun House, is now the North Devon Maritime Museum. A thousand years of local seafaring history is shown in models, documents and photographs.

On the steep slopes below, the maze of streets – some too narrow for cars – were built to house more humble seamen and fisherfolk. Cobble gutters run down the centre of the streets and occasionally garden walls are built from sea cobbles. Tucked away from the larger streets are tiny courtyards – called 'drangs' by the locals – ringed with small houses. Few of the houses have space for gardens, but many are decorated with hanging baskets and pots of colourful plants.

Elizabeth I is said to have been so impressed with the courage of Appledore's seamen at the time of the Spanish Armada in 1588 that she made the village a free port for all shipping – as it is still to this day.

It has a large shipbuilding industry, and a vast hangar beside the estuary south of the village is one of the largest covered shipyards in Europe. Two ships of 5000 tons each can be built side by side beneath its roof.

In total contrast, to the west of the village and facing the open sea, a more modest shipyard builds wooden vessels. Fishing boats are the mainstay of this firm's work, but they have also built full-scale working replicas of historic ships, such as Sir Francis Drake's flagship the *Golden Hind*. Like the original, the modern *Golden Hind* has sailed around the world without mishap. It docks nowhere permanently and visits ports all over the world – from San Francisco to Liverpool.

Chittlehampton DEVON

16 miles east of Bideford (PAGE 39 Db)

With the heather-clad uplands of Exmoor only a buzzard's flight to the north-east, Chittlehampton snuggles down in a more intimate landscape of rolling green hills. The narrow winding lanes approaching the village are sunk beneath high leafy banks, decked with flowers in summer and offering an occasional glimpse of an impressive many-pinnacled church and tower that appear to rise in isolation out of the fields.

The hedge banks that divide the country into a variegated green jigsaw of small fields are a clue to the great age of the farms around Chittlehampton; and a clue to the antiquity of the village itself is the arrangement of cottages huddled tightly together in a steep-sloping square below the church.

About 1200 years ago a Saxon settlement occupied this same site. There are no signs of the original Saxon houses, but the present buildings are an attractive blend of 16th to 19th-century styles, some built in stone, some in whitewashed cob. Several cottages in the square and in the main street of the village are thatched; some even have thatched porches.

The square is the hub of the village, with the post office, the Bell Inn, the Wesleyan chapel of 1858 and the village school facing the cast-iron village pump that stands in solitary splendour on a raised cobbled plinth in the middle. Commanding the square on the north side is the Church of St Hieritha, crowned by a magnificent tower built in the 16th century that soars to a height of 115 ft.

In the churchyard an avenue of lime trees, their branches woven together into a tunnel, make a guard of honour that invites the visitor inside. Rebuilding in the late 15th century and restoration in Victorian times have hidden almost all the evidence that the church was a place of pilgrimage in the Middle Ages.

The faithful came here from far and wide to visit the shrine of Chittlehampton's own saint, Hieritha, or Urith. Tradition has it that she was a Celtic girl, born in the 6th century at East Stowford, a mile to the north of the village. She was converted to Christianity by missionaries from Glastonbury, but as a Christian she was made a scapegoat for a severe drought.

Goaded by Urith's jealous stepmother, the Saxon villagers butchered her with haymaking scythes. Inside the church a curious recess on the north side of the sanctuary is all that remains of Urith's shrine, and there is a rustic carving of the saint on the pulpit that dates from about 1500. At the eastern end of the village a modest little well, with a stone slab set into a modern wall, is known as St Teara's (yet another version of Urith) Well. It was at this spot that she fell, and legend says that as she died water gushed out of the ground and flowers blossomed all about.

Hartland DEVON

14 miles west of Bideford (PAGE 39 Bb)

At the extreme north-west tip of Devon the rocky coastline dips to the south, creating a corner of land which is occupied by the huge parish of Hartland. Atlantic waves beating against the western shore with furious power have smashed the cliffs into strange configurations of rock. Gales have bent the trees into an attitude of submission, so that they cower away from the sea even on the calmest day.

The village stands 2 miles inland, on high ground between two wooded valleys. Terraces of stone and whitewashed cob houses line the long main street, which opens into a small square. The most handsome houses in the village face the square – one of them Georgian, stone-built with shutters. A chapel in the square is now used as the village music and arts centre. The clock above the door is dated 1622 and is the oldest

UNDER A CANOPY OF LIMES

From every approach to Chittlehampton, the soaring tower of St Hieritha's Church catches the eye. In the churchyard, a shady avenue of limes forms a green canopy overhead. The cottages near by are a fine advertisement for the resident thatcher, whose skills are in demand not only in the village, but all over the West Country.

Churchyard avenue of limes

St Hieritha's Church, Chittlehampton

Cottages in the village square

in North Devon. Hartland is largely an agricultural community and a stronghold of Devon custom. Craftsmen in the village include a chair-maker and potters, and there has been a blacksmith hammering away here for generations.

The parish church of St Nectan is over a mile from the main village, at the pretty hamlet of Stoke. Its 128 ft tower can be seen from far out to sea, standing sentinel behind the cliffs – it was a landmark for mariners before Hartland had its own lighthouse.

A huge ash tree, gnarled and contorted by the wind, guards the gate to the church. The interior is magnificent. Dating from the 14th century, the spacious south aisle is roofed with bold and richly painted stars. The 15th-century screen is outstanding, 45 ft long and intricately carved. Steps from the north porch lead up to a little 'Pope's chamber', where the priest or sexton used to sleep in pre-Reformation days to guard the church and its treasures; it is now a small museum, and among its more fascinating exhibits are, of all things, fox traps.

From the churchyard, by the wicket gate to the east, a marked path drops down to St Nectan's Well. St Nectan, as legend tells, was a Celtic missionary from Wales who reached Hartland in about AD 500. Leaving his hermit's hut one day he was beset by robbers in the woods and one of them cut off his head. The saint proceeded to pick up his head and carry it back to the spring near his hut. One happy detail of this macabre legend is that every drop of blood that Nectan spilt sprang up into a foxglove – an explanation for the profusion of these flowers in June along the leafy lanes of Hartland.

West of Stoke the road ends at Hartland Quay. A few local boats can be launched from a slipway here, but the quay itself was broken up by storms in the 19th century – its great stones, weighing several tons each, were tossed along the shore like so many marbles. A museum at the Hartland Quay Hotel charts the eventful history of this coast.

A coastal footpath leads $2\frac{1}{2}$ miles north to Hartland Point – or the Promontory of Hercules as the Romans called it. Standing about 350 ft above the sea, it commands fine views to Bideford Bay in the east, the island of Lundy in the north-west and south-west to Cornwall. Below the headland is Hartland's lighthouse and a mile east Shipload Bay, with a pebble beach backed by cliffs owned by the National Trust.

Welcombe DEVON

18 miles south-west of Bideford (PAGE 39 Bc)

Tucked away in the 'farthest corner of Devon', tiny Welcombe is bordered to the west by the wild Atlantic and to the south by a stream across which Cornwall begins. The scattered farmhouses, built of stone and cob for the most part, crouch low against the winds which whip up the valley from the sea.

There is no village street, only a sprinkling of houses in isolated clusters, linked by high-banked lanes which are ablaze with primroses and violets in spring, pink campion and foxgloves in summer.

The venerable little church is, like that of Stoke (see above), dedicated to St Nectan. It has a 14th-century screen said to be the oldest in Devon – and is floored with 17th-century gravestones. There is also some 15th-century paintwork in the roof. Below the church, beside the lane leading to the beach of rocks and sand, is another St Nectan's Well. Its clear, cold and delicious spring waters were believed to have healing properties. If so, Welcombe must have been as healthy as its name before mains water reached the village in about 1960 – until then the well was the only water supply for the cottages near the church.

A mile west of the village is Welcombe Mouth, a cove of rocks and pebbles and a narrow strip of sand where a stream runs through a valley before cascading down to the beach. The valley was the haunt of 'Cruel' Coppinger, a smuggler and wrecker who terrorised the district in the 18th century. He was the leader of a wild gang which is said to have lured ships onto the rocks with lights, then plundered the wrecks. The authorities nearly caught up with him once, but in the nick of time Coppinger escaped onto a ship – never to be seen here again. From Welcombe Mouth the Somerset and North Devon Coast Path leads 5 miles north along the cliffs to Hartland Quay.

WATCHET

SOMERSET

19 miles west of Bridgwater (PAGE 39 Fa)

The Ancient Mariner is thought to have set out on his 'fateful voyage' from this small and attractive port. The poet Samuel Taylor Coleridge (1772 – 1834) visited Watchet while holidaying in the area with William Wordsworth and his sister Dorothy. Coleridge almost certainly based his famous poem – *The Rime of the Ancient Mariner*, published in 1798 – on one of the old salts whom he met by the harbour.

The port was founded by the Saxons, and during the 19th century it flourished by exporting locally mined iron ore. But in 1894 the iron mines were closed and in the winter of 1900 the harbour was wrecked by a fierce storm, tidal waves washing away the wooden piers. Nonetheless, the present harbour was built immediately afterwards and today the port does a brisk trade. It deals in cargoes that include wine and steel.

WHITE WALLS, WHITE WATER

Spanned by a weathered stone bridge, the Washford river foams and froths its way past the thatched and whitewashed Waterloo Cottages at Watchet. The aristocratic Wyndham family has several brass monuments in St Decuman's Church – including one to John Wyndham and his wife Florence, who both died in the late 16th century. A niche in the church tower contains a figure of St Decuman, who was murdered in the 6th century.

Waterloo Cottages, Watchet

Watchet is a pleasing mixture of old stone houses and cottages, studded with handsome, late Georgian or early Victorian mansions. These include Market House on the corner of the harbour and Market Street, and the National Westminster Bank in Swain Street. The town climbs up to grassy high ground overlooking the seafront, on which stand a Baptist chapel and a 15th-century Anglican church.

The chapel was built in 1824 and is painted a fetching pale blue and cream. The church is dedicated to the 6th-century Welsh monk Decuman, who, according to legend, sailed to north Somerset on a raft – accompanied by a cow which gave him milk during the voyage. Settling in the district, he lived the life of a hermit, bothering no one and communicating only with God. One day, while kneeling at prayer, he was decapitated for no known reason by an unknown assassin. A figure of the murdered saint is set in a niche in the church tower.

St Decuman's has a fine Jacobean pulpit and a wagon roof supported by figures of angels. There are also some monuments to the local Wyndham family who originally lived at nearby Kentsford Farm. Among the monuments are some 16th-century brass likenesses of the major members of the same family mounted on the walls. The grandest monument is to Sir John Wyndham, who died in 1574.

● **Parking** Anchor Street; Market Street; Swain Street (all car parks) ● **Early closing** Wednesday ● **Event** Carnival (July) ● **Information** TEL. Watchet 31824 (summer) ● **AA 24 hour service** TEL. Taunton 73363.

Crowcombe SOMERSET

7 miles south-east of Watchet (PAGE 39 Fb)

The top of what was once the church spire lies half forgotten and gathering moss in the churchyard here – a relic of a dramatic December afternoon in 1725. Worshippers were just arriving for evensong amid a gathering storm when a great bolt of lightning struck the church. The top of the spire was brought crashing through the roof, causing much damage. But the worshippers, who had taken shelter in the porch, were unharmed. They set the fallen top of the spire where it has remained ever since – you can find it just beyond the east window. The Church of the Holy Ghost – duly repaired after the incident – has a splendidly carved late 14th or early 15th-century font, and the now spireless red-sandstone tower is 14th century.

There are many who consider Crowcombe to be the fairest of the Quantock Hills villages. A delightful ribbon of stone and cob (a mixture of mud and straw) cottages, many with thatched roofs, it slumbers contentedly on the lower slopes, looking across rich farmland to the Brendon Hills. Most visitors reach the village from the Taunton to Williton road, which passes half a mile to the west. But the best approach is over the Quantocks from Nether Stowey, 5 miles to the north-east. As you descend into Crowcombe a canopy of trees frames a glorious view over the surrounding countryside.

In medieval times the village was an important junction on the hill crossing from Taunton to Bridgwater Bay. It had a market as long ago as 1226, and a stone market cross that still stands at the centre of the village served also as a focal point for the annual fair, which began in 1234. Sadly, there is neither market nor fair nowadays, but the steps of the cross bear the marks of wear from those who, all those centuries ago, traded and roistered here.

Close by, opposite the church, is the 15th-century Church House, with mullioned windows and a Tudor door. It served originally as a sort of parish hall, where villagers could hold meetings and celebrations. Holy ale was brewed and holy bread baked for medieval church suppers; travelling tradesmen could sell their wares here and seek shelter for the night. For almost 200 years, up to 1871, the building was used as a school and almshouse, and, stout as ever, still serves the parish as a village hall.

Across the road, at the end of a long drive, is the huge, red-brick mansion, Crowcombe Court. The house was begun about 1725 by a Devon architect, Thomas Parker, who was later sacked for theft. Building was eventually completed ten years later by a Wincanton man, Nathaniel Ireson, for the lord of the manor, Thomas Carew.

Wyndham family memorial brass, Watchet

Dunster SOMERSET

7 miles west of Watchet (PAGE 39 Ea)

Dunster is a dream of a West Country village, watched over by an ancient castle, full of old buildings with intriguing nooks and crannies, and possessed of a venerable church whose quirky history reflects the salty character of the local people. Add to these the Bristol Channel and Exmoor as backdrops, and you may understand why there is a story that the Victorian hymn-writer Mrs Cecil Alexander composed the words for *All Things Bright and Beautiful* while walking on nearby Grabbist Hill.

The Norman Mohun family built Dunster's first castle shortly after the Conquest, on the natural hill overlooking the High Street. They died out after 300 years and it was then bought by the Luttrell family, who in turn owned it for six centuries until 1976. Their occupation was continuous except for short periods

Dunster Castle and Yarn Market

The Nunnery

Monks' dovecote

Inside the dovecote

Gallox Bridge

Old water mill

ASPECTS OF DUNSTER

Three thousand pounds may not sound much today, but it was enough in the late 14th century to pay for the building of Dunster Castle. Below it, equally eye-catching, is the Yarn Market, where merchants once came to buy Dunster cloth. Visitors to the priory stayed at the slate-hung house called The Nunnery. The monks' circular dovecote is another memento of the Middle Ages—as is the Gallox Bridge over the River Avill. Near by stands a 17th-century water mill, still used to grind flour.

when the family chose the losing side in civil wars.

Sir James Luttrell died after the second Battle of St Albans in the Wars of the Roses, and his family lands were taken over by Yorkist enemies until Henry VII came to the throne in 1485 and restored them. The second time round, the family were even luckier. Thomas Luttrell held the castle for the Roundheads in the Civil War, then handed it over to the Cavaliers, who were eventually besieged. For 160 days the Royalists under Colonel Francis Wyndham fought off their enemies. The Roundhead general, Robert Blake, is said to have threatened to put Wyndham's mother between the firing lines to force a surrender, but backed down when the grand old lady urged her son to do his duty regardless. Eventually, in 1646, the defenders of the last Royalist stronghold in Somerset marched out battered and ill, but with drums beating and colours flying, in honourable surrender.

Cromwell had much of the castle pulled down, but the Luttrells returned at the Restoration of Charles II and turned what remained into a magnificent house. To this period belong the oak and elm staircase, carved with lively hunting scenes, and the splendid plaster ceiling of the dining room. Later centuries, too, brought their additions – a chapel in the 18th, two new towers and living accommodation in the 19th. The 20th century brought death duties which finally led to the National Trust taking over the castle.

As lords of the manor, Luttrells were dispensing local justice in the 15th century – which may have been something of a headache if surviving records are true. In 1493 John Huyshe and Jerard Goldesmyth were ordered to stop their wives quarrelling and abusing neighbours, goings-on which cost them a fine of one pound. On another occasion, no fewer than 86 people were fined 6d ($2\frac{1}{2}$p) for brewing ale at home – a prerogative the lord liked to keep to himself.

The villagers' contentiousness led, ironically, to the finest feature in St George's parish church. The living had been given to Benedictine monks by William de Mohun (1138 – 50), and the villagers were eternally squabbling with them about which bit of the church belonged to whom. In 1498, after centuries of quarrels, a rood screen was built to form a new choir where the villagers could hold their own services. The screen, 54 ft long, fan-vaulted and with richly carved friezes, is one of the country's finest.

Within 50 years the monks were swept away by the Dissolution, but remnants of their buildings include a circular dovecote with a revolving ladder. There is also the Old Priory, now a private house, and a tithe barn.

Among other fine buildings is the Luttrell Arms, which was altered between 1622 and 1629 by George Luttrell. It has a hall, probably dating from the 15th century, which was a guesthouse for the Cistercian monks from nearby Cleeve. The hall has a hammer-beamed and vaulted ceiling and an ancient fireplace. There is also a gatehouse with openings for arrows. In Church Street is another venerable building misleadingly called The Nunnery – a name given to it in the 18th century. This three-storey, slate-hung house was built at the end of the 14th century and originally known as the Chantry of St Lawrence. It served as a guesthouse for visitors to Dunster Priory and was owned by the Benedictine monks. In the market place the Yarn Market, an octagonal structure built about 1590, reflects the old industry of the village. Merchants would arrive here to buy the local cloth, called Dunsters, which was noted for quality and strength.

Old-world images are everywhere in Dunster – lattice windows, odd chimneys, doors on medieval hinges, a churchyard yew tree said to be 1000 years old, a restored water mill. Only one place is not what it seems; Conygar Tower, the landmark facing the castle from the opposite end of the High Street. It is not medieval but, that most English of buildings, a folly, built in 1775 as one of the improvements then being made to the castle and its estate.

Exford SOMERSET

17 miles west of Watchet (PAGE 39 Eb)

Exford's glory is not the usual rich historic sense of continuity built up over the centuries but an instant treasure, acquired with the help of a tape measure and the collecting plate.

In 1857, the old Church of St Audrey at West Quantoxhead was pulled down for rebuilding and its superb 15th-century fan-vaulted rood screen packed away in pieces in a barn. It lay there for 40 years until Church authorities realised they had a masterpiece on their hands. It was unpacked with a view to putting it together again in Williton church, near Watchet. However, it would not fit, and so was sent to South Kensington, London, for possible display in the Victoria and Albert Museum. This proved impractical, so a search was started for a church of the right size that was willing to pay for the screen to be put up. St Mary Magdalene, Exford, proved inch-perfect, and the villagers generous – they collected £700. So the perfect match was made and the screen looks now as if it has been there for centuries, although it was only installed in 1929.

The church itself is half a mile outside the village, on the Wheddon Cross road. It is mid-14th century with clustered pillars and a quaint carved group of a demon and angels outside the west window. The village is on lower ground, with Georgian and Victorian cottages of brick and stone, many painted cream, grouped round a green.

Exford is in hunting and fishing country, and the Exe is a youthful river here, yet still making an impressive sight after heavy rains as it rushes under the stone bridge near the gabled White Horse inn. The village is the centre of the Devon and Somerset stag hunt and the kennels, stables and houses for the hunt servants are here. The blacksmith's forge is largely kept busy shoeing horses for the hunt. In the Auction Field by the river, sheep auctions are held three times a year. Although the village is set in pleasant fields, there is bleak moorland only a mile from the centre.

The churchyard gives a fine view over the moors and the Exe Valley, to the hills along which a prehistoric route ran from Bridgwater to Barnstaple. This route kept to the hilltops as the valleys were densely forested – the blackened trunks of ancient oaks are still found only a few feet beneath the soil.

Luccombe SOMERSET

17 miles west of Watchet (PAGE 39 Ea)

A modest plaque on the north wall of Luccombe church commemorates a hero who might have stepped from the pages of a West Country romance – perhaps *Lorna Doone*, which brought fame to the combes and moorland a few miles beyond Porlock.

Henry Byam was born in the village rectory and succeeded his father as rector. He was chaplain to the exiled Charles, Prince of Wales, and he took up arms in the Civil War, with his five sons as captains. However, he was defeated and captured in 1643 by Robert Blake, Parliament's all-conquering general in the West. Byam escaped to rejoin the fighting again,

Cottage with bread oven in Stony Street

Stream and cottage with bread oven

TALL CHIMNEYS AND FRESH BREAD

A growing taste for freshly baked bread in the 17th century and onwards resulted in many West Country cottages having bread ovens bulging from their walls. This is so in Luccombe, where some of the cottages also have tall chimneys on their sides — a building fad of the time. The village's prettiest little houses — some with thatched and others with tiled roofs — are found in and around Stony Street. By itself, the name Stony Street might suggest a bleak, unfriendly road. But no street with a stream chuckling through it, and with so many cheerful flowers, could be anything but pleasing. Just beyond the cottages, casting an approving eye on the scene, is the Church of St Mary.

Stony Street and St Mary's Church

but his wife and daughter were drowned fleeing across the Bristol Channel. After the Royalists' defeat, Byam shared the exile of Charles II while his arch-enemy Blake went on to glory as Cromwell's 'General at Sea', defeating the large and hitherto all-powerful Dutch fleet three times between May 1652 and June the following year, although he had almost no previous naval experience to call on.

But Byam returned to England when the king was restored three years after Blake's death in 1657. He lived out his days until 1669 as rector of Luccombe once more. Byam's Church of St Mary was old when he was the incumbent, dating from the 1200s and with a fine original carved roof. Let into the floor is a brass effigy of 1615, depicting in all his finery a local worthy, William Harrison. In the churchyard are the remains of a cross, which was damaged by the Roundheads.

The name Luccombe means either 'enclosed valley' or 'courting valley', or it derives from the name of a 13th-century landowner, John de Lucume. Accessible only along narrow lanes banked with hedges, the village is set in a deep hollow between the high moor and soft pastures on which cattle and sheep graze. Many of its cottages are thatched and painted cream and some have old bread ovens in their walls.

A stream rising on Dunkery Hill flows through the village, skirting the front doors of many of the cottages before disappearing under a low sandstone bridge. Its gentle burble is frequently the loudest noise in this peaceful scene.

MAP 5

HARDY'S WESSEX AND CRANBORNE CHASE

Storybook towns and villages are dotted through this rich, pleasant land, which has its own peaceful way of life that has flourished undisturbed over the centuries. According to legend, Arthur built his Camelot on the earthworks overlooking the Cadburys. Here, too, the novelist Thomas Hardy (1840–1928) immortalised people and countryside in a Wessex of his own creation. Stylish Sherborne, for example, where Sir Walter Raleigh paid court to Elizabeth I, became Hardy's Sherton Abbas, while the models for some of the chief characters of *Tess of the D'Urbervilles* lived at Melcombe Bingham in the manor house, the Bingham's family home for over 600 years.

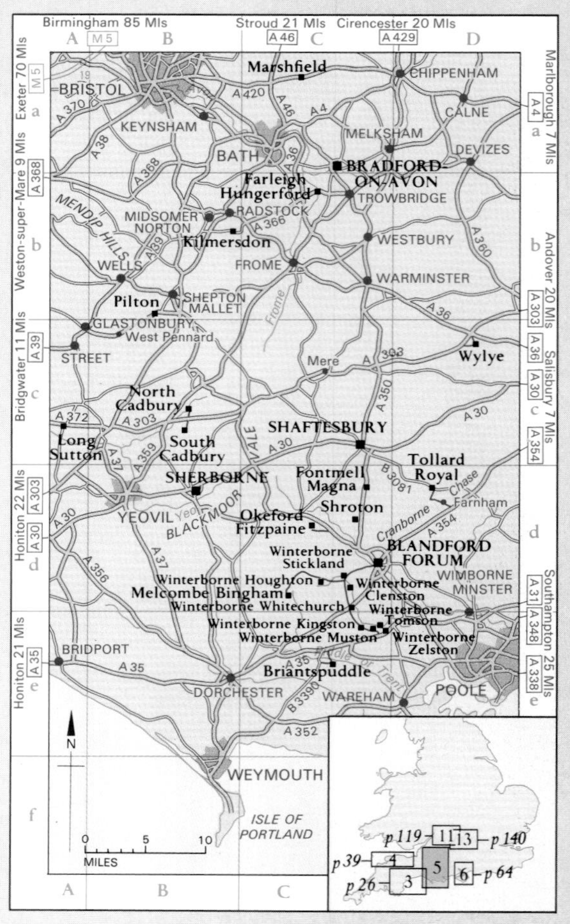

MAP 5: NEIGHBOURING AREAS – MAPS 3, 4, 6, 11, 13

BLANDFORD FORUM	BRADFORD-ON-AVON
Briantspuddle	Farleigh Hungerford
Melcombe Bingham	Kilmersdon
Okeford Fitzpaine	Marshfield
Shroton	
The Winterbornes	

SHAFTESBURY	SHERBORNE
Fontmell Magna	The Cadburys
Tollard Royal	Long Sutton
Wylye	Pilton

BLANDFORD FORUM

DORSET

20 miles north-west of Bournemouth (PAGE 48 Cd)

The elegant Georgian appearance of Blandford Forum is the result of a fire which devastated the centre of the town in the summer of 1731. The fire started in a tallow-chandler's house in the middle of Blandford, and quickly spread from one thatched building to another. The primitive, wooden fire engines were destroyed by the flames, and a strong, high wind carried pieces of blazing thatch to the neighbouring villages of Bryanston and Blandford St Mary – parts of which also burnt down.

A nationwide appeal to rebuild the town was then launched. George II gave £1000 to the fund, and two local builders, William Bastard and his brother John, were commissioned to supervise the work. They began immediately and by 1760 the 'new' Blandford had risen from the ashes of the old.

The brothers cleared many old buildings from the Market Place, and rebuilt the Town Hall and the large and handsome parish church of St Peter and St Paul – whose churchyard now contains the Bastard family tomb. Working mainly in red brick, they also rebuilt the almshouses, the grammar school and many dignified town houses.

In 1760, to commemorate the completion of the work, John Bastard designed and built the Portland stone Fire Monument – complete with Grecian columns and a triangular gable-end – which stands on its own in the Market Place. Known in the town as 'Bastard's Pump', it was meant to supply water for fire hoses in the event of a future blaze.

Part of an inscription on the back of the monument reads, 'in grateful Acknowledgement of the DIVINE MERCY, that has raised this Town, like the PHAENIX from it's ashes, to it's present beautiful and flourishing State . . .'

Not all of Blandford dates from Georgian times, however. Among the few buildings which survived the Great Fire are the mid-17th-century Old House, in The Close; Dale House, dating from 1689, in Salisbury Street; and the Ryves Almshouses, built in 1682 with money left by George Ryves, Sheriff of Dorset. East of the town are the remains of Blandford's only medieval building, St Leonard's Chapel. It was built in the 13th century as a leper hospital and rebuilt in the 15th century to house the old and infirm. A museum of local history in East Street is open daily, except Mondays, from Easter until the end of September.

Damory Street and Damory Court Street owe their names to the French nuns of Ste Marie. In the 13th century, the nuns were given this part of Blandford, which came to be known as Dame Marie's Manor. Bryanston, with its famous public school, takes its name from Brian de Insula, a wealthy Dorset landowner in the reign of Henry III (1216–72).

Blandford Forum is set at an important crossing of the River Stour and was listed in the Domesday Survey of 1086 as Blaneford, meaning 'the place by the ford'. In the 13th century it was called Cheping Blaneford until its name was changed by Latin-speaking tax officials, who translated *cheping*—the Saxon word for 'market'—into forum, or public meeting-place. The town appears in the Wessex novels of Thomas Hardy (1840–1928) as Shottsford Forum.

• **Parking** West Street; Market Place; Church Lane; Langton Road; Sheep Market Hill (all car parks) • **Early closing** Wednesday • **Market days** Thursday, Saturday • **Museum** Old Coach-house, Bere's Yard, East Street • **Events** Raft Race (June); Town Criers' contest (June); Fire Engine Rally (July); Carnival (September) • **Information** TEL. Blandford Forum 51989 (summer) • **AA 24 hour service** TEL. Bournemouth 25751.

Briantspuddle DORSET

10 miles south-west of Blandford Forum (PAGE 48 Ce)

Narrow lanes hemmed in by tall hedges crisscross the mid-Dorset countryside. They skirt the sides of grassy combes and trace a splattering way through muddy farmyards, leading the visitor suddenly to a series of hidden villages. Briantspuddle is one of these. It has no church and no inn, and consists solely of a string of whitewashed cottages with thatched roofs.

Between the two world wars Briantspuddle was part of a remarkable agricultural experiment. Sir Ernest Debenham, head of the large London store at the time, tried to bring scientific methods and factory-style efficiency to agriculture in the area, with intensive pig, poultry and dairy farming. The experiment was ahead of its time, but Sir Ernest's legacy lives on in the cottages—some of which were restored and others newly built. The Ring, for example, a group of cottages with two turrets capped with thatch, was built in 1919 as a dairy farm.

A few hundred yards west of the main street lies Bladen Valley, a hamlet purpose-built for estate workers during the First World War. Broad green verges,

Cottage and garden

On the way to milking, Briantspuddle

Thatched turret, The Ring, Briantspuddle

HIDDEN CHARMS

Hidden in the depths of mid-Dorset, Briantspuddle has a quiet charm all of its own. Like many of the surrounding villages, it owes its name to the River Piddle—'a small stream'—that flows through it. The village itself is made up of attractive whitewashed cottages, the survivors of an early attempt at scientific farming between the wars. Though that experiment was not a success, farming is still the main occupation here today. Just outside the village, in the hamlet of Bladen Valley, stands a war memorial sculpted by the artist-craftsman Eric Gill and modelled on a market cross.

War memorial, Bladen Valley

studded with clumps of daffodils in spring, sweep up past colour-washed cottages with thatched roofs. At one end of the hamlet is a war memorial sculpted in Portland stone by the artist-craftsman Eric Gill. Although it was modelled on a medieval market cross, it is entirely modern in feel. Around the base run the comforting words of the 15th-century mystic Juliana of Norwich: 'It is sooth that sin is cause of all this pain, But all shall be well and all shall be well and all manner of thing shall be well.'

Melcombe Bingham DORSET

10 miles west of Blandford Forum (PAGE 48 Cd)

Gateposts, crowned by heraldic eagles, announce the entrance to the manor house called Bingham's Melcombe and the footpath to the Church of St Andrew. Walking towards the manor house and its church is like stepping into the heart of a 19th-century romance. Indeed, the author Thomas Hardy immortalised several of the names associated with Bingham's Melcombe in his novel *Tess of the D'Urbervilles*.

One of the Bingham family married Lucy Turberville – from the family whose name Hardy altered to D'Urberville. Another Bingham, who was the rector of St Andrew's Church, appeared in the novel as Parson Tringham.

Straight ahead from the gateway stands the 14th-century gatehouse, with the church to one side. At the bottom of the churchyard Mash Water, a small stream also known as Devil's Brook, meanders slowly through woodland gardens beneath the grassy slopes of Combe Hill.

The Bingham family lived at Bingham's Melcombe for more than 600 years until 1895. The present Purbeck and Ham stone house, breathing an air of well-preserved prosperity, dates mostly from the Tudor period, but parts were refurbished in about 1720. It is not open to the public, but, from the path to the church, visitors can glimpse the terraced garden which rises behind it and which has one of the finest yew hedges in England. It was planted in the reign of Elizabeth I, and is more than 20 ft high and 20 ft wide. The ghostly Turberville coach is said to drive through the garden on Midsummer night.

The 14th-century Church of St Andrew houses many memorials to the Bingham family – one of them

Village centre, Okeford Fitzpaine

to Thomas Bingham, 'deare childe', who died aged seven months in 1711. A touching plaque dedicated by his mother expresses the wish that his dust might never be disturbed.

The village of Melcombe Bingham itself lies a mile to the north-west and can be reached by road or by public footpath. It is a happy gathering of Dorset roadside cottages – some of them thatched – which straggle along to join up with the hamlets of Higher and Lower Ansty.

Okeford Fitzpaine DORSET

7 miles north-west of Blandford Forum (PAGE 48 Cd)

Locals persist in telling the story of how an orphan was adopted by the nearby village of Child Okeford. Shilling Okeford, now the village of Shillingstone, is said to have contributed a shilling towards the child's upkeep while Okeford Fitzpaine gave five pence. Though this is a charming explanation for the names of the three villages, 'Fitzpaine' is not, in fact, a corruption of 'five pence'; the village owes its name to the Fitzpaine family, who were lords of the manor in the 14th century.

Parts of the Church of St Andrew, including the west window, date from this period, although most of the church was rebuilt in 1866, using fragments from the older church. Inside, there is a fine 15th-century stone pulpit and an east window dedicated to the memory of George Rivers Hunter, rector of the parish for 52 years from 1820 to 1872.

The church clambers up a mound overlooking the 18th-century rectory and a jumble of thatched village roofs. Behind immaculately tended borders stand cottages built of a whole range of different materials. One cottage in particular, St Lo House, is composed of distinct sections: a flint wall, then a stone section with mullioned windows and, finally, a section of timber-framed red brick. The different types of construction and the uneven lie of the land on which the village is built lend Okeford Fitzpaine a charmingly individual character.

The heart of the village is called The Cross; and here, next to the school, a tiny and venerable fire engine is preserved in a purpose-built shelter. Dated 1895, it belonged to the Okeford Fitzpaine Parish Council and was operated by the see-saw action of shafts on either side driving a pump.

Okeford Hill towers behind the village. It is linked by a ridge to Bulbarrow Hill, at 901 ft the second highest hill in Dorset. From here it is possible, on a clear day, to see the Needles, off the Isle of Wight.

Thatch and wisteria

Fire engine, 1895

PHONE RINGS IN HARMONY

Not much has changed in Okeford Fitzpaine over the centuries – and when the present intrudes in the shape of a telephone box, it is painted green to blend with the surroundings. The object is harmony rather than conformity – as can be seen from the wide range of materials used in building the village's houses and cottages. However, even here, red is the only colour for a fire engine.

Darknoll Farm, Okeford Fitzpaine

Shroton DORSET

5 miles north of Blandford Forum (PAGE 48 Cd)

It could be said that the Heights of Abraham were stormed on the grassy slopes of Hambledon Hill. For it was here that General Wolfe trained his troops before his successful attack on Quebec in 1759. A mile from the village stand three cottages that are still known as The Lines, after the army lines where Wolfe pitched his camp.

Hambledon Hill, the site of both a Neolithic and an Iron Age camp, towers more than 600 ft above Shroton – a corruption of 'sheriff's town' – which is also known as Iwerne Courtney. The village of stone, flint and brick cottages sprawls along the valley. At its southern end the Church of St Mary is flanked on one side by the garden wall of Ranston House, built in the 18th century but recently remodelled, and on the other by a magnificent thatched barn.

The church tower dates from the 14th century, but the nave and aisles were substantially rebuilt by Sir Thomas Freke in 1610. A memorial to him and his wife, erected by their sons in 1654, proclaims that 'They saw Jerusalem in Greate Prosperitie all their life long: they saw their children's children and peace upon Israel.'

This is somewhat surprising, as only nine years before – in 1645 – Hambledon Hill had witnessed a bloody skirmish. The Dorset Clubmen, a large body of some 2000 defiant Dorset men who were fed up with both the Roundheads and the Cavaliers, had banded together under the leadership of a Mr Bravel, rector of Compton Abbas, to prevent plundering by either side. They were swiftly rounded up by the Parliamentary forces, however, and 300 prisoners were secured within the church for a night.

The Winterbornes DORSET

5 miles south-west of Blandford Forum (PAGE 48 Cd/e)

The streams which run from springs high up in the chalk hills of Wessex are not really streams at all in the conventional sense of the word, since they usually flow only when the water level is high after the autumn rains. They are called winterbourns, locally. Today, however, the spring waters which feed the Winterborne river near Blandford Forum have been tapped by wells drilled through the bedrock, and the stream flows freely throughout the year.

Before joining the River Stour, the Winterborne describes a semicircle along a small, sparsely wooded valley. For most of its journey it trickles beside the grass verges of the road, dissecting the pastureland and linking a series of villages and hamlets: Winterborne Houghton, where it rises, Winterbornes Stickland, Clenston, Whitechurch, Kingston, Muston, Tomson, and – appropriately at the end of the alphabet and of a no-through road – Winterborne Zelston.

With the exception of Winterborne Zelston, none of the villages has the studied prettiness of some of the more famous Dorset villages. Apart from Winterborne Muston, each has its church and thatched cottages built of brick, stone or cob; but, because they are all workaday farming villages, they have modern houses too. This mixture is part of their charm.

All the Winterbornes have something special to offer – Winterborne Stickland has a 13th-century church, for instance – and each has a story to tell. The 11th-century Church of St Andrew in the middle of a farmyard at Tomson is the smallest in Dorset, measuring only 23 ft by 14 ft, and seating between 50 and 60 worshippers in Georgian box-pews. It was much loved by the author Thomas Hardy, the sale of whose manuscripts raised money for its restoration in 1932. The Church of St Mary at Whitechurch has a fine 15th-century pulpit, a treasure discovered purely by chance a century ago. It had come originally from Milton Abbey where, during the Commonwealth, it had been plastered over to preserve it from destruction. When the abbey was restored two centuries later, the pulpit was thrown out into the yard as worthless. It was from here that the church at Whitechurch acquired the pulpit, still covered in plaster, in 1867. One day, as the rector tried to remove a nail from it, chalk and plaster came away in his hands, revealing the carving beneath.

A series of manor houses lines the stream. At Clenston, the Tudor house has not been bought or sold since it was built, but has been passed down through the branches of the de Winterborne family. Next to it, beside the road, stands a magnificent barn with a hammerbeam roof of lavishly carved timbers. Higher Whatcombe lies a mile downstream and then, south-east of the main road, is Anderson Manor – a 17th-century mansion partly designed by Inigo Jones. Clenston Manor can be visited by arrangement and all the manors are clearly visible from the road.

Any journey through this group of Winterborne villages should end at Zelston – the most picturesque of them all. By this stage the stream which began as little more than a trickle is much broader. Willows arch gracefully over it as it passes between the Church of St Mary and Bridge Cottage – originally a row of three thatched 17th-century cottages.

Winterborne Stickland

The church at Winterborne Stickland, with its striking, high nave, dates from the 13th century. Its mellow exterior blends in well with the attractive thatched cottages and colourful gardens. The village's name is derived from the Saxon Stickel-land, *which means 'steep land'.*

Winterborne Clenston

The manor house at Winterborne Clenston has been owned by the de Winterborne family since 1230 and is largely Tudor. The roof of the barn near by is supported by seven gigantic hammerbeams.

FOLLOWING THE STREAM

In many parts of Dorset there are villages which share the same main name, which is usually derived from a prominent natural feature in the locality. The 'piddles', for example, are grouped around the River Piddle as it flows through its valley, though in some cases local custom – or propriety – has softened the original to 'puddle'. The Winterbornes, too, get their name from water – in this case, the sparkling River Winterborne, fed by springs which rise high in the Wessex hills and which once flowed only in winter. But, despite this common factor, each of the villages is still unique, with its own points of interest, character and individual charm, along the crescent course of the stream.

Winterborne Zelston

Fittingly enough, Zelston, the last, but most picturesque, of the Winterbornes is situated at the very end of a no-through road.

Winterborne Tomson

The novelist Thomas Hardy loved the 11th-century Church of St Andrew at Winterborne Tomson, and a sale of his manuscripts helped to pay for its restoration in 1932.

Winterborne Kingston

Well maintained domestic thatch and medieval church architecture combine to make a delightful grouping in this quiet corner of Winterborne Kingston.

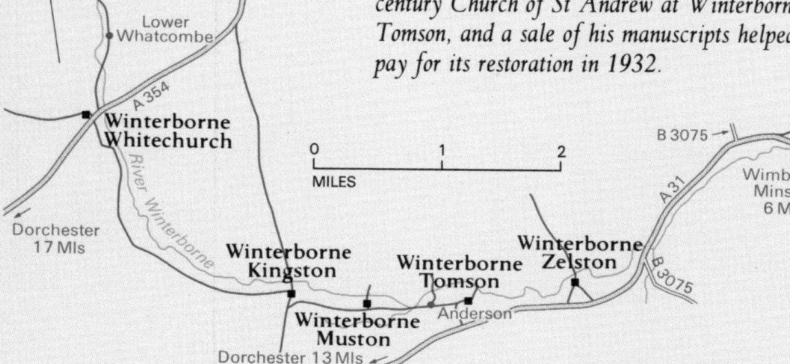

Winterborne Whitechurch

The 15th-century pulpit in St Mary's, at Winterborne Whitechurch, was discovered by chance when a 19th-century vicar dislodged some of the plaster put on to conceal its decoration at the time of the Commonwealth. In fields close by is a more traditional sight – an animal shelter.

Town Bridge, Bradford-on-Avon, and its jail

BRADFORD-ON-AVON

WILTSHIRE

9 miles south-east of Bath (PAGE 48 Ca)

One day in 1856 workmen making repairs to some cottages in Bradford uncovered two carved angels. The vicar of Holy Trinity Church, Canon William Jones, had long suspected that there was a Saxon church hidden in the town and had noticed the cruciform shape of the cottages being repaired. So, seeing the two angels, he realised that they must be Saxon and that this was probably the church he had been looking for. But he had to wait some 14 years for final confirmation. Then at last a cluster of surrounding buildings was cleared away and a pure Saxon church revealed.

The Church of St Laurence had been built about AD 700 by St Aldhelm, the Abbot of Malmesbury, Frome and Bradford. The church belonged to a monastery which was destroyed by the Danes. St Laurence's then 'vanished' for 11 centuries. A plain and simple building, made of rough-hewn stone, it is only 38 ft long. During its 'lost' years it had been used as a school, a charnel house where the bodies of the dead were left, and finally as a house. At the same time it had also been gradually hemmed in by other buildings. St Laurence's was fully restored during the 1870s and today it is one of the town's chief treasures.

Set in the green Avon valley, Bradford rises above the river on a steep limestone slope. Its terraces of houses and cottages seem to grow out of the hillside, and the buildings are mostly made of the local limestone. This gives Bradford a unity which has developed over the last 300 to 400 years.

The highest of its three main terraces is Tory, from the word 'tor' meaning 'high place'. It originally consisted of more than 30 weavers' homes; some have been restored or replaced, especially at the eastern end. Until the 1950s, the 18th-century houses at the western end had kitchens hewn out of caves in the rocky hillside. Near by, the Chapel of St Mary was originally a hospice for Glastonbury-bound pilgrims.

Lower down is the second main terrace, Middle Rank, whose late 17th-century weavers' cottages have also been rebuilt or renovated. And farther down again is Newtown, linked to the higher terraces by a steep road called Conigre Hill. 'Conigre' is an old word which means 'rabbit warren'.

Newtown can be reached by climbing up Barton Steps, which leads from Barton Orchard, another terrace of weavers' houses. Built in the 18th century as a unit, these were recently saved from falling into ruin and renovated. Just behind the terrace is Lady Well, a spring which bubbles from beneath a house built in the 17th century.

A walk across the nearby meadow takes you to the early 14th-century Barton Bridge, and to Barton Farm Country Park beyond. The farm originally provided food for Shaftesbury Abbey and, after the Dissolution of the Monasteries in the 1530s, it continued to be worked until 1971, when the farmland was made into a country park.

Close by is Bradford's other main stone-walled treasure – the 14th-century Tithe Barn. It also belonged to the abbey and housed farm produce and the tithe (one-tenth) of its yearly output which went to the nuns. Almost 170 ft long and 33 ft wide, it is one of the largest tithe barns in England. Its steeply pitched roof is supported by massive timbers.

Bradford's centre lies to the north-east. There, the name of Barton, meaning farm, is found in Dutch Barton, a block of houses in Church Street which were the homes of 17th-century Dutch weavers who brought great prosperity to the town. The chief shop-

Tithe Barn

BRIDGE THAT HAS A LOCK-UP

Though the curious domed building at one end of Bradford's Town Bridge is known as the Chapel, it was for many years the town jail. The great Tithe Barn is one of the largest in England.

ping areas are Market Street and Silver Street, which are joined by The Shambles – a narrow lane for pedestrians. It contains two fine timber-framed buildings and its post office has a rare Edward VIII monogram.

Spanning the River Avon, the Town Bridge connects the north side of Bradford to the south. The bridge has nine short arches and dates mostly from the 17th century, though two of the arches are 13th century. A small, dome-shaped building at the south end of the bridge is called the Chapel, but despite its name it was, in fact, a lock-up.

Bradford's only 'country house' is The Hall, an Elizabethan-style building near the river in the east of the town. Built in the early 17th century by a clothier named John Hall, it was restored in about 1850. The gardens are open all year. There, the main attractions include the Tudor-style stables, two temples – one probably Georgian, the other probably Victorian – and an eight-sided dovecote.

• **Parking** Bridge Street; St Margaret's Street; Station; Market Street; Tithe Barn (all car parks) • **Early closing** Wednesday • **Market day** Thursday • **Information** TEL. Bradford-on-Avon 2224 • **AA 24 hour service** TEL. Bath 24731.

Farleigh Hungerford SOMERSET

5 miles south-west of Bradford-on-Avon (PAGE 48 Cb)

A mighty castle, owned by an ancient family who were as rich, dynamic and sometimes unscrupulous as any in an American television saga, once dominated Farleigh Hungerford.

The remains of Farleigh Castle appear almost intact as you approach the village from the Trowbridge road – an immense range of towers and curtain walls rearing from the green valley of the River Frome. But entering from the Radstock road, on the western side, opposite, all is seen to be a façade. Behind the imposing front are just a few low ruins and the foundations of walls carefully preserved amid noble trees and the greensward.

The castle was started by Sir Thomas Hungerford, first Speaker of the House of Commons, whose family boasted they could ride to Salisbury and back without leaving their own lands. Sir Thomas bought the old manor from the widowed daughter-in-law of a crony of his, Lord Burghersh. He then laid out a 180 ft courtyard and surrounded it with 6 ft thick walls topped with four 60 ft towers.

The Hungerfords survived here for 250 years, weathering the turmoil of the Wars of the Roses and the Tudors – although one Hungerford was beheaded by Henry VIII on charges of treason and unnatural vice. The tower in which this wayward lord is believed to have locked up his wife for four years is still standing. Another of Henry's many axe victims was Margaret, Countess of Salisbury, who was born in the castle. She had too much royal blood to be allowed to live as a possible rival.

The castle was held for King Charles in the Civil War, but fell to the Parliamentarians without a fight. From this time on, the family went into decline and the castle, though still intact, was 'very ruinous', until in the 1730s it was acquired by a Trowbridge family, the Houltons. They were interested in it more as a quarry than as a home, and they carted away hundreds of tons of stone to embellish and develop their Gothic-style house – now a school – on the other side of the village. Nor were they the only ones to use the castle in this way; many of the village houses are built with its stone.

In 1891 the Houltons sold the sadly battered castle to Lord Donington, whose wife was Baroness Hungerford in her own right. But the re-established family connection was destined not to last, and the castle was sold again. The place is now owned by the Department of the Environment.

But the Hungerfords still make their presence felt. The family Chapel of St Leonard, intact within the protecting wall, contains an awesome throng of tombs, beginning with the plain, solid one of old Sir Thomas and going on to the grandiose marble extravaganzas of the later Hungerfords.

In the crypt are the lead coffins of six adults and two children. The adults' coffins are in human form, four with portrait heads moulded on them, giving an eerie effect in the half light. Much else from the earliest period still survives in the chapel, including a magnificent 15th-century mural of St George and some fine stained glass. The priest's house also survives near the chapel, and is an excellent little museum.

To make up for the village church which they appropriated to create this chapel, the Hungerfords provided a new one in 1443 – another St Leonard's. It is simple, but with a splendid stained-glass glowering portrait of the great Sir Thomas in armour.

Though it is at least three centuries since a Hungerford ruled this part of Somerset, the church rather touchingly maintains a 'living' representation of their coat of arms – a real wheatsheaf and two practical-looking sickles in heraldic form.

Near by is the local inn – popular in summer, for its garden gives a superb view across a valley – the village itself lying at the junction of two combes, the wooded ravines so typical of the county.

Kilmersdon SOMERSET

12 miles south-west of Bradford-on-Avon (PAGE 48 Bb)

Kilmersdon is an estate village, mostly owned by Lord Hylton of Ammerdown House, a mile to the east. It lies tucked neatly away in a combe, with a little brook forming the northern boundary, creating a delightful break with the world beyond.

There are a handful of new houses, but these are visible only from the surrounding hills. From road level, the village appears as a symphony of grey and green, the silvery stone of the buildings blending with the rich green of the meadows and, in spring, contrasting with the dandelions that bloom in profusion or the occasional yellow field of rape on the hills.

Its brightest gem is the Church of St Peter and St Paul. Even a casual glance shows that both money and care have been lavished on it over the centuries, and the 20th-century contribution is an unusual triangular lych gate designed by the architect Sir Edwin Lutyens (1869–1944). But happily the church has not been 'improved' out of recognition by its benefactors. The result is that it constitutes a practical guide to church architecture over the centuries, with work from almost every period – a Norman window, door and frieze; a 97 ft medieval tower with carved angels and fearsome beasts; a door with its date studded in nails in 1766 and Pre-Raphaelite stained glass of 1878. The highlight is the 15th-century screen in front of the north chapel.

Kilmersdon is a village for drifting round on a somnolent summer's day. There is, apart from the church, a plain, handsome Nonconformist chapel, a quaint disused lock-up – a temporary jail for drunks and other minor miscreants – and an 18th-century inn, the Jolliffe Arms.

But it is the total ambience that stays in the mind. Climb the steep hill on the far side of the brook for a general view. From here, too, you can see the neighbouring farms linked by a barely visible network of lanes, as well as the bulk of Ammerdown House. Lutyens also designed the gardens at Ammerdown, which are periodically open to the public.

The house itself was built in 1788 to the design of the architect James Wyatt, and Thomas Samuel Jolliffe, MP, moved here in 1791. He is commemorated by a stone column, 150 ft high with a lantern at the top, across the valley. It was built by his family in the 1850s and to make trebly sure that the Jolliffe name is never forgotten, the inscription on the base is carved in three languages.

SOMERSET GEM *The tiny village of Kilmersdon sparkles in the sunlight. Its church reflects the building styles of practically every historical period from the Norman onwards.*

Marshfield AVON

14 miles north of Bradford-on-Avon (PAGE 48 Ca)

A remarkable village shop existed in Marshfield until 1983. Bodman's Grocery and Drapery Store had been run by the same family since at least 1870, and the last Mr Bodman continued trading up to his death at the age of 90, having inherited the shop from his father.

In his last years, however, the place was more of a museum than a shop. The fixtures and fittings were unchanged from the early 1900s, and if Mr Bodman did not want to part with something in his stock that he had grown to like, he would simply refuse to sell it. So he preserved a little corner of old rural England.

On his death, villagers hoped that Bodman's might become an official museum, but market forces prevailed and antique dealers and curators moved in and the place was stripped. It stayed empty for a year and was sold to a local businessman who expressed the wish to retain 'the unique charm' of the shop.

The whole village is itself a remarkable survival. Its high street must be one of the longest in Britain, running for almost a mile, with the parish church at one end and the walled Crispe almshouses of 1619 – they are still in use – at the other.

Ranks of grey stone buildings, Georgian or Georgian-style, face each other across the street with scarcely a break along its length and without a hint of green. The effect could be claustrophobic, but it escapes this, probably because no two houses are exactly alike. They are large houses in the Cotswold manner, with door lintels and window frames seemingly designed to withstand a siege.

Two factors created Marshfield's prosperity: its position and its industry. The village lies along a ridge like a grey cap on the green head of the combe. Once there were 13 inns along its length, and even now three survive in a community of 1300 people.

Most of these hostelries were coaching inns – one survivor, the Catherine Wheel, is particularly stylish – for the village lay on the main Bristol to London road, a fact betokened by the precision of an 18th-century signpost which proclaims that it is '103 miles to London; 12 miles and one furlong to Bristol'.

Wool was the original creator of Marshfield's wealth and, later, malting the local grain for brewing. So skilled did the maltsters become that they were in demand for miles around – not simply because they knew their trade, but because they knew how to deal with excisemen. A house in the High Street has peepholes through which, it is said, the excisemen could be observed as they snooped around.

Although the main part of the village is a conservation area, a large new development is tucked away behind the imposing Church of St Mary, which has two choir chapels and a spectacular tower with a pierced open parapet.

The name Marshfield seems odd for a place perched on high ground, but 'marsh' is derived from march, or border. Until 1974 the borders of Wiltshire, Somerset and Gloucestershire met near by.

Shaftesbury from above

Gold Hill, Shaftesbury

In Shaftesbury Museum

THE TOWN AT THE TOP OF GOLD HILL

The hilltop town of Shaftesbury grew up around its abbey, which, in medieval times, was one of the richest in England. Trade flourished, while the rich farmland around the town fostered a way of life that remained virtually unchanged for centuries, as exhibits in the town's museum show (they even include a farmworker's smock). The pretty cottages of stone and thatch that stagger up steep Gold Hill are equally well preserved, as is the ancient public pump in St Andrew's Pump Yard.

St Andrew's Pump Yard

SHAFTESBURY

DORSET

20 miles west of Salisbury (PAGE 48 Cc)

Standing more than 700 ft high on a ridge of green sandstone, Shaftesbury is the only hilltop town in Dorset. Its summit can be reached by way of Gold Hill – steep, curved and cobbled – with old stone cottages on one side, a buttressed, medieval wall on the other, and breathtaking views of the surrounding countryside.

Perched at the peak is St Peter's Church, dating partly from the 14th century with later additions. It has fine 18th-century panelling and a 17th-century iron poor box. The church is also used for music recitals and concerts.

The Town Hall, next to it in the High Street, was built in the 1820s in semi-Tudor style. A small passageway leads from the High Street to Park Walk, which contains the ruins of a Benedictine abbey for nuns founded in about AD 888 by Alfred the Great. The

HOTSPUR GOES TO WAR ON THE SIDEBOARD

The Chevy Chase sideboard, on display at the Grosvenor Hotel in The Commons, Shaftesbury, is one of the town's chief treasures. The sideboard gets its name from the dramatic woodcarvings which decorate it, showing the rout of the English army under Henry Percy – Shakespeare's Hotspur – by the Scots at the Battle of Chevy Chase. The sideboard was made by a carpenter from Newcastle upon Tyne between 1857 and 1862, but it found its way to Shaftesbury by coincidence. The hotel owners bought the masterpiece in a sale in 1919.

king's daughter, Aethelgifa, was the first abbess, and she is thought to have presided over about 100 nuns.

The assassinated Anglo-Saxon boy king, Edward the Martyr (about AD 963–78), was buried in the abbey and thousands of pilgrims visited his tomb which they believed had miraculous healing powers. After the abbey's dissolution in the late 1530s, Edward's relics were thought to be lost. But in the 1930s the ruins were excavated, and a lead box was found containing the bones of a teenage boy. They were assumed to be those of Edward, and there is a small shrine to commemorate him on the site.

Below the abbey ruins is the parish of St James. It is named after St James's Church, built in the late 1860s at a cost of £3350. Close by is St James Street, with its terraces of stone cottages. It opens into St Andrew's Pump Yard, where an ancient pump stands.

As well as elegant town houses, Shaftesbury has its share of pretty thatched cottages – many of which are on Gold Hill, and in Bell Street, Angel Lane and St James Street. The Westminster Memorial Hospital, between Abbey Walk and Magdalene Lane, was built in the 1870s in memory of a local landowner, Richard, 2nd Marquis of Westminster.

Shaftesbury also has two unique historical attractions: the Byzant and the elaborately carved Chevy Chase sideboard. The Byzant, a curious ornamental relic, was carried by the townsfolk when they paid an annual courtesy visit downhill to the lord of the manor of neighbouring Gillingham; Shaftesbury's water came from springs at Enmore Green which fell within the borough of Gillingham. The Byzant was decked with ribbons, feathers and up to £200 worth of jewellery. The ceremony ceased in 1830 and the Byzant can now be seen in the museum. The Chevy Chase sideboard, housed in the Grosvenor Hotel, celebrates the Battle of Chevy Chase, which took place near Otterburn, Northumberland, in 1388.

• **Parking** Bell Street; Coppice Street (both car parks) • **Early closing** Monday, Wednesday • **Market day** Thursday • **Theatre** Shaftesbury Arts Centre, Bell Street • **Event** Carnival (September or October) • **Information** TEL. Shaftesbury 2256 • **AA 24 hour service** TEL. Yeovil 27744.

Fontmell Magna DORSET

5 miles south of Shaftesbury (PAGE 48 Cd)

Every three hours the church clock at Fontmell Magna chimes the time to the tune of the hymn *O Worship the King*. It inspired a villager to write:

I shall turn again to Fontmell
In the Autumn of my days,
And I'll walk among the hollows
And narrow winding ways
Which from Fontmell Wood to Compton
And from Twyford back to Pen,
Are within the sound of Fontmell
Bells, and dear to Fontmell men.

The verse of this charming poem is as true now as it ever was. At the heart of the village and its 17th-century cottages the clear waters of a chalk stream dive down a mill-race and under the road. They pass Holbrook, a cottage built of grey stone and the alternating bands of flint and red brick that are so typical of Dorset.

Springhead

On a mound above towers the Church of St Andrew, which dates from the 14th century but was extensively rebuilt in 1863. The large cross in the churchyard commemorates a local hero – Philip Salkeld, the son of a former rector of the parish. As a lieutenant in the Bengal Engineers he was mortally wounded during the Indian Mutiny of 1857 while blowing up the Cashmere Gate at Delhi.

An inscription explains how it was he 'who personally fastened the powder bags to the gates, fixed the hose, and although fearfully wounded continued to hand to a non-commissioned officer the light to fire the train'. For his heroism he was awarded the Victoria Cross.

Until the 19th century, Fontmell Magna was a self-supporting community of some 800 people. With the arrival of modern farming methods and machinery, the population declined; and by 1906 a guide book described the village as 'one of those peaceful retreats from the excitement of cities and great towns which the wearied crave and the invalid rejoice in'.

This is now only partly true. For Fontmell Magna is still at the heart of a prosperous farming community. It has its own carriage-builder and, a mile away at Bedchester, a maker of traditional harpsichords. Next to the Crown Inn, a large red-brick building which now houses the thriving Fontmell Potteries was once a brewery belonging to the Flower family. It drew its water from the stream whose spring gives the village part of its name.

The name Fontmell comes from *funta*, Old English for 'spring' and *mael*, Celtic for 'bare hill'. The stream rises east of the village at Springhead. Here, at the foot of a grassy chalk hill, there has been a mill ever since the time of the Domesday Survey. Springhead consists of a fine white-walled thatched house with a mill-building at right angles to it. Behind it stretch splendid gardens – weeping willows, herbaceous borders and a Venetian rotunda on the edge of the millpond.

In 1933, Springhead was bought by Rolf Gardiner, who promoted summer music schools at Springhead until his death in 1973. The Springhead Trust continues to develop his work. It runs courses for all ages in subjects ranging from painting to prayer, and from archaeology to environmental studies. The gardens are open to the public twice a year.

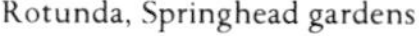

Rotunda, Springhead gardens

Fosse Cottage, Fontmell Magna

View from the church tower, Fontmell Magna

THE MUSICAL WATERS OF SPRINGHEAD

A clear, sparkling stream runs through Fontmell Magna, rising just east of the village. Here, amid spacious gardens and beside the quiet waters of a millpond, stands a house that is appropriately named Springhead. And here the owner, Rolf Gardiner, held a celebrated summer music school from 1933 until he died in 1973. A plaque in the village church commemorates him as a 'visionary and man of action, farmer, forester and writer, poet and lover of music'. In the late 19th century the famous Flower family of brewers lived in the house, and the inventive J. W. Flower, who was more interested in engineering than brewing, patented and manufactured corking and bottling machines at his Springhead works.

Tollard Royal WILTSHIRE

8 miles south-east of Shaftesbury (PAGE 48 Dd)

The village tumbles down the side of a valley in the heart of Cranborne Chase, an undulating tract of downland lying between Salisbury, Wimborne Minster, Blandford and Shaftesbury. Tangled copses and a belt of woodland running through the landscape are all that remain of forest which once covered the area. It was a forest often hunted by King John, who had a small estate at Tollard – and so the village came to be called Tollard Royal.

His name is also commemorated in the village inn, King John's Hotel, and in King John's House which dates from the 13th century. The house was once the king's hunting lodge, and owes its present superb condition to General Pitt-Rivers, who owned it in the late 19th century. It is an elegant part stone and part timber-framed building, standing in well-kept gardens behind the low green wall of an immaculately clipped box hedge. There is still a member of the Pitt-Rivers family living in the house.

General Pitt-Rivers, sometimes called the 'father of English archaeology', inherited the surrounding Rushmore Estate in 1880, and devoted the last 20 years of his life to excavating its many Bronze Age earthworks. He also laid out the park on the Wiltshire border called Larmer Tree Gardens – the Larmer Tree being the spot where King John and his huntsmen used to gather. The original tree was probably a wych elm, but there remains only the stump, from which an oak tree now grows.

A lane leads up from the village to the Church of St Peter ad Vincula ('in chains') – one of only three such dedications in England, one of the others being the chapel at the Tower of London. The village church dates from the late 13th century and houses the tomb of General Pitt-Rivers.

The general's finds were exhibited in a museum in the village of Farnham, 3 miles south-east, until the 1960s when the museum was closed and the exhibits dispersed. Most went to Oxford, but in the South Wiltshire Museum in Salisbury there is a Pitt-Rivers Gallery with some scale models and finds from Cranborne Chase. The days when Farnham's Pitt-Rivers Museum was one of the most important in the country are commemorated by the local inn, the

ROYAL RETREAT *King John's House, in Tollard Royal, was used by the king as a hunting lodge in the early 1200s. In the 19th century it was lovingly restored by General Pitt-Rivers, whose 20-year series of archaeological excavations won him the title of 'father of English archaeology'.*

Museum Hotel, and by the museum building, which was originally a school for gypsy children and is now a private house. Outside the hotel stands the village stocks where miscreants were punished.

The whitewashed and thatched cottages of Farnham are in neat rows, their backs to the north winds and their lattice windows glinting as they reflect the late morning sunlight.

An ancient cedar dominates the churchyard of St Laurence's Church, which has a 12th-century nave and 15th-century tower. Flint and green sandstone have been used to give the tower an attractive chequerboard appearance.

Wylye WILTSHIRE

16 miles north-east of Shaftesbury (PAGE 48 Dc)

Until the 1970s, Wylye was on the main road from London to Exeter. Now a bypass leaves the village in peace. It is a well-earned respite. For centuries Wylye was a major staging point between Amesbury and Mere. The Bell Inn, built in the 14th century, is now the only survivor of nine pubs in the village.

As the road winds into the village, it crosses the Wylye – the river which gave Wiltshire its name. From the bridge it is just possible to glimpse downstream a lead statue of a boy blowing a horn in the waters beside the red-brick mill building. This commemorates a post-boy who, in the days when there was a ford at this point, saved several of the passengers of a stage-coach which had overturned in the floods. He drowned in the act of doing so.

The road then curves into the main street and its row of cottages which lead to the 14th-century Wylands Cottage. Several have mullioned windows and the chequered walls of flint and Chilmark stone that are typical of this part of Wiltshire. Since 1924 many have had tiled roofs. In that year a blaze started at a farm in the village and, fanned by a strong westerly wind, set fire to the original thatched roofs as it raged along the street. Wylands Cottage hardly fits the dictionary definition of 'a small house'. Originally two cottages, it now dominates a road junction with its part stone, part timbered frontage, massive gable and steep, red-tiled roof.

The Church of St Mary the Virgin, which has a 15th-century tower, stands next to the Bell Inn. It has a richly carved oak pulpit dated 1628 and, by the south gate of the churchyard, an ostentatious tomb framed by wrought-iron railings. Tradition claims that it was built by a 'man of mean extraction' named Popjay, for his mother and sister. He left the village before he had paid for it and so, it is said, the rector settled the bill and had himself buried in the tomb.

There has long been a close association between the inn and the church; indeed, the 19th-century bell clappers from the church still hang in the fireplace of the Bell Inn.

During the Roman occupation, the valley was one of the main farming areas producing food for the

BOY HERO *This cherubic statue, on private land near Wylye bridge, commemorates the heroism of a post-boy who saved several passengers when a stagecoach overturned while fording the river.*

legions. Excavations at Bilbury Farm, a mile away, have revealed grain pits; and large edible snails imported into the country by the Romans can still be found on the southern ridge of the Wylye valley.

SHERBORNE

DORSET

6 miles east of Yeovil (PAGE 48 Bd)

The Elizabethan courtier, writer and explorer Sir Walter Raleigh had close associations with Sherborne's two castles – the old and the new. The Old Castle, set on a rocky knoll to the east of the town, was leased to Raleigh by Elizabeth I in 1592, and seven years later she gave him the freehold. At first Raleigh tried to convert the 12th-century fortress into a suitable home, but he found it impractical for his needs and decided to build himself a new castle instead.

He chose a site some 400 yds south of his original residence, and put up the present Sherborne Castle where an earlier Tudor hunting lodge once stood. The new building, dating from 1594, had four elaborate storeys, with tall chimneys and mullioned windows. One day, while sitting in the castle grounds quietly smoking his pipe, Sir Walter is said to have had a bucket of ale poured over him by an over-zealous servant. The man thought that his master – who a few years previously had popularised the smoking of tobacco from Virginia – was on fire.

Raleigh's castle looked like something out of a fairy tale, and later additions made it look even more romantic. In 1625 its owner, Sir John Digby, 1st Earl of Bristol, added four wings and four turrets. This gave the castle an 'H' shape – said to be in honour of Prince Henry, James I's gifted eldest son, who died in 1612. Then in the 18th century the celebrated gardener Capability Brown laid out 200 acres of wooded grounds, flooding Sir Walter's formal gardens to make a serpentine lake between the two castles. The Old Castle was destroyed by Parliamentary troops in the Civil War, but its ruins are still here. Sherborne Castle is open on weekend and Thursday afternoons from Easter to the end of September.

Sherborne lies amid green countryside on the north bank of the River Yeo. The town dates from the 8th century, and is a gracious blend of mainly Georgian, Regency and Victorian buildings. Since the mid-16th century, when Sherborne public school was refounded in part of the abbey buildings, the town has been noted for its fine schools. There are ten of them in all, including Lord Digby's School for Girls, which occupies a handsome Georgian house in Newland.

The town's main shopping area is Cheap Street, at the bottom of which is The Conduit, used by the Benedictine monks as a wash-house and moved to its present site after the Dissolution in 1539. From there Church Lane leads past the abbey to the Almshouse of St John the Baptist and St John the Evangelist. Henry VI granted the Bishop of Salisbury a royal licence to build the almshouse in the mid-15th century, and the bishop appointed a 'Perpetual Priest' to pray for the souls of its inmates – 12 poor men and four poor women. The almshouse's chaplain is now the vicar of Sherborne Abbey, whose choir and nave have superb fan-vaulted ceilings – the choir's fan vault is the earliest in England.

The abbey contains all the 35 available colours (flags) of the Dorsetshire Regiment (now the Devonshire and Dorset Regiment). It also has the world's heaviest ring of eight bells – a total weight of nearly 8 tons. The tenor bell is thought to have been given to the abbey by Cardinal Wolsey in 1514.

At the bottom of the town, near the railway station, are Pageant Gardens. These were laid out with the profits of the Sherborne Pageant of 1905. This grand affair, master-minded by Louis Napoleon Parker, dramatist, composer and master at Sherborne School, had an immense cast of 900 and was the mother of all modern pageants. In the 1960s Sherborne was the setting of the film musical *Goodbye Mr Chips*. Sherborne also appears in the novels of Thomas Hardy (1840 – 1928) as Sherton Abbas.

• **Parking** The Old Market; Coldharbour; Acreman Street; Culverhayes, off Long Street (all car parks) • **Early closing** Wednesday • **Market days** Thursday, Saturday • **Events** Carnival (August); Pack Monday Fair (October) • **Information** TEL. Sherborne 815341 (summer) • **AA 24 hour service** TEL. Yeovil 27744.

The Cadburys SOMERSET

7 miles north of Sherborne (PAGE 48 Bc)

On a morning when haze engulfs the low-lying Somerset Levels, the view from Cadbury Castle shows Glastonbury Tor and other hills rising like islands from the swirling mist. This is how the Levels must have looked in the Dark Ages when the sea covered much of the land farther west, between the sweep of the Quantocks and the Mendip Hills. It is easy, then, to understand what a strategic position the massive earthworks occupied; and why it is thought that Cadbury Castle may be the site of King Arthur's legendary Camelot. This tradition has been kept alive for centuries. Even in the 16th century, when the antiquarian John Leland visited the sleepy little village of South Cadbury, he was told that the villagers had 'hard say that Arture much resortid to Camalat'.

Until the 1960s there was no evidence to support this theory, but then archaeologists began to excavate the flat-topped hill. Their work showed that in the 5th and 6th centuries – the time when King Arthur was said to be fighting the Saxons – Cadbury Castle housed a community wealthy enough to trade. It was not conclusive proof of Camelot, but it has certainly allowed the legend to live on.

Cadbury Castle is reached by a footpath from South Cadbury. In the village purple aubrietia spills over honey-coloured stone walls, and straw storks perch on the thatched roof of a cottage. There is an 18th-century former rectory, and a house with a bell on its roof which used to be the school. Castle Farm House, with its mullioned windows and thatched roof, dates from 1687.

The Church of St Thomas à Becket was built in the 14th century; in a niche in the south wall there is a faded wall-painting of a bishop in a cope and mitre which may represent the saint himself.

North Cadbury lies a mile or so away. Its cottages, with roofs of tile, slate or thatch, are mostly built of a grey stone which has weathered over the centuries to a mellow sandy colour. An avenue of beech trees leads to North Cadbury Court, an Elizabethan mansion, and to the churchyard which is flanked on one side by the house's stable block. This dates from 1715.

The large Church of St Michael was built in about 1417 by Lady Elizabeth Botreaux, whose tomb lies inside. Among the most remarkable features of the church are its 16th-century bench ends, which are thought to have been carved by continental craftsmen.

Many bear heraldic devices, such as the Tudor Rose, or religious emblems, such as that of St Joseph of Arimathea – a ragged cross and two cruets with drops of blood. But others are simply fun: a flute player, a couple kissing and a cat catching a mouse which has escaped the mousetrap below. The letters of the alphabet are painted on the vestry wall, which was probably once the village school.

Long Sutton SOMERSET

17 miles north-west of Sherborne (PAGE 48 Ac)

Sleepy Long Sutton lies a quarter of a mile south of the Yeovil to Taunton road, and is typical of this low-lying part of Somerset. The cottages have walls built of local lias, a grey stone tinged with blue, and windows dressed in honey-coloured Ham stone. The heart of the village has everything you would expect to find in the heart of rural Somerset; a green, a church, a manor house farm, a school, an inn – the Devonshire Arms – and a post office. The inn, facing the green, has more the appearance of a manor house than a country inn, even to the coat of arms of the Dukes of Devonshire above the porticoed entrance.

Like the rest of the village, the 15th-century Church of the Holy Trinity is built of lias stone with Ham stone dressings. Inside, it is a blaze of colour, for the 15th-century pulpit and rood screen have been gaily painted in red, green, gold and blue; not even the Jacobean font cover has escaped the restorer's brush. The nave is spanned by a magnificent timber roof supported by carved wooden angels carrying shields.

On the main road, north of the village, stands the Friends' Meeting House. It is dated 1717 – a time when the Quakers formed the strongest nonconformist movement in Somerset. The immaculately scrubbed benches and panelled screen at the entrance create an atmosphere of order and peace. The Court House, which dates from the Tudor period but was altered in 1658, stands a few hundred yards to the west. It has mullioned windows, set at different levels, and a porch with a rounded arch.

Pilton SOMERSET

21 miles north of Sherborne (PAGE 48 Bb)

Although almost 20 miles inland, Pilton – or Pooltown as it was called in Saxon times – was once a harbour on the edge of a low-lying tidal lake which stretched to the sea. Legend claims that Joseph of Arimathea, who came from the Holy Land in the 1st century to convert the British to Christianity, landed here and built a small mud-and-wattle church on the banks of the Whitelake, which courses through the village.

The present Church of St John the Baptist, said to stand on the site of Joseph's church, dates from the 12th century. Its churchyard clambers up the steep dip in which the village is set – a haphazard assortment of greystone cottages on either side of the stream. The Whitelake gurgles alongside cottage gardens, passes under a stone bridge and then opens out under the shade of chestnut trees in the meadows of the Manor House grounds.

Silhouetted against the sky on the other side of the hollow stand the gaunt remains of a medieval tithe barn which once belonged to the Abbey of Glastonbury. Although its thatched roof was destroyed by lightning and fire in the early 1960s, the stonework is in good repair. Its gables still carry the carved emblems of the four Evangelists – the God-man for St Matthew, the lion of Judah for St Mark, the sacrificial ox for St Luke and the eagle for St John. The barn lies on private property but may be visited by written application to Mr Peters, of Cumhill Farm.

From the barn, there are fine views of the village and the surrounding countryside – west towards the tower which caps Glastonbury Tor, 6 miles away, and north back over the village and its pinnacled, turreted church. The Norman south door to the church was taken down in the 19th century and the present replica later installed. The bottom stage of the tower was built in 1196 and the top part was added in 1490. But the church's greatest treasure is the 15th-century timbered, tie-beamed roof, which is bathed in light by the clerestory windows. Carved wooden angels with wings outspread hover at the centre of each beam, which is itself supported by an angel carved in stone.

Beneath the church stands the Manor House – in a curious and capricious blend of styles. The front is Georgian with a Venetian window, castellations and corner pinnacles; while Gothic windows on the south side overlook the stream. The manor has a vineyard, planted in 1966 and 1968, and produces three white wines which have achieved international recognition. In a good year such as 1976, with its long, hot summer, 17,000 bottles are produced. Villagers help to harvest the grapes in late autumn, and the vineyard is open to the public at times during the summer.

MAP 6

VICTORIA'S ISLAND AND HISTORIC HAMPSHIRE

Queen Victoria came to the Isle of Wight and her devoted subjects followed – in their thousands. It has been a holiday isle ever since – and Britain's yachting capital. The Solent that divides it from the mainland offers an irresistible challenge to sporting skippers. But an earlier monarch came too – Charles I, seeking refuge from Parliament and leaving only to face trial and execution. Across The Solent, history took a gentler turn as Izaak Walton fished trout streams among Hampshire villages and welcoming inns where The Compleat Angler lives still.

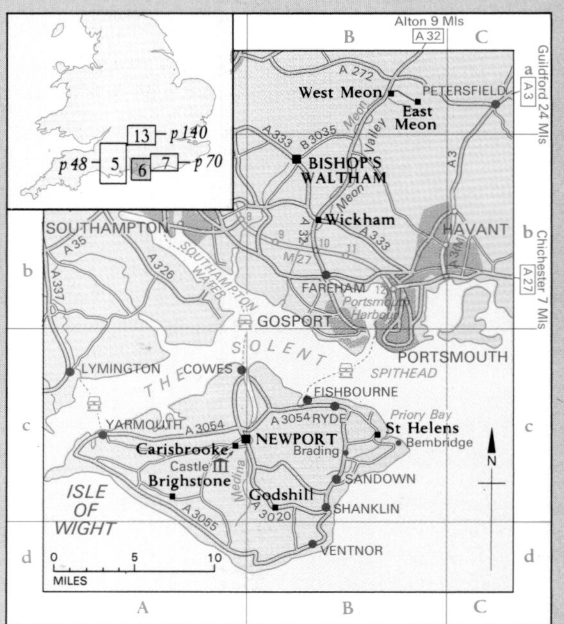

MAP 6: NEIGHBOURING AREAS – MAPS 5, 7, 13

BISHOP'S WALTHAM

HAMPSHIRE

10 miles north-east of Southampton (PAGE 64 Bb)

At first sight, Bishop's Waltham appears to be a typically Georgian town – and a pleasant one, too. But its history can be traced to prehistoric times and a fine Bronze Age burial mound has been found near by. In Saxon times the town was known as 'Wealdham' or 'Wealtham', and in AD 904 King Edward the Elder exchanged it for an estate owned by the Bishop of Winchester – hence Bishop's Waltham.

Invading Danes destroyed the Saxon settlement in 1001, but the town soon grew again, this time around a fortified palace built by Henri of Blois, Bishop of Winchester, in the 12th century. The palace became the seat of several later Bishops of Winchester, and was visited by a succession of kings and princes; Henry II held a council there to organise his Crusade, Richard I was entertained there after his coronation at Winchester, Henry V was there in 1415 and Henry VIII in 1532. Its most celebrated resident was William of Wykeham, 14th Bishop of Winchester, Lord Chancellor of England and founder of Winchester College and New College, Oxford. He died at the palace in 1404.

The palace's days of glory ended in 1644, when Parliamentarian troops laid siege to Bishop Curll and a force of Royalists. It is said that the bishop escaped in a dung cart, disguised as a farm labourer. The palace was largely destroyed and never restored, although a significant ruin remains. It includes part of a 12th-century tower, the tall traceried windows of the Great Hall, part of the moat and sections of a brick wall built by Bishop Langton in 1501. Most of the town lies to the north of the ruined palace, and is centred around St George's Square. From it runs the High Street which has a fine show of Georgian houses, including the three-storeyed Barclays Bank building. Most of the surrounding streets are narrow and contain groups of attractive 18th-century and 19th-century houses and a scattering of timber-framed cottages.

St Peter's Street leads to the Church of St Peter, which dates from the 12th century but was extensively restored in the 19th century. It retains what is believed to be the original Saxon font – found in a garden in Houchin Street in 1933 – and a fine Jacobean pulpit of 1626. The west wall bears the arms of Bishop Langton, together with three Cromwellian cannon balls found on the palace site. The chancel is probably the work of Bishop Wykeham, whose badge, the Hampshire Rose, appears above the east window.

● **Parking** Houchin Street; Lower Lane (both car parks) ● **Early closing** Wednesday ● **Events** Carnival and Fair (June); Agricultural Show (July) ● **Information** TEL. Southampton 21106 ● **AA 24 hour service** TEL. Southampton 36811.

The Meons HAMPSHIRE

8 miles north-east of Bishop's Waltham (PAGE 64 Ba)

When Rudyard Kipling wrote that 'East is east and west is west, and never the twain shall meet', he certainly did not have East and West Meon in mind – but the phrase fits them perfectly. For although the two villages are only 3 miles apart, the people seem to have quite different temperaments, and a traditional rivalry exists between them that has lasted for more than a thousand years. Indeed, this pocket of 'clan warfare' deep in rural Hampshire is said to date from the 6th century, when a tribe of Jutes, the Meonwara, colonised the Meon Valley as far as West Meon, expelling the native Celtic people eastwards. Two separate and distinct cultures continue to this day.

Local cultural differences apart, both villages are extremely attractive. East Meon lies at the head of the valley, and the springs which feed the river rise less than a mile away. The waters form little more than a chalky stream ambling gently under a series of four small flint-built bridges at the heart of the village, and past a string of cottages (two dating from around 1350), a couple of 18th-century houses and the Izaak Walton inn. The author of *The Compleat Angler* had no connection with the village, but he probably fished the lower reaches of the river for trout. The village lies beneath the steep grassy mound of Park Hill, so called because it once formed part of the Bishop of Winchester's 500 acre deer park. It protects the village from the north winds, and the Church of All Saints fits snugly into its lower slopes. The magnificent church dates from the 11th century and possesses a rare font, sculpted from a single block of Tournai marble. It was a gift to the church from Henri of Blois, Bishop of Winchester, in the 12th century, and there are few others like it in Britain. Its elaborate carvings depict the Creation and the Fall of Man. A replica of the font is displayed in the Victoria and Albert Museum, London.

Dating from about 1400, the superb Court House stands opposite the church. Its thatched Court Barn was once the manorial court of the Bishops of Winchester who were lords of the manor of East Meon for almost 800 years, until 1851. Below East Meon the river

All Saints, at East Meon

The Tournai font – carved with the Creation and Fall of Man

MEDIEVAL MASTERPIECE

Tournai, in Flanders, was famed throughout medieval Europe for the skill of its sculptors, who carved the superb font at All Saints, East Meon, from a single block of their local marble. Henry of Blois, Bishop of Winchester (the Conqueror's grandson), gave it to the church around 1150. All Saints itself is 11th century, and below it the Meon chalk stream, where Izaak Walton fished, flows under four little bridges past ancient cottages, handsome houses – and a pub named after the great angler-author.

Village cottages . . . . . . Meon-side terrace

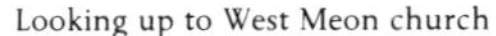

Looking up to West Meon church

Wall of squared flints

Thomas Lord's tombstone

LORDLY CELEBRATION

Thomas Lord, who founded Lord's cricket ground in 1787, is buried in West Meon churchyard. He spent his last two years in the village. The Victorian church, faced with beautiful, squared local flints, cost £12,000 – most of it paid by the rector, Henry Vincent Bayley. Local workers, given a day off to celebrate its foundation in 1843, did so to such good effect that they were off for a week.

---

winds through sparsely wooded pastureland on its way to The Solent, murmuring gently between flint walls as it passes through West Meon. Beetle-browed thatched cottages are tucked away in quiet side roads; just below the church stands the Georgian Red Lion Inn, once the rectory; and the village cross stands sentinel over all. On its site St Wilfrid is said to have preached Christianity to the heathen Meonwara in the 7th century.

West Meon's Church of St John the Evangelist was rebuilt in the early 1840s by George Gilbert Scott, and is a fine example of the Victorian Gothic style. Thomas Lord, founder of Lord's cricket ground, is buried in the churchyard. He lived in West Meon for two years before his death in 1832, and every few years the Marylebone Cricket Club sends someone to the village to clean his grave.

Another grave holds the ashes of the traitor and spy Guy Burgess, who defected to Russia in 1951 and whose family once lived in the district. He died in 1963 and was cremated in Moscow. Enquiries as to his grave's exact location in the churchyard are met with silence or polite evasion: West Meon prefers to forgive, forget and let his remains rest in peace.

Wickham HAMPSHIRE

5 miles south of Bishop's Waltham (PAGE 64 Bb)

Timbers from an American frigate captured by the Royal Navy after a bloody action have found a peaceful resting place beside the tranquil waters of the Meon at Wickham. They form the floor beams of a fine, three-storey mill named after the USS *Chesapeake*, taken by the British frigate HMS *Shannon* off Boston, Massachusetts on June 1, 1813.

As he lay dying in his shattered vessel, the gallant American captain, James Lawrence, cried out: 'Don't give up the ship!' His plea was in vain, but his fighting words became the famous rallying cry of the US Navy.

The Royal Navy, too, found inspiration in the ringing call of Captain Philip Bowes Vere Broke of the *Shannon*, as he drew his sword and leapt on board the *Chesapeake* crying, 'Follow me who can!'

The American frigate ended up in a British breakers' yard, where some of its timbers were sold to the Wickham mill owner who used them in building the three-storey Chesapeake Mill in 1820. It stands beside the River Meon, near the red-brick former brewery.

From this point, Bridge Street, with its pleasant cottages, curves up the hill to the Square, passing on the way a row of cottages called The Barracks.

The Square is a delightful mixture of large and small buildings, their rooftops forming an erratic line. The style is mostly Georgian, particularly the Old House Hotel and its neighbour Wickham House. Both are built of local grey and red brick. Several of the buildings in the Square have steeply pitched roofs, suggesting that earlier timber-framed construction hides behind their Georgian façades.

Wickham was granted a Market Charter in 1269. The market is no longer held but an annual fair takes place in the Square on May 20, the eve of the Feast of St Nicholas, to whom the church is dedicated.

The village is separated from its church by the river and by the course of the Meon Valley Railway. Although the line is now disused, there is a pleasant walk along its embankment, with fine views across the village. The Church of St Nicholas is mainly 19th century and houses a small display commemorating William of Wykeham, who was born in the village in 1324 (see also Bishop's Waltham, page 64).

NEWPORT

ISLE OF WIGHT

5 miles south of Cowes (PAGE 64 A/Bc)

Newport, established on the River Medina as a 'new port' in 1180, is almost in the centre of the island, yet coasters occasionally still make their way up to its busy harbour. But despite its modern preoccupation with trade and commerce, this attractive town retains historical links with the past – most notably with Charles I.

In September 1648, the king was paroled from Carisbrooke Castle (see page 68), overlooking the town from the south-west. He came to the heart of Newport and for nearly three months reputedly lived with Sir William Hopkins, master of the Old Grammar School which was built in 1614 with mullioned windows and tall gables.

Near by is the parish church – dedicated to St Thomas the Apostle and St Thomas Becket – its steepled tower thrusting over the surrounding shops and offices. It was built in the 1850s on the site of a much older church, whose oak pulpit is still in use. The foundation stone was laid by Queen Victoria's consort, Prince Albert. The queen herself gave a statue in white marble of a sleeping princess – a memorial to Charles I's second daughter, Elizabeth, who is buried in the church beneath the high altar.

St Thomas Square contains the dignified God's Providence House, built in 1701 on the site of the only house in Newport not touched by death during the plague of 1583–4. In the High Street is Newport's oldest inn, The Castle. Built in 1684 it staged cock fights until the 19th century. On a corner of the High Street is the Guildhall, built in 1814–16 to a classical design by the great architect and town planner John Nash. He also designed the elegant County Club in nearby St James Square.

In Pyle Street, running parallel to the High Street, is the early 17th-century Chantry House of chequered brick. The remains of a Roman villa can be found in Cypress Road, on the south side of Newport. It is open to the public from Easter until the end of September except on Fridays and Saturdays.

A marina was opened about 2 miles downriver in 1982. Berthed there, along with modern yachts, is an old paddle-steamer – now a floating restaurant.

• **Parking** Lugley Street; Chapel Street; Orchard Street; Coppins Bridge; St John's Road; Town Lane; Royal Exchange; Carisbrooke High Street; Medina Avenue (all car parks) • **Early closing** Thursday • **Market day** Tuesday • **Theatre** Apollo, Pyle Street; Mountbatten Theatre; Fairlee Road • **Cinema** Studio One, High Street • **Events** Royal Isle of Wight County Show, Northwood (July); Carnival (August) • **Information** TEL. Newport 524343 • **AA 24 hour service** TEL. Newport 522653.

Brighstone ISLE OF WIGHT

7 miles south-west of Newport (PAGE 64 Ac)

Brighstone must have one of the prettiest post offices in England. Set in a row of terraced cottages built of chalk and with trimly thatched roofs, its bright red little sign hangs above a low doorway which, like all the other cottages, has roses climbing almost to the tiny casement windows of the upper floor. A little farther along is Ye Olde Shoppe, not thatched but with a mossy tiled roof, and that, more or less, is Brighstone except for some buildings in the main street, a tea-garden, the village pub and the church.

St Mary's Church and The Three Bishops have something in common, for the pub's name celebrates the fact that three rectors of the church went on to become bishops. Their names are recorded on a handsome marble memorial in the church: Bishop Ken of Bath and Wells, who was rector in 1667–9; Bishop Wilberforce of Oxford and Winchester, rector in 1830–40; and Bishop Moberley of Salisbury, rector in 1866–8. The church is built of local limestone and flint and dates from the late 12th century. It was extended in the 16th century, when the north aisle was demolished and the Norman arches filled in. But in 1852 the aisle was rebuilt and the arches opened up, so that now they can be seen properly – bowed with age but still vigorously supporting the roof.

The sea is visible a mere three-quarters of a mile away, and seems to play no particular part in the life of Brighstone, but that is misleading. As in many other seaside villages, smuggling was once a flourishing occupation, with French brandy from Cherbourg the main 'import'. On the walls of one cottage are carved the rough outlines of ships, said to indicate to smugglers what kind of contraband was currently the most profitable.

An ex-smuggler named James Buckett was the coxswain of Brighstone's first lifeboat. The station, established in the 1860s, was also the first on the island and remained in service until 1915, when its work was transferred to Yarmouth lifeboat. During that time 433 lives were saved – sometimes at the cost of the lifeboatmen's lives. In March 1888 the lifeboat capsized when going to the assistance of an American barque. The coxswain and a crew member were lost, but the boat was righted and carried on.

DOWN THE THATCH *The mossy tiles of Ye Olde Shoppe harmonise with the deep thatch next door in peaceful Brighstone. But it was not always so calm – smuggling was once rife here.*

Carisbrooke ISLE OF WIGHT

1 mile west of Newport (PAGE 64 Ac)

In terms of history, architecture and topography Carisbrooke is undoubtedly the most important village on the island. Romans, Normans, Stuarts and Victorians have all left their marks here in what was for centuries the island's capital – once called Buccombe, or Beaucombe, 'the fair valley'. Fair it still is, with a long winding street of colour-washed houses running uphill from a brook, and overlooked by the island's finest church, set high above the road.

St Mary's Church began life as part of a Benedictine priory, established by French monks about 1150. The priory was dissolved by Henry V in 1415 during the French Wars, and the church was substantially reduced in size. Neglect over the centuries took its toll, but in 1907 the church was restored to its full glory.

Its most striking feature is the 14th-century tower, rising in five stages with a turret at one corner and a battlemented and pinnacled crown. Inside the church are Norman windows, nave and arches, a Cromwellian pulpit and a low-relief sculpture of the Virgin and Child made in 1969 by John Skelton.

But though St Mary's is beautiful, and its surrounds are delightful, pride of place in Carisbrooke must go to its great castle, which stands 150 ft above the village. On foot it is best approached along Castle Street, opposite the church, which crosses the brook and then winds upwards to the greensward bank below the castle walls.

It was begun by William Fitz-Osborne, the first Norman commander of the Isle of Wight, on the site of a Roman fort, traces of which can be seen near the castle entrance. The Norman keep stands on a 58 ft mound within the walls and is reached by 71 steps. It is the oldest part of the castle, for the massive outer walls and gateway were built in the 1590s. The castle well, 161 ft deep, was sunk in 1150 and is still operated by donkeys working a treadmill.

Carisbrooke's most famous association is with Charles I who came here in 1647 to seek refuge from Parliament but was later imprisoned by the castle's governor, Colonel Robert Hammond. The Great Hall where the king was imprisoned can still be seen, also the window through which he tried to escape – an attempt foiled because his body would not pass through the bars. The room and others adjoining it now house the Carisbrooke Castle Museum which includes the king's Book of Common Prayer, part of the cravat worn at his death and the cap he wore on the night before his execution.

Charles left Carisbrooke in 1648 for his trial and subsequent execution, but the castle's association with the Stuarts did not end. In 1650 the king's children, Prince Henry and Princess Elizabeth, were imprisoned there. For the princess it was but a short stay – she died a month later and was buried in Newport's parish church. Prince Henry was released in 1652 and died six years later.

In 1896 Princess Beatrice, Queen Victoria's youngest daughter, was made Governor of the Isle of Wight. She took up summer residence in the castle and used to stay there from time to time until her death in London in 1944.

Before his attempted escape, Charles I was allowed to play bowls on a green prepared for him outside the castle walls, on the site of the old tilt yard. It can still be seen from the ramparts which allow visitors to walk the entire length of the castle walls. The views are magnificent, taking in the village below, the rooftops of Newport and the rolling green hills of the Bowcombe valley.

Godshill ISLE OF WIGHT

5 miles south of Newport (PAGE 64 Bc)

Godshill is one of the prettiest villages on the island and is, therefore, a popular tourist attraction. And because tourism is the island's major industry there is much in Godshill designed to part the visitor from his money – in other words it is commercialised. But the village manages to avoid the vulgar excesses of some other tourist spots, and has much to offer a discerning visitor.

The heart of the village is a sudden, very steep hill on top of which is perched All Saints' Church, on the site of a pagan shrine, hence the village's name. The church rises majestically above a cluster of thatched cottages which stand like well-groomed attendants to their regal neighbour and form a group that few photographers can resist.

The churchyard occupies the entire crest of the hill, which is carpeted with thick turf speckled with snowdrops in early spring and studded with sombre gravestones – one dating back to the 14th century.

DONKEY WORK *Prisoners used to work the treadmill at Carisbrooke Castle, drawing water from a well 161 ft deep. Nowadays a placid donkey turns the wheel, which was made in the 16th century when the massive outer walls and gate were also built. Royalty have been frequent – and sometimes unwilling – guests in the castle. Charles I sought refuge here in 1647, but was imprisoned by the governor. Queen Victoria's daughter Princess Beatrice made it her summer residence when she was governor of the island.*

Thatch, stone and daffodils at Godshill

Model village at the Rectory

WHAT'S IN A NAME

Thatched roofs groomed to crew-cut neatness, crowning ancient cottages of barely bearable perfection, all winding up past verges aglow with daffodils to a church with impeccable 15th-century credentials . . . This is Godshill – like its name, almost too good to be true; but as nice as it looks, mirrored admiringly in miniature by a model of itself among the lawns of the Rectory.

Most of the woodland on the hill is outside the boundary of the churchyard which is a little overgrown, with narrow, twisting paths sometimes crossing partly hidden graves. Yet it is a serene spot despite the crumbling monuments to the long-departed.

All Saints dates from the 15th century and later, its buttressed tower crowned by eight pinnacles. Inside, a unique medieval wall painting shows Christ crucified on a branched lily, and All Saints is often called the 'Church of the Lily Cross'.

Below the hill the winding main street is lined on both sides by cottages of every age from the 16th century onwards. Most are thatched and all are as neat as their lofty neighbours up on the hill. Teashops abound, one in a conservatory housing two vast, 100-year-old grape vines; gift shops supply curios and pottery and the Old Smithy now sells brass, copper and wrought-iron ware. Its deep well stands near by, inviting the superstitious to make a wish.

There is a model village in the Rectory garden at the western end of the main street, and Godshill also boasts its own Natural History Museum, based on a private shell collection and now including everything from piranha fish to butterflies. A glittering array of replicas of the Crown Jewels demonstrates varieties of precious stones.

St Helens ISLE OF WIGHT

12 miles east of Newport (PAGE 64 Bc)

Since the 12th century, homecoming sailors have had good reason to bless St Helens, for it has a landmark that signposts the way to the waters of Spithead and Portsmouth Harbour. Standing right on the water's edge the ruined tower of the Old Church – all that remains of a priory founded more than 800 years ago – is now purely a navigational aid, its seaward side bricked up, whitewashed and visible for miles.

The sea and Henry V both contributed to the priory's downfall; the main body was demolished when the king dissolved the priory in 1414, and erosion by the tides did the rest. Not far from the tower is Priory Bay, where in 1545 a French fleet anchored while waiting to attack Portsmouth. It was in the subsequent battle with the British fleet that Henry VIII's *Mary Rose* was lost, and lay on the bottom at Spithead until 1982 when she was raised and taken to Portsmouth. Farther offshore lie St Helens Roads, much favoured by Nelson as an anchorage that gave protection from the south and south-westerly winds.

St Helens was once a significant little port, its entrance protected by a large spit of land, called the Duver, which created a haven from north-easterly gales. The village stands north of St Helens Quay at the mouth of the River Yar, which runs inland to Brading and was navigable for merchant vessels until silting in the 17th century reduced its importance.

There are quite a few modern houses in the village, but also a number of older buildings in stone and thatch and some later Georgian houses, standing around a large green. One 18th-century cottage in Upper Green Road was the home of the locally famous Sophie Dawes, a smuggler's daughter who became the mistress of the Duke of Bourbon and earned herself the title 'Queen of Chantilly'. Sophie, who died in 1840, is remembered by a plaque displayed on a wall of her home.

In summer a ferry runs from the tip of the Duver to Bembridge on the other side of the harbour. Alternatively, there is a pleasant walk around the harbour which leads through Brading Haven where an odd assortment of houseboats line the shore.

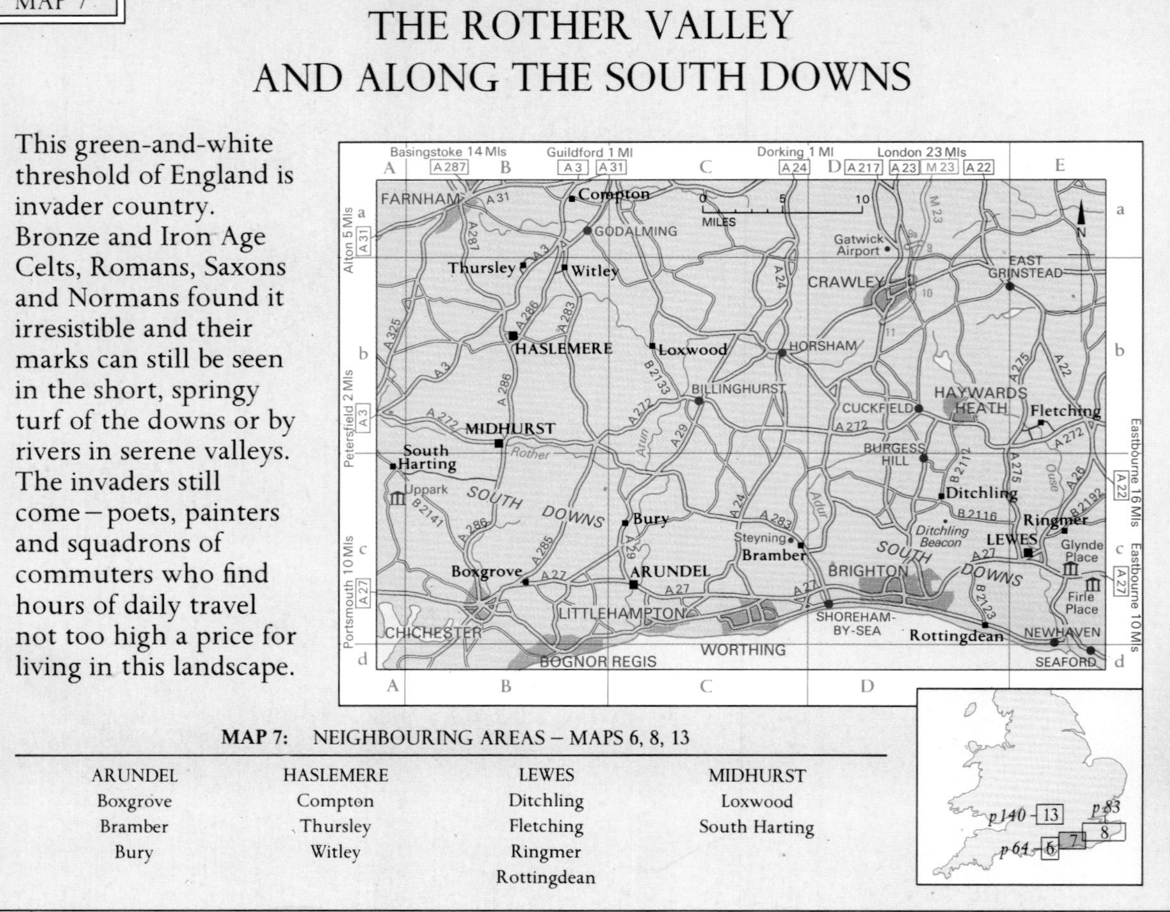

THE ROTHER VALLEY AND ALONG THE SOUTH DOWNS

This green-and-white threshold of England is invader country. Bronze and Iron Age Celts, Romans, Saxons and Normans found it irresistible and their marks can still be seen in the short, springy turf of the downs or by rivers in serene valleys. The invaders still come – poets, painters and squadrons of commuters who find hours of daily travel not too high a price for living in this landscape.

MAP 7: NEIGHBOURING AREAS – MAPS 6, 8, 13

ARUNDEL	HASLEMERE	LEWES	MIDHURST
Boxgrove	Compton	Ditchling	Loxwood
Bramber	Thursley	Fletching	South Harting
Bury	Witley	Ringmer	
		Rottingdean	

ARUNDEL

WEST SUSSEX

4 miles north of Littlehampton (PAGE 70 Cc)

Three majestic buildings – a castle, a cathedral and a church – watch over the ancient town of Arundel.

The castle has stood above the River Arun since the 11th century, but much of the present fortress was built in the 18th and 19th centuries although the Norman keep and the 13th-century barbican were retained. It is the home of England's premier nobleman, the Duke of Norfolk, and in 1890 more major restoration work was undertaken by the 15th Duke. Castle and grounds are open on most afternoons between April and October, and visitors can see armour, art treasures, rare books and Tudor furniture.

The 15th Duke also sponsored the building of the Roman Catholic Cathedral of Our Lady and St Philip Howard, which sits on the crest of a hill to the west of the castle. Built originally as a church, it became a cathedral only in 1965. St Philip Howard was the 13th Earl of Arundel, sentenced to death in the reign of Elizabeth I for his staunch Catholicism but not executed as he died in prison. His bones lie in the cathedral, with an imposing shrine to his memory.

Between castle and cathedral is the parish church of St Nicholas, which houses the tombs of the Dukes of Norfolk and the Earls of Arundel. It was built of knap flint and sandstone in the late 14th century, and although Church of England it has a private Roman Catholic chapel which is open to the public.

Arundel lies snugly below its three great landmarks, and is a dignified mixture of Victorian and Georgian houses. The sloping High Street contains the Norfolk Arms, an 18th-century coaching inn, and by the bridge over the nearby River Arun are the remains of Maison Dieu, a group of 14th-century almshouses. The High Street also has three contrasting museums: the Arundel Museum and Heritage Centre, with exhibits of the town's eventful past; the Toy and Military Museum; and the Museum of Curiosity, whose Victorian tableaux of stuffed birds and animals show such scenes as the Kittens' Tea Party and the Guinea Pigs' Cricket Match (see Bramber, page 72).

● **Parking** Crown Yard; Mill Road; Castle car park, off Mill Road (all car parks); High Street ● **Early closing** Wednesday ● **Events** Grand Arun Bathtub Boatrace (August); Arundel Festival (August and September) ● **Information** TEL. Arundel 882268 ● **AA 24 hour service** TEL. Brighton 695231.

Boxgrove WEST SUSSEX

8 miles west of Arundel (PAGE 70 Bc)

Content with a quieter pace of life, this scenic village has long enticed travellers away from the busy main road to Chichester, which runs a little to the south. Chunky flint walls are softened by such charming

NORFOLK'S SUSSEX *Arundel, principal home of the Dukes of Norfolk, is indeed a fairytale place, in that little about it is quite what it seems. The medieval bridge is modern, the Tudor cottages Victorian, and this view of the castle a 19th-century confection, though it masks an older and more purposeful fortress – built to defend the Arun valley. But the overall effect is a sheer delight.*

sights as the timbered Nightingale Cottage, and in Church Lane, Thatched Cottage contrasts with flint-and-tile neighbours. But such delights may seem trivial, almost, alongside the magnificence awaiting visitors who open a gate in the lane and enter the great Church of St Mary and St Blaise.

The village lies beneath the sheep-rearing South Downs, and St Blaise, martyred in the 4th century by having his flesh torn by iron combs, is the patron saint of woolcombers. The sheer size of the church is impressive, but the squat Norman tower and heavy buttresses give little hint of the splendours within. It was once part of a rich Benedictine priory, and though large sections of the monastic building have crumbled or been demolished, what remains is still magnificent.

The house was founded around 1115 as a cell of the Abbey of Lessay, some 35 miles south of Cherbourg in France, which sent three monks to supervise the small community. Its numbers rose during the Middle Ages, and in the time of Edward I (1272 – 1307) the monks were warned against over-lavish hospitality to visitors. By 1518, Bishop Sherbourne was denouncing archery contests, the keeping of hawks and dogs, and playing at cards and dice on the property.

The lord of the manor, Earl de la Warr, built a private chapel there as a future resting place for himself and his wife. At Henry VIII's Dissolution of the Monasteries in 1536, he was allowed to buy the whole monastery and pulled down a number of buildings. The king later forced him to dispose of Boxgrove, so when he died he was not buried there but at Broadwater, a village just north of Worthing.

However, de la Warr's chapel remains, an empty but dazzling extravaganza in blue, white, gilt and terracotta red, with fan vaulting, dragons, cherubs and a wealth of curlicues.

The original nave was partially demolished and the present nave was once the choir. In its vaulted roof are arms, crests and delicate floral decorations commissioned by de la Warr from Lambert Barnard, one of the first known English painters in this style. Many of the memorials portray military figures and deeds of valour. There is a life-size recumbent figure of Nelson's great-grandson, Admiral Philip Nelson-Ward, who died in 1937.

Less than a mile north of Boxgrove, on the continuation of the village street, lies de la Warr's old manorial village of Halnaker (pronounced Hannaker). Below it the admirably restored 18th-century Halnaker Mill was a ruin when Hilaire Belloc wrote a poem about it in 1912.

Bramber WEST SUSSEX

15 miles east of Arundel (PAGE 70 Cc)

An imposing Norman castle once dominated the hill above Bramber; and though the castle has long been a ruin, a 76 ft high, jagged sliver of the massive gatehouse-keep still looks just as menacing as the original keep and walls must have been.

After his victory near Hastings, William the Conqueror gave Bramber to William de Braose, who built a wooden fortification above the River Adur, with a central man-made mound which may have supported a Saxon castle; the mound still rears up from the grassy crown of the hill. On the sides not defended by the river, de Braose built a defensive moat, later adding a stone keep and curtain walls. The few remains that can be seen today are managed by the National Trust.

Clinging to the slope just below the castle ruins is the Church of St Nicholas, with a squat Norman tower and a nave from the days of de Braose, who originally conceived it as his chapel. Much damaged through neglect and the side-effects of Parliamentarian assaults on the castle, it has been rebuilt several times since the 18th century and a vestry was added at the west end in 1931.

Throughout the Middle Ages, ships brought supplies up the tidal river to quays at Bramber and Steyning, half a mile to the north-west. Bramber was important enough to have two MPs until the Reform Act of 1832 swept away 'rotten' and 'pocket' boroughs. In those declining years, when only 32 Bramber folk were entitled to vote, the social reformer William Wilberforce was given the seat as a reward for his anti-slavery measures and philanthropy. Apparently, he only saw the village once, while driving through it. On being told its name, he marvelled: 'Bramber? How interesting – that's the place I'm Member for.'

A stone bridge that spanned the river in Henry III's time had a chapel, and both were rebuilt towards the end of the 15th century by William Waynflete, Bishop of Winchester. The bridge stood a few yards west of the present bridge, and though it fell into disrepair as the river silted up it was there when Charles II passed through Bramber on his flight into exile after the Battle of Worcester in 1651. Near it stands a 15th-century building that probably housed the monks who were bridge wardens, and was also a hostel for pilgrims and other travellers. The building is now called St Mary's and has a 'King's Room' in which it is claimed that Charles II spent his last night in England before going into exile.

However, this does not fit the record. The memoirs of Colonel Gounter, who arranged the king's escape, state that they reached Bramber around 4 p.m. on October 6 to find Parliamentary troops crowding the streets. Rather than draw attention to themselves by turning back, they boldly crossed the bridge, reached Brighton by nightfall and then escaped by ship to France.

The house, with its sturdy oak frame, commanding frontage and fine garden, was a private residence by the time of Elizabeth I, when fireplaces and chimneys were added. It passed through many hands and was allowed to deteriorate badly during and after the Second World War.

An unusual museum was opened by a local amateur taxidermist, Walter Potter, in the main street in 1861. It featured, among other bizarre exhibits, tableaux in glass cases showing animals engaged in human activities. His family carried it on until 1970, and the collection can now be seen in Arundel. Two years later the museum was reopened as the House of Pipes, with 38,000 exhibits of 'Smokiana' – smoking implements and souvenirs including old tobacco tins, cigarette cards and cigarette rolling machines, collected from many parts of the world.

Bury WEST SUSSEX

5 miles north of Arundel (PAGE 70 Cc)

Approached from either the gentle slopes of the north or the wonderful descent from the heights above Arundel Park, Bury seems too shy to show itself in its entrancing surroundings. The main road to Arundel rushes past within a few hundred yards, but only a lazy drift of chimney smoke or a hint of red roofs reveal the presence of a village. Bury remains unspoilt and uncluttered, hugging a slope down to the River Arun as if trying to avoid detection.

Sandstone houses and cottages with tiled roofs lurch their way down between trees and steeply banked gardens to the grassy bank by the water. Here a ferry once crossed to the Amberley side; but no longer – the landing area was informally landscaped in 1977, with riverside seats where strollers can rest and enjoy the view.

Close to the river and a pool among the reeds is the Church of St John the Evangelist. The Domesday Survey records a church here in 1087, suggesting that the sturdier, later building was added to a Saxon foundation. The nave and aisle roofs carry the weight of 'Horsham slabs', heavy greystone tiles taken from a quarry, on the site of which Christ's Hospital now stands, near Horsham. Inside the church, the war memorial, a Crucifixion set on the rood screen in 1948, is carved from local Sussex oak. The square tower is 13th century, but the shingled, octagonal spire rising from it was added about 400 years later. Beside the church is 17th-century Bury Manor, part of which was once a priest's house. In the heart of the village, next to the village shop, Bury House is partly timbered and plastered, but in essence is a golden stone building like those the Wealden ironmasters used to make for themselves. It was built in 1910 and was a home of John Galsworthy, whose novels include *The Forsyte Saga.* A modern house opposite has appropriated the name of Forsytes.

The contemporary village hall makes imaginative use of decorative flinty pebbles, matching the side wall of the massive Fogdens, a few paces away. Beyond, attractive thatched cottages cluster around the Black Dog and Duck, the village inn; among them is Prattendens Cottage, for some years the home of Mabel Constanduros, a popular radio personality during the Second World War.

Throughout the village, almost every step reveals glimpses of the sheltering downs, some bare and others softened by clumps of trees. The South Downs Way climbs past ancient mounds on Bury Hill to offer a magnificent panorama of fields and woods, with bright little villages and hamlets snug under the windbreaks of their trees.

HASLEMERE

SURREY

11 miles south of Farnham (PAGE 70 Bb)

The French-born musician Arnold Dolmetsch settled in Haslemere towards the end of the First World War, and opened his now world-renowned workshops for early musical instruments in 1921. Since then he and his family after him have produced beautifully crafted viols, lutes, recorders, spinets, harpsichords and clavichords – and visitors can make appointments to watch the instruments being made. In 1925 the Dolmetsch family founded the Haslemere Festival of Early Music, which is held in the town each July. Arnold Dolmetsch died in Haslemere in 1940 aged 82, and was buried in nearby Shottermill cemetery.

Haslemere is set among the hills and woods of the Surrey-West Sussex border, and its spread of late-Victorian country houses blends harmoniously with the surroundings. In the centre of the town, some of the plain red-brick buildings are Georgian. There are also 17th-century and 19th-century tile-hung buildings, and in Lower Street there is a pretty, 17th-century, tile-hung cottage, Yew Tree Cottage. Climbing above Lower Street is Shepherds Hill, with its curved terrace of houses and cottages in a pleasing patchwork of styles – including tile-hung, brick and stucco. Down below, the sturdy Town Hall was rebuilt in 1814 – although it looks much older – and near it, in the long sloping High Street, are three outstanding Georgian buildings. They are the Town House, its third storey added around 1800, and two handsome hotels, the Georgian and the White Horse. Another fine building, Church Hill House, dates from the early 1700s – although its porch was added about 1910. Next to it stands the parish church of St Bartholomew, which – with the exception of its 13th-century capped tower – was totally rebuilt in 1871.

Alfred, Lord Tennyson, the Victorian Poet Laureate, attended the church when he lived at his house called Aldworth, 2 miles to the south-east in Sussex. There is a stained-glass memorial window to him in the north aisle, designed by the 19th-century painter Sir Edward Burne-Jones. Another window commemorates the poet and Jesuit priest Gerard Manley Hopkins (1844 – 89), whose parents lived in the area. Tennyson and Hopkins were not the only literary figures connected with Haslemere. The creator of Sherlock Holmes, Sir Arthur Conan Doyle (1859 – 1930), played cricket for the town in his youth and the playwright Sir Arthur Wing Pinero (1855 – 1934), author of *The Second Mrs Tanqueray*, stayed here in 1890.

Until the 19th century leather-tanning and iron-smelting flourished in the town, and a toll was gathered on market days, the profit from which went into the building of Tolle House, a group of late 17th-century almshouses in Petworth Road. Not far away, the Educational Museum in the High Street contains collections of zoology, geology, local history and British birds, and has a display of live amphibians.

• **Parking** High Street; Cheshunt Avenue; Tanners Lane; Lion Green; Wey Hill (all car parks) • **Early closing** Wednesday • **Cinema** Rex, Shottermill TEL. Haslemere 2444 • **Event** Haslemere Festival (July) • **Information** TEL. Haslemere 54305 • **AA 24 hour service** TEL. Guildford 572841.

Compton SURREY

12 miles north-east of Haslemere (PAGE 70 Ba)

Though far from the sea, Compton was once a transit centre for smuggled goods, and numerous cellars and passages lie hidden beneath its older red-brick and tile cottages. Near the church is a striking timbered Tudor building, with a fine overhanging first floor. Many apparently mellow old houses actually belong to the 19th and 20th centuries, yet fit companionably into the long curve of the village street.

The Church of St Nicholas, half obscured by two huge cedars on its abrupt hillside, has a Saxon tower and other Saxon parts which may date from at least 50 years before the Norman Conquest. The Normans adapted the building to their own style and were responsible for the leaf-decorated pillars in the aisle.

Scratched on the south side of the chancel arch is the figure of a late 12th-century Norman knight,

DOUBLE SANCTUARY *The Norman sanctuary in Compton church is on two levels – and said to be the only example in England. The upper level may have been a private chapel.*

Watts Mortuary Chapel, Compton

EVERY ANGLE HAS A STORY

The Mortuary Chapel of G. F. Watts, a well-known Victorian painter, looms over Compton Cemetery like a lost double-decker bus. It was designed by his widow, Mary Fraser-Tytler, herself an artist, and as was fairly usual at the time, the monument is heavily charged with symbolism. Even the lines of the building are said to represent the Circle of Eternity with the Cross of Faith running through it, while some of the art nouveau angels within 'look downwards in sympathy' and others 'look upwards in hope'. In addition, there is a Garment of Eternity, a Tree of Life and various other allegories. The work was brilliantly executed in terracotta by Mary Fraser-Tytler with the help of a local builder, a blacksmith and a number of villagers whom she had trained. Building was completed in 1904, shortly after the death of her husband. She died 34 years later, and they lie together in the churchyard near the chapel. The Watts Gallery in the village shows many of the artist's works, and those of his contemporaries. At the far end of the gallery is a house where some of Mrs Watts's pottery workers used to live.

Terracotta angels

Inside the Mortuary Chapel

holding a cross of St George superimposed on that of St Andrew. It may have been carved by a Crusader observing a vigil here before leaving for the Holy Land. Above the heavy arch, with its zigzag decorations, 12th-century lozenge-pattern murals were revealed in 1966. A sanctuary beyond the arch is on two levels, unique in England. The upper storey has a balustrade that is one of the oldest examples of Norman woodwork in the country. This upper sanctuary may have been a private chapel housing a holy relic. Certainly such a relic would have attracted travellers along the nearby Pilgrims' Way from Winchester to Canterbury. Almost at floor level inside the chancel, an aperture looks into a former anchorite's cell – dating from Saxon times and only discovered in 1929 – where a hermit was walled up and fed by villagers in return for his prayers, advice and comfort.

In Down Lane are two notable buildings – the Watts Gallery and the eccentric red-brick and terracotta Mortuary Chapel on the slope of the new village cemetery. G. F. Watts, born in 1817, was a largely self-taught painter, best remembered for his statue *Physical Energy* in Kensington Gardens, London. In 1864 he married the actress Ellen Terry, 31 years younger than himself, but they separated after a year.

He married again 22 years later, this time successfully, to a woman 33 years his junior. An artist herself, Mary Fraser-Tytler was overwhelmed by her husband's genius. They lived happily together in a house called Limnersease, which Watts built beside the Pilgrims' Way. Before he died, she had constructed the art gallery which now displays much of his work. It is open on Wednesday and Saturday mornings and every afternoon except Thursday.

Below this building, Mrs Watts installed a workshop where she taught pottery. Her pupils helped to build the extraordinary red Mortuary Chapel which she had designed and almost completed building before her husband's death. The interior was restored in the 1960s with financial help from the Pilgrim Trust. The chapel has strong Celtic and art nouveau influences, and is open daily until dusk. The couple now lie in a grave on the crown of the hill.

Thursley SURREY

6 miles north of Haslemere (PAGE 70 Bb)

A gravestone in Thursley churchyard tells the sad story of a 'generous but unfortunate sailor, who was barbarously murder'd on Hindhead on Sep. 24th 1786 by three villains'. It seems that the sailor, while on the road to Portsmouth, came across three travellers apparently in need of help, and good naturedly went to their aid. Far from being grateful, they murdered him. The tragedy touched the hearts of the villagers – they never discovered the sailor's name, but gave him a decent burial and raised the memorial which still stands over his grave. The murderers were eventually brought to justice and duly hanged at Gibbet Hill on Hindhead Common, in chains made at Thursley's forge.

The 'hammer ponds' to the east of the village testify to its former importance as a centre of the great Wealden iron industry that thrived in the region for centuries. These artificially dammed streams provided the power that drove the trip hammers and worked the bellows of the village's forges until late in the

The Corner, Thursley

THE ARCHITECT AND A VICTIM

The Corner, a pretty, tile-hung house at Thursley, was one of Lutyens's first designs. He created it out of a row of cottages when he was 19, and was no doubt aided in getting the job by the fact that his aunt lived in the village. An unusual tombstone in Thursley commemorates a sailor who was 'barbarously murder'd' on Hindhead Common in 1786. His attackers were hanged at the place where he died, now called Gibbet Hill.

The victim's grave

1700s. Today the tiny village, set in a vast common of splendid heather and gorse studded with silver birch and pine trees, centres on the green, with two streets, The Lane and The Street, running off it. Much of the common is a nature reserve, home to 26 species of dragonfly – the largest number in England. Overlooking the green is an acacia tree, planted in memory of the traveller and writer William Cobbett (1762 – 1835).

He encouraged the extensive planting of the acacia, an American tree. Cobbett, the author of *Rural Rides* (1830) which described horseback tours of England, was a frequent visitor to Thursley. Street House, originally called The Cottage, was owned by the aunt of the architect Sir Edwin Lutyens (1869 – 1944) who lived there for a short time. He converted a row of cottages into a house, The Corner. It is part stone, part brick and tile-hung.

The Church of St Michael and All Angels probably got its name because St Michael was the closest Christian equivalent to the Norse god Thor, both being entrusted with care of the dead. The name Thursley means Thor's Leah (grove). Although much restored in the 19th century, the basic building is Saxon, and the two small windows retain their original oak frames. The wooden belfry and spire were added in the late 18th century. Their builders seemed determined that they should stand for ever: the whole construction rests on a complex platform of massive beams, supported by four huge tree trunks.

Beside the church is the 16th-century Old Parsonage, a half-timbered house filled in with bricks, and tile-hung. Hill Farm near by dates from 1530 and is based on a four-bay, timber-framed hall. In The Street, the timber-framed, white-painted Sunset Cottage, once a bakery, is similarly based on a medieval hall and still has two large inglenook hearths. Wheeler's Farm, opposite and also timber-framed, has a nice Elizabethan front.

Witley SURREY

7 miles north-east of Haslemere (PAGE 70 Bb)

Witley was once a fashionable summer retreat for artists and writers escaping the heat and dust of London. The novelist George Eliot made The Heights, now a nursing home, her country home from 1874 to 1876, and wrote her last novel, *Daniel Deronda*, here. The house was built by the Victorian architect Sir Henry Cole, whose other works include the Royal Albert Hall. The poet Tennyson was a neighbour, and the American novelist Henry James was one of many distinguished visitors.

Lloyd George, Prime Minister from 1916 to 1922, sought refuge in Witley from the stresses of high office and later bought a house here, Timbers, which was sold by one of his daughters in 1983.

But Witley was favoured by the king himself seven centuries ago: Edward I gave the royal manor, now called the Old Manor, to his beloved queen, Eleanor of Castile, and in 1283 she persuaded him to grant the villagers a charter to hold a market each Friday 'against the White Hart' – the village inn which still thrives and is one of the oldest in England. A hundred years later, Richard II paid several visits to the manor. His guests stayed at the White Hart – where Richard himself may well have joined them.

Today, Witley, with its half-timbered and tile-hung houses, retains its charm. At the heart of the village is the Church of All Saints. Built by the Saxons around 1050, it has been added to by succeeding generations in a variety of styles. The original simple Saxon structure can be seen in the nave. The Normans added the chancel and transepts around 1180, and there are 12th-century frescoes on the life of the Virgin on the original south wall. The 13th-century font is finely carved.

A 16th-century vicar, the Reverend Lawrence Stoughton, preached there for 53 years and died in office at the age of 88. Meanwhile, he married five times – and outlived all his wives.

Beneath the Church of All Saints are Old Cottage and Step Cottage, dating from the 15th and 16th centuries, with timber frames filled in with brick, and tile-hung upper storeys. Near by, in similar style, is Red Rose Cottage, given its name when Thomas Stynt, a weaver, granted a lease to Richard Payne at Christmas 1580, for an annual rent of one red rose.

LEWES

EAST SUSSEX

9 miles north-east of Brighton (PAGE 70 Ec)

When Henry VIII divorced his fourth wife, Anne of Cleves, in 1540 he gave her the house now called Anne of Cleves' House, in Lewes. It was built about 1500 and added to at the end of the century, with materials that

Step Cottage and All Saints, Witley

HIS RENT WAS JUST ONE RED ROSE

Witley is a village superbly English even in this era of commuterdom. The tile-hung, 16th-century Step Cottage—once the Rectory—partly hides All Saints' Church, that was 50-odd years old when the Normans arrived. Even now the interior is not too unlike that looked upon by the original worshippers. The village pub, the White Hart, is claimed, with some probability, to stand on the site of a Saxon inn, though the present building is mostly Elizabethan. So is Red Rose Cottage, a timber-framed building in The Street which got its name in a mysteriously delightful way. It is on record as having been leased at Christmas 1580 to a man named Richard Payne by Thomas Stynt, a weaver, for the surprisingly small annual rent of a single red rose.

Red Rose Cottage

included Caen stone taken from the nearby Priory of St Pancras. The priory was destroyed by Henry in 1537, during the Dissolution of the Monasteries. The porch was added in 1599 (42 years after Anne's death), but the house has changed very little since then.

It is now a folk museum with a fascinating collection of old iron. Known as the Every Collection—after a local ironmaster, Alderman John Every, who died in 1941—it includes embossed firebacks, chimney-cranes, spits, ladles and stewpans dating from the early 15th century.

The house also contains furniture exhibits, a bone model man-o'-war made by Russian prisoners from the Crimea who were held at Lewes, and numerous exhibits of Sussex arts and crafts. The town's other museum, Barbican House—a 16th-century, timber-framed building in the High Street—is the headquarters of the Sussex Archaeological Society. It has collections of local flints, swords, pottery, glass and tiles from prehistoric times to the 19th century.

Lewes is the county town of East Sussex and stands on a hillside between the River Ouse and the remains of a castle, built by William de Warenne, a henchman of the Conqueror. In May 1264, it withstood an assault by Simon de Montfort and other barons who opposed the supreme rule of Henry III. However, they then marched on Lewes, captured Henry's headquarters in the priory and put his troops to flight. After the Battle of Lewes, Henry signed a treaty which is held by many authorities to have marked the beginning of parliamentary government. Lewes Castle was not lived in after the death of the last de Warenne, the Earl of Surrey, in 1347. Later it was broken into, looted and finally dismantled. Today only the massive keep and the barbican maintain their watch over the now peaceful area.

The town is split from east to west by the long Georgian High Street with its attractive array of buildings, such as Shelleys Hotel, a former Elizabethan inn built in 1577. Another old building, Bull House, now a restaurant, was the home of the revolutionary writer Thomas Paine. Paine worked in Lewes as an excise officer from 1768 to 1774, and married the daughter of his landlord, a tobacconist named Samuel Ollive. In 1774 Paine went to America, where he supported the American Revolution in such pamphlets as *The Crises* series (1776 – 83), and defended the French Revolution in *The Rights of Man* (1791 – 2).

Lewes has a number of 'twittens', or footpaths, which connect its steep and narrow side streets. Church Twitten, with high flint walls and overhanging trees, leads south from High Street to Lansdown Place. The ruins of St Pancras's Priory stand on grassland at the south end of the town. The priory, like Anne of Cleves' House, was built by William de Warenne, who lies buried with his wife Gundrada in the nearby parish church of St John the Baptist – originally a rest-house at the gates of the priory.

Southover Grange, in Southover Road, was built in 1572 and was the boyhood home of the 17th-century diarist John Evelyn. Like the castle, Southover Grange was built of stones taken from the priory. It is set among beautiful floral gardens which are open to the public.

• **Parking** Cliffe High Street; East Street (2); High Street; North Street; Phoenix Causeway; Mountfield Road; South Street; West Street; Westgate Street (all car parks) • **Early closing** Wednesday • **Market days** Monday (cattle), Tuesday (fruit and vegetable) • **Event** Bonfire Night (November 5) • **Information** TEL. Brighton 471600 • **AA 24 hour service** TEL. Brighton 695231.

Ditchling EAST SUSSEX

8 miles north-west of Lewes (PAGE 70 Dc)

On a sandstone rise between the lofty South Downs and an undulating common of ragged gorse, Ditchling clusters around a busy crossroads, yet tranquillity reigns among the old houses and cottages down its back lanes. Less peaceful but much grander are some of the buildings in the main street.

A majestic timber-framed 16th-century building, part plaster, part weathered brickwork, stands on the south-west corner of the crossroads. It is now one of many antiques shops in the village. Past it, along West Street, is a splendidly uneven jumble of Tudor brickwork and timber with a precarious outer flight of steps to the first floor, complemented by timber and plaster in a gabled wing. This is Wings Place, more generally known to locals as Anne of Cleves' House because it stands on land given by Henry VIII to his fourth wife, as part of his divorce settlement. Despite the name, there is no evidence that Anne ever lived here.

A little farther along West Street, Cotterlings, a stylish Regency house, has a gleaming façade of glossy black-fired tiles, patterned with red-brick corner stones and window surrounds. Nearly opposite, on a steep mound, stands the Church of St Margaret of Antioch, its 'Sussex cap' spire restored with cedar shingles in place of the original oak. Caen stone, shipped from Normandy, was used with local flint and chalk for the mainly 13th-century building.

The high flint wall of what was, until 1965, Court Farm, now provides a sheltering arm round the neat village green, broken by the preserved foundations of an old tithe barn. One of the cattle sheds is still there, too, and a renovated wagon shed stands beside the duckpond. Beyond the wall, on a detached triangle of green, is the stark monolith of a war memorial by Joseph Cribb, a pupil of Eric Gill, the sculptor, typographer and writer.

Gill was one of several artists who lived and worked in Ditchling in the 1920s. Soon after he married he moved from London to Sopers, a red-brick house where the High Street begins to slope. His mentor, the calligrapher Edward Johnston, spent some years at Cleves, on the Lewes road, and the painter Frank Brangwyn once lived at The Jointure, in South Street.

Ditchling has a long tradition of religious nonconformism. In 1665, when the Five Mile Act forbade Dissenters to worship within 5 miles of a town, strict General Baptists walked from Lewes to hold services in the village. Their well-protected Old Meeting House in The Twitten (a Sussex word for a narrow path or alley) is now used by the Unitarians.

The smart, modern Emmanuel Chapel stands in South Street; and in East Gardens a private house still has a tethering ring in its wall and a peg for holding a saddle – it used to be a saddler's shop. Candles, a weatherboarded house, was once a candlemaker's.

South Street leads to the 813 ft high summit of Ditchling Beacon, reached by footpaths or a narrow winding road with parking at the top, near the remains of a Neolithic hill-fort.

The main road north crosses over 2 miles of Ditchling Common, and beside a tight curve in this road is the Royal Oak inn, scene of a particularly brutal murder. In 1734 the landlord, his wife and a maid had their throats cut by Jacob Harris, a pedlar who came to rob the inn. He was hanged, and his body was displayed on a gibbet on the common. The original wood was gradually chipped away by villagers who believed a fragment would cure toothache and other ailments. The remaining stump of the gibbet hangs in the Royal Oak; and preserved in Chichester House, a High Street picture gallery, is the iron cock which once crowned it. A replica of what became known as Jacob's Post stands just south of the inn.

Fletching EAST SUSSEX

10 miles north of Lewes (PAGE 70 Eb)

Fletching seems such a compact, demure little place that it is difficult to associate its trim houses and sylvan surroundings with violent moments in history. Yet in the Middle Ages it was a supply centre for highly regarded arrowheads; its name could derive from its village fletchers, or arrow-makers. However, the name is more likely derived from that of a Saxon settler Fleece – Fletching meaning 'family of Fleece'.

Baron Simon de Montfort's troops assembled in the village in 1264 when he prepared to fight Henry III (see Lewes). In May of that year, Henry established his

Wings Place, Ditchling

Edward Johnston's house

Tudor tenement

GOING-AWAY PRESENT

Wings Place in Ditchling used to be called Anne of Cleves' House, since it was built on land given to her to sweeten the bitter pill of her divorce from Henry VIII, who unkindly dubbed her 'the Flanders mare'. The antiques shop at the village crossroads was a Tudor tenement; it contrasts oddly with the 1920's house that was the home of Edward Johnston, the famous calligrapher. The Twitten, with its tile-hung cottages and a rare private graveyard, is one of several pretty Ditchling lanes.

The Twitten, Ditchling

headquarters in the Priory of St Pancras, just outside Lewes. De Montfort reconnoitred from Fletching Common in his manor of Sifelle near by (which later became the village of Sheffield), and planned a surprise attack along an old sunken track. On the eve of the Battle of Lewes, he kept vigil with his supporters in Fletching's Church of St Andrew and St Mary the Virgin.

Henry was defeated and his son (later Edward I) taken hostage. De Montfort established a representative assembly on which today's Houses of Parliament are based. It is said that some knights who died in the conflict are buried in full armour below the nave of the church.

The lovingly maintained church houses some imposing monuments – and a delightful small one. This is a delicate brass of two gloves, in memory of Petrus (Peter) Denot, a glove-maker who took part in a rebellion against Henry VI in 1450 – one of many outbreaks which culminated in the Wars of the Roses. Denot was pardoned along with other Fletching men. A more impressive brass is a memorial to the 14th-century Sir Walter Dalyngrygge, one of the family who built Bodiam Castle (see page 94), and his wife. The church also contains the mausoleum of the Sheffield family, in which lie the bones of their friend Edward Gibbon, author of *The Decline and Fall of the Roman Empire*.

In 1769, John Baker Holroyd, MP, bought Sheffield Park, the estate to the west of the village. Created Baron Sheffield and then Earl of Sheffield, he engaged the architect James Wyatt to design his house and Humphry Repton to landscape his parklands. His close friend Gibbon often came to stay, and wrote much of his celebrated book in the library. The 3rd Earl had different interests. A keen cricketer, he organised the earliest Australian Test Tours and for 20 years, from 1876 onwards, the opening game was played at Sheffield Park against the Earl's Eleven.

A private carriageway into the estate begins through a stone gateway – closed to the public – at the foot of Fletching's main street. At the far side of Sheffield Park is an entrance for visitors wishing to see the wonderful expanse of woods, lakes and gardens, famous for their rhododendrons and colourful shrubs set against a backdrop of dark conifers. Run by the National Trust, the house and gardens are open from April to mid-November, Tuesday to Saturday, and on Sunday and Bank Holiday Monday afternoons. The Bluebell Railway, with its old steam trains, is another attraction, just across the road from the entrance to the gardens.

From the gateway of Fletching Lodge, the eye is coaxed up the inviting village street. Corner Cottage's stonework perfectly matches that of the lodge and gateway. Next door, St Andrew's House, with a timbered upper storey complementing its neighbour's, is a 19th-century reconstruction by Norman Shaw, the architect who designed the old New Scotland Yard building in London.

It was once a home of the Maryon-Wilson family who almost matched the Sheffields in local landowning. The two families did not get on, and the story goes that during the 3rd Earl's day, one Maryon-Wilson refused even to set foot in Sheffield Park. But he was such a cricket enthusiast that he watched matches there through a telescope from Fletching windmill, which was demolished in 1950.

To the north of Fletching lie the slopes of Ashdown Forest's coppices and heathland, with plenty of picnic areas and long walks.

Ringmer EAST SUSSEX

3 miles north-east of Lewes (PAGE 70 Ec)

The brightly coloured village sign commemorates two historic marriages which link Ringmer to the United States, and, in striking contrast, the life of a lowly tortoise. In 1636 Ann Sadler, the vicar's daughter, married John Harvard and went with him to America, where he founded the university bearing his name. The other wedding was that of Guglielma Springett, daughter of a local knight, and William Penn, the Quaker founder of Pennsylvania.

Timothy the tortoise belonged to Mrs Rebecca Snooke, wife of a later vicar, who lived at Delves House near the church. Her nephew was the naturalist Gilbert White, a frequent visitor. He recorded Timothy's activities in *The Natural History of Selborne*, and after his aunt's death in 1780 took the tortoise home. He wrote that the 80 mile coach journey to Hampshire 'so perfectly roused it that when I turned it out on a border it walked twice down to the bottom of my garden'. Delves House has stood above the vast village green since at least 1340, though the present building is partly Queen Anne.

The green gives Ringmer, winner of a best-kept-village award in 1982, its shape and character. Grassy expanses, including a cricket pitch and bowling green, roll one after another, with views towards the Weald and a ridge of the downs above Lewes. Beside the bowling green is the Victorian village pump, protected by a pert little shelter.

For generations, the Springett family lived at Broyle Place, once a bishop's palace, a mile east of the village. After their time it was used simply as a farmhouse, but was restored to its original glory in 1955 – 7. Sir William Springett and his friend Colonel Morley, from nearby Glynde Place, served with Cromwell's Parliamentary forces besieging Arundel in December 1643. Sir William developed a deadly fever, and his pregnant wife made a hazardous journey over wintry roads to be with him.

But he died, only 23 years old, soon after she reached him. His body was carried home in his ammunition wagon, and a monument to him was erected in the church. It was their daughter, Guglielma Maria Posthuma, who became Mrs William Penn.

The Church of St Mary the Virgin owes much to the Christie family of Glyndebourne, the house just over a mile south in which an opera festival, launched in 1934, has since become world famous. The stained-glass window of the Nativity is in memory of W. L. Christie, who paid for the building of the present tower. John Christie, the festival founder, gave large donations towards the church organ and also built the present gallery.

Rottingdean EAST SUSSEX

9 miles south-east of Lewes (PAGE 70 Dc)

The Saxon clan of Rota's people lived in what was then a secluded 'dene' or hollow in a fold in the South Downs, some distance from the sea. Coastal erosion brought the sea closer until, in the 1930s, a promenade and groynes were built to protect the cliffs. The

LIONS' RETREAT *A prime minister, great artists and famous authors—among them Rudyard Kipling—have all lived in the village of Rottingdean, attracted by its old-world charm.*

promenade now links the waterfront to the resort of Brighton, but behind the coastal road the village keeps much of its old character.

Rudyard Kipling was the village's most famous resident, but in 1902 he fled to Burwash about 25 miles to the north-east to escape celebrity hunters.

Many of Kipling's relatives had associations with Rottingdean, and they formed a small community around the green and village pond. The Pre-Raphaelite artist Sir Edward Burne-Jones spent his last 18 years at North End House, on the west of the green, and designed some fine stained-glass windows for the Church of St Margaret.

His wife was one of five beautiful sisters—among them Kipling's mother and the mother of Prime Minister Stanley Baldwin. It was in Rottingdean that Baldwin met and married Lucy Ridsdale, of The Dene.

Kipling himself lived at The Elms, dignified and Georgian behind a high, flinty wall. He was devoted to his aunt, Lady Burne-Jones. After her death, North End House was occupied by Sir William Nicholson, the painter, who moved there from The Grange. Then in 1923 it was taken over by Lord Roderick Jones, whose wife Enid Bagnold wrote the novel *National Velvet*, set in a village similar to Rottingdean. The Grange now houses the public library, a local museum, art exhibitions and a toy museum—open daily except Wednesday and afternoons only on Sundays.

South of the pond, Whipping Post House, a Tudor building, was formerly flanked by a post from which it took its name, the village stocks and an enclosure for cattle. It was once the home of the legendary Captain Dunk, who engaged in Rottingdean's most profitable trade—smuggling. Beneath Challoners, the oldest house in the village, secret passages, now blocked, probably had smuggling connections, too.

Among monuments in the church is the bust of Thomas Hooker, vicar from 1792 to 1838, who would act as lookout for smugglers heading for the caves and passages leading up to the village. The church is largely Norman on a Saxon base. In the 14th century it was set ablaze by French pirates, and many villagers hiding in the belfry were burnt alive. The intense heat left scorchmarks that are still visible.

Baldwin and his wife presented the sanctuary with a chair in 1942, to commemorate their golden wedding anniversary. Outside, to the south of the west door, rest the ashes of Sir Edward and Lady Burne-Jones and their celebrated grand-daughter, the novelist Angela Thirkall. Elsewhere is the grave of a very different artist—the music-hall entertainer G. H. Elliott, billed as 'The Chocolate-Coloured Coon'.

MIDHURST

WEST SUSSEX

12 miles north of Chichester (PAGE 70 Bb)

The novelist H. G. Wells went to school in this pretty little market town. 'I found something very agreeable and picturesque in its clean cobbled streets,' he wrote later in *Tono-Bungay*, in which Midhurst becomes Wimblehurst, '. . . its odd turnings and abrupt corners, and in the pleasant park that crowds up one side of the town.'

In 1881 the 15-year-old Wells was apprenticed to a chemist on Church Hill—the shop is still there—off the Market Place. In those days apprentices had to pay for their position and after a month's trial he could no longer afford the cost. Instead, he became a pupil at Midhurst Grammar School and stayed in the headmaster's house. However, six weeks later, his mother—housekeeper at nearby Uppark House (see South Harting, page 82)—got him another apprenticeship in Southsea and he left. But he returned to the school two years later as student assistant and lodged over the sweetshop in North Street.

The school, founded in 1672, stands in North Street. Lower down the street is the curiously named Knockhundred Row. Its timbered workshops were once part of an ironmonger's, but are now occupied by a number of shops. The name is thought to derive from medieval times when Midhurst had a castle, and the owner could call upon 100 men to defend it—which was done by knocking on 100 households. The tile-hung public library in North Street was built in the early 16th century and was probably first used as a storehouse or granary. From there, a short walk down Church Hill leads into Market Square, in which a weekly market was held from the Middle Ages to the turn of the century.

On the north side of the square is the parish church of St Mary Magdalene and St Denys, mostly 19th century but with earlier traces. Close by is the half-timbered Elizabeth House, a recently restored Tudor building which is now a restaurant with an inglenook fireplace. The Old Market Hall, on a corner near by, was built in the 16th century and was the Grammar School's first home in 1672. Below the Old Market Hall is South Street, flanked by South Pond, a calm oasis of water and grass, and the Spread Eagle Hotel, a coaching inn dating from 1430. Elizabeth I is said to have visited it while staying at Cowdray House, and Edward VII stayed at the inn at the turn of the present century.

Rising above the town is St Ann's Hill, site of a long-vanished Norman castle. The River Rother curves past the hill on its way to the majestic ruins of Cowdray House. The ruins can be reached either by way of Queen's Path, a favourite walk of Elizabeth I along the river, or by a causeway branching off North Street near the Grammar School. The path is now part of a nature trail leading past South Pond, populated by mute swans, Canada geese, mallards—and even gulls.

The house was built about 1530 by the Earl of Southampton, but the interior was destroyed by fire in 1793. However, visitors can still see around the rooms—including the Great Chamber, the Great Parlour and the Chapel. The wainscoting in the hall still bears charred evidence of the fire. Lord Cowdray has turned the surrounding parkland into sports fields, where you can sometimes see Prince Charles playing polo – and even mingle with royalty when an appeal is made for everyone present to stamp down the turf at the end of a chukka.

● **Parking** North Street; Grange Road (both car parks) ● **Early closing** Wednesday ● **AA 24 hour service** TEL. Guildford 572841.

Loxwood WEST SUSSEX

17 miles north-east of Midhurst (PAGE 70 Cb)

In the 13th century the thickly wooded region around Chiddingfold, Fernhurst, Wisborough Green and Loxwood became a busy industrialised complex. Finding the local sands ideal and fuels from the Wealden forests plentiful, French and Flemish settlers introduced new glass-making techniques. They prospered until 1616, when rival claims by shipbuilders and ironmasters led to an Act being passed which forbade the use of wood as fuel in glass manufacture. The once bustling villages sank back again into rural tranquillity, though even today there are enough plantations and woods in this gently rolling landscape to keep a timber depot active.

Beside the pond, Loxwood's village stores used to be run by disciples of a puritanical evangelist who came here in 1850. John Sirgood pushed his belongings on a handcart from London, occasionally allowing his wife to ride as well. He chose Loxwood as his base and gathered about him The Society of Dependants. They became known as Cokelers because of their teetotal preference for cocoa. They established a meeting house and gradually built up influence here, in neighbouring villages and as far away as Hove on the coast. The Cokelers' local co-operative stores included a bakery and a butcher's, and eventually a garage. They also operated the first taxi service in the region. The store survived until 1980, but now stands empty.

The Cokelers' austere philosophy, which banned sport, the theatre, music in the home, and refused to solemnise marriage in their chapel, may have contributed to their decline; but many locals – even those not sharing their beliefs – regret their passing. They did a great deal of quiet charitable work in the region, and 'Nobody ever went hungry if the Cokelers heard about it,' reminisced one villager in 1984.

The single-storey chapel along Spy Lane is neat and unpretentious. John Sirgood lies in the peaceful graveyard behind, but no headstone marks his grave. For many decades the sect identified their little burial mounds with simple numbers. These have been replaced by a set of stone 'Grave Measuring Points' which indicate the general grouping of the graves. The few remaining members of the sect live in retirement houses opposite the chapel.

The parish church of St John the Baptist, built in 1900, has a bright, red-brick interior. On the bend below it stands The Onslow Arms, with part of the Wey and Arun Junction Canal, opened in 1816, running behind it. The canal was meant to link the two rivers to make a continuous waterway from London to Littlehampton, with spurs to Chichester and Portsmouth. It was completed between Newbridge and Shalford but was soon doomed to extinction by the newly expanding railways, and closed in 1871. Canal enthusiasts work intermittently to revive a sizable section for recreational use, and the stretch behind The Onslow Arms is occasionally cleared of reeds.

South Harting WEST SUSSEX

9 miles west of Midhurst (PAGE 70 Ac)

The bridle path of the South Downs Way loops around Beacon Hill and Harting Downs, south of the groups of Harting villages which crouch below slopes of beech and ash. From the north, South Harting is reached by a tortuous switchback of twisting lanes. 'Of all the downland villages it is to my mind the most attractive,' wrote the naturalist W. H. Hudson in *Nature in Downland*.

The two roads which approach from the south climb and then plunge to a junction on the edge of the village. Here, ancient cottages, with moss-stained thatch and slyly peeping dormer windows, appear to have been roughly assembled and patched with any wood, chalk and brick that was available.

An unexpectedly wide main street descends between Georgian and older restored houses. On the left, the timber jetty of the upper storey of 'ffowlers' Bucke' is attractively exposed, and the brass plaque of its wine-dealing occupant is as discreet as the tasteful decoration of the plastered façade. The neighbouring White Hart, with two sets of steps up from the sloping road, contains massive timbers.

The 19th-century novelist Anthony Trollope lived the last two years of his life in the village, and his pen and paperknife are displayed in the church. In the churchyard is a slender war memorial in Portland stone, the work of the modern sculptor and typographer Eric Gill, who used to live at Ditchling (see page 78). Just outside the churchyard, near the gate, are the parish stocks and a whipping post equipped with three sets of wrist irons.

The Church of St Mary and St Gabriel is cruciform, with a spire of green copper shingles. Inside are memorials to the Fords and Fetherstonhaughs of Uppark, a mansion over the hill a mile south.

Commanding magnificent views towards the coast, this house, in its landscaped grounds, was built around the end of the 17th and beginning of the 18th centuries, on 15th-century foundations. During the Civil War its owner was Sir Edward Ford, a Royalist who nevertheless managed to become First Lord of the Works under Cromwell. He invented a water pump to raise water to his property – the little pump house is 200 yds south of South Harting church. Ford then successfully applied its principles in London in 1656, pumping Thames water through four 8 in. pipes.

Uppark's most colourful owner, however, was Sir Harry Fetherstonhaugh, who imported French furniture and ornaments still on display in the mansion's spacious rooms. He also installed 15-year-old Emma Hart and her illegitimate baby for a year. Emma – future wife of Sir William Hamilton and mistress of Lord Nelson – used to entertain his male guests by dancing on the dining-room table.

When he was over 70, Sir Harry married his dairymaid and they spent 21 years together. His widow continued to live at Uppark with her sister, who in turn inherited and stayed until 1895 with her former governess as her companion. Both ladies are depicted in the writer H. G. Wells's *Autobiography* – his mother was housekeeper at Uppark for 13 years (see Midhurst, page 81). The National Trust now administers the property which is open Wednesday, Thursday, Sunday and Bank Holiday Monday afternoons from April to the end of September.

MAP 8

GARDEN OF ENGLAND AND THE PILGRIMS' WAY

A front line of defence against invaders, yet always fulfilling its role as the peaceful Garden of England . . . This dual personality sits lightly upon a countryside ripe with orchards, heady with hop gardens and graced by the Pilgrims' Way, winding past old Wealden towns and villages towards Canterbury, as it did in Chaucer's day.

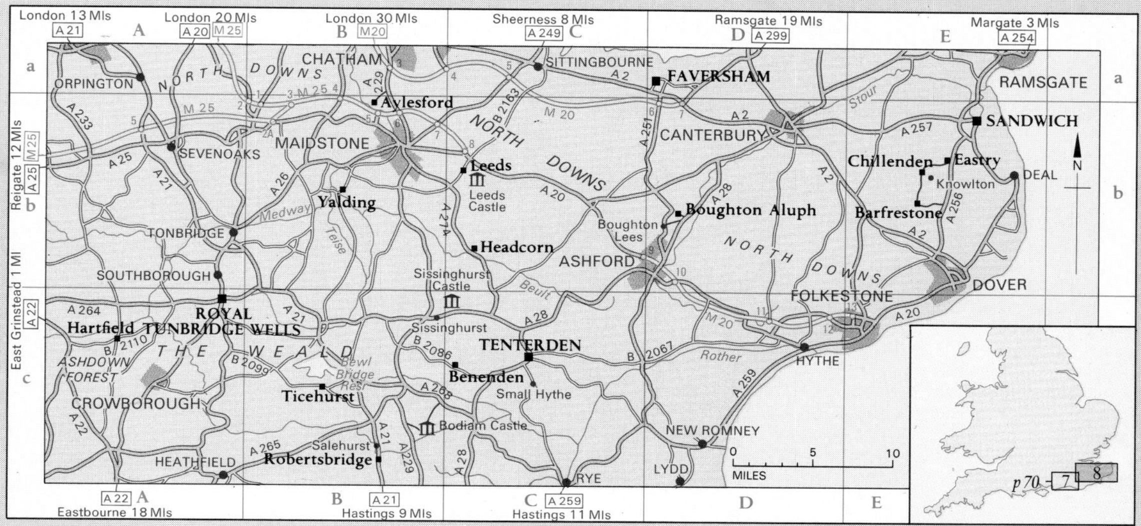

MAP 8: NEIGHBOURING AREA – MAP 7

FAVERSHAM Aylesford Boughton Aluph
ROYAL TUNBRIDGE WELLS Hartfield Leeds Ticehurst Yalding
SANDWICH Barfrestone Chillenden Eastry
TENTERDEN Benenden Headcorn Robertsbridge

FAVERSHAM

KENT

10 miles west of Canterbury (PAGE 83 Da)

On February 15, 1551, at 7 p.m., Thomas Arden, one of Faversham's leading citizens and a former mayor, was murdered by his wife's lover, Thomas Mosby, and two accomplices, all of whom were later convicted and executed. The crime – a sensation at the time and later the subject of the Elizabethan drama *Arden of Feversham* – was committed in Arden's own home. This large timber-framed house, incorporating the only remains of Faversham's medieval abbey, still stands in Abbey Street. The former Fleur de Lis inn, where the crime was plotted, has also survived and is now Faversham's excellent Heritage Centre.

The town combines architecture of different eras into a harmonious whole – most clearly seen in the Guildhall, with its unlikely but successful combination of a rough 16th-century timber arcade and an elegant Regency superstructure. It dominates the Market Place which, with the streets radiating from it, houses a superb assembly of buildings of every century from the 15th onwards. Also noteworthy in the Market Place is No. 10, an overhanging black-and-white timber-framed building, dated 1570. Near by, No. 12 was once an inn, where James II, captured while trying to flee the country in 1688, was held by local fishermen. In West Street, No. 121, dated 1697, has three fine panels of ornamental plasterwork. The late 19th-century offices of Shepherd Neame, the brewers, in Court Street, is decorated with brightly coloured reliefs of hops and poppies in the doorposts.

Faversham, though, is no mere showcase town. By the 12th century it had risen to prominence as a manufacturing centre and a port. It is also a member of the Confederation of Cinque Ports, one of many towns supporting the five main ports entrusted with the defence of the South-East coast. A walk by the creek, where sailing barges are moored alongside, confirms that the town still has a busy commercial life. The continuity is symbolised by the warehouse on Standard Quay at the far end of Abbey Street. It was built in the 17th century, probably with 14th-century materials salvaged from the abbey, and is still in use. One industry, important from the 16th century to the 1930s, was the manufacture of gunpowder in the marshy land to the west. The 18th-century Chart Gunpowder Mills have now been restored.

The parish church of St Mary of Charity is large and impressive. Surprisingly, the clearly Gothic building turns out to have a Georgian nave, built after the original Norman nave was declared unsafe in the 1750s.

HARMONY OF HISTORY *Faversham's Market Place, with the town pump in the foreground. Buildings from many periods and a variety of styles manage to harmonise delightfully in the town.*

In the west end, above a strongroom for storing valuables, is an intriguing watch-room with small windows from which most of the building could be seen during an emergency. Fourteenth-century paintings of New Testament scenes have survived on an octagonal pillar in the north transept. Another 18th-century addition was the open spire built in 1797 in imitation of Wren's St Dunstan-in-the-East in London. Beside the church is the original Elizabethan grammar school of 1587, now the Masonic Hall.

In the western outskirts of Faversham, overlooking the creek, stands the 12th-century Davington Priory, restored in the 19th century. The domestic quarters are now a private house, and the church is the parish church for the suburb of Davington. In another suburb, beside the main road to London, is Maison Dieu, a fragment of a 13th-century hostel for Canterbury pilgrims, now a museum.

● **Parking** Bank Street; Forbes Road ● **Early closing** Thursday ● **Market days** Thursday, Friday, Saturday ● **Theatre** Arden Theatre, Bank Street ● **Cinema** New Royal Cinema, Middle Row ● **Museum** Maison Dieu Museum, Ospringe Street ● **Events** Swale Festival Week (March); Sailing barge race (August); Carnival (October) ● **Information** TEL. Faversham 534542 ● **AA 24 hour service** TEL. Maidstone 55353.

Aylesford KENT

22 miles west of Faversham (PAGE 83 Bb)

Floodlit by night, the Norman tower of the Church of St Peter and St Paul glows like a beacon to travellers on the M20 motorway, which runs just south of this large village. The church stands on a steep, walled bank, and beneath it the jumbled rooftops of Aylesford stagger down the hillside towards a large medieval bridge spanning the River Medway.

English history starts early here. *The Anglo-Saxon Chronicle*, a 9th-century record started by Alfred the Great, tells how in AD 455 the warrior mercenaries Hengest and Horsa fought Vortigern, king of the Britons, in Aegelsthrep, as Aylesford was called then. Horsa was killed and Hengest and his son Aesc 'received the kingdom'. Aegel's threp, or ford, was one of the earliest crossings over the Medway. The Romans used it, and the ancient Britons before them.

A charter to hold a weekly market was granted in the 13th century, and what is now The Little Gem inn was probably built then – possibly as a market house.

The 16th-century Chequers Inn was built as a merchant's house, and along Rochester Road is a row of almshouses built in 1605, with a fine 19th-century pump in front. On Cage Hill there is a plaque where a cage was built into the ragstone wall to hold felons in custody to await trial.

Next to the Chequers, a lane leads to a riverside quay, and half a mile downstream is The Friars where, once again, ancient and modern meet. A religious settlement was founded here in 1242, when the crusader Richard de Grey returned from the Holy Land with a dozen hermits from Mount Carmel and gave them his manor. At the Dissolution of the Monasteries in 1539, the priory was sold off and remained in private hands for 410 years.

In 1949 it was put up for sale, and Carmelites all over the world subscribed to buy it. Monks led by Father Malachy Lynch returned on the Vigil of All Saints Day, October 31, that year. The Friars, now much restored, has an open-air church, a medieval courtyard and Rosary Way, a garden set aside for prayer and meditation. Guests staying at the priory dine in its oldest building, the galleried, 13th-century Pilgrims' Hall.

On the downs just north of the village are the standing-stone remains of Neolithic communal burial chambers, Kits Coty House and Little Kits Coty House. They are about 5500 years old. The names probably derive from *Kid Coit*, Celtic for 'tomb in the wood'.

The vicar at Aylesford from 1902 to 1909 was the Reverend Arthur Thorndike. His daughter, the late Dame Sybil Thorndike, became one of the great actresses of the 20th century. She was married in St Peter and St Paul's in 1908, and died in June 1976.

Boughton Aluph KENT

10 miles south of Faversham (PAGE 83 Db)

Boughton Aluph lies hidden in the folds of the North Downs, amid rich arable farmland laced by narrow, hedge-banked lanes. The village is in two parts – a cluster of farm buildings around the lonely, little-used Church of All Saints, and the houses lining the large triangular green at Boughton Lees, a mile to the south-west.

A curious feature of the flint-walled church is a chimney sprouting beside the stocky tower. Once it carried away smoke from a fireplace built into the southern porch, where people on the ancient Pilgrims' Way from Winchester to Canterbury could rest and warm themselves.

King Harold owned the village before he died at Hastings in 1066, but its name derives from a later lord, Alulphus of Boctune, who built the north-east chancel of the church early in the 13th century. All Saints was much enlarged over the next two centuries, and its stained-glass windows bear the arms of three sons of Edward III – the Black Prince, John of Gaunt and Lionel, Duke of Clarence.

A natural son of Richard III – therefore the last of the Plantagenets – is thought to be buried in the

REFLECTED BEAUTY *Clouds, a medieval bridge, a timbered house and a church tower pleasingly reflect in the Medway at Aylesford.*

church grounds. Surrounding fields such as 'The Danes' are still known by names unchanged since Norman times. The elegant manor, Boughton Court, is mostly 18th century, but was built above a rib-vaulted 14th-century crypt.

The major part of the village is grouped around the green and cricket pitch – a string of red-brick and weatherboarded cottages, the inn and the converted tithe barn where most of the village's church services are held in winter. Opposite is the 17th-century manor house and the gateway to Eastwell Park and Manor – a Jacobean-style mansion largely rebuilt in the 1920s and now a hotel set in 3000 acres of parkland.

ROYAL TUNBRIDGE WELLS

KENT

12 miles south of Sevenoaks (PAGE 83 Ac)

Set in a beautiful corner of the 'Garden of England', this historic spa town only dates from the early 17th century. It was then that Lord North, a rakish young nobleman staying in the district, refreshed himself at a spring on the edge of the forest. He took a sample of the sparkling water back with him to London, where it was found to be rich in iron.

It soon became fashionable to visit the rustic 'wells' and take the medicinal water as an aid to recovery from the excesses of court life. At first, noblemen pitched tents on the surrounding grassland, but by the late 1630s the village of Tunbridge Wells had sprung up, with market booths and taverns.

Among its first royal visitors was Princess (later Queen) Anne. One day in 1697 her son, the Duke of Gloucester, slipped on the grassy banks around the spring – and she gave £100 to have the place paved. The work was done three years later, when the inhabitants laid down square, baked tiles known locally as 'pantiles'. The area became called The Pantiles and although the tiles were replaced in 1793 by Purbeck flagstones, 14 of the original red tiles can be seen by the steps on the west side of Bath Square.

The spring is now in the portico of the old Bath House at the north entrance to The Pantiles. Between Good Friday and mid-October, the traditional 'dipper', or serving lady, hands out glasses of water, in which you really can taste iron. The dipper is usually there from Wednesday to Sunday, and you have to make a small payment for the water.

Visitors to the town usually make straight for The Pantiles – a shopping centre known for its antiques showrooms. Film sequences were shot here for the musical *Half a Sixpence* (1967), starring the cockney singer Tommy Steele. The Upper Walk contains the 18th-century Assembly Rooms, now converted into shops and a post office, where the dandy Beau Nash (1674 – 1761) presided over gambling tables; he was Master of Ceremonies from 1735 until his death. The 'new' Lower Assembly Rooms are in the Lower Walk.

With its elegant colonnades and wrought-iron balconies The Pantiles forms 'old' Tunbridge Wells; the 'new' town stretches away to the north. It was started in the 1820s when the London architect Decimus Burton (1800 – 81) was commissioned to build an estate of Grecian mansions and villas. His ornate and stylish houses are set near the Calverley Hotel, which was once a private house in which the young Princess Victoria often spent her holidays.

The princess and her mother, the Duchess of Kent, attended the town's oldest church, that of King Charles-the-Martyr, between 1827 and 1834. A brass plaque marks the pew in which they sat. Built in the late 17th century, the church's modest exterior gives no indication of the delights inside – the chief of which is a magnificent Baroque plaster ceiling.

In 1630, royalty first visited Tunbridge Wells – 24 years after Lord North discovered the spring – when Queen Henrietta Maria, wife of Charles I, took a course of the waters. She was followed by so many other crowned heads that in 1909 the Mayor and Burgesses petitioned Edward VII for permission to add the prefix 'Royal' to the town's name. The king gave his consent and since then the town has officially been called Royal Tunbridge Wells. Its two halves, the 'old' and the 'new', have joined harmoniously together, and the borough is noted for its broad, tree-lined streets and expanses of greenery.

Among the many famous writers to visit the area was William Makepeace Thackeray (1811 – 63), author of *Vanity Fair*. In 1860 he stayed for some months in

'Thackeray's House', a white clapboard building, on the London Road, where he wrote the essay *Tunbridge Toys* – which tells of his delight in the town.

Just south-west of the town are the popular High Rocks – a sandstone outcrop which can be explored by walking and climbing enthusiasts throughout the year.

● **Parking** Crescent Road; Goods Station Road; Victoria Road (3); Beech Street; John Street; Eridge Road; Little Mount Sion; Warwick Road; Major Yorks Road (all car parks) ● **Early closing** Wednesday ● **Market day** Wednesday ● **Theatre** Assembly Hall, Crescent Road ● **Cinema** Classic 1, 2 and 3, Mount Pleasant Road ● **Information** TEL. Tunbridge Wells 26121 ● **AA 24 hour service** TEL. Maidstone 55353.

Hartfield EAST SUSSEX

8 miles west of Royal Tunbridge Wells (PAGE 83 Ac)

Millions of readers are unwittingly familiar with the wooded countryside around Hartfield, for it has been immortalised by A. A. Milne and the artist E. H. Shepard in the tales of *Winnie the Pooh.* Milne lived at Cotchford Farm, half a mile south of the village and the wooden bridge where his son (Christopher Robin) and his companions liked to meet.

A glance at a local map will transport many visitors back to their childhood: Gill's Lap is Galleon's Lap in the Pooh books, and Five Hundred Acre Wood is One Hundred Acre Wood.

Hartfield stands on the borders of Ashdown Forest, the largest area of land in the south-east never to have been under the plough. In the Middle Ages the forest, larger than now, was a royal hunting ground – hence the village's name, a hart being a stag. Since then, the village has been moderately prosperous through farming, timber and, until the 18th century, ironfounding – which used charcoal produced in the forest as fuel and iron from the local ironstone quarries. Fields to the north of Hartfield slope down to the River Medway, along which the industry's products were transported.

The Hay Wagon and the Anchor Inn, two oak-beamed pubs on the main road, are at the centre of the village. The 16th-century Anchor was once a workhouse for women requiring 'correction'. A lane of weatherboarded cottages leads up to a lych gate, partly overhung by the upper floor of a half-timbered 16th-century cottage. The ironstone Church of St Mary the Virgin, with its tall shingled spire, is framed by this attractive black-and-white entrance.

The 13th-century church has one particularly intriguing wall tablet with a Latin verse inscription. It is dedicated to the memory of Richard Rands, Oxford scholar and rector of Hartfield from 1622 to 1640. He apparently experienced a late religious conversion and his epitaph – composed by himself – says: 'He lived obscure and always shunned the vulgar throng, that is wont to reek of the odours of the vine-crowned Bacchus. But alas! He who lived in retreat lived badly . . . before my death I had almost become prey of the Red Dragon (i.e. the Devil) but the Lord Jesus looked on me and delivered me.' Practical results of his deliverance included the establishing of a parish school.

Visitors can wander at will in Ashdown Forest, with its open heathland, beech glades and clumps of Scots pine. The wide variety of birds to be seen there includes the hobby, kestrel, nightjar and tree pipit.

Ticehurst EAST SUSSEX

11 miles south-east of Royal Tunbridge Wells (PAGE 83 Bc)

Cottages of gleaming white weatherboard and glowing russet tiles stand around the Square, with a group of chestnut trees in its centre. St Mary's Church forms a buttress on the south side of the village, on the ridge between the valleys of the rivers Bewl and Limden. An ancient track once ran along this ridge, following today's road through Ticehurst. Centuries later, the Romans had ironworks in the district – in 1968 the remains of a Roman 'bloomery', or iron-smelting furnace, were excavated at Holbeam Wood, some 2 miles away.

There is a good view of the church from the bottom of St Mary's Lane which leads up past a grassy close where there was once a pond. Smugglers, according to local tradition, once used the pond as a hiding place for kegs of brandy. Opposite, the weatherboarded

Shaping up the iron

The shoe is hammered out

THE SMITH FAMILY

Four generations of the Stern family have been village blacksmiths at Yalding, and two of them – Edgar Stern and his son Trevor – are now working there together, forging shoes for export and shoeing local horses. Here, amid flying sparks and the sizzle of hot metal, Edgar shoes a horse at the old forge. First he heats up the shoe and beats it into shape, then the horse stands calmly as he ensures a comfortable fit.

wall of Whatman's curves curiously away from the lane. It was built around the turn of the century by a carpenter who wanted a storeroom for his timber. He therefore extended the cottage to the limit of his land, which happened to follow the bend in the road.

One of the best features of the 14th-century Church of St Mary is easily missed. A window in the north end is made up of fragments of medieval glass. It is a Doom – a lurid and radical representation of the Last Judgment – which shows the damned, and a bishop's mitre and a pope's triple crown being dragged in a cart by devils down to Hell. In the floor of the south chapel stands an iron tombstone, bearing the arms of the May family. Such tombstones were very popular in the 17th and 18th centuries when the Wealden iron industry was thriving.

There are splendid walks along footpaths in the surrounding countryside, one leading through a nature reserve and along the banks of the Bewl Bridge reservoir. Dunsters Mill, a 15th-century house beside the reservoir, was moved about 200 yds, brick by brick, from its original site, which is now under water.

Yalding KENT

12 miles north-east of Royal Tunbridge Wells (PAGE 83 Bb)

Seen from the ridge to the north, Yalding is surrounded by a sea of hop gardens, broken by the white, sail-like cowls of oast-houses where the hops are dried. Rows of hop poles and orchards of apple and pear march into the distance. Yalding is one of the largest hop-growing parishes in England. Until the 1950s it was invaded every summer by up to 2000 hop-pickers from London's East End, who stayed in the squat rows of red-brick huts which line the nearby lanes.

Folk memories die hard, and even today many of the trippers who fish or swim at The Lees – meadows between the rivers Medway and Beult – are former hoppers returning to the village of their early summers, before machines took over hop-picking. Yalding remains a working village. From the lych gate of the Church of St Peter and St Paul, the ringing of iron and

Ensuring that the shoe is a comfortable fit

POET'S WINDOW *Laurence Whistler engraved this beautiful window in Yalding church, in memory of his friend, the poet Edmund Blunden, who was brought up in the village and described it in verse.*

the clatter of horses' hooves can be heard on the other side of the High Street. The sound comes from the forge of the farriers Stern and Sons. Edgar Stern's son Trevor is the fourth generation of farrier in the family, and father and son together have 'shoed' for England and won many major prizes. They are always pleased to welcome visitors.

Perhaps inevitably in such a bustling little place, some recent buildings and conversions show scant respect for the traditional style of the weatherboarded or tile-hung cottages which are interspersed with batteries of barns and red-brick oast-houses.

The village stands where the rivers Beult and Teise join the Medway. When the rivers flood, they deposit the rich alluvial soil which has made the farmland around so fertile. The village is approached from the south-west over two long medieval bridges, the second of which, Town Bridge, leads into the High Street.

The church, on a mound at the south end, dates from the 12th century with 13th and 14th-century additions. A small window in the south wall of the chancel commemorates Edmund Blunden (1896–1974), the 'poet of peace and war' who was brought up in Yalding and who described the life and landscape of Kent in verses such as:

Here they went with smock and crook,
Toiled in the sun, lolled in the shade,
Here they mudded out the brook
And here their hatchet cleared the glade:
Harvest supper woke their wit,
Huntsman's moon their wooings lit.

The window, which was engraved by Blunden's friend Laurence Whistler, reconciles the two themes of the poet's work, with living briar coiled like barbed wire and a bombshell bursting into bloom like a tree.

From the church, the High Street curves gently up a slope past Court Lodge, an imposing red-brick mansion of the late 17th century, past old cottages towards Cleaves, the former grammar school. South-east of the village lies Wade's Moat, an elegant Georgian house surrounded – for no other reason than caprice – by a moat. Near by is Cheveney House, black and white, timber framed and partly 16th century.

SANDWICH

KENT

12 miles east of Canterbury (PAGE 83 Eb)

In 1573 Elizabeth I paid a four-day visit to Sandwich, and the town has several reminders of the event. She stayed in Strand Street, in the King's Lodging, named after her father, Henry VIII, who was also a guest here. The building's original timber frames are now hidden behind a brick front. During her visit, the queen inspected the Sir Roger Manwood School (now Manwood Court) in Strand Street which had been founded in 1564. According to a contemporary chronicler, while she was there she 'did make merrye and did eat of dyvers dishes'.

The half-timbered Guildhall, in the town centre, was built in 1579. The courtroom, still in use today as a magistrates' court, has changed little since Elizabeth's time. The panelling, installed in 1607, includes a jury-box which can be folded into the wall when not in use. On either side of the 13th-century entrance to the courtroom are two carved figures. They represent the lion of England and the Tudor dragon, and both were part of the original decorations when Elizabeth visited the town. The stained-glass window, put up in 1906, shows the Mayor and Jurats (municipal officers) receiving Elizabeth at Sandown Gate.

In the Council Chamber above the court hangs a portrait of Edward, 1st Earl of Sandwich and Admiral of the Fleet (1625–72). He was killed at the Battle of Sole Bay, off the east coast during the Anglo-Dutch war. Painted wooden panels beside his portrait depict the battle (see also Southwold, page 182).

As one of England's original Cinque Ports – a medieval group of five ports which defended the South-East coast – Sandwich has long associations with the sea. The town lies some 2 miles inland on the River Stour, and its life as a port ended in the 16th century when the harbour silted up. Around the same time the town was inundated with Flemish clothworkers. Having fled from their Spanish oppressors, they transformed Sandwich into a thriving market town.

The Flemish influence can be seen in buildings such as Manwood Court, the White Friars in New Street, and the Dutch House in King Street. The refugees also rebuilt the tower of St Peter's Church, which collapsed after an earth tremor in 1661. The role of parish church was taken over in 1948 by St Clement's, with its robust Norman tower. Almost opposite the King's Lodging is the town's third church, St Mary the Virgin, which was damaged by another earth tremor in 1668. However, it was restored recently and is usually open.

Sandwich has two surviving town gates, both on the banks of the Stour. The Barbican, now a private residence, stands at the end of the toll bridge. Henry VIII built it in 1539 to guard the approaches to Sandwich Haven. Fisher Gate, a short distance to the east, dates from 1384. Running parallel to the river is Upper Strand Street, at the end of which is The Salutation, a house in the Queen Anne style designed in 1911 by Sir Edwin Lutyens, whose work included the Whitehall Cenotaph. At the opposite end of the town, in Strand Street, are two 15th-century houses called The Pilgrims with their black-and-white upper floors overhanging the pavement.

The old roofs and chimneys are best seen from

PORT OF THE PAST *Sandwich, a town rich in history, lies 2 miles inland. But it was a port until its harbour silted up in the 16th century. Elizabeth I was a visitor.*

the town walls (particularly from The Butts) which now comprise an elevated walk curving around the town. On the outskirts is St Bartholomew's Hospital on the Dover road, founded about 1217 as a wayfarers' hostel. Farther out are Sandwich's two famous golf courses and the Gazen Salts Nature Reserve. This was created in 1973 and its central lake is the habitat of nesting warblers, moorhens and tufted ducks.

• **Parking** The Quay; Cattle Market (both car parks) • **Early closing** Wednesday • **Market day** Thursday • **Information** TEL. Sandwich 617106 (summer) • **AA 24 hour service** TEL. Thanet 81226.

Barfrestone KENT

9 miles south-west of Sandwich (PAGE 83 Eb)

A village pond, a couple of farms and a clutch of thatched cottages conceal a surprise for the visitor: one of England's finest very small Norman churches. To push open the gate into the churchyard is to enter a fantastic world of angels and armed warriors, dragons and dancing girls. The outside walls of the tiny Church of St Nicholas are a riot of elaborate 12th-century carving in stone imported from Caen, in Normandy.

In the round arch above the south door, amidst a swirling confusion of foliage, sits Christ with four legendary beasts at his feet: the Sphinx, symbolising the world with its riddles, two mermaids typifying temptation and passion, and a griffin, who is meant to depict the Devil.

Surrounding this scene is a series of 12 niches depicting the lighter side of life – a love scene, a drinking party, a falconer and a figure dancing to a tune played on a harp by a bear. Finally, 14 stones that form the outer semicircle of the arch represent every-day activities of the manor house and estate. Gargoyles peer from under the eaves; they are said to represent

THE CHURCH WHERE FANTASY RUNS WILD

A world of strange beings awaits the visitor to the ancient little Church of St Nicholas at Barfrestone. On its outer walls is an assortment of 12th-century carved stone figures – including dancing girls. Christ, the Sphinx and the Devil are featured in a group above the south door. The church also boasts a fine wheel window with eight stone spokes, surrounded by a frieze.

St Nicholas Church, Barfrestone

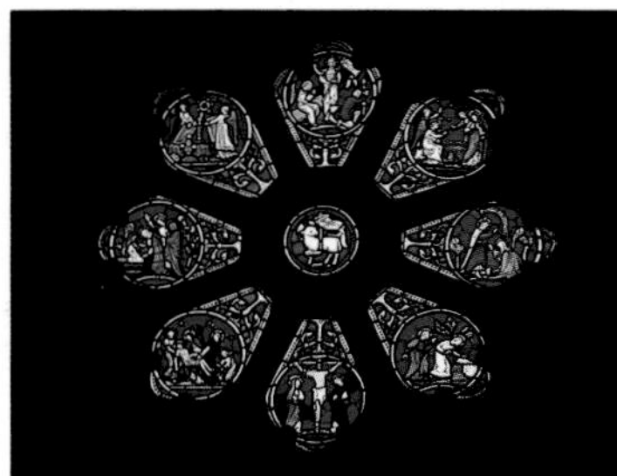

The wheel window

Gargoyle group

The church's south door

malignant spirits exorcised from the building at the time of its consecration, and exhibited as a warning to evil powers to stay outside. The east end of the church has a magnificent wheel window divided by eight stone spokes and encircled by a frieze. Lions stand on stone brackets gazing eastwards. According to medieval bestiaries – books professing to describe the nature and significance of animals – lions sleep with their eyes open. They are therefore ideally suited to watch for the Second Coming.

A more recent feature which adds to the general air of unreality is the bell suspended, almost out of sight, from a yew tree in the churchyard. The bell is rung from inside the church by a rope that passes through the wall and into the tree. Behind the church, a narrow lane winds past cottages whose attic windows peep out from beneath eyebrows of thatch.

Chillenden KENT

6 miles south-west of Sandwich (PAGE 83 Eb)

A well-restored 19th-century post-mill stands above the gentle dip in which Chillenden rests. The village is typical of this part of east Kent: fields around once belonged to the large estates of Knowlton and Goodnestone, and farming still provides the life blood of the area. A pond, a few farm buildings and two rows of 19th-century estate cottages bear witness to this.

Farming also endowed the region with its legacy of churches. The small flint-walled Church of All Saints has two Norman doorways, one surmounted by carved chevron moulding.

Half a mile east, past the timber-framed Griffin's Head inn, lies Knowlton. The tiny box-pewed Church of St Clement stands beside Knowlton Court, with its cluster of stables and octagonal 18th-century dovecote. Keys to the church can be obtained from the office at the back entrance to Knowlton Court, a part-Elizabethan part-Queen Anne red-brick house.

Among several marble monuments inside the church is a magnificent 18th-century tomb chest commissioned by a loving mother, Lady Narborough, to commemorate her two sons lost in a Scilly shipwreck. The carved relief shows a three-masted ship striking a rock, with an inscription above describing the brothers as 'happy in their inclinations, happy in their fortunes, unhappy only in their fates'.

Eastry KENT

3 miles south-west of Sandwich (PAGE 83 Eb)

In 1979 Eastry celebrated its millennium, but more than a thousand years of history are packed into the lane which runs past the Church of St Mary the Virgin. Eastry was the capital of the eastern district of the kingdom of Kent during the Dark Ages, and the Saxon kings had a royal hall which stood beside the church, on the site of Eastry Court. It was here, too, that Archbishop Thomas Becket, fleeing from Henry II, sheltered while a boat was found to take him from Sandwich to France. While in hiding at Eastry Court, he is said to have heard Mass in secret in the church.

The church has a solid Norman tower and a 13th-century clerestory – the high pointed windows which bathe the interior with light. On the north wall, an angel clutching a victor's palm floats over a marble relief of a naval battle. The monument commemorates Captain John Harvey, who died in 1794 from wounds received in the victory over the French off Brest on the 'Glorious First of June'. Captain Harvey lived at Heronden, a charming 18th-century plum-brick house a mile to the south-west of Eastry. A more poignant monument in the church shows a child reaching out in vain towards a woman by an urn. She is his mother, Sarah Boteler, who died in childbirth in 1777.

Church Street, with its row of 18th and 19th-century cottages, leads to the church and towards the early 18th-century front of Eastry Court. The village contains several other interesting buildings. Although very well preserved, Fairfield House, a 15th-century timber-framed building south of the church, is beginning to betray its age; both corners of the front lean spectacularly away from each other. In Mill Lane there is the 19th-century workhouse, now a hospital, whose dour grandeur greets visitors approaching from the south. Farther on stands the black stump of a windmill, now without its sails.

TENTERDEN

KENT

12 miles south-west of Ashford (PAGE 83 Cc)

From the tower of St Mildred's Church, rising more than 100 ft above its unusual twin doors, it is possible to see the coast, the shipping in the Channel beyond and, on a clear day, even the coast of France. But the sea and ships were once more than just a distant prospect from Tenterden. Until the River Rother's original course silted up in the 17th century, the town had its own port at Small Hythe, 2 miles south. In the 15th century, Tenterden – with its outlying villages – was, indeed, such an important port and shipbuilding centre that it was admitted to the Confederation of the Cinque Ports. It is still a member, but has left its maritime past far behind. Straggling out along a broad High Street, it is now a picture of rural charm.

Standing centrally near the church, the 15th-century Tudor Rose Cafe is one of the few early timber-framed buildings in Tenterden which has escaped being refaced with weatherboarding, hung tiles or mathematical tiles (which give the appearance of brick). These 'brick' tiles can be seen on shops at Nos 19-21 High Street, on the large 18th-century East Hill House, on the town's eastern outskirts, and on more than 20 other buildings. In Oaks Road, near East Hill House, Hales Place has an Elizabethan walled garden, open to the public three or four times a year. At the western edge of the town is the William Caxton Inn – named after the father of English printing, believed to have been born in Tenterden. Beyond the inn are two fine 18th-century houses: the Cedars and the imposing red-brick and sandstone Westwell House, dated 1711.

The modest-looking Old Meeting House beyond East Cross has some well-preserved 18th-century woodwork. The American statesman and philosopher Benjamin Franklin worshipped here in 1774, while staying with friends. Although now a Unitarian chapel, it was founded in the late 17th century by a Presbyterian former vicar of Tenterden, who had been removed from his post after the Restoration. A later vicar, from

ELLEN'S PLACE *The actress Ellen Terry lived in Smallhythe Place, and it is now a theatrical museum open three afternoons a week, April to October. She is pictured in 1897, in an English version of the French* Madame Sans-Gêne *at London's Lyceum.*

1830 to 1858, was Nelson's son-in-law, the Reverend Philip Ward. He married Horatia, the admiral's daughter by Lady Hamilton, and is buried in the churchyard in a barrel tomb – a family vault built of brick. After her husband's death, Horatia moved to Pinner, near London, where she died in 1881.

Below the knoll on which the church stands is Tenterden Town Station, the headquarters of the Kent and East Sussex Railway. In 1974 volunteer steam enthusiasts reopened a stretch of the line from Tenterden through the beautiful Rother Valley.

Sadly, nobody could save the port of Small Hythe – its last link with the sea ended earlier this century when the drainage system was changed and barges could no longer sail up to the wharf. All that remains of the once busy port is a charming hamlet of timber-framed houses around the 16th-century Church of St John the Baptist, and the excavated repair dock in the grounds of Smallhythe Place.

This 16th-century farmhouse, set in flat grassland on the edge of the hamlet, was chosen by the great actress Dame Ellen Terry as the place 'where I should like to live and die'. She bought it in 1899 and died there, as she had wished, in 1928.

• **Parking** Recreation Ground Road; Station Road; Bridewell Lane • **Early closing** Wednesday • **Market day** Friday • **Museum** Station Road • **Ellen Terry's House** Smallhythe Place, Small Hythe • **Event** Gala (August Bank Holiday) • **Information** TEL. Tenterden 3572 (Easter – September only) • **AA 24 hour service** TEL. Maidstone 55353.

Benenden KENT

6 miles west of Tenterden (PAGE 83 Cc)

Fewer village greens provide a more perfect setting for playing or watching cricket than Benenden's. From the weatherboarded former post office, a triangular expanse of grass, fringed by chestnuts, slopes up to the pale sandstone Church of St George. The houses scattered around the green are a happy blend of different architectural styles. Near the post office, now a private house, the row of tile-hung cottages was once a school, founded in 1609. The present primary school, on the other side of the green, was built by the Victorian architect George Davey in 1861. It is an adventurous building of sandstone and red brick.

On December 30, 1672, a bolt of lightning set fire to the steeple of St George's. The blaze melted the church's five large bells, razed five houses adjoining the churchyard and left the interior of the church in ruins. Fortunately, many of the best 15th-century features were saved, particularly the north porch with its gargoyles and stone-vaulted ceiling. Restoration immediately after the fire and in the 19th century has left the church as handsome as ever.

Benenden is probably more famous for its girls' school than for its village green. The large Elizabethan-style house where Princess Anne was educated stands in parkland half a mile from the village. Sissinghurst Castle is about 4 miles to the north. When

ANNE'S PLACE *Well-groomed young ladies on well-groomed ponies stroll past an immaculate old post office by an immaculate village green in Benenden, where Princess Anne went to school.*

FORTRESS OF LOVE *Medieval Leeds Castle, which was built on two islands in a lake, makes a dreamlike picture. Fittingly, its history is steeped*

writer Vita Sackville-West first saw it in 1930, she described it as 'but a castle running away into sordidness and squalor, a garden crying out for rescue'. Nevertheless, she fell in love with it, bought it and, with her husband Harold Nicolson, transformed what was a cabbage patch and rubbish dump into one of England's loveliest gardens.

It is difficult to imagine that, between 1756 and 1763, the name of Sissinghurst terrified French soldiers captured in the Seven Years' War. For what is now a garden was then a jail for prisoners of war.

Edward Gibbon (1737–94), author of *The History of the Decline and Fall of the Roman Empire*, once had the unenviable job of guarding them. 'The inconceivable dirtiness of the season, the country and the spot,' he wrote later, 'aggravated the hardships of a duty far too heavy for our numbers.'

Headcorn KENT

9 miles north-west of Tenterden (PAGE 83 Cb)

Bustling fairs and markets used to be held regularly in Headcorn, the heart of an agricultural community which is still busy today. Low-ceilinged shops, with awnings stretched over the pavement, line one side of the High Street, leading straight to the focal point – the Church of St Peter and St Paul.

Until 1815, when French prisoners of war completed the present main road, the road between Tenterden and Maidstone ran straight past the church, instead of stopping short of the churchyard and describing a dog's-leg northwards as it does today.

in royal romance, which began in the 13th century when Edward I made a present of the castle to his well-loved queen, Eleanor of Castile.

Church Walk, a string of cottages leading towards the church, was once a continuation of the High Street.

An avenue of chestnuts, planted to commemorate Queen Victoria's Diamond Jubilee, flanks the other side of the churchyard. At the end, an ancient oak stands by the church – a lonely survivor of the days when Headcorn was a clearing in the great Wealden Forest. A young villager, John Hensell, owed his freedom to this tree. In 1776 he was locked in the little room above the south porch of the church, awaiting trial falsely accused of sheep-stealing, which was then a capital offence.

However, aided by his sweetheart Charity Byrd, he succeeded in loosening the bars in the window. When night fell, he reached out, grabbed a branch and slithered down the oak to freedom. The real thief was later caught and sentenced to seven years' penal servitude – and the couple were wed in the church.

Headcorn has rows of weatherboarded and tile-hung cottages, and several half-timbered houses. Two fine examples are Shakespeare House, a 15th-century weaving house with steep gables, and Headcorn Manor, built in the 15th century as a parsonage.

Leeds KENT

15 miles north of Tenterden (PAGE 83 Cb)

Motorists who suddenly catch a glimpse of a fairytale castle floating on a lake beside the main Maidstone to Ashford road might well not believe their eyes. For Leeds has all the ingredients of a mythical medieval stronghold. It is built on two islands joined by a bridge. On one stands the 13th-century Gate Tower, the walled Inner Bailey, the Maiden's Tower built by Henry VIII and the main building, which was skilfully reconstructed in 1822. On the second island is the oldest part of the castle, the medieval Gloriette.

Building was started in 1119 by a Norman baron, Robert de Crèvecoeur. In 1278 the stone castle was transferred to Edward I, and gradually the castle was transformed from a fort into a palace, partly because of its close association with the queens of England.

The castle has long been enchanted by romance. Edward I started a tradition when he gave the castle to his beloved Spanish queen, Eleanor of Castile. He also established a chantry in the castle chapel where a Mass was celebrated daily for her soul.

Leeds was the scene of another royal romance. Here, about 150 years later, Queen Catherine – widow of Henry V – fell in love with and married her Clerk of the Wardrobe, Owen Tudor. The grandson of this scandalous liaison, for which both were imprisoned, was Henry VII, who founded the Tudor dynasty.

The castle passed through royal grant and subsequent purchases into private hands. The graceful touch of the last private owner, Lady Baillie, ensured that the interior of Leeds should become as elegant as the exterior. In 1926 she fell in love with the castle and bought it. A Gothic oak staircase was imported from France; rooms were hung with Flemish tapestries and paintings that included Impressionist and Italian masterpieces. Lady Baillie's mother was a member of a wealthy American family, the Whitneys, renowned for their philanthropy in contributions to medicine. The tradition has continued, and the castle is now run by the Leeds Castle Foundation and is a centre for medical research seminars.

The parkland surrounding the castle contains a nine-hole golf course, an extensive garden, aviaries and the oak-beamed Fairfax Hall, which houses a restaurant. In the castle is an extraordinary collection of dog collars, including fearsome spiked specimens.

Leeds village lies a mile to the west. The massive ragstone tower of the Church of St Nicholas, with its impressive arch, dates from the 11th century. The interior is mostly 14th and 16th century.

From the church the road dips, twists and climbs through the village – a typical Kentish straggle of red brickwork and white weatherboarding, interspersed with modest 18th-century houses, a clutch of old oast-houses and groups of timber-framed cottages.

Robertsbridge EAST SUSSEX

17 miles south-west of Tenterden (PAGE 83 Bc)

Neat rows of half-timbered houses and weather-boarded cottages line the rising High Street here. Over the rooftops, occasional views open up towards a patchwork of fields sloping down the sides of the valley to the River Rother. The village got its name either from the river – a corruption of Rother bridge – or from its first abbot, Robert.

A no-through road leads to the ruins of a Cistercian abbey in a field a mile to the east. Christmas carol services are still held occasionally in its crypt. The abbey was founded in 1176 and had for its guest house the building in the High Street which is now the Seven Stars Inn. Like all good inns, this one boasts a resident ghost – the Red Monk, who was said to have been walled up here by Cromwell's men. Robertsbridge is also the home of Gray-Nicolls, a firm that has made cricket bats since 1875.

The River Rother divides the village from its parish church of St Mary, at Salehurst, which dates from the 13th century. A grateful Richard the Lionheart presented the font. The Abbot of Robertsbridge negotiated Richard's ransom when he was taken prisoner in Germany while returning from the Crusades in 1192.

Bodiam Castle stands just 5 miles north-east of the village, four-square in the valley of the Rother. Bodiam was built as part of a coastal defence scheme against the French, who had already sacked Rye and Winchelsea. The Rother, navigable as far as Bodiam, was of great strategic importance, so Richard II granted Sir Edward Dalyngrigge a licence to 'strengthen and crenellate' his manor house in 1385.

Instead, Sir Edward built a castle, with massive walls around a courtyard, round towers at the corners, a square tower on each side and a gatehouse. Openings above the gateway were made so that defenders could pour boiling oil or lime on their attackers. But the castle was never put to the test – damage to its interior was probably caused in the Civil War.

KING WILLOW'S CASTLE

Any one of these rough-hewn pieces of willow could be destined to make a century in a Test Match or a duck on a village green – when it takes final, elegant shape as a cricket bat. The transformation is made at Robertsbridge, by a firm that created the bat with which the great W. G. Grace scored his 100th century in first-class cricket, in 1895. Willow logs are split down the grain into sections called 'clefts' – an operation requiring rare skill and judgment. Each cleft is then sawn into the rough shape of a bat blade, and stacked with others for seasoning – a process which can take a year. When the handle of split cane has been fashioned and fitted, the final critical shaping and finishing is done by hand.

MAP 9

THE WELSH LAKELAND AND DYLAN'S SANDS OF TIME

The broad sweep of south-west Wales embraces a stunning variety of mood and landscape, from the 'lake district' around Rhayader, with its vertiginous mountain roads, through scholarly Lampeter to the brooding hillsides and secret trout streams of the Brechfa Forest. And so to the long, long sands of the Dyfed coast, where Dylan Thomas reigned among the ghosts of speed kings.

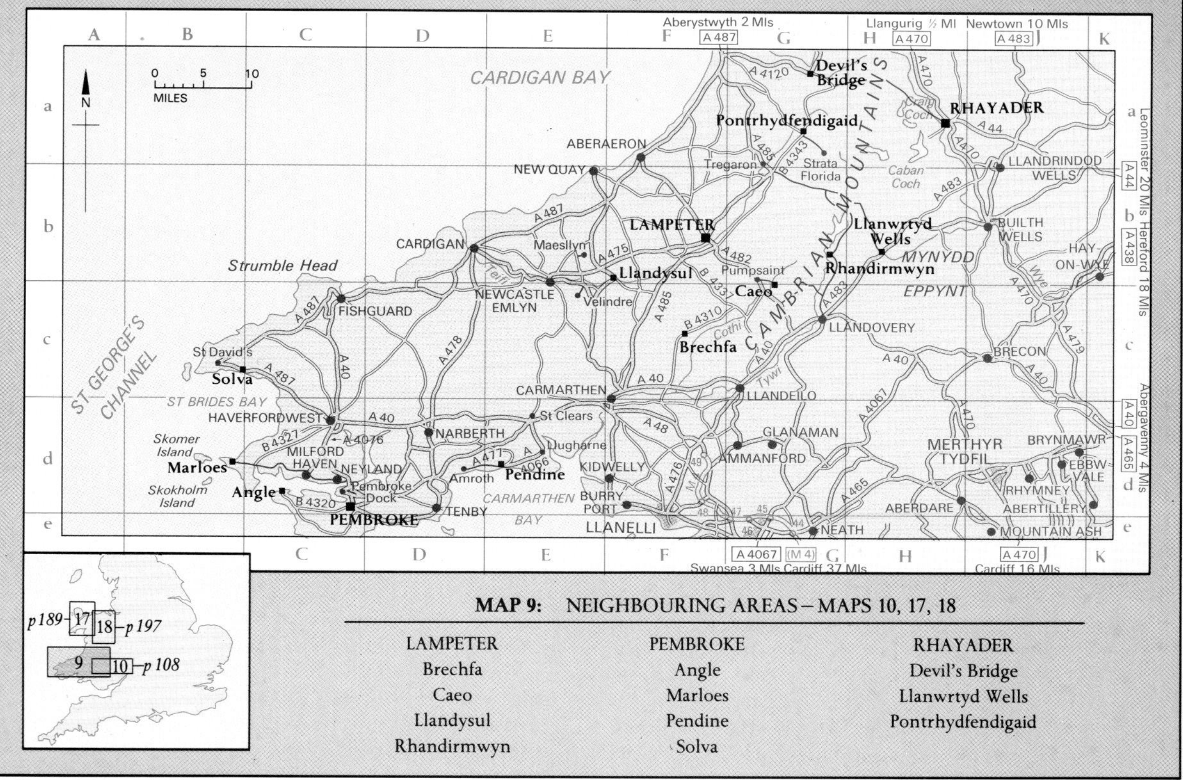

MAP 9: NEIGHBOURING AREAS – MAPS 10, 17, 18

LAMPETER	PEMBROKE	RHAYADER
Brechfa	Angle	Devil's Bridge
Caeo	Marloes	Llanwrtyd Wells
Llandysul	Pendine	Pontrhydfendigaid
Rhandirmwyn	Solva	

LAMPETER

DYFED

23 miles north-east of Carmarthen (PAGE 95 Fb)

Farmers and scholars fare well in this secluded little town. Lampeter's busy cattle market has flourished since the 13th century; and St David's University College, founded originally in 1822 for training students in the arts and sciences, is now part of the University of Wales.

Set among wooded hills in the valley of the Afon Teifi, Lampeter is a neat and attractive place with rows of trim, stone-built and slate-roofed terraced houses and the 17th-century Black Lion Royal Hotel.

In term time it is awash with students. The college was the creation of an Englishman, Thomas Burgess, Bishop of St David's in the early 19th century. Determined to found his own educational institution, he set aside part of his income each year to help pay for the building costs. His clergy followed suit, and George IV made a special grant of £1000.

The main block was designed in neo-Gothic style and the building was added to in 1880 and again in recent years. The college grounds contain the overgrown remains of a 12th-century fortress.

About 4 miles east of Lampeter is part of a Roman road called Sarn Helen. Some historians believe that the road was named after Helen, the Welsh wife of Magnus Maximus, the self-proclaimed Roman emperor who ruled Britain from AD 383–8.

• **Parking** The Rookery; The Common (both car parks) • **Early closing** Wednesday • **Market day** Alternate Tuesdays • **Events** Agricultural Show (August); Pantyfedwen Eisteddfod (August) • **Information** TEL. Lampeter 422426 (summer) • **AA 24 hour service** TEL. Aberystwyth 4801.

Brechfa DYFED

22 miles south of Lampeter (PAGE 95 Fc)

Almost lost in the vast conifer forest which takes its name, Brechfa is a village the uninitiated are likely to find only by chance. Canny fishermen have known it for ages, but tend to keep quiet about the plentiful sewin (sea trout) in the clear, fast-flowing waters of the Afon Cothi and its tributary, the Afon Marlais.

Those who find Brechfa discover a welcoming little place, composed of the charming Victorian bell-cote Church of St Teilo, built in 1891, a fishing pub covered with creeper, stone houses facing each other with their backs to the forest, and the 16th-century manor house of Ty Mawr – Welsh for 'Big House'.

The house stood empty and neglected for decades, and was so near-derelict that in the 1970s it was condemned. However, it has now been restored with great care and turned into a hotel.

Most of the surrounding countryside is run by the Forestry Commission. Conifers sweep over the 1200 ft high hillsides and moorlands to the north of the village. They look impenetrable, but there are car parks, picnic sites, and walks laid out across one of the most relaxing and unpeopled parts of Wales.

Caeo DYFED

10 miles south-east of Lampeter (PAGE 95 Gc)

Improbable as it may seem strolling through the hushed countryside into Caeo's sunlit main street, Roman legions marched there 1900 years ago in search of gold. They found it in the hillside of Dolaucothi, a bare mile outside the village. Their open-cast workings, much overgrown now and looking like part of a disused quarry, burrow into the hill just off the main road to Pumpsaint.

Roman chisel marks in the rock can still be seen; so can the path of a Roman aqueduct which carried water to the mines from the Afon Cothi. The best of the gold was shipped to Rome before the empire collapsed, but the mines were still being worked on a more modest basis as recently as 1938.

The gold left no lasting marks on the village itself, and the painted stone cottages, the chapel and the solid 13th-century Church of The Virgin and St Cynwyl merge gently into the valley.

Caeo is a contented, self-sufficient community of sheep farmers, and woodmen tending the ubiquitous conifers of the Forestry Commission. Since the Romans left, history and the roads have bypassed Caeo, though local records do show that the village sent nine archers to Agincourt in 1415. The mounted archers were paid 6d per day, the others 4d.

For such a tiny place, the village and surrounding area have some famous sons. Lewis Glyn Cothi, a 15th-century Welsh bard was born here. Roger Williams (1604 – 83), who was born in the parish, sailed to America in search of religious freedom and founded Rhode Island. Joshua Thomas, another villager, published in 1778 a *History of the Baptists in Wales*.

In the National Trust woodlands behind the old gold mines is the farm where once lived the self-styled 'Doctor' John Harris – 'Astrologer, Wizard and Surgeon'. In the 1830s he was famed throughout Wales for his knowledge of herbalism and his power to 'charm away the pain'. Many claimed that, with little medical training, he did just that. Others whispered that he practised black arts in the woods.

Judge John Johnes is also remembered – though for somewhat macabre reasons. The judge, a member of a prominent local family, was the victim of a notorious murder in August 1876. A villager named Henry Tremble, in dispute with him over the running of a pub, murdered the judge in the study of the family home at Dolaucothi, and then committed suicide. The judge is buried in the churchyard.

The Methodist Chapel, founded in 1777 and rebuilt in 1907, stands beside the road to the neighbouring village of Pumpsaint. Off the road, in a clearing opposite Ogafau Lodge, stands an unusual stone monument to the Welsh quintuplets who were all made saints – Ceitho, Celynin, Gwyn, Gwyno and Gwynoro. They are said to have rested with their heads against the stone while a fierce storm raged, blowing so hard it pressed their heads into the stone, leaving five indentations. The saints are believed to be one of the first quintuplet births ever recorded. Pumpsaint takes its name from the legend – *pump* being Welsh for 'five'.

SANCTUARY FOR QUINTUPLET SAINTS

Conifers stride over the hills above Caeo, where the Romans once marched in search of gold. A sturdy, 13th-century church looks out over colour-washed cottages and quiet pastures. In a clearing near neighbouring Pumpsaint is a stone which has five curious hollows, said to have been made when five unique saints – they were quintuplets – took shelter by the stone during a fierce storm.

Caeo and 13th-century church

Stone of the quintuplet saints

Massive mill machinery

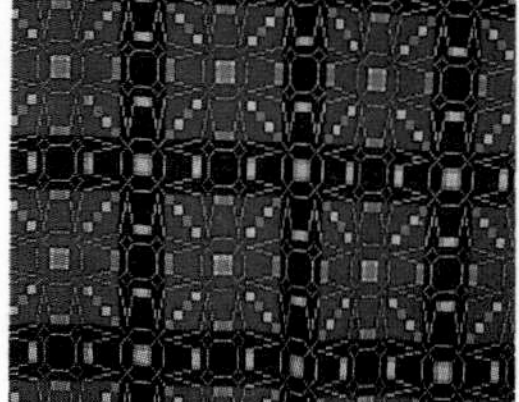
Esgair Moel

Meirion

A SOFT SPOT
FOR WOOL

The tall old mill at Maesllyn, deep in the country north-west of Llandysul, becomes even taller reflected in the quiet waters of the Teifi. The water is soft enough to wash the wool of local sheep, yet has strength enough to drive the massive machinery of the mill. Although no longer working at full capacity, the mill is still turning out some woollen cloth and visitors can see the processes by which it is woven.

Maesllyn mill

Wernant

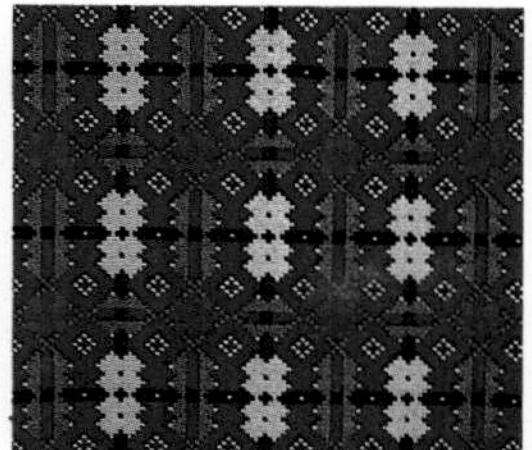
Brynkir

PATTERNS OF HISTORY

South-west of Llandysul, at Velindre, the Museum of the Woollen Industry shows weaving techniques from the Middle Ages to modern times. It also shows samples of traditional Welsh patterns with names such as Esgair Moel, Meirion, Wernant and Brynkir.

Llandysul DYFED

14 miles south-west of Lampeter (PAGE 95 Fb)

The Afon Teifi loops its way around Llandysul and gives the village its character and its life. The water is soft enough to wash the wool of the sheep from the surrounding countryside, and the river also rushes fast enough down the hillside to turn a mill wheel.

Once Llandysul resounded to the clatter of woollen mills. Most have gone, though 5 miles north-west at Maesllyn an old mill still turns out a distinctive local weave and, as a working museum, demonstrates the processes to visitors. Downstream from Llandysul, at Velindre, is a museum to the whole woollen industry, showing techniques from medieval times to the present day.

There are still sheep in the hills, and the farmers come from the valleys every other week to a market in the old station yard. But many people staying at the inns and guesthouses in the two village streets, stepped one above the other on the hillside, are there for the fishing – salmon and sewin (sea trout) – or canoeing.

The Teifi, flowing gently past the 13th-century St Tysul's Church, with its square, battlemented Norman tower, rounds a bend, sweeps under a bridge, then rushes down a half-mile, narrow, rocky chasm. The white-water rapids here offer a real challenge to the finest canoeists, who pit themselves against it in their thousands each year.

Art and craft workshops have sprung up – there is spinning and woodworking and a skilled boatbuilder from Northumberland makes traditional wooden craft. The village has also started a biannual arts festival in Welsh and English, with theatre, jazz, poetry and art exhibitions. It takes place in October in years ending with an odd number.

BUILDING BOATS
THE OLD WAY

John Kerr, a Northumbrian boatbuilder whose graceful craft are always made of wood, has now settled in Llandysul. He displays his philosophy in a notice on his workshop wall. It reads: 'If God had meant us to build fibre-glass boats He would have grown fibre-glass trees.' The boats John makes are clinker-built – a traditional form of construction in which the planks are overlapped. Their comfortable curves contrast with those of the super-slim canoes which are brought here to tackle white-water rapids that foam outside the village, down a half-mile-long chasm dotted with dangerous rocks.

Rhandirmwyn DYFED

20 miles east of Lampeter (PAGE 95 Gb)

Two of Wales's natural resources have given Rhandirmwyn a lease of life twice in its long history – the first was lead, the second was water. Translated from the Welsh the name Rhandirmwyn means 'lead mining area', and for hundreds of years lead was mined in the district, reaching a peak in the 18th and 19th centuries when it had one of Europe's largest mines. But by the 1930s the last of the mines had closed and Rhandirmwyn sank into obscurity, a remote village in the upper Tywi valley reached only by a narrow lane that eventually petered out into a rough track.

Then, in the 1960s, the expanding city of Swansea needed a new water supply, and 4 miles up the valley from Rhandirmwyn the Afon Tywi was dammed to form Llyn Brianne. The reservoir was opened in 1973, and now the road to the village goes on up the valley, running high above the lake's eastern shore.

The road provides a highway to some of the finest scenery in Wales, where sometimes the rare red kite can be seen soaring overhead. It also gave new life to Rhandirmwyn once again. The village, a scattered settlement of cottages and farms, is itself in a setting of great natural beauty, and the Royal Oak, in the centre, now describes itself as the 'Inn with a View'.

Nearly all traces of the old lead workings have disappeared, and a steep, narrow lane climbing up from the Royal Oak leads to a hillside once riddled with levels but now clothed with conifers. The only evidence of Rhandirmwyn's industrial past lies at the bottom of the valley, where the ore was washed and crushed. A man-made pond still survives, while a large, grey area of wasteland – spoil heaps on which nothing will grow – intrudes among the pastoral banks of the Tywi. Near by stands a white-painted house called Nant-y-Mwyn, the 'stream of the mine', which was once the mine manager's home. Now it is used by a religious community.

Next door is the Towy Pottery, housed in a group of red-washed stone buildings. The shop was once the storeroom for the mine and now displays a wide range of stoneware and earthenware.

The little Church of St Paulinus stands on the roadside leading to the dam. It was built in 1117 as a resting place for Cistercian monks making their way to their abbey at Strata Florida, 15 miles to the north, along the trail that led over the 'Roof of Wales'. Much of the old trail now lies beneath the waters of Llyn Brianne, but the church still stands, though it was rebuilt in the 1820s by the Earl of Cawdor.

Rhandirmwyn has a place in Welsh folklore, for it was in the hills north of the village that Twm Sion Cati, the 'Welsh Rob Roy', hid from the Sheriff of Carmarthen during the 17th century.

His name was Thomas Jones, and the cave in which he is said to have hidden is high on the densely wooded, boulder-strewn slopes of Dinas Hill, now a nature reserve. A signposted path leads around the hill and up to the cave entrance, a difficult climb but worth the effort for the views the cave commands, looking down on the Tywi as it tumbles through a rocky gorge. The walls of the cave, at the far end of a narrow entrance, are decorated with an old and elegant form of graffiti – names dating back to the 18th century, skilfully carved into the stone.

Pembroke Castle – fell to Cromwell's men

PEMBROKE

DYFED

32 miles south-west of Carmarthen (PAGE 95 Cd)

A castle has stood guard at Pembroke since about 1093, but the rugged fortress that now overlooks the town dates mostly from the following century. Set on a tree-fringed headland jutting into the Pembroke river, the castle became an important stronghold of Cromwell's Parliamentary forces during the Civil War. But in 1648, John Poyer, Mayor of Pembroke and governor

Old Monkton Hall

IMPREGNABLE, BUT . . .

Pembroke Castle, on its limestone headland, looks every inch the impregnable fortress. But Cromwell's men took it, and destroyed the gates and six towers. Major repairs were made in 1928. Old Monkton Hall, with its curious chimney, is 15th century, built as a priory guesthouse. The Church of St Nicholas near by was part of the priory. It has been restored.

St Nicholas's Church – once part of a priory

THE MOBILE ART OF THE GYPSY

Romanies have a tradition of burning a caravan when its owner dies. Happily this is not always done, so there are some superb four-wheeled homes of the 'travelling people' to be seen in the National Museum of Gypsy Caravans, Romany Crafts and Lore, in Pembroke. Intricately carved and painted wagons demonstrate the artistry and skill of their builders, one of whom 'signs' his work with a golden horse motif. The museum is in Commons Road, by the Town Wall, and is open to the public daily from Easter through to September.

Golden horse 'signature'

Detail carving on a wagon

Romany home on wheels

A showman's wagon at Pembroke gypsy museum

of the castle, went over to the Royalist cause and fortified the castle and town against Cromwell. In July the castle fell to the Roundheads, and Cromwell blew up its gates and six outer towers to prevent further trouble. Pembroke Castle – birthplace in 1457 of the future Henry VII – then lay derelict until 1880, when some restoration work was done; major repairs and rebuilding came in 1928. The circular keep, over 75 ft high and about 20 ft thick at the base, is the oldest part of the castle and dates from the beginning of the 13th century. The turreted gatehouse, looking down on the narrow canyon of Main Street, was also part of the medieval defences.

The town stretches along the banks of the Pembroke river, and though largely rebuilt in the 18th and 19th centuries it boasts several fine buildings of much greater age. St Nicholas's Church, just beyond the town walls in Monkton, was part of an 11th-century Benedictine priory, and what remains of the priory walls can be seen near by. Also near by is 15th-century Monkton Old Hall, built as a guesthouse for the priory, and the 17th-century Priory Farmhouse, with its slate roof and pointed windows.

A variety of waterfowl – including swan, mallard and moorhen, coot and wigeon – add life and colour to a mill pond formed by damming the river with a sluice gate. A stroll along Mill Pond Walk is a pleasant way to see them.

The stone, two-storeyed Town Hall in Main Street has rounded arches and was built in the 18th century. Westgate Cottages on Westgate Hill are partly medieval. One cottage has a vaulted storeroom which was formerly used as a lock-up, and the rings to which the prisoners were chained are still in the wall.

The neighbouring town of Pembroke Dock was built by the Admiralty in a chessboard design in the 19th century. A government dockyard flourished here until the mid-1920s, but the area was revitalised during the Second World War when it became a base for the Sunderland and Catalina flying boats which flew over the Atlantic, protecting convoys and hunting German U-boats. After the war, the RAF kept a flying-boat station there until 1958. Since then Pembroke Dock has become a base for engineers and geologists exploring the Irish Sea for oil and gas. A car ferry service also operates from here to Rosslare in Ireland.

• **Parking** The Quay; Long Entry; Commons Road; Station Road; St Michael's Square (all car parks, Pembroke); Meyrick Street; Upper and Lower Meyrick Street; Commercial Row; Gordon Street; Albion Square (all car parks, Pembroke Dock) • **Early closing** Wednesday • **Market day** Friday (Pembroke Dock) • **Event** Michaelmas Fair (October) • **Information** TEL. Pembroke 682148 (summer) • **AA 24 hour service** TEL. Swansea 55598.

Angle DYFED

9 miles west of Pembroke (PAGE 95 Cd)

Standing in the single street of this small coastal village, visitors could be forgiven for thinking themselves suddenly transported across the world. For here are buildings which would not look out of place in the India of the Raj. This unexpected – even bizarre – effect was created by a 19th-century local landowner named Richard Mirehouse who had, indeed, spent time in India. When he returned he proceeded to build a series of two-storey, flat-roofed houses.

His most fanciful confection is now the Globe Hotel, decorated with delicate wrought-iron balconies and converted from two houses around 1904. A pink-washed ground floor, complete with an overhanging pavement passageway of arcaded columns, supports three further storeys, all topped by a flat roof with frontier-fort battlements.

Angle is out on a limb, at the far end of a peninsula on the southern entrance to Milford Haven. The region is rich in names which can be traced to Norse invasions in the Dark Ages (Skomer and Skokholm, for example).

Angle may have similar roots (*nangle* is Norse for 'sheltered haven'). A more prosaic explanation is based on the village's location *in angulo* (Latin for 'in a corner'), at an entrance to the haven.

Sea trading was once the main occupation, reaching a peak in the 18th century, when traders based at Bristol would call at Angle to sell cloth, ironware and general goods. For the return trip they would buy local agricultural produce. The waters outside yielded rich catches for fishermen, but the industry has now declined, and most of the small lobster and mackerel boats are worked only part-time.

In summer, however, the two harbours – West Angle Bay and Angle Bay to the east – are still busy with yachts and other pleasure craft.

Behind the parish church of St Mary stands the Fishermen's Chapel – a small, stone building, with room for only 14 worshippers. Its doorway, set high up a stone staircase, leads to a delightful interior dedicated, as a stone tablet proclaims, 'to St Anthony and founded by Edward Shirburn of Nangle, AD 1447'.

A ruined rectangular tower in the fields behind the church is what remains of a Norman strongpoint, and close by is a medieval dovecote. On Thorn Island, just off the headland, stands a huge 19th-century fort – built to protect Milford Haven from the French.

The Rocket Cart House, a three-storey square tower that is now part of a private residence outside the village on the Ridgeway, was an important lookout post in the last century, where rescue rockets and lifelines were stored ready for use in case of shipwreck.

West Angle Bay is a sheltered sandy beach and quayside, along a road leading west from the village.

Marloes DYFED

14 miles north-west of Pembroke (PAGE 95 Bd)

Marloes is an old fishing village with a difference, for the sea is nowhere to be seen. The village is about 2 miles from the little cove of Martin's Haven on St Brides Bay, lying in a remote corner of the Pembrokeshire Coast National Park.

Marloes declined with the fishing industry, and agriculture has taken over in the form of early crop potatoes and dairy farming. But there are still reminders of links with the sea – notably the modern Lobster Pot inn.

The large, square stone clock tower looks somewhat out of place, with the clock faces set in green-painted woodwork. It was built in memory of a local landowner, Lord Kensington, who died in 1896. The Kensingtons lived in St Brides, an estate 2 miles north.

The road west passes typical old Pembrokeshire cottages, with black-painted slate roofs. It runs along a ridge of high land with magnificent sea views, including Martin's Haven, equipped with just a slipway and winch. During the holiday season, from Easter to the end of September, ferry boats run to Skomer Island, about a mile offshore. Skomer is a nature reserve, renowned for its puffins and other seabirds, and for a superb display of bluebells in May.

Landlubbers can explore the Deer Park peninsula around Martin's Haven. This rugged finger of land, managed by the National Trust, has an Iron Age fort and some exceptional cliff and beach scenery. The Pembrokeshire coast long-distance footpath follows the windy, clifftop route. Visitors must also walk about half a mile from the car park to one of Wales's most beautiful beaches, Marloes Sands.

This long stretch of firm, golden sand, interrupted by weirdly shaped rocky outcrops, is backed by a natural amphitheatre of red and pale yellow cliffs. But the remoteness of the place discourages crowds, and visitors are few – other than scientists studying the cliffs and rock strata, which embrace many different geological eras. Here film-makers were able to shoot the opening sequence for *The Lion in Winter*, the story of Henry II and his queen, Eleanor of Aquitaine.

The villagers of Marloes once enjoyed a dubious reputation as smugglers and wreckers of ships. In fact, many of them earned a legitimate, if unappetising, living collecting leeches from the marshlands of Marloes Mere. Records reveal that Harley Street doctors were among their best customers, buying leeches at four a penny to 'bleed' patients.

Nowadays a few locals work at gathering edible seaweed, both at Marloes and nearby Musselwick Sands. The weed is washed, boiled until it becomes a black, shiny mass, then shaped into small cakes and fried as the traditional Welsh laver bread.

Back inland, the stone bridge across the stream at Mullock has fanciful historic associations. Henry Tudor, who became Henry VII and founded the Tudor dynasty, came this way in 1485. He landed at Milford Haven and started a march that culminated in his victory over Richard III at Bosworth. The story goes that when he reached Mullock Bridge he found a local nobleman, Sir Rhys ap Thomas, lying beneath its arch. The pragmatic Sir Rhys had his reasons: he was preserving both life and honour – for he had promised Richard III that Henry Tudor would enter Wales only over his body.

Pendine DYFED

20 miles north-east of Pembroke (PAGE 95 Ed)

The golden sands at Pendine have a reputation for being unkind to motorists. More than 5 miles long, they stretch to Ginst Point on the Taf estuary near Laugharne, adopted home of the poet Dylan Thomas. A notice on the slipway at Pendine reads: 'DANGER. Do not drive or park near the water's edge. On average ten cars a year get submerged by the sea.'

These sands have claimed more than machinery. In the mid-1920s, they saw a hectic period of landspeed record-breaking as Sir Malcolm Campbell, in *Blue Bird*, and the Welsh ace J. G. Parry Thomas behind the wheel of *Babs*, vied to become the fastest man on four wheels over the flying kilometre and mile. In 1927 Campbell reached a speed of 174.88 mph. In the same year, while attempting to regain the title, Parry Thomas veered out of control in *Babs* and was killed – possibly because the car's drive chain broke.

His grieving mechanics buried *Babs* in sand dunes behind the beach, but in 1971 the car was dug up and restored to full working order. It made a commemorative run along the sands in 1977.

Between the First and Second World Wars, Pendine attracted other record-breakers. Motorcyclists raced there and in 1933, aviator Amy Johnson took off from the beach on her daring flight across the Atlantic.

The red-painted Beach Hotel on the seafront was usually the base for the teams making record attempts. A plaque outside lists drivers, dates, cars and speeds achieved during the duels between Campbell and Parry Thomas. Inside the hotel, photographs of monster racing cars decorate the walls, recalling those heady days. Access to the sands beyond Pendine is now limited – much of the area is a Defence Ministry 'Proof and Experimental Establishment'. Past the Beach Hotel the sands stop abruptly at the base of a rocky, bracken-covered headland. The village, a loose collection of houses and cottages, spreads along the dunelands below and up into the hillside. There are caravan parks, and a small promenade leads to the inevitable ice-cream parlour – but one with perhaps the most spectacular coastal view in Wales: to the west, the coast curves around to Caldey Island and the headlands beyond Tenby; to the east, across the sands and waters of Carmarthen Bay to the tip of the Gower peninsula.

Solva DYFED

25 miles north-west of Pembroke (PAGE 95 Bc)

There is a building in Solva known as the Nectarium. The word is not in a dictionary, for it was invented by the owners as a suitably evocative title for the Tropical Butterfly Farm, established here in the late 1970s. Species from all around the world – including the rain forests of India, Malaysia and the Amazon – can be seen flying and breeding in a specially designed glasshouse. The Nectarium is open from Easter to the end of September.

Solva comes in two parts. Upper Solva is built around a hill just inland from the northern shores of St Brides Bay. As the road slopes down the hill, Lower Solva and the sea come into view.

Lower Solva is the smaller of the two settlements, but is the place most visitors head for. The village sits at the mouth of a sheltered creek where the River Solfach tumbles from the hills, a pretty cluster of cottages and houses secure beneath the steep-sided, wooded slopes.

Solva Creek, a tidal inlet half a mile long, is a haven from the open waters of St Brides Bay. This sheltered waterway is by far the best natural harbour

Yachts in Solva's creek

House with outside stairs

FOR MANY, THIS WAS THE LAST OF WALES

Yachts and pleasure craft crowd Solva's sheltered creek – but 200 years ago the scene was very different, for this was a busy port, packed with tall-masted ships. Many an emigrant saw the last of Wales here, as he – or she – sailed away to a new beginning in America with a £3 10s. one-way ticket . . . perhaps saying goodbye to a house with an outside stairway to the upper floor.

on this stretch of coast. During the 18th and 19th centuries Solva was a busy port, because overland transportation – especially to somewhere as remote as Pembrokeshire – was a daunting prospect: the sea route was the easiest way until the railway arrived in the area. It was much easier, for example, to take a ship to Bristol, Liverpool or London, than to travel by any other method. This was all to Solva's advantage. Its harbour became busier as cargoes – ranging from beer to ladies' hats, and from donkeys to honey – were shipped in. Corn was sent out to Bristol, while limestone was imported. The old lime-kilns can still be seen along the harbour walls.

The port had its own shipbuilding industry and a fleet of more than 30 vessels. Trading links were extended to many parts of the world, and from here this part of Pembrokeshire had its first taste of oranges, tobacco, sultanas and cloves. A regular service from Solva carried Welsh emigrants to America for the modest sum of £3 10s. per person. Today the harbour is busy again with fishing boats and holiday craft. A regatta takes place every August.

As early as 1773 the harbour had its own lighthouse, constructed of oak on a reef known as the Smalls, 18 miles out to sea. This potentially precarious beacon was replaced by a permanent granite building in 1861, erected by Trinity House.

Solva's prosperous past is reflected in the architecture of large houses along the single main street, built by the wealthy merchants and shippers. Old three and four-storey warehouses, also along the main street, have since been restored and converted into attractive craft shops and living accommodation. The Old Pharmacy, also converted, still preserves its delightful wrought ironwork.

The use of colour on even the smallest cottages is a constant delight to the eye. Some houses are whitewashed, with yellow door and window frames, others pink-washed with contrasting green decoration. Next to the Cambrian pub is an interesting two-storey cream-painted house. Although modernised, it retains the traditional concrete-washed slate roof and a crude, roughcast outside stairway leading to a door in the loft.

A footpath leads out of Solva from The Harbour House Hotel on the quayside and around the headland known as the Gribin. There is a fine view of the village from this path as it climbs high above the harbour.

RHAYADER

POWYS

15 miles north of Builth Wells (PAGE 95 Ha)

Rhayader is the gateway to the Elan Valley – the Welsh 'Lake District' – and the man-made dams and reservoirs to the west of the town are a spectacular tourist attraction. The five reservoirs – four opened in 1904 and the fifth in 1952 – provide fine trout fishing, and form some 10 miles of sweeping lakeland from the high moorlands above Craig Goch to the woodlands of Caban Goch.

Sheltered on all sides by mountains, this small market town is itself 700 ft above sea level and lies on the River Wye. Its setting makes it a centre for pony-trekkers, fishermen, campers and hikers.

The four main streets form a crossroads, and an attractive clock tower crowned by a cross stands in

BLACK BOARD BEAUTY *Weatherboarding takes the form of great, blackened planks on Rhayader's oldest building, the Cwmdauddwr Arms in West Street. This handsome pub was built in the early years of the 17th century.*

East Street. It was built in 1924 on the site once occupied by an 18th-century Town Hall. On the corner of South Street and Bridge Street is the timber-framed Old Swan, built in 1683 as an inn and now a tourist information centre.

Rhayader is *Rhaeadr Gwy*, Welsh for 'The Cataract on the Wye', and a cataract there was until 1780, when a single-span bridge was built. The present arched bridge dates from 1929, and all that remains of the cataract are some modest rapids.

The town's 12th-century castle was destroyed in the Civil War, but its location is marked by the parish church of St Clement, which stands near the site of the castle's chapel. St Clement's has been rebuilt since Norman times, but still has its 12th-century font.

• **Parking** Dark Lane (car park) • **Early closing** Thursday • **Market day** Wednesday (stock) • **Event** Carnival Week (begins last Saturday in July) • **Information** TEL. Rhayader 810591 (summer) • **AA 24 hour service** TEL. Brecon 2015.

Devil's Bridge DYFED

18 miles north-west of Rhayader (PAGE 95 Ga)

There are 'works of the Devil' scattered all over Britain, his punch bowls, gorges, dykes and cauldrons appear everywhere, and in Wales he is credited with, among other things, a bridge. In fact, Devil's Bridge, spanning a narrow, 300 ft deep chasm through which flows the Mynach, was built by Cistercian monks in the 12th century. Local legend, however, tells a different and more lurid story. It seems that the Devil built the bridge to enable an old woman to get her cow across the gorge, on condition that he might own the first living creature that crossed. But the woman outwitted him by throwing a piece of bread across the gorge, and her dog ran after it – so Satan became its owner. A very similar tale is told about the Devil's Bridge over the River Lune at Kirkby Lonsdale (see page 302).

Legend apart, nevertheless, the views from a platform below the bridge are awe-inspiring. The bridge, called *Pont-y-gwr-Drwy* or 'Bridge of the Evil One' in Welsh, is topped by two more bridges, one built in

Gorge and River Mynach

Rheidol Railway locomotive

DOGGED BY THE DEVIL'S LUCK

Monks built the Devil's Bridge in the 12th century. But if local legend is to be believed, the Devil put it there so that he could have the first being to walk across. Unluckily for him, the first was only a dog. Two more bridges now stand above the original one, and below is a gorge where the River Mynach runs. A more cheerful attraction in this region of diabolic names is the Vale of Rheidol Railway which climbs through delightful woodland scenery from Aberystwyth. The narrow-gauge track was built in 1902.

Devil's Bridge, with later bridges above

1753 and above it an iron bridge of 1901. Below, in another diabolic association, is the Devil's Punch Bowl where the river has carved strange shapes into the rocks. The platform is reached by an easy path, but there is also a steep footpath and a flight of 100 steps which lead down to a metal footbridge at the bottom of the chasm. Here the falls come into view, brimming over the edge of the Punch Bowl in a cascade of seething water to join the Afon Rheidol.

The Hafod Arms, otherwise known as the Devil's Bridge Hotel, is a handsome early 19th-century inn with an ivy-covered façade, gabled roof and huge eaves. The gorge is directly beneath, while across the valley the Rheidol and its own torrent, the Gyfarllwyd Falls, cut through hillsides.

This scene of great natural beauty is served by one of Wales's 'Great Little Trains', running along the Vale of Rheidol Railway which climbs the 12 miles from Aberystwyth through woodland to Devil's Bridge. The track used to carry ore from local lead mines.

Llanwrtyd Wells POWYS

14 miles south-west of Rhayader (PAGE 95 Hb)

It may be hard to believe that a once sleepy village became a prosperous resort through the hale and hearty fitness of the local frog population, yet that is the story of how Llanwrtyd Wells joined the ranks of the booming spas in the 18th century. It all started, according to local history, in the 1730s when the Reverend Theophilus Evans, vicar of nearby Llangammarch, concluded that the rude health of the local frogs was due to the quality of the local waters. Humans, he decided, might also benefit from drinking the water of the sulphur, chalybeate (iron-bearing) and saline springs. Evans suffered from chronic scurvy and was apparently completely cured by the water. Rightly or wrongly, thousands believed him and the

village flourished as a spa for more than 150 years.

The village now stands as a poignant testament to the spa boom. Like an ageing duchess, remembering girlhood with a wistful smile, Llanwrtyd Wells reclines in its valley between the Cambrian Mountains and the Mynydd Eppynt moors, and gently tolerates the touring motorists who come to tackle the spectacular Abergwesyn mountain road. The road starts from the village and winds its way to Tregaron, 20 miles away, following an ancient drovers' route.

An attractive little square forms the centre of the village. From one side of it a stone road bridge crosses the Irfon river; shops, chapels and tall Victorian and Edwardian houses are grouped around the other sides.

A number of hotels and guesthouses survive from the days when visitors came to take the waters at one penny a glass. They cannot do so now, and the old well house, about half a mile from the village centre, stands neglected in the beautiful park behind the Dol-y-Coed Hotel. A long avenue of chestnut trees leads to the well, a handful of grey buildings known locally as *Y Ffynon Ddrewllyd*—'The Stinking Well'. An overpowering sulphurous smell rises from its bluish waters, held within a circular wellhead decorated with mosaic patterns. Remnants of a once-elegant building lie around and, though few of the original fittings remain, there are plans to restore the well.

Originally built as a farmhouse in 1532, the ivy-covered Dol-y-Coed Hotel is delightfully situated on the banks of the clear-flowing Irfon. On the opposite bank, the site once occupied by the old Victoria Wells is now a modern holiday centre. Another hotel is the rather grand Abernant Lake, standing in fine grounds and still with its large boating lake and island.

On the eastern approach to Llanwrtyd Wells is the Cambrian Factory, a woollen mill started in 1918 to provide work for the disabled of the First World War. The British Legion still maintains an interest in the mill, which produces Welsh tweeds. Visitors can see the various stages of production.

Pontrhydfendigaid DYFED

22 miles west of Rhayader (PAGE 95 Ga)

This isolated village, miles from any major town, has two attractions that span 800 years; one is the ruined Strata Florida Abbey founded in the 12th century by Cistercian monks; the other is the annual eisteddfod started this century by a local man who made good.

Strata Florida (the name means 'The way of the flowers') stands at the foot of green hills south-east of the village, and wild flowers can still be seen growing in the water meadows beside the Afon Teifi that flows through the valley.

Once the abbey was the political, religious and educational centre of Wales, but over the years it was steadily reduced to a ruin by natural and political disasters. Lightning badly damaged it in 1284, Edward I set fire to it ten years later and Henry IV's troops vandalised it when garrisoned there during Owain Glyndwr's fight for Welsh independence. All that remains now is a striking archway set in crumbling walls which mark the outlines of this once impressive building.

The village, on the edge of a flat, upland plain, is a traditionally Welsh community – sturdy granite

Archway of Strata Florida Abbey

Tiles on abbey floor

ARCH OF TIME

An impressive archway is a reminder of the lost glory of Strata Florida Abbey at Pontrhydfendigaid. Once the abbey, founded in the 12th century, was a great centre of learning. Beautiful floor tiles can still be seen. In the local churchyard, near the abbey, is a bizarre tombstone above a grave in which rests the left leg of a man named Henry Hughes, which was amputated and buried here in 1756. Henry, minus his leg, went to America.

Here lies Henry's leg

houses and cottages of the Victorian and Edwardian eras, slate-roofed and colour-washed in shades of white, cream and blue. The main street winds away from a stone, hump-backed bridge that gives Pontrhydfendigaid its name, which means 'The bridge of the blessed ford'.

Just outside the village is Pantyfedwen, birthplace of Sir David John James (1887-1967) who made his fortune in London, selling milk and building cinemas, and devoted part of it to inaugurating the eisteddfod. He built a barn-like pavilion seating 3000 for the musical and literary event, which attracts entrants from all over Wales and beyond.

Sir David is buried in the churchyard of the small church built in 1700 close to the ruins of Strata Florida, and his grave is marked by a massive, 15 ft black marble memorial. Another great Welshman rests near by, the 14th-century lyric poet Dafydd ap Gwilym whose body is said to lie beneath the gnarled old yew tree next to the church.

Headstones of polished grey or black slate stand in rows in the churchyard, interspersed by humbler memorials. One is decorated with an amputated leg and the inscription reads: 'The left leg and part of the thigh of Henry Hughes, cooper, was cut off and interred here June 18th 1756.' Henry later emigrated to America, so exactly where all the other parts of his body have been buried is anyone's guess.

MAP 10

BRECON BEACONS AND THE WYE VALLEY

Here is drama, among the high vistas of the Black Mountains and Brecon Beacons. Castle and abbey ruins by haunted lake and tumbling torrent tell of ancient, unforgotten battles. But peace is almost palpable where the lovely Wye bends through meadows dotted with red-and-white Hereford cattle, and a rolling, green landscape beyond is dotted with black-and-white towns and villages.

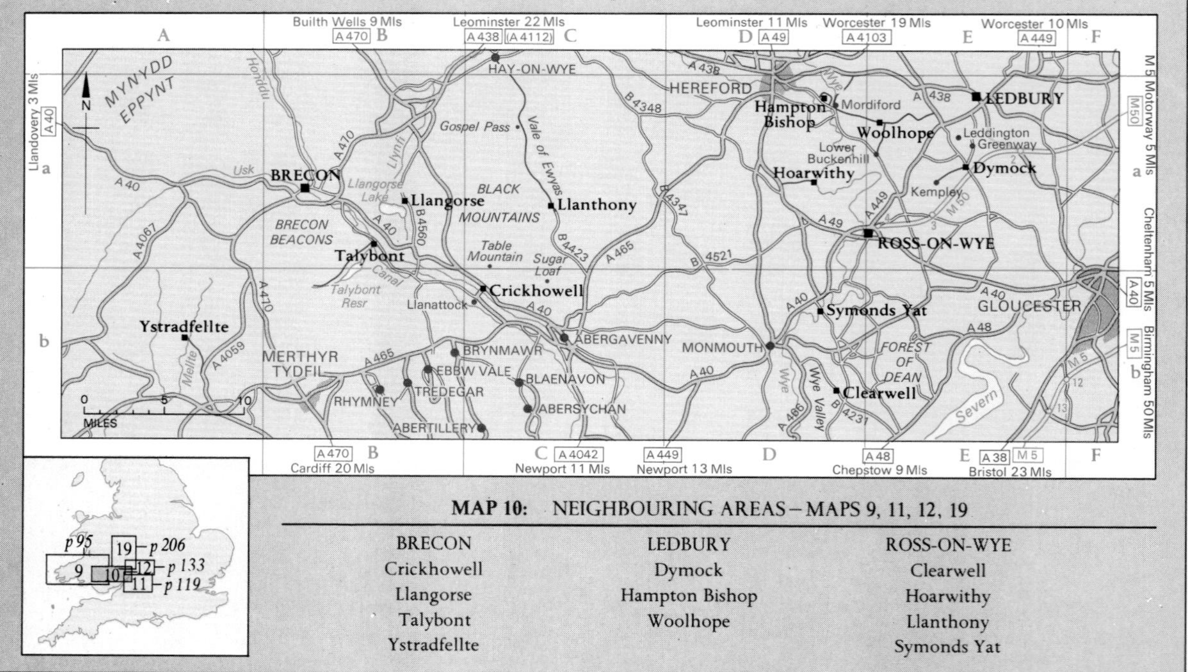

MAP 10: NEIGHBOURING AREAS – MAPS 9, 11, 12, 19

BRECON	LEDBURY	ROSS-ON-WYE
Crickhowell	Dymock	Clearwell
Llangorse	Hampton Bishop	Hoarwithy
Talybont	Woolhope	Llanthony
Ystradfellte		Symonds Yat

BRECON

POWYS

18 miles north of Merthyr Tydfil (PAGE 108 Ba)

Two rivers, the Usk and the Honddu, meet in the centre of Brecon and provide a fascinating contrast of surroundings and views. The Usk, the broader of the two, is spanned by a five-arched bridge and flanked by a tree-lined walk, the Promenade. This is one of Brecon's main leisure areas, with tennis courts, bowling and putting greens, and a boathouse from which rowing boats and canoes can be hired. From the walk the peaks of the Brecon Beacons can be seen about 5 miles away.

Branching off the Promenade, the Honddu curves past a grey stone tower and battlemented wall – the remains of Brecon Castle. The fortress was built in 1093 by a Norman baron – Bernard de Neufmarché, who came to England with William the Conqueror – and it was demolished by the townsfolk during the Civil War to avoid attack by Cromwell's troops.

Higher up is the Cathedral Church of St John the Evangelist, originally built by de Neufmarché as a Benedictine priory. Parts of the present building date back to the 12th century, but most of it – including the chapels, choir, nave and tower – were added over the following 200 to 300 years. St John's was the local parish church until 1923, when it became the cathedral of the newly formed diocese of Swansea and Brecon.

The Honddu is crossed by three bridges, the middle one of which leads into the first of Brecon's two High Streets – High Street Superior. It is joined by High Street Inferior, and between them the two streets contain a colourful mixture of period houses – mostly of the 17th, 18th and 19th centuries. These include the old Shoulder of Mutton inn, now called the Sarah Siddons in honour of the renowned tragic actress who was born here in 1755. Her brother Charles Kemble, equally famous on the stage, was also born in Brecon. Near by, the Brecknock Museum in Glamorgan Street has a fine collection of local artefacts, including an 8th-century lake-dweller's canoe from Llangorse (see page 110), and complete settings for a Welsh farmhouse kitchen and a gallery containing a splendid 17th-century four-poster bed.

A short distance away, in the Watton, is the Regimental Museum of the South Wales Borderers, displaying weapons, uniforms and medals. It has 16 of the 23 Victoria Crosses won by the Borderers – a record for a line regiment. Nine VCs were won in one day – January 22 to 23, 1879 – at the battles of Isandhlwana and Rorke's Drift, during the Zulu War.

• **Parking** Cattle Market; Struet; Bridge Street; Watergate (all carparks) • **Early closing** Wednesday • **Market days** Tuesday,

Friday ● **Cinema** Coliseum 1, 2 and 3, Wheat Street ● **Events** Fair (May and November); Agricultural Show (August) ● **Information** TEL. Brecon 4437 ● **AA 24 hour service** TEL. Brecon 2015.

Crickhowell POWYS

13 miles south-east of Brecon (PAGE 108 Cb)

This prosperous and handsome village has a distinctly cosmopolitan air – probably because it stands on a long-established road (now the A40) between England and west Wales. It stands also at the foot of the towering Black Mountains, on a small hill intruding into the sheltered lowlands of the Usk valley. Approached from the lofty perspective of a minor road through the mountains to the west, the village comes suddenly into view, spreading from the riverside meadows of the Usk into the lower slopes of the Sugar Loaf and Table mountains.

Two village landmarks stand out – the tall, needle spire of St Edmund's Church, and the long bridge over the Usk. In the porch of the 14th-century church there is an engraved stone slab of the 1800s laying down a matrimonial blacklist of 30 blood relations that men and women were forbidden to marry.

A maze of small side streets radiates from the centre of Crickhowell. A row of stone cottages in Standard Street leads to an old malt house and brewery, now converted into a craft workshop specialising in handmade furniture, including Welsh dressers. Bridge Street, which drops down to the river, has delightful bow windows, and elegant Georgian façades decorate High Street, the main shopping area.

Spire of St Edmund's Church, above the rooftops of Crickhowell

Bridge and Table Mountain

Norman castle ruins

A BRIDGE TOO FAR

The riverside meadows of the Usk form a lush, green backdrop to the stern slate roofs of Crickhowell and the sharp, lofty spire of St Edmund's Church. The village is spread over the lower slopes of the Sugar Loaf and Table mountains. The flat-topped Table Mountain is also known as Crug Hywell, or Hywell's Fort – hence the name Crickhowell. It still bears the marks of ancient earthworks built by the Welsh. The remains of a Norman castle stand in a park where sheep graze in the shadow of a ruined tower. However, the best-known local landmark is, perhaps, the long bridge spanning the River Usk. Built in the 16th and 17th centuries and widened in 1810, it often baffles visitors. From the eastern end all 13 of its sturdy arches can be seen, but from the west it appears to have only 12.

The Bear Hotel in the village centre was an important coaching inn, with a narrow archway leading to a courtyard. The nearby Coffee Tavern, a few doors away, is strictly teetotal. It was left in trusteeship to the village in 1903 by Mr and Mrs Percy Davies, the local couple who founded it, on condition that the genteel custom of coffee drinking continues, as the plaque set into the front wall puts it, 'to the general welfare of the inhabitants'.

Activities available in the district range from pony trekking to potholing, and canal cruising to fishing. Just beyond the village is a fine Georgian house, Gwernvale, which is now a hotel. It was once the home of Sir George Everest, Surveyor-General of India, who gave his name to the world's highest mountain.

Llangorse POWYS

12 miles east of Brecon (PAGE 108 Ba)

It is easy to see how myth and legend surround little Llangorse, settled, as it is, within a sudden and unexpected bowl on the edge of the Black Mountains. They and Pen y fan – at 2906 ft the highest peak in the Beacons – tower over it. Stone cottages cling together around the church and a little stone bridge over Nant Cui brook, which runs into Llangorse lake, a mile long and half a mile across – the largest stretch of natural water in South Wales.

On a mist-shrouded morning it is not difficult to imagine voices rising from the reedy shallows, as legend claims. Or to believe, as villagers say, that an ancient city lies sunken in its marshy waters.

If there is a submerged city, it is most likely the remains of a lakeside prehistoric settlement of raised huts. A small island banked and stockaded with stones and wood piles can still be seen. In the 1920s a primitive canoe, dug out of a single tree trunk, was found. It is now in the Brecknock Museum, Brecon.

The only voices rising above the water today are those of happy visitors. Llangorse and its lake – called Syfaddan in Welsh – is a sailing and water sports centre with facilities for campers, caravanners and walkers. You can also go caving and pony trekking close by. Fishing is popular too, mostly for pike and perch.

The village has its origin in the distant age of saints. Paulinus, tutor to St David, set up a community of monks here. In the 6th century a place of worship existed roughly on the site of the present church, now dedicated to St Paulinus. The square-towered building is mainly 15th and 19th century.

The village lies about half a mile from the lake, safely above its flood level. On the common land between them are car parking and a picnic site. Near by, in the dark Afon Llyfni, may lie the key to another Llangorse medieval myth – that blood once flowed into the lake. Its water runs over a red clay bed, which is sometimes washed into the lake as a thick silt.

Talybont POWYS

6 miles south-east of Brecon (PAGE 108 Ba)

Talybont is named Talybont-on-Usk by the locals – just as well, for there are many Talybonts scattered across Wales – but it is linked with another waterway, the Monmouthshire and Brecon Canal. The canal cuts right through the village, often above roof height, the waterway supported by huge, moss-covered retaining walls. It was built between 1797 and 1812 to carry lime, coal and wool the 33 miles from Brecon to Newport and the Severn estuary. The wool and coal came from villages around Brecon. The lime, from the Trefil quarries south of Talybont, was carried by tramway to the village and shipped in barges.

A fragile-looking swing bridge carries traffic across the canal, and remains of limekilns can be seen near the stone bridge south of the village. A tall, canal-company house stands near by, like a bizarre sleeping-beauty's tower. This was where the company's office work was done.

The trade vanished half a century ago. But the canal and the village were saved from decline by canal-loving visitors: cruisers and pleasure craft moor here while their crews enjoy the luxuriant countryside around, or the refreshments of the Star Inn.

The old steam trains from Merthyr to Brecon used to stop at Talybont. The line is closed now, and the station has been turned into a centre for outdoor pursuits. There are pleasant towpath walks to north and south, and a spectacular minor road runs south-west, through the forested Caerfanell valley and past the 2 mile long Talybont reservoir. From there it climbs steeply past the tree line and the Blaen-y-glyn waterfall to a summit of 1400 ft, on the edge of the Brecon Beacons.

Ystradfellte POWYS

18 miles south-west of Brecon (PAGE 108 Ab)

This hamlet, almost lost in the grandeur of the surrounding countryside, is a Welsh village in miniature. The classic ingredients are here – a church, white-washed pub, post office, and a handful of houses, all within a few yards of each other.

The New Inn is a meeting place for the local farming folk. The church, also a focal point for the community, was built by enterprising Cistercian monks in the 12th century. It has been improved over the ages but keeps its medieval character – a row of ancient yew trees in the grounds, said to be more than 800 years old, are taller than the tower.

Ystradfellte, meaning 'Way over the Mellte river', is one of only a handful of settlements in a remote, fascinating southern corner of the Brecon Beacons National Park. Here, the otherwise smooth and rounded outlines of the Beacons are broken by rugged outcrops as red sandstone gives way to magnificent limestone country. The landscape is riddled with caves, cleft by secluded, wooded valleys and alive with waterfalls and cascades.

The cave systems range from narrow potholes to vast chambers. A mile downstream from Ystradfellte, the Mellte disappears into the huge mouth of the Porth yr Ogof cave, to reappear about 500 yds away in a deep and dangerous pool. From here it takes a more leisurely course before plunging down a series of spectacular waterfalls – Sgwd Clun-gwyn, Sgwd Clun-gwyn Isaf and Sgwd y Pannwr – into wild and wooded gorges.

The waterfalls can be visited by following a lovely riverside footpath from the car park at Porth yr Ogof. A connecting path also leads to perhaps the most celebrated waterfall in the area, Sgwd yr Eira ('The Spout of Snow'). This waterfall on the Hepste, a tributary of the Mellte, overhangs so much that you can walk behind it without getting wet.

Walkers can also follow the Sarn Helen Roman road across windswept, open moorlands north of Ystradfellte to the Roman fort of Y Gaer, near Brecon.

LEDBURY

HEREFORD AND WORCESTER

12 miles east of Hereford (PAGE 108 Ea)

Black-and-white half-timbered buildings abound in Ledbury, and those in the High Street include an old coaching inn, The Feathers Hotel, and the 17th-century Market House. The Market House stands upon 16 stout timber pillars, and over the years it has served as a corn store, the town hall and a theatre for travelling players. An open market is still held in the sheltered space inside the pillars.

At the corner of Worcester Road and The Southend is Ledbury Park, a house which Prince Rupert of the Rhine used as headquarters when he occupied the town during the Civil War. In April 1645 some of his troops clashed with Roundheads under General Massey in the dining room of the gabled Talbot Hotel, in New Street. A running fight raged through the streets and churchyard, during which Rupert's horse was killed beneath him, and his Cavaliers finally drove the Roundheads from the town. There are small

TIMBERED TREASURE *Crooked, half-timbered houses and an ancient pub lean over cobbled Church Lane in Ledbury, a rural market town full of history and mellow black-and-white buildings.*

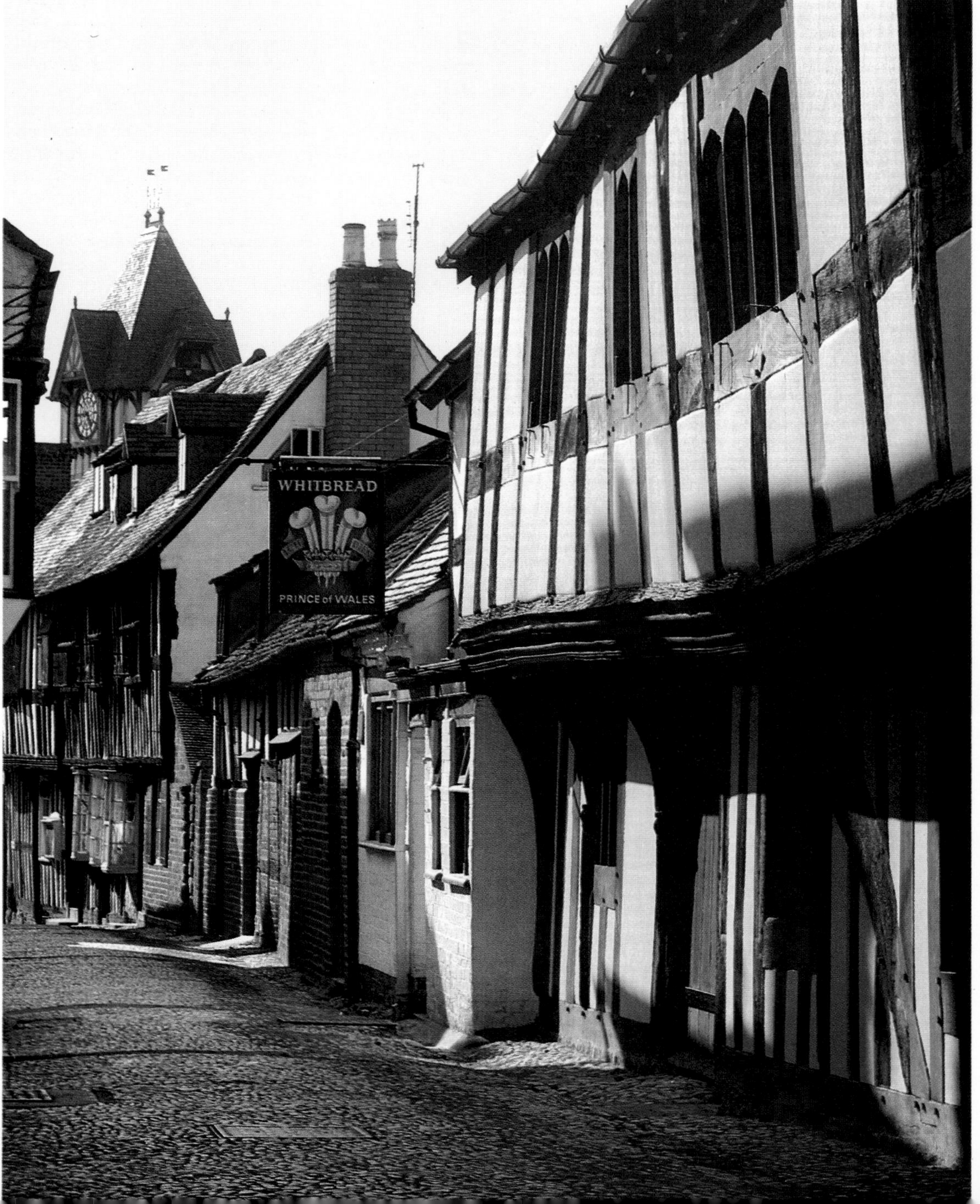

reminders of the fracas still to be found, including bullets embedded in the north door of the 12th to 14th-century parish church of St Michael and All Angels, which has more bullets on display inside. A soaring (126 ft) steeple was added to the church's detached tower in the 18th century, and it looks down on the cobblestones and crooked, black-and-white cottages that border Church Lane. Horse-drawn carriages rattled past to the church until the 1740s, when iron posts were put up to stop the traffic.

Two poets, John Masefield and Elizabeth Barrett Browning, are commemorated in this market town. Masefield, Poet Laureate from 1930 until he died at the age of 89 in 1967, was born in a house called The Knapp in The Homend. He celebrated his home town in several epic poems, including *The Widow in the Bye Street,* a dramatic story of a mother's devotion to her murderous son. But at 14 he had rounded Cape Horn in a windjammer, and the sea was his great passion. He is best remembered, perhaps, for works such as *Cargoes* and *Sea Fever*.

Elizabeth Barrett Browning grew up at Ledbury, and her childhood home, turreted Hope End – rebuilt by her father in Moorish style, but later destroyed by fire – stood in a tree-studded park 2 miles north of the town. She had her own bower of white roses in the grounds, which she described later in her poem *Lost Bower*. The Barrett Browning Memorial Institute, with a clock tower, is on the corner of The Homend and Bye Street. Built in the mid-1890s, it became a public library in 1938 – opened by John Masefield, on his last official visit to the town.

On the west side of the High Street is St Katharine's Hospital, founded in 1232 for the relief of the poor. Of the medieval buildings, only one wing, containing the chapel and the great hall, remains. The chapel is in regular use, and the great hall with its timber roof was restored in 1971 for use as a parish hall. The separate Master's House near by dates from the late 15th century, with 18th and 19th-century additions, and now houses the Tourist Office and a doctors' surgery. The row of almshouses next to St Katharine's was entirely rebuilt last century, and now contains 16 flats for elderly people.

● **Parking** Bye Street (2 car parks) ● **Early closing** Wednesday ● **Market days** Tuesday, Wednesday (cattle), Saturday ● **Event** Carnival (August) ● **Information** TEL. Ledbury 2461 ● **AA 24 hour service** TEL. Worcester 51070.

Dymock GLOUCESTERSHIRE

5 miles south of Ledbury (PAGE 108 Ea)

Set on a small hill, Dymock rises serenely out of the delightful undulating countryside. In the few years before the First World War, the village and its surroundings were much loved by the Dymock poets, whose quarterly magazine *New Numbers* was sent throughout the world from Dymock post office. Rupert Brooke was one of their number, and many of his most famous poems were first published in *New Numbers*. So, too, were those of John Drinkwater, the American Robert Frost and his close friend Edward Thomas, who first contemplated writing poetry while staying in the village. Brooke and Drinkwater had been drawn to Dymock by their friend, the poet Lascelles Abercrombie who in 1911 took up residence in the tiny hamlet of Ryton, which is about $2\frac{1}{2}$ miles to the east.

Abercrombie's home was The Gallows, a timber-framed cottage below Ryton Woods. Here, a figure of local folk history, Jock of Dymock, was hanged for poaching the king's deer. Jock is famed for an alarming custom. On wild nights he used to jump out from a tunnel near Dymock church, with a stag's antlers on his shoulders, and scare passers-by. His tunnel has long since disappeared, but the fine early Norman Church of St Mary and the shady Wintour's Green in front still make a delightful centre to the village. Inside, the church has some interesting relics, including the last Dymock railway ticket, issued September 1959.

Beside the church is the 18th-century, red-brick Old Rectory and, farther down the main street, the Old Cottage still shows its A-shaped cruck beams at the side. The red-brick White House, opposite the church, was the birthplace in 1637 of John Kyrle, the Man of Ross (see Ross-on-Wye, page 114).

Many of Dymock's most delightful houses lie scattered in the countryside round about. The red-brick Old Grange stands three-quarters of a mile north-west, off the Preston road. The core of the house, which once belonged to the Cistercian abbey of Flaxley, is probably medieval, although it was altered in the 18th and 19th centuries. The Welsh rebel leader Owain Glyndwr is believed to have sought refuge here in the early 15th century, and the house still has some secret chambers where he could have hidden.

Beyond The Old Grange, in the tiny hamlets of Greenway and Leddington, are the delightful timber-framed cottages named Little Iddens, home of Robert Frost from 1914 to 1915, and The Old Nail Shop, where his friend Wilfred Wilson Gibson, the sixth of the Dymock poets, lived. It was at Gibson's encouragement and suggestion that Frost came to live here.

The old Church of St Mary, Kempley, 2 miles west, has an almost complete set of 12th-century frescoes, and between Kempley and Dymock, the delightful Dymock Wood is rich in all kinds of wild flowers, including, in the spring, daffodils and bluebells.

Hampton Bishop

HEREFORD AND WORCESTER

12 miles west of Ledbury (PAGE 108 Da)

The half-timbering, thatched roofs and lovingly tended gardens of Hampton Bishop lie strung out along the village street, and are perhaps best appreciated on foot. The handsome, frequently photographed church makes the best starting point. The tower and almost half the walls are original Norman, well integrated with 13th and 14th-century additions. The most striking feature, the black-and-white timber-framed belfry with its six bells, is perched atop the tower. Inside, behind the altar, is a red-sandstone canopied screen of the 15th century.

The small thatched cottage next to the church is typical of many in the village. Box Tree Cottage, some distance away, still has original 15th-century timber crucks supporting it. The Old Court Cottage's 16th-

MATCHED PAIR *Church and cottage are matched for perfection at Hampton Bishop, a village of half-timbering and thatched roofs. The church's pyramid-topped belfry stands on a Norman tower.*

century timbers also still support a neat thatched roof.

Farther down the road at Pentilo, a 300-year-old house, the skill of the thatcher becomes a work of art, with the roof sweeping down in a series of waves almost to the floor, hooding upstairs windows with beautifully cropped overhangs.

The village has been saved from flooding by the rivers Wye and Lugg through the recent construction of huge earth banks, known as The Stanks. The Wye at this point has some of its best salmon beats – 40 pounders have been landed – while walkers can follow a scenic riverside path to the confluence with the Lugg just below the village of Mordiford.

Woolhope HEREFORD AND WORCESTER

10 miles west of Ledbury (PAGE 108 Ea)

A dome of limestone rising to 500 ft above the face of green borderland country has literally put Woolhope on the map. Woolhope Dome, laid down more than 400 million years ago, has a complex geology of alternate shale and limestone outcrops which create an unusual mixture of ridge and vale scenery. All main roads go around rather than over the dome, but a minor road from Hereford follows a steep and narrow route through woodland and across an open common to reach the village perched on a south-eastern slope. Here, in 1851, was founded the Woolhope Naturalists' Field Club, devoted to studying the natural history and archaeology of this fascinating area. Today the club is a national body and is world famous.

Woolhope is sometimes called 'the walled village', because of its preference for stone walls rather than garden hedges. It has two attractive pubs: the black-and-white Butcher's Arms and the Crown Inn, its whitewashed walls and grey roof standing out among handsome red-brick houses. On the outskirts of the village is Wessington Court, a 19th-century Gothic mansion set high on a hill overlooking green fields and pastures. Its brick and stone lodge gatehouse stands beside the road behind tall spike railings and massive stone gateposts.

A fine timber-framed black-and-white house called Terrace Hall stands in Wessington, a mile down the road. It is the home of the Polish sculptor Walenty Pytel, and one of his creations, a 6 ft tall metal flamingo, stands in the forecourt. Near it stands a Victorian lamp post, a piece of metalwork by an earlier, unknown artist.

Woolhope's Church of St George is a red-sandstone building with some 13th-century work, but with a modern stained-glass window which reveals the origin of the village's name. It depicts Lady Godiva and her sister Wulviva who gave the manor of Wulviva's Hope (hope meaning 'valley') to Hereford Cathedral in the 11th century. By 1234 the village had become known as Wulvivehope, which later became abbreviated to Woolhope.

The churchyard has a lych gate, a rickety but noble timber structure erected in Tudor times and known by its Herefordshire name, The Skallenge. From the steps just below it there are views across farmlands and fields to Holling Hill.

Woolhope exists mainly as a farming community, and at Lower Buckenhill, a mile south, a working farm with a farmhouse pure Tudor in style proudly displays its date, 1592, on the black-and-white front wall. Ancient grazing rights still exist on the common, Broadmoor, which is clothed on its northern slopes by Haugh Wood, a mixed forest of broadleaf and conifer trees. It is part Forestry Commission and part National Trust property, and has a small herd of fallow deer.

ROSS-ON-WYE

HEREFORD AND WORCESTER

11 miles north-east of Monmouth (PAGE 108 Ea)

The heart of Ross-on-Wye is the 17th-century Market House, built of the district's red sandstone, which presides over the crowded Market Square. For the past 800 years farmers and their families from outlying villages have converged each week on the market, with its colourful jumble of stalls, to shop and catch up on local gossip. The ground floor of Market House is open; the upper floor is supported by weathered pillars and arches.

Market House is now the library. Here are displayed two mementoes of the town's allegiance to Charles II and the Royalist cause. A bust of the monarch is shown on a white stone medallion on the east wall, and the south-east corner of the building has the curious monogram 'FC', intertwined with a heart. The device is generally taken to mean 'Faithful to Charles in Heart', and was put there by the town's greatest benefactor, a wealthy barrister named John Kyrle (1637-1724).

He restored the tapering spire of the medieval Church of St Mary and gave it a magnificent tenor bell. He also sponsored the causeway to the nearby Wilton Bridge and donated the town's main public garden, The Prospect, with its unbroken views of the surrounding woods and mountains.

No one knows where John Kyrle is buried, but there is a tombstone to him inside the church. His former home is opposite the Market House, but the half-timbered Elizabethan building is now divided into two shops. At the back of one of them, a chemist's, is an old garden laid out to Kyrle's original design, with a maze of box hedges about 12 in. high. Visitors are allowed to see the garden on request. The 19th-century summerhouse here has a most unusual floor; set into it is a mosaic, commissioned by Kyrle, of a swan made from horses' teeth.

Flanking the other side of Market House is a splendid black-and-white building with heads carved on its beams. In coaching days this was the Saracen's Head inn, and today it is an estate agent's office. Another coaching inn, the 19th-century Royal Hotel, is still a hostelry, and a plaque records that it was where Charles Dickens and his future biographer John Forster met in 1867. The Man of Ross inn in Wye Street is another reminder of John Kyrle, who was nicknamed 'The Man of Ross' by the poet and essayist Alexander Pope (1688-1744). The name was also later used by the poet Samuel Taylor Coleridge (1772-1834), who stayed at Kyrle's old home when it served as an inn and wrote there his *Ode to the Man of Ross*.

In the 1830s a new road was built beside the River Wye, and the area was 'decorated' in a medieval style. This accounts for the deceptively old-looking round tower and red-sandstone walls with arrow slits.

• **Parking** Henry Street; Brook End Street; Wilton Road; Millpond Street; Kyrle Street; Edde Cross Street (all car

Ross-on-Wye, reflected in its river

A MAN'S TOWN

Stroll along the broad banks of the Wye and the Man of Ross's town can be seen rising in tiers above its bend in the river. The slim, elegant spire of the Church of St Mary, reflected in the placid river, is but one of the glories owed to the Man. His name was John Kyrle, and more than 300 years ago he lived near the red-sandstone Market House, which is also 17th century.

A view through the pillars of Market House

parks) • **Early closing** Wednesday • **Market days** Thursday, Friday (cattle), Saturday • **Cinema** Roxy, Broad Street • **Events** Raft race (May); Carnival (August) • **Information** TEL. Ross-on-Wye 62768 • **AA 24 hour service** TEL. Worcester 51070.

Clearwell GLOUCESTERSHIRE

16 miles south of Ross-on-Wye (PAGE 108 Db)

Clearwell's castle has a fairy-tale all to itself – a modern one with a happy ending. Built around 1727 by landowner Thomas Wyndham, it was England's first neo-Gothic mansion. But it burnt down in 1929 and, despite renovation, went into decline until 1953, when an unlikely saviour appeared – Mr Frank Yeates, son of the castle gardener.

He spent his boyhood at Clearwell, then went on to become a successful baker in Blackpool. But he returned finally to his roots, bought the derelict shell of the great house where his father had worked, and spent the last 20 years of his life restoring it to its former glory.

The castle and its grounds are now open to the public from Easter to October. The house has an elegant main hall of Elizabethan origin and, upstairs, rooms with merman motifs, incorporated from an earlier building on the site. It was used by the infamous Judge Jeffreys when he toured the countryside, hanging and transporting followers of the Duke of Monmouth after the unsuccessful 1685 rebellion.

The village itself, on the fringes of the Forest of Dean, was a mining community for 3000 years, until the 1940s. Iron ore was dug in prehistoric times; Roman quarrymen left oak shovels behind in caves – or 'churns' as they are known locally. In Puzzle Wood, to the north, is a 2000-year-old open-cast iron pit and, beneath it, the Clearwell Caves, a 600 ft deep labyrinthine mining complex which is being developed as a museum.

Relics of this eventful past are the large, white-painted Wyndham Arms inn, which has a sign proclaiming it as 'c. 1340'; and a 14th-century sandstone cross where wandering friars would preach. Tudor Farm is said to have been occupied at one time by Oliver Cromwell. On the outskirts is the oddly named Stank Farm. The name means fishpond, and this was probably where the lord of the manor kept his carp.

The Church of St Peter was built by Caroline Wyndham, Countess of Dunraven, who lived in the castle during the 19th century – the last in her family line to do so. The church is large and exuberantly decorated, and some locals describe it as 'a fancy layer cake'. The countess was also responsible for building the village school and the cemetery chapel on the site of the original St Peter's, at the other end of the village.

Hoarwithy HEREFORD AND WORCESTER

7 miles north-west of Ross-on-Wye (PAGE 108 Da)

A little corner of Italy stands in the Wye Valley water meadows of Hoarwithy. On a hilltop above the old stone buildings is the Church of St Catherine, which has a fine bell tower, arcades and mosaic floors that

A TOUCH OF TUSCANY FROM THE PARSON

An exercise in rich English eccentricity has turned part of the Wye Valley village of Hoarwithy into a small corner of Tuscany. A wealthy Victorian parson arrived there in 1854, decided he did not care for the 'ugly brick' church he found, and spent 40 years creating a new one to his Italianate taste – complete with tiled and mosaic floors, arcades, a bell tower and a white marble altar.

The Reverend William Poole's Italianate Church of St Catherine, Hoarwithy

Sunlight streams across the cool mosaic floor of a colonnade in St Catherine's

would fit in quite well amid the cypresses of Tuscany.

The church was the work of a wealthy Victorian parson, the Reverend William Poole. He arrived in 1854 to find his chapel 'an ugly brick building with no pretension to any style of architecture'. Over the years he changed all that, building a new church around the existing chapel. He brought in craftsmen from near and far, including Italy, and employed his own architect, J. P. Seddon. The result is a magnificent folly, a unique parish church with intricate tiled floors, a domed ceiling supported by columns of grey French and Cornish marble, a white marble altar inlaid with lapis lazuli, superb choir-stall woodcarvings showing 12 British saints and rich stained-glass windows.

St Catherine's is set off by the Englishness of the rest of the village. Tresseck, a black-and-white 16th-century building with a stone-gabled wing, a quarter of a mile to the west, is still a working farm. The cornmill, below the church, was working until the 1940s and is now a private house. It is distinguished by an old iron wheel set into the stonework.

On the southern approach to the village stands Bark House, a reminder that this was once a centre of an industry based on the oak trees which were plentiful in the area. Their bark was shipped by barge to Hereford where it was used for tanning. The riverbanks are lined with willow trees, and the village's name means white willow. Another reminder of old times is the tall, angular cottage – built as a toll house in 1856 – beside the iron bridge spanning the Wye. A horse-drawn ferry operated until 1856 when it was replaced by a bridge – the present one was built in 1876. The pink-washed Upper Orchard Hotel dates from 1700 and was one of Hoarwithy's first inns.

Hoarwithy comes within the parish of Hentland, where on Palm Sundays there is a distribution in church of pax cakes – biscuits decorated with the legend 'peace and good neighbourhood'. The custom dates back to the 16th century.

Llanthony GWENT

30 miles west of Ross-on-Wye (PAGE 108 Ca)

Llanthony's Abbey Hotel is a rarity among village inns. It is part of a ruined 12th-century priory, and it puts up visitors in an original tower. The licence for this 'pub in a priory' was granted when the hotel became a shooting box in the 18th century.

The priory itself was founded on the site of a lonely chapel dedicated to St David 1400 years ago. This chapel was discovered by a Norman knight, William de Lacy, during a hunt. He was impressed by its austere setting and, renouncing worldly pursuits, founded a hermitage which became an Augustinian monastery in about 1118.

Marauding Welsh drove the monks to a more comfortable berth – another Llanthony Priory, in Gloucestershire. But in 1175 they returned and a new church was built, then added to over the next 50 years. The spot was 'truly calculated for religion and more adopted to canonical discipline than all the monasteries of the British Isles', wrote the medieval chronicler Gerald of Wales – though he admitted its remoteness might mean the monks were 'singing to the wolves'.

The austere beauty that made Llanthony so attractive to de Lacy is still much in evidence. A superb row of red stone arches survived the priory's dissolution in the 16th century and frames mountains populated only by sheep and ponies. This beautiful setting attracted Walter Savage Landor – author of *Imaginary Conversations* – who bought an estate and had a home built. But he became disillusioned with the 'wretched' villagers, complaining of their 'drunkenness', and 'idleness', and saying that they treated him as their 'worst enemy'. He left in 1814 never to return.

The priory now forms the core of a peaceful hamlet. Next to it is St David's parish church, medieval but renovated. All around is pony-trekking and walking country, with footpaths from the priory car park to the Offa's Dyke borderland walk. To the north, the winding road leads out of the Vale of Ewyas, which cuts through the Black Mountains, and climbs to the 1809 ft Gospel Pass with magnificent views. At Capel-y-ffin, on this road, is the confusingly named Llanthony Monastery, where a short-lived 19th-century monastery was founded.

Symonds Yat

HEREFORD AND WORCESTER

8 miles south-west of Ross-on-Wye (PAGE 108 Db)

It takes a 4½ mile car trip to get from one half of the resort to the other, although the two halves are only 100 yds apart. This is because Symonds Yat is cut in two by the River Wye, with no bridge between. Spread out along the craggy slopes of a spectacular wooded limestone gorge, the village is a centre for walking and river cruising amid some of the best scenery of the Wye Valley.

Yat Rock, near by, stands 473 ft above sea level at the neck of a 4 mile loop in the river, giving panoramic views. The Wye Valley Walk passes close by; 2 miles downstream are the Biblins, water meadows with a precarious suspension footbridge across the river. There are also the Seven Sisters Rocks, and the fancifully named King Arthur's Cave – where the remains of Stone Age man and of mammoths and woolly rhinoceroses have been found. To the north is the Queen Stone, strangely indented and probably a prehistoric ceremonial monument.

Regular boating trips are run up and down the river as they have been for centuries (Nelson was a visitor), and the Wye can be crossed in the village by small rope-guided ferries running between two pubs – one on each bank. The riverside church is largely 14th century, with an impressive trussed rafter roof. More interestingly, perhaps, it is dedicated to St Dubricius, a local holy man who converted the Hereford area to Christianity and died around AD 550. Legend has it that he also crowned King Arthur, and that his mother Efrddil, was the subject of a miracle. When Efrddil's father, a local chieftain, discovered that she was pregnant he ordered her to be drowned. She survived, so he ordered her to be burnt. She survived that, too, and was found next day, nursing the infant Dubricius.

The most distinguished old building in Symonds Yat – yat means pass, and there was a 17th-century high sheriff named Symonds – is the Old Court, a 16th to 17th-century stone house with fine timber-and-plaster fittings inside. It is now a hotel, but its delicately finished stonework and mullioned windows capped by a stone tiled roof remain as they were.

MAP 11

THE COTSWOLDS AND THEIR GOLDEN FLEECES

The peaceful parishes of the Cotswold Hills had their character formed largely by the cream and gold local stone. Here the scenery is gentle, even formal-looking, but seldom less than enchanting. Many towns and villages were once centres of the wool trade. Homes built by rich wool merchants and churches that benefited from their charity survive to bear impressive witness to their riches.

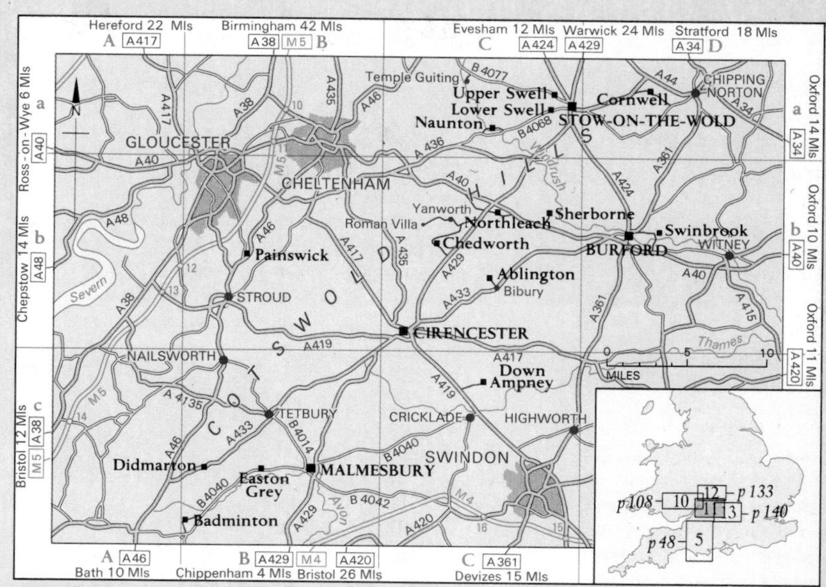

MAP 11: NEIGHBOURING AREAS – MAPS 5, 10, 12, 13

BURFORD Northleach Sherborne Swinbrook
CIRENCESTER Ablington Chedworth Down Ampney Painswick
MALMESBURY Badminton Didmarton Easton Grey
STOW-ON-THE-WOLD Cornwell Naunton The Swells

BURFORD

OXFORDSHIRE

7 miles west of Witney (PAGE 119 Db)

Burford's handsome sloping High Street was originally built as a market place, with narrow plots running back from the broad street, on which the traders pitched their stalls. The plots are still here, but the stalls have been replaced by dignified shops and houses – mostly 17th century and earlier.

In Saxon times Burford – 'the fort by the ford' – was an important crossing place over the River Windrush, which flows past the bottom of High Street. By the early Middle Ages it was a successful market town, and the local Guild of Merchants met in a stone building called the Tolsey, or town hall, and took the payments for the fairs and markets.

The Tolsey, which now houses a museum, stands at the junction of High Street and Sheep Street. The Hill, another street, climbs steeply away south and is lined with fine old buildings – some dating from the 15th century. On the corner of High Street and Priory Lane is Falkland Hall, in warm Cotswold stone, like most of the town's old buildings. The hall – whose original oriel window juts out onto High Street – was built in 1558 as the town house of a local cloth merchant named Edmund Sylvester.

Also in High Street is the Bull Hotel, with a fine stone and brick Georgian front – the hotel was badly damaged by fire in 1982 but reopened in 1984. On the west side of the street, an arch leads to the former George Hotel, now homes for the elderly, where, it is said, Charles II used to stay with Nell Gwynne.

The Bull and the George, with Burford's other inns, thrived during the coaching age of the 18th and early 19th centuries. The town lies on the old main road from London to the West of England and Wales, and many coaches passed through every day.

On Church Green are some almshouses, recently modernised but founded in 1457 by the lord of the manor, Richard Neville, Earl of Warwick – 'the King-maker'. Facing them is the old Burford Grammar School, founded in 1571 by Symon Wysdom, another wealthy cloth merchant.

In 1530 Wysdom was charged with possessing a copy of the Bible in English, probably the banned version by William Tyndale (about 1494 – 1536), but on account of his youth, he was spared the usual punishment – branding on each cheek.

During the Civil War Burford saw the suppressing of a mutiny. In May 1649 Oliver Cromwell entered the town at midnight with 2000 horsemen in pursuit of 800 troopers of the Parliamentary army who had mutinied. Some 340 of the mutineers were rounded up and imprisoned in the beautiful Church of St John Baptist. A few days later three of the ringleaders were shot in the churchyard while the other prisoners, later discharged, looked on from the roof. A fourth ringleader – who was possibly a double agent – was then forced to preach a sermon. He did so 'howling and weeping like a crocodile'. One mutineer cut his name, 'ANTHONY SEDLEY, PRISNER, 1649', on the font. St John's was founded in the 12th century and

The Windrush at Burford

The Lamb inn

A RIVER THAT ROLLS THROUGH HISTORY

The River Windrush rolls serenely past the Church of St John Baptist at Burford – a river linked intimately with the town since there was a ford here in Saxon times. Much of Burford's history is preserved in the church and in the town's many fine houses, such as that of Tudor merchant Symon Wysdom in High Street, and others that climb the Hill. Among the surviving inns is the partly 14th-century Lamb, in Sheep Street.

Symon Wysdom's house

Houses on the Hill

largely 'restored' 300 years later. Inside there is a monument to Edmund Harman (about 1509–76), which he built himself in 1569 to thank God for His goodness – and which, for no known reason, bears a carving of a group of Red Indians.

Harman was born in Ipswich and became Barber Surgeon to Henry VIII in 1540. Later he saved Henry's life when the king suffered an apoplectic fit. As a reward, Harman was granted the lease of The Priory in Burford. It had been founded in the late 12th century and was run by Augustinian canons as a hospital for the aged and sick.

A stone bridge across the Windrush has stood at the bottom of High Street from before the 14th century, but has been restored many times since. In 1945, at the end of the Second World War, the parapet had to be rebuilt because a US Army tank wrecked it.

Every June, schoolchildren march through the town with a mock-up dragon to commemorate a victory by the West Saxons over the Mercians in AD 750. The West Saxons had a dragon banner.

● **Parking** Guildenford (car park); High Street; The Hill ● **Early closing** Wednesday ● **Event** The Dragon Festival (June) ● **Information** TEL. Burford 3590 ● **AA 24 hour service** TEL. Oxford 240286.

Northleach GLOUCESTERSHIRE

9 miles west of Burford (PAGE 119 Cb)

Sheep grazing in the churchyard and sheep depicted on memorial brasses inside the church tell the story of Northleach – a wool centre of the Cotswold uplands which, in medieval times, was as important as Cirencester. As in so many other Cotswold villages and towns, its church is a memorial to the days when the wealthy wool merchants lavished their riches on a place in which they could give thanks for their good fortune, and go to their final rest in suitably splendid surroundings.

The Church of St Peter and St Paul was largely rebuilt in the 15th century, in the delicate Perpendicular style of the period that gloried in pinnacled buttresses, tall windows and lofty towers. At Northleach the tower rises 100 ft above a two-storey south porch which is claimed to be the loveliest in England.

Inside the church there are many brasses, including those of John and Thomas Fortey, who both had a hand in the rebuilding of the nave. The memorial of Thomas Bushe, who died in 1526, includes the arms of Calais in France, a reminder that this was the port to which the fleeces were sent.

Northleach's wool industry declined after the Abbey of Gloucester, which held the manorial rights, was dissolved in the mid-16th century. However, its market, established by the abbey in 1200, went on and the place became a miniature market town with its own annually elected bailiff and constables. For a few years in the mid-18th century the coaching trade brought renewed prosperity.

The High Street is lined with many houses whose fine fronts in pale gold Cotswold stone were added at several dates from the mid-1500s onwards. The Wheatsheaf Hotel is a particularly attractive example.

At the crossroads, where the Foss Way crosses the old Oxford to Gloucester road, stands the grim façade of a House of Correction built in the 1780s. Such establishments were used as an alternative to prison or transportation, and minor offenders were sent there in the pious hope that a short dose of hard labour would make them see the error of their ways. For the

37 inmates the 'short, sharp shock' consisted of various tasks which, in the 1820s, included working on a treadmill. Each prisoner had a ground-floor day cell and a first-floor night cell. He was also allowed to wash. Men did not have such rights in the formal prisons of that time.

The building now houses a fascinating Museum of Rural Life, though it includes one cell block preserved in its original condition. Also on display are farm implements, a superb collection of carts and a steam tractor, and a range of domestic items.

Sherborne GLOUCESTERSHIRE

$5\frac{1}{2}$ miles west of Burford (PAGE 119 Cb)

In early summer there seem to be bees everywhere in Sherborne, buzzing around the colourful cottage gardens and visiting the dazzling yellow fields of rape that chequer the broad Cotswold Hills around the village. There are hives in gardens, and Sherborne honey is often available at one or two cottage doors.

The village sits comfortably beside its stream, the Sherborne Brook, and little terraces of two or three stone cottages are strung out, with plenty of space between them, for almost a mile along the valley. They have stone-slate roofs, stone-mullioned windows and stone hoods above the doors; and they stand back behind generous front gardens crossed by stone paths and framed by stone walls. The gardens are a delight. In season they are filled with neat rows of cabbages, beans and onions intermingled with garden flowers to make a riot of contrasting texture and colour.

At first sight there seems nothing special about the small cottage numbered 88 at the crossroads to the east of the village. But look again. The stone archway around the door, decorated with zigzag patterns, came from a Norman church that once stood in the village.

Midway along the main street is a group of grander buildings around Sherborne House. The monks of Winchcombe Abbey built a small chapel on this site in AD 811. Later a separate monastery was established. In 1552 the site was bought by Thomas Dutton, who had a mansion built on it. The Dutton family became noted for their lavish hospitality in Elizabethan times. On one occasion Elizabeth I was entertained here and the household accounts show that the cost of 'Makynge Readye' for her visit was £5.18s. (£5.90), a princely sum then – equivalent to more than £885 now.

John Dutton, 2nd Lord Sherborne, commissioned the architect Lewis Wyatt to rebuild the house in 1830. Wyatt retained the style of the earlier stone façade, with classical columns separating the tall, mullioned windows. In recent years the house has been a school and a meditation centre. Now it has been divided into flats and is not open to the public. The Church of St

AN UNEXPECTED OASIS AT THE POST OFFICE

At the wisteria-hung post office in Sherborne one can buy not only stamps, but 'Beer, Stout and Cider, to be consumed off the premises' – noteworthy in a publess village. Architectural treats range from the splendours of Sherborne House to the oddity of a cottage with a Norman-arched doorway. Flowers bloom delightfully among vegetables in attractive village gardens.

Sherborne post office

Cottage with a Norman arch

Sherborne House

Flower and vegetable garden

Mary Magdalene, attached to Sherborne House, can be visited by taking the road that passes to the right of the stable blocks. The church houses a remarkable collection of monuments to the Dutton family. A macabre effigy of John Dutton, who died in 1656, is shown in his shroud, but standing upright. An inscription says that he was 'one who was master of a large fortune and owner of a mind aequall to it'.

The sculptor Rysbrack's marble carving of Sir John Dutton, dated 1749, shows him leaning nonchalantly on an urn, wearing a Roman toga and sandals. There must have been some red faces when this memorial was unveiled, for the name of Sir John's grandfather, a Mr Barwick, was wrongly inscribed: the word 'John' is scored out, and 'Peter' carved above it.

Although Sherborne House is now in private hands, the village, surrounding park and agricultural land are owned by the National Trust.

Swinbrook OXFORDSHIRE

2½ miles east of Burford (PAGE 119 Db)

A trio of almost identical Tudor knights in armour, complete with swords, recline stiffly on their sides in Swinbrook's Church of St Mary, each with his head propped on one hand. They await the Day of Judgment stacked one above the other like children on a three-tier bunk. Beside them is a second stack of three effigies, carved later in the 17th century. Less rigid and more relaxed in style, each wears his wig and leans nonchalantly on one elbow, with a knee raised and a helmet at his foot. They were all called Fettiplace, and their monuments occupy most of the chancel's north wall in the 13th to 15th-century church.

The memorials to the Fettiplaces are all that remain in Swinbrook of one of the great families of Oxfordshire, who came to the village around 1490 and built a large mansion south of the church. Of the house not a trace remains, unless some of its stones were re-used to build the cottages around the small green below the church. The family name has vanished from Swinbrook too – the last of the Swinbrook Fettiplaces died in 1805 with no male heir.

In the churchyard there is a row of magnificent stone table tombs, decorated with cherubs and topped by carved cylinders of stone that may represent funeral biers. Slabs of Cotswold stone commemorate members of another Swinbrook family rather better known – the Mitfords. Two of the six Mitford sisters are buried here, the author Nancy and Unity. Their father was Lord Redesdale who, in the 1920s, built the austere Swinbrook House a mile north of the village.

Nancy Mitford described her eccentric and isolated childhood at Swinbrook and, before that, at nearby Asthall in her first novel, *The Pursuit of Love*. Life was seldom dull in the Mitfords' home, it seems. Printed notices in guest rooms warned: 'Owing to an unidentified corpse in the cistern visitors are requested not to drink the bath water.' And the hills sometimes resounded with the screams of the girls being tracked by their father's bloodhounds.

Stone walls enclose the meadows leading down from the church to the River Windrush. Cattle and sheep escape from the sun under tall willows on the riverbank; moorhens scurry for shelter and swallows skim the surface, poaching flies from the trout. A swan or two may swim within neck-stretching reach of food dropped from the garden of the Swan Inn, which occupies the old mill house beside the river.

From the church there is a delightful half-mile walk across meadows to the little Church of St Oswald, Widford. Built on the site of a Roman villa, the church houses fragments of a Roman mosaic floor, medieval wall paintings and box pews.

CIRENCESTER

GLOUCESTERSHIRE

14 miles north-west of Swindon (PAGE 119 Cb)

Beneath the streets of this ancient market town are the remains of the Roman town of Corinium, founded about AD 75. Next to Londinium (London) it was the largest and one of the most important Roman towns in England – and excavations have shown it was built to their classic grid plan of straight streets. It was destroyed by Saxons in the 6th century, but reborn in the Middle Ages as Cirencester (pronounced 'Syren-sester'), when the grid pattern was abandoned and the streets turned and twisted in all directions. Even the Market Place, which replaced the old Roman forum, was given a distinct curve.

Set at the junction of two of the great Roman roads, Foss Way and Ermin Street, Corinium was also planned as an administrative centre for the area inhabited by the Dobunni – a conquered British tribe who lived in the southern part of the Cotswold Hills.

Cirencester's huge 15th to 16th-century parish church of St John the Baptist, in the Market Place, is built of pale yellow stone, and was largely paid for by wealthy wool merchants – it is one of the numerous Cotswold 'wool churches'. The money for its pinnacled tower, however, came unwittingly from the Earls of Salisbury and Kent. They rebelled against Henry IV in 1399, but while passing through Cirencester they were arrested by zealous townsfolk and executed for treason. Grateful Henry allowed the townsfolk to keep the earls' treasure chests – which paid the builders.

Inside the church, the impressive pulpit is shaped like a vast wineglass, and on the wall beside it is a 17th-century hourglass which was used by the preacher to time his sermons. By the door of the south

Swinbrook, across the Windrush

Fettiplace knights in church

A FAMILY OF WARRIORS IN TIERS

St Mary's Church at Swinbrook looks out over sleepy Oxfordshire acres and the gentle Windrush river. Surrounded by nature's beauty, St Mary's guards its own rich treasures. Light from the large east window falls on a strange triple memorial to three armoured gentlemen of an attractively named local family, the Fettiplaces, complete with swords and helmets. The family once lived in a large mansion near by. In the churchyard are some elaborately carved table tombs – and, in striking contrast, the simple headstones marking the graves of two sisters from another local family – the eccentric Mitfords. They were the author Nancy, and Unity who was devoted to Hitler and tried to kill herself when the Second World War was declared.

Table tombs in churchyard

Nancy Mitford's grave

Swinbrook cottages

aisle is a coloured statue of a blue-coated boy, used in the 18th century to 'beg' funds for the church's primary school. The school was founded in 1714 by Rebecca Powell, and is still flourishing today.

On display in the south aisle is the silver-gilt Boleyn Cup made in 1535 for Anne Boleyn, second wife of Henry VIII, the year before she was executed for alleged adultery. Perched on the lid are a falcon holding a sceptre, and a rose tree – Anne's personal emblem. After her death the cup went to her daughter, Elizabeth I, who in turn passed it on to her physician, Dr Richard Master, who later gave it to St John's.

At the top of Cecily Hill, to the south-west, is Cirencester Park, home of the Earl Bathurst. His mansion, hidden behind a 40 ft high yew hedge planted in 1818, is not open to the public. But the park is; you can walk along its 5 mile tree-lined Broad Avenue or ride horseback along part of it.

The 3000 acres of wooded parkland were laid out in the 18th century by the 1st Earl Bathurst and his friend the poet Alexander Pope (1688–1744). At a point where ten rides meet is a summerhouse named Pope's Seat. It was a favourite retreat of the poet.

In Park Street is the Corinium Museum, which houses one of the most valuable collections of Roman antiquities in Britain. The exhibits all come from Cirencester and the Cotswolds, and include sculpture, domestic articles, such as jewellery, pottery and cooking vessels, and magnificent mosaic floors.

• **Parking** Dugdale Road; Beeches Road; Forum, Southway; Cripps Road, off Ashcroft Road; Market Place; The Waterloo; Cattle Market; Tetbury Road (all car parks) • **Early closing** Thursday • **Market days** Monday, Friday (street markets); Tuesday (cattle) • **Theatre** Beeches Barn Theatre, Beeches Road • **Cinema** Regal, Lewis Lane • **Events** Ermin Street Guard (Easter Saturday); Amberley Horse Show (May); Polo (mid May – mid September); Carnival (July); Mop Fair (October) • **Information** TEL. Cirencester 4180 • **AA 24 hour service** TEL. Gloucester 23278.

Ablington GLOUCESTERSHIRE

7 miles north-east of Cirencester (PAGE 119 Cb)

The trout-happy River Coln curls through Ablington, watering a woody dell in which rests a hamlet of stone-built houses. This is but one of a string of pearls along the Coln, among which the best known is Bibury, a mile downstream. Little seems to have changed in Ablington for centuries – except for the

STORY-BOOK ENDING OVERLEAF
The Old Mill House rests from its labours on the green bank of the weed-streaked Coln at Ablington, where J. Arthur Gibbs chronicled daily life in his evocative book A Cotswold Village.

old mill whose forecourt serves as a vestigial village square. It is now a private house with gardens leading down to a millstream where the banks are golden with daffodils in spring.

But the Victorian writer J. Arthur Gibbs – who chronicled Ablington life in his book *A Cotswold Village* – would perhaps applaud improvements made since his time. 'Farms are to be had for the asking,' he wrote then, 'and the country is rapidly going back to its original uncultivated state.'

Now disused barns have been converted to handsome homes, and the gardens around the old houses are immaculate. The Elizabethan Manor House, where Gibbs lived, has huge gardens stretching down to the river, but remains private behind high stone walls. Its doorway, dated 1590, features five elaborately carved heads – one of them Elizabeth I herself. The high gables of 17th-century Ablington House peer over another tall, dry-stone wall. Guarding the iron gate are two rampant stone lions that once graced the Houses of Parliament.

One of the most colourful characters in Arthur Gibbs's book was a gamekeeper named Tom Peregrine. He was based on a real-life gamekeeper, John Brown, whose small cottage sits somewhat unsteadily on the slope above the hamlet.

Chedworth GLOUCESTERSHIRE

8 miles north of Cirencester (PAGE 119 Cb)

West of the Foss Way, where it plunges steeply to cross the River Coln at Fossebridge, the houses of Chedworth stand along the lower slopes of a shallow valley between Pancake Hill and Chedworth Beacon. Here the pale grey limestone of the Cotswolds can be seen at its best, not in grand houses and a soaring 'wool' church, but in simple homesteads and farms, and a Norman church that sits prettily and at ease among its sturdy neighbours.

St Andrew's Church retains its original plan of west tower, nave and chancel, but its plain Norman lines are enhanced by tall windows in the south wall that rise almost from ground level to the battlemented roof parapet. Below the church, in Church Row and Ballingers Row, there are 18th-century cottages, and a little farther to the east Cromwell House and The Old Farm, both with gables and mullioned windows and dating from the 16th or 17th centuries.

A thousand years before the Normans came to the Cotswolds, however, the Romans were here, and using that same limestone to build Chedworth Villa. It was discovered in 1864, about a mile to the north of the village.

The villa's mosaic floors were the first to come to light, and further excavations organised by Lord Eldon, who owned the land, revealed an elaborate range of baths with rooms designed for both humid and dry heat and a cold plunge. Another wing contained a number of living rooms.

The villa's floors are richly patterned and depict the seasons in the forms of figures, such as Cupid carrying a garland for summer. A museum, built in 1866, contains objects found in the villa, including pottery, iron tools and small altars.

By road the villa is most easily reached via Yanworth. Since 1924 the site has been owned by the National Trust who have built a visitors' centre. Above the villa, public footpaths cross mixed woodland, alive with colour in autumn, where edible Roman snails are said to live. There is a large herd of deer in Chedworth Woods, to the west.

About 1½ miles south-east of the village is Denfurlong Farm, a working dairy and arable farm which welcomes visitors from daylight to dusk throughout the year. There is an exhibition explaining different aspects of the working of a farm, and two trails, one round the fields and the other round the buildings. At afternoon milking time the automated milking parlour can be seen in operation from a viewing platform in the cowshed.

Down Ampney GLOUCESTERSHIRE

6 miles south-east of Cirencester (PAGE 119 Cc)

Visible for miles across the flat pastureland through which runs the infant Thames, the 14th-century spire of All Saints' Church, Down Ampney, beckons above the tall trees that surround it. Plump cows champ the grass of the lush meadows in front of the church – a scene so peaceful that it is hard to imagine the whine and roar of Second World War planes taking off from these fields bound for the D-Day invasion and, later, the ill-fated airborne mission to Arnhem.

Every year in September the church, which dates from 1265, is filled to overflowing for a service commemorating the Battle of Arnhem. A stained-glass window preserves the memory of Down Ampney's airmen, among them Flight Lieutenant David Lord who was posthumously awarded the Victoria Cross for bravery when flying in desperately needed supplies.

An earlier warrior, Sir Nicholas de Valers – sometimes spelt Villiers – reclines in effigy in the south transept, his feet crossed. Beside the church a tall yew hedge screens Down Ampney House, a fine stone Tudor building 'modernised' in 1799.

The rest of the village stands apart from the big house and the church, its stone houses – new ones infilled among the old – straddling a long street.

Among them, set back from the road, is the Old Vicarage, which has a tall pine beside its gate. Ralph Vaughan-Williams, the composer, was born here in 1872, when his father was vicar. Later he wrote the music of a tune to the hymn *Come down O Love Divine*, and called it *Down Ampney*.

Painswick GLOUCESTERSHIRE

16 miles north-west of Cirencester (PAGE 119 Bb)

Painswick churchyard is a mass of yew trees in all imaginable shapes and forms. Some have grown together to form multiple arches; others are trained as hedges, skilfully clipped to give square sides. Many are freestanding, some of them proud under bouffant hairstyles sweeping the ground; others are standard trees, clipped to form neat cones above wide trunks. Yews in pairs straddle one path through the churchyard and meet overhead – looking almost like married couples tripping hand in hand from the altar.

As if the yews were not enough, the magnificent stone tombs in St Mary's churchyard confirm that here is no ordinary village. This assembly of mainly

18th-century table and pedestal tombs is unique in Britain; and complemented by the dark foliage of the yews they make the churchyard appear almost like a sculpture garden.

Brass plates on the sides of some are elegantly engraved with the names of their occupants – the Lovedays, the Packers, the Pooles – families of rich merchants and clothiers.

Painswick's heyday was between the 14th and 18th centuries, when the village – a town at that time – grew rich from the wool trade and was a centre of cloth making. The wealthy built magnificent houses in creamy-white stone quarried from Painswick Hill, a mile to the north. Several of the more interesting houses are in Bisley Street.

The elegant 18th-century front of Byfield House masks an earlier building of Tudor origin. Humbler cottages – but still built of the same creamy stone – line Vicarage Street. The street slopes downwards giving views of the Cotswold Hills, where a few sheep graze in hedged fields generously wooded with beech and oak. In medieval times these hills were unfenced, and Painswick merchants could gaze contentedly out at great flocks roaming them under the watchful eyes of their shepherds.

However, the atmosphere was not always one of peace and plenty, judging by the stocks in St Mary's Street. The stocks were put here in the mid-19th century 'for the punishment of those who carry on carousels to the annoyance of neighbours'.

The church manages to hold its own within the incomparable frame of its churchyard. The 15th-century tower, housing a famous peal of 12 bells, was topped in 1632 by a spire which reaches to 172 ft. Annually, on the first Sunday after September 18, a 'clipping' ceremony takes place, when the children of the village hold hands to encircle the church and dance around it, singing hymns. Afterwards the children, who are garlanded with flowers, each receive a traditional Painswick bun and a silver coin.

Half a mile outside the village, on the Gloucester Road, stands the handsome Palladian mansion, Painswick House. It has a good collection of furniture and some fine Chinese wallpaper. The house is open throughout August.

MALMESBURY

WILTSHIRE

15 miles west of Swindon (PAGE 119 Bc)

When Henry VIII abolished the monasteries in 1539, the handsome Benedictine abbey at Malmesbury was sold off for £1517 to a local wool merchant, William Stumpe. He used many of the old abbey buildings for cloth weaving, but two years later presented the abbey's nave to the town as a new parish church.

The abbey had been founded in the 7th century by St Aldhelm, its first abbot, and what remains is impressive. The church's Norman porch is considered one of the finest in England and has a richly decorated arch illustrating various Biblical themes.

The church also contains a 15th-century monument to the first Saxon monarch to rule the whole of England, King Athelstan (AD 925 – 40), who is buried here. In a corner of the churchyard is the tower of the previous parish church, St Paul's, now used as the abbey belfry. St Paul's was already falling into ruin when Stumpe gave the town its new church.

Malmesbury stands between two branches of the River Avon, on the site of a fortified Saxon hilltop town. It claims to be the oldest borough in England – Alfred the Great granted it a charter in AD 880. About 60 years later King Athelstan gave some 500

WOOL LEAVES ITS MARK

Hollyhocks stand like colourful sentinels beside the studded oak door of The Chur, a medieval Painswick house where a rich wool merchant once lived. In those days donkeys would have carried fleeces through the archway. The village churchyard has some splendidly carved table tombs, and in St Mary's Street are iron stocks looking oddly like a pair of spectacles.

Doorway of The Chur, Painswick

Table tombs in the churchyard

Stocks in St Mary's Street

Market Cross gargoyles, Malmesbury

Six of the Apostles at abbey church

SAINTS, SINNERS AND CROSS OLD GARGOYLES

Grotesque gargoyles gape out from the old Market Cross building at Malmesbury, while the Twelve Apostles decorate the richly carved Norman porch of the abbey church, along with Biblical themes that include the Creation of Adam and Eve, the Expulsion from Paradise and the battle between David and Goliath.

acres of land to a number of townsmen who helped him defeat Norse invaders. This land, known as the King's Heath, is still owned by about 200 men living in Malmesbury who can trace their ancestry back to those who fought for Athelstan.

At the centre of the town is the elaborate late 15th-century Market Cross, which is not just a cross but a building. According to one chronicler, 'it is curiously voulted, for poore market folkes to stande dry when rayne cummith'. The fine vaulting remains and people still take shelter here. Near by are Abbey House, built by William Stumpe on the site of the old abbot's house, and the arched Tolsey Gate, whose two flanking cells served as the town prison in the 18th and 19th centuries.

Most of the older buildings are made of locally quarried stone. They include, at the bottom of the High Street, the mainly 17th-century St John's Almshouse, which has a late Norman arch. The Old Bell Hotel may have belonged to a Saxon castle, demolished in 1216, and incorporates what could be some walls of a 13th-century abbey guesthouse.

An 11th-century monk of Malmesbury, named Elmer, once tried to fly. He fastened home-made wings on his feet and hands; then he jumped off the abbey tower, frantically beating the air. It is said that he flew some 200 yds before crashing, breaking both legs and laming himself for life. Brother Elmer's epic flight of fancy has been commemorated in the abbey by a modern stained-glass window.

• **Parking** Cross Hayes; Horsefair; Market Cross; Station Yard (all car parks) • **Early closing** Thursday • **Event** Carnival (August) • **Information** TEL. Malmesbury 2143 • **AA 24 hour service** TEL. Swindon 21446.

Badminton AVON

10 miles south-west of Malmesbury (PAGE 119 Bc)

As you approach the rolling parkland of the Duke of Beaufort's estate at Badminton, the place seems at first sight to be guarded by a series of forts and small castles. Closer scrutiny reveals that the forts are farm buildings, disguised by turrets and castellations; and the little castles are lodges with miniature round towers at each corner. These charming 'follies' date from the 1750s when the estate was decorated by the architect Thomas Wright. More of Wright's eccentric work can be seen on the edge of Badminton village. One cottage looks like an upturned boat.

The village centre is more restrained, as befits a village that was largely built to house estate workers. The main street flanks the gates of Badminton House, the cottages standing back at a discreet distance. Some are in terraces, some freestanding; some in stone, some rendered. They were built at different periods between the 17th and 19th centuries, but all share the same colour scheme – dark cream front doors, and battleship grey for the gates and low palings that surround many of the front gardens.

The 18th-century almshouses have leaded-light windows and are topped by pediments decorated with the Beaufort family crest. You enter the post office through a grandiose iron arch supporting a handsome lantern; and to step inside the two delightful village shops is to return to the era of personal service, before supermarket was even a word. In the village centre there is a fine cricket ground, where matches are played on most weekends in the summer.

The parish church of St Michael and All Angels is attached to Badminton House. Built in a classical style in 1785, it is filled – as might be expected – with Beaufort memorials. Among them is a marble monument by the sculptor Grinling Gibbons (1648 – 1721) to Henry Somerset, the 1st Duke, who died in 1699. The effigy, brought here from St George's Chapel, Windsor, shows the duke in garter robes. The elaborate memorial is topped, 25 ft up, by a coronet on a tasselled cushion. The 2nd, 3rd and 4th Dukes are commemorated with monuments by the Flemish sculptor Michael Rysbrack (about 1693 – 1770).

The dukedom was created in 1682 in recognition of the Somerset family's descent from John of Gaunt, Duke of Lancaster. Naturally, they supported the Lancastrian cause in the Wars of the Roses, and were Royalists in the Civil War. Recent dukes have been great horsemen. The 10th Duke, who died in 1984, was known simply as 'Master' by his many friends. He was for many years Master of the Queen's Horse, and even in his eighties, rode to hounds several days each week as Master of the Beaufort Hunt. He created the three-day Badminton Horse Trials, a highlight of the equestrian year held each April, when top horsemen

'Boat' house at Badminton

Post office and archway

BOAT OF THATCH

Stout wooden posts help to bear the weight of a great sweep of thatch that roofs a cottage shaped like an upturned boat at Badminton. An iron arch with a lantern leads into the post office. And a village cat contemplates the wonder of it all.

compete on a gruelling cross-country course through the park.

Little Badminton is a smaller village on the estate, beside the western wall of the great park. Its cottages – several of them very old and some thatched – are scattered in a wide circle around a large green. The little church of St Michael, dating from the 14th century, is shaded by large yews.

A handsome round dovecote stands at one side of the green; it is said to have 365 nesting boxes – one for each day of the year. A wicket gate leads into the beautifully wooded grounds, where visitors may walk.

Didmarton GLOUCESTERSHIRE

9 miles west of Malmesbury (PAGE 119 Bc)

Cotswold stone houses of the 18th and 19th centuries line the busy road winding through Didmarton. But the heart of the village is at the foot of a hill, where the Church of St Lawrence is shaded by a tall Wellingtonia tree, with, set back behind it, a 17th-century manor house and its huge barns.

The church is disused but kept open, a rare example of a building that was originally medieval, and has remained unaltered since the 18th century. Instead of their usual restoration job, the Victorians built a whole new church, St Michael's, a few hundred yards up the road. Now the airy interior of St Lawrence's is disturbed only by the rhythmic tick of the church clock. Box pews, painted a subtle shade of Georgian green, are overlooked by a three-decker pulpit, set high between two windows. A row of hatpegs is set 16 ft above the floor at the back of the church: one might think that a race of giants worshipped here. The prosaic explanation is that there was once a gallery.

Across the road from the church, a semicircle of stones encloses St Lawrence's Well. Village legend tells that in the 6th century St Lawrence himself visited the place and blessed the well, promising at the same time that it should never run dry.

Halfway up the village street, near St Michael's, Chapel Walk leads past a terrace of tiny cottages to a pretty little Congregational chapel, set somewhat incongruously among the cabbages and cauliflowers of the village allotments. From here there is a view across fields, separated from one another by stone walls, to an isolated hamlet – Oldbury on the Hill with its little Church of St Arild and the ancient stone Manor Farm peeping out from behind it.

Easton Grey WILTSHIRE

3½ miles west of Malmesbury (PAGE 119 Bc)

The young River Avon sketches a curling silver line through the meadows of Easton Grey early on its journey to Bath and Bristol. Ponies come down to drink from the shallow river beside the 16th-century stone bridge, built with five low arches.

Set around the bridge and climbing a short, curving street is an intimate huddle of houses in mellow grey stone. Windows are mullioned; lichened roofs are steeply pitched to bear the weight of stone tiles; and gardens are bordered by dry-stone walls from which purple aubrietia cascades in early summer.

Since 1236 the lords of the manor have looked down on the little hamlet over which they held sway from a succession of manor houses set back on a rise above the river.

In the 14th century John de Greye held the manor in exchange for maintaining one of the king's falcons. The present Easton Grey House is a handsome early 18th-century mansion with a classical façade and portico, surrounded by elegant gardens. Herbert Asquith, later 1st Earl of Oxford and Asquith (1852 – 1928), spent his summers here when he was Prime Minister (1908 – 16). The house was occupied then by his sister-in-law, and he used it as a country retreat – rather as modern prime ministers use Chequers in Buckinghamshire.

The late Duke of Windsor, when Prince of Wales, appreciated the fine stabling facilities at the house and its proximity to the Duke of Beaufort's hunt at Badminton (see page 128). He spent the hunting season at Easton Grey in 1923.

Just inside the iron gates of the house is a little church with a squat Norman tower; the interior, apart from the Norman font, was extensively restored in

AVON CALLING *The charm of Easton Grey, with its winding street and cottage post office, beckons across an ancient bridge over the Avon.*

1836. The prime local attraction for visitors is the Westonbirt Arboretum, 2 miles north-west. It is a large park containing rare trees, many of them planted in the 19th century and now gloriously mature.

STOW-ON-THE-WOLD

GLOUCESTERSHIRE

9 miles west of Chipping Norton (PAGE 119 Ca)

Stow is set on a round hill some 750 ft above sea level. From here the ancient wool town looks south-west to the Cotswolds. Apart from the Roman Foss Way, four other roads meet at Stow – which has been an important junction since pre-Roman times.

The town is built mainly of Cotswold stone, and its buildings are grouped around a series of spaces – which give Stow a gracious sense of openness and comfort. In old English, the town's name means 'the meeting-place on the hill', and from 1107 to the turn of the present century a Thursday market attracted farmers and traders, as well as travellers.

Daniel Defoe (1660 – 1731), author of *Robinson Crusoe*, once attended one of the twice yearly Sheep Fairs in the late 17th century, and recorded that more than 20,000 sheep were sold. The Sheep Fairs later became Horse Fairs, and are still held in May and October.

The Square has a medieval cross, with a carved headstone added in 1878. The carving on the cross's north face shows Robert de Jumiges, Abbot of Evesham, receiving the town's charter from William Rufus in the late 11th century.

The town stocks once stood near the cross, but were moved a short distance away to the Green in the 1870s when the civic centre, St Edward's Hall, was being built. The Gothic-style hall has a figure of St Edward the Confessor in a niche above the main door. The hall cost just over £4000 to build – and the money came from unclaimed deposits in a local savings bank.

The nearby Talbot Hotel was built before 1714 and acted for a time as the Corn Exchange. The brass box on the front of the hotel was where farmers used to leave packets of grain to be tested for quality. On the left of the hotel is one of the narrow alleys known locally as 'tures'. Several tures lead into The Square – on market days sheep were brought through them in single file so that they could be counted.

Two of Stow's main thoroughfares – Sheep Street and Shepherds Way – are reminders of the days when sheep were the town's main livelihood. Branching off Sheep Street is Church Street, on the bend of which is the Masonic Hall, built of rubble masonry in 1594 to house St Edward's Grammar School. The school had been founded in 1475 and stayed here until 1848.

Behind it stands the parish church of St Edward – this could be the St Edward who, according to local legend, lived a hermit's life on the hill, long before the town existed. The church was built by Normans and was added to in the following centuries, giving its interior a variety of architectural styles. In the churchyard the graves of three wool merchants are topped with wool bales carved in stone.

A walk through the churchyard and back into The Square leads to Stow's most unusual building – known as the Crooked House, dating from about 1450 and now an antiques shop. Because of subsidence, the upper part of the house leans steeply to one side as though about to collapse of old age.

• **Parking** Park Street (car park); The Square • **Early closing** Wednesday • **Events** Horse Fair (May and October) • **Information** TEL. Stow-on-the-Wold 30352 • **AA 24 hour service** TEL. Gloucester 23278.

Cornwell OXFORDSHIRE

5 miles east of Stow-on-the-Wold (PAGE 119 Da)

Perhaps the best way to approach Cornwell is from the east, along a little road that wanders down from the broad bare hills near Chipping Norton into the rolling valley where the village lies. This way you pass the Manor House first and it never fails to take the breath away, coming unexpectedly into sight beside the road. Magnificent limes, hollies, horse chestnuts and hawthorn hedges, laced in spring with cow parsley, hide the house until you are almost upon it. An elegant wrought-iron gate is set into a long stone wall, and there beyond it is one of the most charming views in the Cotswolds.

The Manor House, built in mellow stone in the perfectly proportioned style of the 1750s, is set on high ground, with steps leading down through terraced gardens to a pool in a dip below. At the centre of the pool a little statue of a cherub on a scallop shell surveys the shimmering reflection of the house; a weeping willow, yews, flowering crab apple and cherry trees make a riot of colour round the pool.

The garden is a masterpiece of landscape art. It was laid out in 1939 by the architect Sir Clough Williams-Ellis (1883–1978), famous for his Mediterranean-style village of Portmeirion in Gwynedd, North Wales. He also restored the interior of the manor, adding a ballroom, and completely rebuilt the small estate village beyond.

The village huddles on the slopes rising from a brook that feeds the pool in the manor gardens. Williams-Ellis channelled the brook itself, which is no more than a trickle here, under a curving cobbled footpath and across the road, creating a shallow ford. The village green he enclosed with unusual curving stone walls. The shape is echoed in the round arch above one of the garden gates, the round window in a stone garden shed, and the curved walls of the school building, now used as an estate office.

Most curious of all is the stone bell tower he built above the school. It has an oblong bell opening which makes it look like an open fireplace and chimney perched on top of the roof. Some would call these details precious, but they have been immaculately done in stone, and have weathered well.

Before Williams-Ellis set to work on the village, the cottages had low thatched roofs and small windows. One with a partly thatched roof remains much as it was, but the rest now have stone slates.

The little Church of St Peter is set apart from the village in the middle of a field within the manor grounds. To reach it, pass the farm buildings to the north of the village and, beside a tall pine tree, take the track that leads to a gate into the field. The church, which has a little belfry, is screened by a fine group of trees, some of them yews.

A simple Norman doorway opens into an interior which was restored in Victorian times. There is a fine pulpit with carved heads of lions at its base. The most rewarding part of a visit to the church, however, is another view of the Manor House, standing at the other side of the field against a backcloth of magnificent trees – copper beeches, willows and pines.

Naunton GLOUCESTERSHIRE

5 miles west of Stow-on-the-Wold (PAGE 119 Ca)

The north Cotswold Hills are almost bare of trees along the tops, but miles of dry-stone walls follow their contours, giving some shelter to the wheat crops that in summer shimmer like a yellow eiderdown from one horizon to the other. The Stow to Cheltenham road runs along the top of a high ridge, and Naunton looks like a child's model village in the dip below. The little Church of St Andrew stands at the west end, and stone cottages are threaded like beads along the fine string of the River Windrush.

Local lore tells mischievously that Satan and his devils founded Naunton when they flew over the Cotswold Hills and let fall an imp. Unable to fly because of a broken wing, the imp built himself a cottage from local stone.

A more likely story, based on archaeological finds, is that Naunton's sheltered and well-watered site was first settled in Neolithic times. The Saxons called the place *Niwetone* – New Town – and a relic of their settlement is a small Saxon cross, carved in stone and set into a wall below the tower in St Andrew's. Do not miss the pulpit of about 1400, carved in stone with patterns of Gothic arches and tracery.

The little green outside the church is shaded by huge beech trees growing from the gardens of two large houses. The infant Windrush, clear, gravel-bedded, and fast-flowing, is channelled under a bridge and then between stone walls before emerging to run through little paddocks, dotted with cowslips in spring, where ponies, cows and sheep graze.

A footpath, starting almost opposite the Black Horse Inn, follows the river as it weaves through the village, past several cottage gardens and orchards. Many of the stone cottages are hung with roses, wisteria and pears trained to grow against their walls.

One of the oldest of the buildings is the square and gabled dovecote which stands beside the river. It was probably built in the 15th century and can accommodate up to 2000 doves.

Naunton's long main street often echoes to the clatter of horses' hooves, for no fewer than three packs of foxhounds hunt in the area. The Cotswold Farm Park, 2 miles north at Temple Guiting, contains a unique collection of rare breeds of domestic animals that include some sheep called Cotswold Lions.

DEVILISH MYTH *Naunton lies like a model village beneath a rolling Cotswold landscape. Local legend holds that it was founded by one of Satan's imps who fell to earth while flying over the spot.*

Millpond and cottages at Upper Swell

Abbotswood house and garden

Manor house, Upper Swell

The Swells GLOUCESTERSHIRE

1½ miles west of Stow-on-the-Wold (PAGE 119 Ca)

An elegant bridge, an old mill still with its wheel, and an attractive millpond make a charming introduction to Upper Swell, which has even more of interest to offer in the shape of its manor house and tiny church at the centre of the village.

The manor house dates from the 17th century and has a fine Jacobean, two-storey porch with columns, mullioned windows and a roof of Cotswold stone. Only a few feet away stands St Mary's Church, mostly Norman with its original plan of chancel, nave and porch, and crowned with a bellcote. The River Dikler flows behind church and house, reappearing at the millpond.

Another mill is the Donnington Brewery, 1½ miles north of Upper Swell, which has been a brewery since 1827 and was a flour mill and a cloth mill for 150 years before that. Its brew can be sampled at the Golden Ball in Lower Swell, a village larger than its neighbour and also boasting a hotel, the Old Farmhouse. In the early 19th century, Lower Swell might have become a 'spa', had not the local chalybeate (iron) spring lost its strength. Dating from that time are Spa Cottages, a group of three houses with a carved façade, standing on the east side of the Dikler and, like all the houses in Lower Swell, built of Cotswold stone.

The road climbing to Upper Swell leaves the village by the Church of St Mary the Virgin, a Norman building extended northwards in the Victorian period. Between the two villages there is a view, restricted in summer, across the valley to Abbotswood, a grand house of 1902 by the architect Sir Edwin Lutyens.

HIDDEN PLEASURES

A delightful millpond hides just beyond a little bridge over the River Dikler, where the narrow, winding road dips into Upper Swell. Swans, coots and ducks may be seen there, and close by is the village's 17th-century manor. Between the Swells stands Abbotswood, a fine house designed by the architect Sir Edwin Lutyens. He also designed the garden, noted for its flower displays and shrubs, which is open to the public several days each year.

OLD CURIOSITY

Some curious cottages were built at Lower Swell when hopes were high that the village would become a spa. The more traditional local pub—selling local beer—and hotel are neighbours just up the road.

Pub and hotel, Lower Swell

Cottage at Lower Swell

MAP 12

SHAKESPEARE COUNTRY AND A MARRIAGE OF RIVERS

The Avon is a modest river compared with the mighty Severn, yet perhaps more famed because of one man – William Shakespeare, immortalised as the Swan of Avon. Here, where both rivers run, is the kind of scenery to nurture genius. The Avon flows on from Stratford to join the Severn near the abbey town of Tewkesbury.

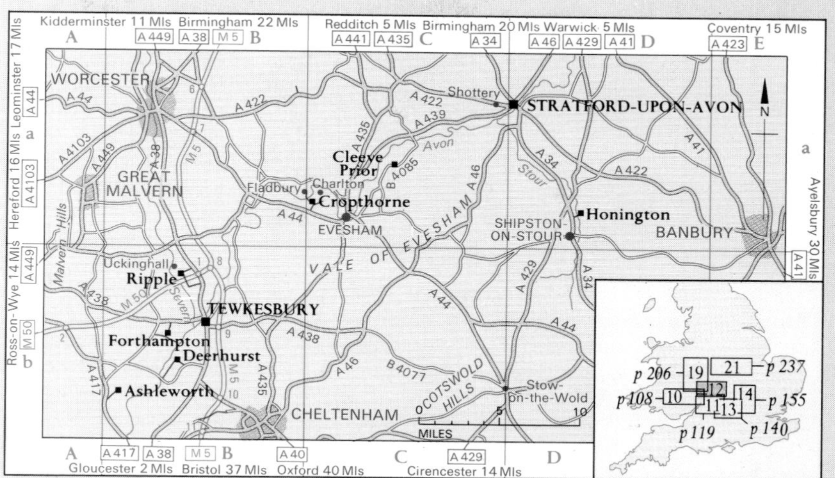

MAP 12: NEIGHBOURING AREAS – MAPS 10, 11, 13, 14, 19, 21

STRATFORD-UPON-AVON Cleeve Prior Cropthorne Honington
TEWKESBURY Ashleworth Deerhurst Forthampton Ripple

STRATFORD-UPON-AVON

WARWICKSHIRE

8 miles south-west of Warwick (PAGE 133 Da)

People from many parts of the world visit Stratford to pay homage to its most famous son, William Shakespeare. The playwright was born here on St George's Day, April 23, 1564, in a gabled Tudor house in Henley Street, near the town centre. His father was a bailiff and the family home is open to the public. Furnished in authentic period style it is a picture of middle-class stability and security. There are reminders of the Bard everywhere in Stratford, but – Shakespeare apart – this is the very model of a thriving market town, with roots lying deep in the Middle Ages.

To the east of Henley Street is Chapel Street, where in 1597 Shakespeare bought his own substantial home, New Place, from the proceeds of his early plays, such as *Titus Andronicus*. The house, which cost him £60, was demolished in 1759 by a subsequent owner, and the place where it stood is now a restful garden, which incorporates an Elizabethan formal garden.

Next to the garden in Chapel Street stands New Place Museum, devoted to the history of the town. It was once the house of Thomas Nash, first husband of the playwright's grand-daughter Elizabeth Hall. The bookshop next to it was the home of one Julius Shaw, who witnessed Shakespeare's will in which he gave 'unto my wife my second-best bed, with the furniture'. The will was signed on March 25, 1616, less than a month before the playwright's death on his 52nd birthday.

On the corner of Chapel Street and Church Street is the Guild Chapel, founded in the 13th century but having a 15th-century tower and nave – as proud and attractive as it was in Shakespeare's day. Beside the chapel stands the old Grammar School which Shakespeare is thought to have attended. The school may date from the 13th century and was refounded in 1553 by Edward VI. It is usually open to visitors in the Easter and summer holidays. Beneath the school is the Guildhall, which was occasionally used as a theatre in Shakespeare's time.

A street called Old Town contains Hall's Croft, the 16th-century timber-framed house of Dr John Hall, who married Shakespeare's elder daughter, Susanna, in 1607. The street leads to Holy Trinity Church, where Shakespeare is buried. The partly 13th-century church backs onto the River Avon. On the north wall of the chancel is a life-size bust of the playwright with his coat of arms and motto *Non Sans Droict* – 'Not Without Right'. The church has a copy of the parish register recording Shakespeare's baptism and burial, and the font in which he was probably baptised still exists. Shakespeare's wife, Anne, and Susanna and her husband, Dr Hall, are also buried in the chancel.

A pleasant riverside walk from the church leads through the gardens of the Royal Shakespeare Theatre. Built in 1932, the theatre replaced one from the late 19th century, which was destroyed by fire six years earlier. Made of brash red brick, the new theatre's modernity caused controversy in the 1930s; but today it fits naturally into its leafy surroundings. It has a restaurant overlooking the river.

Shakespeare's influence extends to the town Information Centre, on the corner of Bridge Street and High Street. It is in the former home of his younger daughter Judith and her husband Thomas Quiney. Not far away is the Georgian Town Hall, which looks onto Harvard House. Built in 1596, it was the home of Katherine Rodgers, whose teacher son John Harvard emigrated to America at the beginning

ANNE'S OWN PLACE *This thatched cottage is probably as well known to millions of tourists as it was to young Shakespeare. Anne Hathaway lived here until she married the Bard in 1582.*

of the 17th century and was the first benefactor of Harvard College – later Harvard University. Adjoining the house is The Garrick Inn, named after the famous 18th-century actor-manager David Garrick, whose three-day festival of Shakespeare's plays in September 1769 set a fashion for theatrical seasons.

Just over a mile west of the town centre, in what was once the hamlet of Shottery, is Anne Hathaway's Cottage, a thatched, timber-framed building that was actually a 12-roomed farmhouse. It was her home before she married Shakespeare in November 1582. It has been carefully preserved, as have some of the surrounding cottages.

Stratford's annual Mop Fair began during King John's reign (1199 – 1216). Like other Mop Fairs, it was the day on which apprentices, farmhands, serving maids and other workers put themselves up for hire. The pig-roasting, country dancing and merrymaking are as popular as ever. The charter for the weekly market – still held in the town – was granted by John's elder brother, King Richard the Lionheart, towards the end of the 12th century.

• **Parking** Windsor Street, Rother Street, Bridgeway, Arden Street (all car parks) • **Early closing** Thursday • **Market day** Friday • **Theatres** Royal Shakespeare Theatre, Waterside, TEL. Stratford-upon-Avon 295623; The Other Place, Southern Lane, TEL. Stratford-upon-Avon 295623 • **Events** World Homage to Shakespeare (April); Mop Fair (October 12) • **Information** TEL. Stratford-upon-Avon 293127 • **AA 24 hour service** TEL. Birmingham 550 4858.

Cleeve Prior

HEREFORD AND WORCESTER

9 miles south-west of Stratford-upon-Avon (PAGE 133 Ca)

Cleeve Prior's fine manor house was the birthplace of an extraordinary man named Thomas Bushell. In 1609, at the tender age of 15, he joined the household of the philosopher and statesman Francis Bacon, and when Bacon became Lord Chancellor, Bushell went with him to court. There he ran up debts – which Bacon paid off for him – and attracted the notice of James I because of the richness of his dress. However, when Bacon died in 1626, Bushell elected to spend his next three years on a tiny Manx island, the Calf of Man, living austerely on herbs, oil, mustard, honey and water. This, he said, was 'such a repentance as my former debauchedness required'.

Returning to the mainland, he soon rose to prominence at the court of Charles I, and on a number of occasions entertained the king and queen at his house at Road Enstone, in Oxfordshire, with ingenious displays of fountains and other waterworks. In 1636 the king granted Bushell the right to exploit the royal silver mines in Wales. He was outstandingly successful, devising new methods of mining and ventilation, reclaiming flooded mines and extending others.

When the Civil War broke out, a few years later, Bushell supported the king. But following the Royalists' defeat he had to return to his family home in Cleeve Prior, where he hid from the victorious Parliamentarians in a secret chamber. However, he was later restored to his important positions, and when he died in 1674 he was buried in Westminster Abbey.

The manor, with its fine porch and avenue of yew trees representing the 12 apostles, stands on the northern edge of the village. Just south of it, the main road passes a charming row of stone houses set back on a green. Among them stands the King's Arms pub, built in 1542, with a large stone dovecote in its yard; and opposite is the fine Queen Anne Vicarage. At the back of the Vicarage is the Church of St Andrew, set secluded behind walls and poplars.

A yew tree outside the church porch probably dates from the 14th century, and its wood was once used to make arrows. There are deep grooves in the south-west corner of the tower beside it, where archers are said to have sharpened the arrows. A tombstone near by displays an intriguing slip of the carver's chisel. It commemorates Sara Charlett, who according to the stone, died in 1693 at the age of 309.

Sara Charlett's family lived in Cleeve Prior from at least 1280. Their home latterly was Prior House, a Jacobean building now demolished. Opposite the present building named Prior House is Cleeve Barn, an interesting modern conversion.

Cropthorne

HEREFORD AND WORCESTER

17 miles south-west of Stratford-upon-Avon (PAGE 133 Ca)

Cropthorne's tiny Church of St Michael contains two large 17th-century tombs. On one, the figure of Edward Dingley, who died in 1646, kneels facing his wife. His parents lie side by side on the other under an inscription that boasts their noble descent from the kings of England and Scotland and many ancient families. All four figures have a reposed and noble dignity. Nothing in them suggests the history of violence and insanity that brought their line to an end within three generations, after Edward's daughter Eleanor, who married Sir Edward Goodere, inherited estates in Cropthorne and neighbouring Charlton.

Of Eleanor's five sons, two died young and the others all came to violent ends, starting with Francis who was killed in a duel. His death left only John and Samuel, and these brothers were deadly rivals. In 1733 they both stood for election as mayor of Evesham. When both received exactly the same number of votes,

Samuel, the younger, had his brother forcibly thrown out of the church where the investing ceremony took place. Eight years later, when John was threatening to cut Samuel out of the inheritance, the younger brother, by then a captain in the Royal Navy, took more effective action in Bristol where he was based in his ship, the *Ruby*. There, a friend, hoping to reconcile the brothers, had invited them both to dinner. All seemed to go well at the meal, but afterwards, as John was walking back through the streets of Bristol, he was seized and dragged on board the *Ruby*, where Samuel had three hired accomplices ready to strangle him.

But the foul murder came to light, and, a few months later, Samuel and the three assassins were hanged. Samuel left two sons. The elder boy, Edward, was 12 at his father's death and died insane in 1761. Samuel's younger son John then ran through the entire fortune within a few years of inheriting it, and spent the rest of his life as a poor knight at Windsor. There he became well known for presenting rich heiresses with written marriage proposals. He died in 1809, aged 80.

Cropthorne today is a quiet village of mostly thatched and timber-framed cottages stretched out along a ridge above the River Avon. At the centre is St Michael's, which is partly 12th century. Apart from the Dingley tombs, it also houses the magnificently carved head of a Saxon cross, decorated with delightful scenes of birds and animals. On either side of the church are the Manor and the Court, both dating from the 18th century. The Court stands on the site of a summer palace of Offa, an 8th-century king of Mercia. Beyond it is the long, thatched and timber-framed Holland House, converted from a row of cottages. Its gardens were laid out by the early 20th-century architect Sir Edwin Lutyens.

At the north end of the village, the road forks at an attractively shady green, overlooked by a timber-framed cottage. One branch of the road leads to Charlton, once the home of the Dingleys, a mile north-east. Today, Charlton is a group of houses around a charming green with a brook running through it. The other branch of the road leads across Jubilee Bridge – built in 1933 to replace a 19th-century bridge which marked Queen Victoria's Jubilee – to Fladbury, a mile north-west. This large village has a number of fine buildings. On its southern edge, by the Avon, is the well-preserved, red-brick Fladbury Mill. In the centre, the Church of St John the Baptist has some good 15th-century brasses to the Throckmorton family. Standing near by is the Manor, which was built in the early 18th century.

Honington WARWICKSHIRE

11 miles south-east of Stratford-upon-Avon (PAGE 133 Da)

On a gentle slope, rising from the River Stour where it meanders through a flat green valley, stands Honington Hall, one of the finest mansions to survive from the Restoration era.

Built in the 1680s of red brick, the hall – which is open to the public in the summer on Wednesday afternoons – has an imposing series of busts of Roman emperors set in niches over the ground-floor windows. Inside is a superb display of mid-18th-century plasterwork in the flamboyant rococo style. At the turn of the century, the Australian opera singer Dame Nellie Melba, a regular visitor to the hall, used to give private recitals in the majestic octagonal saloon.

Honington Hall was built by Sir Henry Parker, a royalist alderman of the City of London, who profited from the restoration of Charles II. He and his son Hugh are commemorated in an impressive monument in the stone Church of All Saints, just across the drive from the front of the hall. Although the tower dates

FLOWERS AND FLAMBOYANCE

Fronted by rich greensward and fine arrays of flowers, cottages wind gently up Honington's sloping main street. This attractive little village has a magnificent Restoration mansion, Honington Hall, with some flamboyant touches to the decoration inside. The hall stands impressively on a slope rising from the River Stour. Visitors approaching the village from the main Oxford to Stratford road pass through a fine pair of 18th-century gateposts and cross the Stour by the graceful 17th-century bridge.

Bridge over Stour

Cottages in Honington's village street

Honington Hall

from the 15th century, the rest of the church was built by Sir Henry in the 1680s. The spacious village street, with ample greensward on either side, is dominated by the gateway to the hall. From here, fine stone cottages are scattered up a slight slope and, below, a shady lane runs to the church. Magpie House, opposite, has fine diagonal timbers.

TEWKESBURY

GLOUCESTERSHIRE

9 miles north-west of Cheltenham (PAGE 133 Bb)

A tragic young Prince of Wales and a royal duke who may have helped to murder him lie entombed amid the splendours of Tewkesbury Abbey – possibly the finest parish church in England. Some historians believe that the 17-year-old Prince Edward died during the Battle of Tewkesbury in 1471. Others think he was captured, taken to the Cross House, at the corner of Tolsey Lane, and stabbed to death. The duke who was alleged to have been one of his attackers was George, Duke of Clarence – himself supposedly murdered six years later when he drowned in a butt of malmsey wine.

The main battle was fought in a field now called Bloody Meadow, off Lincoln Green Lane in the south of the town. Here most of the Lancastrians were massacred, but some fled to the nearby abbey – where they were butchered in the aisles by the Yorkists despite the pleas of the abbot.

Tewkesbury Abbey was founded by a Norman lord, Robert FitzHamon, at the beginning of the 12th century. Stone from the Cotswolds was used, and the abbey's massive tower is 132 ft high and 46 ft square. The arch on the West Front rises 65 ft, the largest of its

AN ABBEY WHERE BLOOD FLOWED

Imposing Tewkesbury Abbey was the scene of a vicious massacre of Lancastrians by Yorkists during the Wars of the Roses. Many reminders of that conflict can still be seen inside, but some of the abbey's glories – such as the 17th-century West Window and the Milton Organ – date from a later period. The town is noted for its black-and-white timbered houses and medieval character.

Tewkesbury Abbey gate

Ironmonger's sign

Inn sign

Abbey chancel roof

Houses in St Mary's Lane

kind in Britain. But the abbey's greatest glories are the seven 14th-century stained-glass windows in the choir.

By the West Front stands Abbey House, the former lodging of the abbot. It is probably late 15th century, but was restored in the late 18th century and returned to the abbey in 1883. It is now the vicarage. Beyond Abbey House is the 16th-century Gate House, restored in 1849.

The townsfolk were so proud of the abbey – properly called the Abbey Church of St Mary the Virgin – that in 1540 they bought it from Henry VIII for £453. This saved it from destruction at the Dissolution. Since then it has been sympathetically restored, and the medieval glass painstakingly cleaned.

Tewkesbury lies where the Severn and Avon rivers meet in the valley between the Malvern and Cotswold Hills. It has numerous black-and-white timbered houses with leaded-light windows and overhanging eaves, balustrades and gables.

The town's three main streets – High Street, Church Street and Barton Street – form a 'Y'. They are surrounded by a maze of small courts and narrow alleyways containing tiny, medieval cottages. Many of the inns and houses look much as they did at the time of the battle, and the conflict between the Yorkists and the Lancastrians is commemorated in The Ancient Grudge Hotel in the High Street. The building dates from shortly after Prince Edward's death. Farther along the High Street is the House of Nodding Gables, once a depot and ticket office for stage coaches. A break in the supports has made one of its gables lean crookedly sideways, as if nodding off to sleep.

In Church Street, the carefully restored Abbey Cottages originally consisted of 23 shops, built about 1450. During the day the shops were open to the street, and at night their counters were raised to act as shutters. One, the Little Museum, is furnished to show how the original occupants lived. Another is the John Moore Museum. Its timbered galleries display farm tools, old domestic utensils and other countryside mementoes. The museum is named after the local author and broadcaster John Moore (1907 – 67), whose many books include the autobiographical *Portrait of Elmbury*, a lightly disguised Tewkesbury.

The town's literary associations go back to Charles Dickens, who set part of his *Pickwick Papers* in the 16th and 18th-century Royal Hop Pole Hotel. Here Mr Pickwick and his friends did themselves well on bottled ale, Madeira and five bottles of port. The Victorian writer Mrs Craik (1826 – 87) visited Tewkesbury several times. Her novel *John Halifax, Gentleman*, published in 1857, was woven around the town and its people.

• **Parking** St Mary's Lane; Gander Lane; Spring Gardens; Swilgate Road; Gloucester Road (all car parks) • **Early closing** Thursday • **Market days** Wednesday, Saturday • **Theatre** Roses Theatre, Sun Street • **Events** Carnival (July); Mop Fair (October) • **Information** TEL. Tewkesbury 295027 (summer) • **AA 24 hour service** TEL. Gloucester 23278.

Ashleworth GLOUCESTERSHIRE

9 miles south-west of Tewkesbury (PAGE 133 Bb)

The Jelf family have lived by the Severn at Ashleworth Quay since the 17th century at least. During the Civil War, an ancestor is believed to have ferried Charles I across the river and received, as a reward, a charter granting his family a perpetual monopoly of the ferry at this point. From that day to this, the Jelfs have been identified with the varying fortunes of the tiny riverside community.

In the 19th century, when the quay was the point where horse-drawn barges had to change from one side of the river to the other, to avoid cliffs upstream near Tewkesbury, it had two pubs. One of them, the Boat Inn, belonged to the Jelfs, and today the charmingly old-fashioned pub, having outlived its rival, remains within the family. However, the busy quay of a century ago now presents a picture of perfect tranquillity, disturbed only by an occasional angler waiting patiently for a bite.

Near the quay, another exceptional group of buildings, all medieval, clusters round the Church of St Andrew and St Bartholomew, which has some ancient herringbone masonry dating from the early 12th century. Beside the church looms the immense 15th-century Tithe Barn, which is owned by the National Trust. This huge building has two vast doors on one side, to let loaded wagons in, and two much lower ones on the other side, through which they would roll out after their high loads had been removed and stored away in the barn.

An outstanding stone house, Ashleworth Court – occasionally open to the public – is set back on a lawn adjoining the churchyard. It was built in 1460 by the Abbey of St Augustine, Bristol, which owned the manor, and it has remained almost unchanged. At about the same time, the abbey also built Ashleworth Manor, a short distance away across the flat riverside meadows. This fine timber-framed house, discreetly enlarged in the 19th and 20th centuries, was the abbots' summer residence.

A noble avenue of poplars leads from the church to the main part of the village, set on higher ground to avoid flooding. At the centre is a large green with a fine stone cross – probably 12th century – its four-sided head showing a figure of Christ.

There are also some charming timber-framed cottages, and, on a rise behind the village, the Gothic-style mansion Foscombe, built in the late 19th century. For a number of years this elaborate mansion, with its fantastic turrets and tower, was the home of Charlie Watts, drummer in the Rolling Stones rock group.

Deerhurst GLOUCESTERSHIRE

4 miles south-west of Tewkesbury (PAGE 133 Bb)

Deerhurst was once an important settlement of Hwicce, the Anglo-Saxon sub-kingdom of the lower Severn valley. Here was the little kingdom's most important monastery, where, during its decline in the 10th century, the martyr St Alphege was a monk. Later, as Archbishop of Canterbury, Alphege was taken by the Danes and killed because he refused to allow himself to be ransomed, knowing that the poor would bear the burden of raising the ransom money.

Here also, some years later in 1016, on a nearby island in the Severn, the English king, Edmund Ironside, made a treaty of friendship with the Danish Canute, who was later to succeed him.

Nowadays the village is a tiny group of largely timber-framed cottages and farmhouses clustering round the Priory Church of St Mary, which stands out from the flat surrounding countryside of the Severn valley. This fine Saxon church dates in part from the 7th century, when the monastery was near the height of its prosperity and importance. High in the east wall of the tower, overlooking the nave, is an elaborate double window with triangular heads. The window resembles nothing else surviving from Saxon England, but is said to be remarkably similar to a window in the Ethiopian monastery of Debra Damo in Africa.

There are also some notable Saxon carvings: a haunting, probably 9th-century angel in the apse; some delightful animals on several arches; a plaque of the Madonna and Child in the porch; and what some consider to be the finest Saxon font in existence. Moving forward in time, there is the only animal to be named in any medieval memorial brass. This is Terri, the pet dog of Alice, Lady Cassey, who, with her husband Sir John – the Chief Baron of the Exchequer from 1389 to 1400 – is commemorated in the north aisle. The Casseys lived in a house on the site of the 16th-century Wightfield Manor, a mile south.

Adjoining the church is the stone, mostly 14th-century, Priory House and near by stands the timber-framed Abbot's Court, with, at its north-west corner, the remarkable Odda's Chapel. This simple little stone chapel dates from 1056, and inside is a copy of the Odda Stone – a dedication stone found close by in 1675 and now in the Ashmolean Museum, Oxford.

Its inscription, translated from the Latin, opens: 'Earl Odda has this royal hall built and dedicated in honour of the Holy Trinity for the soul of his Brother Aelfric which left the body in this place.' Earl Odda was an important local noble and a friend and kinsman of the Saxon king of England, Edward the Confessor (1042 – 66).

Forthampton GLOUCESTERSHIRE

4 miles west of Tewkesbury (PAGE 133 Bb)

Forthampton is a tiny village of outstandingly fine timber-framed cottages and farmhouses scattered in the green and gently undulating countryside of the Severn valley. At its centre is a high knoll topped by the partly 13th-century Church of St Mary; at the foot of the hill are stocks and a whipping post – which still has the iron manacles that held its victims.

Near these relics stand some of the village's most delightful buildings. Vine Farm, nearly opposite, is a timber-framed and stone farmhouse of the 16th and 17th centuries. Down a lane, running north-east, is the 17th-century Alcock's Farm; and another lane, running south-west, leads past the timber-framed Hill Farm House and The Sanctuary, which has a 15th-century hall, to the large 18th-century red-brick Forthampton House.

Beyond the church, a road leads from the village centre to the charming Lower Lode Inn, a mile south-east on the banks of the Severn. From the inn there are fine views over the river and across the flat meadows beyond to Tewkesbury and its abbey. On the way, the road passes the fine early 18th-century Southfield House, with a large elegant dovecote beside it, both built in warmly mellow red brick; and, set back in its park, the long, low Forthampton Court, whose grounds are occasionally open to the public. It was originally the country retreat of the abbots of Tewkesbury, and it still has a late 14th-century hall, a chapel

THE RURAL YEAR: A CALENDAR THAT

THE SUN – with a half-smile

The annual round of country life in the Middle Ages is the subject of a remarkable series of 14th-century misericords – the carved backs of choir seats – in St Mary's Church, Ripple. The carvings, believed to be by local craftsmen, add up to a country calendar with religious overtones, showing the tasks of husbandry month by month. In March, seeds are being sown; in April, men are scaring birds from the fields; and May sees the Virgin Mary blessing the crops. June gives a glimpse of sporting activity, as a man goes hunting on horseback with his hawk. In July, the scene is a bakery on Lammas (Loaf-mass) Eve, with armed figures ready to keep order if a

JANUARY – collecting dead boughs

FEBRUARY – hedging and ditching

MARCH – sowing

JULY – Lammas (Loaf-mass) Eve

AUGUST – reaping

SEPTEMBER – corn for malting

with a 13th-century picture of Edward the Confessor, and a 14th-century tomb of a crusader. At the end of the 19th century, the court and the chapel were altered by the architect and designer Philip Webb.

Ripple HEREFORD AND WORCESTER

5 miles north of Tewkesbury (PAGE 133 Bb)

HEART OF A VILLAGE *In the peaceful centre of Ripple, a small green is surrounded by attractive whitewashed cottages. It is hard to believe now that this was once on a major coaching route.*

A local story tells how in 1437 a farmer's attempt to spite the rector ended in ignominious failure and exposure. Apparently, the rector or lord of the manor once had the right to take the best cow of a herd when the owner died. This farmer, however, was determined that the rector of Ripple – with whom he was on bad terms – should in no way benefit by his death. So, falling dangerously ill and sure that death was close, he sold his entire herd, rather than let the rector take even one of his cows.

But instead of dying, he recovered. The rector heard about his plan and dragged him before a court. There, the unfortunate farmer was sentenced to walk, carrying a candle, three times round the churchyard on a cold winter's night, dressed only in a nightshirt.

The largely 12th-century Church of St Mary has scarcely changed since it was built. Inside is a marvellous series of carvings on the backs of the choir seats (misericords) which have survived intact from the 14th and 15th centuries. Outside, the churchyard looks onto the handsome 18th-century red-brick Rectory, and the grounds of Ripple Hall, partly 17th century but with a fine new front added a century later. Near by lies the tomb of Robert Reeve, known as the Ripple giant and said to have been 7 ft 4 in. tall. He died aged 56, in 1626, from over-straining himself while mowing a meadow for a bet, according to a local story. The inscription on his tomb runs:

'As you passe by, behold my length,
But never glory in your Strength.'

The centre of the village is the tiny green, with its ancient stone cross, overlooked by whitewashed cottages. Manor Cottage, built in the 18th century, was once an almshouse; and close by the former Nag's Head Inn, now Ripple Cottage, is a reminder of days when the road through Ripple was an important coaching route. North of the village, this road runs past the scene of the Battle of Ripple in 1643.

HAS SURVIVED FOR SIX CENTURIES

row breaks out between the baker and the villagers — as often happened when the weight of a loaf was questioned. When November comes, pigs feasted with acorns the previous month are slaughtered. The year ends with a peaceful December picture in which spinners sit beside a fire. The carvings also pay tribute to the forces of nature. A benevolent Sun, framed in blazing rays, half-smiles on the world; the Moon is a crescent with a man's face cradled in it. Altogether, the carvings present a fascinating glimpse of country living 600 years ago. Life was harder then, but essentials of the farmer's year were much the same as they are now.

THE MOON – with a man's face

APRIL – bird scaring

MAY – crops blessed

JUNE – hawking scene

OCTOBER – acorns for pigs

NOVEMBER – pig killing

DECEMBER – spinning by the fire

MAP 13

THE VALE OF WHITE HORSE — SOURCE OF LEGEND

Nobody knows who carved the fantastical horse into the chalk at Uffington, though it may well be the emblem of the Celts who built the huge earthworks above it. But it gave the vale a name—and, perhaps, its aura of legend: St George slaying the beast on Dragon Hill, and Arthur's victory at Mount Badon. Then there are the near-legends of the area, the novels of Thomas Hardy.

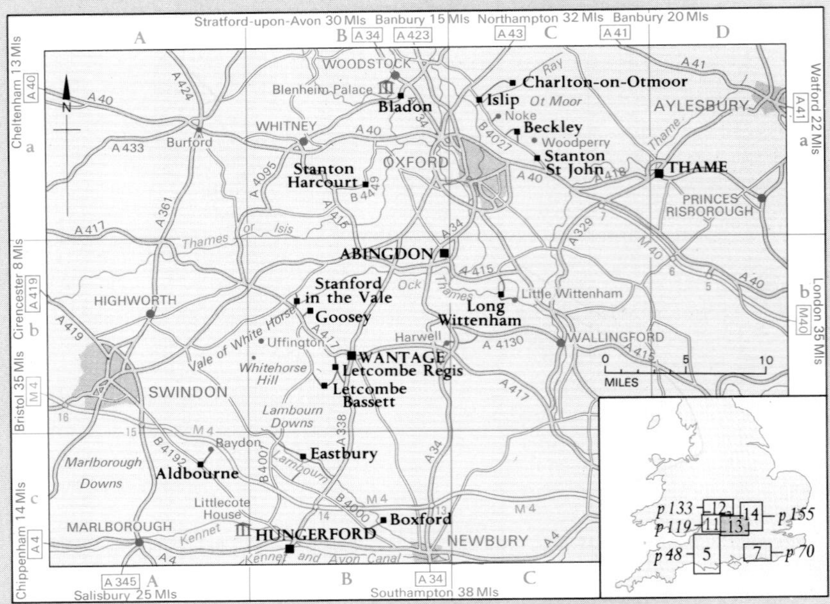

MAP 13: NEIGHBOURING AREAS—MAPS 5, 7, 11, 12, 14

ABINGDON Bladon Long Wittenham Stanton Harcourt
HUNGERFORD Aldbourne Boxford Eastbury
THAME Beckley Charlton-on-Otmoor Islip Stanton St John
WANTAGE Goosey The Letcombes Stanford in the Vale

ABINGDON

OXFORDSHIRE

8 miles south of Oxford (PAGE 140 Bb)

Abingdon grew up around its great abbey, founded in about AD 700 and destroyed in 1539, at the Dissolution of the Monasteries. Nothing remains of the abbey church, but a plan of the abbey and the approximate site of the Saxon and Norman altars have been put on the lawn. The ruins in the grounds are fragments of medieval churches, erected in the 19th century by a Mr Trendell of Abbey House as an ornament to his garden.

Several of the abbey's outbuildings, including the battlemented Gateway and the Granary, are still intact. The room above the Gateway was used as a prison from 1560 until the early 19th century. Today it is called the Abbey Room and can be entered only through the adjacent Guildhall. The Granary, at the foot of Thames Street, is one of four abbey buildings standing cheek by jowl. The other three are the Bakery, the Checker Hall and the Long Gallery, at the east end. The Long Gallery, with its oak-beamed roof, dates from the late 15th or early 16th centuries—and was the last building to be added.

Just below the 15th-century Gateway is the Church of St Nicolas, built in the 12th century for the abbey's lay servants. It contains the tomb of John and Jane Blacknall, dated 1684. Until recently, in accordance with John Blacknall's will, loaves of bread were put on the tomb each week for the poor.

Abingdon is a pleasant mixture of mostly Georgian and Victorian buildings, sprinkled with timber-framed medieval houses. The town centres around the pedestrians-only Market Place, whose south side is dominated by the dignified County Hall. This was completed in 1682 by Christopher Kempster, one of Sir Christopher Wren's masons on the building of St Paul's Cathedral.

Each Monday a covered market is held on the ground floor of the County Hall; the first floor houses the Abingdon Museum, which has some nostalgic souvenirs of the MG sports cars that were made in the town until 1980, and a fine silver collection.

South of the Market Place is the Old Gaol, built by Napoleonic prisoners of war in 1805–11, when Abingdon was the county town of Berkshire. Until 1867, when the town lost its title to Reading, it was also the county prison. It was renovated in the mid-1970s at a cost of £1¼ million, and is now a leisure, entertainment and sports centre. Abingdon remained part of Berkshire until a boundary change in 1974 placed it in the Oxfordshire district of the Vale of White Horse.

At the bottom of Bridge Street there is a stone bridge over the Thames. A short way downstream is a group of mellowed almshouses: Long Alley, Brick Alley and Twitty's. Long Alley was built in 1446, while Brick Alley and Twitty's date from the early 18th century. On a visit to the almshouses in 1668 the diarist Samuel Pepys put a donation in the almsbox: the almshouses are still in use and you can look around them by arrangement.

In front of them stands the partly 13th-century Church of St Helen, which is 108 ft wide and only 97 ft long. It has a 200-year-old candelabra, a fine medieval painted ceiling in the Lady Chapel, and the tomb of John Roysse. The tomb is a stone slab specially brought from his garden in London. In 1563 Roysse founded the former Grammar School, near the Gateway, and he is also remembered in the name of Roysse Court near by. Alongside the court is the Crown and Thistle, a beautiful coaching inn dating from about 1605. The name and sign mark the union of England and Scotland under James I.

From St Helen's churchyard, a walk over a small iron bridge leads to the narrow River Ock, named from the pre-Saxon word *ehoc* meaning 'salmon'. Just above it, Ock Street is the traditional home of the morris dancers, who elect their own mayor each June when they dance here and also in the Market Place.

• **Parking** West St Helen's Street; Stert Street; Vineyard (all car parks) • **Early closing** Thursday • **Market day** Monday • **Theatres** Little Theatre, Old Gaol Sports Centre; Unicorn Theatre, Thames Street • **Cinema** Little Theatre • **Events** St Edmund Fair (June); Michaelmas Fair (October) • **Information** TEL. Abingdon 22711 • **AA 24 hour service** TEL. Oxford 240286.

Abbey's Checker Hall with rare 13th-century chimney

CHANGE AND CONTINUITY

The surviving outbuildings of Abingdon's now-vanished abbey have been lovingly restored and converted to a number of uses very different from those they were built for — the old Granary has become a theatre, for example. However, the medieval almshouses, given by a guild of town merchants, still house old people.

Bladon OXFORDSHIRE

15 miles north of Abingdon (PAGE 140 Ba)

Since 1965 St Martin's Church at Bladon has become a place of pilgrimage for visitors from all over the world. Here, on a cold day in January, Sir Winston Churchill was laid to rest beside the graves of his parents and within sight of the great park that surrounds his birthplace, Blenheim Palace.

He had expressed the wish to be buried at Bladon after visiting his father's grave in 1895, and wrote to his mother: 'I went this morning to Bladon to look at Papa's grave . . . I was so struck by the sense of quietness and peace as well as by the old-world air of the place that my sadness was not unmixed with solace.' There is still a consoling peace about this simple country churchyard. Its grass is immaculately mown and planted out with lilacs and flowering cherries. In season martins twitter as they dive low into the church porch to their nests in the eaves.

Churchill's grave is simplicity itself — a flat stone slab plainly engraved with his names and dates, and those of his wife Clementine who died in 1977. Other

Long Alley almshouses, Abingdon

members of the Spencer Churchill dynasty are buried close by, including Winston's son Randolph and two of his daughters, Sarah and Diana.

There is a delightful carved statue of St Martin of Tours on horseback above the porch of the church, which was largely rebuilt in 1891. Fortunately the early 19th-century charity boards were retained, and among the inscriptions is one that records a bequest by William Hopkins in 1681 to 'a manservant or maidservant in the town of Bladon who has served for the space of three years or more in one service'.

Clematises and rambling roses wreathe the doors and windows of the stone cottages around the church. One cottage is called King's View and has a weather vane showing a crowned head. Its name may refer to the fact that the royal palace of Woodstock once stood near where Blenheim Palace stands now.

It was in 1702 that Winston's illustrious ancestor John Churchill was created Duke of Marlborough. He was presented with the vast estate between Bladon and Woodstock by Queen Anne and the nation, in gratitude for victories that included the Battle of Blenheim. The grand entrance to Blenheim Palace is in Woodstock, a mile or so north, but the older settlement of Bladon provided most of the men who built the palace between 1705 and 1722, and the village still houses many estate workers.

A tiled roof shelters the village pump, beside the main road below the school. There is a pedestrians-only entrance to the park, opposite the pump, with the White House Inn near by. Bladon's oldest house, the Old Malthouse, stands just outside the park walls. Stone-built, with mullioned windows and stone tiles, this 15th-century house has curious round chimneys.

Inside the park gates a breathtaking view unfolds – copses of copper beeches, fir trees and horse chestnuts are lined along the River Glyme, which was landscaped by Capability Brown to form a limb of Blenheim's great lake.

In the distance the broad façade of the palace forms a romantic silhouette of towers and pinnacles. The palace itself – the baroque masterpiece of the soldier-playwright-architect Sir John Vanbrugh (1664 – 1726) – is best approached from Woodstock and is open daily from late March to October.

Long Wittenham OXFORDSHIRE

5 miles south-east of Abingdon (PAGE 140 Cb)

The urge to conform has been stoutly resisted in Long Wittenham. Half-timbered cottages have their frameworks filled in, sometimes with bricks in herringbone patterns, sometimes with plaster, sometimes with stone – and a wing of one leans at an improbable angle.

Many of the cottages are overhung with a soft fringe of thatch, but among the thatch there are gables and porch roofs picked out with red tiles, mellowed by a covering of yellow lichen. Then there are places built of lapped timber, while others, like The Plough – which is still a pub – have walls of hung tiles.

A grassy enclosure behind palings is the village pound, where stray animals were shut up to await collection. Near by, a lane to St Mary's Church passes between the thatched wooden barn of a farm and a timber-framed house with an overhanging first floor.

There has been a church here since the 7th century when St Birinus, Bishop of Dorchester, brought Christianity to the district. The present building was begun by the lord of the manor, Walter Giffard, in about 1120, and a fine rounded Norman arch divides the nave from the chancel.

The church's greatest treasure is a rare 12th-century lead font, embossed with 30 figures of archbishops, each standing beneath a pointed arch and raising his right hand in blessing. It would have been melted for bullets by Cromwell's troops but for the churchwardens, who hid it within a wooden case packed with rubbish. Another rarity – in the south chapel, now used as the vestry – is the miniature effigy of a crusader knight in armour. He was Gilbert de Clare, Earl of Gloucester, who died in 1295.

Long Wittenham has further delights for lovers of miniatures – the Pendon Museum, at the western edge of the village, houses a unique model village as well as a collection of railway models and full-scale locomotive and railway bygones. Based upon actual buildings in villages within the Vale of White Horse, the tiny cottages, pubs and farms are perfect in every detail, from the thatch – made from human hair – to the tiny flowers and shrubs in the gardens. Each building took at least 500 hours to model, and the project was begun in 1931 by an Australian named Roye England. The museum is open afternoons only at weekends, and on summer Bank Holidays.

Behind Long Wittenham's main street the Thames laps grassy meadows, its gentle curve defined by a line of tall willows across the flat country. The path beside the road to the north of the village is raised on planks – an indication of frequent flooding.

A footpath from the riverside village of Little Wittenham, a mile or so south-east, climbs up a hill known as the Wittenham Clumps. From here there are magnificent views to the Vale of White Horse in the west, and to the Chilterns in the east.

Stanton Harcourt OXFORDSHIRE

12 miles north-west of Abingdon (PAGE 140 Ba)

Both halves of its name tell of Stanton Harcourt's venerable history. Stanton comes from Saxon words meaning, 'the settlement near the stones', and may have referred to three prehistoric stones called the Devil's Quoits, which used to stand to the south-west. During the Second World War, they were buried close by so that an aerodrome could be built. One of the county's oldest families, the Harcourts, came from Normandy and gave their name to the Manor of Stanton when they acquired it in the 12th century.

The village retains fascinating remains of the Harcourts' feudal estate, and is best visited on one of the three or four afternoons each month in summer when the Manor House is open.

Three great towers of mellow stone rise among trees above a flat landscape of wheatfields and meadows through which the Thames, or Isis, meanders. Attractive stone houses, many thatched, are spread out along the road that winds through the village, past the Harcourt Arms Hotel to the Manor House at the centre.

Two of the towers are in the walled garden of the manor, and are the most complete remaining portions of the medieval house begun by Thomas Harcourt in the late 14th century. The Harcourts abandoned the house in 1688, so it was a picturesque ruin when the

Cruck-built cottage, Long Wittenham

The 800-year-old font

Shield of hanging tiles

Timber framing with herringbone brick infill

SELF-ASSERTION AND SURVIVAL

Long Wittenham's houses are among the most individualistic in the area, ranging from medieval cruck (curved beam) construction with thatch to hung tiles and brick infilling. The late Norman font in St Mary's Church is also unique, and bears a moulded frieze of bishops. It is made of lead, and narrowly escaped being cast into bullets by Roundheads in the Civil War.

poet Alexander Pope spent most of 1717 and 1718 in an upper room of the surviving central tower, to complete his translation of *The Iliad* by Homer.

It is called Pope's Tower in commemoration of his stay, but the building dates from 1470. The room on the ground floor, which can be visited on open days, is an exquisite little family chapel with a fan-vaulted ceiling.

The second tower is occupied entirely by the most spectacular room of the original house – the great kitchen – and has an octagonal pyramid roof topped by a lead griffin. A cook accustomed to modern gadgetry might well boggle at the crude simplicity and vast scale of the kitchen. Smoke from centuries of open fires has blackened walls that rise more than 30 ft. There never was a chimney – smoke escaped through shutters under the roof which could be adjusted according to wind direction.

The fires must have turned the kitchen into one vast oven, roasting the cooks almost as crisply as the beef and lamb carcasses they turned on the huge spits. Little wonder that villagers believed witches haunted the place and kept their sabbat here; and that once a year, as Pope wrote: 'the Devil treats them with infernal venison, viz. a toasted tiger stuffed with tenpenny nails.'

After the Second World War the Harcourts returned to the manor and restored the beautiful gardens that surround the house and run down to a large pool, where fish were stocked to feed the medieval household. A smaller pond, the Lady Pool, lies to the east. It is said that when this runs dry the ghost of Alice Harcourt – murdered by her chaplain centuries ago – wanders to and fro between chapel and pool.

The third tower is that of St Michael's Church, huddled against the manor walls, but entered from the road outside. The doorways and windows remain from the original Norman building of about 1140.

TALE OF THREE TOWERS

OVERLEAF

The lowest of Stanton Harcourt's three towers covers a kitchen where mighty medieval banquets were prepared, and the middle one contains a room where Alexander Pope made his famous translation of The Iliad. *Beneath the tower of St Michael's Church, there lies a member of the Harcourt family who was Henry Tudor's standard-bearer at Bosworth in 1485. The tattered standard which he carried into battle hangs over his tomb.*

HUNGERFORD

BERKSHIRE

10 miles west of Newbury (PAGE 140 Bc)

A turning off the main road from London to Bath takes you across an old canal bridge, under an iron railway bridge and out into Hungerford's broad and handsome High Street.

This ancient market town was built on the old Roman road to Bath. Later it became a major staging post on the Great West Road, and by the 1950s the town was jammed with vehicles going to and from Bath. But with the opening of the M4 motorway in 1971 the congestion was relieved, and Hungerford was able to breathe again.

The turning into the town is by The Bear Hotel. Probably built in the late 1200s, the inn was once the haunt of highwaymen – and in the 16th century Henry VIII settled the property in turn on five of his six wives, the exception being Anne Boleyn.

Many of Hungerford's shops and houses date from the 17th and 18th centuries. A supermarket in the High Street has a window in the shape of the door of the 18th-century Manor House that stood here until 1965.

Farther along the High Street is a house with an iron bridge leading to the first floor. The house's stout bow windows face onto the Kennet and Avon Canal, which cuts through the town. Hungerford's other waterways are the rivers Kennet and Dun, a byword among fishermen for their multitude of trout.

The fishing rights were granted to the townsfolk in 1364 by John of Gaunt, Duke of Lancaster, whose first wife, Blanche, inherited the manor of Hungerford. The nobleman's action is commemorated each year on the second Tuesday after Easter, when the centuries old Hocktide Festival is held in the town. At 8 a.m. a blast on a replica of the duke's hunting horn summons the townsfolk to the Commoners' Court, held in the Town Hall an hour later. There the various town officials – Constable, Portreeve, Bailiff, Water Bailiff, Keepers of the Keys of the Common Coffers, Ale-Tasters and Tutti-men – are elected for the coming twelve months.

Armed with Tutti-poles – long beribboned staffs decorated with tuttis, or nosegays – the Tutti-men tour about 100 households demanding a kiss from the ladies. Every lady who gives a kiss receives an orange from the Orange-man. At lunchtime the Court gathers in the Corn Exchange for a meal. The Ale-Tasters judge the quality of the beer that is served and a toast is drunk in hot punch to the memory of John of Gaunt. Afterwards comes the Shoeing of the Colts, when those who did not attend the lunch have nails driven into their shoes until they agree to contribute to the supply of punch.

Hungerford is also noted for antiques fairs that are held regularly in the Corn Exchange, and for its numerous antiques shops that have sprung up in recent years. Most of these are in the Hungerford Arcade, in the High Street, which has more than 70 shops and showcases.

Three miles west of Hungerford, on the banks of the Kennet, is an unspoilt Tudor manor, Littlecote House. It has a unique collection of Cromwellian arms and armour and a complete Cromwellian chapel. A Roman villa in the grounds is still being excavated, but visitors can see the fully restored Orpheus Mosaic – the largest coloured Roman mosaic in England. It was unearthed in 1730 but soon covered by the owner, who hated publicity, and remained hidden until 1976.

• **Parking** Church Street (car park); High Street • **Early closing** Thursday • **Market day** Wednesday • **Event** Hocktide (second Tuesday after Easter) • **Information** TEL. Newbury 30267 • **AA 24 hour service** TEL. Swindon 21446.

Aldbourne WILTSHIRE

7 miles north-west of Hungerford (PAGE 140 Ac)

A little before the hour of evening opening, the landlord of The Crown often rides a fine horse into his car park, and ties it up where the coach horses stood in the 18th century. In a way, this pleasant ritual symbolises Aldbourne, for though progressive and large as villages go – it has several shops, a restaurant, a minuscule bank and a number of other pubs as well as The Crown – it also possesses a strong sense of continuity and tradition.

Aldbourne has two focal points, The Green and The Square. The Green is a turf slope with a stone cross in the middle and a framing of ancient cottages, Georgian houses and the Blue Boar pub, on whose site an ale and lodging house has stood since 1460 at least.

Standing above all, on a higher mound still, is the truly majestic Church of St Michael, a building that is a conglomeration of all kinds of periods from the Normans on; it probably stands on the foundations of an earlier, Saxon church. The interior is equally magnificent, and presents an extraordinarily vivid picture of Aldbourne's history. There is a lively alabaster portrait of John Stone, a vicar who died in 1524, and numerous monuments to Goddards and Walronds. An early Walrond was Ranger of Aldbourne Chase in the days of William the Conqueror. The Goddard monument of about 1616 shows husband, wife and four children in decreasing sizes; the three small boys, curiously, have beards and moustaches.

Near by is the splendid tomb of two Walrond brothers – benign, bearded old gentlemen who also died at the beginning of the 17th century. One is described as a 'lover of hospitality and entertainer of many friends', and looks it. All the monuments, Goddards and Walronds alike, have had their praying hands knocked off, presumably by Parliamentarian troops during the Civil War. Also in the church are a pair of 18th-century fire engines, known affectionately as Adam and Eve. They served the village well through a number of serious conflagrations, the last in 1921, before going into honourable retirement.

Behind St Michael's, along a rocky causeway high above the road, and around The Square are a number of good-looking Georgian houses, recalling the days when Aldbourne was an important place, noted for its bell-founding, the weaving of fustian – a coarse cloth – and its hats of plaited straw and willow. Many of the houses are in a local mixture of red brick and rough stone blocks, offset by dark pink, tiled roofs.

The Square is also a green, with a perfectly round pond at its centre. A notice board tells of the several occasions on which Aldbourne has been judged the best-kept village in Wiltshire, and beneath it there is a monument to a dog called Rover, 'a faithful worker for Savernake Hospital', who died in 1933. Rover used

St Michael's Church, Aldbourne

Goddard monument

Old cottages, Aldbourne

Old Malthouse, Aldbourne

OLD WARS, OLD PEACE

King Alfred once owned Aldbourne, William the Conqueror seized it from the niece of King Canute, and fleeing Cromwellian troopers broke the hands off the effigies in the church. But the village, with its pretty cottages under the guardianship of a Norman church, serenely absorbed all vicissitudes, and went back to important things like smuggling, bell-founding and malt-making.

to carry a collecting box at Aldbourne's carnivals, and raised a lot of money for the hospital.

High on a ridge to the north is the little village of Baydon. No architectural gem, it has a fair share of modern buildings, but the views to the Marlborough Downs on one side and the Lambourn Downs on the other are breathtaking. The road that runs through the village is the great Roman Ermin Way, which linked the towns of Corinium (Cirencester) and Calleva (Silchester).

Boxford BERKSHIRE

9 miles east of Hungerford (PAGE 140 Bc)

The first line of defence against casual intruders is some pre-war red-brick houses and a big, mock-Tudor pub of about the same period. But press on beyond these, deeper into the village, past the supports of a

Boxford Mill

long-defunct railway bridge, and a Boxford of more antique charm begins to reveal itself.

The street divides into a curving 'Y', the left fork of which is announced as a dead end; and so it is, fading out in a farmyard, beyond which the M4 motorway gathers itself for a leap across the Lambourn valley. But between the junction and the farmyard there is a large number of pretty, thatched cottages. Some are of brick, some of plaster with timber framing, and each is an individual, like Stream Cottage – blue and white, with a dark wooden bay added on.

Mingled with the cottages are some 18th-century houses and farms, of which the grandest and probably the oldest is Westbrook House, a miniature stately home of blue and red brick. Some of the corrugated farm buildings show an ascendancy of the practical over the picturesque, but this is a workaday village that makes its living from the land. Cottages, houses and all are knitted together by a dreamy little stream that idles its way by clumps of flowers, through rushes and waterweeds, and beneath ancient, tumbled willows to the Lambourn.

The other branch of the 'Y' has a different character, more typical maybe of the villages of the southern chalk. A brick bridge spans the Lambourn that runs glassy and swift, waving long waterweeds in its depths. On one side of the bridge there is a magnificent old red-brick mill pouring white water through its mill race. On the other, the river washes the end of a perfectly shaved cottage lawn, decorated with old, espaliered fruit trees and immaculately edged flower beds. Behind the mill is St Andrew's Church, part 17th century, part Victorian and all attractive in a livery of split flint patterned with brick.

The river curves round the churchyard, running not quite so swiftly, since it has yet to be accelerated by the mill race. Deep-thatched cottages are gathered about, and some modern houses too, and in season the gardens everywhere are full of flowers.

A WORKADAY PLACE

Boxford is a village of unpretentious permanence, of old farms, old cottages, and an old water mill on the Lambourn river. It is a place where people have always lived and always will, it would seem. By way of confirmation, there are the Stone Age axe heads and the Iron Age pottery that often turn up at spring ploughing.

St Andrew's Church and cottages, Boxford

Eastbury BERKSHIRE

7 miles north of Hungerford (PAGE 140 Bc)

In the plain Victorian Church of St James the Greater there is a particular jewel, a window engraved by Laurence Whistler. Installed in 1971, it is a symbolic portrait of the high chalk country, and a celebration of the lives of the poet Edward Thomas and his wife, Helen. Thomas, killed near Arras in 1917, never lived in Eastbury; but his widow, who survived him by 50 years, spent the last 12 here, rejoicing in the things that pleased them both:

. . . willows, willow-herb and grass,
And meadowsweet, and haycocks dry,
No whit less still and lonely fair
Than the high cloudlets in the sky.

Helen died in 1967, and is buried by the row of beech trees at the top of the churchyard.

It seems a pity that Edward Thomas, one of the greatest of war poets, did not know Eastbury, for there could scarcely be a finer subject for a home thought from abroad. The village is bisected by the Lambourn, clear as molten glass and waving banners of weed from its gravelly bed. Its waters run beneath the walls of red-tiled or deeply thatched cottages, so that it is possible, in theory at least, to catch a trout from a kitchen window.

At one end of the street, by the Plough Inn, there is a bridge of strawberry brick, and beside it a little square of mown turf. Behind is Pigeonhouse Farm which dates from 1620 and has a dovecote incorporating, so it is said, 999 nesting holes.

Balancing Pigeonhouse Farm at the other end of the village is Manor Farm, hidden away behind vast barns of black timber and heavy thatch; the partly 15th-century house itself is of a glorious local mixture of split-flint walls and tall, dark red-brick chimneys.

In the heart of the village is a large stable, out of whose loose boxes protrude the slim, aristocratic heads of racehorses, as a reminder that this is the edge of the Lambourn Downs, training ground of champions. Not far off along the stream is a little red-brick smithy with a large, neat pile of rusty horseshoes stacked against one wall. These are roadshoes, worn by racehorses during training – for races they are re-shod with light aluminium shoes called plates.

The smith is quite happy to shoe the donkeys that live in a field up the road, or a child's pony. But his true vocation is apparent in the two racing plates that he keeps nailed above his door: one from the 1974 Derby winner, Snow Knight, and the other from Ayala, who won the Grand National in 1963.

THAME

OXFORDSHIRE

13 miles east of Oxford (PAGE 140 Da)

When John Fothergill bought the 18th-century Spread Eagle Hotel in Thame in 1922, he found a traditional market-town pub – empty every day of the week except for market day. When he sold it in 1931 it was

Church Road almshouses, Thame

Prebendal House, Thame

Richard Quatremain

THAME, FAITH AND CHARITY

Richard Quatremain, whose likeness in brass may be seen in Thame church, acquired the market town and the country about it through marriage in 1415. He signified his gratitude by endowing the almshouses in High Street – rebuilt in the following century by another benefactor – and by the chapel at his home at nearby Rycote. The pews he installed are still there. The 13th-century Prebendal House, now private, was a priest's house when Thame was a prebend, or dependency, of Lincoln Cathedral.

Original pews in Rycote chapel

one of the most famous inns in England. Customers included the authors H. G. Wells, G. K. Chesterton, Grahame Greene and Evelyn Waugh; the painter Augustus John; and prominent politicians.

Fothergill achieved this remarkable transformation by an extraordinary mixture of excellence and rudeness. Customers he approved of he provided with only the best. Food, for example, was brought specially from Jaffa, Athens, France, Norway and Italy. But those he disapproved of – such as farmers or commercial travellers and rich Oxford undergraduates – he would go out of his way to insult.

The imposing red-brick inn stands on Thame's broad High Street, opposite another pub, the 15th-century timber-framed Bird Cage Inn. Hampden House near by used to be The Greyhound Inn. John Hampden, a former pupil of Thame grammar school and a Parliamentary leader at the beginning of the Civil War, died here in 1643 from wounds suffered at the Battle of Chalgrove Field in south Oxfordshire.

Also outstanding in the High Street, which grew up around a 13th-century market, are two 16th-century timber-framed cottages, The Cruck and Thatcher's – now a restaurant – and, at the other end of the street, the fine 18th-century Moat House, with its ornate doorway and carriage entrance. The Old Maltings is an interesting modern conversion.

At the west end of the High Street, Priestend turns off towards The Prebendal, a former priest's house, partly dating from the 13th century and restored in the 19th century as a private home with beautiful grounds down to the River Thame. The church opposite has some good brasses, especially those of the Quatremain family, and in the centre of the chancel is the impressive tomb of Lord Williams of Thame and his wife. Lord Williams was an astute 16th-century courtier who survived, with profit, the reigns of Henry VIII, Edward VI and Mary I. The 16th-century former grammar school and almshouses in Church Road were endowed from his fortune.

After Henry's Dissolution of the Monasteries, Williams acquired Thame Abbey. The present (mostly 18th century) Thame Park, built by his descendants, incorporates some of the abbey's 13th-century buildings. Williams also owned Rycote Park, 2½ miles south-west of Thame. Of this mansion little remains; but the charming Rycote chapel, founded by the Quatremain family in the 15th century, still stands and is open to the public. Inside are the original pews and some 17th-century decorated woodwork. The yew outside was planted, it is believed, in 1138 to mark King Stephen's coronation.

• **Parking** Upper and Lower High Street • **Early closing** Wednesday • **Market day** Tuesday • **Theatre** Thame Players Theatre, Nelson Street • **Events** Thame Festival Week (July); Thame Agricultural Show (3rd Thursday in September) • **Information** TEL. Thame 2834 • **AA 24 hour service** TEL. Oxford 240286.

Beckley OXFORDSHIRE

11 miles north-west of Thame (PAGE 140 Ca)

In the late 1860s a ridge known as The High Ground of Beckley was a favourite retreat of Charles Dodgson, better known as Lewis Carroll. Standing there, overlooking the flat 4000 acre expanse of Ot Moor below, with its intermingled patches of coarse grass, sedges and rushes, he is said to have envisaged the giant chessboard in his second Alice book, *Through the Looking Glass*. Much of Ot Moor has now been reclaimed for agricultural use; but the ridge still commands a spectacular view from the parklike grounds of the fine late Georgian Grove House, in the west, to an old Roman road which disappears into the moor to the east.

The village's centre is the Church of St Mary, from which the main street of thatched and delightfully crooked stone cottages leads to the Abingdon Arms. St Mary's, an attractive little church standing well up on the ridge, has some good 14th and 15th-century stained glass, including a minute but touching depiction of the Assumption of the Virgin. It also has the remains, above the tower arch, of a 14th-century wall painting of the Last Judgment. The large and awe-inspiring figures of St Peter and St Paul are still clearly visible.

In the 13th century the manor of Beckley was given to Henry III's younger brother, Richard, Earl of Cornwall. He built a hunting lodge, of which nothing now remains, and a walled hunting park, whose limits can still be seen from the field boundaries. Later, Henry VIII gave the manor to Lord Williams of Thame (see Thame), who probably built the present Beckley Park on the site of the previous royal hunting lodge in 1540.

The brick house – a private home – is set on its own in the moor, a mile east of the village, and stands within the remains of three concentric moats, which possibly protected a Saxon castle. It is the most complete Tudor house in England, even its doors and hinges being original 16th century. There are some good views of the house from a stretch of the Oxfordshire Way that runs east of the village, up beyond Cripps Cottage – setting of the 19th-century novel *Cripps the Carrier*, written by R. D. Blackmore, who was also the author of *Lorna Doone*.

Standing out on the moor, 1½ miles north-west of Beckley, is the hamlet of Noke. Its inhabitants once, apparently, had a reputation for being taciturn, giving rise to the traditional local rhyme:

> '*I went to Noke and nobody spoke,*
> *I went to Beckley and they spoke directly.*'

Today, charming thatched cottages and some good modern housing spread out from the tiny Church of St Giles and the partly 16th-century Manor Farm. A 17th-century tomb in the church commemorates Benedict Winchcombe, who lived at Manor Farm. Winchcombe was a great huntsman, and locals will tell you that, if you listen hard, you can still sometimes hear him riding through the village with his hounds on cold winter nights.

Charlton-on-Otmoor

OXFORDSHIRE

17 miles north-west of Thame (PAGE 140 Ca)

On May Day morning a custom dating back to pagan times takes place in Charlton-on-Otmoor. A procession of children carrying a May garland, a rope of flowers and foliage some 12 ft long, winds its way from the village school to the church. Here the parish priest blesses the garland, which is then hung along the top of the magnificent 16th-century rood screen. Above the screen stands a cross made from the evergreen foliage of the box tree. It is believed that this once represented the Virgin Mary – the cross still spreads out at the bottom like a skirt. The cross is known as Our Lady of Otmoor, and until the 19th century it, too, was carried in the procession. The foliage is renewed for each May Day and for the Feast of Mary in September.

Like many May Day festivities around Britain the custom has pagan origins. These are usually related to fertility ceremonies which have been adapted to a Christian celebration. At Charlton there is dancing in the streets after the church ceremonies.

There could be no finer setting for this typically English tradition than Charlton. The colourful procession threads its way along streets lined with cottages of stone and thatch, and the dancing takes place at a crossroads in the village centre. Close by is the 17th-century former Rectory and the 13th-century Church of St Mary the Virgin, standing on a knoll.

The moor itself is reached by a lane running south from the Crown Inn. Although enclosed now and mostly drained, a mysterious and wild aura still clings to the heart of Ot Moor. Its 6 square miles of marsh and swamp have been described in the past as 'bewitched' and 'cast under a spell of ancient magic'. There is said to be a legendary Lady of Otmoor who granted the people of the moor's 'seven towns' – Charlton, Fencott, Murcott, Studley, Beckley, Noke and Oddington – their grazing rights. The story goes that she rode around the area while an oat sheaf was burning, saying that all the land she covered while the sheaf burnt should become common land.

A marshy area called Fowl's Pill remains much as the moor has always been, and the Spinney is part of a nature reserve of the Berkshire, Buckinghamshire and Oxfordshire Naturalists' Trust. The reserve is home to some pairs of nightingales and about 265 species of wild flower have been found here.

Islip OXFORDSHIRE

12 miles north-west of Thame (PAGE 140 Ca)

Until the 19th century Islip was an important market for neighbouring Ot Moor and the surrounding region. It lies where the River Ray flows into the Cherwell, and on the old London to Worcester road.

Monks' Cottage, Islip

FISHING FOR A FAVOUR

A local boatman was given exclusive fishing rights in the River Ray for ferrying Parliamentarian troops during the Battle of Islip Bridge in 1645. The skirmish is almost forgotten, but the bridge still serves the village of Edward the Confessor's birth.

Mill Street, Islip

Islip Bridge over the River Ray

From here Islip eels, caught in the Cherwell and Ray, were sent as far afield as the Ship Inn in Greenwich; and water lilies from the marshy lands of Ot Moor were sent to Covent Garden. Islip also has a long association with Westminster Abbey, dating to the Saxon era when the village had a royal palace.

This palace, which was used by Ethelred the Unready (*c.* AD 978-1016), was birthplace of the Saxon king, Edward the Confessor. Edward, in his will, left 'ye little town . . . wherein I was born' to the monastery he had founded at Westminster, and the links between them have remained strong ever since. The last abbot of Westminster, before the Dissolution of the Monasteries in 1539, was an Islip man, and Westminster still appoints the parish's rectors.

The best approach to Islip is across the bridge over the Ray – the scene of a battle during the Civil War. Arriving from that direction you find the beautiful and immaculately kept village, rising impressively on a hillside before you. Many of its fine stone houses are 17th and 18th century, and in pride of place, near the top of the hill, stands the superb old Rectory, which looks out from an imposing bayed front and has a fine hooded doorway and a walled garden sloping down steeply towards the river. The Rectory was built in 1689 by one of the village's most notable benefactors, Dr Robert South, rector of Islip from 1678 until his death in 1716.

Dr South, who had also been a chaplain at the Court of Charles II, did much good work in the parish. Out of his own income he provided for the education and apprenticing of the children, and in 1680 he paid for the restoration of the chancel of the Church of St Nicholas. The church was later restored and remodelled by the Victorians, but standing in its well-kept graveyard, overhung by the thatched eaves of the ancient Monks' Cottage, it still makes a charming centrepiece to the village.

Outside its east end a large crucifix under thatched roofing overlooks the small Crosstree Green, where the market used to be held. Dr South's old School House, built in 1710, stands near by, and the attractive Middle Street, with its unusual Gothic-style Tompkins Terrace runs down the hill opposite. A stroll down to the river leads to Mill Street, with its many pretty houses and cottages. Near by, just below the old Rectory, stands Wooster Arms. It is now a private home, but used to be one of several pubs that thrived in Islip in the days when coaches rolled through on their way to Worcester and beyond.

Stanton St John OXFORDSHIRE

10 miles north-west of Thame (PAGE 140 Ca)

A plaque over the door announces that the village's Rectory Farm House was the birthplace in 1575 of the Reverend John White, 'chief founder of the colony of Massachusetts in New England'. Although not himself one of the colonists, White, who became a Fellow of New College, Oxford, was one of the prime movers behind the founding of the Massachusetts Company in 1628, to help Puritans escape religious persecution.

At roughly the same time – a further connection with the Puritans – Stanton St John was the home of the poet John Milton's grandparents, and he is believed to have spent much of his childhood here. Stanton St John is a village of simple but handsome stone cottages – some of them thatched. It stretches along a street, from the 17th-century George Inn, on what used to be the main road from London to Worcester, down a steep hill, past the late 19th-century Stanton House, standing four-square in its grounds on the hillside, to the old Mill House at the bottom. Its centre point is the little green knoll on which stands the Church of St John the Baptist. From here, in the churchyard, there are fine views of the elegant, early 19th-century College House; the back of Manor Farm House, dating from the 16th century at least; and tucked cosily into the hillside below, White's birthplace – its mellowed stone walls reflecting the centuries of warmth and protection they have given to the families living there.

Holly Wood, Stanton Great Wood – part of a former royal hunting forest – and the Forestry Commission's Bernwood Forest, lie to the east of the village. All are crossed by attractive footpaths, and are home to a wide variety of plant and animal life. Large numbers of the tiny muntjac deer roam wild. They were introduced into Britain from Asia in the 19th century and are only 20 in. high fully grown. The unusual black hairstreak butterfly can be seen on the blackthorn bushes at the edges of the woods. Above all, this is one of the few places where the rare wild service tree still grows. The small, grey-barked tree, which has clusters of white flowers in May and small edible berries in October, was once used to make charcoal, with the result that it is now extremely uncommon and survives only in ancient woodland.

A footpath from the centre of Stanton St John leads across the fields to Woodperry, 2 miles to the north-west. It used to be a separate village, but was abandoned – possibly after the Black Death in the 14th century. Now all that remains is the magnificent early 18th-century Woodperry House, standing at the end of a fine tree-lined avenue. The stone mansion has two curved Palladian-style side wings, formerly stables, which stretch out to form an elegant semicircle in front. At the back, it looks out onto an enormous walled garden built on a ridge.

WANTAGE

OXFORDSHIRE

17 miles south-west of Oxford (PAGE 140 Bb)

Alfred the Great, King of Wessex, was born at Wantage in AD 849 – and there is a 19th-century statue of him in the Market Place. The Saxon settlement where historians believe that Alfred was born stood about half a mile to the north of the present town. Alfred united much of what is now England against the Danish invaders, but in 1006, about 100 years after he died, Wantage with other towns in the area was probably sacked by the Danes.

Much of the town was rebuilt during Norman times, and in the Middle Ages it became a prosperous market centre. But by the late 18th century an agricultural slump had set in and, as its fortunes declined, the town was dubbed 'Black Wantage'. Its nickname came from the numerous villains of various kinds who crowded the inns and made the streets unsafe for respectable folk after dark.

Wantage regained its decorum in the 19th century, and many of its buildings – with roofs of Welsh slate – are Victorian. Some older timber-framed houses have façades of red and blue brick from the century before. There is also a row of probably 16th and 17th-century black-and-white cottages, believed to have been weavers' workshops.

Wantage is set in the glorious Vale of White Horse, with the rolling downs to the south; and the district's long and eventful history is recorded in the Vale and Downland Museum in Church Street. The building was originally a 17th-century cloth-merchant's house, and as well as display galleries it now has a refreshment area and a shop. The exhibits depict the history of the area since the end of the Ice Age – and show how the local occupations changed from hunting and fishing to farming and the wool trade.

Opposite the museum is the Church of St Peter and St Paul – mostly late 13th century – which contains a magnificent chandelier made in 1711 and some fine stained glass of 1848. A silver plate in the church is said to have been owned by Peter the Great, Tsar of Russia from 1682 to 1725. Among the tombs are those of the Fitzwarin family, one of whose members, Alice Fitzwarin, married Sir Richard ('Dick') Whittington who was three times Lord Mayor of London in the late 14th and early 15th centuries.

• **Parking** Limborough Road; Portway (both car parks) • **Early closing** Thursday • **Market days** Wednesday, Saturday • **Cinema** The Regent, Newbury Street • **Event** Spring Festival (May) • **Information** TEL. Wantage 3456. • **AA 24 hour service** TEL. Oxford 240286.

Goosey OXFORDSHIRE

4 miles north-west of Wantage (PAGE 140 Bb)

The village with the nursery-rhyme name consists of little more than a vast green surrounded by a scattering of handsome stone buildings, some modern bungalows, a church and a pub. The name is perfectly serious; the suffix 'ey' signifies that it was an island once – in this case an island in a swamp, on which geese were bred. The breeders were the monks of Abingdon, who were presented with the land by King Offa of Mercia in AD 785, and continued to hold it until the Reformation. The site of their cell is now occupied by the big Abbey Farm.

The pretty stone church is painted white with a 19th-century wooden belfry crowning its lichen-encrusted stone slates. The interior is simple, like a small stone barn. Massive timbers support the slates, and the building is lit by narrow windows sunk deep in the 13th-century walls. There is a small pulpit, two crosses intricately woven in straw and an appliqué altar frontal depicting cheerful monks attending geese.

Tiny in the wide, flat valley below Whitehorse Hill, Goosey would seem to be gently fading away. Its school is long closed, its village shop and post office are gone, and many of its young people have left. Soon, perhaps, it may cease to exist as a community, and become no more than a few isolated houses. This, at any rate, was the conclusion reached by the brewers who owned The Pound, Goosey's only pub. In 1978, feeling that future profits would be most unlikely to balance the cost of refurbishment, they decided to close the pub down.

It was as though they had raised a battle flag. Violent objections to the loss of the last community centre came not only from the villagers but from people in outlying farms, cottages and houses. Under the leadership of some retired farm workers and a scientist from Harwell atomic research centre, about 10 miles to the east, a village resistance movement was started – in the best traditions of the English at bay.

First they offered to take over the pub and, when this came to naught, raised a clamour that reverberated through the national newspapers, radio and television. For the first time in its 1200 year history, Goosey was famous. The furore continued for over a week until the brewers relented and promised to keep the pub open. It is open still, and Goosey is itself again.

The Letcombes OXFORDSHIRE

2 miles south-west of Wantage (PAGE 140 Bb)

Horses have been popular hereabouts for a very long time, as is apparent from the fantastical galloping horse – a god or a war emblem – that the Atrebates, the local Celtic tribe, carved into the hillside about 3 miles west at Uffington, some 2000 years ago. It lies by the Ridgeway, the track that was ancient long before the White Horse was cut; and also from the Ridgeway can be seen the creature's spiritual descendants, the strings of racehorses out on exercise in the early morning mists, or galloping as single, tiny figures in the vast chalklands of the Lambourn Downs.

As likely as not, the horses are stabled at Letcombe Bassett or Letcombe Regis, two villages below the Ridgeway at the point where it touches upon the great Iron Age hill-fort of Segsbury. Letcombe Bassett, the nearer to the high downland track, has a strong flavour of the idyllic. Racehorses in green canvas overcoats lean over paddock rails beside thatched, colour-washed cottages and the Church of St Michael, part of which dates from Norman times.

About and through the village wanders the little Letcombe brook in its surprisingly deep valley, sometimes opening out into watercress beds and crossed by concrete walkways raised above the level of the stream. High above the brook, and the road, is the little Yew Tree pub, with the old smithy behind. Below it, by the Letcombe, is a cottage picturesque almost to the point of overstatement; this is said to be the model for Arabella's cottage in Thomas Hardy's novel *Jude the Obscure*, just as the village is the model for Cresscombe in the same book.

All about the cottage is a delightful water garden of little grassy isthmuses, yellow and gold with daffodils in spring; while Holborn Farm, with its curving thatch, makes a pleasant balance near by.

Letcombe Regis, also overlooked by the ancient trackway, is a mixture of thatched black-and-white cottages, small Georgian houses and a good deal of modern red brick, producing some uneasy contrasts.

But much of the older Letcombe Regis remains – The Old House, for example, with its inscription 'HKM 1698', and switchback thatched roof whose hillocks and dips match those of the Ridgeway itself. There is, too, the big Georgian pub which has an Aunt Sally pitch; this is an old Oxfordshire game in which batons are thrown at a wooden dummy.

The Church of St Andrew, high on a mound filled with tombstones and flowers, is a patchwork of the ages from the 12th century onwards. The stump of a medieval cross stands by the gateway into the churchyard, and beneath the yews by the porch lies a

'Arabella's Cottage', Letcombe Bassett

RESCUED FROM OBSCURITY

Letcombe Bassett becomes 'Cresscombe' in early scenes of one of Thomas Hardy's best-known Wessex novels, the unrelenting tragedy Jude the Obscure. *A cottage by the brook was a model for the home of Arabella, Jude's future wife. Hardy says: 'A smell of piggeries came from the back and the grunting of the originators of that smell'; no one, however, would recognise it from that description now. It is a neat, freshly painted, desirable cottage with not a pig in view or hearing. No doubt the whole area surrounding Letcombe Bassett and the neighbouring village of Letcombe Regis is cleaner and tidier than it was in Hardy's day, and probably less rural. But watercress can still be found growing in the Letcombe brook, and the villages are just as attractive as they were 100 years ago.*

St Michael's Church, Letcombe Bassett

The Old House, Letcombe Regis

Maori chieftain. He was George King Hipango, who died aged 19 of consumption in 1871 while staying with a friend in the village. More typical of the district, perhaps, are the monuments in the church to the Piggotts, forebears of the jockey Lester Piggott.

Stanford in the Vale

OXFORDSHIRE

6 miles north-west of Wantage (PAGE 140 Bb)

The vale is that of the Vale of White Horse, a wide, flat landscape with the hazy ramparts of the Lambourn Downs and Whitehorse Hill to the south, though the horse itself cannot be seen from this angle. It is a pleasant, easy-going landscape, crossed by streams that mostly flow to the River Ock that in turn makes its vague way to the Thames at Abingdon. Stanford lies between streams and the river, and is a big, casually put-together village, mostly of stone, and gathered about two greens. These were markets once, noted for a sage-flavoured cheese that was shaped in moulds in the form of a hare.

Upper Green has Stanford House in red and blue patterned brick, and there is an 18th-century house whose stone front is dripping in early summer with the dark pink and purple of japonica and aubrietia. All the rest about this green is modern, built of rectangular blocks which, though they are the same colour, still contrast oddly with the small, uneven stones of the older buildings.

The green by the church, on the other hand, is almost a village in itself, with its Anchor pub, village stores and rows of pretty stone cottages, some thatched, some tiled, and with attractively out-of-proportion dormer windows. At the back there is a very grand group indeed, consisting of the early 18th-century Manor Farmhouse in stone elegantly patterned with brick, the big Church of St Denys and, separating them, a vast stone barn of 1618.

St Denys is an unusual dedication for an English church, and where it occurs it usually implies an early Norman founding. St Denys was a Bishop of Paris who, after his execution in Montmartre in AD 250, walked with his head under his arm to his chosen place of burial, and afterwards became the patron saint of France. His church in Stanford dates from the 12th century at least and contains among its many treasures a brass to Roger Campedene, who was rector there in the 1390s.

The speciality of the village, however, is the grandeur of its farmhouses that argue considerable agricultural prosperity over many centuries. There is Penstones Farm which, big though it is, is only a part of a much larger 16th-century building. It has windows in all sorts of sizes and shapes, including an intriguing one high up in the middle that has been merely painted in. Then, too, there is dignified Coxe's Hall with its roughcast front and drainpipe bearing the date 1739; and Spinages, whose enormous thatched roof is enough to take the breath away.

MAP 14

THE CHILTERNS AND THAMES VALLEY

Since prehistoric times man has roamed through the green vales and russet beechwoods of the Chiltern Hills – the chalk ridge that sweeps dramatically through the lower part of Buckinghamshire. Today, people can still travel along the ancient track of the Icknield Way, as our ancestors did more than 4000 years ago. In the Chilterns, expect to find the unexpected . . . the only country hall by Sir Christopher Wren that remains as he built it . . . the village where the much-loved Mrs Miniver lived. And in the lush Thames Valley, a visitor may follow in the wake of the *Three Men in a Boat* – not forgetting the dog, Montmorency.

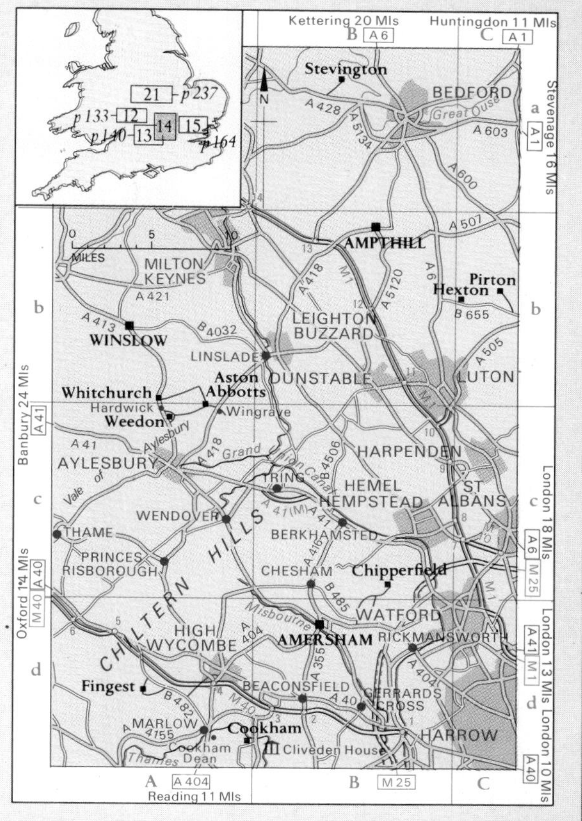

MAP 14: NEIGHBOURING AREAS – MAPS 12, 13, 15, 21

AMERSHAM	AMPTHILL	WINSLOW
Chipperfield	Hexton	Aston Abbotts
Cookham	Pirton	Weedon
Fingest	Stevington	Whitchurch

AMERSHAM

BUCKINGHAMSHIRE

11 miles west of Watford (PAGE 155 Bd)

Set in the 'Gateway to the Chilterns', this ancient market town consists of two pleasantly contrasting districts: Old Amersham and 'new' Amersham-on-the-Hill. Old Amersham lies below wooded hills in the valley of the River Misbourne. The town was once a staging post on the coach road which ran from London to Aylesbury, and its collection of old coaching inns bears witness to this. The Crown Hotel, The Griffin, Red Lion House, the Elephant and Castle, the Swan and The King's Arms all date from the 16th, 17th or 18th centuries.

The coach road – now the broad and spacious High Street – still runs through the town. It goes past the medieval market area, where produce has been sold since 1200 – when King John granted the town its charter. He also sanctioned an annual, two-day fair which is held on September 19 and 20 when the stalls and attractions stretch the length of the old town.

On the north side of the street is the timbered, early 17th-century building which housed the Robert Challoner Grammar School – long since removed to Amersham-on-the-Hill – and which is now shops. Next door are an art gallery and restaurant. Most of the surrounding timbered cottages and black-and-white houses date from the 16th century. However, many of them were given a 'face-lift' in the 18th century, when new brick fronts were added, disguising their true age.

To the west of the High Street is Shardeloes House, the former home of the local Drake family. The mansion was completed in 1766 and contained some of the earliest work of the architect Robert Adam (1728 – 92). The house, which has now been converted into flats, is on the site of a manor house where Elizabeth I once stayed.

Branching off the High Street is Church Street, in which stands the parish church of St Mary, partly 12th century but extensively added to since. The grey flints which give an attractive sheen to the exterior were put there in 1870. Inside are some impressive monuments to the Drakes.

In Market Square is one of Amersham's finest buildings – the elegant Market Hall. At the top of Church Street the road broadens and becomes Rectory Hill, which climbs past the 18th-century Old Rectory and on to Parsonage Wood. Running parallel to Rectory Hill is Station Road, which links the old town with the new.

Amersham-on-the-Hill grew up around the railway station that was built there in the 1890s. On a footpath off Station Road stands the Martyrs' Memorial, a monument to seven Nonconformists killed in Amersham in the 16th century for their religious beliefs. In particular, the followers of the religious reformer John Wycliff (1329 – 84) were savagely persecuted. In 1506, a Wycliff supporter named William Tylsworth was burnt alive and his daughter was forced to light the faggots. Fifteen years later the children of another offender, John Scrivener, also had the grim

Amersham – general view

King's Arms hotel

Market Hall

Town pump

Lock-up

KEEPING IT IN THE FAMILY

Amersham is its own monument to the past. The town and the land around it were once owned by the aristocratic Drake family, who built the 17th-century Market Hall. The market was held on the central flagstones, and the old lock-up is set among the ground-floor arches. The town pump was added in 1785. In the High Street is the black-and-white King's Arms hotel.

task of lighting a fire under their father. Off Station Road is a white house named High and Over, built in 1929 of concrete and glass. It was the first house in Britain to incorporate the 'functional' ideas of the Swiss-French architect Le Corbusier (1887 – 1965).

• **Parking** The Broadway, Old Amersham; Sycamore Road, Amersham-on-the-Hill (both car parks) • **Early closing** Thursday • **Market day** Tuesday, Amersham-on-the-Hill • **Event** Carnival (July), Amersham-on-the-Hill • **AA 24 hour service** TEL. London 954 7373.

Chipperfield HERTFORDSHIRE

7 miles north-east of Amersham (PAGE 155 Bc)

All about the village are London's northern attendants – the industrial spread of Watford and the dormitories of the Chalfonts, Rickmansworth, Latimer and the rest, whose histories are inseparable from those of the Quaker founders of America, and the Metropolitan Railway. Chipperfield has nothing to do with any of them, and is really quite difficult to find – so difficult, in fact, that it is easy to suspect that the inhabitants have removed all signposts.

No doubt it has its quota of commuters, but it is totally – even typically – English rural. It is a little place arranged about a green that has grown into a 116 acre common with a ring of venerable trees, chestnuts, beeches and limes, in the background. One Spanish chestnut, with writhing hoary limbs, is reputed to be 300 years old, and Apostle's Pond has 12 limes grouped about it; or rather had, until one of them blew down in the 1970s.

There is a cricket pitch of the delicately nurtured sort in the middle of the green and the scene is overlooked by the Two Brewers, a long, low pub with a little white fence and seats behind. It is a classic place to watch a cricket match on a long, lazy, hot summer afternoon. At the edge of the green there is a neat flint church of 1837, and in the background, some flint cottages to match. They are set off by others which are timber-framed, in red brick, and in pink or white plaster; Tile Cottage, reasonably enough, is hung all over with red tiles. Down The Street, there is The Pale Farm, very big and handsome among its mown lawns. As its old timbering and overhanging storey suggest, it dates from the 16th century, though it also has a delicate and Victorian-looking conservatory – built, however, in 1983 – peeping over the fence. A few yards farther on is the cheerful and tempting village shop; a notice says that it was established in 1897.

The Manor House, at the far end of the green from the church, is one of those loved English houses that grew gradually down the years as the needs of its residents dictated. Part of it was built in the 16th century or earlier, and added to in the 17th, 18th and the present one. The owners presented much of the common and the woods to the village, on the condition that the elms in front of the house were preserved. But, alas, they were dangerously close to the road and have been replaced by lime saplings.

Cookham BERKSHIRE

10 miles south-west of Amersham (PAGE 155 Ad)

It is not too easy to tell where Maidenhead's modern fringes end and those of Cookham begin, but once into the village proper it is apparent, and heart-warming to see, that nothing has really changed, and that the latter part of the 20th century has done little more than to add a smart veneer. The pubs are still there that have been used by generations of pleasure-seekers from London – The Ferry, the Bel and the Dragon, the King's Arms and the Royal Exchange, among many.

The village centre is undoubtedly the road junction by the river end where three roads meet. Here sits the Tarry Stone, a smallish, brownish sarsen boulder about which village games were played until the 16th century. There are some good-looking 18th-century houses facing a former Nonconformist chapel that the artist Sir Stanley Spencer (1891 – 1959) attended when he was a boy. Spencer was born in Cookham, a couple of doors from the King's Arms, and spent most of his life there. The chapel is now a gallery devoted to his works, and is open to the public at weekends and Bank Holidays throughout the year.

Between this group and the river there is the partly Queen Anne vicarage and Holy Trinity Church in its large churchyard that, in season, is awash with daffodils. The church dates in part from the 12th century, and contains all manner of interesting things. There is a copy of Spencer's *Last Supper* – the original is in the gallery – and a spirited painting of *East Indiamen at Sea*, by Nicholas Pocock (1741 – 1821). Pocock is buried in the church and was a master mariner – and what would now be termed a war artist; his depictions of Nelson's ships and battles are accounted to be the most authentic marine paintings of the period.

Behind the church is the River Thames and the Victorian iron bridge that gives marvellous views in either direction. On one side, the eye is drawn over stately cabin cruisers to smooth lawns and a smoother golf course; and on the other there is the Ferry Inn (where waterborne seekers after refreshment can tie up), the weir, and the steep climb of Cliveden Woods to Cliveden House on its majestic terraces.

In *Three Men in a Boat*, Jerome K. Jerome described this as 'the sweetest stretch of all the river', and recorded that the immortal trio stopped off and made tea by Cookham backwater. Quarry Wood, near Cookham Dean, is thought to be the model for the Wild Wood in Kenneth Grahame's *The Wind in the Willows*; it still has a menacing air.

At the other end of Cookham High Street, away from the Thames, there are more pubs, and a common, the Moor, where stray animals used to be kept.

One other thing should be noted, a warning affixed to a cottage wall by the Bel and the Dragon. It announces: 'All Fighting to be Over by 10 p.m.' It is a relief to learn that this was a parish commandment applying only to the bygone sport of cockfighting. Nowadays, Cookham is much kinder to birds, and signifies it by being the centre of the annual Swan Upping, or counting, on the Thames, in late July.

Fingest BUCKINGHAMSHIRE

15 miles west of Amersham (PAGE 155 Ad)

A tiny and secret place in a deep bowl in the Chilterns, its concealment is made all the more effective by the tall beechwoods that spill over the rim of the bowl and down the steep meadows. This is an extremely attractive village of flint and rosy brick and timber framing; pretty Fingest House adds a pale blue gate to the colour scheme, and the Chequers pub is suitably

Holy Trinity Church

PORTRAIT OF A PLAYGROUND

In Victorian times, Cookham and the upper Thames were a favourite playground for Londoners. Cookham has grown since those days, but its past remains very much alive in the present. Villas with ornate boathouses line the riverbank, while pleasure-boats pass dreamily by. The partly medieval Holy Trinity Church, built of flint and stone, overlooks the river. Much older is the Tarry Stone, a prehistoric boulder lying opposite Tarry Stone House. In recent times, the Cookham-born artist Sir Stanley Spencer depicted the village in many of his paintings, drawing inspiration from the river, the village and surrounding countryside. The view of Cookham from Englefield was completed by Spencer in 1948.

The Tarry Stone

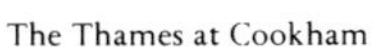

The Thames at Cookham

'Cookham from Englefield'

picked out in a chequerboard pattern of blue and red bricks. Manor Farm is solidly handsome and is surrounded by low, massive barns in dark flint.

Over all is the mighty tower of St Bartholomew's Church, whose unique double-saddleback roof gives the whole village a slightly foreign air. The tower is early Norman, with tiny windows like those of a fortress in its 4 ft thick walls. The nave, too, is Norman, but looks ridiculously tiny for its tower. It has been suggested that once the whole thing was worked the other way around – that the tower was actually the nave, and the present nave was the chancel. The interior is cool and plain behind the thick walls, and the only decoration is the Royal Arms of Queen Anne. The font, however, dates from the 14th century.

Fingest is small, but a peaceful and pleasant spot in which to spend an hour or so, especially in spring when the may is coming into flower and the rooks sail in fleets to their nests in the tall trees about the church. Their chatter is a raucous overlay upon the gentle undertone that drifts from hundreds of sheep with their new lambs high up on the meadows.

AMPTHILL

BEDFORDSHIRE

7 miles south of Bedford (PAGE 155 Bb)

The pride of this serene and historic market town is the 300 acre park which overlooks it. First enclosed in the mid-15th century, Ampthill Park later became the hunting ground of Henry VIII. His first wife, Catherine of Aragon, lived in a castle in the grounds in 1533 during the king's divorce proceedings against her.

Although not a trace of the castle remains, its site is marked by a Gothic cross. This was put up in 1773 at the suggestion of the writer Horace Walpole, who penned the verse inscribed on its base, recalling the 'mournful refuge of an injur'd Queen'.

The grounds of the park were laid down by Capability Brown, who also masterminded the tree-fringed artificial lake, The Reservoir, which the townsfolk affectionately call The Rezzy. Close by is the handsome Ampthill Park House, the steward's lodge in Tudor times. It has been remodelled and enlarged on several later occasions – notably by Lord Ossory in the late 18th century.

Ampthill stands on the slopes of a hill above the Great Ouse valley. To the west lies wooded countryside, and to the east stretch miles of market gardens. The town, which has many Georgian and Victorian buildings, is divided by its four main streets – Woburn Street, Bedford Street, Dunstable Street and Church Street, which cross each other at the Clock House.

Woburn Street, which climbs westwards past the foot of the park, has several half-timbered thatched cottages built in the early 19th century by the same Lord Ossory for the workers on his estate.

Bedford Street, running north out of the town, has a group of mid-19th-century estate cottages. At the top, a track leads to the ruins of Houghton House, a Jacobean mansion which is said to have appeared as the 'House Beautiful' in John Bunyan's *Pilgrim's Progress*, published in 1678–84. Dunstable Street, south of the Clock House, is lined with 18th and early 19th-century houses. One of these, The Cedars, built as a workhouse, is now an old people's home.

Church Street, going east, is rich in Georgian buildings, some of them sheltering more recent façades. In it stands Avenue House, No. 20, built in red brick between 1790 and 1819 for a local brewer, John Morris. On the other side of the street is a Jacobean house with an overhanging first storey. It was the home of a local Member of Parliament, Edmund Wingate, who taught English to Henrietta Maria (1609–69), the French wife of Charles I.

To the side of the street, in a close-like square, is the parish church of St Andrew, built of local stone in the 14th and 15th centuries. Among its several fine monuments is one placed near the north side of the altar bearing the flags of Great Britain and the USA. It is a memorial to Colonel Richard Nicolls, an Ampthill man sent by Charles II to reclaim the American colonies from the Dutch. In August 1664 Colonel Nicolls received the surrender of New Amsterdam, which he renamed New York in honour of the king's brother, James, Duke of York. The colonel stayed in America until 1667 when he returned to Ampthill.

Georgian house, Church Street

SAFE IN TRUST

Some of the Georgian houses in Ampthill's Church Street hide their good looks beneath modern façades. But there is no false modesty about No. 28, elegant behind a fine pair of wrought-iron gates dating from the early 19th century. The parish church of St Andrew, built in the 14th and 15th centuries and which has a roof that is a modern copy of the medieval original, is set back from the street. Next to it are the white-fronted Feoffee Almshouses, which have been maintained by the Town Feoffees (Trustees) since the 15th century.

Church and white-fronted almshouses

Five years later, he was slain by a cannon shot while serving on board the Duke of York's flagship at the Battle of Sole Bay (see Southwold, page 182). The cannon ball that killed him is fixed on his memorial.

• **Parking** Bedford Street; Church Street; Woburn Street (all car parks) • **Early closing** Tuesday • **Market day** Thursday • **Event** Festival (July) • **Information** TEL. Ampthill 40205 • **AA 24 hour service** TEL. Bedford 218888.

Hexton HERTFORDSHIRE

10 miles south-east of Ampthill (PAGE 155 Cb)

So swiftly does the traffic move along the road towards Hitchin that it is quite easy to miss Hexton. Look out for a curiously ornate signpost, where the village's main street branches off. Closer inspection reveals the signpost to be a pump presented 'for the use of Hexton villagers' in 1846 and cunningly converted to its present use at a later date. One side of the main street is bordered by a rose-red brick wall, which shelters fruit trees growing on its garden side and encloses the grounds of the manor house. The other side of the street, and much of the rest of the village, consists of big, comfortable, mock-Tudor estate cottages, with gardens surrounded by trim hedges.

The Church of St Faith is endearing. Its tower presents a big, bold, battlemented front to the road, but a glance behind reveals that it is a propped-up shell; the back wall fell down after eight weeks of severe frost and snow in 1947. A good deal of the church is medieval, including the angel roof, but the general appearance is of the early 19th century, when considerable renovations took place. The raised pew for the occupants of the manor house and the double-decker pulpit belong to this period. A stone in the churchyard commemorates John Elliot, the parish clerk and village blacksmith who died in 1795. His epitaph, which is considerably worn, reads:

My sledge and hammer lie reclined,
My bellows, too, have lost their wind,
My fire's extinct, my forge decayed,
And in the dust my vice is laid,
My coal is spent, my iron's gone.
My nails are drove, my work is done.
My rusted corpse is here at rest.
My soul, smoak-like, soars to be blest.

The real charm of the village is its setting, under the glorious Barton Hills, which are part of the Chilterns. Cloud patterns chase each other across great sweeps of wheat, like huge ski runs curving down, through and around steep woods of tall beeches. One of the woods partly hides the mighty ramparts of Ravensburgh Castle, an Iron Age hill-fort, whose still impressive earthworks enclose some 22 acres.

Pirton HERTFORDSHIRE

14 miles south-east of Ampthill (PAGE 155 Cb)

Long ago, this was a fortified village owing allegiance to – and claiming protection from – a Norman knight named Ralph de Limesi, who built a timber castle here, quite possibly on the site of prehistoric ramparts. The knight is forgotten, but the village thrived upon the broad, beech-clad bosom of the Chilterns, as is apparent from the wide range of buildings, ancient, old, and those of yesterday all happily co-existing. About the green there are black-and-white timbered cottages, others decked out in colour-washed plaster, Victorian houses in mustard brick with darker, ornamental bands, and modern buildings in the dusky red brick that has recently found much favour hereabouts.

There are three pleasant pubs, the Cat and Fiddle, the Fox, and the Motte and Bailey. The name of the last is a reference to the remnants of the Norman fortifications; the church is built within the bailey, or courtyard, of the castle, while the motte, or mound, on which the building stood, is a worn, grassy hummock – called Toot Hill – to the rear. A notice proclaims that it is a protected monument.

St Mary's Church, like its village, belongs to all kinds of periods from the 12th century to the 19th. It has the jaunty little spike on top of the tower that is characteristic of many Hertfordshire churches, and between the church and the motte there are the remains of the castle's moat, still full of water. There is a pretty pair of cottages by the gate, one pink and white, the other black and white; and round the corner there is a willow-hung pond full of ducks.

Large, prosperous-looking farms are a special feature of Pirton, and all are of considerable age. Rectory Farm, built of massive stone blocks, is particularly attractive, with tall brick chimneys and vast, accompanying tithe barns. Hammonds Farm makes a fine contrast in old brick and timber framing. Away to the south at the edge of a wood, there is the lovely, late-Elizabethan manor of High Down. It belonged to the Docwra family, one of whom – Jane, who died in 1645 – has a monument in the church. The ghost of a headless horseman, a Cavalier named Goring, is said to ride around Midsummer's Day from High Down to Hitchin. During the Civil War he hid at High Down, but he was caught and beheaded by the Roundheads.

Stevington BEDFORDSHIRE

14 miles north of Ampthill (PAGE 155 Ba)

'Now I saw in my dream that the highway up which Christian was to go was fenced on either side with a wall, and that wall is called Salvation. Up this way therefore did burdened Christian run, but not without great difficulty, because of the load on his back. He ran thus till he came at a place somewhat ascending, and upon that place stood a cross, and a little below in the bottom, a sepulchre . . .' All the things that John Bunyan wrote about in that famous passage in *Pilgrim's Progress* can still be seen at Stevington.

The ancient cross stands by some limestone cottages and in these prosaic days sometimes carries announcements of the Cricket Club's Wine and Cheese evenings. The sepulchre is not really a sepulchre – that was poetic licence on Bunyan's part – but a holy well or spring that was a place of pilgrimage for those suffering from eye diseases in the Middle Ages.

Its cold, clear waters still bubble forth from a dark hole at the foot of the limestone outcrop on which the church stands. They feed a bright little bog where the rare butterbur or bog rhubarb flourishes, under the care and protection of the Bedfordshire and Huntingdonshire Naturalists Trust. The modern successor to Bunyan's wall is a massive, buttressed thing of rough limestone. It is a wonderful wall to sit upon and look out over the meadows to shadowy arcs of woodland beyond.

There is some uneasy modern building in Stevington, but lots of bright paint and individual touches like a polished plough used as a garden ornament go far to redeem it, and many of the houses stand upon banks festooned with green willow. In their midst are some pretty cottages of old, worn stone and there is a fine stone group of Manor House, Manor Farm, Rectory and St Mary's Church.

The church, parts of which are at least 1000 years old, witnessed and survived the successive invasions of Danes, Norsemen and Normans along the Great Ouse valley. It has two chapels that have been roofless, for no particular reason, since the days of Elizabeth I, and the interior is plain and airy. There is a brass monument to Thome Salle who died in 1422, and a massive, iron-bound parish chest of about the same vintage.

The figures on the ends of the pews – two men kneeling and drinking from a bowl, another writing, and assorted weird animals – still raise a grin, 600 years after they were carved. A man with the curious name of Nisephros Betts, who died in 1713, is buried in the churchyard.

An 18th-century post mill, the only complete windmill in Bedfordshire, still points its arms at the eastern sky.

WINSLOW

BUCKINGHAMSHIRE

10 miles north of Aylesbury (PAGE 155 Ab)

Sir Christopher Wren (1632 – 1723) was the chief designer of stately Winslow Hall, the jewel of this tiny market town. It is the only country house of Wren's not to have been 'improved' over the years, and it retains its dignified, red-brick front, high narrow windows, and four tall chimneys in line.

The hall was built between 1698 and 1702 as a manor house for Sir William Lowndes, Secretary of the Treasury to William III. The tree-studded grounds were laid out by the king's gardeners, and the royal carpenter and joiner did all the woodwork and panelling in the house.

For more than 230 years the hall remained a private home. Then, during the Second World War, it became the headquarters of a Royal Air Force bomber group. Today it is once again privately owned. Rising majestically from behind low creeper-clad walls, Winslow Hall is open to the public from the beginning of July until the middle of September. It contains early 18th-century English furniture and several outstanding examples of Chinese art – particularly of the Tang dynasty (AD 618 – 906). Among the magnificent rooms on show are the oak-panelled Morning Room and a bedroom – the ornately decorated Painted Room.

Life in Winslow revolves around its small, attractive Market Square, which has two charming old-world pubs – The George and The Bell. Built in the 18th century, The George has an ornate wrought-iron balcony which once graced a local private house.

Many of the town's red-brick houses are Victorian, and they lend an air of solidity and well-being. The broad and busy High Street runs through the middle of Winslow, and has the parish church of St Laurence at one end. Built mainly in the 14th century, the church has a richly carved Jacobean pulpit and some 15th-century wall paintings showing the murder of Archbishop Becket at Canterbury in 1170.

The High Street is surrounded by a warren of narrow, twisting lanes lined with timbered houses and thatched and red-roofed cottages. In one of these lanes, Bell Alley, is a tiny, 17th-century Baptist chapel called Keach's Meeting House. It was founded in 1695 by a Baptist preacher named Keach, who upset the London Baptist Association by introducing community hymn singing. The association thought that the idea of people standing up and raising their voices – even in praise of God – was unseemly.

• **Parking** Market Square; Greyhound Lane (both car parks) • **Early closing** Thursday • **Market days** Monday, Thursday • **Event** Winslow Show (August) • **AA 24 hour service** TEL. Luton 419549.

Aston Abbotts BUCKINGHAMSHIRE

10 miles south-east of Winslow (PAGE 155 Ab/c)

Aston Abbotts was a seat of government during the Second World War. Dr Eduard Beneš, former President of Czechoslovakia and leader of its government-in-exile, found refuge in this village deep in the green and rolling Buckinghamshire countryside.

Here, and in neighbouring Wingrave, he and his fellow exiles stayed for most of the war. Finally, in 1945, they returned home to establish a government which Beneš led until 1948.

Just outside Aston Abbotts, a bus-shelter at the Wingrave crossroads bears testimony to the warm relations that grew between the Czech exiles and their English hosts. The shelter was a parting gift from Dr Beneš himself, for the comfort of the villagers he used to see waiting in all weathers for a bus.

His home in those years was The Abbey, which has a fine tree-lined drive, wrought-iron gates and a thatched white lodge overlooking the spacious, well-shaded village green. The house stands on the site of a country retreat of the Abbots of St Albans, and the present, mostly 19th-century mansion probably incorporates some of the original building. Its grounds go down to a lake which has two small islands and was once part of a moat.

The 19th-century navigator and discoverer of the magnetic pole, Rear-Admiral Sir James Clark Ross, once lived at The Abbey and lies buried in the village churchyard. He named the two lake islands Erebus and Terror, after the two ships he took on a voyage of exploration to the Antarctic between 1839 and 1843.

From the green, the Wingrave road leads past 19th-century brick cottages to a long row of timber-framed buildings that includes the general stores and the thatched Royal Oak Inn. A gated road leads from the south-west corner of the green past The Abbey's grounds to Line's Hill, from which there are fine views of the Vale of Aylesbury and the Chiltern Hills beyond. This is also the best point from which to see the outlines of the lost medieval village of Burston, in a field immediately below. Burston flourished until the early 16th century, when the villagers were summarily evicted and the houses demolished by the lord of the manor. He had decided to raise sheep on land which the villagers had always cultivated in common. The land has probably never been ploughed since then, so the foundations of houses and walls are clearly visible as humps in the ground – especially when the sun is low. The Science Museum in London has a model of the Burston remains, to show how oblique lighting can reveal sites of archaeological interest.

Weedon BUCKINGHAMSHIRE

7 miles south of Winslow (PAGE 155 Ac)

The view south from Weedon's Methodist church, over sheep-filled fields to the Vale of Aylesbury, is like looking into a pastoral painting of the 18th century. On the far horizon rise the rolling Chiltern Hills. Immediately to the east the timber-framed Chestnuts Farmhouse stands among trees. Colourful cottage gardens lie just below the churchyard to the west and the red-brick 19th-century church itself rises attractively on the slope behind.

Weedon, which won the county's Best Kept Village award in 1976, stands on a rise on the edge of the Vale of Aylesbury. Its centre, just below the Methodist church – Weedon has never had an Anglican church – is a crossroads with a green in the middle. This tiny green is overlooked by the Five Elms Inn and a cottage called The Royal George, both of which, in common with many of the cottages and farmhouses here, are thatched and have timber frames with the brick infilling known as herringbone nogging.

East of the crossroads, on rising ground, is the part of the village called East End, where Lambsquay House has a fine gabled brick windowhead and East Gate House has exceptionally good herringbone nogging. Set back from the road is the imposing late 18th-century Weedon Lodge.

One of the oldest houses is the 17th-century Manor Farmhouse in the High Street, which runs north of the crossroads. The street also passes Tumbling Acre and the former Wheatsheaf pub – both thatched and timber-framed – and The Lilies.

This red-brick mansion was built in 1870 on the site of the home of Lord Nugent, a 19th-century antiquarian. The superb grounds, planted with fine spreading cedar trees, still have Lord Nugent's 'Circle of Friends'. This is a circle of stone seats, each dedicated to one of his distinguished friends, who included the novelist Charles Dickens, and W. Harrison Ainsworth, author of *The Tower of London*. Sadly, the stone believed to have been dedicated to Dickens has been stolen.

Opposite the entrance to The Lilies, a footpath leads across the fields to Hardwick – a mile north-west – where Weedon's Anglican villagers have to go for their church. Noteworthy in Hardwick, which spreads out around two large triangular greens, are Hardwicke Place, parts of which may date from the

Lambsquay House

CRESTED FRIENDS

No truly English village is complete without ducks and a duck pond – and the ducks in Weedon are rather special. By a quirk of nature, what were ordinary mallards have, in generations of inbreeding, developed jaunty crests. The ducks are so tame they often sit contentedly on the doorsteps of nearby cottages. Two of Weedon's finest private houses are Lambsquay House and Tumbling Acre.

Duck pond

Tumbling Acre

General view of Hardwick from Weedon

St Mary's Cottage, Hardwick

Sir Robert Lee Memorial, Hardwick

A VILLAGE LINK WITH GENERAL ROBERT E. LEE

The tranquil parish church of St Mary's at Hardwick, across the fields from Weedon, may seem remote in time and distance from the battlefields of the American Civil War. But an ancestor of the Southern general Robert E. Lee is commemorated by a monument. He was Sir Robert Lee, who died in 1616. His wife and 14 children are commemorated, too. By the church is St Mary's Cottage.

16th century, although the front is 18th century; the early 17th-century Manor Farm House; and the delightful St Mary's Cottage beside the church. The Church of St Mary has a Saxon north wall in its nave.

A large tomb under the south side of the church tower is said to contain the bodies of 247 soldiers of the British Civil War – Royalists and Parliamentarians alike. They were found in a communal grave near the site of a Civil War skirmish at Holman's Bridge, near Aylesbury, and reburied here in the 19th century by Lord Nugent. Recent scholarship, however, has concluded that they could equally well be victims of the plague or even of an 8th-century tribal skirmish.

Whitchurch BUCKINGHAMSHIRE

6 miles south-east of Winslow (PAGE 155 Ab)

Whitchurch, with its many outstanding old buildings and rural tranquillity, provided the inspiration behind a film classic, *Mrs Miniver*. A patriotic portrayal of English middle-class country life at the beginning of the Second World War, the film became one of the war's great box-office successes, winning an Oscar award for itself and its star, Greer Garson. The collection of sketches, from which the story of the film was taken, was written by the poet and novelist Jan Struther, who grew up in Whitchurch and based her sketches on the village life around her.

Jan Struther and her family – her real name was Joyce Anstruther – had the good fortune to live in one of the village's most outstanding houses. This is the 15th-century Priory, probably the oldest building in Whitchurch. The Priory – which was a courthouse rather than a priory, and is now a hotel – still stands prominently in the High Street, built, like many of the village's old houses, of timber, brick and stone. Near by in the street are a number of other fine houses, including the timber-framed cottage at No. 28; and the early 17th-century Kempson House – one of the large village's two manor houses. Behind a high hedge, near by, is The Old House, parts of which probably date from the 15th century, although the fine front was greatly extended in the 1950s.

Opposite The Old House is Market Hill, and halfway up the hill, Castle Lane forks off to run past a mound which is all that now remains of the 11th-century Bolebec Castle, near which the village grew.

Both Market Hill and Castle Lane are lined with a number of delightful thatched cottages and houses. The Fairings, in Castle Lane, has a particularly fine gabled brick doorhead.

At the top of the slope, Market Hill joins the Oving Road, and near by stands Bolebec House, home of the 20th-century artist Rex Whistler, who painted the murals in the restaurant of the Tate Gallery in London. The 17th-century Whitchurch House, which was also once a home of Jan Struther's family, stands across the street. Its fine front, with an imposing coat of arms over the door, is 18th century.

The Church of St John the Evangelist, in whose graveyard Jan Struther is buried under her married name of Jan Plachzek, has a memorial to John Westcar, a local farmer who died in 1833. Westcar took advantage of the Grand Union Canal, which ends at Aylesbury 5 miles south, to ship his livestock directly to Smithfield Market in London. He also founded the Smithfield Cattle and Sheep Society and won several prizes at the Smithfield Shows. His memorial shows him with one of his prize oxen and some sheep.

His home was the imposing Creslow Manor, at the end of a private road a mile north-east of Whitchurch. It is the oldest inhabited manor house in Buckinghamshire, dating in part from the 14th century and added to in the mid-17th by Cornelius Holland, one of the men who signed Charles I's death warrant. Its farm buildings include the remains of a church probably built by the Knights Templar.

DIALLING TIME AT THE TOP OF THE HILL

Walkers in Market Hill, Whitchurch, almost rub shoulders with the cottages lining the steep and winding street where each May a market and fair is held. At the top, Whitchurch House has a neatly kept sundial on its roughcast walls. The stone and timbered front of The Old House, near the church, has recently been restored. The new thatch on a snug cottage awaits a final trim.

Market Hill

Sundial, Whitchurch House

Untrimmed thatched cottage

The Old House

MAP 15

MOTORWAY RETREATS AND THE BLACKWATER ESTUARY

Hertfordshire and Essex both have suburban London nibbling at their borders, yet both still fight a successful rearguard action to retain their rural character. Off the motorway, among the rolling Hertfordshire and north Essex wheat fields, there are small towns, river ports and villages, many of whose buildings, crafts and traditions are as old as those of London.

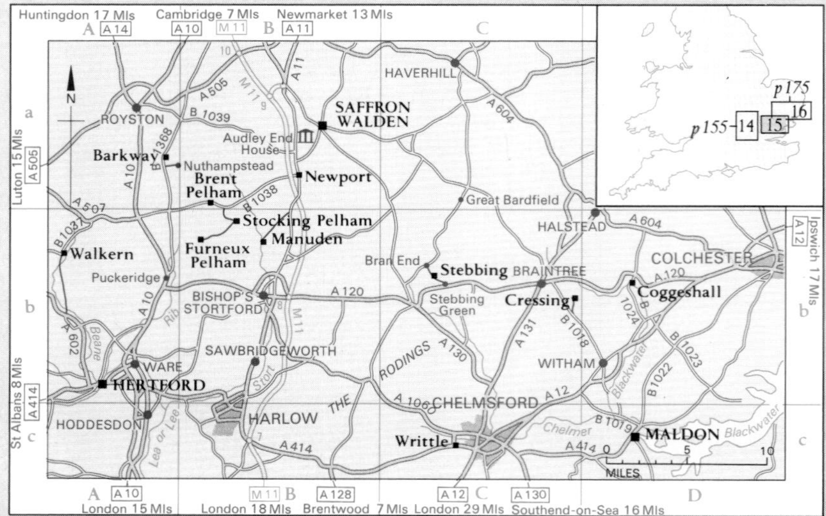

MAP 15: NEIGHBOURING AREAS – MAPS 14 AND 16

HERTFORD Barkway The Pelhams Walkern
MALDON Coggeshall Cressing Writtle
SAFFRON WALDEN Manuden Newport Stebbing

HERTFORD

HERTFORDSHIRE

22 miles north of London (PAGE 164 Ab)

For more than 900 years the castle at the heart of this pleasant county town has been in constant use. It has served as a fortress, royal palace, hunting lodge, prison, family home – and now council offices.

The site was originally fortified in AD 911 by King Edward the Elder to defend the northern approaches to London against the Danes. A stone castle was built by the Normans, and the impressive gatehouse was added in the 15th century by Edward IV. Elizabeth I frequently stayed in the castle as a child, but most of the old buildings were demolished in 1609, during the reign of James I, as they had fallen into decay. Now only the gatehouse – expanded in the 18th century – is intact, and is used for council offices.

The River Lea cuts through the trimly kept grounds, past a tree-covered mound – this is all that remains of the Norman fortress – and beyond a massive 12th-century wall and two 20th-century round towers. The grounds are open to the public, and the Gatehouse (now known as 'the castle') is open in the afternoon on the first Sunday of the month, May to September.

Until about 1850 the town could not grow, because of the surrounding cornfields, so many of the buildings had extra storeys added – which accounts in part for the higgledy-piggledy rooftops that are a feature of Hertford. Two elegant and comparatively modern squares, Salisbury Square and Parliament Square, house some of its most fascinating buildings.

In Salisbury Square is the oak-timbered White Hart inn, which has been so named for the past 350 years. Close by the square is the old Lombard House (now the Hertford Club), former home of Sir Henry Chauncy (1632 – 1719), the local historian and magistrate. In 1712 he was involved in the last witchcraft trial held in England (see Walkern, page 168).

Fore Street contains the late 16th-century Salisbury Arms Hotel, built around a courtyard. It faces a line of shops which have flamboyant displays of the decorative plasterwork known as pargeting. Dating from the 17th century, they show trailing vines and enormous clusters of flowers. Farther on is Barclays Bank, formerly a private house and the birthplace of Samuel Stone, who in 1636 founded Hartford, Connecticut, which, despite the difference in spelling, is named after his home town.

The town's most ancient house, now an antiques shop, is the Old Verger's House in nearby St Andrew's Street. The timber-framed building dates from about 1450, and was restored in 1970. On its first-floor wall is a link extinguisher (a link was a pitch torch used by pedestrians to light their way at night); and farther along the wall is a plaque issued in 1720 by the Royal Exchange Assurance Company showing that they had insured the building against fire.

Hertford's oldest religious building is the Friends' Meeting House in Railway Street – the oldest purpose-built Quaker meeting house. It has been in regular use since 1670. Both George Fox (1624 – 91), founder of Quakerism, and William Penn (1644 – 1718), who established the American state of Pennsylvania in 1682, visited and worshipped there.

The town has two Victorian churches: Hertford St Andrew, the bulk of which was built in nine months in 1870, while the tower was added five years later; and All Saints, built in the 1890s. All Saints has an avenue of chestnut trees in its churchyard, which were probably planted in the late 17th century.

Four rivers flow into Hertford – the Mimram, the Beane, the Rib and the Lea – and converge near its centre. The Lea once formed the boundary between Saxon and Danish England.

• **Parking** Gascoyne Way; St Andrew's Street; Old London Road; Railway Street (all car parks) • **Early closing** Thursday • **Market days** Monday and Thursday (cattle); Saturday • **Events** County Day (May); Horse Show (August); Carnival (September) • **Information** TEL. Bishop's Stortford 55261 ext. 487 • **AA 24 hour service** TEL. Hatfield 62852.

Barkway HERTFORDSHIRE

18 miles north of Hertford (PAGE 164 Aa)

Conservation is the theme at Barkway, whose keynote is at once set at the northern end of the High Street by a group that almost defines conservation. There is a late 17th-century cottage, a much brightened 18th-century pub, a late medieval house restored by the Hertfordshire Preservation Trust in 1978, an early enamel sign advertising petrol from the pump and,

HARKING BACK AT BARKWAY

The peace of the past lingers on in Barkway, where many periods – some fairly recent – furnish reminders ranging from picturesque cottages to an early enamel petrol-pump sign. In coaching days, the village was a regular stop on the Ware to Cambridge road, and a milestone gives the distances to both. At the Clockhouse Cottage, time appears to stand still – at 10.24.

Barkway's pond flanked by Manor Farm and the churchyard

Clockhouse Cottage

Early petrol sign

Village milestone

occasionally, a well-polished vintage tractor. These obviously represent labours of love, and similar things may be found at intervals down the long, lazy 'S' of the lawn-verged main street.

A few years ago, there were still some cottages of unconserved shabbiness, now all their pargeted plaster is of biscuit-like crispness; and their thatch, mostly reed, is a model to the craft.

The country round about is great, rolling billows of cornland that turns a creamy-brown – because of the chalk – when ploughed. There are reefs and clumps of chestnut and beech which, at Barkway's northern approach, become a grand avenue separating two large estates – Newsells Park, open and sweeping, and Cokenach, buried in secret woods. Long, and mostly spread out beside a single street, the village grew and prospered as a handy stopping-place between Ware and Cambridge.

The names of the pubs are horsey, the Tally Ho! and the Chaise and Pair, and at the southern end there is Clockhouse Cottage, with its clock frozen at 10.24, and a small cartwheel sunk into the wall as a frame to hold in place the panes of a window. Next door is Turnpike Cottage, and all are reminders of the village's importance to traffic on the old road. So, too, is the milestone which, worn though it is, still shows the inscription London 36, Ware 14, Cambridge 16, and the crescent-moon badge of Trinity College, Cambridge. It was erected in 1728 under the terms of wills left much earlier by two Fellows of Trinity named Hare and Mouse.

There are only three side turnings off the High Street. One is Burr's Lane, which leads to a small housing estate, stables and a footpath through fields to Nuthampstead where, after a lengthy and bitter wrangle, the third London airport was never built. Another is Church Lane where some sturdy walls of dark flint lead to an attractive grouping of pond, church and Jacobean Manor Farm, whose mullioned windows and fine ornamental gables are now partly obscured from view by the great branches of an ancient cedar tree.

The partly 13th-century Church of St Mary Magdalene is big and dim and quiet, with the thumping tick of the tower clock like a heartbeat, felt rather than heard. Among its many monuments is one by Rysbrack, the best-known sculptor of his day, to Admiral Sir John Jennings, who died at his house in Newsells Park in 1743. He 'so happily improved the great endowments he owed to nature, that he bore the highest commands' and was Member of Parliament, Governor of Greenwich Hospital and a few other things. His bust is flanked, rather oddly considering the martial nature of his attainments, by a charming pair of cherubs.

In 1928 a peal of Grandsire triples, involving 5040 changes, was rung from the tower in 2 hours 58 minutes; the deed was only matched in 1936 by a Bob Major, also of 5040 changes, taking 3 hours 11 minutes. No mean feats, as connoisseurs of campanology will probably confirm.

The Pelhams HERTFORDSHIRE

About 15 miles north-east of Hertford (PAGE 164 Ba/b)

The three villages of Brent, Stocking and Furneux Pelham make a little triangular constellation upon the great backdrop of the rolling Hertfordshire wheatlands. They are connected by footpaths, the best way to come to them, and all should be visited, since despite their closeness in geography and name, each is a complete and endearing individual.

Deeply sunken lanes lead up to Brent Pelham, past a pub called The Black Horse, whose sign depicts the animal with a rider in pink, for this is hunting country. Next door is a pretty quadrangle of cottages in the Hertfordshire mixture of thatch, plaster and timber cladding, and, on top of the hill, as pic-

VILLAGE VICE *A crime wave of up to six persons – but no more – could be accommodated by Brent Pelham's stocks and whipping post.*

Furneux Pelham church

FLYING HIGH

Angels soar at Furneux Pelham – though confined within the 13th-century Church of St Mary the Virgin. These happy-faced, brilliantly clad figures spread their wings beneath the roof beams while holding their musical instruments or heraldic shields. Outside, on the church tower, is a clock bearing a Father Time figure and the edict: 'Time Flies, Mind Your Business.' The village has many unusual features, including a huge topiary chicken and its own small brewery. The popular local ale can be tasted by regulars and visitors alike at The Star, The Brewery Tap and other pubs in the area.

Angels soar roof-high

turesquely English a group as anyone could wish.

There is a post office and general store that sells everything from paraffin to champagne, cottages with deep straw thatch, and a Jacobean manor house with aristocratic hunters grazing in its paddocks. But for most people, it is the little Church of St Mary that is the chief attraction, since it is there that the last dragon-slayer in England – so they say – is buried.

His name was Piers Shonks, and shortly after the Norman Conquest he speared a dragon that had for long been plaguing the neighbourhood. It seems, however, that the creature was a special pet of the Devil who, much aggrieved, demanded the warrior's body and soul in reparation, 'whether you are buried within church or without'. 'Not so,' quoth Piers stoutly, 'for my soul is God's, and as for my body, you shall not have that either, since it will be buried neither inside nor outside the church.'

Sure enough, on his deathbed in 1086, he drew a bow in his house, a reputed mile from Brent Pelham, and commanded he should be interred wherever the arrow fell. It flitted through the church window and struck the opposite wall, within whose thickness his tomb may be seen to this day. Stretching the imagination a little, the slab does indeed depict an impaled dragon, though prosaic scholars have said that it shows nothing but somewhat unusual symbols of salvation. The inscription is quite definite, however:

> *'Shonks one serpent kills, t'other defies*
> *And in this wall as in a fortress lies.'*

The story may be doubtful, but surely no one could have invented a name like Piers Shonks?

His hunting tradition is maintained in season when the Puckeridge meets outside the church and the green is crammed with horses, hounds and pretty girls in mud-splashed boots. Also outside the church is a whipping post with irons to suit the wrists of malefactors of three different sizes, and stocks to take 3 pairs of feet. Altogether a village of robust pursuits.

Stocking Pelham lies to the south-east, across the billowing countryside given shape and dimension by dark, curving bands of woods. It is the smallest of the three villages – really not much more than a little flint church with a wooden belfry, and a grouping of farm buildings about a neat green.

Furneux Pelham (pronounced 'Furnix' or 'Furnex', as it was sometimes spelt) is the largest, and is named after the de Furneux family who owned all three villages in the 12th century. Of more widespread fame than any Norman, however, is the small, unobtrusive brewery in Furneux Pelham, whose products may be sampled at a little pub opposite called The Brewery Tap. But the brewery modestly hides itself away; and much more noticeable is the great and beautiful Elizabethan Hall, tucked behind crags of shaven yew, with peacocks posed on the ornamented gable ends, uttering their haunting, arrogant screams.

There is something exuberant and pleasantly humorous about Furneux Pelham. It has some wonderful cottages, pargeted, pink-washed and deep-thatched. One of them is almost overwhelmed by a weathercock on its roof that adorned the church spire until it fell off some years ago.

The Church of St Mary the Virgin is mostly of the late 15th century and the interior is glorious. The roof beams are supported by golden-haired, cheerful-faced angels, sumptuously clad in scarlet, blue and gold and carrying musical instruments or shields bearing coats of arms. All the paintwork in the church was renewed between 1963 and 1964. Until then, nobody had realised that the figures holding up the roof were meant to be angels because their wings had been removed. It was during the restoration that the wings were added. On the tower's exterior is a clock with the gilded figure of Father Time.

Walkern HERTFORDSHIRE

10 miles north of Hertford (PAGE 164 Ab)

In the Middle Ages, when Boxbury was a village instead of the few slight hummocks that it is now, its people began to build a church, but each night their carefully laid stones whizzed off to reassemble themselves on a site by the River Beane. It was, of course, the work of the Devil, who was heard to encourage the movement of the building materials with the cry 'Walk on, walk on!' But, this being Hertfordshire, what he said was 'Walk ern!' Thus, when the villagers thought it prudent to adopt the Devil's choice of site, the new settlement already had a name.

But the Devil had not finished with Walkern, if the trial in 1711 of Jane Wenham, the last person to be condemned to death for witchcraft in England, is any evidence. Jane was a middle-aged woman who lived in a hovel, now long vanished, in Church End. She was accused, among other things, of bewitching sheep – and a farm labourer – to death, flying about, appearing in the guise of a cat, and setting demons onto a servant girl.

The terrible witch mania that had gripped eastern England in the previous century was still within living memory, and the village well knew how an interrogation should be conducted. Jane was pricked with needles and ducked in the river, after which she was ready to confess to anything and was sent for trial in Hertford.

Mr Justice Powell, a man of the dawning Age of Reason, crisply told the jury that, so far as he was aware, there was no law against flying and directed them to dismiss the case. They insisted on finding her guilty, however, and the judge had no option but to sentence her to death. Nevertheless, he managed to obtain a stay of execution, and in 1712 Jane received a pardon from Queen Anne. Too terrified to go home, she was given a cottage at Hertingfordbury by a kindly squire, and there she spent the remainder of her life. Nowadays, Walkern is quite proud of Jane, and even put on a play about her a few years ago.

As is not unusual in this part of Hertfordshire, the village consists mostly of a single street; in this instance, a street something over a mile long. The introductions at either end are remarkably attractive – from the north, the Georgian Old Rectory, with the branches of a grave and dignified cedar caressing its pink-washed walls; and from the south, a water mill dating from the 1880s, admirably converted into flats. The mill race has become a feature of the garden.

It would be a lot to ask that the intervening mile should be of the same perfection, but in fact, among the garages and nondescript Victorian and modern, there are some fine 17th and 18th-century houses. The star is Manor Farm, a large Georgian building, with a vast late 17th-century dovecote beside it. The dovecote is patterned in red and blue brick, and daylight is admitted to the interior through a glass cupola.

The prettiest part is Church End, almost a separate village behind the Old Rectory. It is a grouping of a farm and some pleasant houses beside a shallow, tree-draped ford. Over all, the church clock strikes out the hours and the quarters with sweetly unusual chimes. St Mary's itself is an encyclopaedia of English ecclesiastical architecture. The walls of the nave are Saxon (so predating the Devil's work), other parts are early Norman, and from then until the 15th century, each generation added something; the chapel, originally a private family pew, is a late thought by the Victorians. There is a Saxon crucifix that portrays Christ robed and with a moustache, and a marble effigy of a knight recumbent in an uncomfortable cross-legged sprawl.

No one knows who he is, but he is thought to be one of the Lanvaleis, the Norman lords of the manor. After them came the Humbarstons, and their monuments are here too, spanning the years from the 15th century to the reign of Charles I.

MALDON

ESSEX

10 miles east of Chelmsford (PAGE 164 Dc)

Tall-masted sailing barges moored at Hythe Quay bear witness to Maldon's maritime past and present. The Hythe is Saxon for 'wharf', and was a port and landing-place on the River Blackwater before the Normans came. Its Maritime Centre has graphic displays and information about the barges, the port and the river. Behind The Hythe stands the Church of St Mary, its 17th-century tower topped by a tiny timber turret and spire, added in 1740. Farther along the reach, boat-building yards flourish.

Across from St Mary's, the High Street stretches up to the 13th-century Church of All Saints, which has the only triangular church tower in England. Near by is the Moot Hall, built about 1440 by the MP for the borough, Sir Robert D'Arcy, as his town house. In 1576 it became the local council headquarters, and the Council Chamber and Old Courthouse are preserved.

A pillared balcony over the pavement was added in the 19th century, and the building is still used for some meetings. Just below it is St Peter's Tower – all that remains of a church that collapsed in the 1660s – and the brick library built onto it by a local cleric, Dr Thomas Plume, later that century. He was Archdeacon of Rochester when he died in 1704 and left his vast library and paintings to Maldon.

Immediately below the Plume Library is Maldon Museum, which has mementoes of the town's most unusual native son, Edward Bright. Born in 1721, Bright grew to weigh almost 42 stones and was the heaviest man then known to have lived in Britain (the heaviest ever was a Scot, William Campbell, 1856 – 78, who weighed 53½ stones). Bright died at 29 and is buried in a vault at All Saints. The parish burial register notes that he was 'comely in his person, affable in his temper, a tender father and valuable friend'.

• **Parking** White Horse Lane; Butt Lane; Marine Parade (all car parks) • **Early closing** Wednesday • **Market days** Thursday, Saturday • **Event** Barge match (June or July) • **Information** TEL. Maldon 56503 • **AA 24 hour service** TEL. Chelmsford 261711.

Barges moored in Maldon harbour

Church of All Saints

BARGES ALONG THE BLACKWATER

Sailing barges with tall masts and furled sails line the quay in Maldon harbour on the Blackwater estuary. Once they were commercial vessels on regular hauls to London and beyond. Now they give youngsters adventure holidays. Maldon has been a port since Saxon times. It is a pleasant town, of long memories, but living much in the present, with a thriving boat-building industry. The church behind the quay is St Mary's. Another church, the 13th-century All Saints in the High Street, has England's only triangular church tower – and the tomb of Edward Bright, who weighed 42 stones.

Coggeshall ESSEX

11 miles north of Maldon (PAGE 164 Db)

One of England's finest half-timbered buildings, the house in West Street called Paycocke's is probably more famous than Coggeshall itself, but visitors find much else to admire in this large village. Wool and lace-making gave Coggeshall its prosperity in medieval times, and wool merchant John Paycocke built his house there early in the 16th century. It was first mentioned in 1505, when John Paycocke willed it to his son Thomas, whose initials together with those of his wife, Margaret Herrold, can still be seen carved on a breast beam.

The house has had a chequered history, passing from the Paycockes in 1584 to a series of owners over the next three centuries. It was allowed to deteriorate so badly that in 1890 it was sold for demolition. But it was saved from this sad fate by a Coggeshall antiquary, Mr G. F. Beaumont, who managed to cancel the sale. In 1904 it was bought by Edward Noel – later Lord Noel-Buxton – and restored to plans approved by the architect Sir Edwin Lutyens. It is now owned by the National Trust and is open to the public three days a week. Heavily beamed and panelled, with elaborate woodcarvings, the house contains a collection of period furniture.

Paycocke's is one of many old buildings in the village, including the 15th-century Woolpack, which has been an inn since the 17th century, and the 12th-century Grange Hill barn, used by monks who introduced sheep into the region and so started the wool trade upon which Coggeshall's prosperity was built.

Coggeshall Abbey was founded in 1140 by King Stephen, then taken over by Cistercian monks, who learnt the art of brick-making from sister houses on the Continent and thus re-established brick manufacture in England for the first time since the departure of the Romans. The arches of Long Bridge, in Bridge Street, are made of abbey bricks, and it is now claimed to be the oldest brick bridge in the country.

On the south side of the bridge is Monkwell, the lower portion of which served as the abbey brewery. Its brick-lined well is still there, in the garden. The house later became a silk works, and then the home of a French immigrant named Drago who introduced lace-making to Coggeshall early in the 19th century. The industry prospered until the First World War and Coggeshall lace is still made.

Coggeshall's Church of St Peter ad Vincula stands on the site of a Norman building and was rebuilt in the 15th century. Much of the building was destroyed by a lone German bomb during the Second World War; repair work took six years to complete. Brasses of the Paycocke family survived, and in the south chapel is a monument to Mary Honywood who died in 1620 and left no fewer than 367 descendants.

The early Georgian Congregational church in Queen Street was opened about 1715. There are other

Tudor house from Cistercian abbey

Coggeshall water mill

Paycocke's carved tapestry

Coggeshall reflections

MEDIEVAL IMAGES AND THE WONDER OF WOOL

Coggeshall's abbey church disappeared at the Reformation, but some of its outbuildings remain – its tithe barn, for example, and many of the abbey's bricks were incorporated into a Tudor house. The decoration on Paycocke's in West Street shows what style a late-medieval wool merchant could afford, while the water mill, of similar vintage, completes a perfect Essex idyll.

attractive Georgian and later buildings in East Street, which follows the line of the Roman Stane Street; and round the corner in Stoneham Street is the hexagonal weatherboarded Clock Tower, which was built in 1787 and was then restored a century later.

Cressing ESSEX

9 miles north-west of Maldon (PAGE 164 Cb)

The village is probably known best for the huge, ancient barns in the grounds of Cressing Temple, part of a farmhouse on the road towards Witham. This land once belonged to the Knights Templar. When their order was outlawed in 1312 – on the grounds of heresy, blasphemy and immoral practices – the place was handed to the Knights Hospitaller.

Evidence of the Hospitallers' vast wealth is displayed in the magnificence of the great barns. The huge-aisled barley barn is weatherboarded and 120 ft long; the narrower, 140 ft long wheat barn has brick infilling around its massive timbers.

For many years the barns were thought to be 14th or 15th century, but radiocarbon dating has proved that timber in the barley barn is more than 800 years old, and that in the wheat barn about 700.

In 1623 a third barn was added, and this one is whitewashed. Although the barns are on private ground, admission is obtained by arrangement with the farm manager.

But Cressing has more than its barns to be proud of – it has a hero, Sir Henry Evelyn Wood, whose exploits in numerous wars were the stuff that Victorian imperialism was made of. Born in 1838, Wood joined the navy as a midshipman at the age of 14 and served on HMS *Queen* during the Crimean War. Despite being wounded while with a landing party, Wood decided that fighting on land was more to his liking than a life at sea and in 1855 he transferred to the army. As a lieutenant with the 17th Lancers he was mentioned in dispatches many times for his gallantry and zeal during the Indian Mutiny, and in 1860 received the supreme award, the Victoria Cross, for defeating, the year before, a band of some 80 rebels in dense jungle with a force of just 11 men.

During the Zulu Wars, Wood distinguished himself again when a column he was leading was attacked by the Zulu army. The battle raged for 5½ hours and, although outnumbered by 12 to 1, Wood's men put the Zulus to flight. In 1879 Wood's commander, Sir Garnet Wolseley, wrote of his 'genius for war' – a genius that was to serve him well during the Egyptian campaign of 1882 when he commanded a brigade and stayed on to become the first British Sirdar (commander-in-chief) of the Egyptian army.

In 1903 Sir Henry Evelyn Wood, VC, CM, GCB, GCMG, became Field-Marshal. He died in 1919 and has a fittingly impressive memorial in Cressing's All Saints' Church. All Saints stands on a site where there was once a pre-Roman tribal settlement and then a Saxon building. A wooden bell turret tops the small, flinty church which has a part-Norman nave, 12th-century chancel and early 15th-century roof.

The village takes its name from the watercress that provided a thriving industry until about 200 years ago. The tiny main street has houses with moulded plaster panels – called pargeting – and small front lawns open to the road.

Writtle ESSEX

12 miles west of Maldon (PAGE 164 Cc)

Rich parklands and fragments of ancient forest abound in Writtle parish, the largest in Essex. It was once a royal manor, passing from King Harold to William the Conqueror, and later became one of King John's hunting lodges. In 1204 he granted its revenues to the Hospital of the Holy Ghost in Rome. Then, in 1391 it was sold to William of Wykeham, Bishop of Winchester and founder of the school, who used it as part of his endowment of New College, Oxford.

Drivers heading up the long slope into Chelmsford will be aware of the high brick wall climbing the hill beside them. This is part of the perimeter of Hylands Park, much of which lies within the parish. At the heart of its 400 acres of woods and lakes is an early Georgian manor.

The central green of Writtle slopes gently towards its pond, which originally supplied water for traction engines. All around the green are houses of different styles, from the Tudor-timbered splendour of Aubyns, near the church, through elegant Georgian brickwork to varieties of pargeted plaster. Some of the pargeting boasts sizable relief bosses; other examples, like a pair of 1787 cottages, have simpler, incised panels.

The Church of All Saints was built around 1230, but tiles dating from Roman times are incorporated into the structure, and an earlier church stood there at the time of the Conquest.

The tower is of rough stone and rubble, with narrow red-brick buttresses and a brick parapet. Inside are medieval stone angels on the roof supports, recoloured in recent times, and decorative shields down the centre roof beam.

Parts of the building have been replaced or restored because of two local catastrophes. In 1802 a gale tore out one wall of the tower and left the bells swinging in the wind. Within a day the whole tower had collapsed, bells and all. The entire west end of the church had to be rebuilt, and stones from the wreckage were used in houses on the north of the green.

Then in 1974 a disastrous fire destroyed the chancel roof and the vestry and damaged much of the east end. Motifs on the wall above the west door, and embroidered ones in front of the altar commemorate this blaze. Outside, the large wooden cross in the churchyard was fashioned from charred chancel beams.

Down the road by St John's Green is a Marconi Research Establishment. In 1899 Guglielmo Marconi, the inventor of radio, set up his first workshop in an old silk factory in Chelmsford. Soon after, he began making transmissions from Writtle, raising his aerials on the flat land by the River Wid.

SAFFRON WALDEN

ESSEX

15 miles south of Cambridge (PAGE 164 Ba)

Although the saffron crocus is no longer grown commercially in the district, carvings of it can be seen around the town. It forms part of the coat of arms in the Town Hall portico and appears on decorations in the vast parish church of St Mary the Virgin. The bright yellow dye extracted from the golden stigma of purple crocus (*Crocus sativus*) was used to colour cloth until the end of the 18th century, when it was replaced by artificial dyes. Even so, the crocus brought prosperity to the town for some 400 years.

The crocus is also incorporated in some of the elaborate decorative plasterwork called pargeting, to be seen on a number of buildings. A particularly fine design enlivens the front of the medieval Sun Inn – now an antiques shop and bookseller's – in Church Street. It shows a legendary local hero, Tom Hickathrift, a carter of immense strength, overcoming the legendary Wisbech giant.

Running parallel to Church Street is Castle Street, which has the remains of the castle keep – all that is left of a fortress built by Geoffrey de Mandeville in the 12th century. In the grounds of this ruined castle, near the church, is the Town Museum, built in 1834. Among its exhibits is Prince Charles's xylophone.

Opposite the foot of Castle Street is the town's finest medieval building, timber-framed and built about 1500 as a malt house, but now a youth hostel. Much of its plasterwork has worn off, revealing the original window frames. In the middle of the town are the Market Square and its old Corn Exchange, built about 1850 and converted in the mid-1970s into a library and arts centre.

On the outskirts of Saffron Walden are two of its prize attractions: the largest earth maze in England, and the mansion of Audley End. The maze, of

Saffron Walden High Street

Cricket on the green

Oval window in High Street

The Sun Inn – now an antiques shop

THE TOWN THAT LIVED ON CROCUSES

The saffron crocus brought prosperity to Saffron Walden for 400 years. It was grown for the yellow dye extracted from it, which was used to colour cloth and cakes until the end of the 18th century. Saffron Walden has many buildings bearing plasterwork designs, like those on the medieval Sun Inn. Other ancient features in the town include a mysterious maze of unknown origin.

unknown date and purpose, is about 40 yds in diameter, but its path coils and twists for almost a mile on the Common. It was first documented in 1699. Audley End was built in 1603 by the first Earl of Suffolk, and its grounds were landscaped in the 1760s by Capability Brown. The 18th-century architect Robert Adam added to it later. The mansion and grounds are open in the afternoon from April to September, but closed on Mondays except Bank Holidays.

• **Parking** Common Hill; Fairycroft Road; Catons Lane; Market Square (all car parks) • **Early closing** Thursday • **Market days** Tuesday, Saturday • **Information** TEL. Saffron Walden 24282 • **AA 24 hour service** TEL. Chelmsford 261711.

Manuden ESSEX

9 miles south-west of Saffron Walden (PAGE 164 Bb)

The little River Stort and streams such as Wicken Water, which is often dry in summer, wind between some of the prettiest villages and hamlets in Essex. Walls of flint taken from the chalkland riverbeds give way to timbered and plastered houses on the arable farmlands of the boulder clay. One snug little settlement is echoed within a few miles by another.

Manuden is such a village, giving an immediate impression of whiteness – very white plaster and whitewashed brickwork. A house on the corner of Mallows Green Road combines pargeted panels of almost classical formality with white weatherboarding. But across the lane two superb barns in the farmyard of The Bury provide a contrast, with massive thatch above timber and brick. Peeping from the houses along the road and lanes are profusions of little dormer windows with tiled caps.

The Church of St Mary the Virgin has been much restored but still contains a medieval chancel screen and some interesting memorials; a 17th-century one to Sir William Waad gives a list in Latin of all the many important posts he held. Waad's family home was Battles Hall, near to a hamlet with the undignified name of Maggots End. Battles is a corruption of Bataille, the name of the manorial family who for generations used a church transept as their chapel.

Facing the churchyard gate to The Street, a sagging house with a wavy roof and similarly undulating timbers along its overhanging upper storey was built in the 14th century, then rebuilt during the reign of Elizabeth I. Farther along, Yew Tree Inn took its name from a spreading yew tree growing in its courtyard, now replaced by a neat, conically trimmed descendant. In coaching times, the original alehouse had its own wheelwright's shop, run in conjunction with a cobbler's and a bakery.

Manuden House, a Queen Anne mansion with a 19th-century stucco coating, stands on a tight bend in The Street behind impressive iron railings, with gilded owls peering down from the gates. The red brick of its equally imposing Georgian neighbour is complemented by a cheerful red stable block, detached to form a private house around a cobbled yard, with a smartly repainted clock.

Manuden Hall, across a narrow, humped bridge carrying a minor road north towards Saffron Walden, is a mixture of Tudor brickwork and restoration, including Victorian windows and a slate roof, introduced after a fire started by a drunkard in 1888.

Newport ESSEX

2 miles south-west of Saffron Walden (PAGE 164 Ba)

Lying near a motorway and bisected by the Bishop's Stortford road, Newport has always been affected by roads, as a scale of charges ('For every ass . . . ½d') by the old Toll Bridge bears witness. Yet much of the village is tucked away from the main road, looped back in charming, narrow streets, with only a glimpse of traffic at their ends.

In the 13th century, Newport had a market, mills, numerous inns for travellers, and gave work to furriers, dyers, vintners and even a goldsmith. At that time, it was held by the King of the Romans, an archaic title for King John's second son. He was heartily detested by the great landowner, Roger Bigod, who seriously damaged Newport's trade by opening a rival market at Great Chesterford, 6 miles north. But like Saffron Walden, Newport began to grow the saffron crocus and entered a long period of prosperity.

Most of Newport's splendours belong to this time. The church was developed and the humbly named Monk's Barn, in the main street, was built in the 15th century. No one should miss Monk's Barn. Composed of dark red bricks, laid in herringbone pattern, it has a crumbling oak carving under one window of the Virgin in Heaven. Far from being a barn, it was the summer holiday retreat of the monks of St Martin-le-Grand in London. By The Green is a delightful group of houses. Three late medieval buildings particularly leap to the eye – Martin's Farm, with its tall pedestal of patterned Tudor chimneys, the Old Three Tuns and the Crown House, which has wonderful plasterwork and, over the door, a hood shaped like an oyster-shell and dated 1692.

To the north is the park of Shortgrove Hall, a mid-17th-century house burnt down in 1966 and, opposite, high on a hillock once occupied by a Norman castle, is the grammar school, founded in 1588, although the present buildings are mostly Victorian.

The Church of St Mary stands on another hill in the heart of the village. Gathered round it are pleasant cottages, some Victorian, others much older; these are swaybacked, with dormer windows, and roofed with an unusual combination of thatch and tile – the thatch thrown around the shoulders of the cottages like old and friendly shawls. The church is grand, dating mostly from the 13th to the 16th centuries. Its chief treasure is an extremely rare 13th-century altar chest – a kind of travelling altar with compartments for vestments and plate. Its lid bears some of the earliest known oil paintings in the country.

Beside the road, almost opposite the grammar school, lies a very large brown boulder which holds a special place in Newport's affections. It is called the Leper Stone, and the grooves cut in its surface are said to be where alms were left for lepers; the ancient masonry in the wall beside may be part of a medieval hospice for poor travellers, or perhaps lepers.

Matters medical have frequently engaged the interest of the village. In the 1670s, Mistress Hannah Wooley, the wife of a schoolmaster, published her *Gentlewoman's Companion*, and enjoyed a considerable local reputation for her medicines. For everyday maladies she prescribed snail water, whose recipe begins 'Take a peck of snails with houses on their backs . . .' But for really serious illnesses, she advises woodlice.

Stebbing ESSEX

15 miles south-east of Saffron Walden (PAGE 164 Cb)

Rising from the grounds of Stebbing Park, on the approach to the village from Bran End, is an impressive conical earthwork known as the Great Mount. Towering 44 ft high and stretching no fewer than 225 ft across, the mound is reached by a causeway across its moat. There is thought to have been a small fortification here before the Norman invasion. It was then replaced by a more substantial defensive motte by Ranulf Peverel – one of the lords among whom the Conqueror shared out local manorial rights. Peverel married one of his king's mistresses, and their son founded the priory of Hatfield Peverel 12 miles south-east of the village.

Another moat surrounds Porters Hall, an early 17th-century farmhouse on Stebbing Green, built to an L-shaped plan with two front gables and retaining one of its original chimney-stacks. A great deal of Roman pottery and traces of a Roman building have been found close by. Porters Hall is only one of many admirably preserved buildings in the village. Most of those dating from the Middle Ages were extended or altered in the 16th, 17th or 18th centuries and, like Butlers Cottage in the High Street, many are decorated with pargeting on their façades.

Below the church, sprawling across the end of the main street beyond the war memorial, is Church Farm, an early 16th-century building now plastered over. Farther down the steep hill stands the breathtaking Priors Hall or Parsonage Farm, another of the village's former manorial seats.

At the top of the hill above the church, the frame of an old inn sign, hanging empty, and a red emblem over the door are the only reminders that the Red Lion, now a private house, was once a pub. It was built in the 16th century and extended later.

The Church of St Mary the Virgin with its shingle-tiled spire has altered little since the 14th century, when it replaced an earlier foundation. Its window tracery is a delight and the interior is enhanced by the chancel's later roofing and repairs made to the nave in 1825. The greatest revelation is the mighty rood screen filling the chancel opening, carved not in wood, as is usual, but in stone.

A stroll down Mill Lane to the Stebbing Brook gives glimpses of Stebbing Park's imposing manor house between attractive cottages, including Mill Cottage, the smallest in the village. The weatherboarded water mill itself is 18th century. It still works, though powered by electricity except on occasional festive days when the miller sets the original machinery in motion.

THE OLD, OLD MIXTURE

Because Stebbing is so old, it contains an unusually wide variety of building styles, ranging from medieval half-timbering to 18th-century weatherboarding. Here, too, are splendid examples of pargeting – the decorative plasterwork on outside walls.

Pargeted wall

Houses with pargeting

Water mill and timbered cottage

MAP 16

THE SAXON SHORE AND THOROUGHBRED COUNTRY

The peaceful landscapes of Suffolk, where life seems to amble along at nature's own pace, have seen their share of strife. Saxon and Danish invaders have raided these shores, and Dutch men-o'-war have pounded British ships off the coast. Today's battles are of a different kind, as thoroughbred horses thunder down the straight at Newmarket.

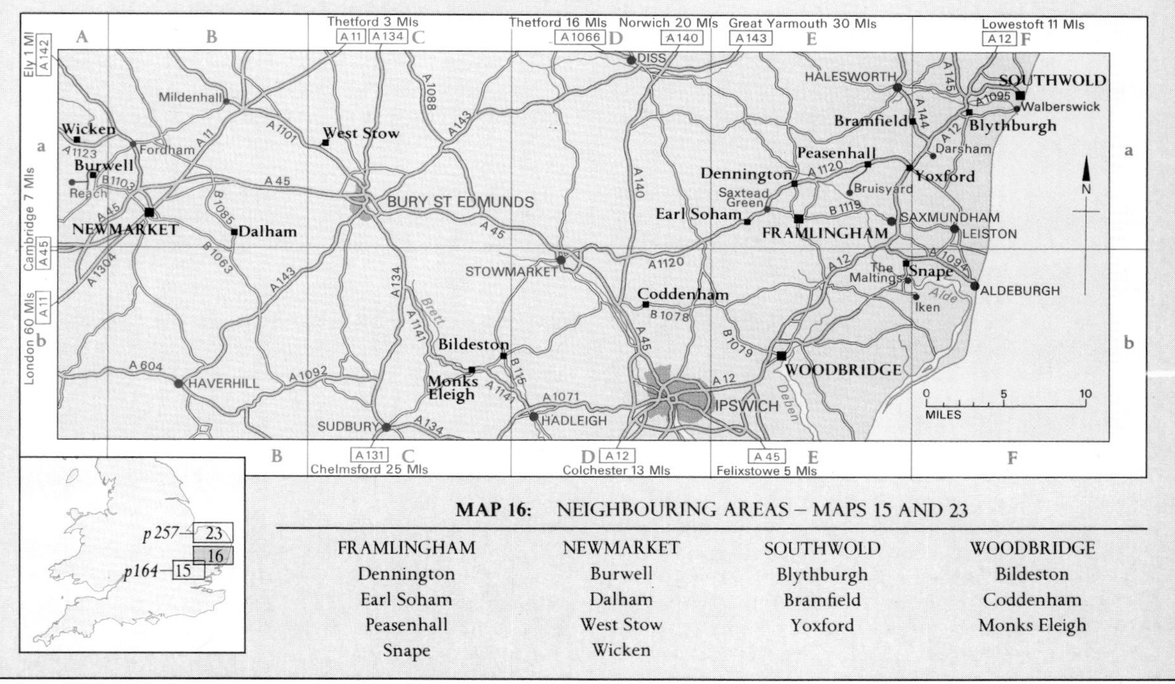

MAP 16: NEIGHBOURING AREAS – MAPS 15 AND 23

FRAMLINGHAM	NEWMARKET	SOUTHWOLD	WOODBRIDGE
Dennington	Burwell	Blythburgh	Bildeston
Earl Soham	Dalham	Bramfield	Coddenham
Peasenhall	West Stow	Yoxford	Monks Eleigh
Snape	Wicken		

FRAMLINGHAM

SUFFOLK

19 miles north-east of Ipswich (PAGE 175 Ea)

Framlingham Castle, built in the 12th century by Roger Bigod, Earl of Norfolk, stands a little way outside the town, but its rugged walls and battlements dominate the area. The most notable of its towers is the Prison Tower, which has no outside entrance to its ground floor. The only way in is by a door on the first floor of the west wall, then down through a trapdoor to the dungeon-like room below.

The original Great Hall, once the scene of splendid banquets, was razed in the early 18th century and replaced by a poorhouse – which still stands. Framlingham spreads between the castle and Mills Almshouses, named after Thomas Mills, a wealthy wheelwright who left the money to build them when he died in 1703. The almshouses stand back from Station Road – the station is now a garage and the railway was closed to passengers in 1952. The town's other group of almshouses, Hitcham's Almshouses, was built in 1654 with money bequeathed by Sir Robert Hitcham, the Attorney-General to Anne of Denmark, wife of James I. Sir Robert, who died in 1636, is buried in a black marble tomb in St Michael's Church.

On the east side of Market Hill is the Mansion House, built in the 16th century and later faced with special tiles – known as mathematical tiles – that look like bricks. They are also on the house next door. At the top of Market Hill a narrow lane called Queen's Head Passage runs down to Fore Street. The monarch concerned was Mary Tudor (1516–58) who owned the castle and was staying there when she heard that she had been declared queen in July 1553. Later she paid a state visit to the town with her husband, Philip II of Spain.

The parish church of St Michael, built between the 14th and 16th centuries, has one of the few pre-Civil War organ-cases in England that escaped destruction by Oliver Cromwell's Commissioners. The organ itself, built in 1674, originally belonged to Pembroke College, Cambridge, who gave it to the church in 1708. The church also contains the tombs of several members of the Howard family, including that of Thomas Howard, the 3rd Duke of Norfolk, who in 1547 was sentenced to be executed for treason. His neck was saved by the death of Henry VIII the night before the execution, and the duke died seven years later in his bed. To the east of St Michael's is Double Street, with its early Victorian pillar box – one of two in the town. The street was the first in Framlingham to have houses and shops on either side – hence its name.

As a market town, Framlingham has a number of fine inns – once used by the farmers and their wives who came by horse and carriage on market days. The oldest of these which is still a pub is the Crown Hotel on Market Hill – now modernised, but with parts that date back to the mid-16th century.

• **Parking** Fore Street; New Road (all car parks) • **Early closing** Wednesday • **Market day** Saturday • **Event** Framlingham Gala (Spring Bank Holiday) • **AA 24 hour service** TEL. Ipswich 214942.

Dennington SUFFOLK

3 miles north of Framlingham (PAGE 175 Ea)

A farming community in the middle of fertile, heavy clay lands, Dennington was for generations a centre for horse and cattle dealers. Until some years after the Second World War there were regular parades of Suffolk heavy horses and horse-drawing team contests on the village green. This became so trampled by horse and man that all traces of green vanished and its bare surface has become known simply as 'The Square'.

Behind it, The Queen's Head inn, bought by the parish in 1694, has records dating back to 1483. Only the addition of a porch in 1961 and tiles instead of a once thatched roof have changed its original appearance. Until the beginning of this century, the poor received bread and coal at the inn, which also held 'largesses' – celebrations at which local landowners and farmers treated their men to harvest suppers, when ale was 2 shillings (10p) a gallon and whisky 3s 3d (just over 16p) a bottle. The square in front is still the 'meet' for the local hunt and for most other village events.

An oak seat in the square was put there to mark the Silver Jubilee of King George V and Queen Mary in 1935. Two years later, an oak tree was planted for the coronation of George VI, and at the same time the horse pond was filled in and replaced by a shelter.

The flint Church of St Mary the Virgin has a sturdy tower with a turret on top, and a superb interior. Its late 14th-century benches have ends carved with geometrical designs, broken only in the centre aisle by one depicting a Sciapod, a mythical creature supposed to have lived in the desert. It hopped about on its single foot until, wearying, it lay down and used that huge foot as a sunshade. This is the only known representation of the creature in Britain.

Armrests are fashioned into other mythical figures and more ordinary beasts, including a hare, a pelican and a mermaid. In front of the benches are Georgian box pews, watched over by a 1625 pulpit later converted into a three-decker. The church houses two ornately screened chapels. The one dedicated to St Margaret of Antioch was lengthened between 1440 and 1450 to accommodate the Bardolph tomb. An alabaster effigy of Lord Bardolph, who fought with Henry V at Agincourt, lies with its feet on a hawk, while beside him the feet of his wife's effigy rest on a wyvern, a two-legged dragon with wings.

In the north aisle a 19th-century sand table is preserved. Here, schoolchildren practised writing and sums by making marks in the sand with their fingers. Beside the table is an 18th-century bier (on which coffins used to be placed before burial), a 19th-century reading desk for use in the choir, and the mechanism of a 17th-century clock which was replaced in 1948 by a memorial clock in honour of those who died during the Second World War.

Earl Soham SUFFOLK

4 miles west of Framlingham (PAGE 175 Ea)

The village sits on a most unusual feature in a Roman road – a kink in the otherwise ramrod-straight highway. The Romans' practice of building roads along a more or less unswerving line was foiled here by a large lake. Over the centuries, the lake has almost completely disappeared. Not so the road: from the east, it dips into a shady hollow and along Earl Soham's main street, twists past the banks of the old lake, then climbs back up to the open farmland through Pettaugh to Coddenham.

At the eastern end of the village, a private drive and footpath turn off the road to a moated farmhouse, Earl Soham Lodge. The moat – like others in the area – was dug for comfort rather than defence. The earth removed was used to make a raised platform for the house, and the moat itself helped to drain the clayey ground. The aim was to help keep the building free of damp.

The present lodge dates mostly from the 18th century, but it probably stands on the site of an earlier hunting lodge built for the Bigod family of Framlingham Castle – Earls of Norfolk in the 13th century, from whom the village is said to get its name.

The Bigods must have enjoyed falconry, for Earl Soham has two reminders of this ancient form of hunting. The 15th-century timber-framed inn is called The Falcon; and on the triangular green there is a striking carving of a falconer, presented by the Women's Institute in 1953 to mark the coronation of Elizabeth II. The green used also to be the site of an annual sheep and cattle fair. Near by, in Victoria Street, is a row of timbered cottages, converted towards the end of the 19th century from disused malt houses.

The village is overlooked by the 17th-century tower of St Mary's Church. Inside the church is some superb woodwork: a double hammerbeam roof spans the nave, and the bench-ends are elaborately carved with poppy-heads and a rich variety of birds, beasts, angels and men. The nearby rectory, looking almost grander than the church itself, dates from Tudor times but has been added to, with Georgian windows at the front and a coat of white plaster.

In Saxtead Green, a mile to the north-east, is a working windmill – open to the public – on a site where there has been a mill since the 13th century.

Peasenhall SUFFOLK

7 miles north-east of Framlingham (PAGE 175 Ea)

No hint of mystery lurks behind the friendly shops fronting The Street in peaceful Peasenhall. Yet the village was the improbable scene of one of the most celebrated unsolved murders of the century.

In 1902, Rose Harsent, a maid at Providence House – now called Stuart House – became pregnant. Gossips guessed that a local carpenter, William Gardiner, already a father of six (and a Sunday School teacher) was responsible. On the morning of June 1, Rose was found dead at the foot of the stairs in Providence House. She had savage neck wounds and burns, as if someone had tried to set fire to her body.

Saxtead Mill – still working

Carved bench-end in church

BY MILL AND MOAT

Images of Earl Soham reflect centuries of peace and prosperity – prosperity enough to endow the village church with a superb timbered roof and richly carved bench-ends; peace enough for the moat of an elegant farmhouse to have been dug for drainage rather than defence. The equally elegant white windmill at neighbouring Saxtead Green is in working order and open to the public. A mill has stood here for about 700 years.

Earl Soham Lodge – moated farmhouse

Gardiner, an obvious suspect, was arrested, and magistrates sitting at the Swan Inn sent him for trial to Suffolk Assizes. There was evidence about the state of the body and much circumstantial evidence besides. But the jury could not agree on a verdict and Gardiner was acquitted. After the trial, he and his wife moved to London where they opened a shop, resisting advice to go and live abroad.

The Swan, much modernised, but retaining some old timbers inside, stands on the north side of The Street. Customers there still argue about whether the carpenter was guilty or not.

The Street was originally a Roman village, built on either side of a river, and the Roman road from Saxmundham to Norwich crossed the village to the west of the church. South of The Street, a wide, shaded ditch follows the road out across the landscape.

Fine 15th-century linenfold panels, stripped out of the Swan during renovations, were rescued by the vicar and are now fitted in the parish church of St Michael. The church has an unusual welcome above the porch; a carved dragon and a woodwose – a mythical half-human woodland creature – whose origins remain a mystery.

Peasenhall's past, like its present, has centred on the land. Its only concession to industry lies behind the church, in the remnants of a factory where an ingenious corn seed drill was made. James Smyth, the village wheelwright, designed it in the early 19th century, and it proved so much more efficient than others that it is still used today by many farmers in Suffolk. One of the last of Smyth's 'Nonpareil' drills is exhibited in the Abbot's Hall museum at Stowmarket.

A footpath to the east of the village passes the jagged fragments of Sibton Abbey, founded in 1150 – the only Cistercian house in Suffolk. The abbey monks developed the wool trade in Peasenhall and their timber-framed Wool Hall, overlooking the tiny green at the eastern end of the village, has recently been restored by the Landmark Trust and converted into three flats around the central hall.

About 2 miles south-west of Peasenhall, near Bruisyard Church, a successful vineyard was established in 1974, and its acres of Müller-Thurgau vines usually yield around 17,000 litres of white wine a year. Visitors are welcome from May to mid-October.

ENTER A WOODWOSE *This figure of a woodwose – a mythical half-human creature of the forest – is carved above the porch of St Michael's Church, Peasenhall. A mythical dragon confronts him.*

DAWN PATROL *Hoarfrost sparkles in the early light as stable lads exercise their aristocratic charges on Newmarket Heath. Steam wreathes*

Snape SUFFOLK

10 miles south-east of Framlingham (PAGE 175 Eb)

Unique among villages as an international centre of music, Snape is alive with opera, jazz, The Maltings Proms and concerts from April to October, and antique fairs, television and recording sessions are taking place throughout the year.

Centrepiece of the activities is The Maltings concert hall, home of the Aldeburgh Festival since 1967. It was burnt out after the opening night of the 1969 season – probably due to an electrical fault – but was restored and reopened by Elizabeth II a year later. The acoustics are as fine as in any concert hall in Europe.

The Maltings complex includes shops, galleries, wine and coffee bars, a centre for activity holidays, and the Suffolk Piano Workshop, which repairs old instruments and welcomes visitors. Here also is the Britten-Pears School for Advanced Musical Studies, named after the festival's founders, composer Benjamin Britten and singer Peter Pears. Britten fell in love with Snape and lived in a converted windmill north of the bridge in the 1930s and 1940s, composing his opera *Peter Grimes* there. Master classes held in the school are open to casual observers for a small admission charge.

The creeper-covered 19th-century brick maltings buildings were originally used to prepare fine Suffolk barley for brewing, the malt produced being shipped out via the River Alde. The combination of farming and shipping gave the nearby Plough and Sail pub its name. Departing seamen used to drop barley seeds into cracks in the bar and find them sprouting on their return to port.

The malting business was started by Newson Garrett in 1841. He was the father of Elizabeth Garrett Anderson, Britain's first woman to qualify as a doctor and first woman mayor (of Aldeburgh).

Salt marshes adjoining The Maltings are the home of many species of wild birds and are the starting point for walks and river trips along the Alde to Aldeburgh and Iken. There is an old smugglers' inn, The Crown, which used to have peepholes allowing watch to be kept over river and countryside, and a windowless upstairs room for use as a hideaway.

At a crossroads stands Snape church, a flint and brick building dating from the 13th century and with a 15th-century carved font. Just east of the church, a 48 ft ship dating from around AD 625 was unearthed in 1862. A Saxon gold ring, now in the British Museum, was found on the site and all around was a cemetery of burial urns.

rippling flanks as a gallop slows to a canter; breath condenses in clouds. Work well done, a fortune in horseflesh strolls home over the skyline.

NEWMARKET

SUFFOLK

13 miles east of Cambridge (PAGE 175 Ba)

The headquarters of British horse racing since the 17th century, Newmarket houses two of the turf's most revered institutions: the Jockey Club and Tattersalls. The Jockey Club, in the High Street, was founded in 1752 by a group of racehorse owners and it now governs every aspect of racing, including the licensing of jockeys, trainers and racecourses. The present building, next door to the fascinating National Horse Racing Museum, dates from 1882. However, its handsome red-brick front was added in 1933. Tattersalls – with its bowling-green turf, pristine stabling and magnificent covered sale ring, is just off the High Street in The Avenue. Horse sales – which are open to the public – have been held here since the 1880s, and in 1983 there was a record turnover of more than 64 million guineas (more than £67 million).

Monarchs from James I to the present Queen Elizabeth have gone to Newmarket races. When Charles II was there in March 1683, a fire broke out which destroyed most of the town. Among the surviving buildings is Nell Gwynne's House in Palace Street, where the king's mistress is said to have stayed whenever Charles visited Newmarket.

The town, with its two racecourses, stables, horse-breeding and training establishments, is flanked by the vast expanse of Newmarket Heath. During peak periods, there may be some 2000 horses exercising on the 2500 acres here at any one time. Beside the heath is the 500 acre National Stud which houses some of the world's finest stallions. About 20 miles of fencing have been put up to form paddocks, and thousands of trees provide shelter from the winds that can whip across the open country. The stud is open by appointment in August and September.

In Newmarket itself other 'monuments' to the sport of kings include two old coaching inns in the High Street at which racegoers stay – the Rutland Arms Hotel and the White Hart Hotel opposite the Jockey Club. Just off the High Street is the traffic-free Rookery Shopping Precinct, in which a twice-weekly market is held.

• **Parking** Fred Archer Way; All Saints Road; Church Lane; Grosvenor Yard (all car parks) • **Early closing** Wednesday • **Market days** Tuesday, Saturday • **Events** Race meetings held from April to October • **Information** TEL. Newmarket 661216 • **AA 24 hour service** TEL. Mildenhall 712928.

Burwell CAMBRIDGESHIRE

5 miles north-west of Newmarket (PAGE 175 Aa)

Among the trim lawns of Burwell's churchyard stands a poignant memorial to a sad episode in the long history of the fenland village. A tombstone, carved with a flaming heart, marks the grave of 82 people who died when what had begun as a joyous occasion ended in tragedy. On September 8, 1727, a travelling puppet showman set up his theatre in a barn, and people came from far and wide to enjoy the entertainment. But there were more spectators than the barn could hold, so the doors were closed. A few moments later a fire started which quickly engulfed the trapped audience. The doors were found to have been nailed shut, and later a man was accused of starting the fire. He was acquitted at Cambridge Assizes, but in 1774 the local press reported that a man from Fordham, 4½ miles north-east of Burwell, had confessed to the crime on his deathbed, saying that he had set fire to the barn to spite the showman.

The soaring 100 ft tower of St Mary is an unmistakable landmark above the fenland fringes, its octagonal upper section clearly influenced by the tower of Ely Cathedral.

To the west of the church is the site of Burwell Castle, built during the 12th century by the villainous Geoffrey de Mandeville who used it as a base for his plundering exploits. But Geoffrey overstepped the mark when he rebelled against King Stephen, who gave him the choice of the gallows or surrender of the castle. Wisely he gave up the castle, but still continued to ransack the surrounding countryside until an arrow from Stephen's troops occupying the castle put an end to his infamous career. He is remembered in Burwell by a lane, The Mandeville, which leads from a dried-up moat – all that remains of the castle.

But Burwell's history stretches back far beyond the Middle Ages – back to the Dark Ages and the Devil's Dyke which ends at the village of Reach, 1½ miles west of Burwell. The dyke was a massive earthwork defence system which included Fleam Dyke, the Brent Ditch and the Bran Ditch, and although these might have been Roman defences against Anglo-Saxon invaders they were more probably barriers between the rival kingdoms of Mercia and East Anglia.

Burwell today is a sprawling village with a wide main street running for about 2 miles. Most of its buildings date from the 17th and 18th centuries, but in High Street a building numbered 4 and 6 was originally a hospice built in the 14th century by the Knights Hospitaller for travellers journeying to the Crusades. It is now a private residence. At Malting Corner, at the southern end of the village, a stone barn and malt house probably served the Priory of St John, established around 1100 where the vicarage now stands.

The tiny village of Reach was once the Roman river port for Cambridge. It was fed by a canal from the River Cam at Upware and its quays were in use through medieval times. Once a year the village celebrates Reach Fair, a colourful event of gaily painted swings and roundabouts held on Fair Green and opened by the Mayor and Corporation of Cambridge. A symbolic figure of the fair is 'The King of Reach', a tradition stemming from a charter given by King John which granted Reach perpetual freedom and therefore, villagers argue, the right to have its own king.

MEMORIAL FLAME *Beneath a flaming heart on this Burwell tombstone lie 82 arson victims. In 1727 a man set fire to a barn as they watched a puppet show inside – confessing only when he died.*

Dalham SUFFOLK

6 miles east of Newmarket (PAGE 175 Ba)

Here the River Kennett meanders between the grass-fringed village street and a cluster of thatched and white-plastered cottages with trim gardens, reached by smart little white footbridges and sometimes backed by orchards. A footpath from the Affleck Arms inn leads to stepping stones through the water. Opposite the lane to the church, a jaunty conical oasthouse, once used for drying hops, stands in the garden of Malting Farm, now a private house.

The 14th-century Church of St Mary stands in manorial grounds, up a steep avenue of overarching yews and on the site of an earlier Saxon church. In 1303 the manor was presented by Edward I to his second wife, Margaret, daughter of Philip the Bold, King of France. She appealed formally to him at the church door for the manor as a marriage settlement – though they had been wedded for four years, and her demand seems somewhat belated.

The tower was rebuilt in 1627, with the injunction KEEP MY SABBATHS carved on the parapet. It had a wooden steeple which blew down in a storm on September 3, 1658 – the night Oliver Cromwell died. Within the church are memorials to the Stuteville family, who owned the manor for nearly 300 years. There is one to Sir Martin Stuteville, who 'visited the American world with Francis Drake'.

The last Stuteville sold the manor to Simon Patrick, Bishop of Ely, who between 1704 and 1705 built a new red-brick mansion, Dalham Hall, in the adjoining parkland, on medieval foundations whose stone vaults remain below the house. He added an extra storey from which he may have been able to see his cathedral in Ely, some 16 miles away. Although the hall burnt down and was rebuilt with only two storeys, it is still the highest point in the county, looking across the Kennett Valley to a ridge topped by a white windmill.

In the late 18th and 19th centuries the Affleck family were the landowners, giving their name and coat of arms to the inn sign. The estate was bought in 1900 by the statesman Cecil Rhodes (Rhodesia, now Zambia and Zimbabwe, was named after him) for his retirement. But he died in 1902, without returning to England. His brother inherited, brought home Rhodes's horse, and built a village hall in his memory.

West Stow SUFFOLK

13 miles north-east of Newmarket (PAGE 175 Ca)

Scanty West Stow looks as if it has never been anything more than a tiny village among the inhospitable sandy heaths, known locally as Breckland. Its long and crowded past lies buried beneath 3 ft of sand, residue of a violent 14th-century sandstorm that swept over the district – a common hazard in Breckland until the Forestry Commission recently laid down trees which keep a firm hold on the soil.

An archaeologist's treasure trove is now being uncovered here. Ever since Stone Age man dug for flint, West Stow had – until that sandstorm – been a busy community. Hunters and Bronze Age farmers camped in the valley beside the River Lark, where the Romans later built pottery kilns. And between AD 450 and 650, a small Anglo-Saxon settlement was established. It was probably peopled by farmers, who came over from Denmark and Germany.

The traces of about 80 wooden buildings – now simply dark stains in the ground – have been so well preserved in the sand that it has been possible to reconstruct some of them on their foundations. These huts were made of split tree trunks, and roofed with thatch. Pottery, bronze jewellery, spinning tools and bone combs found on the site are now on display in Ipswich Museum.

The reconstructed village – open from April to October, except on Mondays – is the main attraction in West Stow's 125 acre country park and nature trail. The path includes a walk beside the river, and on the approach road from the village are picnic sites.

The few cottages that make up West Stow today are mostly of mellow white Suffolk brick, so West Stow Hall stands out as a surprise. Its three-storey red-brick gatehouse, dating from the 1520s, has turrets and pinnacles and carries the arms of Mary Tudor, sister of Henry VIII. She became the wife of Louis XII of France, and, after his death, Duchess of Suffolk. She is buried in St Mary's Church, Bury St Edmund's.

West Stow Hall – the brick-and-timber gatehouse

TALL STOREYS

Timbered, turreted, pinnacled and three storeys tall, the amazing gatehouse of West Stow Hall soars above the Breckland village it has overlooked through over four centuries. Nothing could contrast with it more than the primitive Anglo-Saxon homestead that has been reconstructed in the country park near by. Foundations of a small settlement of AD 450–650 have been excavated.

Anglo-Saxon hut – rebuilt with logs, mud and thatch

Wicken CAMBRIDGESHIRE

9 miles north-west of Newmarket (PAGE 175 Aa)

Wicken, with its four village greens, stands beside Britain's oldest nature reserve – and the last stretch of natural, undrained fenland in East Anglia. Wicken Fen, just a step from the main street, is 600 soggy, peaty acres of old England. Before Roman times the Great Fens covered 2500 square miles.

The Romans raised a network of causeways and opened drainage channels through the treacherous marshes. Draining has continued since the 13th century across the whole area. Now only Wicken is left in its original state, a treasureland of sedges, reeds and many other marsh plants, with 5000 species of insects, and a great variety of birds including warblers and breeding snipe, all jealously guarded by the National Trust, which has managed the fen since 1899.

Wicken Fen stands out like an island above the surrounding peatland, which has shrunk as it has been drained. The water level in the reserve is kept high by a unique windpump with a scoop-wheel – carrying out a task which is the reverse of that for which it was designed.

Until the 1820s there were about 700 such pumps draining water from the fenlands. They were mostly replaced by steam pumps, but a few, like Wicken's, were used well into the 20th century. The Wicken Fen Mill, a four-sided timber building standing on a brick base and with a boat-shaped cap, was built in 1908 and has been restored on a new site to pump water back into the fen. A 2 mile nature trail wanders around the reserve, and there is a hide for birdwatching.

The village is at the other end of Lode Lane from the fen. One village green lies beside the main road, scattered about with houses. Another, Pond Green, has a duckpond and is surrounded by cottages and farm buildings. The William Thorpe Building, at the foot of Lode Lane, has displays recounting the history of the nature reserve.

St Laurence's Church stands to the east of Wicken. A chancel screen was presented to the church as a memorial to Henry, the fourth son of Oliver Cromwell, who lived at Spinney Abbey after the Restoration. Its stones were reused in building what is now a farmhouse set back from the road to Stretham, a mile to the north-west of the village. Henry is buried beside the altar with another Oliver Cromwell, one of the Lord Protector's grandsons.

SOUTHWOLD

SUFFOLK

12 miles south of Lowestoft (PAGE 175 Fa)

The imposing white lighthouse which rears 100 ft above Southwold is visible from almost every part of the town. It was built in 1890 and its beam can be seen 17 miles out to sea. Even during the day the lighthouse serves as a very distinctive landmark for passing ships.

NIGHTLIGHT *You can plot your course through Southwold by the lighthouse, visible from every part of the town; and from as far out to sea as 17 miles, sailors have taken bearings on it since 1890.*

The town is a pleasant mixture of period houses and cottages, many painted in the old Suffolk colours of pink and pale blue, with roofs of black or red pantiles. Dotted among them like scatter cushions are nine greens of varying shapes and sizes. Some of these mark places where buildings were destroyed by a fire that engulfed the town in 1659.

Southwold began its long history as a Saxon fishing port, became a sizable harbour in medieval times, then declined as the seaward approaches silted up. Today it thrives as a holiday resort, but a reminder of its maritime past can be seen in Park Lane, where a ship's figurehead of a girl holding a bunch of grapes stands outside Park Lane Cottage.

There are several more figureheads in the Sailors' Reading Room at the seafront end of East Street. On Gun Hill, farther along the front, stand six cannon thought to have been presented to the town by the Duke of Cumberland – who landed there from Flanders in October 1745 on his way to Scotland to fight Bonnie Prince Charlie.

The town is spread around the large and splendid Church of St Edmund, which houses Southwold Jack, a realistic 15th-century mechanical figure of an armoured foot soldier, made of painted oak. Jack holds a short axe with which he strikes a bell before each service and whenever a bride arrives for her wedding. The paintwork is original, and endows him with a dark stubble of beard and blood-flecked eyes.

To the west of the church, in High Street, is a restaurant called Sutherland House that was the headquarters of the Duke of York (later James II), England's Lord High Admiral during the 17th-century wars with the Dutch. At the Battle of Sole Bay, fought off the town on May 27, 1672, the Dutch fleet took the duke's squadron by surprise and the battle raged all day. The English ships were badly battered, but as the Dutch withdrew and did not return to the attack, the honours were thought to be even. A panorama of the battle can be seen in the town museum – a pretty Dutch-styled cottage facing the church. To the north of the church is Station Road, where George Orwell, author of *1984* and *Animal Farm*, lived in Montague House for a time in the 1930s.

Southwold has had its own brewery since the 16th century, and the present one – Adnams, in East Green, in the town centre – incorporates the original building. It recaptures the spirit of the past by using horse-drawn drays to deliver barrels of real ale.

• **Parking** Pier; The Common; Ferry Road; Harbour Quay; Gardner Road (all car parks) • **Early closing** Wednesday • **Market days** Monday, Thursday • **Events** Trinity Fair (Monday and Tuesday after Trinity Sunday); sailing regattas (May and August) • **Theatre** St Edmund's Hall, Cumberland Road TEL. Southwold 722389 (summer only) • **Information** TEL. Southwold 722366 (summer only) • **AA 24 hour service** TEL. Norwich 29401.

Blythburgh SUFFOLK

4 miles west of Southwold (PAGE 175 Fa)

An explosion rent the sky above Blythburgh on August 12, 1944, and remnants of a shattered aircraft fell to earth. One of the victims was the pilot, Joseph Kennedy, elder brother of John F. Kennedy, who was to

Holy Trinity, Blythburgh and (below) one of its roof angels

MARSHLAND MAGIC

Easy to see why the beautiful Church of the Holy Trinity at Blythburgh has been called the 'Cathedral of the Marshes'. Outlined against a violet sky at sunset, and reflected among reedy water margins, its huge bulk becomes perfectly in scale with the wide landscape that surrounds it. Wait a little longer for darkness . . . then floodlights bathe the whole building in a magical glow. Inside is just as rewarding: carved angels soar among the rafters and roof beams, and services are heralded by a 17th-century Jack-o'-the-clock.

become President of the United States. The cause of the wartime blast remains a mystery, but windows damaged by it in Blythburgh's lovely Church of Holy Trinity bear witness to its ferocity.

The village, now so peaceful, has known other hectic times. The quiet River Blyth once bustled with ships, winching cargoes of fish and salt from the Continent onto wharves now long vanished. Wool was exported from the surrounding pasturelands and the port minted coins – and had its own jail.

Trade fell away in the late 15th century as medieval shipwrights launched vessels too big to navigate the river, which silted up until even the fishermen went. A disastrous fire raged through the village in 1676, and left only part of an old Augustinian monastery, a courthouse which had been converted into an inn – and Holy Trinity.

The church remains Blythburgh's glory, visible for miles across the marshes, floodlit at night and reflected in the high tide. Locals call it the 'Cathedral of the Marshes', and it is huge for a village – but then Blythburgh was big, too, when work began on the church in 1412. Its tie-beam roof, jointed without a single nail, covers a nave 127 ft long. The tower, a century older, belonged to an earlier church and once had a steeple.

During a fearful storm in 1577, lightning struck Holy Trinity during a service, and toppled the steeple into the nave, killing a man and a boy. Scorch marks on the church door were believed by frightened villagers to have been made by the Devil's claws. The marks can still be seen.

A more earthly shock struck the church in 1644, when Cromwell's reformer William Dowsing and his followers smashed ornaments, windows and statues, and blasted shot into the carved, wooden angels soaring along the roof beams. Haltermarks and hoofmarks in the nave still show where the Puritans tethered horses.

As in Southwold, services are still started by a 17th-century Jack-o'-the-clock. Above the south porch an ancient private room for the priest has been restored, with an altar made of wood from Nelson's flagship *Victory*.

The Dutch-styled gables of the old White Hart Inn show East Anglia's long links with the continental lowlands. Inside, panelling and moulded ceilings survive from its days as a courthouse for Quarter Sessions. A path along the riverbank below the inn winds to Walberswick, skirting a nature reserve. A mile south of the village are the undulating heathlands of Toby's Walks, where there is a picnic area and parking place.

Bramfield SUFFOLK

9 miles west of Southwold (PAGE 175 E/Fa)

An acorn fell to the ground in Bramfield at about the time that Alfred the Great was burning cakes. It grew into a sapling as the Vikings were driven out of eastern England, and was a sturdy oak when the Normans conquered the Saxons in 1066. Soon afterwards, Bramfield and its oak became part of the feudal estates of the Earl of Richmond, son-in-law of William the Conqueror.

The tree was a majestic local landmark when it was mentioned in a Suffolk ballad about a fractious earl fleeing the wrath of Henry II in 1174. Pursued by the king's 'Baily' (bailiff), the earl, Sir Hugh Bigod, thundered through Bramfield to the safety of his castle at Bungay, about 12 miles north:

'When the Baily had ridden to Bramfield Oak,
Sir Hugh was at Ilksall Bower.
When Baily had ridden to Halesworth Cross,
He was singing in Bungay Tower.'

The road he took through Bramfield is still known as Earlsway, and memories of Earl Bigod survive also in a local dialect word, 'biggotty', meaning proud or stuck up. The word bigot may also be linked to his family name: the Old French word *bigot* was a disparaging term for a Norman – and most noble families in England at the time were Norman.

Bramfield built its own defensive sanctuary in the 13th century – a massive round tower with walls 5 ft thick in places, which is now the tower of St Andrew's Church. Unusually, tower and church are set apart, and the 14th-century church building is thatched. Inside is a magnificent rood screen, elaborately carved and with painted panels, which was made in the 15th century – while the old village oak thrived on.

Sir Edward Coke (1552 – 1634), who owned the neighbouring manor of Huntingfield, became Lord Chief Justice and champion of the rule of law against the whim of the current monarchs. His son and daughter-in-law, Arthur and Elizabeth, who both died in the 1620s, can be seen in effigy in St Andrew's, with Arthur kneeling in full armour and Elizabeth holding a baby in her arms.

Twenty years later, while the Civil War raged, the Puritan William Dowsing descended on the church and destroyed '24 superstitious pictures: one crucifix and picture of Christ: and twelve angels on the roof'. Happily, Arthur and Elizabeth were not disturbed.

Meanwhile, during the 16th century a family named Rabett had moved into Bramfield Hall, across the road from St Andrew's, and become custodians of the oak – by then the oldest resident of the hall's grounds. The Rabetts stayed for more than 300 years, and four of their coats of arms still hang in the church. The rabbits on their painted shields are a pun on the family name.

Also in the church, a tombstone tells the melodramatic story of Bridgett Applewhaite, who 'after the enjoyment of the Glorious Freedom of an Easy and unblemisht Widowhood for four years . . . resolved to run the Risk of a Second Marriage Bed. But DEATH forbad the Banns'. She collapsed in the arms of her husband-to-be and died soon after in 1737, aged 44.

In the same century the Rabetts built the 'crinkle-crankle' brick wall which now encloses Bramfield Hall. The serpentine wall was designed to shelter fruit trees within its curves, but the family could not preserve for ever the village oak. On a calm, June day in 1843 its last two branches fell. Now only the stump remains – monument and witness to more than a thousand years of village history.

Yoxford SUFFOLK

11 miles south-west of Southwold (PAGE 175 Ea)

In the 18th century, coaches travelling between London and Yarmouth turned off the Yarmouth road to call at the Three Tuns Hotel at Yoxford, a village set in a wooded hollow of the Yox Valley. Sadly the hotel burnt down in 1926 – its visitors' book is reputed to have included the signatures of Lord Nelson and Charles Dickens. A restaurant now stands on the site.

Although with the loss of the inn Yoxford has lost much of its stagecoach-days character, travellers will still find it worthwhile to make the small diversion from the London to Yarmouth road, guided by the 17th-century spire of St Peter's Church which stands out as an unmistakable landmark. Further guidance is obtainable in the village itself, given by a cast-iron signpost opposite the church, said to be one of only two such signposts in England. It dates from about 1830 and its arms, pointing to London, Yarmouth and Framlingham, are set at the height of a stagecoach driver's seat.

The High Street has a medley of styles and periods, with colour-washed cottages, Georgian balconies, Dutch gables and two 17th-century inns, mingling with the butcher's, the general store, an art gallery, the inevitable antiques shops and other tradesmen's premises. Milestone House, which takes its name from a 150-year-old milestone outside, is a particularly ornate 18th-century building with two porticoed porches topped by an elegant hooded iron balcony. The building now houses a pottery.

Embracing the village are the luxuriant parklands of three large mansions, Rookery Park, Grove Park and Cockfield Hall – parklands that have given Yoxford the title 'The Garden of Suffolk'. Cockfield Hall has been the home of the Blois family since the 17th century, and their name appears on one of the village inns, the Blois Arms. A Victorian lodge guards the entrance to Cockfield Hall, itself much remodelled but still bearing traces of its ancestry in a Tudor wing and gatehouse.

In Tudor days, Lady Catherine Grey was held in custody at the hall after imprisonment in the Tower of London. She was a sister of the tragic nine-day Queen of England, Lady Jane Grey, who was beheaded in 1554. Lady Catherine died in 1568 and was buried in Cockfield Chapel. Later, in the reign of James I, her body was taken to lie beside her husband's in Salisbury Cathedral.

Satis House, on the edge of the Cockfield grounds and now a hotel, was the home of the wealthy Mrs Clarissa Ricketts. In 1887 she lost all her money gambling at Monte Carlo and died shortly after her return to Yoxford. Mystery surrounds her funeral, which she is said to have arranged herself and which took place at nightfall. The mystery is further deepened by the rumour that she was seen leaving Darsham railway station disguised as a man after the funeral, and was later reported in Egypt.

WOODBRIDGE

SUFFOLK

8 miles north-east of Ipswich (PAGE 175 Eb)

When yeoman farmer John Sayer died in 1635, he left a sum of money to pay for bread to be distributed each week to the town's poor. The bread is still distributed, though the loaves his money buys now are few, and they go to the first-comer rather than the most poor But each week a Woodbridge baker comes to the church and leaves some bread in an elegant cupboard of polished wood, purpose-built into the stone of the porch to contain it. During the Second World War, however, recipients of the bread were obliged to surrender their ration coupons.

Traditions last long in Woodbridge, which stands at the head of the Deben estuary, 9 miles from the North Sea. Down beside the river, boatbuilders and sailmakers have been at work for at least six centuries. But where their 14th-century predecessors built vessels used as warships by Edward III, they now turn out craft devoted to pleasure.

The former Boat Inn – now a private house – has stood on the Quayside since 1530, and near by is the 17th-century Ferry House. The row of cottages at Nos 1–5 Quayside used to be the Ship Inn, built in the 16th century. The Congregationalists once held their meetings in the Ship, then in 1688 they built their own church around the corner in Quay Street. The present Quay United Reformed Church, which was formerly the Congregational Church, was built on the original

A house that deceives the eye

Cottages in the pink

FALSE FRONT

The elegant frontage of one house in Yoxford is not quite what it seems. A local artist has painted a blank wall of the house with an eye-deceiving doorway and windows. Not to mention a very realistic peacock. Other cottages preen in the colour known locally as Suffolk pink, once concocted by mixing pig's blood or sloe juice into the plaster.

site in 1805. But the most eye-catching riverside building is the weatherboarded tide mill. Built in the 18th century, it was working until 1957, when the oak shaft attached to the water wheel fractured.

In Woodbridge, it is difficult to escape reminders of the town's greatest benefactor, Thomas Seckford, a 16th-century MP and barrister, who commissioned the first systematically surveyed maps of England. He founded the Seckford Almshouses to look after 13 poor men – although the present almshouse buildings date only from Victorian times – and built the Shire Hall. This fine building, ornamented with curly gables in the Dutch manner, still looks out on the main square, called Market Hill, making a fitting memorial to its builder. An ornate Gothic pump and drinking trough in front of it were added in 1876.

Seckford was buried in 1587 in the parish church of St Mary the Virgin, connected to Market Hill by cobbled footpaths. The church also has a remarkable three-tiered monument to Jeffrey Pitman, a local tanner and haberdasher who became High Sheriff of Suffolk and who died in 1627. In the monument, Pitman kneels piously on the top tier with his two wives and two sons kneeling facing one another in the tiers below.

As lord of the manor, Thomas Seckford lived with his family at The Abbey, just below the church. The earliest parts of the house – now a school – were

built on the site of an Augustinian priory and date from 1564. However, the building has been much altered in the centuries since then.

Another Seckford family home – once connected to The Abbey by a secret tunnel – is the fine Elizabethan Seckford Hall. The hall stands a mile southwest of Woodbridge, on a site which was owned by the Seckfords for 520 years, and is said to be haunted by Thomas Seckford's ghost. In 1940, it was bought derelict by Sir Ralph Harwood, a former secretary to George V. He restored it and made it into a hotel, with some interesting furniture from Windsor Castle and Buckingham Palace, including the winged chair in which Edward VII died in 1910.

TURN OF THE TIDE *The sparkling waters of the River Deben, where it flows past Woodbridge, give life to a tide mill that is the last of its kind still working in England. These days it works only in the summer months and then mostly for the benefit of visitors, driven as it has been since the 18th century by the surging power of the tidewater as it ebbs and flows. The massive, white, weatherboarded mill was in daily use until 1957, and was rebuilt in the 1970s.*

• **Parking** New Street; Lime Kiln Quay Road; Station Road; Turban Shopping Area; Theatre Street • **Early closing** Wednesday • **Market day** Thursday • **Cinema** Quayside • **Event** Woodbridge Regatta (July) • **AA 24 hour service** TEL. Ipswich 214942.

Bildeston SUFFOLK

24 miles west of Woodbridge (PAGE 175 Cb)

A doctor's generosity probably saved Bildeston from a lethal epidemic in the late 19th century – but he could not save his own children from the same disease. In 1877 diphtheria – often fatal in those days – struck the villagers. The local physician, Dr Grouse, spotted an open drain running from the butcher's slaughterhouse, and realising that it was probably polluted and the source of the disease, he paid for a new covered drain to be built.

The doctor's diagnosis proved to be correct: once the drain was covered, the threat of an epidemic faded away. But it faded too late for Dr Grouse's own family. Two of his children had already died.

The good doctor's large, yellow-brick house stands in a corner of the market place. In the churchyard a stone screen, accompanied by six small crosses, tells the story of the family.

Long before Dr Grouse's time, in the 13th and 14th centuries, Bildeston was a wealthy wool town, especially noted for making blankets and blue cloth. Although competition from the Cotswolds later killed the industry, the village retains traces of its former greatness. Fine old half-timbered houses, plastered in many colours and built as homes for wealthy merchants, line the streets that radiate from the market place. On a steep hillside just outside the village, the unusually large 15th-century Church of St Mary Magdalene stands with its original carved door intact – a reminder of Bildeston's medieval grandeur.

The church had until recently a tower at its west end, but on May 31, 1975 – Ascension Day – a corner of the tower collapsed, and most of the rest was pulled down to make the other parts of the building safe. Inside the church is a memorial to Edward Rotherham, captain of Collingwood's flagship *Royal Sovereign*, which led the British fleet into action at Trafalgar in 1805.

Down in the village, a row of 15th-century cottages still lines Chapel Street. At one time all the attics formed a long, single common room, used for manufacturing coconut fibre and matting by workers who moved in after the wool industry moved out. Not far away stands what was once a wool merchant's fine timbered home, built in 1495. When the trade died it became a pub – The Crown. Over the centuries since, stories have been told of ghostly footsteps pacing the pub corridors at night. Some people staying at The Crown have even reported ghosts entering their bedrooms and touching them with chilly fingers. The stories were so persistent that in 1982 a team of ghost-hunters, sponsored by a whisky company, went to Bildeston to investigate. The result of their researches was that The Crown was named one of the 12 most haunted pubs in England.

Coddenham SUFFOLK

11 miles north-west of Woodbridge (PAGE 175 Db)

Tucked snugly away in a wooded hollow amid rolling acres of wheat, barley, sugar beet and pastureland, Coddenham has a Saxon name but an older ancestry. It was the Roman settlement of Combretovium, guarding an important road junction from Cambridge towards the east coast, and from London by way of Colchester to Caistor St Edmund. Traces of small Roman villages have been found in the neighbourhood, but none has yet been thoroughly excavated, and outlines of the Roman fort have been revealed only by aerial photography in this century.

The parish church of St Mary is a typical Suffolk rough flint building, tilted gently upwards to the east by the slope of the knoll on which it stands. The 15th-century timbered roof was restored in the 19th century and is decorated with flights of angels.

The narrow main street also slopes, though a lot more steeply, through an almost unspoilt ascent of imposing old houses, some with overhanging upper storeys. No two are the same and each is lovingly painted, plastered and cared for. Gryffon House at the bottom was once part of an inn, licensed in the early 17th century. It is said to be the home of an archer named Wodehouse, who was knighted by Henry V after the Battle of Agincourt. A few steps up the hill is another inn, built in about 1500 and now the post office, with a frontage of timber and pink-washed plaster adorned with 17th-century geometrical pargeting – a technique of raising or indenting designs by means of a comb or trowel. The regional colour, known as Suffolk pink, was obtained by mixing white plaster with pig's blood or the juice of sloes.

Monks Eleigh SUFFOLK

24 miles west of Woodbridge (PAGE 175 Cb)

The main road – The Street – follows one bank of the meandering River Brett, while the thatched and timbered houses of Swingleton Green stand in graceful seclusion higher up on the opposite bank. The two parts of the village are linked by an old footpath known as The Causeway, which incorporates a Victorian footbridge.

In Saxon times, the settlement was that of a leader called Illa and so became Illanlege – Illa's wood – and eventually Eleigh. The monks were those of Canterbury, into whose hands the property came in medieval times. During the 14th and 15th centuries the inhabitants shared in the prosperity of neighbouring wool and cloth towns and had a guildhall on The Street. Dating from 1400, it has been a builder's workshop in modern times and is now a private house.

The imposing outline of St Peter's Church, with its buttresses and stair tower – once a familiar sight on railway posters advertising the area – crowns a rising triangular green complete with Victorian parish pump. On one side, Hall Farm shelters behind trees, on the other lies a wavering rank of variegated cottages, thatched and tiled, and at different pitches and angles, which spill down towards The Street. The house called Hobarts is a sturdy survivor of the early 15th century and The Fenn is a 16th-century building with an elegant Georgian frontage grafted on.

On a hill south-east of the village stands Bridge Farm. Among its crops are varieties of maize developed over years of research to produce cobs coloured light and deep purple, brown and ivory. A small showroom in The Rise, by the crossroads, displays maize dolls and traditional corn dollies, the corn also being cultivated in different varieties on the farm. Visitors are welcome and may see dolls and straw decorations being made.

MAP 17

SNOWDONIA AND THE DRUIDS' LAST REFUGE

The majestic, often mist-shrouded peaks of Snowdonia are the natural bastions of North Wales. The vast, complex castles of Edward I are the man-made ones, built to hold it for England against the stubborn refusal of Wales to be conquered. The rugged mountains, precipitous valleys, high lakes, dark forests and isolated farms remain one of Britain's most dramatic landscapes. But the mighty castles are now just romantic backdrops to friendly towns and villages roofed with the slate of great quarries that have sliced away whole hillsides. Across the superb Menai Bridge lies Anglesey, centre of pre-Christian culture and the Druids' last refuge from the Romans. The landscape is gentler here. Small farms thrive around snug villages, and the coastline embraces tall cliffs, sandy coves and fine beaches.

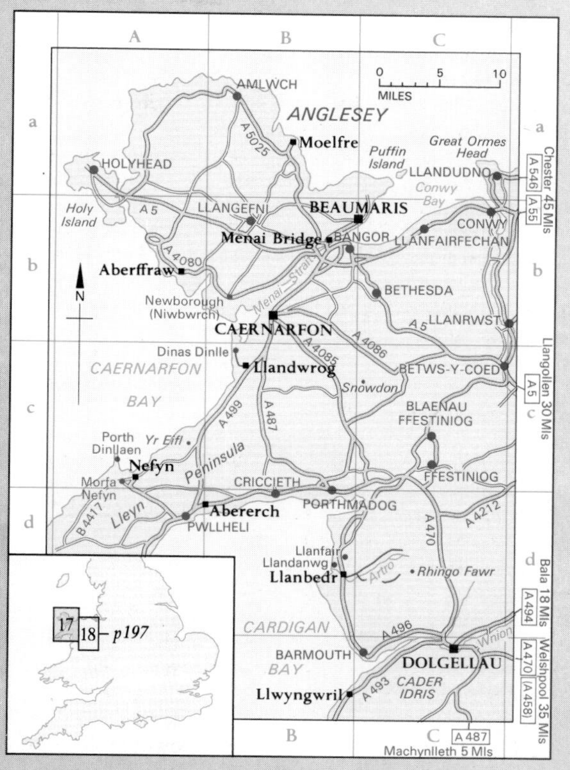

MAP 17: NEIGHBOURING AREA – MAP 18

BEAUMARIS	CAERNARFON	DOLGELLAU
Aberffraw	Abererch	Llanbedr
Menai Bridge	Llandwrog	Llwyngwril
Moelfre	Nefyn	

BEAUMARIS

ANGLESEY

7 miles north-east of Bangor (PAGE 189 B/Cb)

The town looks across the Menai Strait to Bangor and the far-off mountains of Snowdonia, and its small, narrow streets crowd around a massive but unfinished medieval castle.

Gracious Regency and Georgian houses are reminders of the days when Beaumaris was the home of Anglesey's gentry, and the place has a very English atmosphere. The town grew around the castle, which was built by Edward I in 1295. He chose the site on a *beau marais* – the Norman French for 'beautiful marsh' – and this was the last castle he built in Wales.

It is noted for its complex defences, designed by Edward's military architect, James of St George. These included a moat and drawbridge, portcullises, towers, outer and inner walls and about 300 places from which arrows could be fired. Even so, only lack of funds stopped the walls from being even higher and the defences more numerous.

Near the castle is the old Grammar School, founded in 1603 by David Hughes, a wealthy Anglesey landowner. The school closed in 1962 and the building is now a community centre and library. Close by is the early 17th-century courthouse, in which the assize courts were held until 1971. It was said to be the only court in Britain in which the jury sat higher than the judge. Today it is used as a magistrates' court and is open to the public.

Beaumaris has a small, attractive seafront, behind which stretches The Green – the original 'beautiful marsh'. The town is a major yachting centre, and during the annual yachting fortnight at the beginning of August hundreds of colourful sailing craft criss-cross the Strait and nearby Conwy Bay.

The main street is Castle Street, in which stands the handsome Bulkeley Arms Hotel. From its balcony, on the morning after the annual Hunt Ball, the Lady Patroness of the Anglesey Hunt used to throw down pennies – heated so that the members of the hunt would be amused when the locals burnt their fingers. Farther along is the Old Bull's Head, built in 1472 and rebuilt in 1617, which has the largest hinged door in Britain (11 ft wide and 13 ft high), through which mail coaches passed in and out of the courtyard. Near by is the town's oldest house, the half-timbered Tudor Rose, built in the 15th century with wood from a 12th-century building. The house is open to visitors by appointment in the summer, and the Tudor Rose from which it gets its name is carved on a boss in the hall.

The parish church of St Mary and St Nicholas was built for the use of the English garrison in the early years of the 14th century. It has been much added to and restored since then, particularly in the 16th, 19th and present centuries. In the south porch is the stone coffin of Princess Joanna, wife of Llywelyn the Great and daughter of King John. She died in 1237, and her coffin was used as a horse-trough before the church rescued it. In the north aisle is the impressive alabaster tomb of Rowland Bulkeley, a member of a prominent North Wales family and constable of the castle, who died in 1537.

Across from the church are the tall forbidding walls of Beaumaris Gaol, built in 1829 as a 'model' prison. Its inmates had single cells and were visited regularly by a surgeon and chaplain. Women prisoners, too, had their own separate cells and were attended by a matron. The prisoners were expected to work, and the cleaning of the cells was left to the warders. The prison is now a museum, and among its exhibits are the drunks' cell, a treadmill, the punishment cell, the condemned cell and the gallows.

• **Parking** The Green; The Castle • **Early closing** Wednesday • **Event** Menai Strait Regatta (August) • **Information** TEL. Llangefni 724666 • **AA 24 hour service** TEL. Caernarfon 3935.

STRONG STUFF *Massive though it is, Beaumaris Castle was meant to be even larger — but money ran out before it could be completed. This was the most complex of the chain of castles Edward I built in Wales, with inner and outer walls, a drawbridge, portcullises, drum towers and a moat with a sea gate through which the fortress could be supplied. Nevertheless, the walls were designed to be even higher, and with more strongpoints.*

Aberffraw ANGLESEY

20 miles south-west of Beaumaris (PAGE 189 Ab)

A single-arched packhorse bridge of grey stone, built in 1731 and now closed to traffic, takes walkers over the tidal Afon Ffraw to the sleepy little village where cottages huddle behind stone walls. Bridge Street climbs gently up to Bodorgan Square. Before tackling the hill, thirsty travellers can drink from a Victorian lion-head well, if they care to ignore a notice warning that the water should first be boiled. Or they can call at the smart-as-paint Crown Inn which stands in bright contrast to the sombre grey chapel which, in 1887, rose on foundation stones laid by no fewer than seven local dignitaries. The square itself wears an air of sedate calm, and gives no hint that Aberffraw was once the capital of North Wales.

The village has links with the legendary Cadfan – 'wisest and most renowned of all kings' – who is said to have ruled in the 7th century; and with King Rhodri the Great who reigned over Gwynedd, Powys and Ceredigion before he died in battle in AD 877. In the 13th century Llywelyn the Great and his grandson Llywelyn the Last held court here, both taking the title of Prince of Aberffraw. Then in 1282 Llywelyn the Last was killed in a skirmish with the forces of Edward I and the village's 700-year-old status came to an end. No trace of the Llywelyn palace remains, and nobody has yet been able to identify its site, but a street, a pub and a garage now proudly bear the name of Llywelyn.

Above the square, the twin-naved St Beuno's Church stands at the start of a narrow lane, squeezed between stone walls, which zigzags down to Porth Cwyfan. This rocky bay embraces an islet on which stands a tiny, little used church dedicated to St Cwyfan. A narrow causeway linking the islet to the mainland vanishes beneath the waves at high tide, and in the old days, when the church was used regularly, the services often ended abruptly when strong winds brought the tide racing in faster than expected, and the congregation fled home.

The main road between Aberffraw and Menai Bridge passes through Newborough, a village founded by people who were driven from Beaumaris when Edward I built his castle there in 1295. It is sheltered from the prevailing winds by Newborough Forest and Newborough Warren, one of the largest expanses of sand dunes in Britain. The dunes, driven inland by medieval storms, cover the 'lost' village of Rhosyr and overlook the 4 mile sweep of sands bounding Llanddwyn Bay. Much of the area, including Malltraeth Sands to the north, is now a nature reserve.

Menai Bridge ANGLESEY

5 miles south-west of Beaumaris (PAGE 189 Bb)

Menai Bridge grew around the great suspension bridge built by Thomas Telford between 1819 and 1826. Before then it was known by its Welsh name, Porthaethwy, and was the departure point for a ferry to the mainland. The buildings are mostly Victorian, and there is a delightful Museum of Childhood in Water Street which displays many of the toys in use at the time when the bridge was built.

The museum was opened in 1973 by the Marquis of Anglesey and the collection spans about 150 years, from Victorian times to the age of Walt Disney and the Beatles. One of the six rooms contains 'magic lanterns' and musical toys, and another has the largest collection of children's money boxes in Britain, together with penny-in-the-slot machines from seaside piers and amusement arcades.

Telford's bridge was the last and most vital link in his new road between London and Holyhead, now the A5. The great towers and abutments were built of limestone quarried at Penmon, near Beaumaris, while the massive suspension chains were shipped by canal, river and sea from the ironworks of William Hazeldine at Shrewsbury. The chains were anchored to huge cast-iron frames buried in tunnels blasted 20 yds into solid rock. The raising of the first chain in 1825 was an occasion for great celebration, and the first people to cross, high above the seething waters of the Menai Strait, were three intrepid workmen who ran the entire length of the chain, which is only 9 in. wide.

What was then the longest bridge in the world – 579 ft between the piers and 1265 ft overall – was completed in January 1826, and the first London to Holyhead mail coach made the first crossing on the last day of the month. Within 25 years the mail coaches had been replaced by the railways, and in 1850 Telford's bridge was joined by Robert Stephenson's Britannia Bridge, a mile to the south. It carried the Chester and Holyhead Railway in cast-iron tubes which were badly damaged by fire in 1970. The bridge had to be rebuilt and is now a double-decker, with the

SOARING GRACE *Set on a grassy islet, the 15th-century Church of St Tysilio looks across the Menai Strait to Telford's graceful suspension bridge, which soars 100 ft above the water.*

railway below a road, having been reopened in 1980.

Menai Bridge's origins can be traced back to the 7th century, when St Tysilio built a small church on a tiny island now linked to Anglesey by a causeway. Its 15th-century successor stands surrounded by a graveyard with many slate headstones, and overlooked from a hillock by a war memorial in the shape of a Celtic cross. The church is reached by the Belgian Promenade, built by Belgian refugees who settled in Menai Bridge during the First World War.

A colourful reminder of the past is the annual Ffair y Borth, which dates from the 16th century. It is held on October 24 each year and was once a cattle and pony fair. Nowadays it is a festive event of sideshows, stalls and fairground amusements, and is the largest of its kind in Wales.

MAGICAL MEMORIES FROM A VICTORIAN CHILDHOOD

A Victorian dolls' house, complete with perfect period furniture – and occupants – is just one of the many enchanting exhibits in the Museum of Childhood at Menai Bridge. The museum's six toy-packed rooms contain delights that include wasp-waisted Victorian ladies in miniature and rare black baby dolls, alongside modern television puppets and Disney characters.

Moelfre ANGLESEY

11 miles north-west of Beaumaris (PAGE 189 Ba)

A street of sturdy stone-built cottages, their fronts colour-washed in pastel shades, winds down to a small, sheltered beach where shingle crunches underfoot and the sea curls creamy tongues around seaweed-draped rocks. From the beach there are fine views across Conwy Bay to Great Ormes Head – rising to almost 700 ft above Llandudno on the mainland – the majestic peaks of Snowdonia, and Puffin Island off the eastern tip of Anglesey. Opposite the beach a shop caters for the needs of the many sailing enthusiasts who visit Moelfre each year, and if they are English their spiritual needs are attended to in the little chapel, where services are conducted in English during the summer months.

A five-minute walk from the beach along low cliffs leads to a small, unpretentious building which, nevertheless, is steeped in drama. Moelfre's lifeboat house has been the centre of heroic sea rescues for a century and a half, with more than 1000 lives saved during that time. Richard Evans, coxswain of the lifeboat in the 1950s, was awarded his second RNLI gold medal after he and his crew rescued the eight crew members of the 650 ton *Hindlea* in 1959. The rusting remains of the coaster, driven ashore by 100 mph winds, can still be seen on the rocks near a coastguard lookout station.

A century earlier, almost to the day, a fierce storm smashed the iron-hulled sailing ship *Royal Charter* on to the rocks just north of Moelfre. Homeward bound for Liverpool from Australia with a cargo of gold the ship quickly broke her back, and despite the gallant rescue of 39 people by villagers and the lifeboat crew, more than 460 men, women and children were drowned. Many are buried at Llanallgo, on the road from Moelfre to Amlwch, and there is a memorial to them on the clifftop where the rescuers tried in vain to save them with a line and breeches buoy.

The lane from Moelfre to Lligwy Bay passes a Stone Age burial chamber where the remains of 30 people were found in 1908. The massive capstone is believed to weigh 25 tons. Near by, a short walk across fields leads to Din Lligwy, the well-preserved remains of a 1600-year-old fortified village where huge slabs of pale stone surround the ruins of nine buildings.

CAERNARFON

GWYNEDD

9 miles south-west of Bangor (PAGE 189 Bb)

For 700 years the massive bulk of Edward I's mightiest castle has loomed over the walled market town of Caernarfon. Built in stages between 1283 and 1327, it is the only castle which Edward built in Wales as both a fortress and a palace.

Visiting the castle in 1774, Dr Samuel Johnson called it 'an edifice of stupendous majesty and strength'. He was thinking mainly of its seven major and two minor towers, and two huge double-gatehouses. Part of the Queen's Tower (named after Edward's wife, Eleanor) is now the regimental museum of the Royal Welch Fusiliers. Its exhibits fill three floors

Caernarfon and its castle

Remains of Segontium

PALACE FORT

Edward I built Caernarfon Castle as a fortress and a palace – and in 1301 he installed his son here as the first Prince of Wales. In 1911 the first investiture was held, when the future Edward VIII became the new prince. And 1969 saw the investiture of the present Prince of Wales. Outside the town are the remains of a much older fortress – Roman Segontium.

and include eight Victoria Crosses won by members of the regiment. From the top of Queen's Gate – also named after Eleanor – there are magnificent views of Snowdonia.

Although the castle was gradually strengthened and enlarged, the Old Town was kept the size that Edward had planned it. Its walls extend from those of the castle, and built into them is the Church of St Mary, whose vestry fits snugly into a corner tower. The surrounding network of narrow streets centres on Castle Square, which has a statue of David Lloyd George, Prime Minister from 1916-22, brandishing his fist. He was MP for the town from 1890 until 1945, and was also the constable of the castle from 1908. His greatest achievement as constable was to persuade George V to introduce the public investiture of the Prince of Wales at the castle.

The first Prince of Wales was the son of Edward I. Born in the castle in 1284, the prince was granted the title at the age of 16 – seven years before he became Edward II. It was not until 1911 that the castle staged its first investiture – thanks to Lloyd George – when the future Edward VIII received the title. Then, in 1969, the present Prince of Wales was ceremonially invested at Caernarfon.

Much of Caernarfon has a solid Victorian appearance. The railway arrived in 1852, providing a second valuable outlet for slate quarried in the area – it was also shipped from the harbour. The imposing County Hall, now the courthouse, with its four tall, fluted pillars, dates from the early 1860s; and the large, handsome Conservative Club in Market Street was built in the early 19th century.

Just beyond the town walls, on Llanbeblig Road, are the remains of the Roman fort of Segontium. It protected the approach to the Menai Strait and nearby Anglesey before being abandoned in about AD 383, shortly before the Romans left Britain. The fort has a museum exhibiting remnants of tools and equipment used by the soldiers, and some coins. Like the castle, the fort is open to the public all year.

Caernarfon's long association with the sea is recalled in the Maritime Museum, beside Victoria Dock. Among its exhibits are a restored steam dredger of 1937. In the museum itself is a pictorial history of Caernarfon's role as a port since Roman times. There are also navigational instruments, shipwrights' and sailmakers' tools and numerous models of ships. The museum is open every afternoon during the summer.

• **Parking** Slate Quay; Pool Side; Bangor Road; Crown Street; Pavilion Road; St Helens Road (all car parks) • **Early closing** Thursday • **Market day** Saturday • **Events** Festival (July); Menai Strait Regatta (August) • **Information** TEL. Caernarfon 2232 (summer) • **AA 24 hour service** TEL. Caernarfon 3935.

Abererch GWYNEDD

19 miles south of Caernarfon (PAGE 189 Bd)

Though not at the mouth of the Afon Erch, as its Welsh name suggests, Abererch is nevertheless very much a riverside village, enfolded in a loop of the river as it meanders to meet the sea at Pwllheli, 2 miles to the south-west. The main street runs down to the river between cottages of rough-hewn stone, their four-square frontages toeing narrow pavements and their painted doors and windows adding stabs of colour against a mottled grey background. At Ty Gwyn Farm the farmhouse walls are built of huge boulders and are whitewashed, giving a quaint snowhouse effect, and throughout the village there is an air of neatness and pride. Small wonder that Abererch is a winner of best-kept village awards.

On high ground above the village stands a medieval church dedicated to St Cawrdaf. The church is a distinguished double-naved building of pale grey stone with a small bell-cote and a slate roof. Grey, blue and purple slate tombs and headstones, mostly 19th century and inscribed in Welsh, dot the churchyard.

About a mile south-east of the village, the wide and lonely beach of Morfa Abererch runs for about 2 miles to the headland of Pen-y-chain. The beach is backed by dunes and marshland and at its western end, beyond the headland, the rocks of Cerrig y Barcdy standing out of the sea are the haunt of seals.

In a narrow, leafy lane 1½ miles north-west of Abererch stands Penarth Fawr, a house believed to date from the 15th and 16th centuries. The rough stone exterior is plain and undistinguished, but the interior is impressive: a framework of heavy beams supports the roof and a large fireplace dominates a room with a flagstone floor. The house was altered in the 17th century and was restored in 1937.

Llandwrog GWYNEDD

6 miles south-west of Caernarfon (PAGE 189 Bc)

Estate villages are rare in Wales, but Llandwrog was built in the 19th century by the Newborough family whose home, Glynllifon Park, is hidden by a high wall flanking the main road between Caernarfon and Pwllheli. It is now a college. The Newboroughs housed their tenants well, in solid cottages which are attractive examples of the art of building with rough-hewn stone. They are also in a variety of styles, avoiding the uniformity of many other estate villages. The splendid Harp Inn has the air of a country mansion with its two massive bays and tall, double chimneystacks. A ground-floor window in one of the bays has been sealed with a slab of slate inscribed with a verse, in Welsh and English, which extols the virtues of drinking in moderation. The last couplet reads:

'Enjoy your life, but don't betray
The good old beer, come what may.'

The inn shares the centre of the village with the church, originally built in the 6th century by St Twrog. The present-day building dates from the early 1860s and is the work of Henry Kennedy, an architect who settled near by in Bangor. It is a superb example of Victorian architecture, with a buttressed tower, belfry windows and a slender octagonal spire soaring to 110 ft. To the right of the porch a gravestone commemorates Daniel Thomas, the village blacksmith who died in 1776. His epitaph, complete with poetic licence, reads:

'My anvil and hammer lay declined,
My bellows too have lost their wind.
My fire extinguished, my forge decayed,
And in the dust my vice is laid.
My coals are spent, my irons gone,
My nails are drove, my work is done.'

Inside the church the stalls face each other, rather than the altar, in the style of a collegiate chapel. The small south chapel has memorials to Thomas Wynn, 1st Lord Newborough, and to his father, an MP who held a string of resounding offices, recorded in stone. They include Constable of Caernarfon Castle, Forester of Snowdon, Steward of Bardsey Island and Clerk of the Green Cloth to the Prince of Wales.

A narrow lane winds westwards from Llandwrog

COTTAGE INDUSTRY *This attractive stone cottage is one of a number built by a 19th-century landowner for his tenants at Llandwrog.*

to Dinas Dinlle, where waves pound the crumbling base of a steep, grassy mound that was an early British fort. It stands 100 ft above the sea and commands fine views of Anglesey and of Yr Eifl, the clustered peaks which dominate the Lleyn Peninsula. North of Dinas Dinlle the western end of the Menai Strait, barely 300 yds wide at this point, is guarded by Fort Belan, built around 1776 by the 1st Lord Newborough.

His lordship correctly foresaw that unrest in the North American colonies was bound to boil over into a full-scale conflict – the War of Independence. Also, the daring Scottish privateer John Paul Jones, who had joined the US Navy, was rumoured to be leading a squadron in British waters and to have sunk two ships carrying mail.

The fort was manned until the war ended in 1783, and was 'manned' again by the Loyal Newborough Volunteers when Napoleon began to threaten Europe. The Volunteers were not the military force they might have seemed, but were a group of Lord Newborough's cronies and a few local estate workers who were enlisted to swell their number.

Nefyn GWYNEDD

20 miles south-west of Caernarfon (PAGE 189 Ac)

In 1284 Nefyn echoed to the thunder of horses' hooves and the clash of sword, lance and shield when Edward I held a tournament here to celebrate his conquest of North Wales. Edward dedicated these colourful festivities to King Arthur and his Knights of the Round Table, and the tournament lists can still be seen in a field at the foot of Mynydd Nefyn, one of the conical hills that rise to almost 1000 ft above the village. In 1355 Edward's son, the Black Prince, made Nefyn a borough, and it remained one until 1883.

In the village, traditional Welsh cottages built with massive, rough-dressed stone mingle with prim and proper 19th-century architecture. At the top of Stryd y Ffynnon in the centre of the village a stone edifice with a pyramid-shaped roof guards St Mary's Well. It was rebuilt in 1868 by the local authority. St Mary's Church, tucked away behind the main streets, was restored in 1825 and now houses the Lleyn Museum. Its slender tower is topped by a large weathervane shaped like a ship in full sail.

On the outskirts of the village a lane hairpins down to a small, sandy bay backed by 100 ft high grassy cliffs. The road west from Nefyn leads to Morfa Nefyn, which stands on high ground above a cliff-backed crescent of sand with the tiny hamlet of Porth Dinllaen tucked away under a headland. Porth Dinllaen is small and beautiful, with sugar-white cottages sparkling beside a tidewashed satin-smooth beach which serves as the hamlet's only street.

Crumbling cliffs on the edge of a golf course tower above the Ty Coch Inn, and the road down to the hamlet is open only to residents and golf-club members – visitors must leave their cars at Morfa Nefyn. Such isolation is hard to equate with Porth Dinllaen's past as a busy port, yet in the days of sail many vessels called there – 700 were recorded in the early 19th century – and the port also had a small herring-fishing fleet. In 1837 there were plans to make Porth Dinllaen the railway terminus for the ferry service to Ireland, but the line was never built and Holyhead was chosen instead.

DOLGELLAU

GWYNEDD

18 miles south-west of Bala (PAGE 189 Ce)

Tucked between towering hills and narrow valleys in Snowdonia National Park, Dolgellau is a mecca for hikers and anglers. Walkers can explore a number of well-maintained mountain paths near the town, and anglers can fish for salmon in the nearby rivers and streams. Looming over the scene is Cader Idris (The Chair of Idris), 2927 ft high, whose slopes and ridges spread out behind the town. Local legend holds that anyone who spends the night on Cader Idris will, by morning, be either a poet or a madman.

Dolgellau – always pronounced 'Dolgethlay' – is a friendly maze of grey buildings, winding streets, crooked lanes and small, mellow squares. Many of the houses are made of square-shaped and oblong boulders, cemented together. Even so, there are crooked stone cottages leaning this way and that, as though kept upright only by optimism.

The town unfolds from Eldon Square, the original market place – the market is now held in Farmers' Mart, Bala Road – but the Market Hall, built in 1870, was not used for the weekly markets. Instead, it served as a public assembly hall and is now a community centre. Leading off the square is Queen's Square, smaller and quieter, in which stands the Royal Ship Hotel. Lion Street funnels off to the north and contains the Golden Lion Royal Hotel. Both hotels are large, imposing and smothered in Virginia creeper.

Near by is the parish church of St Mary, rebuilt in 1716 on the site of a 13th-century church. Its short, massive tower has a fort-like parapet, and inside there are four oak pillars on each side of the nave. The pillars came from trees felled at Dinas-Mawddwy, 10 miles away, and brought to Dolgellau by teams of oxen. The west wall has two small, high windows containing rare 18th-century stained glass.

Dolgellau was once Merionethshire's county town, and the County Hall, built in 1825, stands at its northern end, overlooking Y Bont Fawr, a six-arched stone bridge across the Afon Wnion. The original bridge was built in 1638, but it has been improved and strengthened several times since then – particularly after flood damage at the beginning of this century.

Gold has been mined near Dolgellau since the 1840s – and local gold was used to make the wedding rings of Queen Elizabeth in 1947 and the Princess of Wales in 1981.

• **Parking** The Marian; Aran Road (both car parks) • **Early closing** Wednesday • **Market day** Friday (cattle) • **Events** Spring Fair (April); Autumn Fair (September) • **Information** TEL. Dolgellau 422888 (summer) • **AA 24 hour service** TEL. Caernarfon 3935.

Llanbedr GWYNEDD

16 miles north-west of Dolgellau (PAGE 189 Bd)

Trim slate-roofed houses, their grey stonework brightened by flowers in summer, line the main street of this pleasant little village set on the swift-flowing Afon Artro, 1½ miles from the sea. Hill-walking and

SOURCE OF BEAUTY *A lane from Llanbedr runs beside the Afon Artro to its source – the lonely Llyn Cwm Bychan, beneath Rhinog Fawr.*

canoeing attract many visitors in the summer, some of whom stay in the red-brick and whitewashed youth hostel, for this is the gateway to some of the most memorable scenery in North Wales.

A lane runs seawards from Llanbedr to the tidal causeway to Mochras, a peninsula formed in the 19th century after the Artro's course was diverted to reclaim land. It is generally known as Shell Island, because of the 200 or so different varieties of seashell found on the sandy beach. The peninsula protects a large lagoon where small boats ride at anchor and herons hunt for fish. Visitors must pay a small toll.

Behind the village a lane follows the Artro to its source, Llyn Cwm Bychan, a lovely lake below the craggy slopes of the 2362 ft Rhinog Fawr. Another lane leads to Cwm Nantcol and passes the 18th-century Salem Baptist Chapel, where the Edwardian artist Sydney Curnow Vosper painted his famous picture of a Welsh lady in traditional dress. The picture, hung at the Royal Academy in 1909, is now in the Lever Gallery at Port Sunlight, on Merseyside. It was reproduced as a print, and copies hang in thousands of Welsh homes in many parts of the world.

Maes Artro, on the southern edge of Llanbedr, is a craft village where goods are made in leather, slate, wool and many other materials. To the north, at Llanfair, there are guided tours of lofty caverns where slate was quarried until 1906. A lane from Llanfair leads to the shore at Llandanwg where drifting dunes almost bury the tiny Church of St Tanwg, parts of which date from the 6th century. Services are held here during August, after volunteers clear all the sand out of the church.

Llwyngwril GWYNEDD

11 miles south-west of Dolgellau (PAGE 189 Be)

Clad with gorse, bracken and huge boulders, the western slopes of Cader Idris rise so steeply that the road and railway below are squeezed onto narrow terraces above Cardigan Bay. Llwyngwril, near the mouth of a small, fast-flowing river, is the only place for miles with enough level ground for a village.

It developed in the 19th century, when it was the terminus for the Aberystwyth and Welsh Coast Railway, but many cottages – built with huge, uncut stones taken from streams and hillsides – are considerably older. The most attractive of them all, T-shaped and painted white, dates from 1732 and stands next to the stern Salem Methodist Chapel built 150 years later. Meirion Terrace, by the bridge over the Afon Gwril, also dates from the 1870s and is much more formal than the village's older buildings. They include the Garthangharad Hotel, whose five-gabled façade dominates the centre of Llwyngwril and bears the date 1736.

To the north, a footpath to the sand and shingle beach passes a walled graveyard where Quakers have been buried since about 1650. Llangelynin church was built in 1843 to replace its 12th-century predecessor, dedicated to St Celynin, which hugs the shore 2 miles south of Llwyngwril. It contains a horse-powered bier, used to haul coffins up steep slopes, and the grave of Abram Wood, an 18th-century 'King of the Gypsies' who died near by in 1799.

MAP 18

GREEN BORDERS AND THE VALE OF LLANGOLLEN

A calm beauty pervades the borderlands where England's green counties of Cheshire and Shropshire merge into the Wales of poets and princes, castles and cascades. Here, in the lovely Vale of Llangollen, a grand eisteddfod draws dancers, musicians and aspirants to bardic honours from far afield. Here reigned the last prince of Welsh blood acknowledged by England. Here, too, a controversial genius was a pioneer of the Industrial Revolution, in a village that has long since reverted to rural isolation. And here is a rare, rustic racecourse – one of only two in Wales.

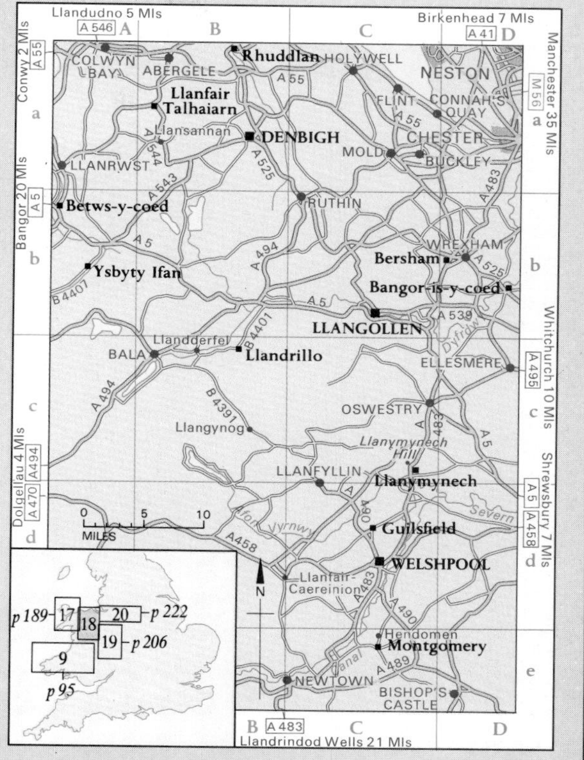

MAP 18: NEIGHBOURING AREAS – MAPS 9, 17, 19, 20

DENBIGH	LLANGOLLEN
Betws-y-coed	Bangor-is-y-coed
Llanfair Talhaiarn	Bersham
Rhuddlan	Llandrillo
Ysbyty Ifan	

WELSHPOOL
Guilsfield
Llanymynech
Montgomery

DENBIGH

CLWYD

8 miles north-west of Ruthin (PAGE 197 Ba)

Denbigh Castle was built by order of Edward I in 1282, and its ruins now overlook this market town set in the peaceful meadows of the Vale of Clwyd.

The hilltop castle was part of Edward's strategy to control Wales, and he appointed Henry de Lacy, Earl of Lincoln, to supervise the work. The castle took 40 years to complete, and some 3000 skilled and unskilled workmen – ranging from carpenters to sappers – were employed. The impressive triangular Gatehouse, made up of three octagonal towers, still bears witness to this great labour. Above it is a battered statue which could be either Edward or de Lacy.

A short distance away is the tower of St Hilary's Church. The church was built about 1300 as the castle's chapel, but everything except the tower was demolished in the 1920s. Farther along the hill is the skeleton of another church which the Earl of Leicester started building in 1579. He meant it to replace St Asaph Cathedral, but Leicester's Church, as it is called, was abandoned on his death in 1588 and never completed.

Denbigh clusters on the northern slopes of the castle's hill, and at the foot of the street called Tower Hill stands the 13th-century Burgess Gate, once the main entrance in the town walls. From here, Broomhill Lane – with a profusion of staggered rooftops – leads into the broad High Street, where the weekly market is held.

Here, in contrast to the quiet grey of the castle and the town walls, the brickwork of many shops and houses is a warm and friendly red, and the roofs are mostly of green, blue and purple slate. The buildings stand casually out of line, and some of them overhang the pavements, supported by pillars.

At the top of High Street is Crown Square, which contains the sober and bulky Victorian Town Hall. Just behind it, in Hall Square, is a building which the Earl of Leicester did manage to complete – the stately County Hall, whose ground floor was once open and housed a weekly market. The building dates from 1572, but was largely restored in 1780, when the ground-floor archways were walled up. Behind Hall Square is Bull Lane, climbing steeply to the castle. The narrow road is squeezed between tall buildings of red brick from Ruabon, 35 miles to the south-east. At the top of the lane are breathtaking views of the Clwydian Hills, presided over by the majestic 1817 ft high Moel Fammau, which means 'mother mountain'.

In the north of Denbigh is St Mary's Church, made of local limestone and consecrated in 1875. Off the Ruthin road, about a mile outside the town, is the medieval Church of St Marcella. A brass tablet inside is in memory of Richard Myddleton, Governor of Denbigh Castle in the mid-16th century. Here also is the splendid alabaster tomb of Sir John Salusbury, a chamberlain of North Wales who died in 1578, and his wife. The figures of their eight sons are carved on one side of the tomb, and their four daughters on the

WATER WONDERLAND

Bridges, waterfalls, rushing torrents and deep, tranquil pools play their part in the fascination of Betws-y-coed. The boldly lettered Waterloo Bridge over the Afon Conwy commemorates the battle, and is the work of the great engineer Thomas Telford. In contrast, above the waterfalls of the Afon Llugwy, is a 15th-century stone bridge with five arches, and yet another delight is a small suspension bridge across the Conwy. The village, bright with flowers in season and surrounded by woodlands, was often painted by the landscape artist David Cox.

Afon Llugwy bridge and falls

Waterloo Bridge at Betws-y-coed

Clematis on a local cottage

other. Thomas Edward, called in Welsh Twm o'r Nant, the first Welsh playwright of note, is buried in the churchyard. He toured Wales acting in his own plays at fairs, festivals and in farmhouses, and died in 1810.

The journalist and explorer Sir Henry Morton Stanley (1841 – 1904) grew up in Denbigh, where his house was near the castle Gatehouse. In 1871 he found the lost explorer David Livingstone at Lake Tanganyika. He also explored equatorial Africa and founded the Congo Free State for Leopold II of Belgium.

• **Parking** Barkers Well Lane; Vale Street; Post Office Lane; Crown Lane • **Early closing** Thursday • **Market days** Tuesday (cattle); Wednesday • **Cinema** Futura, Love Lane • **Theatre** Theatre Twm o'r Nant, Station Road • **Events** Carnival (July); Flower Show (August) • **AA 24 hour service** TEL. Llandudno 79066.

Betws-y-coed GWYNEDD

23 miles west of Denbigh (PAGE 197 Ab)

The London to Holyhead road runs through increasingly spectacular scenery as it enters the Snowdonia National Park near Betws-y-coed. It plunges down a wooded gorge, carved by the energetic River Conwy, and zigzags into the village over a graceful iron bridge whose single span bears the date 1815 and the words: 'This arch was constructed in the same year the Battle of Waterloo was fought.' It is called, not unexpectedly, Waterloo Bridge, and is decorated with roses, thistles, shamrocks and leeks – the national emblems of England, Scotland, Ireland and Wales. Small letters, picked

out in white on the south side, recall the man who built it – the engineer Thomas Telford.

Some years after the bridge was built, Betws-y-coed inspired the landscape painter David Cox (1783 – 1859). He paid regular yearly visits between 1844 and 1856, staying at the Royal Oak, whose signboard he repainted in 1847 – it can still be seen inside the hotel. Thanks to his oil paintings and drawings, the village and its surroundings became a famed beauty spot. Visitors are still drawn to this beautiful region whose sights include the Fairy Glen and Conwy Falls to the south, and the spectacular Swallow Falls, which tumble between wooded banks, 2½ miles west.

The village itself lies beneath steep, wooded crags which rise majestically above the Afon Llugwy's confluence with the Conwy. Right in the centre, oaks thick with moss and lichen overlook waterfalls which foam into a deep, dark pool immediately below a 15th-century five-arch stone bridge. The village also has a delightful little suspension footbridge which crosses the Conwy by a 14th-century church dedicated to St Michael and All Angels. The church – now disused – stands amid ancient yews and slate gravestones mottled with lichen. Its stark, whitewashed interior shelters the armoured effigy of Gruffydd ap Dafydd Goch, a 14th-century knight who served with the Black Prince in France during the Hundred Years' War. He was a great-nephew of Llywelyn ap Gruffydd (died 1282), the only Welshman whose right to be called Prince of Wales was officially acknowledged by England.

The nearby railway station, built of grey stone embellished by red-and-yellow brickwork, overlooks the Conwy Valley Railway Museum. Most visitors now arrive by car and coach, flooding the long main street with colour during the holiday season. Many shops specialise in goods made by Welsh craftsmen, and the village has its own potters and weavers on the road to Capel Curig, 5 miles or so to the west.

Llanfair Talhaiarn CLWYD

13 miles west of Denbigh (PAGE 197 Ba)

The road along the River Elwy's lovely valley skirts this small village enfolded in a crumpled quilt of steep hills and hidden valleys webbed by narrow lanes. Two pubs – the Black Lion and the Swan – a 19th-century school and other buildings of dark stone cluster round a small square overlooked from a cliff-like slope by a church whose origins go back to St Talhaiarn's time in the 6th century. The hillside is so steep that the north-east corner of the churchyard is on the same level as a cottage chimney some 10 ft away.

Two ancient yews flank the path to the porch, while inside are memorials to members of the Wynne family whose 18th-century home, Garthewin, is on the opposite side of the valley. A tablet, hidden away behind the organ, recalls Robert Wynne, who died in 1682: 'He was partaker with his Brother in his Loyalty and sufferings for ye Royal cause during ye Great Rebellion, being with him when he was killed at Wem.' The rebellion was the Civil War which swept Charles I from his throne to the scaffold in 1649.

The village was the birthplace of John Jones, a Victorian poet writing largely in Welsh, who adopted Talhaiarn as his bardic name. Born in 1810, he became an architect and worked under Sir Joseph Paxton on the building of the Crystal Palace for the Great Exhibition of 1851. He is buried beneath a yew tree in the churchyard.

Five other local writers whose careers spanned 500 years are commemorated at Llansannan, 4 miles away in the valley of the Afon Aled. One was William Salusbury who helped Bishop William Morgan translate the Bible into Welsh in the 16th century. The others are Tudor Aled, a poet born in the late 1400s, and three 19th-century writers, Lonwerth Glan Aled, and the brothers Henry and William Rees. Llansannan also has a small, traditional pottery where hand-thrown domestic stoneware is shaped, glazed and fired in what used to be the village bakery.

Rhuddlan CLWYD

8 miles north of Denbigh (PAGE 197 Ba)

The impressive ruins of a 13th-century castle, perched on grassy slopes above the River Clwyd, symbolise the period when this large main-road village was one of the military keys to North Wales. Rhuddlan's history is studded with such names as King Harold, Edward I, and Owain Gwynedd – ruler of North Wales in the 12th century.

The village stands on the east bank of the river whose broad, boggy estuary once formed a formidable natural barrier for armies advancing into Wales along the narrow coastal plain. In AD 796 an English army defeated the Welsh at Rhuddlan, but by 1063 it had become the base from which Gruffydd ap Llywelyn ruled his kingdom and raided its enemies. In that year, however, his stronghold fell to Earl Harold, the Saxon king-to-be whose brief reign ended at Hastings in 1066. A few months after Harold took Rhuddlan in 1063, Gruffydd was killed by his own followers.

William the Conqueror ordered a castle to be built above the river by Robert of Rhuddlan, a kinsman of Hugh the Wolf, Earl of Chester. Its site, a steep mound known as Twthill, still stands some 60 ft above the river on the southern outskirts of the village. It changed hands several times during the Anglo-Welsh wars before being granted to Llywelyn ap Gruffydd, or Llywelyn the Last, in 1267 under the terms of the Treaty of Montgomery. Ten years later, Edward I marched into North Wales with an army supported at sea by a fleet of ships. He captured Rhuddlan and forced Llywelyn to pay homage.

Edward immediately set about building a new castle and a town whose gridiron of streets still forms the old part of the village. The king, determined that his fortress could be supplied from the sea, also spent an estimated three years diverting and canalising the Clwyd between Rhuddlan and the coast, 2 miles away near the modern resort of Rhyl. The 'great dyke' eventually turned the waterlogged estuary into fertile farmland whose patchwork fields spread westwards.

Parliament Building, now a private house in High Street, incorporates part of the building where Edward is said to have held a parliament which passed the Statute of Rhuddlan after Llywelyn the Last's death. Its measures included establishing in Wales English-style shires which survived until local government was reorganised in 1974.

In 1400, when Owain Glyndwr launched the last great bid for Welsh independence, Rhuddlan was sacked by the rebels – but they failed to take the castle. During the Civil War it was held for Charles I, but surrendered to General Thomas Mytton in 1646. Parliament later ordered the castle to be demolished and, like many others, it became a convenient source of dressed stone for local buildings. But what remains is still impressive, the great drum towers standing boldly against the skyline above the Clwyd.

Rhuddlan's 16th-century bridge and its main street are usually busy with traffic, but the old part of the village retains a more peaceful atmosphere. Its buildings include the double-naved Church of St Mary, which dates from the 14th century, and, near the castle, a whitewashed cottage whose thatched roof is a rare sight in a region known for its slate.

Ysbyty Ifan GWYNEDD

20 miles south-west of Denbigh (PAGE 197 Ab)

Small, isolated, peaceful and picturesque, Ysbyty Ifan stands nearly 800 ft above sea level in a valley carved by the River Conwy, whose source is a small lake some 4 miles away to the south-west. The village is part of a huge National Trust estate whose 25,820 acres spread south and west from the London to Holyhead road at Pentrefoelas to the wilderness of Migneint.

An ancient bridge, just wide enough for a car, crosses the Conwy to the village. Stone cottages with walled and hedged gardens flank the river's western bank and others line the main street, their slate rooftops rising against a serene background of steep, green fields dotted with sheep. Rural tranquillity is rarely broken by anything louder than the chuckling river and the singing of birds. But towards the end of the Middle Ages this apparently idyllic place was a notorious 'wasp's nest, which troubled the whole country' and was feared as 'a receptacle of thieves and murderers'.

Ysbyty Ifan's history goes back to about 1189 when the Knights of St John of Jerusalem founded a lodging place for travellers in what is still a remote part of North Wales. Fugitives were granted rights of sanctuary which were grossly abused in later years. It was said that no place within a day's march was safe from the brigands of Ysbyty Ifan, but they were eventually hunted down at the end of the 15th century.

The Church of St John the Baptist has equally unexpected links with the past. It contains three mutilated effigies. One is believed to represent Rhys ap Meredydd who carried Henry Tudor's standard at the Battle of Bosworth in 1485, where Richard III's defeat paved the way for the Tudor dynasty. Another is said to commemorate his wife, while the third is of their son, Robert, who was chaplain to Cardinal Wolsey.

CELEBRITY HOUSE *Castell Dinas Brân — sometimes called Crow Castle — looks down to Plas Newydd, where the Ladies of Llangollen entertained such celebrities as the Duke of Wellington.*

LLANGOLLEN

CLWYD

11 miles south-west of Wrexham (PAGE 197 Cb)

The town has a charming Victorian air. The police station is Victorian, and so are many of the rows of immaculate terraced houses — some with rounded arches over their doorways, toothed brickwork at the eaves, and carved bargeboards on gabled roofs.

Princess Victoria paid a visit in 1832, five years before she became queen. She stayed in Bridge Street at the King's Head Hotel, which to commemorate the event changed its name to the Royal Hotel. Beside the hotel, which overlooks the River Dee, is the stone Llangollen Bridge known as one of the 'Seven Wonders of Wales'. It has four graceful arches of different sizes and heights, and was originally built in the 14th century by John Trevor, Bishop of St Asaph and Chancellor of Cheshire, Flint and Caernarfon. It was rebuilt in Tudor times, and in 1873 its width was doubled to cope with ever-increasing traffic. Just below the bridge is a salmon leap, where during the salmon season the fish fight their way upriver to its source in Bala Lake, 22 miles to the west. Victoria Promenade skirts the tree-lined river west of the bridge. In contrast to the surrounding greenery, the promenade wall is a chessboard of blue and red bricks. It stretches to Riverside Park — where there are bowling greens and tennis courts — and curves past a weir and an 18th-century corn mill.

On the opposite side of the river are the remains of Castell Dinas Brân, probably built in the 13th century by Gruffyd ap Madoc, Lord of Lower Powys.

The town, a vigorous mixture of black-and-white, roughcast and red-brick buildings, grows out from Market Street, where a Tuesday market has been held

MAJESTIC VIEW *Llangollen's 'wonder' bridge over the River Dee, flanked by a hotel where Princess – later Queen – Victoria once stayed.*

since the 13th century. Overlooking the area is the 1069 ft high Barber's Hill, thought to be named after a barber who hanged himself on the summit after murdering his wife.

Each July Llangollen stages a giant eisteddfod – an international folk song and dance festival which attracts more than 10,000 competitors from some 30 countries. On the north side of the Dee is the Canal Wharf, from which horse-drawn boats take passengers through the unspoilt Vale of Llangollen.

The Church of St Collen dates from the 13th century and has an 18th-century tower. It was restored and enlarged in 1863. The ceiling, richly carved with angels, beasts and flowers, is said to have come from Valle Crucis (Valley of the Cross) Abbey, whose ruins lie about 1½ miles west of the town.

Buried in the churchyard are the renowned 'Ladies of Llangollen', Lady Eleanor Butler and the Honourable Sarah Ponsonby, who held court in the area for more than 30 years. They came to Llangollen in 1780 from their native Ireland, and lived in Plas Newydd (New Place), a large house off Butler Hill.

There they entertained literary celebrities such as Sir Walter Scott, William Wordsworth, Percy Bysshe Shelley – and also the Duke of Wellington. Most of their guests brought them a gift – a piece of elaborately carved oak, stained glass, china and so on – which they collected. The house, its treasures and landscaped gardens are open to the public in the summer.

• **Parking** Market Street; East Street (summer); Brook Street (all car parks) • **Early closing** Thursday • **Market day** Tuesday • **Event** International Musical Eisteddfod (July) • **Information** TEL. Llangollen 860828 (summer) • **AA 24 hour service** TEL. Llandudno 79066.

Bangor-is-y-coed CLWYD

12 miles east of Llangollen (PAGE 197 Db)

Also known as Bangor-on-Dee, the village is a cheerful medley of brick and sandstone buildings. The sandstone church has a tower built in 1726 by Richard Trubshaw, an architect who was also a champion wrestler. John Douglas restored the church between 1868–77. Among Douglas's patrons was the Duke of Westminster, whose Eaton Hall estate flanks the River Dee on its way to nearby Chester.

On the outskirts of the village, in Malpas Road, is the home of a basket-making business which has been in the same family for four generations. It was started by James Johnson in the 18th century. Visitors can watch while willow is weaved using traditional skills.

Farmers often flock across Bangor's medieval five-arched bridge for the races at the village's Deeside track, one of only two courses in Wales (the other is at Chepstow). The battles fought here are the only ones Bangor has known for more than 1300 years.

The last clash of arms was the final rout of Celtic Christianity in Britain. If local history is correct, a monastery was set up in Bangor in AD 180. By AD 596, it had 2400 intransigent monks who refused to accept the authority of Rome, as Augustine demanded. Most of them were slaughtered at the command of the Anglo-Saxon Aethelfrith, King of Northumbria, who regarded their prayers for his defeat as an act of hostility. The surviving monks fled to Bardsey Island, where they established an abbey. Nothing of the monastery at Bangor remains today.

Bersham CLWYD

10 miles north-east of Llangollen (PAGE 197 Db)

John Wilkinson, the great ironmaster, died in 1808 and the Industrial Revolution passed away from Bersham with him. An old octagonal building that housed his foundry by the River Clywedog was recently being used as a barn, and there is little trace of his other works, across the river. Nature has reclaimed Bersham from its improbable past.

A carefully laid out industrial trail through the woodlands, meadows, hedgerows and wild flowers is the only reminder that Wellington's guns, Watt's steam engine, and much of the motivation for the whole Industrial Revolution owe something to this Welsh borderland – and to Wilkinson.

Born in 1728, son of a Cumberland farmer, Wilkinson was energetic, opinionated and argumentative. He married wealthy women to finance his ideas, kept his second wife a virtual prisoner, and was 79 when a servant girl gave birth to his third illegitimate child. A contemporary wrote: 'I do believe him to be one of the most hard-hearted, malevolent old scoundrels.'

But he was also inventive. He and his brother William set up the New Bersham Company in 1762. This was a perfect spot for a foundry. There was iron ore at nearby Llwyneinion and Ponciau; charcoal from the woods at Coedpoeth for the furnaces; limestone from Minera; water power for the mill wheel from the Clywedog; and later, again from Llwyneinion and Ponciau, coal to make coke for even hotter furnaces.

Wilkinson made iron church pews and vats, and invented a water-powered boring machine that produced superbly accurate cannon – used by Wellington in Spain and reputedly sold to both sides during the American War of Independence (1775–83). His machine was also precise enough to make the cylinders for Watt's first steam engine workable. Wilkinson also patented a technique for making lead pipes, and in 1787 launched what was possibly the world's first iron boat, a barge to carry coal on the Severn.

In 1776 his brother William went to France where he managed the state ironworks at Indret, near Nantes, and Le Creusot, teaching the French how to cast near-perfect cannon that would one day fire at his own countrymen.

John Wilkinson bought up coal mines and even issued currency, bearing his profile, which could be traded only with the company, or at approved shops.

Wilkinson left his own epitaph: 'Delivered from Persecution of Malice and Envy . . .' His industrial empire was not. It collapsed in a haggle among his nephews and illegitimate children that lasted seven years. And now just an occasional incongruous name, like Machine House, recalls Bersham's brief burst of energy 200 years ago.

Llandrillo CLWYD

16 miles west of Llangollen (PAGE 197 Bc)

An 18th-century stone bridge spans the fast-flowing Afon Ceidiog, and cottages of the same period line the quiet road that runs through Llandrillo. Its setting is superb, with the tree-clad slopes of the Berwyn mountains plunging from nearly 3000 ft to the beautiful upper valley of the River Dee.

There are also rewarding walks along ancient tracks running eastwards into the mountains, whose northern slopes rise to the ragged crests of Moel Sych (2713 ft) and Cadair Fronwen (2572 ft). South of the village a lane petering out to a rough track follows the course of the Afon Ceidiog, climbing to 1600 ft and joining the spectacular mountain road between Bala and Llangynog.

But Llandrillo itself has much to offer the visitor, from buying a stamp in the 300-year-old post office to relaxing in the 18th-century Dudley Arms. Most of the village is Georgian, but its Presbyterian chapel of 1840 is a splendid building with a white façade and tall, arched windows. The parish church, dedicated to St Trillo, was rebuilt in 1877 in the Gothic style.

Across the river from the village stands Pale – pronounced 'palais' – a mansion built in 1871 for Henry Robertson, who constructed the long and lofty viaduct that carries the railway line across the River Dee east of Llangollen.

Llandderfel, 4 miles west along the Dee valley, is an equally delightful little place facing south-west to the Aberhirnant Forest. Stone cottages are overlooked by the Church of St Derfel, dating from 1636. According to legend, Derfel was a 6th-century warrior who founded the village.

WELSHPOOL

POWYS

19 miles west of Shrewsbury (PAGE 197 Cd)

The town possesses an extraordinary relic of a cruel sport long outlawed: a complete cockpit building, still on its original site. The six-sided pit, built in the early 18th century of red brick, was in regular use until 1849 – when cock-fighting was banned.

In the 1970s the cockpit – after serving, among other things, as headquarters of a poultry business – fell into disrepair. But in 1978 it was restored with the help of local authorities and a bank. Ten high windows flood the ring with light, and there are shelves and alcoves where bets were counted. The building is off New Street, and is open to the public on weekdays from April to September.

The town is set in the beautiful Severn Valley overlooked by handsome Powis Castle, built of red gritstone. An earlier castle, the Castle of La Pole or (Welsh) Pool, was a stronghold of Gruffyd, the pro-English Prince of Upper Powys. But it was destroyed in 1275 in one of Gruffyd's struggles with other Welsh princes. Gruffyd's family built the present castle in the remaining years of the 13th century. In 1587 it was bought by Sir Edward Herbert, whose descendants became Earls of Powis, and the castle was transformed into an imposing and comfortable home. Superb hanging gardens – red-brick terraces overhung with clipped yews – were added in the 17th or early 18th centuries.

A Douglas fir more than 160 ft high grows in the castle park and is one of the tallest trees in Britain. The building houses a fine furniture collection, tapestries and pictures from the 17th and 18th centuries. Many of these were inherited from Clive of India, whose son married a Powis heiress in 1784 and later became Earl of Powis. The castle has been occupied continuously for 700 years, and the present earl still lives here, leasing it from the National Trust.

The town has had a Monday livestock market since the 13th century. The broad, pleasant streets – where black-and-white timber-framed buildings mingle with elegant Georgian houses – are backed by narrow 'shuts' or alleys.

A plaque on an office at the corner of Church Street and Severn Street dates from 1692 and proclaims that this was the home of Gilbert and Ann Jones, whose 16th-century ancestor Roger is said to have been the first Welsh Jones. A black-and-white cottage in Red Bank is named after Grace Evans, a local heroine who in 1716 helped Lord Nithsdale escape, disguised in hood and cloak, from the Tower of London, where he was awaiting execution the next day for his part in a Jacobite uprising. Grace is buried in the 13th-century Church of St Mary of the Salutation.

Welshpool was the western terminus of the old Shropshire Union Canal, which closed in 1936. However, in 1969 the $1\frac{1}{2}$ mile Welshpool stretch was re-opened, and it is now used for summer pleasure trips on a traditional canal narrowboat.

Trips can also be made on the narrow-gauge Welshpool and Llanfair Light Railway. The line opened in 1903, closed 53 years later through lack of passengers, but was re-opened in 1963. Now steam and diesel locomotives carry passengers the 16 miles to Llanfair-Caereinion and back to the Raven Square terminus.

• **Parking** Church Street; Berriew Street; Union Street (both car parks) • **Early closing** Thursday • **Market day** Monday • **Cinema** Pola, Berriew Street, TEL. Welshpool 2145 • **Event** County Show (May) • **Information** TEL. Welshpool 2043 (summer only) • **AA 24 hour service** TEL. Shrewsbury 53003.

Guilsfield POWYS

3 miles north of Welshpool (PAGE 197 Cd)

Gentle Guilsfield hugs the Welsh Marches with a faintly uncertain air. In this hazy division of the borderlands, it seems unsure of which country it belongs to. The village has a distinctly English air, but the dedication of its church to St Aelhaiarn suggests that it rightly belongs to the Principality. Aelhaiarn is a very Welsh saint, one of three sons of a family that ruled Powys and the borders in the 6th century.

However, the church itself looks English, with battlements, corner buttresses and squared-off windows. The houses, too, are English, mostly brick Georgian or black-and-white timbered. Only a few slate-hung walls give a hint of the Welsh connection.

There is, however, a strong sense of Welsh respect for the faith and the dear departed in Guilsfield. The church clock, with its unusual slate face and numerals of gold leaf, ticks off the hours above an inscription warning: 'Be diligent; Night cometh'. The big bell in the tower beneath the small but jaunty spire, is boldly inscribed: 'May all I summon to the grave enjoy everlasting bliss.'

Parish records show that in 1811 there were 2049 people in 410 families living in 362 houses: 'Of these 975 were employed in agriculture and 162 in trade.' Working the land is still the main occupation in Guilsfield and the broad, shallow, fairly fertile valley that flanks it. The outside world reaches no nearer than a little-used branch of the Shropshire Union Canal that peters out about a mile from the village.

Guilsfield's Welsh name is *Cegidfa*, meaning 'the place of Cegid'. Cegid is hemlock in Welsh, and although hemlock itself is rare, tall clumps of similar white-flowered plants, such as hogweed and cow parsley, grow in abundance in the meadows and along the paths and streams that meander through the valley. You can see the name, Cegidfa, beneath Guilsfield on the signpost as you enter the village.

Llanymynech POWYS AND SHROPSHIRE

10 miles north of Welshpool (PAGE 197 Cc)

Listen carefully on a still night beside the long-disused lead and copper mines pockmarked into Llanymynech Hill and, so they say, you will hear the plaintive music of a blind fiddler lost for generations in the subterranean maze. He wandered, says a local legend, into the Ogof, the most extensive of the old workings, and fiddles despairingly in his search for a way out.

That may be, but there are other, perhaps more real, secrets in this mysterious borderland between England and Wales; more than just a lone fiddler lost among the rocks that look down on Llanymynech's winding street of stone houses.

Roman coins were found in the Ogof in 1965, and there is no doubt that their legions were plundering its mineral riches, including silver, around AD 100. Could this be the lost site of a Roman camp, known to have existed somewhere along the ordered supply line of the Welsh border from Chester in the north to Caerleon in the south?

This would fit in with the Roman scheme of things, and in Llanymynech's Lion Hotel you can hear – no names, of course – of a local farmer, who, ploughing a long-neglected field, found the remains of a Roman fort. He covered them up again quickly, thinking the land better to farm than to quarrel over with archaeologists.

People have fought long and often enough over these marches in the past. The border between England and Wales, not settled until 1535, now winds its way up Llanymynech's main street and cuts clean through the Lion. You can order a pint in the Principality and drink it in England. A plaque marks the borderline in the bar. Before Welsh licensing law was changed in 1960, you could drink on a Sunday in the English bar, but not in the lounge just a step away.

Llanymynech stands by the Afon Vyrnwy just above the point where it joins the Severn. For all its long past, the village has an early 19th-century look as if, during profitable years of mining and limestone quarrying, it decided to update its image and identify with the solid prosperity of the Industrial Revolution.

Now the ruins of the village potteries and the North Wales Railway hide near by behind screens of wild flowers, and 50 years of disuse has clogged the local stretch of the Shropshire Union Canal – known as the Montgomery Branch – which is now being restored.

Only the Church of St Agatha, alongside the Lion, proudly reflects its lost age. It was rebuilt in 1843–4 by Thomas Penson, surveyor for the former counties of Montgomeryshire and Denbighshire. He was inspired by Norman architecture, but he embellished it with incongruous pointed arches in the tower.

The interior resounds to the ticking of a clock

designed by local inventor Richard Roberts, who died in 1864. Its faces on the outside were made big enough to be seen by the quarrymen about a mile away on Llanymynech Hill, where Roberts worked as a boy. Final incongruity – the church is in England, so Welsh parishioners must enter another country to worship.

The greens and fairways of an international golf course dodge about among the mine workings. There are three holes in England and 15 in Wales – you can tee off in Wales and land out of bounds in England.

Montgomery POWYS

8 miles south of Welshpool (PAGE 197 Ce)

Age hangs gracefully on this ancient village. It has fine Georgian buildings and a lofty air of having played its part in history, come what may in the 20th century. How many villages have a town hall and a county jail?

But the centuries-old weekly cattle market moved to Welshpool years ago with the railway; and the fair, granted by charter of Henry III in 1227, has gone, too. The modern roads into Wales sweep away to the north, bypassing the valley and the wooded hills in which Montgomery sits.

It owes its name to a powerful friend of the Conqueror, Roger de Montgomery, Earl of Shrewsbury and Arundel, who was trusted to remain in Normandy as regent when William set out for Hastings in 1066. His reward was vast tracts of land in England, and the task of holding a strategic pass through the border hills against the troublesome Welsh.

Earl Roger built a castle a mile from the heart of present-day Montgomery, at a place called Hendomen, or the old mound. The original mound, 30 ft high and 22 ft across, can be clearly seen. For the best part of the following 500 years, Montgomery was a key defence post of the Welsh Marches.

The stark stone ruins remaining on an outcrop above the village are all that is left of the last castle built here, started by Henry III in 1223. There, 42 years later, at what became known as the Treaty of Montgomery, Henry accepted Llywelyn ap Gruffydd's right to be called Prince of Wales. He was the first and last full-blooded Welshman whose claim to the title was recognised by the English.

From 1541 Montgomery Castle was occupied by the Herbert family. It included the gifted brothers Edward, Lord Herbert of Cherbury (1582 – 1648), philosopher, historian, poet, soldier, diplomat and courtier; and also George Herbert (1593 – 1633), religious poet and hymn-writer. Edward occasionally lived at the castle, and George was born in Montgomery.

Montgomery became officially Welsh when the border was settled in 1535. Its strategic importance led to its name being given also to the county, formed from part of the medieval Welsh region of Powys. Montgomeryshire became part of the modern county of Powys when the boundaries were changed in 1974.

In September 1644, Parliamentary troops besieged the castle. Lord Herbert, a lukewarm Royalist, surrendered it in return for his safekeeping and that of his people. In 1649, Parliament ordered its demolition.

However, Montgomery remained a county town long after the castle had gone. Its frontages, mostly Georgian, still follow the medieval street pattern set when Henry granted the charter. Farmers crowded there then for business from the castle, and sheep and cattle were traded in Broad Street.

The old Town Hall, built in 1748, once had an open, arcaded ground floor where the market was held. The arches have now been filled in. Halfway up the hill behind the Town Hall is a terrace of three cottages converted from the old House of Correction – the original town jail, built in 1740. Its most celebrated occupant was John Davies, who spent his last night there after being sentenced to death for stealing a watch and five pence (about 2p).

He was hauled to the gallows in 1821, vehemently protesting his innocence, and swore from the scaffold that God would not let grass grow on his grave as proof of his innocence. A wooden sign marks the Robber's Grave by the north gate of St Nicholas's churchyard. A few sparse tufts of grass cling to it . . . but for more than 100 years a 3 ft long strip on the grave remained as barren as Davies had promised.

In 1830, a new county jail was built at the other end of the village. It was closed in 1878, and all but one of the three cell blocks were demolished.

WINDOW WATCH *Black-and-white timbered houses contrast with a mellow brick neighbour in this Montgomery terrace – though the distinctive upper windows of all three are almost identical.*

MAP 19

ON WENLOCK EDGE AND THE WELSH MARCHES

What are those blue remembered hills,
What spires, what farms are those?

The poet A. E. Housman was no Shropshire lad, but the beauty of Wenlock Edge and the Welsh Marches moved him to some memorable lines. Wenlock's heights stretch 16 miles; breathtaking vistas of woods and fertile farmlands lie below. Black-and-white buildings grace town and village; castle ruins and the great rampart of Offa's Dyke bespeak ancient battles along disputed borders.

MAP 19: NEIGHBOURING AREAS – MAPS 10, 12, 18, 20, 21

BEWDLEY	CHURCH STRETTON	LUDLOW
Abberley	Condover	Clungunford
Great Witley	Leebotwood	Dilwyn
Hartlebury	Munslow	Stokesay
	Pitchford	

MUCH WENLOCK	WEM
Leighton, Morville	High Ercall
Tong	Loppington

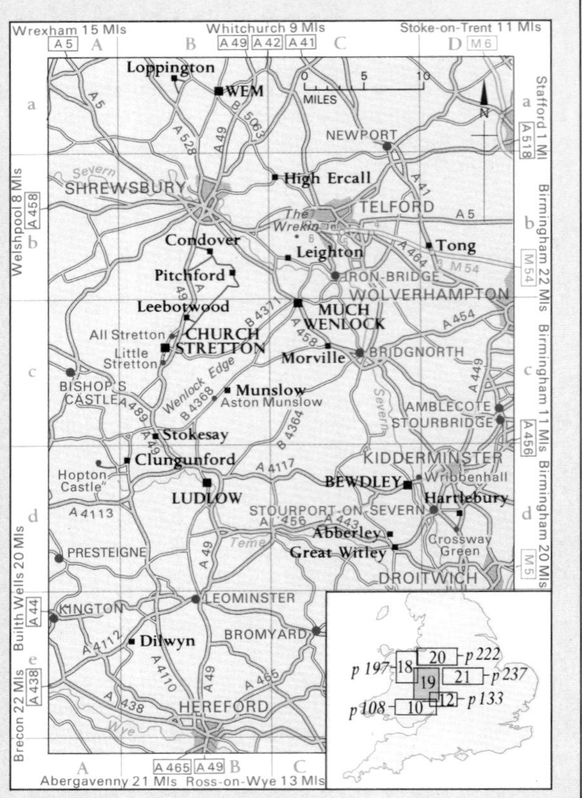

BEWDLEY

HEREFORD AND WORCESTER

4 miles west of Kidderminster (PAGE 206 Cd)

The medieval trades that brought prosperity to Bewdley – charcoal-burning, basket-making, tanning and saddlery – live on in the Shambles, a cobbled street in the centre of the town. Built in 1783 on the site of a butchers' market, the Shambles has two arcades of brick arches with market stalls inside. In the late 19th century three of the arches were demolished to make way for a police station, and in 1972 Bewdley Museum was opened here underneath the Guild Hall.

The museum galleries show displays of the various trades and their tools, and the building also houses the studios and workshops of local craftsmen, which are open to the public from March to November. At the bottom end of the Shambles are the cells and exercise yards of the town's former jail, built in 1802. The original prison cells were razed when a 15th-century bridge over the River Severn on which they stood was replaced in 1798.

This 'new' sandstone bridge was designed in three graceful arches by the great engineer Thomas Telford (1757 – 1834), with smaller arches on either side of the bank. On the west bank the bridge leads into the short but wide main street, Load Street – which, like the entire town centre, is a conservation area.

Load Street is lined by large Georgian houses, among which stands the dignified Guild Hall, built in 1808 by the Earl of Dudley. Next door is a 16th-century, timber-framed house which is the old post office. Beyond it, the street slopes up to the parish church of St Anne, built in the 1740s on the site of a medieval chapel. The peal of eight bells hung in the square tower in 1780 is still in use. On the corner of Lower Park and Lax Lane is an imposing Georgian house that was the birthplace of Stanley Baldwin (1867 – 1947), three times Prime Minister and later Earl Baldwin of Bewdley.

Across Telford's Bridge, in Wribbenhall, is the Severn Valley Railway and the West Midland Safari and Leisure Park. The railway runs a fleet of jaunty steam locomotives, which make the 25 mile round trip to Bridgnorth in Shropshire and the $3\frac{1}{2}$ mile trip to Kidderminster. The 200 acre safari park is set in the grounds of Spring Grove House, built in 1790.

• **Parking** Dog Lane; Load Street; Westbourne Street (all car parks) • **Early closing** Wednesday • **Market day** Saturday • **Events** Carnival (June); Regatta (July) • **Information** TEL. Bewdley 403303 • **Museum** TEL. Bewdley 403573 • **AA 24 hour service** TEL. Birmingham 550 4858.

Abberley HEREFORD AND WORCESTER

8 miles south-west of Bewdley (PAGE 206 Cd)

In the 16th century, Abberley's rector was a saintly man named John Blamyre. He came from an old Cumberland family and had been the abbot of a monastery in the north of England. But when he was deprived of his position, at the Dissolution of the

RIVERSIDE REVERIE *Small, colourful boats nose contentedly against an ancient hull by a riverside pub on the tranquil Severn at Bewdley.*

Monasteries, such was the unquestionable uprightness of his life amid the general corruption rife in many monasteries, that Henry VIII was obliged to give him some compensation. This the king did by appointing Blamyre rector of the parish of Abberley, at the southern end of a lush, undulating valley. A large bell, now cracked, still stands in a corner of the Church of St Michael to remind us of the former abbot. He had brought it from his monastery in the north.

The fine Rectory where Blamyre lived may date partly from the 14th century and, together with the 12th-century church beside it, stands on a little knoll in the centre of the old part of the village. Of the church, only the chancel is still intact, but the ruins of the nave have been well preserved and form part of a charming little garden overlooking the village square. Opposite the garden, on the other side of the square, is the imposing red-brick, 18th-century Jaylands, and a Dutch gabled, partly 16th-century building, which is now the village shop. Near by is the superb, timber-framed Town Farmhouse, probably 17th century.

Just behind the square rises the rich green Abberley Hill. Near the top is Abberley Hall, now a private school for boys – which includes among its former pupils the politician Sir Geoffrey Howe and the actor Anthony Quayle. The present house was built in the mid-19th century for the Moilliets, an Anglo-Swiss banking family. Later owners of Abberley Hall were the Jones family, who had made a fortune in the Lancashire cotton industry. They built the tall Gothic-style clock tower at the top of the hill.

Abberley's second church, dedicated to St Mary, was built by James Moilliet. It stands near the early 18th-century Tump House, across a small valley from the old church and the village square.

Great Witley

HEREFORD AND WORCESTER

8 miles south of Bewdley (PAGE 206 Cd)

Lying in the remains of a park on Great Witley's south-eastern edge, the ruins of the palatial Witley Court present a scene of eerie, desolate grandeur. A noble portico built by the Regency architect John Nash in the early 19th century, the arches of an orangery which once housed exotic plants, and the immense ballroom where such guests as Edward VII when Prince of Wales and probably the actress Lillie Langtry were entertained – all lie empty and open to the elements. Below them, on the south terrace is a colossal fountain, depicting the classical hero Perseus and Andromeda, his wife. It stands in a dried-up miniature lake, where once the fountain's main jet soared 90 ft high.

Witley Court, never restored after a disastrous fire in 1937, was once a modest manor house bought in the mid-17th century by the Foley family, ironmasters from Stourbridge. From that time on, successive owners added to the building, until it became a palace fit for a queen – Queen Adelaide, widow of William IV, who lived here between 1843 and 1846. Later in the 19th century it was embellished even further by the Earls of Dudley.

The only part to survive the fire and remain in use is the Church of St Michael and All Angels, built onto Witley Court itself in 1735. Its builder, the 1st Lord Foley, is commemorated in a superb memorial, in the south transept, by the 18th-century Flemish sculptor John Michael Rysbrack. The church's other most outstanding features – fine Venetian paintings on the ceiling, painted glass windows and the case of an organ used by the composer George Frederic Handel – were bought by the 2nd Lord Foley. They came from the chapel of Canons, a long-demolished 18th-century villa at Edgware, Middlesex.

Beyond Witley Court's North Lodge, the village of Great Witley lies scattered over the green plain at the foot of the hills of Abberley, Walsgrove and Woodbury. At the crossroads marking the village centre is the imposing 18th-century Hundred House Inn, with a fine double-bow front. From here, the Stourport road passes the former Rectory and an old mill house down in a dell. A lane off the Droitwich road goes past the fine red-brick Hillhampton House, to the south-east, and other roads from the village centre lead up the hills behind. From the edges of the wood on top of Woodbury Hill, superb views look south-east over Worcestershire and west into Wales. Woodbury Hill also bears the remains of ancient British earthworks.

Hartlebury HEREFORD AND WORCESTER

5 miles south-east of Bewdley (PAGE 206 Dd)

On the northern edge of the village and rising serenely from a moat, Hartlebury Castle serves as a permanent reminder of an era when the Bishops of Worcester, whose official residence it is, were military as well as ecclesiastical figures. The present castle was built on a site that has belonged to the bishops since it was given to them by the King of Mercia in the 9th century. It incorporates remains of a 13th-century castle and centres on a 15th-century great hall. But most of the elegant building of warm red sandstone and brick dates from the 17th and 18th centuries, when it was added to by a succession of bishops.

The castle has striking pointed-arch windows on the ground floor. Its state rooms, including the late 18th-century Bishop Hurd's Library, are open to the public on Wednesdays in summer. In the north wing, the Hereford and Worcester County Museum – open on weekdays and Sunday afternoons from March to October – houses a collection of carriages, bright gypsy caravans and old costumes.

Beyond the castle park, which has a small nature reserve, Hartlebury village rises up the side of a steep hill. About halfway up is the 19th-century Church of St James, which has a 16th-century tower. The timber-framed Church Cottage lies just below the church, and standing back from the road is the late 17th-century Rectory. This red-brick house, with a shell-shaped hood over the front door, is in the style of Sir Christopher Wren, and was built for the son of Bishop Stillingfleet, one of the Worcester bishops.

CHURCH STRETTON

SHROPSHIRE

13½ miles south of Shrewsbury (PAGE 206 Bc)

The town looks old – which it is. Its many black-and-white buildings look medieval, which most of them are not, having been built around the turn of the century when the town was enjoying a new vogue as a health resort.

Church Stretton is actually three settlements in one. Little Stretton stands 1½ miles south of the town and the village of All Stretton lies to the north. It is said that James I distinguished between the three when he arrived first at Little Stretton, and gave it that name; then he went on to name Church Stretton because of its Norman church; and finally reaching the next village, he remarked: 'It's all Stretton about here.' An unlikely story, perhaps.

King John granted Church Stretton a Market Charter in 1214, and a small market is still held every Thursday in the square. Remains of the medieval town are in High Street, once part of the old Bristol to Chester road, an important coaching route. It is here that some genuinely old buildings are found. Most of the 18th and 19th-century buildings are also in High Street, both half-timbered and more conventionally Georgian and Victorian.

The Church of St Laurence, just behind High Street, was built on the site of a Saxon foundation. Its nave is Norman and the tower was built about 1200. Above the doorway in the north wall there is a well-worn medieval fertility figure. A poignant memorial to a tragic event of 1968 hangs over the aisle; it takes the form of a gridiron with twisted flakes of copper simulating flames, and is dedicated to three boys who died in a hotel fire. The gridiron is the symbol of St Laurence, who was burnt to death on one in AD 258.

In the south transept is a small memorial window to the Victorian novelist Sarah Smith. She was a constant visitor to All Stretton and wrote under the name of 'Hesba Stretton'. A figure in green on the window represents her book *Jessica's First Prayer*.

Victoriana at its most decorative can be seen along the wide and pleasant Sandford Avenue, which was created in 1884 by the Reverend Holland Sandford. At one end, The Hotel – originally an extension of The Crown inn – was where the boys died. Most of the building is now converted into shops and flats, but a pub still called The Hotel has survived.

All Stretton has a couple of black-and-white houses, while Little Stretton has a number of fine timber-framed buildings, some genuine and some, like All Saints' Church, not all they seem. The church with its trim thatch, Gothic windows and close-set timbers is a picture, but was built as recently as 1903.

Shops, hotels and restaurants are reminders of the town's growth in the late 19th and early 20th centuries, when it was vigorously promoted as a 'health resort with natural springs of pure water second to none in the country'. However good the water, the Victorians came also to enjoy the 'very bracing and exhilarating surroundings', and for once the publicity men did not exaggerate. True an old guidebook went a little over the top when it described Church Stretton's location as being within the 'Highlands of England', for the surrounding hills are barely 1700 ft high. Yet what they lack in size they make up for in scenic grandeur. Carding Mill Valley between The Long Mynd to the west and Caer Caradoc, opposite, is particularly attractive. Carding Mill Valley belongs to the National Trust. It takes its name from an old mill, now demolished, and lies about a mile from the town centre. It is reached along a cul-de-sac road that winds its way up the hillside.

• **Parking** Easthope Road (car park) • **Early closing** Wednesday • **Market day** Thursday • **Event** Arts Festival (July/August) • **Information** TEL. Church Stretton 722535 (summer) • **AA 24 hour service** TEL. Shrewsbury 53003.

Condover SHROPSHIRE

8½ miles north of Church Stretton (PAGE 206 Bb)

A quiet country road snakes through this pretty village, its houses tucked away behind neat hedgerows, grassy banks and red-sandstone walls. There are several attractive old brick and timber-framed houses, a post office, a shop and a church which, standing back from the road, harmonises well with its surroundings. This handsome building of creamy-red sandstone is dedicated to St Andrew and St Mary.

A church has stood here for more than 1000 years, from the times when Condover was a Saxon settlement. The present building dates from Norman times, though much was rebuilt after a disaster in 1660 when, as the parish records have it, 'the steeple and church came all down and fell on heaps'. It has no steeple now, but the simple buttressed and castellated tower has a black-and-gold clock face.

In complete contrast to the rural simplicity of the village is Condover Hall, a magnificent Elizabethan house which is now a school run by the Royal National Institute for the Blind. Educationalists from many parts of the world came to study the techniques used here to assist blind and handicapped children.

The hall was built for a wealthy merchant, Judge Thomas Owen, who died in 1598 before it was completed. It is not open to the public, but can be seen, framed by its stone archway, at the edge of the village. Made of the same creamy sandstone as the church, it is a monument to the art of its stonemason builder, Walter Hancock, from Much Wenlock – a perfect blend of gables, windows, bays and towers, topped by groups of tall chimneys.

Condover has another Elizabethan connection, for here lived Richard Tarlton who was jester to Elizabeth I. It is said that he was Shakespeare's inspiration for the character of Yorick, the 'fellow of infinite jest, of most excellent fancy', whose skull features in the graveyard scene in *Hamlet*.

Leebotwood SHROPSHIRE

4 miles north of Church Stretton (PAGE 206 Bc)

Motorists purring along the trunk road that cuts Leebotwood in two are often oblivious to the existence of the village, so spread-out are its buildings. Occasional glimpses of black-and-white houses and red-brick farms scattered among fields and hedgerows are all that most travellers see, yet there is a rich store of history hereabouts.

The best starting point is the church, a plain and simple building dating from the 13th century and standing on a hill overlooking the village, which lies in a wide valley. In the 12th century the whole area was thickly forested and was known as Botwde, or Botwood. These lands were granted to the Augustinian canons by Henry II (1154 – 89), together with a chapel at Lega – hence Leebotwood.

The valley was an important thoroughfare even in Roman times. Watling Street, its route still clearly visible, forms the eastern boundary of the village. Caer Caradoc, rising in the south to 1506 ft, is said to be one of the last strongholds of the native chief Caradoc, or Caractacus, who held out against the Roman invaders. Castle Hill, on the opposite side of the valley, has a 260 ft long mound which was possibly a Saxon fortification built over a prehistoric barrow.

The village began to assume its present shape in the mid-16th century, and some houses probably date from that period, although red-brick walls now disguise the timber-frame core. The Pound Inn, however, proudly displays its gleaming white walls to passing traffic on the main road, and even has white-painted chimneys poking up from a thatch that looks as though it had been flung over the building like a thick blanket. Although the inn bears the date 1650, the building actually dates from around 1480 and was a farmhouse, not an inn, until 1804.

Horseshoe Corner, farther down the road, was once an inn, too, which closed after the coming of the railway in 1852 and is now a private house. Its size, courtyard and exposed timbers are evidence of its age and previous use, and it keeps its name.

Munslow SHROPSHIRE

8 miles south-east of Church Stretton (PAGE 206 Bc)

The village, strung out along a sharp S-bend in the road running below Wenlock Edge, is pretty enough, with a terrace of gabled cottages, stone houses and a high stone wall oozing aubrietia, stonecrop and toadflax. The best of Munslow, however, lies off the road in the direction of the church, reached by a twisting lane that winds among steep little hills.

St Michael's Church sits in a wooded hollow and is surrounded by immaculate houses and barns, all built with Wenlock limestone. The elegant Georgian rectory, now a private house, has a fine front porch supported by two pairs of columns, with mature lawns leading down to a small pool. St Michael's has a Norman tower, topped by an 18th-century parapet, a splendid 14th-century wooden porch, and some 500-year-old stained-glass windows.

Aston Munslow, a mile to the south-west, has also developed away from the main road and is graced with several black-and-white buildings, including the Swan Inn, which has a dormer-like storey nodding forward over steps leading to the entrance.

But of all the charming buildings tucked away along a maze of back lanes, the most interesting is the White House. This has Norman foundations – possibly even earlier – a 14th-century hall, an Elizabethan timbered wing and a Georgian wing.

These additions, seemingly made with little regard to blending with the previous styles, give the White House a rather rambling appearance, but therein lies its charm: there can be few places where so many contrasting styles can be seen under one roof.

In every room the skill and craftsmanship of the original builders can be seen. All the original woodwork is still there, down to the locking pegs in the beams, and the medieval hall has a ceiling supported by a magnificent cruck frame. The fine state of preservation is undoubtedly due to the fact that the house has been lived in continuously for 900 years or more.

There are other interesting buildings in the grounds, including 17th-century coach and cider houses, a granary, a 16th-century stable block and the ruins of a 13th-century dovecote. The White House now contains a Country Life Museum, established by the present owner, and is open to visitors from Easter to the end of October, usually on Wednesdays, Saturdays and sometimes on Thursdays.

Pitchford SHROPSHIRE

7 miles north-east of Church Stretton (PAGE 206 Bb)

This typical Shropshire farming village, where red-brick houses complement the red sandstone of solidly built Pitchford Farm, lies on a quiet back lane and has no shops or pubs. It has, however, one of the most

WOODEN WONDER OVERLEAF

The dazzling patterns of diamonds and chevrons that decorate the front of Pitchford Hall represent a peak of timber-framed construction in England. The 16th-century house was built before the growing demands of Elizabethan shipwrights made timber less plentiful.

notable Elizabethan houses in England, Pitchford Hall.

The hall was built between 1473 and 1549 for the Ottleys, members of a wealthy Shrewsbury family which acquired the estate in 1473, then lived there for 300 years. The hall represents the peak of the timber-frame building period, and is a riot of black and white. From their stone foundations to the stone-tiled roof, the walls are a maze of beams forming diamond and chevron patterns.

One of the best views of the hall is from the lodge at the northern end of the village, when all the superb details come into perspective, particularly the elegant star-shaped chimneys and the pretty roof gables. A closer view can be gained from the drive that leads from a second lodge, half a mile north of the village, to the Church of St Michael and All Angels which stands on a slight rise next to the house. Near the church a giant lime tree supports a timber-framed 'tree house' of 1714 in its massive branches.

St Michael's is considerably older than the hall, dating partly from the 12th century but mostly from the 13th. It is a small, unpretentious building of red sandstone with buttressed walls and a steeply sloping roof topped by a weatherboarded belfry. In the north wall, Norman herringbone stonework can be seen below a blocked window. Inside the church is an oak effigy – measuring 7 ft – of the Knight Templar Sir John de Pitchford (1237 – 85).

The Row Brook flows through a wooded hollow in the parkland below the hall, and an old stone wall stands beside a disused bridge. This is the site of the bituminous well, which still produces pitch, and the ford from which the village and the hall took their names.

LUDLOW

SHROPSHIRE

27 miles south of Shrewsbury (PAGE 206 Bd)

Two imposing buildings break the skyline above the beautiful border town of Ludlow: the sand and limestone castle and the spacious Church of St Laurence.

The castle was built between 1086 and 1094 by a Norman knight named Roger de Lacy. He chose the site shrewdly, so that the fortress had towering cliffs on two sides. From its lofty vantage point, the castle helped to hold down the conquered Welsh and the rebellious men of the border.

The outer bailey is the size of a sports field, and may have been used as a refuge by the townspeople during times of strife. The massive keep was built up from the original gatehouse tower in the early 12th century, and the domestic buildings were added in the late 13th and early 14th centuries, mainly by the Mortimer family, who inherited the castle from the de Lacys. The Elizabethan buildings came when the castle became the seat of the Council of the Marches, set up to govern Wales and its wild borderlands.

Ludlow town grew up on the east side of the castle, and its magnificent jumble of medieval, Tudor, Stuart and Georgian houses is overlooked by the 135 ft tower of St Laurence's Church. Built mostly in the 15th century, it is one of the largest parish churches in England. But its special glories are the beautifully carved misericords (backs of choir seats) in the chancel.

Next to the church, in the Garden of Rest, is the Reader's House, so called because it was the home in

Broad Gate, Broad Street

The Reader's House – the porch

the 18th century of the Reader, the Rector's chief assistant. West of the church are Hosier's Almshouses, originally endowed in 1486 by a rich local wool merchant, John Hosier. The present buildings, however, date from 1758.

Near by is a classically designed 18th-century stone building, the Butter Cross, which lies at the heart of Ludlow's market place. The Butter Cross once housed a school but is now the town museum.

North of the Butter Cross, in the Bull Ring, is The Feathers Hotel, one of the finest timber-framed buildings in England. Enlarged in 1619, its front is a rich profusion of ornamental carvings – and its interior contains carved overmantels, embossed plaster ceilings and panelling. An ornate, first-floor balcony was added in the mid-19th century.

South of the Butter Cross is Ludlow's most impressive thoroughfare, Broad Street. The Angel Hotel, an old coaching inn, has a back room called the Nelson Room. Lord Nelson was a hereditary burgess of Ludlow, and it was in this inn, in 1802, that his title was formally confirmed and he was given the freedom of the town.

At the foot of Broad Street – with its ranks of black-and-white, timber-framed shops and houses – is the Broad Gate. It was built in the 13th century, and is

Butter Cross, timbered shops and St Laurence's Church

FINE FEATHERS FOR THE FESTIVAL

The Broad Gate is the only surviving medieval gate into Ludlow. Uphill from it, the stone Butter Cross is flanked by half-timbered shops—while St Laurence's Church peeps over its shoulder. Next door to the church, the Reader's House has a fine Jacobean porch, which was added in 1616. Each June, the Feathers Hotel and other buildings in the town centre wear bunting to celebrate a festival of music and art.

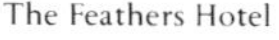

The Feathers Hotel

the only one of Ludlow's seven town gates to survive. Below it, Lower Broad Street, once an important cloth-making area, dips down to the River Teme, which flows by the town and the castle. The river is crossed by the 15th-century Ludford Bridge.

In the summer, Ludlow holds a festival of music, drama and art. Among its highlights is an outdoor production of a Shakespeare play, staged within the inner bailey of the castle.

• **Parking** Castle Street; Lower Galdeford; Upper Galdeford (all car parks) • **Early closing** Thursday • **Market days** Monday, Friday, Saturday • **Event** Festival (June/July) • **Information** TEL. Ludlow 3857 (summer) **AA 24 hour service** TEL. Shrewsbury 53003.

Clungunford SHROPSHIRE

10 miles west of Ludlow (PAGE 206 Bd)

As far as this timeless little village is concerned, the words written by the poet A. E. Housman in *A Shropshire Lad* still apply:

'Clunton and Clunbury, Clungunford and Clun,
Are the quietest places under the sun.'

Clungunford, once known and still sometimes called by its Saxon name of Gunnas, takes its present name from the Saxon lord, Gunna or Gunward, and his 'ford over the river Clun'. From the small village centre, on the slopes above the church, you can see the river meandering among rolling hill country close to the English-Welsh border. Offa's Dyke, the huge 8th-century earth bank which served as the first official border, straddles the hills only a few miles away. Behind the church is a Norman motte – a mound that carried a rough-and-ready castle.

Red-brick houses and older, more traditional cottages are scattered around the village. Clungunford House, a fine Georgian mansion, is hidden among trees and gardens. Splendid though it may be, however, its desirability as a residence is today matched by what was once a far humbler home – The Thatched Cottage on Beckjay Lane, built probably in the 14th century as a farm labourer's home.

Skilfully restored with an eye to authenticity, the timber-framed cottage even retains some of the original wattle-and-daub (woven twigs plastered with mud) filling between the timbers. A stepped chimney, built onto the end wall, is a rare example of Welsh influence in these parts.

Clungunford's Church of St Cuthbert is a grand affair, in an interesting mixture of styles, from the mid-13th century onwards. The tower looks Norman, but in fact was built in 1895, at the same time as the splendid timber porch. Near the porch there is a circular, three-tiered mound of stones – the remnants of an ancient preaching cross.

In a hollow among wooded hills 3 miles west of the village stands Hopton Castle, a square Norman keep three storeys high that was given to the de Hoptons in 1165 by Henry II. During the Civil War, a

small garrison of 29 Parliamentarians held out against a superior Royalist force. When the castle fell in March 1644, the defenders were clubbed to death and their bodies thrown into a nearby pond.

Dilwyn HEREFORD AND WORCESTER

18 miles south-west of Ludlow (PAGE 206 Be)

Dilwyn, set in the peaceful Herefordshire countryside, is a study in black and white, for around the pretty little village green stand timber-framed houses that dazzle the eye when the sun catches their chequered façades and is mirrored in the polished glass of casement windows. Karen Court is particularly fine and a credit to the restorers who, quite recently, turned a ramshackle collection of farm buildings into a long row of pristine cottages. Behind the cottages is a well kept courtyard and gardens, with a massive stone cider press, a reminder that this is cider country.

Not every building in Dilwyn is timber-framed, though that is the first impression; others of later periods blend well with their comely neighbours. The Old Police Station is one, pretending to be timber-framed with black timbers set into the stonework of its gable end; another is Townsend House, a rather grand mostly 17th-century residence with an ornate canopied verandah.

Of much greater age, yet hardly showing it, is St Mary's Church which stands on slightly raised ground. Mainly 13th century, it has a squat Norman tower topped by a spire thought to have been added in the 18th century. St Mary's lists every one of its vicars on an inside wall, from Thomas of Colchester in 1275 to the present day.

Outside the village there are more black-and-white buildings, red-roofed and gabled, and contrasting vividly with the soft green of the surrounding low hills and farmland. Over a mile to the north is Luntley Court, a 17th-century manor house with a superb two-storey porch. Even the dovecote is timber-framed. It stands in a field opposite the house and is a squat building, looking rather like a house of cards about to collapse. Pitch Farm, about a mile from Dilwyn on the Leominster road, is another black-and-white house dating from the 16th and 17th centuries.

Though its name is Welsh sounding, Dilwyn is as English as the cider for which the county is famous. Cider apples and hops are still grown, and the beef cattle known as Haven Herefords originated at the local Haven Farm.

Stokesay SHROPSHIRE

8 miles north-west of Ludlow (PAGE 206 Bc)

The few houses and farm buildings that make up Stokesay, live in the shadow of a perfectly preserved piece of medieval England – Stokesay Castle, one of the oldest surviving fortified manor houses in the

FORTIFIED IN THE GRAND MANOR

The incredible Stokesay Castle rears from its rural setting like some fairytale fastness, defying both time and enemies. What began as a stark Norman stronghold was transformed between 1285 and 1305 into a grand manor house – but one that could still defend itself. Elizabethans added the timbered gatehouse.

Stokesay Castle

The castle gatehouse

country, which has remained almost unchanged over seven centuries. The settlement, originally known as Stoke (meaning 'dairy farm'), became the property of the de Say family following the Norman Conquest, and Stokesay, as it eventually became known, was their home until about 1240.

Although the lower two storeys in the north tower survive from this early period, Stokesay as it now stands was largely the work of Lawrence of Ludlow, a wealthy wool merchant who probably bought the castle in 1281 and set about turning it into a grand country residence. He demolished much of the older building and put up a cavernous great hall, comfortable living quarters, south tower and a protective wall. The manor house, one of the first of its kind, was built between 1285 and 1305 and was the home of Lawrence's descendants for the next 300 years. Its superb condition today is due largely to the care given it by successive owners, and to the fact that it has changed hands only five times in 700 years. During the Civil War, it escaped virtually undamaged after being surrendered to Cromwellian troops in 1645.

The result of Lawrence's handiwork is an extremely attractive building which, nevertheless, gives the impression that its creator was not sure what he wanted it to be. The south tower is very much fortress-like with its buttressed walls and battlements. The north tower, however, is domestic and has a timber-framed projecting upper storey and a steeply sloping roof. Between the two towers the great hall has tall Gothic windows and pointed gables, facing the courtyard on one side and open country on the other.

Near fantasy is added by the Elizabethan gatehouse which, with its timber-framing, overlapping upper storey and leaded windows, is as unfortress-like as the main entrance to a castle could be. It is, for all that, a superb structure with close-set timbers in the lower floor, diamond-shaped strutting on the upper and much carving – all in natural-coloured wood.

Stokesay Castle is open daily between March and October, except on Tuesdays, and in November at weekends. Worth seeing are the massive roof of the great hall, with timbers made from whole trees, a timber staircase set into the wall and the oldest of its kind in the country, and the Flemish carved overmantel fitted over a medieval fireplace. The overmantel was brought over from Flanders by the Baldwyn family, who lived in the castle in the 17th century.

Stokesay's parish church, dedicated to St John the Baptist, was partially destroyed by Cromwell's men. It was rebuilt in the mid-17th century and is, therefore, that rarity, a Commonwealth church. Inside there are elegant canopied pews where sat the gentry, and plain box pews for humbler folk.

MUCH WENLOCK

SHROPSHIRE

13 miles south-east of Shrewsbury (PAGE 206 Cc)

Set in a dip to the north-east of Wenlock Edge, the tiny market town of Much Wenlock is a friendly patchwork of twisting streets, half-timbered houses, black-and-white cottages and limestone buildings.

The town grew beside a priory dedicated to its first abbess, St Milburga. Milburga came from a family of saints – her mother and two sisters were all saints and her father, Merewald, King of Mercia, founded the priory about AD 680 as a nunnery. Two centuries later the priory was disrupted by the Danes, and 200 years after that it was rebuilt by Lady Godiva's husband, Leofric. Finally, in 1540, it was closed by order of Henry VIII, and its extensive ruins, which are open to the public, lie at the end of the Bull Ring. Adjoining the priory is an L-shaped, early 16th-century building that was once the infirmary and the Prior's Lodge. It is now a private house.

In the middle of the town is the mainly 16th-century Guildhall, its overhanging first floor held up by stout oak pillars. One of these pillars was the town

Looking down on Much Wenlock

whipping post, and still carries the iron staples to which the prisoners' wrists were tied. Beside the whipping post are the wheeled stocks in which wrongdoers were carted about the town. The last time this happened was in 1852.

The Guildhall has three gables, one of them over a passageway leading into the yard of Holy Trinity Church. The Norman church, with its stubby, battlemented tower, has a Jacobean pulpit whose carved panels include, somewhat oddly, some two-tailed mermen. On the other side of the street, opposite the Guildhall, is the local museum, and farther along in Sheinton Street are the Old Gaolhouse, which was a prison in the 18th century, and the timber-framed, mainly 17th-century Manor House. The only exposed cruck-framed building in the town is St Owen's Well House, in Queen Street. It is next to a well, dedicated to the 6th-century Welsh saint, who may have visited the area.

In the High Street is Raynalds' Mansion, built in about 1600 and which takes its name from John and Mary Raynalds who lived there. The timbered building has three steep gables with carved balconies in each of its bays which John Raynalds added in 1683. Across the road, a medieval timber-framed building that was once the old Falcon Inn is now a bank.

A native of Much Wenlock, Dr William Penny Brookes, introduced physical education to British schools. In 1850 he also started his Olympian Games in the town. The annual event became so famous that in 1860, when games modelled on those of ancient Greece were held near Athens, the marathon winner's trophy was called the Wenlock Prize. Sadly, the doctor died in 1895, a year before the modern Olympic Games were started at Athens. An athletics meeting is still held annually at Much Wenlock in his honour.

• **Parking** St Mary's Lane; High Street; Back Lane; Bull Ring (all car parks) • **Early closing** Wednesday • **Event** Wenlock Olympian Games (July) • **Information** TEL. Much Wenlock 727629 (summer) • **AA 24 hour service** TEL. Shrewsbury 53003.

Leighton SHROPSHIRE

6 miles north of Much Wenlock (PAGE 206 Cb)

Any village with the wooded Wrekin, the high escarpment of Wenlock Edge and the twisting River Severn as companions starts with a huge advantage, and Leighton must be a contender for the title of Shropshire's loveliest village. There is not much of it, but in such a setting the church, pub, hall and a few houses are just enough to make a discreet blend of rural community and unspoilt countryside.

Several black-and-white cottages line the Shrewsbury to Iron-Bridge road that runs through the village. Each cottage has its own style, but all have their gables and dormer windows decorated with a carved sawtooth design and a wooden spike at the apex. The windows themselves are decorated with a distinctive latticework pattern.

Trees border both sides of the road, some forming part of the park of Leighton Hall, a red-brick house of 1778. Leighton Lodge stands near the entrance to the hall, and was the birthplace in 1881 of Mary Webb, the author of *Precious Bane* and other stories about life in Shropshire.

The village church, St Mary's, is also in the park and predates its neighbours by some 60 years. It contains many memorials to the Leighton family, including an effigy, probably dating from the 13th century, of a knight in chain mail, and others to the Kynnersley family.

The road east of Leighton Lodge climbs a small hill and, emerging from the trees, brings into view a green-baize landscape of water meadows with the Severn carving a silvery loop and Wenlock Edge ascendant on the skyline. The road then drops down to Buildwas, where the impressive remains of a 12th-century abbey stand by the river. Near by, the Severn is spanned by an arch built in 1906 to replace Thomas

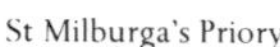
St Milburga's Priory

Raynalds' Mansion

Limestone cottage

MARKET TOWN THAT HAS A VILLAGE AIR

Rising above rooftops on the edge of Much Wenlock, the Church of Holy Trinity dates from Norman times. Norman, too, are the remains of St Milburga's Priory, founded as a nunnery in the 7th century. The priory flourished until it was dissolved in 1540, and now its impressive ruins tower more than 70 ft above immaculate expanses of lawn. The High Street, not far away, is so narrow you might think yourself in a village. Among its fine timbered houses is the late 17th-century Raynalds' Mansion. Limestone from the hillside quarries of Wenlock Edge was used to build the priory and many of the town's neat little cottages.

Leighton Hall

STOUT BRICK, TRIM TIMBER

Glinting through parkland greenery stands Leighton Hall, built of red brick in the late 18th century. Just as decorative, though not so grand, is one of Leighton's trim, black-and-white cottages.

Telford's first cast-iron bridge of 1795–8. A section of the old bridge remains as a tribute to the engineer who was 'Surveyor of Public Works for Shropshire' from 1786 until 1793.

Morville SHROPSHIRE

5 miles south-east of Much Wenlock (PAGE 206 Cc)

The steep, wooded slopes of Meadowley Bank provide a green velvet setting for this scattered limestone village on the main road between Much Wenlock and Bridgnorth. From the road the view is inviting, with a church and a hall facing each other across a wide lawn and the gilded domes of two rooftop cupolas rising above the trees.

Closer inspection reveals that the cupolas crown the stable pavilions of Morville Hall, an Elizabethan house extensively rebuilt in the 18th century. They stand facing each other across the broad sweep of grass in front of the hall, to which they are connected by curved walls. The hall itself is in unpretentious Georgian style, with lattice windows, a parapeted roof and porticoed doorway. The only ornamentation is on the faces of the two projecting wings, where four columns, each topped by a stone ball, rise to the level of the third storey.

Much of the stone is from the Benedictine priory buildings which once stood on the site and there is evidence of the original Elizabethan staircases. Morville Hall is owned by the National Trust, but can be visited only by written application to the tenant.

The village church is the only one in Shropshire dedicated to St Gregory. After the dedication ceremony, performed in 1118 by the Bishop of Hereford, lightning killed two women and five horses in the village. Most of the church is Norman, and the south door has 12th-century ironwork. The nave has 17th-century woodcarvings of St Matthew with an angel, St Mark with a lion, St Luke with an ox and St John with an eagle. There is little more to Morville other than the church and the hall, but what there is completes the picture of rural charm. The village school is a rugged Victorian building watching over the weathered remains of a sandstone whipping post. Near by is the Acton Arms, as smart as the pale beige paint that decorates its outside walls.

Black-and-white cottage, at Leighton

Aldenham Park, a few miles west of the church, was built at the end of the 17th century by Sir Edward Acton. His family lived there from the 14th century and includes a number of remarkable men. One was Sir John Acton, who went to seek his fortune in Italy before inheriting Aldenham. He ended as Prime Minister to King Ferdinand IV of Naples during the

Napoleonic Wars. There he reorganised the navy and army. At the time it was rumoured in Naples that he had arranged the murder of Prince Caramanico, who was one of his rivals.

Sir John's son Charles was a cardinal of the Roman Catholic Church. A cousin was the Victorian historian, the 1st Lord Acton, who also lived at Aldenham. He was a friend of Gladstone and wrote the much-quoted words: 'Power tends to corrupt, and absolute power corrupts absolutely', in a letter to Bishop Mandell Creighton.

Another member of the family is the 20th-century man of letters Sir Harold Acton, friend of the writers Evelyn Waugh and Nancy Mitford. Sir Harold is reputed to have started the fashion for baggy trousers known as Oxford Bags in the 1920s.

Tong SHROPSHIRE

17 miles north-east of Much Wenlock (PAGE 206 Db)

There can be few villages in England that have had their place of worship compared with Westminster Abbey. Perhaps the American consul to Birmingham in 1868, Elihu Burritt, was overstating it a bit when he called Tong church a 'little Westminster', but certainly it has a wealth of beautiful and impressive monuments to noble families.

Pride of place goes to the Vernons, whose tombs include that of Sir Richard, a 15th-century Speaker of the House of Commons, and his wife Benedicta. Close

The 'Westminster' church at Tong

NOBLY RESTING IN PEACE

The alabaster effigies and vast tombs of some notable local families lie in Tong's ornate, red-sandstone church. These striking monuments have been compared to those in Westminster Abbey.

Effigies and tombs in the church

by lies Sir William, a Knight Constable of England, and his wife Margaret. The oldest tomb is that of Sir Fulke de Pembrugge, who was Lord of Tong from 1371 to 1409. His second wife, Isabella, lies beside him, and it was she who founded the church in 1410 so that Masses could be said for Sir Fulke, and for her two other husbands, Thomas Peyteveyne and John Ludlow.

The Church of St Mary and St Bartholomew is a Collegiate church, though the college buildings for 'a warden and four priests, two clerks and thirteen poor people' have long since gone. Built of red sandstone it has a central tower rising to a pinnacled spire.

Another link with the Vernons is the Great Bell of Tong, given to the church in 1518 by Henry Vernon. Recast twice in the centuries since, it now weighs 2 tons. A notice in the porch lists the special occasions on which it is rung – including royal births, royal visits to Tong, and visits by the head of the Vernon family.

Tong village is small and attractive with three red-brick Georgian houses, a large Victorian one, only a couple of new houses and several black-and-white cottages tucked away in quiet corners. It was here that Charles Dickens (1812–70) set the closing chapters of *The Old Curiosity Shop*. Beyond the main road an ornamental lake is all that remains of the landscaped park of Tong Castle, remodelled by Capability Brown in 1765. The castle was demolished in 1954 and the M54 motorway goes through the middle of the ruins.

Relics of two wars, some 300 years apart, can be found near Tong. At RAF Cosford, 2 miles south, are aircraft and other exhibits of the Second World War. Boscobel House, 3 miles east, is where Charles Stuart hid in an oak tree after his defeat at the Battle of Worcester in 1651. The present 'Royal Oak' is said to have sprouted from an acorn of the original tree.

WEM

SHROPSHIRE

11 miles north of Shrewsbury (PAGE 206 Ba)

The infamous Judge Jeffreys, of the 'Bloody Assizes', once owned this small and peaceful market town. He bought it – and several nearby hamlets, including Aston and Wolverley – for £9000 in 1684. Although he does not seem to have visited the town, he chose its name when, in the following year, he was made the 1st Baron Jeffreys of Wem. As James II's Chief Justice, Jeffreys held his notorious assizes in the West Country, when he condemned to death some 150 followers of the rebel Duke of Monmouth after their defeat at the Battle of Sedgemoor in July 1685.

Wem was largely destroyed by fire in 1677, and the oldest surviving building, other than the parish church, is Dial Cottage in the High Street. In the centuries after the fire, the cottage was protected by an insurance company fire mark (badge) high up on the front wall, but no longer there. The badge was to ensure that in the event of another blaze, the cottage would be saved by the company's local fire-fighters.

Set among the shops in the High Street are some half-timbered houses which give the street a somewhat medieval look. This is also true of the parish church of St Peter and St Paul, which has a 14th-century doorway and lofty tower with battlements, buttresses and pinnacles. The rest of the sandstone church is more recent, and inside is an early 18th-century brass chandelier and a Victorian wrought-iron pulpit.

To one side of the church is the old Market House, built in the early 1800s. Its upper floor stood on a series of stone columns, but the spaces between them are now bricked in and rendered. To the other side is the red-brick Town Hall, built in 1905 and with a Cheese Hall added 23 years later. A cheese fair was held there about every month until 1937. Not far away, in New Street, is The Hall, a fine Georgian house of mellow red brick; and the Conservative Club in Noble Street is also Georgian.

Farther along Noble Street is Hazlitt House, the boyhood home of the essayist and critic William Hazlitt (1778–1830). He had fond memories of the small cream-coloured house and wrote later: 'If I see a row of cabbage-plants or of peas or beans coming up, I immediately think of those which I used so carefully to water of an evening at Wem when my day's tasks were done . . .'

● **Parking** High Street (car park) ● **Early closing** Wednesday ● **Market day** Thursday ● **Event** Carnival (September) ● **Information** TEL. Whitchurch 4577 ● **AA 24 hour service** TEL. Shrewsbury 53003.

High Ercall SHROPSHIRE

10 miles south-east of Wem (PAGE 206 Cb)

The sandstone and brick houses of the village cluster around a T-junction near High Ercall Hall, the impressive remains of what was once a magnificent nobleman's mansion. It was built in 1608 for Sir Francis Newport, 1st Earl of Bradford, and the village – say it Arkle, like the great steeplechaser – grew with it.

With the exception of Ludlow, High Ercall was the last garrison in Royalist Shropshire to hold out against the Roundheads. Little is recorded of what damage was done in the conflict, but since then all but two wings of the house, forming an L-shape, have vanished. The ground floor is of local red sandstone, and the upper storey's brickwork has weathered badly. The old entrance cannot be recognised, and the moat and drawbridge which so patently failed to defend the hall against Cromwell's men have vanished.

In a garden behind the house stands an arcade of four arches mounted on round piers. There is nothing to show what they were for, but most likely they formed part of an inner courtyard, which the hall was known to have, or a loggia.

St Michael's Church stands next to the hall, still mostly medieval, despite the Puritans' exaggerated claims in 1646 that it was 'demolished'. The tower dates from the 14th century. The base is badly worn, possibly by the weather, though parishioners say that it was caused in olden times by people sharpening their spears on it – and they may be right.

In the churchyard is an 18th-century sundial which, surprisingly, records the time not only in High Ercall, but also in Jerusalem, Rome and Plymouth in Massachusetts, though nobody seems to know why.

About 200 yds from the T-junction, there are some almshouses of 1694, rather severely built in brick with dormer windows. But there is a certain dignity in their functionalism, and in that of the mid-19th-century façade of the local pub, the Cleveland Arms.

Loppington SHROPSHIRE

4 miles west of Wem (PAGE 206 Ba)

They are not given much to change in Loppington. This is old farming country, and novelty is viewed with suspicion. You can see all around the stamp of conservatism, not least in St Michael's Church.

Roundheads garrisoned it during the Civil War, entrenched behind its battlemented tower. Local Royalists stormed it, and drove them out regardless of the damage done to their own church in the process. Records show that St Michael's was badly burnt and the roof ruined. However, the church was completely replaced in 1656.

In the renovated south porch an inscription notes that the churchwarden at the time was Nicholas Dickin, one of a notable family of local landowners, after whom the village pub, the Dickin Arms, is named. However, if the Royalists celebrated after their victory – and it was a rare one for the Royalists around here – it was most likely to have been in the Blacksmith's Arms, which is much older. And they probably did it in much the same way as the regulars did until quite recently.

The pub was always what its name proclaims it as: the village blacksmith's. While horses were shod, beer was served. There was never a bar until 1984, when the building was renovated. Until then barrels were racked in the cellar and the ale hand-pumped upstairs on demand.

Subtle renovation and a thatched roof have kept its character. Even the villagers agree that the thatch is an improvement on the corrugated-iron roof, fitted in the 19th century, that replaced an earlier thatch.

An iron ring, 3 in. in diameter, is set in the middle of the road outside the Dickin Arms. It is the last bull ring in Shropshire. Until as recently as 1835, bulls were tethered there and baited as sport for the young bloods. A plaque in the pub wall tells of its use. They keep it not so much to celebrate an ancestral barbarity, but because to move it would mean change.

Loppington Hall, an 18th-century brick building with five bays and three storeys, contrasts rather harshly with the softness of the village, where the other houses are mostly brick and half-timbering, many with the cruck frame exposed.

One of the most attractive is The Nook, down the lane from the church, which for all its coy name is a working farmhouse. Its brick is mellowed by centuries of sunlight, yet the timbers are barely weathered. The churchyard has a well-worn look. In the interests of conservation the grass is kept uncut for most of the year, making it seem truly ancient rather than simply untidy. It fits in with the stone arches and Loppington's general air of changelessness.

MAP 20

THE PROUD PEAKS AND THE CHARM OF CHESHIRE

The Peak District is an oasis of beauty in England's industrial heartland. Its towns and villages speckle a landscape which offers windswept moors to the walker, lofty crags to the climber, sparkling streams to the angler – and peace to all. Below lies the Cheshire Plain, where cattle graze in black-and-white harmony with the timber-framed houses that adorn every village.

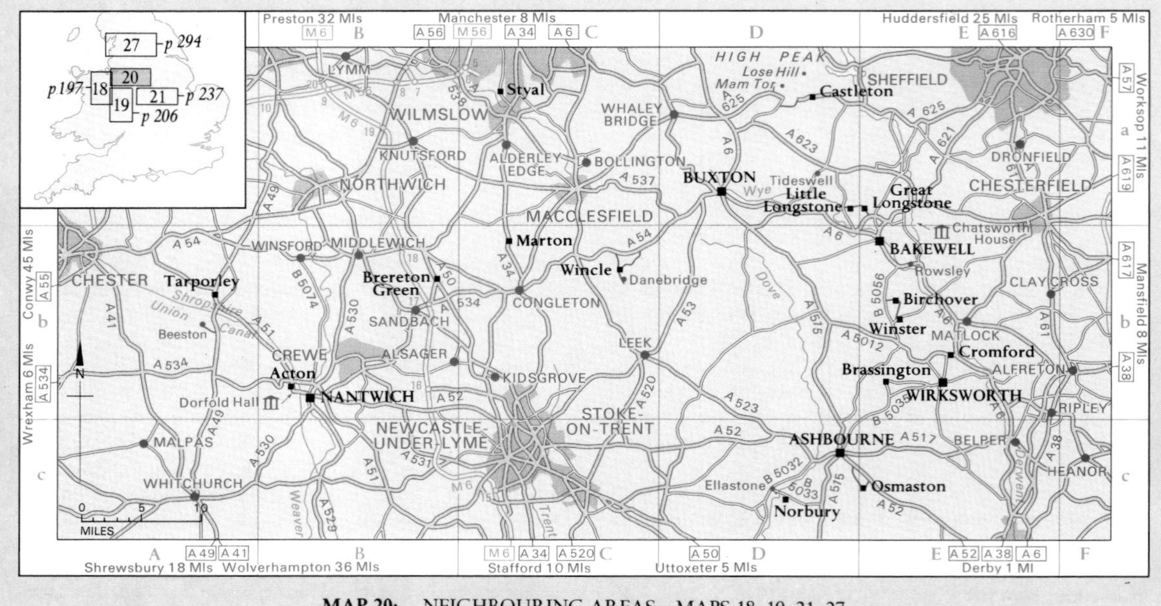

MAP 20: NEIGHBOURING AREAS – MAPS 18, 19, 21, 27

ASHBOURNE	BAKEWELL	BUXTON	NANTWICH	WIRKSWORTH
Norbury	Birchover	Castleton	Acton	Brassington
Osmaston	The Longstones	Marton	Brereton Green	Cromford
		Styal	Tarporley	Winster
		Wincle		

ASHBOURNE

DERBYSHIRE

21 miles east of Stoke-on-Trent (PAGE 222 Dc)

The 19th-century novelist George Eliot (Mary Ann Evans) used to visit Ashbourne, which she described as a 'pretty town within sight of the blue hills'. These hills, some up to 600 ft high, ring the town on the border of what is now the Peak District National Park. Ashbourne is Oakbourne in George Eliot's *Adam Bede* and the surrounding district, with its 'wide-scattered grey stone houses', is Stonyshire. She was particularly impressed by the 212 ft tapering spire of the parish church of St Oswald, which she called the finest single spire in England.

Dating from 1241, the church is noted for its host of ornamental tombs – the most impressive being those of two influential local families, the Cokaynes and the Boothbys. One outstanding monument, in white marble, is by the 18th-century sculptor Thomas Banks, and commemorates five-year-old Penelope Boothby, only child of Sir Brooke Boothby. She died in 1791 and is shown life-size, lying on her side, hands clasped and feet crossed, as if asleep. The church also has a wealth of stained glass, and three cannon balls, said to have been fired at the building by Parliamentary troops during the Civil War. The dents the cannon balls made can still be seen in the west wall. The lectern and pulpit are decorated with Blue John stone from Castleton (see page 226), and the stone churchyard gateposts have a most unusual design of obelisks resting on skulls and flames.

Near the church is Ashley, the house where George Eliot sometimes stayed. She was not the only writer fond of Ashbourne. Izaak Walton frequently fished in the area and set some of *The Compleat Angler* at the Talbot Inn in the Market Place – the town hall is now on its site. Dr Samuel Johnson, the writer and lexicographer, often stayed with his friend Dr John Taylor in The Mansion, a 17th-century building in Church Street which has a Georgian front. Opposite is the Old Grammar School, chartered by Elizabeth I and built between 1585 and 1610. The Mansion is now a boarding-house for girls who attend the new Queen Elizabeth Grammar School in Green Road.

Ashbourne is remarkable for its abundance of old almshouses. The oldest are Owfield Almshouses, in

Church Street, dated 1640 but with an upper storey added in 1848. Next to them are the single-storeyed Pegge's Almshouses, built about 1669 of local sandstone and now private homes. Also in Church Street are the Clergy Widows' Almshouses, built in 1753 as 'four neat and pretty houses' for Anglican clergymen's widows. The buildings are now converted into flats, but are still used as almshouses. Near St Oswald's churchyard are Spalden's Almshouses, which date from 1723.

The Memorial Park, off Cokayne Avenue, has a bust of Catherine Booth, co-founder of the Salvation Army, with her husband General William Booth. She was born in the town in 1829. Opposite the park is Ashbourne Hall, where Bonnie Prince Charlie, the Young Pretender, stayed for a night on his retreat from Derby to Scotland in 1745. For many generations Ashbourne Hall was the seat of the Cokayne and later the Boothby families, but it passed into other hands in the mid-19th century. It was closed after the First World War and later reopened as the County Library.

Visitors to Ashbourne on Shrove Tuesday and Ash Wednesday can witness a free-for-all football game played on a pitch that is 3 miles long. The game originated in the Middle Ages and is between the Up'ards (those who live to the north of Henmore Brook, which runs through the town), and the Down'ards (those who live south of the brook). The goals were once marked by millwheels, but today the Up'ards' goal is the spindle of the old wheel, and the Down'ards' goal is a stone plaque. There is a separate match on each day, and each game can last up to eight hours – from 2 to 10 p.m.

• **Parking** Market Place; Cattle Market; Cokayne Avenue; School Lane; Shaw Croft (all car parks) • **Early closing** Wednesday • **Market days** Thursday, Saturday • **Events** Royal Shrovetide Football Match (Shrove Tuesday and Ash Wednesday); Carnival (July) • **Information** TEL. Ashbourne 43666 • **AA 24 hour service** TEL. Nottingham 787751.

Norbury DERBYSHIRE

5 miles south-west of Ashbourne (PAGE 222 Dc)

The combination of ancient church, manor house and cottages high on the banks of the River Dove makes Norbury one of the most beautiful villages in Derbyshire, and one of the most peaceful. Indeed it can hardly fail to be so, for its setting in the wooded Dove valley is as serene and tranquil as anyone could wish.

The village is tiny but has an aristocratic air, for it has been the home of the great Derbyshire family, the Fitzherberts, since medieval times. Their manor house as it now stands is just one wing of a long-since demolished Tudor mansion, to which has been added a neat brick building of about 1680. The present owner has lovingly restored the house, and it blends perfectly with its close neighbour, the impressive Church of St Mary and St Barlok.

The church, whose enormous chancel is almost as big as the nave, is more than just a parish church. In it lie Fitzherberts going back over 600 years. Sir Henry has been lying there since 1315; his effigy, cross-legged in chain mail, is carved in gritstone. Nicholas and Ralph, who died within ten years of each other in the 15th century, lie with their wives, all richly carved in Derbyshire alabaster. The chancel was built in the 14th century by a rector of Norbury, and its great traceried

FAMILY HERITAGE *The noble Fitzherbert family lived at Norbury in the Middle Ages – and their descendants still do, in the gracious part Tudor, part 17th-century manor house.*

windows fill the church with light. Later additions to the building include the south tower, which is placed above the entrance porch.

The Norbury area has several literary and musical associations. A mile or so to the west is Ellastone, which was 'Hayslope' in George Eliot's *Adam Bede*, and a mile farther on is Wootton Hall, built in the early 17th century and for a year the home of the French philosopher Jean-Jacques Rousseau. Across the valley from Norbury, by the Dove, are the ruins of Calwich Abbey. Here, it is said, George Frederick Handel may have composed some of his *Messiah*.

Osmaston DERBYSHIRE

3 miles south-east of Ashbourne (PAGE 222 Ec)

An extraordinary piece of Victorian architecture in Osmaston's park is all that remains of a huge mock-Tudor mansion built by Francis Wright, principal owner of the Butterley Iron Works, near Ripley. Wright's architect, H. I. Stevens, hit upon the idea of incorporating all the mansion's chimneys into a single tower. The idea never worked and eventually conventional chimneys were installed, but when the house was demolished in 1966 the tower was left standing.

The Walker family of Liverpool, benefactors of the city's Walker Art Gallery, bought Osmaston Manor and it was their descendant, Sir Ian Walker, who pulled down the house and moved to Okeover Hall, at the same time changing his name to Walker-Okeover – Okeover being his wife's maiden name. But his name is remembered in Osmaston along with that of Wright and Stevens – inscribed on an altar-like memorial that stands on the terrace.

Undoubtedly Francis Wright made a wise decision in the choice of a site, if not in the choice of an architect, for the views from the terrace are magnificent, embracing woods, pastures and rolling countryside. Stevens did a better job with St Martin's Church, a grand building faced with stone and containing many inscriptions to the Wright family. The village it serves is a credit to the Walker-Okeovers who provided their estate workers with picturesque cottages of brick and thatch.

River Wye scenery

Rutland Arms, Bakewell

Old plough at the Folk Museum

WYE'S QUIET WATERS

Trees bend gracefully over the River Wye at Bakewell – a warm and welcoming town famed for its pudding, which was the result of an error in the Rutland Arms Hotel kitchen. Bakewell's Folk Museum contains craftsmen's tools, farm implements and lacework.

BAKEWELL

DERBYSHIRE

9 miles west of Chesterfield (PAGE 222 Eb)

Rich brown stone houses and buildings give Bakewell an overall appearance of warmth. The largest town in the Peak District National Park, it retains a rural atmosphere – particularly on Mondays when the weekly market is held, as it has been since the 13th century. Hundreds of cattle are sold each week in the market just behind the 17th-century Old Market Hall, now the local Information Centre.

A short distance away is the dignified Rutland Arms Hotel, where, in 1859, the cook made a mistake while making a strawberry tart. Instead of pouring the egg mixture into the pastry, she poured the jam in first and then put the egg on top. The would-be tart became a pudding and, as such, was greatly enjoyed by the guests. They complimented the landlady, Mrs Greaves, on the tasty new dish – and she duly told the cook, 'Keep on making them that way!' Today the pastries are sold in The Old Original Bakewell Pudding Shop farther along spacious Rutland Square.

The hotel was built in 1804 on the site of a former coaching inn. Seven years later the novelist Jane Austen was one of its guests. She used the Rutland Arms as the setting for two tender scenes in *Pride and Prejudice*, and called the town 'Lambton'.

Around the corner from the hotel is King Street, in which stands the 18th-century old Town Hall, now an antiques showroom. Its lower floor was once a hospital for the poor and, until 1796, the upper floor served as a courthouse. Its stone bell tower was added around 1880 to alert the fire brigade, which was based there from 1880 to 1885.

King Street leads into South Church Street, where stands the vast parish church of All Saints. Building began in the early 12th century – it was later altered by the Victorians. Its slender spire, rebuilt in the 19th century, is a landmark for miles around. Among its many fine monuments is the table-tomb of Sir George Vernon, who died in 1567. He was known as the 'King of the Peak' because of his lavish entertaining at Haddon Hall – visible from the churchyard on a clear day. The Vernon Chapel also contains the tomb of Sir George's grandson, Sir George Manners, whose wife Grace founded the Lady Manners School in 1636. A statue of Lady Manners is on her husband's tomb, and her school is still open – although on a different site. Behind the church, a Folk Museum in the Old House, dating from 1534, is open in the afternoon from April until October.

Bakewell has two mills that are very much part of its heritage, but not open to the public. The first, the Victoria Corn Mill, built in the late 18th century, belonged to the Duke of Rutland. It ground corn until the end of the Second World War, and the millwheel now stands to the right of the building. The second, Lumford Mill, was built in 1777 by Sir Richard Arkwright, inventor of a cotton-spinning machine. The mill was one of his first factories, employing 350 people, but much was later demolished. Houses he built for some of his workers can be seen in Arkwright Square.

Two bridges span the River Wye at Bakewell. The older one, at the foot of Bridge Street, was built in the 13th century but widened in the 1800s and has five graceful arches. The younger, Holme Bridge, dates from 1664 and was originally meant for packhorses.

• **Parking** Granby Road; Market Place; New Street; Smith Woodyard (all car parks) • **Early closing** Thursday • **Market day** Monday • **Events** Well-dressing and carnival (July); Bakewell Show (August) • **Information** TEL. Bakewell 3227 • **AA 24 hour service** TEL. Sheffield 28861.

Birchover DERBYSHIRE

6 miles south of Bakewell (PAGE 222 Eb)

Spectacular rocks and tors surround this simple village, whose houses lie back from its one main street. At the foot of Birchover is The Druid, an inn named during the 18th-century craze for linking strange groups of rocks with the Druids' rituals. Behind the pub, a footpath leads to where Rowtor Rocks and Eagle Tor stand.

The tors are massive gritstone boulders, up to 50 ft high. Some were shaped into seats by an 18th-century clergyman, Thomas Eyre, who used to invite friends to sit there with him to enjoy the wonderful view of the wooded hill and the valley below. Near his house, in the shade of these rocks, Eyre built Jesus Chapel. He died in 1717 and, during the next century, both house and chapel fell into ruin. But in 1869 the chapel was rebuilt and became the parish church of St Michael. Only a short distance away, just south of the village, are two gritstone pinnacles separated by a 20 yd gap. They are known locally as Robin Hood's Stride, because the fabled outlaw of Sherwood Forest is supposed to have jumped the distance between them.

From The Druid, the village street climbs past quarries, where pinkish gritstone is still extracted for special building purposes or for making grindstones. The road leads to Stanton Moor, where there is a magnificent Bronze Age (2000 – 600 BC) burial ground with stone circles, grave mounds and standing stones. Many of these are named: a sandy path north leads to the Nine Ladies, a circle of rocks standing like a miniature Stonehenge; slightly to the west is the King's Stone. The moor is littered with burial mounds, often hidden by heather. Many of them have been excavated, revealing urns, flints and pottery fragments which are now on display at Sheffield City Museum.

There are dramatic views from the edge of Stanton Moor, although it is only about 1000 ft above sea level. The walk up the Derwent Valley towards Chatsworth is well worth the effort. On the eastern edge of the moor, a tower commemorates the passing of the Great Reform Act in 1832 – which changed the existing electoral system – by the Whigs under Earl Grey, who is perhaps better known for having a blend of tea named after him.

The Longstones DERBYSHIRE

3 miles north-west of Bakewell (PAGE 222 D/Ea)

The two villages are strung along a minor road running east-west at the foot of Longstone Edge, a 1300 ft high escarpment more than 3 miles long which offers splendid views.

Great Longstone, as its name implies, is the larger village. It climbs gently up a street and has some attractive 18th-century houses. At the higher, western end is a small triangular green where worn steps lead up to the shaft of a preaching cross.

The Crispin Inn bears the sign and name of the patron saint of shoemakers, whose craft once thrived in the village. A far more important local industry, however, was lead mining. Fields around the Longstones are sprinkled with old mine shafts, their spoil-heaps long grassed over. The mounds are quite small, because the miners worked in a special way: they would sink a shaft, dig out only the ore that was easily reached, then move along the seam or 'rake'.

St Giles Church in Great Longstone, built between the 13th and 15th centuries, was extensively restored in 1872 – 3 by the Victorian architect Norman Shaw. However, he preserved some windows, the 15th-century wooden ceiling, a sturdy, heavily studded oak inner door to the porch and a private chapel dedicated to the local Eyre family. The family coat of arms is still on the wooden screen dividing chapel from chancel.

The pulpit pedestal is built up with pieces of red, iron-stained marble, known as the Duke's Red Marble. In 1831 the 6th Duke of Devonshire ordered the whole deposit at nearby Youlgreave to be quarried. He then stored the marble in the cellars of his mansion, Chatsworth, and presented small quantities for work in a number of local churches. Only a little of the marble still remains.

Church Lane, at right angles to the main street, divides the churchyard. The oldest part is around the church where there are some ancient gravestones and a cross carved with the date 1656. At the western end of the village are a restored manor house and the 18th-century Longstone Hall.

Little Longstone, farther up the hill to the west, is a pleasant, quiet hamlet from which you can enjoy one of the finest views in the Peak District. This is at Monsal Head, by the hotel of the same name, high above Monsal Dale where the River Wye threads through a deep, steep and winding limestone gorge. Other beauty spots worth visiting in the area are Hassop, just to the east, and Tideswell, about 4 miles north-west, as well as the continuation upstream of Monsal Dale into Miller's Dale.

BUXTON

DERBYSHIRE

12 miles east of Macclesfield (PAGE 222 Da)

Buxton's popularity as a spa grew in the late 18th century, when the local landowner, the 5th Duke of Devonshire, wanted to attract more people to the town. He commissioned a leading architect, the Yorkshireman John Carr, to design a place where visitors could stay. The Crescent, with its sweep of elegant arches and 378 windows, was built to this purpose between 1780 and 1784. Originally there were three hotels, with shops in the arches below; today the building houses a hotel and council offices. It also contains a magnificent Assembly Room – now a reference library – with an Adam-style ceiling. Beneath the building the pale blue waters of the thermal springs bubble up from 3500 ft to 5000 ft below ground, at a constant temperature of 82°F (28°C).

Behind The Crescent, John Carr built the Great Stables, with room for 110 horses around an open exercise yard. This was later covered by a huge slate dome with a span of 156 ft. When it was built in 1881, it was the largest dome in the world, and it is still one of the largest in Europe. The Great Stables now houses the Devonshire Royal Hospital, which, among other things, treats rheumatic patients with spring water.

Buxton's graceful new look extended to precincts such as The Colonnade, whose original verandahs have recently been restored; the majestic Palace Hotel, opened in 1868 in time to accommodate railway travellers; the glass-and-iron Octagon designed as an entertainment centre – which it still is – and the Pump Room, presented by the 7th Duke of Devonshire in 1894. The building contains the world's first Micrarium, in which you can explore the hidden natural world through microscopes.

Near by is St Ann's Well, from which the water can be drunk, though you have to take something to drink it from. Standing some 1000 ft above sea level,

Buxton is the second highest town in England, and is noted for its pure air. It is overlooked by a ring of even higher hills, on one of which, Grin Low, stands a circular folly, Solomon's Temple. This was built in 1895 by public subscription, as a means to provide the unemployed with some work.

Below the temple is Poole's Cavern, named after a 15th-century robber who is supposed to have lived in it. Inside is the source of the River Wye, which emerges to zigzag through the town before flowing east and joining the River Derwent at Rowsley, about 15 miles south-east. The cavern was inhabited by Stone Age man and known to the Romans, who built the first baths in the area. They called the settlement *Aqua Arnemetiae*, 'The Water of the Goddess of the Grove'. Roman coins and items of jewellery are in Buxton Museum.

From 1573 to 1584 the captive Mary, Queen of Scots was periodically allowed to visit Buxton to take its medicinal waters. She stayed at Buxton Hall and there she scratched a couplet, probably in Latin, on a window pane. The original pane has gone, but in the 19th century another pane, now on show in the Poole's Cavern Museum, was engraved with an English version of her couplet, which runs:

'Buxton, whose fame they milk-warm waters tell,
Whom I, perhaps, no more shall see, farewell!'

The Old Hall Hotel is now on the site of Buxton Hall.

Also in the town centre is Buxton Opera House, built as a theatre in 1903–5. All Edwardian opulence and marbled splendour, the theatre was the final part of the Pavilion Gardens complex, and since 1979 has staged a summer festival of opera, music and drama.

• **Parking** Sylvan Park; Wye Street; Pavilion Gardens; Burlington Road; Market Place; Market Street (all car parks) • **Early closing** Wednesday • **Market days** Tuesday, Saturday • **Theatre** Opera House, The Pavilion Gardens • **Cinema** Spa One and Two, Spring Gardens • **Events** Well-dressing carnival (July); Buxton Festival (July/August) • **Information** TEL. Buxton 5106 • **AA 24 hour service** TEL. Manchester 485 6299.

Castleton DERBYSHIRE

10 miles north-east of Buxton (PAGE 222 Da)

The castle from which the village takes its name has stood on the edge of a limestone cliff for 900 years. William Peveril, a bastard son of William the Conqueror, built it in 1086 and Henry II added the keep in 1176. Until the 14th century it was one of the strongest fortresses in Derbyshire, commanding the western entrance to the Hope Valley – which it still does, with imposing grandeur. Since the 17th century it has been a ruin, but a romantic ruin which inspired Sir Walter Scott's novel *Peveril of the Peak*.

After the castle came the village – and not too long after, if the mostly Norman St Edmund's Church can be taken as evidence. However, much of the church was restored and rebuilt in the early 1800s. Many of the houses date from the 18th century or a little earlier – solidly built of pale grey limestone and lining narrow-pavemented streets.

Castleton is well adapted to the needs of visitors – it lies in the heart of that area of the Peak District National Park famous for its limestone caves, and six of its pubs offer accommodation. The largest cave, Peak Cavern, is at the foot of the cliff on which the castle stands, and its entrance is said to be the biggest of any cave in Britain – about 60 ft high and 120 ft wide. The cave was used by ropemakers for more than 500 years, and some of them lived in cottages inside the mouth of the cave. The cottages are gone now, but the ropewalks remain. There are conducted tours through the cavern daily in summer.

Three other caverns around Castleton can also be visited – Speedwell, Treak Cliff and Blue John. All are noted for the banded veins of the blue, yellow, red and purple mineral known as Blue John, found only in Derbyshire. It has been prized for making jewellery and ornaments since Roman times.

One of the best walks in the National Park begins

A NIGHT AT THE OPERA IN A SPA OF STYLE AND SPARKLE

The elegance of the late 18th century and the lavish splendour of Edwardian times are both strikingly represented in Buxton. The Crescent was built in the 1780s as part of the 5th Duke of Devonshire's plan to attract more people to the spa town. The ornate early 20th-century Opera House, in the town centre, is now the dazzling setting for an annual music and drama festival.

The Crescent, Buxton

Inside the Opera House

The crumbling face of Mam Tor

Castle seen through trees

Rope workings in Peak Cavern

CLIMBS, CAVES AND A CASTLE AMONG THE PEAKS

Mam Tor, rising impressively above beautiful Peak District countryside, is a magnet for ramblers and climbers. It is best approached from Castleton, a village which also gives access to the area's famous limestone caves. One of these, Peak Cavern, has relics of the ropemaking craft once carried on inside it. The village takes its name from a Norman castle.

about 2 miles west of Castleton – the 2½ mile ridge walk from Mam Tor to Lose Hill. Mam Tor rises to 1700 ft and is known as the 'Shivering Mountain' because of the landslips on its eastern face caused by unstable strata in the rock. The views from the summit and along the ridge walk are tremendous.

Marton CHESHIRE

20 miles west of Buxton (PAGE 222 Cb)

A church that has claims to be the oldest of its kind in regular use in Europe, and a giant oak tree in which a farmer used to pen his bull are Marton's two unique features. The rest of the village is a charming example of a scattered community sprinkled with delightful disorder in green and wooded countryside.

Marton has its share of pretty black-and-white houses, some of them thatched, but it is the Church of St James and St Paul that catches the eye. This, too, is timber-framed, and a board by the entrance proudly proclaims that it is 'the oldest half-timbered church in use in Europe'. The building dates from 1343, when it was founded by Sir John Davenport, and it has been superbly preserved. The evenly spaced timber uprights and white infill almost dazzle beneath a stone slabbed roof that rises to a shingled tower and spire topped by a weathercock. Inside the church are two stone effigies, believed to be of Sir John and his son, Vivian.

The manor of Marton was once held by the Davenports, ancestors of the Bromley-Davenports of Capesthorne near Macclesfield, and the village still has

Remains of giant oak

Black-and-white painted cottage

Marton's parish church

A CHERISHED CHURCH

The people of Marton are proud of what is claimed to be Europe's oldest half-timbered church still in use. It dates from 1343 and is wonderfully preserved. Marton also has some delightful houses and an oak tree once reputed to be the biggest in Britain. At its base the tree has a girth of 58 ft, and the girth of its largest limb was 11 ft 6 in.

its Davenport Arms, an old brick-built inn where once the manor courts were held.

The Marton Oak, or what remains of it, stands in Oak Lane and was once reputed to be the largest in Britain. Age has split the trunk into four, so that at first it looks like four trees close together. It was this decayed and empty heart that the farmer of Oak Farm used as a pound for his bull.

Styal CHESHIRE

21 miles north-west of Buxton (PAGE 222 Ca)

In the 18th century this little village, ringed by towns, found itself caught up in the Industrial Revolution that spread a dark cloak across the green and pleasant land of northern England. But in Styal there were no dark, Satanic mills – instead there grew up a factory colony that was, in effect, a miniature welfare state.

The factory, Quarry Bank Mill, was the brainchild of Samuel Greg, a Belfast man who invested an inheritance in the manufacture of cotton cloth. He chose Styal because here the River Bollin provided an ideal head of water for powering a mill.

Greg built not only a mill, but also cottages for his workers, provided a farm to feed them and built an Apprentices' House so that young workers recruited from city slums lived in healthy conditions. He was a humanitarian and a philanthropist who provided decent homes for his workers, and looked after their education and health.

In 1784, when Greg came to the Bollin Valley, Styal was a delightful country village – and it still is. Quarry Bank Mill still stands virtually as it was 200 years ago – a memorial to a more acceptable face of the Industrial Revolution.

Since 1939 the estate has been owned by the National Trust and is leased to the Quarry Bank Mills Trust, an organisation that has turned the mill into a working museum where cloth is still produced on machines of the past, though a giant water wheel no longer powers the mill. The four-storey building is typically Georgian, with rows of latticed windows and a small, rooftop cupola. Close by is Greg's own house, Quarrybank House, and also the Manager's House, while up the hill are the cottages and the Apprentices' House, still used as private residences. In addition there are some 250 acres of parkland in which to wander.

Wincle CHESHIRE

9 miles south-west of Buxton (PAGE 222 Cb)

There is not a lot of Wincle, but what there is has all the charm of an isolated community which has survived for at least 500 years in one of the remotest parts of Cheshire. Its charm is accentuated by its setting, roughly on the borders dividing the rugged grandeur of the Peak District National Park from the richer, gentler countryside of the Cheshire Plain. The village is reached by roads that wind down to the wooded valley of the River Dane and Wincle's sister hamlet, Danebridge.

Wincle's parish church of St Michael was built originally in the 17th century, but was extensively restored in the 19th century. In its early days the church seems to have played little part in parish life; there was no stipend for the parson and parishioners contributed something when they felt like it. Quite often they did not feel like it; nor did the parson often feel like preaching – one bishop went so far as to complain that there had been no sermons in the church for half a year.

There are some attractive houses – one white-painted group with leaded windows stands near the church gate. The Ship Inn and a row of adjoining cottages are of pale red sandstone and have white, iron-studded doors. The inn sign depicts the *Nimrod*, the ship in which the local squire, Sir Philip Brocklehurst, sailed to the Antarctic with Shackleton in 1907.

Wincle Grange, just half a mile away, is now a farm, but in medieval times it belonged to the monks of Combermere Abbey in Cheshire. A religious relic of an earlier period is the tall, round shaft of the 11th-century Cleulow preaching cross, hidden in a clump of trees a mile north-west of Wincle.

Less than half a mile to the south-east, Danebridge has a single-arched stone bridge spanning the crystal-

Wincle church and countryside

Sturdy stone cottages

HIDDEN BELOW THE PEAK

Magnificent wooded country surrounds Wincle, and it is worth leaving the beaten track to visit this remote village with its attractive old houses – though in winter it can be cut off by snow.

clear River Dane and flanked by mossy green banks. From here, splendid walks in all directions are possible, to secret valleys with silvery streams, or moorland tops with fine views.

NANTWICH

CHESHIRE

18 miles west of Stoke-on-Trent (PAGE 222 Bb)

The Elizabethan look which characterises much of Nantwich is largely the result of a fire which devastated the town in 1583. The fire lasted for 20 days, and by the end of it only three of the town's main buildings had been spared.

The first of these is Churche's Mansion in Hospital Street. Built only six years before the fire broke out, the half-timbered house was the home of a wealthy salt merchant, Richard Churche, and his wife, Margery. Their portraits are carved in the porch, and on the front of the house is an emblem of a salamander – a creature which supposedly cannot be destroyed by fire and perhaps protected the house. During restoration work, which began in the 1930s, the mansion's splendid oak panelling was revealed and an Elizabethan well was uncovered, along with the original hearths. A plan to dismantle the house brick by brick and ship it to America was foiled. Today the ground floor is a restaurant and in summer you can also inspect the first floor, which is fitted and furnished in the style of the late 16th century.

Sweetbriar Hall, the second survivor, is close by. Built in 1450 as a half-timbered private home, it was later used as a school and is now architects' offices. The third survivor is the magnificent parish church of St Mary, built in the 14th century of warm, soft, red sandstone and restored in 1854–61 by Sir George Gilbert Scott, who designed St Pancras Station.

Apart from its majesty and size, the church is noted for the number of times the 'Green Man' pagan fertility god appears inside – his head is shown twice in the old glass of the north window, four more times carved on the desk by the south chancel choir stalls, and there are three stone sculptures of him in the north transept and south porch. There is also a sculpture of the Devil catching a woman with her hand in a pitcher.

This is said to have been made by 14th-century workmen who returned to their lodgings one night and found their landlady dipping her hand into the pitcher containing their money. So they decided to immortalise her in stone – outside the church's north transept. The church also has some fine medieval carved misericords (backs of choir seats) which depict, among other scenes, St George and the dragon, and a woman beating a man with a ladle.

After the fire Elizabeth I gave £2000 towards the rebuilding of Nantwich and organised a nationwide collection which raised about £30,000 – a vast sum in those days. In gratitude for this, one of the townsmen, Thomas Cleese, had an inscription carved on the front of his house thanking the queen. It reads:

'God grant our Ryal Queen
In England longe to Raign.
For she hath put her helping
Hand to bild this town againe.'

The building, Queen's Aid House, is in The Square – the heart of Nantwich. Leading from it is the

THE TOWN QUEEN BESS REBUILT

Only three buildings survived the great fire of Nantwich in 1583. They included Richard Churche's fine half-timbered mansion, which was new at the time. Most of the town's Tudor look is the result of rebuilding launched by Elizabeth I – Queen's Aid House and the Crown Hotel are examples. The church – another fire survivor – is noted for images of the pagan 'Green Man'.

Queen's Aid House

Nantwich cottages at sunset

Crown Hotel

Churche's Mansion in Hospital Street, Nantwich

'Green Man' head in church

High Street, in which stands the late 16th-century Crown Hotel. The River Weaver cuts through the High Street. On the east bank, in the south of the town, is the grave of Lieutenant Leslie Brown of the United States Air Force, who crashed his Thunderbolt fighter at this spot in January 1944, during the Second World War. When his plane was in trouble he stayed at the controls and avoided the town centre, where he would undoubtedly have killed many people. Instead, he chose to die himself. The town's Brown Avenue is named after him.

• **Parking** Hospital Street; Beam Street; Love Lane; Snow Hill; Welsh Row (all car parks) • **Early closing** Wednesday • **Market days** Thursday morning; Saturday • **Theatre** Little Theatre, Pillory Street • **Events** Holly Holy Day (January); Nantwich Show (July) • **Information** TEL. Nantwich 623914 • **AA 24 hour service** TEL. Stoke-on-Trent 25881.

Acton CHESHIRE

2 miles west of Nantwich (PAGE 222 Bb)

A mile west of Nantwich the main road passes beneath a fine, cast-iron aqueduct carrying the Shropshire Union Canal, and a few hundred yards later, Acton comes into view. Or in the first instance Acton's parish church of St Mary comes into view, rising cathedral-like across the fields and above the village around it. It is only when the eye ceases to be caught by the square, sandstone tower that the other buildings are noticed, particularly the black-and-white Star Inn standing out among its red-brick neighbours.

This panoramic view occurs because Acton lies on a double bend in the road. At the first bend is a

Dorfold Hall's mastiff guard

A view of the mansion

THE NOBLE HOUSE A KING MISSED

Beyond the splendid, tree-shaded expanse of its pond—which once supplied the whole household with fish—Dorfold Hall catches a shaft of sunlight. A room of this noble 17th-century mansion at Acton was specially decorated by its owners, the Wilbraham family, to accommodate James I. The king did not pay his expected visit, but the room remains a showpiece. Also worth seeing is the Great Chamber with its magnificent plaster ceiling. The hall entrance is guarded by an aggressive-looking stone mastiff—with puppies. In the grounds, look out for a Spanish chestnut tree said to be 1000 years old. Dorfold is open to the public on Tuesday and Bank Holiday Monday afternoons from April to October.

lodge with a pair of handsome wrought-iron gates and brick gate pillars topped by a pair of wrought-iron lions. This is an imposing entrance to an imposing house, the 17th-century Dorfold Hall, which stands in all its Jacobean glory at the end of an avenue of limes.

It is a house of splendid interiors and was the home of the Wilbrahams who built it in 1616 and, a year later, decorated one room in anticipation of a visit by James I. The king never arrived, but the King James Room is one of the house's showpieces, along with the Great Chamber which has one of the finest plaster ceilings in England.

The village itself is small and neat. The Star Inn is half-timbered and has been so extensively restored that its age is uncertain. But clues to its origin lie in the steeply pitched roof, typical of many medieval buildings, and in the well-worn mounting block for horse riders.

The tower of St Mary's Church dates from the 13th century, and inside the church is a Norman font – recovered from a local pigsty. In the chancel are some sandstone blocks carved with medieval figures depicting Christ, angels, a bishop and an eagle. The blocks were discovered during a restoration.

Brereton Green CHESHIRE

13 miles north-east of Nantwich (PAGE 222 Bb)

Cheshire is noted for its fine black-and-white buildings, sometimes called 'magpie' houses, and one of the best examples is the Bear's Head inn at Brereton Green. It is a superb confection of jet-black timbers, the uprights set close together with perfect symmetry, and snow-white infill. The gabled porch bears the date 1615, and a stuffed bear's head glares ferociously from beneath a canopy bedecked rather incongruously with coloured electric lights.

A bear's head was the crest of the Brereton family, who were lords of the manor hereabouts from Norman times until 1679. Their family seat, Brereton Hall, was built in 1586 by the 14th Lord Brereton, and it is said that Elizabeth I laid the foundation stone.

Brereton Hall is now a school – and not open to the public – but its magnificent brick-and-stone façade has remained largely unaltered since it was built. There is superb stone carving surrounding the central, arched doorway, which is flanked by two battlemented towers. It ceased to be the family home when the male line died out in 1679.

The hall stands behind St Oswald's Church, whose key is kept at the Rectory. The only way to reach the church is through the arch of a brick-and-stone gatehouse off a signposted minor road which runs east off the main road north towards Holmes Chapel. Not far from the church there is a small parking area.

The church, to the right of the hall, is partly hidden by trees, but at the churchyard gate the building can be seen in full perspective – an architectural gem of pink-and-grey sandstone standing sedately amid green lawns and lichen-covered headstones. By the gate there is a mounting block, no doubt for the convenience of parishioners who once rode to church wearing their Sunday best.

St Oswald's dates mostly from the 15th century, but has been much restored. It has a buttressed and pinnacled tower, a short nave and tall windows. Inside, the light from large windows picks out the splendid tower arch, the 17th-century font and a few monuments. A medieval altar stone with five incised crosses stands inside the doorway.

There are some pleasant walks around Brereton Green, notably by the tiny River Croco. An insect-trapping white flower called sundew grows beside a pool on the river. This, and other beauties, makes the whole district a special place for naturalists.

Tarporley CHESHIRE

10 miles north-west of Nantwich (PAGE 222 Ab)

Despite a milestone in the High Street that says 'Tarporley Township', Tarporley is a village – and very attractive, too. Its mellowed character was shaped in the days when it was an important staging point for

HISTORY HILL *Towering on the top of a hill near Tarporley, ruined Beeston Castle has a history chiefly bound up with the Civil War. It was built in the 13th century, but saw little action until the forces of Charles I and Cromwell were locked in battle. During the war it changed hands several times. On one occasion eight Royalists seized it from an 80-strong Roundhead garrison – and the Roundhead captain was later shot for letting it happen. In 1646 Parliament ordered the destruction of the castle, reducing it to its present state. From the hill on which it stands, seven counties can be seen if the day is clear.*

the mail coaches on the London to Chester run, and it had a turnpike as early as 1743. The High Street runs north to south and is the backbone of the tadpole-shaped village, with the tadpole's head in the south. The street is wide, elegant, and has many pleasant buildings including Georgian houses and two inns.

The Rising Sun is medieval – long and low, with a porch and wide windows. The Swan Hotel dates from 1769, though behind its brickwork there is probably medieval fabric. Its three storeys, double bay-windowed frontage and archway show that it was once a coaching inn. This is the meeting place of the Tarporley Hunt, which claims to be the oldest hunt club in England. In the first week of November the members gather to take sherry, swallow oysters and sing songs, as they have since 1762.

The club is evidence of Tarporley's past prosperity, when the gentlemen from the great houses rode to hounds. Some of the houses are long gone; others are turned into country clubs, rest homes or in the case of Oulton Park, a motor-racing circuit.

Tarporley's parish church, St Helen's, is in the High Street and, though much altered in the 19th century, bears evidence of its aristocratic past in its wealth of monuments. The Crewe and Done families are well represented.

Though Tarporley may have been an important staging point in the 18th century, it turned its back on the railways when they came. The village voted against having a station and the nearest railway, the Chester to London line via Crewe, runs to the south near Beeston, a scattered jumble of black-and-white timber-framed houses in the shadow of the Peckforton Hills. On a rocky crag rising to 740 ft stands Beeston Castle, built in the 13th century by the Earl of Chester.

WIRKSWORTH

DERBYSHIRE

14 miles south-west of Chesterfield (PAGE 222 Eb)

Surrounded by moorland scarred by limestone quarries, and set in the folds of a deep valley, Wirksworth has all the traditional attractions of a stone-built Derbyshire market town. Overrun with winding alleys, narrow streets crammed with shops and houses that zigzag up hillsides, it has a network of ginnels (passageways) between the homes of the quarry workers. Exploring the twists and turns of the ginnels reveals sudden, dramatic views of the outlying countryside.

By contrast, most of the town's stately Georgian houses are gathered in and around Market Place, the hub of the community. The Red Lion Hotel, a handsome coaching inn rebuilt about 1770, and the Victorian Town Hall, complete with public library, also stand in Market Place. This is the part of Wirksworth in which George Eliot set much of her melodramatic novel *Adam Bede*.

As well as the limestone quarries, Wirksworth is noted for the lead mines that once flourished around it. Lead was first worked in the area by the Romans. At the beginning of the 19th century the industry masked the town in a pall of white smoke, but the last mines closed in 1827 and since then the worst of the pollution has gone. Limestone quarrying, however, still thrives.

Blasting out the big Middle Peak Quarry, which is close to the heart of the town, had a devastating effect in the late 1940s. Wirksworth has only recently recovered through implementation of a three-year Civic Trust plan to 'help the town to help itself'. Special loans and mortgages were arranged so that decayed and tumbledown buildings could be restored. The Wirksworth Project was launched in 1979 and has been so successful that the old, the new and the renovated blend harmoniously.

The town's centrepiece is the glorious 13th-century cruciform Church of St Mary, which was partly restored in the 1870s by Sir George Gilbert Scott, the designer of many famous buildings.

In common with other Derbyshire towns and villages, Wirksworth holds a well-dressing ceremony – even though it has no wells – each Whitsun Bank Holiday to give thanks for its water. Thousands of visitors come to see the nine or ten 'wells' dressed. They are decorated with pictures, usually on a religious theme, made by pressing flower petals, berries and ears of corn into wet clay.

Another Wirksworth custom is 'clypping' the church – 'clypping' means embracing. Each year on the first Sunday after St Mary's Day (September 8) the townsfolk and people from the surrounding villages join hands and completely encircle the building.

• **Parking** Market Place (except on Tuesdays); Barmote Croft, off Coldwell Street (both car parks) • **Early closing** Wednesday • **Market day** Tuesday • **Events** Well-dressing ceremony (Whitsun weekend); Clypping the church (September) • **Information** TEL. Wirksworth 3173 • **AA 24 hour service** TEL. Nottingham 787751.

Brassington DERBYSHIRE

4 miles west of Wirksworth (PAGE 222 Eb)

In the 1720s the author Daniel Defoe discovered a lead miner, his wife and five small children living in a cave at Harboro' Rocks, a mile north-east of Brassington. They eked out a living on the miner's pay of fivepence a day, plus threepence a day his wife sometimes earned by washing the lead ore. Their miserable existence in a cave once occupied by Iron Age people was movingly described by Defoe in his *Tour through the Whole Island of Great Britain.*

Brassington was at the heart of the Derbyshire lead-mining industry which prospered in the 18th and 19th centuries, and died when cheap lead was imported from abroad. Not that there is much evidence of the mining days in Brassington. The village sits on a hillside south of Brassington Moor, looking across to Havenhill. Most of the houses are of local limestone, which gives the place a pearly-grey look.

Some of the houses date from the 17th or 18th centuries, and one or two still have stone slab roofs, though most have blue tiles – the 'Staffordshire blues' made in the Potteries at the beginning of the 19th century. One of the oldest buildings is Tudor House, which dates from 1615 and is a good example of a Derbyshire manor house.

The Church of St James stands in a steep churchyard and is mostly Norman. The west tower is particularly attractive, faced with finely dressed limestone in various shades of grey.

There are superb walks around Brassington. Just to the north the High Peak Trail runs for $17\frac{1}{2}$ miles along the former route of the Cromford and High Peak Railway. It passes below the 1244 ft high Harboro' Rocks. To the west of the village are the Rainster Rocks and the remains of an ancient Romano-British settlement.

Cromford DERBYSHIRE

2 miles north of Wirksworth (PAGE 222 Eb)

Cromford is a mecca for industrial archaeologists, for it was here that Sir Richard Arkwright, developer of the spinning frame, set up the first water-powered cotton mill in England in 1771. For the next 60 years or so he, and his son after him, transformed this little village in the Derwent valley into a thriving industrial centre. Much of their work has survived, and there is hardly a building in Cromford that was not built by Richard Arkwright, senior or junior.

Arkwright was attracted to Cromford by the availability of a good water supply, both from the fast-flowing Derwent and from a channel, called a sough, cut into the hillside to drain the deserted lead mines. There was also a good supply of labour from unemployed local lead miners and their families. Arkwright's first mill still stands, looking darkly satanic. In its day it employed 200, mostly children, working in shifts day and night.

In 1783 Arkwright built Masson Mills, a little to the north of the village beyond a bend in the river. In contrast to Cromford Mill the main building is bright and cheerful. Its red brickwork, mullioned windows with stone lintels and sills and a small rooftop cupola all reflect the late Georgian style more commonly associated with public buildings and country homes.

He invested much of his money in Cromford. He built the Greyhound Hotel in the village square, a splendid three-storey building in pale grey stone and as Georgian in style as they come. He also built the mill manager's house, a place for himself called Rock House, and special houses for his employees, which had three storeys so that the men could work on their knitting frames in the top room while their wives and children went out to work in the mill.

The Cromford Canal was built in 1793 for a consortium that included Arkwright, and at High Peak Junction, a mile south of Cromford, is a stonebuilt aqueduct carrying the canal over the Derwent.

Richard Arkwright junior gave Cromford its school and schoolhouse in 1832, and he also completed St Mary's Church which his father had begun. Both father and son are buried here. Close to the church is a structure that was here long before the Arkwrights – a 15th-century bridge over the Derwent with a ruined chapel at one end. Close by is an 18th-century fishing pavilion bearing the inscription *Piscatoribus sacrum*, meaning 'sanctuary of the fishermen'.

Also overlooking the river is Willersley Castle, a stone mansion that Arkwright senior built for himself. Seven bays wide and two-and-a-half storeys high, it would have made a fitting residence for a man worth almost £500,000. It was completed in 1790, but the interior was burnt out before Arkwright could move in. His son later restored the building.

Winster DERBYSHIRE

6 miles north-west of Wirksworth (PAGE 222 Eb)

Buildings of the 17th and 18th centuries make up much of Winster, which stands on a plateau about 800 ft above sea level. It is a village close to where the limestone uplands of the Peak District meet the gritstone moorland, and these two stones, together with sandstone, have been used in most of the houses and cottages. The effect is charming, the pale limestone of one house complementing the creamy sandstone of its neighbour on one side and offsetting the dark gritstone of its neighbour on the other. It makes for a very pleasant main street which is further enhanced by some fine, large buildings.

The most noticeable is the Market House, partly because it stands forward from the rows of terraced houses and partly because of its obvious great age. Its ground floor dates from the 15th or 16th centuries and has pointed arches, now filled in on three sides and closed by a pair of studded timber doors on the other. The upper floor is of brick, with mullioned windows and leaded panes. It probably dates from the late 17th century or early 18th and may have replaced an earlier timber-framed storey.

In the main street is the Old Hall, a large, elegant three-storey house built entirely of gritstone and dated

Winster cottages and church

Market Hall

A cottage doorway

A SUBTLE WAY WITH STONE

Cottages slope gently down to the church and the open country at Winster. The village, which once prospered from over 20 lead mines in the area, is built in a subtle mixture of gritstone, limestone and sandstone. Its large buildings include the Market House, which boldly adds brick to the local scene. The Church of St John the Baptist has a fine stained-glass window by the Pre-Raphaelite artist Sir Edward Burne-Jones.

1668 and 1715. At the western end is the hall's only rival in size, the 17th-century Dower House, which has two gables facing along the length of the street.

Behind the Dower House is the Church of St John the Baptist—very Victorian though its squat tower was built in 1721. It contains an unusual cast-iron relief, dating from the early 19th century, of Leonardo's painting *The Last Supper*.

Burne-Jones window

MAP 21

HEART OF ENGLAND AND THE HUNTING SHIRES

Here is the prosperous heartland of England – home of the pork pie, Stilton and fine ale. Its towns include Melton Mowbray and Stamford, where comfortable inns have cheered travellers for centuries. Its villages pattern a green countryside where hedgerows live on, and the halloo of the hunt still echoes as it has for generations past.

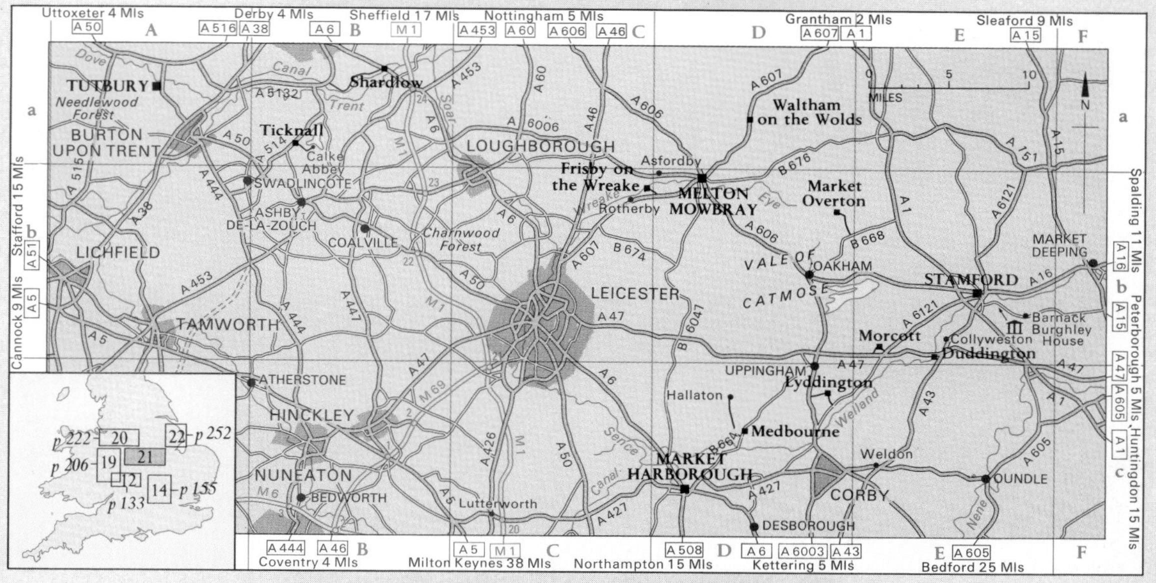

MAP 21: NEIGHBOURING AREAS – MAPS 12, 14, 19, 20, 22

MARKET HARBOROUGH Lyddington Medbourne
MELTON MOWBRAY Frisby on the Wreake Waltham on the Wolds
STAMFORD Duddington Market Overton Morcott
TUTBURY Shardlow Ticknall

MARKET HARBOROUGH

LEICESTERSHIRE

15 miles south-east of Leicester (PAGE 237 Dc)

Two historic buildings in Church Square, the Old Grammar School and the parish church of St Dionysius, form the core of Market Harborough.

The timber-framed school, built in 1614, stands on sturdy posts with an open ground floor. It was the gift of Robert Smyth, a poor local boy who later made good in London as a successful merchant and became Comptroller of the City. He left £20 a year for the upkeep of the school, which occupied the first floor – the ground floor served as a weekly butter market. In 1892 the school left the building, which was substantially restored in 1978. Its Biblical quotations – which Smyth insisted upon – carved above the wooden arches supporting the building still remain. The ornamental gables and pargeting (plasterwork) date from 1869. Meetings and exhibitions are staged here now.

The ironstone church dates from the 14th century and has what is considered the finest broach spire in England, soaring 161 ft above the surrounding rooftops. Very few English churches are dedicated to St Dionysius, and this one is unusual in having no churchyard. During the Civil War, for one night, the church held many of the 4500 Royalist troops captured near by at the Battle of Naseby in June 1645. Shortly before the battle, Charles I made the town his headquarters and held a hasty council of war. Later Cromwell occupied Market Harborough and wrote to Parliament from the Bell Inn, announcing his victory.

Market Harborough was founded about 1170 probably as one of Henry II's new towns, and a market has been held here since 1204. Chains used to be strung between iron bollards in the High Street to keep cattle off the pavement on market days. The cattle market was held in The Square – triangular shaped, despite its name – until 1903, when it moved to its present premises in Springfield Street. In 1938 the weekly produce market also left The Square – for a site in Northampton Road, one of the main streets. In the 19th century the town gained much of its prosperity through the Symington family, whose corset factory stood behind the church. Today the building houses a museum of local history, and council offices.

As a designated Conservation Area, the town centre retains an air of well-bred elegance. Leading off

Old Grammar School

Liberty-bodice advert

OLD SCHOOL TIES AND LADIES' LIB

Stout timber posts and arches carved with Bible quotations support the Old Grammar School at Market Harborough. Walls are pargeted and an ornamental gable bears the date 1614. Lessons continued here until 1892, while a regular butter market was held in the space below. The town's old corset factory is now a museum, but still displays its own splendid little statue of Liberty – the bodice, that is.

The Square is the High Street, with its fine array of Georgian houses, most of which are now shops. Also in the High Street is the Old Town Hall, now a gentlemen's club, little changed since it was built in 1788 as a market hall by the Earl of Harborough. The ground floor was originally used by butchers and the first floor by cloth dealers. Near by in Leicester Road is Brooke House, built in 1708 and the oldest mansion in the town. Now a private school, the building was enlarged in 1807 and named after Lord Brooke's family who lived there in the 19th century. Another imposing building is Catherwood House in The Square, which now houses a bank. It was built in the Gothic style in 1876 by a chemist named William Bragg – whose nephew, the Nobel Prize-winning physicist Sir William Bragg (1862 – 1942), lived there with him when he attended the grammar school.

In the High Street stands The Three Swans Hotel, which dates from the 14th century, although it has an early 19th-century façade and an elaborate wrought-iron sign of three swans. The High Street is turned into a square by The Paddocks, a late 18th-century house at the north end. In keeping with the town's graceful lines is Edinburgh House, built in 1968 on the site of the old Corn Exchange in Abbey Street.

• **Parking** Bowden Lane; Angel Street; Northampton Road (2); St Mary's Road; The Commons (all car parks) • **Early closing** Wednesday • **Market days** Tuesday, Saturday • **Theatre** The Harborough, Church Square • **Event** Carnival (June) • **Information** TEL. Market Harborough 62649 • **AA 24 hour service** TEL. Leicester 20491.

Lyddington LEICESTERSHIRE

14 miles north-east of Market Harborough (PAGE 237 Dc)

On the corner of Church Lane and Main Street you will find the prettiest house in Lyddington. The rich orange and purple blocks of ironstone are laid as precisely as the tiles in a Victorian fireplace, with a single white limestone stripe across the middle of the cottage. This lovely house is still roofed with thatch, but most of the others in Lyddington have lost theirs. Instead they are roofed with less costly slates, pantiles or other materials. You can make out houses which were originally intended for a depth of thatch by their gables, which extend a foot or two above the present roof-line.

The real charm of this village on the edge of the Welland Valley is the great length of its one gently rising street. It is nearly a mile from end to end, takes in two pubs – the White Hart and the Marquess of Exeter – and consists almost entirely of 17th and 18th-century ironstone cottages.

No one is sure why the street is so long and narrow, but there is no doubt that it was there before the village. It is an ancient trackway, and until 1754 was the main road to the south from Uppingham and the Vale of Catmose. In that year a new turnpike road was opened just to the west, and the flow of traffic dwindled to a trickle.

Lyddington is a backwater now, but in the Middle Ages it was extremely important and it is still the only village in the former county of Rutland to boast a palace. The Bishops of Lincoln, whose enormous diocese stretched from the Humber to the Thames, established three separate administrative centres across the country. They maintained a permanent staff, but only occasionally stayed in each place themselves. They chose Lyddington as the site for one of these centres and their palace, standing next to the Church of St Andrew, still forms the heart of the village.

Both church and palace were built early in the Middle Ages, but were radically improved by the bishops in the late 15th century. The church, which has a slightly dumpy broach spire on top of its 14th-century tower, was given a graceful new nave and aisles in the Perpendicular style.

The palace is across the graveyard from the church. Only part of the medieval building survives. The kitchens and stables were probably cannibalised by villagers for stone and timber in the 17th and 18th centuries, but what remains is truly palatial. The grand rooms are on the first floor, reached by a covered stone staircase that leads to two identical nail-studded doors. The one on the left leads into the waiting room, the one on the right into the great hall.

The hall is a room 20 ft wide and 47 ft long. Unusually and luxuriously for the 15th century, it has windows along the length of one side. In use, the stone walls would have been hung with tapestries below the elaborate cornice, which is carved into a sort of fan-vaulting. Its floor would have been laid with rugs, and it was altogether an immensely rich room where the bishop could receive petitioners.

Henry VIII confiscated the palace in 1547 and his daughter, Elizabeth I, gave it to the Cecils of Burghley House near Stamford. In 1602, Thomas Cecil, 1st Earl of Exeter, turned it into the Bede House, an almshouse for ten poor men who were bound to pray for their benefactors. Grim little cells, a few feet square, were constructed for them on the ground floor. The last recipients of this bleak charity were still living in these tiny rooms in the 1930s. The palace is open to visitors from April 1 to September 30 every year.

With the end of the bishop's influence and with the growth of Uppingham just to the north, Lyddington declined. The large fish 'stews', or ponds, which can be seen from the churchyard were neglected, and the little watchtower or gazebo at the corner of the bishop's garden, now called the Bishop's Eye, had its windows blocked up.

The large number of churchmen who had staffed the palace became ordinary villagers, taking the names Pretty (meaning Priest) or the more obvious Clerk. These were still two of the commonest Lyddington names in the 19th century. The village became dependent on Uppingham, and early this century there were four laundries here, all kept busy by washing the linen of the boys from Uppingham School.

Medbourne LEICESTERSHIRE

6 miles north-east of Market Harborough (PAGE 237 Dc)

In summer, kingfishers, swifts and herons can all be seen from the 13th-century packhorse bridge in the middle of Medbourne. It arches over a shallow brook that runs down from the upland pastures of Leicestershire towards the rich flood plain of the River Welland. The village is named after the stream – from the Old English for Meadow-brook – and before the middle of the 19th century the bank of the stream formed the western boundary of a large open green.

Old ironstone houses used to surround this green, but in 1844 it was divided up and the land allotted to various owners in garden-size patches. This has given Medbourne its present rather haphazard appearance. Little vegetable plots and chicken runs, a paddock for ponies and a bowling green outside the Horse and Trumpet pub are all mixed in with each other in the village centre.

Above the jumble rises the 13th and 14th-century Church of St Giles. It too is built in the soft orange ironstone, with some paler limestone for the windows

LOT OF BOTTLE *The small cask at the centre of this melee is known as the bottle. Men of Medbourne and Hallaton fight for it in their Easter bottle-kicking game – which can last for hours.*

and corner quoins. An ambitious plan in the late 13th century to make the church more elaborate was abandoned after a new south transept had been added. But you will find in the transept at least one charming detail – a pair of tiny men bearing the weight of an arch, their arms around each other's backs like undertakers with a coffin.

In the 17th and 18th centuries Medbourne was run by a string of rich yeoman families, and they have left evidence of their passage: half a dozen solid stone houses, each big enough to be a squire's home in a smaller village. The humbler cottages, many of which date from the 17th century, were once lived in by cobblers, saddlers, tanners, weavers and farriers – all occupations of a district devoted to the raising of cattle and sheep.

The unploughed pastures and jumpable hedges made this area perfect for hunting, and between 1871 and 1924 Medbourne was the home of the Fernie Hunt. Red-brick stables, kennels and huntsmen's cottages were all built at that time. The master was Sir Bache Cunard, grandson of the founder of the Cunard shipping line. He wanted to install a horse trough near the church, but the villagers objected. Out of pique, Cunard refused to provide the clock that was meant to grace the new stables at the southern end of the village. And where the clock should have gone, there is still a round hole in the brickwork.

Near the Fernie Stables is the Nevill Arms. A previous pub on the site was burnt down in 1862 when a conjuror displayed his tricks there. An anvil was placed on his chest while Ben Jelly, the blacksmith, forged horseshoes on it. Either sparks from the forging or candles set against the walls started the fire. The pub was rebuilt the next year by a wealthy villager named Captain Nevill, who later went mad, shot at people out of the pub window and was persuaded to go to the asylum only after a villager he was fond of calmed him down by singing to him.

Above the bar in the Nevill Arms is the object of one of Medbourne's strangest customs. It is a small iron-bound barrel called a bottle. Every Easter Monday the men of Medbourne fight with the men of Hallaton, 3 miles away, in an ancient, pagan and traditionally violent game called bottle-kicking.

The game, which has been held in its present form since at least the late 18th century, begins with fragments of hare pie being thrown over the two teams – there is no limit on numbers. The teams then scramble for the best of three bottles, or goals, on Hare Pie Hill outside Hallaton. The battle, which may originally have represented the struggle of winter with spring, can often last four or five hours, with more than 200 players involved at the start. Each team aims to carry the bottle off towards its own village, fighting off the opposing team as it goes. But there are no other rules in the contest and the bottle can disappear under mountainous, heaving scrums for half an hour at a time. The Hallaton men have to carry the bottle about half a mile and over two fields and across a brook. The Medbourne men try to get the bottle about three-quarters of a mile – down the other side of the hill, across three fields, and over a lane and another stream.

MEDIEVAL SHADOWS *Deep shadows delineate arch and buttress of a 13th-century packhorse bridge over the stream that gave Medbourne its name. The ironstone Church of St Giles, across the bridge, has touches of paler limestone and is also medieval, built between the 13th and 14th centuries.*

MELTON MOWBRAY

LEICESTERSHIRE

15 miles north-east of Leicester (PAGE 237 Db)

The saying 'painting the town red', according to one account, was born in Melton Mowbray in 1837, when the eccentric Marquis of Waterford and his cronies rampaged through the twisting streets while celebrating the end of a hard day's fox-hunting. Armed with paint and brushes, they daubed several of the town's dignified stone buildings bright red, painted the toll-gates, long since gone, and even gave the toll-keeper 'a coat of red'.

Melton Mowbray – the virtual headquarters of fox-hunting in England – is the home of three of the smartest hunts: the Quorn, the Belvoir and the Cottesmore. In the 19th century many of those who came to hunt stayed at Egerton Lodge, on the banks of the River Eye which winds through the town. The lodge was the home of the 2nd Earl of Wilton, whose guests included the Empress Elizabeth of Austria, and two prime ministers of Britain – the Duke of Wellington and Benjamin Disraeli. Today the lodge houses the borough council offices.

For more than 200 years the stately Harboro' Hotel in nearby Burton Street has been the place to stay for the fox-hunting fraternity. Its handsome Georgian front has changed little since the days when it was one of the town's two main coaching inns. The other is The George Hotel in the High Street.

Higher up Burton Street is Anne of Cleves House, built in 1384 and now a restaurant. It was given to Anne when Henry VIII divorced her in 1540, but there is no evidence that she ever lived here. Opposite are Bede Houses (also known as Maison De Dieu) dated 1640 and founded by Robert Hudson, a townsman who made his fortune in London as a merchant. He endowed the houses for six elderly men and, in the 18th century, room was made to accommodate six elderly women as well.

At the top of the street stands the gracious parish church of St Mary. Sir Malcolm Sargent (1895 – 1967), the popular conductor, was organist and choirmaster here between 1914 and 1924. Built between 1170 and 1532, the oldest part of the church is the lower section of the pinnacled, 100 ft high tower. Inside, the church has a set of pillars and arches down each side of the transepts – a feature it shares with only three other English parish churches – and each transept has a rare brass candelabra dating from 1746. Its wealth of stained glass is mostly Victorian, but there is some 14th-century stained glass in a window near the font. The magnificent clerestory windows contain more than 15,000 diamond-shaped pieces of clear glass. In the chancel is a memorial tablet to John Ferneley, Leicestershire-born and one of the early 19th century's outstanding horse painters. Some of his canvases are in the Melton Carnegie Museum.

The museum, together with the Information Centre in Thorpe End, also displays the town's most famous products: Melton Mowbray pork pies and Stilton cheese. The pies were first baked in 1831 in a small shop, now a cafe, next to the Fox Inn yard. Ye Olde Pork Pie Shoppe in Nottingham Street, north of the Market Place, has produced the pies since 1850. There, by appointment, you can watch the pies being hand-raised – without baking-tins – on wooden blocks.

St Mary's Church, Melton Mowbray

Lady in alabaster

Pie Shoppe, Nottingham Street

Pies and tools of the trade

NEAR HEAVEN WITH A HAND-RAISED PIE

The so-traditionally English image of an expansive, tree-shaded green and gracious church tower outlined against heavenly cloudlets can seldom be seen to better effect than at Melton Mowbray. The late Sir Malcolm Sargent was once organist at St Mary's Church, which houses the fine alabaster figure of an unnamed woman in 14th-century dress, her hands clasped in prayer. But the town is best known as the unofficial headquarters of fox-hunting, and as the source of the definitive pork pie – hand-raised as ever on wooden blocks, at Ye Olde Pork Pie Shoppe.

Stilton cheese (named after a village in Cambridgeshire where it used to be sold) has been made in the area around Melton Mowbray since at least 1730.

• **Parking** Chapel Street; Mill Street; Scalford Road; Thorpe End; Wilton Road (all car parks) • **Early closing** Thursday • **Market days** Tuesday, Saturday • **Theatre** The College Theatre, Asfordby Road • **Cinema** The Regal, King Street • **Information** TEL. Melton Mowbray 69946 • **AA 24 hour service** TEL. Leicester 20491.

Frisby on the Wreake

LEICESTERSHIRE

5 miles west of Melton Mowbray (PAGE 237 Cb)

An 18th-century vicar of Frisby, the Reverend William Wragge, set up shop in the parish church of St Thomas à Becket marrying couples without the banns being read or a licence being issued. He did a roaring trade for a few years, turning Frisby into the Gretna Green of the Midlands. When at last he was caught, he was sentenced at first to 14 years transportation. But, roguish to the end, he pleaded extreme old age and was let off scot-free.

Frisby was founded by Vikings from the Frisian Islands on the far side of the North Sea, who made their way up the meanders of the River Wreake – the name itself means 'winding' or 'serpentine' – and settled on its banks.

Before 1810, when a turnpike was built, all the traffic from Leicester to Melton went through the village street. The Leicester to Melton canal and the Leicester to Peterborough railway both pass a few yards north of the village, and these trunk routes along the Wreake valley have opened the village up to the world.

Frisby has always been a mixture of styles. Many houses are made of brick, puce-plum in colour, from the yard at Rotherby a mile away. Some of the brick has been painted, particularly on the tall Georgian building opposite the post office and on the old Black Horse Inn. Some of the inn's windows were also bricked up in the late 18th century to avoid window tax, which was introduced in 1777; they were replaced in the mid-1970s.

Apart from the parish church there is little ironstone, but in Mill Lane there is still one short stretch of wall in wattle-and-daub (woven branches sealed with clay), made weatherproof with a small pantile cap. Several houses in the village were built by this ancient technique until quite recently, and this particular wall is now home for a colony of bees.

At the end of Mill Lane and across the railway are the abandoned remains of an early 19th-century canal, the Wreake Navigation. Next to a brick bridge, with its solid, curving ox-horn parapet, there is an old lock choked with driftwood. Beyond are some flooded gravel pits, full of Canada geese, grebes, swans and other water birds.

Before the gravel was dug out of them, the pits were the richest fields in the parish. Now they are good only for dinghy sailing. A footbridge crosses the river, serving the path to Asfordby. This was the route Frisby men used to walk to work in the smelter foundry there. The dross and slag from the iron mills was used to surface Frisby's streets.

Near the village centre, at the corner of Main Street and Wet Lane, are the remains of a 13th-century cross, which used to be the focus of a market. Along the Rotherby road from the cross, at the north end of a large thatched building called Zion House, there once lived a highwayman, who made his living from travellers – including, no doubt, market-goers. He was hanged at Birstall, north-west of Leicester, in 1797.

Waltham on the Wolds

LEICESTERSHIRE

6 miles north-east of Melton Mowbray (PAGE 237 Da)

Standing high on a limestone outcrop in the easternmost corner of Leicestershire, Waltham on the Wolds is chilled by winds off The Wash, 45 flat miles to the east. Villagers say that it is always a topcoat warmer away from the village, but the severe frosts they suffer have given Waltham one of its prettiest features.

Red clay roof tiles tend to crack in frosts, so many of the pale limestone houses are roofed in pantiles which are glazed blue-black. The tiles are both frost-resistant and smart – a serge suit for a house. Villagers say, however, that the secret of making them has now been lost; it died with their last manufacturer in the late 19th century.

Many of the cottages are 400 or 500 years old and new homes were built in the 19th century by the Dukes of Rutland, who live at Belvoir Castle, 6 miles north. They owned most of the village until 1921, when all but one farm and church property was sold.

The dukes' ancestor, Thomas Manners, Earl of Rutland, was given the land by Henry VIII in 1541 after the monasteries were dissolved. The village and its surroundings had belonged to a succession of semi-absent Norman landlords. But from the time of King John (1199 – 1216) most of the land was in the hands of the abbots of Croxton Kerrial and the nuns of Nuneaton. Although all trace of their small nunnery has disappeared, the foundations of a large 13th to 14th-century manor house can still be seen.

There have been racing stables in Waltham since the middle of the 19th century and the racehorses, all thigh and muscle, can be seen walking along the village street and exercising on the old racecourse which adjoins the stables on the village outskirts. The last race meeting was held here in April 1914.

With 560 inhabitants, Waltham has a self-sufficient air of prosperity which stems from the 13th century, when it was designated one of the five towns of Leicestershire, and granted both a weekly market and an annual September fair, neither of which has survived. It was a time of great prosperity, founded on the backs of sheep and on the trade along the Grantham to Melton road which still runs through the village.

The large Church of St Mary Magdalene dates from the 13th century and is now crumbly, leaning and a little decayed. Its crocketed 15th-century spire still dominates the lower end of the village, opposite the two pubs, The Marquis Granby and the Royal Horseshoes. Once there were 17 ale houses here.

The key to the church is in the post office. It is worth collecting. Inside St Mary's, through a plain Norman door, are two lovely 18th-century brass chandeliers hanging from iron chains in the nave, one with a brass dove suspended in flight. The choir stalls are decorated with 19th-century carved foliage, and the Norman font is covered in a jungle of stone leaves and stalks growing in and out of a miniature arcade.

Farther up the High Street, and just off it, is a smock mill – built in 1868 and now converted into a private house, with a white fibreglass skullcap for a roof and no sails. Beyond and above it is Waltham's most modern monument: a television mast 1052 ft high, beaming pictures to the Midlands and the Fens.

CHARM THAT COMES IN FROM THE COLD

A special charm is brought to Waltham on the Wolds by the glazed blue-black pantiles used to roof many of the village's pale limestone houses. The tiles, as well as being attractive to the eye, are frost-resistant – and this matters in Waltham, which suffers chill winds. The parish church shows signs of decay, but it has two beautiful 18th-century chandeliers hanging from iron chains.

Cottages and church lych gate

Chandeliers in church

Glazed tiles on cottage

Stamford High Street and St Martin's Church

THE GEORGE AND CECIL CONNECTION

The old Great North Road snakes into Stamford and under the 'gallows' sign of The George, its famous coaching inn. The main part of the inn was built in 1597 by Lord Burghley, treasurer to Elizabeth I, who also built the palatial Burghley House, south-east of Stamford. His tomb is the most splendid of the Cecil monuments in St Martin's Church, which has a pulpit carved with a figure of St Hugh of Lincoln.

Carving of St Hugh

West front of Burghley House

STAMFORD

LINCOLNSHIRE

14 miles north-west of Peterborough (PAGE 237 Eb)

Arriving in this stone-built market town from the south takes you, in a matter of yards, from the 20th-century countryside to an 18th-century High Street. The shops and houses lining the street date mostly from the 1700s, and the occasional 'intruder' from the 16th or 19th centuries does nothing to spoil the effect.

The River Welland bisects Stamford, and the part of the town south of the river is known as St Martin's. So the main street's full name is High Street, St Martin's, after St Martin's Church, which stands just to the east. Built in 1480, the church is noted for its fine display of stained glass, and some splendid tombs of the Cecil family, the chief of which is that of William Cecil, the 1st Lord Burghley (1520–98), who was Lord High Treasurer to Elizabeth I. He built as his home the palatial Burghley House, which is on the southern outskirts of the town.

The Tudor mansion, set in a deer park, has 18 treasure-packed State Rooms on view – including Elizabeth I's bedroom, in which the four-poster bed and a set of chairs are covered in their original materials. In contrast to this splendour is the below-stairs fascination of the Old Kitchen – a vast room containing more than 260 old copper cooking utensils.

To the north of the river is Stamford's second High Street, which is surrounded by several medieval churches – All Saints, St George's, St John Baptist and, finally, St Mary's.

The spire of St Mary's shoots 163 ft into the sky and can be seen for miles around. It was added in the 14th century to the church's 13th-century tower. St Mary's is regarded as the town's 'mother' church, and among its rich and elaborate carvings is the 15th-century panelled ceiling in the north chapel, decorated with carved bosses depicting grotesque heads, a stag, an angel, foliage and Tudor rose designs.

Stamford's architecture is mainly Georgian, and set among it are a number of imposing buildings from other periods. They include a 17th-century building in the Sheep Market, used as a bus station waiting room. The twin-gabled front originally stood in the High Street as part of the Stamford Mercury building. It was removed to its present site in 1937 when the newspaper's premises were demolished and rebuilt.

Another outstanding building is Browne's Hospital, built in the late 15th century as an almshouse. Its founder, a wealthy wool merchant named William Browne, was six times Alderman of Stamford. Originally the hospital housed ten poor men and two poor women, but it was extensively enlarged and modernised in the 1870s.

The town's most historic inn is The George in High Street, St Martin's. The main part of the hotel was built by Lord Burghley in 1597, and it later became famous as a coaching inn. Its sign is attached to a gallows which stretches across the width of the road, and it was meant to discourage highwaymen.

England's fattest ever man, Daniel Lambert of Leicester, who weighed 52 stone 11 pounds, stayed at the Wagon and Horses, which no longer exists, in June 1809 while touring England on exhibition. There he died suddenly in bed one morning, aged 39, and he is buried in St Martin's churchyard. His walking stick is on display at The George, and his immense suit of clothes can be seen on a life-size model in the Stamford museum in Broad Street.

• **Parking** North Street; Scotgate; Bath Row; St Leonards Street; Wharf Road (all car parks) • **Early closing** Thursday • **Market day** Friday • **Theatre** Arts Centre, St Mary's Street, TEL. Stamford 63203 • **Cinema** Central, Broad Street, TEL. Stamford 63179 • **Events** Festival (July); Burghley Park Horse Trials (September) • **Information** TEL. Stamford 64444 • **AA 24 hour service** TEL. Leicester 20491.

Duddington NORTHAMPTONSHIRE

5 miles south-west of Stamford (PAGE 237 Eb)

The River Welland makes a wide curving sweep under the hillside on which Duddington is settled. Beyond the river, sheep feed on the meadows of the flood plain, which used to be famous for the thickness and richness of its hay crops.

The river once ran in a straighter course across these fields, but in 1664 Nicholas Jackson, the squire of the village and a member of the family that still lives in the 17th-century manor, cut a new line for it. His aim was to provide a weightier head of water for the flour mill he had built at the bottom of the village. The old bed of the river can be made out in the grass from the vantage point opposite the Royal Oak Inn. The river itself now flows through Jackson's cut and under his mill, which is no longer in use.

Duddington used to be on the crossroads of the Stamford to Northampton and Peterborough to Leicester roads. The bridge over this important crossing of the Welland, widened in 1919, dates from the 14th century. By 1972 the combined traffic of the two roads was almost ruining the village, so a double bypass was built. It left Duddington as it is today, weirdly quiet, without a shop, a post office or a school.

It is a Conservation Area and a Heritage Village, and a walk along its streets reveals a strange and stilled perfection. The parish used to have some small quarries – long since closed – which produced limestone roofing slates, but never any building stone for walls. As a result the houses are made in limestone from either Barnack (near Stamford) or Weldon (near Corby). Most have roofs of old slate from Collyweston, only a mile away, where the quarries are now exhausted. Only a few are thatched, since a roof of Collyweston stone-slate used to cost about the same as a thatched roof, and a stone roof lasts longer.

Roses trail around the 14th-century porch of the Church of St Mary, which has a fat little stone spire and thick Norman arches inside, carved with a deep zigzag pattern. The arches were built at about the same time as the nave at the nearby village of Morcott, in the second half of the 12th century. The font, which is also medieval, still has one of the staples used to bolt down the lid so that witches could not steal or defile the holy water.

QUIETLY COLOURFUL OVERLEAF

Dark moss bubbles on the Collyweston slate roof of Church Farm at Duddington and Virginia creeper glows in all its autumnal glory on mellow stone walls. The stumpy little spire of the Church of St Mary peeps between the farmhouse gables. Peace reigns in this crossroads village, rescued from roaring traffic by two bypasses.

STYLISH STREET *Cottages built in varied styles – one of them with a thatched roof – bring a genuine old-world charm to Market Overton. But the once-familiar scent of lavender has gone.*

Market Overton LEICESTERSHIRE

13 miles north-west of Stamford (PAGE 237 Db)

Until the beginning of the Second World War the women of Market Overton used to work at Lady Barbara Seymour's lavender farm, half a mile east of the village. From there in summer, when the wind was right, the scent of the lavender flowers wafted up over the fields, soaking the whole village with their wardrobe smell. The air, sadly, is more ordinary now and the farming a mixture of cereals and sheep pastures.

The pale stone village, on the very edge of the limestone upland, overlooks the clays of the Vale of Catmose. Its one sinuous street slides around a couple of S-bends, narrowing and then encircling small greens as it goes. On one of them, in the churchyard and along the road, trees were planted to celebrate Queen Victoria's Golden Jubilee in 1887. The saplings were carried on foot from Grantham, 15 miles away. The full-grown trees now shelter an older whipping post and set of stocks last used in the early 19th century to punish a villager for drunkenness.

Among the cottages there are several big houses which would not be out of place in a Stamford street. Their names – The Manor, The Old Manor (where Sir Isaac Newton, the discoverer of the law of gravity, stayed as a boy), The Old Hall, The Old Manor Farm House and, the prettiest and most urbane, Market Overton Hall – demonstrate the prosperity that the village has always enjoyed.

It had a market from about 1200 until the 15th century, but its importance is far older. It lies just west of an ancient north-south trackway called Sewstern Lane, which shadowed the Roman Ermine Street and remained in use as a drove road when the Great North Road was made into a turnpike. The Romans also used Sewstern Lane, and a large Roman trading post was discovered on the line of the old road about 1½ miles east of Market Overton.

Many Saxon and Roman objects, now in Oakham Museum, were discovered when the whole area was quarried for ironstone this century. Among the Saxon objects was a primitive clock: a shallow bronze dish with a small hole in it. The dish would be floated in a bowl of water so that it gradually filled and eventually sank. This one, designed to measure an hour, is still remarkably accurate. When it was tested by modern archaeologists, it sank a mere two minutes late. In the early years of quarrying, the ironstone was near the surface and soft enough to dig with picks. The 200 or so men working on the site used to come to the blacksmith's, which is still in the village, for repairs to their picks. There is little evidence of this wide-scale quarrying today, because the soil was replaced as soon as the ironstone was removed, and a crop grown on it within the year.

The mostly 14th-century Church of St Peter and St Paul lies within the outlines of a Roman encampment, faintly visible in the fields to the north and east of it. At the north-west corner of the churchyard there is a stile made of a single slab between two stones, which may be the bases of Roman columns, but are more likely to be parts of a Saxon belfry.

About a mile west of the village, at the bottom of the limestone scarp, you will find the rushy remains of the Oakham to Melton canal.

Morcott LEICESTERSHIRE

9 miles south-west of Stamford (PAGE 237 Eb)

When the open fields around Morcott were enclosed in 1835, the three big landowners of the village marked out their land with different hedgerow trees. The Earl of Ancaster planted elms, the Marquis of Exeter chose oaks and Mr Fydell Rowley planted ash. Many of the trees have now gone, from disease or to be sold for timber, but you can still make out traces of these distinctive boundaries.

The village has the same sort of feudal pattern. Most of the houses are modest, pretty cottages, tucked under heavy Collyweston slate roofs. Their lichened walls are a mixture of white rubble limestone and of the more orange sandstone, called Pilton rag, which is quarried just to the north. But in the middle, opposite the long sloping churchyard, you find the manorial centre of the village. Sideways to the street, and almost concealed behind a high stone wall, is the square-set Manor House (1687), a big hip-roofed building with

Tutbury Castle ruins – north tower and gatehouse

monumental chimneys and open-faced windows. This was good enough for the lords of the manor until the mid-19th century when the Fydell Rowleys built a large new residence just to the east. The old Manor House was let to some farmers named Tyler while the Fydell Rowleys set up in their 'neat modern mansion', as a contemporary guidebook called it.

There are Tylers living and working in Morcott today. The Rowleys, who still own a great deal of the village, live in the United States. Morcott Hall, their mansion, is now a private girls' school.

The Church of St Mary the Virgin is downhill from the hall, at the other end of the crowded yew-filled churchyard. There is a strange and rare circular opening, called a pancake window, in the Norman tower, but the real interest is inside (the key is available from the post office).

Pushing open the door, you find yourself in the heavy dark air of a Norman nave. The massive cylindrical piers and semicircular arches were built between 1150 and 1290, and the capitals are carved with grotesque heads and fir-cones. Notice the mistake on the central pier on the northern side where the mason accidentally knocked off one of the fir-cones and rather crudely recarved the stump. The chancel was extended in about 1320, and new windows that were inserted there in the 15th century made it much lighter, almost a different church from the nave. The narrow lancet window at the south-west corner of the chancel extends almost to the floor so that lepers, who were not allowed in the church, could watch the service from outside.

From many places in the village you can see the windmill high on the ridge to the south-east, past the White Horse Inn. There was a mill there in 1489, but the present building – which was restored in 1968 – dates from 1785. It has always been shared between Morcott and Barrowden, over the ridge in the Welland valley.

TUTBURY

STAFFORDSHIRE

5 miles north-west of Burton upon Trent (PAGE 237 Aa)

Georgian and Regency houses rub shoulders in Tutbury's broad and spacious High Street. The odd building out is the black-and-white, half-timbered Ye Olde

RUINS AND A REGENCY AIR

A royal prison, a royal church and some elegant Regency houses add distinction to Tutbury. Its medieval castle is now a ruin, though an imposing one, with a gatehouse built by John of Gaunt in the 14th century and a north tower which has steps to the top. The parish church, of which Elizabeth II is patron, is entered through one of the finest Norman doors in England. Glass has been made in Tutbury for centuries, contributing to the prosperity demonstrated by the well-preserved old houses lining the High Street.

The glass-blower's art

Norman door of church

Dog and Partridge Hotel. Built in the 15th century, it has served as the town house of the Curzon family and as a coaching inn. The Red Rover, a fast night coach between London and Liverpool, used to call here in the 18th century.

The centre of Tutbury is a conservation area, creating an 'old' town at its heart and a 'new' town on its outskirts. From the old quarter, Castle Street leads up to the ruins of Tutbury Castle, set on an isolated, outlying rock. The present castle dates from various periods in the Middle Ages. The red-sandstone gatehouse was built in 1362 by John of Gaunt, Duke of Lancaster. The south tower, with its winding staircase leading to an ante-chamber and presence chamber, dates from 1442 to 1450. The 15th-century north tower has 67 steps leading to the top, from which there are panoramic views stretching from Needwood Forest – in which guests at the castle went hawking and hunting – to the Low Peak of Derbyshire.

Mary, Queen of Scots (1542–87) was twice imprisoned in the castle, and the remains of her state apartments are in the courtyard. The high north tower contains fragments of rooms used by her secretary, personal physician and chief cook. The dungeons were used as storehouses and later as a prison for those who broke the game laws in Needwood Forest.

Near the castle is the Priory Church of St Mary. Built in the 11th to 12th centuries, the church is under the patronage of the Queen, as Duke of Lancaster. Its chief glory is the magnificent west front, which has a Norman door 14 ft high and $9\frac{1}{2}$ ft wide with seven receding arches. The lectern was carved from a log of black bog oak believed to be some 6000 years old.

The church also contains an early 19th-century notice forbidding people to search for treasure belonging to the Duchy of Lancaster. It refers to the time in 1831 when labourers working near the bridge that spans the River Dove dug up shovelfuls of silver pennies. Altogether they, and the townsfolk, unearthed about 100,000 coins. The money apparently belonged to Thomas, Earl of Lancaster, who was beaten by the forces of Edward II at the nearby Battle of Burton in 1322. The earl fled through Tutbury and his money-chest – containing a fortune in pay for his soldiers – was presumably lost in the confusion as he forded the river. Only 1500 of the coins were handed over to the Duchy – hence the warning notice.

● **Parking** Duke Street (car park) ● **Early closing** Wednesday ● **Information** TEL. Burton upon Trent 45454 ● **AA 24 hour service** TEL. Stoke-on-Trent 25881.

Shardlow DERBYSHIRE

17 miles east of Tutbury (PAGE 237 Ba)

Although some 55 miles from the sea, Shardlow was once a busy port. It had warehouses for such varied goods as iron, cheese, salt from Shropshire and locally grown corn to be shipped to the industrial cities. It also had thriving port industries including ropemaking, sailmaking, crane and boatbuilding. The source of this prosperity, which came to a peak in the early 1840s before the coming of the railways, was the Trent and Mersey Canal. This magnificent waterway was planned by the engineer James Brindley and completed in 1777. Linking the Trent with the Mersey, it connected Hull on the east coast and Liverpool on the west, crossing England's industrial heartland which was developing then. Near Shardlow, the canal joined the River Trent, and the port of Canal Shardlow grew up. Here cargoes were often transferred from river barges to canal narrowboats, or from boats to the main London to Manchester road which also ran through the village.

Today, Shardlow is – with Stourport-on-Severn in Hereford and Worcester – one of the two inland ports to survive almost completely intact, and is finding fresh prosperity as an important centre for canal cruising and the building of pleasure craft. Its most imposing building is the Clock Warehouse which stands, with its distinctive clock, near the bridge where

GHOST PORT *A bridge, old houses and a cluster of canal craft make a pretty picture at Shardlow. Once a busy port on the Trent and Mersey Canal, it is now a cruising and boatbuilding centre.*

Bedroom, with coat laid out

Drawing room, redecorated in 1856

Deer head in bedroom

ABBEY OF THE ECCENTRICS

An old velvet coat is spread out in one bedroom. Deer heads lie about untidily in another – apparently waiting to be mounted on the walls. A splendidly furnished drawing room glows with gilt: it was last decorated in 1856. And a bedroom contains a four-poster state bed, ordered and made in the 18th century, and still in the case in which it was delivered. These are some of the bizarre discoveries made at Calke Abbey by officials of the National Trust, which took over the property in 1984. The house was built in 1703, and until the 1980s it was the home of the Harpur family and their relations, the Crewes. Successive generations produced a number of eccentrics and recluses whose withdrawal from the outside world left the abbey virtually untouched for more than a century. The result is an unrivalled survival of a vanished way of life.

the busy London road crosses the canal. This fine red-brick and tile building has been restored and now houses a restaurant and canal museum. From here boat trips run along the canal and River Trent during the summer. The warehouse was built in 1780 spanning an arm of the canal, so that barges could dock beneath and have their cargoes winched into storage areas.

On the opposite bank of the canal, a towpath leads from a lock, underneath the bridge and into the heart of Shardlow. Here it passes No. 2 Store, a square red-brick building with small semicircular, fan windows. Farther on, a gate in the wall reveals the gardens of the fine 18th-century Lady in Grey Inn – formerly Shardlow Lodge and home of the Soresby family, who, with their rivals the Suttons handled most of the business of the port. Facing it, across the canal, a number of fine, former warehouses and canal pubs stand on The Wharf. Outstanding are the low Iron Warehouse and, beside the Malt Shovel Inn, the Malt Warehouse, with flattened, overhanging corners to avoid damage from wagons. Between them, the former Ship Inn – now Ivy House – and The Firs make a delightful group of red-brick, 18th-century buildings.

Ticknall DERBYSHIRE

13 miles south-east of Tutbury (PAGE 237 Ba)

Set in the gently rolling hills of south Derbyshire, the village of Ticknall owes much of its interest to the unseen presence of Calke Abbey lying amid 400 acres of parkland on its south-eastern edge. Here, in this splendid baroque mansion, the interrelated Harpur and Crewe families have lived since their ancestor Sir John Harpur built it in 1703 to incorporate an earlier 16th or 17th-century house on the site of a 12th-century Augustinian priory. Since then, successive generations of these families, owning vast tracts of south Derbyshire, went on living the life of their ancestors, seemingly oblivious of changes in the world outside, until massive death duties in the early 1980s brought a rude awakening.

Since the late 18th century, when the 'isolated baronet', Sir Henry Harpur, withdrew from all conventional relations with society (eventually committing the social sin of marrying a lady's maid), the owners of Calke Abbey have been distinguished for their rich eccentricity and reclusiveness. In the early 19th century, Sir George Crewe obliged all visitors to Calke to record their name and the purpose of their visit in a special book. His grandson Sir Vauncey Harpur Crewe, who died in 1924, allowed no motor cars within the park boundaries; and he often communicated with his daughters by letters, sometimes delivered to them on a silver salver by a footman, at other times by post. His successor, Mr Charles Harpur Crewe, jealously guarded his privacy until his death in 1981.

The result of this extraordinary history is that today, Calke Abbey, which has now been acquired by the National Trust and will eventually be open to the public, can give an almost unique glimpse into the life of 100 years or more ago. The drawing room remains exactly as it was in a photograph taken in 1886.

Beyond the park's north lodge, Ticknall itself keeps a charming rural character. Its two main streets are lined by many delightful stone and brick cottages and farmhouses. No. 53 High Street shows the remains of its half-cruck timber frame, and Hayes Farm is a fine early 19th-century house, facing the imposing red-brick Methodist Chapel of 1815. Near by is a strange conical lock-up once used for local miscreants. Beside the 19th-century Church of St George, with the remains of the earlier church in its yard, are the Almshouses, built by the Harpurs in the 18th century.

MAP 22

ENGLAND'S HOLLAND AND THE LINCOLNSHIRE WOLDS

Stately windmills, acres of bulb fields and curly Dutch gables in town and village . . . little wonder this part of Lincolnshire is known as Holland, so flat that you seem to see half the county from the top of Boston Stump. But all is quite different a few miles to the north, where sheep graze the rolling chalk downlands of the Wolds and the poet Tennyson invited Maud into the garden.

MAP 22: NEIGHBOURING AREAS – MAPS 21, 23, 29

BOSTON	LOUTH
Burgh le Marsh	Binbrook
Sibsey	Harrington
	Tetford

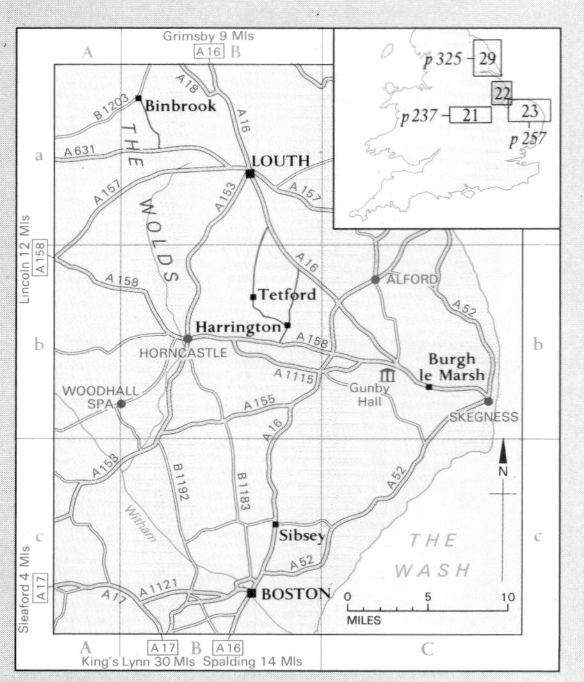

BOSTON

LINCOLNSHIRE

35 miles south-east of Lincoln (PAGE 252 Bc)

The 272 ft tower of St Botolph's Church, on the bank of the River Witham, is known as the Boston Stump. From the top on a clear day you can see Lincoln.

Boston is the port from which a band of Puritans set sail for America in 1630 – ten years after the Pilgrim Fathers made their voyage to the New World. The Puritans founded the settlement of Boston in what is now Massachusetts, and St Botolph's contains a memorial to John Cotton, the 'rebel' minister who led a number of his congregation across the Atlantic. There are also memorials to the five Lincolnshire men who were afterwards appointed Governors of Massachusetts. The elaborately carved misericords (brackets on the choir seats) date from the end of the 14th century, and the chancel has a fine medieval painted ceiling.

To the south of the church is the Queen Anne-style Fydell House, built in 1726 for a former Lord Mayor of Boston, William Fydell. Inside is an American Room for the use of visitors from the town's namesake, and the house itself is sometimes open to the public by arrangement. Next door is another building with an American connection – the 15th-century Guildhall, now a museum. It includes the cells occupied by the Pilgrim Fathers in 1607 after their first – and unsuccessful – attempt to escape to America in search of religious freedom. They were betrayed to the authorities by the ship's captain and arrested, but afterwards they were allowed to go to Holland. Later they returned and in 1620 sailed to America from Southampton on board the *Mayflower*.

Boston's heyday as a port was in the 13th century, when it rivalled London. By the 16th century its fortunes had declined, mainly because of floods and silting of the Witham. But with the drainage of the fens and improvements to the channel such as the opening of the Grand Sluice in the 18th century, trade revived. By the 19th century its docks had once again come into their own – and still do a busy international trade in grain, timber, steel and fertiliser.

● **Parking** Bargate Green; Bargate Bridge; Market Place; Lincoln Lane; Custom House Quay; Doughty Quay; Buoy Yard; Cattle Market; Fydell Crescent; Pump Square; Botolph Street (all car parks) ● **Early closing** Thursday ● **Market days** Wednesday, Saturday ● **Theatre** Blackfriars, Spain Lane TEL. Boston 63108 ● **Cinemas** Haven, South Square TEL. Boston 62961; Regal, West Street TEL. Boston 50553 ● **Events** May Fair; Carnival (June); Festival (June); Horticultural Show (September) ● **Information** TEL. Boston 64601 ● **AA 24 hour service** TEL. Lincoln 42363.

Burgh le Marsh LINCOLNSHIRE

18 miles north-east of Boston (PAGE 252 Cb)

At 8 o'clock in the evening, every Monday to Saturday between Michaelmas and Lady Day, a curfew is rung on the tenor bell of the 14th-century Church of St Peter and St Paul. This custom is thought to date from Norman times, but it was not always carried out. Once, in 1629, a sailing ship in The Wash was driven dangerously close inshore by a gale. The villagers, hoping to profit from the wreck, made no attempt to warn the captain, but the sexton shut himself in the church and rang the bell in time to alert him. The skipper gratefully presented him with a silken rope for the bell. He made a further gift of a piece of land in Orby Field, known as Bell-String Acre.

LANDMARK *The enormous bulk of St Botolph's, one of the largest parish churches in England, dwarfs buildings near by on the bank of the River Witham at Boston. The church tower soars to a height of 272 ft and is known far and wide as the Boston Stump. It is Lincolnshire's best-known landmark and was once a guide for Fenland travellers, as well as ships navigating The Wash.*

The church has an elegant buttressed and pinnacled tower, built of Portland stone, with a brightly painted clockface on one side which bears the faintly ominous message 'Watch and Pray, For Ye Know Not When the Time Is'. Inside are an impressive Jacobean pulpit, traces of medieval wall paintings and a lectern made in 1875 by the local barber, Jabez Good.

The village grew to the size of a small town at the end of the 19th century, with a brisk cattle market and annual foal fair, a number of inns and two breweries. The cattle market site is now occupied by modern flats called Market Close, leading to old people's flats in Dobson's Court, named after the last miller to operate the windmill on the other side of the road. This splendid tower mill, built in 1833, still works and has an unusual feature – its sails turn clockwise instead of anticlockwise. Standing five storeys high it dominates the landscape, its five sails starkly outlined against the sky. Dobson's Mill is maintained by Lincolnshire County Council and is open to the public. At the western end of the village is a sadder relic, the derelict stump of Hanson's Mill, shorn of its sails, its windows

Dobson's Mill

MILL THAT HAS TURNED WITH THE TIMES

The magnificent five-sailed Dobson's Mill at Burgh le Marsh is more than 150 years old, and still in perfect working order, cared for by Lincolnshire County Council and open to visitors. It is named after the last miller to operate it, and is unusual in having sails that turn clockwise, rather than anticlockwise. Possibly the builder was influenced by the exhortation elegantly inscribed on the church clock: 'Watch and Pray, For Ye Know Not When the Time Is.'

Clock with a message

broken and askew, and only the base of its cap crowning the brick-built tower.

Of the two breweries nothing remains except the malthouse of one, which is now a garage opposite Dobson's Mill. The other stood in Brewery Street until 1981, and in the 19th century was known as Matthias Wharram's Steam Brewery. Modern houses now stand on its site. Just around the corner is a complete contrast – Church Street, with a delightful white-washed cottage, West View, dating from 1785 and other buildings of the same period including a shop with a pantiled roof and box dormer windows.

The High Street still boasts three pubs, The White Swan, The White Hart and The Bell Hotel. From the latter, a horse-drawn carriage and omnibus used to pick up guests arriving at the railway station more than a mile to the west. The line is now closed and the station building is an antiques shop. The Market Place is a quiet backwater off the Lincoln to Skegness road that runs through the village. Here is yet another inn, The Fleece, side by side with Georgian buildings and facing the 19th-century County Library which has an attractive bow window, glazed doorway and fanlight.

To the west of the church, alongside the road leading to Lincoln, is Cock Hill, an ancient tumulus from which the remains of a Saxon burial have been excavated. Clay pipes and slate pencils unearthed from a depression in the summit suggest that the mound was once used as a cockpit, hence its name. The soil also contained pieces of Roman pottery and coins. A Roman road from Lincoln ended abruptly at Burgh and it is thought that a Roman ferry ran from near by, taking travellers across The Wash to the junction of Peddars Way and the Icknield Way on the Norfolk shore. Burgh may also have supported a small Roman fort or signal station.

In parkland about 3 miles north-west of the village is Gunby Hall, a manor house built in 1700 in the style of Christopher Wren. It is now administered by the National Trust and is open to the public on Thursday afternoons from April to September.

Sibsey LINCOLNSHIRE

5 miles north of Boston (PAGE 252 Bc)

Like Burgh le Marsh, Sibsey has a magnificent windmill. Beside the road west to Frithville stands Trader Mill, a well preserved tower mill with six sails and six storeys. It dates from 1877 and was probably the last one to be built in Lincolnshire. The mill was working until 1958. It has since been restored by the Department of the Environment and can be visited daily from April to September. A few hundred yards away, flowing under the Frithville road bridge, is a typical fenland drainage channel, running dead straight into the far distance, accompanied by a narrow road with houses and farm buildings huddled under its embankment.

The busy main road between Louth and Boston divides Sibsey, but it maintains a dignified air amid the vast emptiness of the fenland. Its houses are mostly 18th and 19th century, standing in their own grounds. In Chapel Lane there is a friendly blend of old cottages and new bungalows.

The Church of St Margaret has some Norman touches, particularly the north doorway and the nave, which has high arches.

Surrounding the village are acres of sugar beet, potatoes, cabbages and other vegetables. The immense flat landscape, networked by drains, dykes and sluices, is broken only by an occasional farmhouse. Visitors used to rolling hills or softly contoured farmlands ribboned with hedgerows may find this great emptiness intimidating, but for those with an eye for such things, there is an airy magic in the distant horizons and beauty in the constantly changing backdrop of clouds.

LOUTH

LINCOLNSHIRE

17 miles south of Grimsby (PAGE 252 Ba)

A Lincolnshire lad, Alfred Tennyson attended Louth Grammar School – which he loathed – from 1816 to 1820. Later the future Poet Laureate had his first book of verse, *Poems by Two Brothers*, which he wrote with his brother Charles, published in the town by the booksellers J. & J. Jackson. The shop, now called Parkers, still stands in the Market Place. The brothers received £20 for their work – half in books and half in cash.

Louth was an important market centre in the days of the Domesday Survey, and remains so still; on market days the shops and stalls do a thriving trade beneath the shadow of the Victorian Gothic Market Hall. Many streets in the centre have names ending in 'gate' which, as in other northern and east Midland towns, does not mean an opening, but is derived from the Saxon word for a street or walkway.

In May 1920 the River Lud, which winds through the centre of the town, burst its banks after heavy rainfall. Water and mud flooded the lower rooms of many of the houses, and 23 people were drowned. Nearly all of the town's bridges were destroyed and some inscribed stones in Bridge Street, Eastgate and James Street – where three houses were swept away by the torrent – record the height that the flood reached.

From whichever direction Louth is approached, the soaring spire of the 15th-century parish church of St James is an unavoidable landmark. Reaching 295 ft high, it is the tallest spire in Lincolnshire.

• **Parking** Cannon Street; Eastgate (2); Northgate; Kidgate; Queen Street; Eve Street; Bridge Street (all car parks) • **Early closing** Thursday • **Market days** Wednesday, Friday and Saturday • **Theatre** Little, Newmarket TEL. Louth 603549 • **Cinema** Playhouse, Cannon Street TEL. Louth 603333 • **Event** May Fair • **Information** TEL. Louth 602391 • **AA 24 hour service** TEL. Lincoln 42363.

Binbrook LINCOLNSHIRE

10 miles north-west of Louth (PAGE 252 Ba)

Reached along narrow roads, some with squat hedges set back behind wide verges, Binbrook spreads comfortably over a shallow hillside in the northern wolds. Around its wide square, still with a village pump, side lanes lead to pleasant corners and on one side is a late Georgian manor house in stone and glowing red brick.

Two cheerful little inns, the Plough and the Marquis of Granby, owe much of their custom to the nearby RAF airfield now operated by Fighter Command. During the Second World War, units of the Royal Australian Air Force were stationed here, and it was from here that squadrons of No. 1 Bomber Group flew their Lancasters on night raids over Germany. On the night of March 30, 1944, 24 aircraft from Binbrook took part in the raid on Nuremburg; three failed to return.

During the 19th century Binbrook was a centre for the recruitment of agricultural labourers, both men and women, who were employed to work in the fields under intolerable conditions. Their long hours, often dawn until dusk, and miserable pay aroused public reactions that played a part in the formation of the National Union of Agricultural and Allied Workers in 1872.

Binbrook once had two churches, St Gabriel's and St Mary's, but St Gabriel's fell into ruin and was pulled down in 1820.

Set back from the square behind trees, St Mary's ironstone tower and broach spire soar above a church surprisingly large for so small a village. Most of its interior is Victorian, but there are a few relics from the earlier building, including an 18th-century hatchment (a memorial panel bearing his coat of arms) to Richard Bewley Caton of Binbrook, an army major who later took holy orders. In Georgian times the Caton family were substantial landowners in the neighbourhood.

Harrington LINCOLNSHIRE

12 miles south of Louth (PAGE 252 Bb)

'Come into the garden, Maud', wrote Alfred Tennyson, apparently inspired by the secluded walled garden at Harrington Hall. The poet's father knew the Amcotts, who owned the hall, well, and Alfred spent many happy hours here.

Sunk in the embrace of the encircling wolds, Harrington drowses deep in a pocket of woodlands. Every road into and out of the hollow is a leisurely delight, a dip into a fairy dell stockaded by tall conifers that still the north winds to a mere whisper. Along one lane is the old woodman's cottage, single storeyed and steeply thatched, with gleaming white walls and small casement windows peeping out from under the eaves.

Not so easy to find, as it is not visible from the road, is St Mary's Church, a medieval foundation but almost completely rebuilt with greenstone in 1855. It is reached by a path congested with undergrowth and stands dwarfed by the surrounding trees, like a cathedral in miniature with its tower, nave, chancel and porch. The church contains several memorials to

Harrington Hall – and garden

Sundial above the door

DID MAUD EVER COME INTO THIS GARDEN?

The poet Tennyson was a family friend of the Amcotts, who owned Harrington Hall, and was a frequent visitor. He spent many a happy hour in the walled garden there, and it may well have inspired him to write some verses that were set to music by Arthur Somervell in a Victorian ballad that begins: 'Come into the garden, Maud'. The house has the towering porch of an earlier Elizabethan mansion, retained when Vincent Amcott rebuilt the place in 1673. The sundial above the doorway bears the Amcott arms and was put there in 1681.

past lords of the manor, including one of a cross-legged knight of about 1300, thought to have been Sir John Harrington, founder of the church. There are several monuments to the Copledykes who built the Elizabethan Harrington Hall, and to the Amcotts who followed – Vincent Amcott rebuilt the hall in 1673. A gateway leads to it from the churchyard.

The house as Amcott built it includes the original towering porch, and over the doorway is a sundial, installed in 1681, with the Amcott coat of arms above it. On one side of the tower are two rows of seven sash windows, and on the other side two rows of six, splitting the red-brick frontage into pleasing asymmetry. The house, gardens and a garden centre belong to the family of the late Sir John Maitland, MP for Horncastle between 1945 and 1966, and are frequently open to the public.

A mile south along the road to Hagworthingham is Stockwith Mill with its old water wheel and foaming millrace. Apart from a car park and a craft centre, the mill is little changed from when Tennyson wrote about it, in *The Miller's Daughter*:

I loved the brimming wave that swam
Through quiet meadows round the mill,
The sleepy pool above the dam,
The pool beneath it never still.

Tetford LINCOLNSHIRE

9 miles south of Louth (PAGE 252 Bb)

This is the largest village in what is known as 'Tennyson Valley' – the poet was born just over a mile away at Somersby. Tetford lies below the gently billowing Lincolnshire Wolds, with their clusters of beech trees on the skyline and their roads following the contours of leisurely switchbacks, a snug little settlement of mainly red-brick houses and a church built from local greensand stone.

Memories of the past echo in the names of buildings clustered at one road junction. The National School of 1891, a well-proportioned red-brick building with a Georgian rather than Victorian air, is backed by the modernised Old School House. Both are private houses now, and across the road is another – The Old Forge. The manor house on the outskirts of the village is late Georgian and has been restored and extended.

The White Hart Inn was once the meeting place of a Gentlemen's Literary Club, attended by Lord Tennyson and before him by the much-travelled Dr Samuel Johnson, who also played skittles at the inn when staying with his friend Bennet Langton at Langton, a few miles to the south-west.

St Mary's Church dates from the 14th century, though a church at Tetford was mentioned in the Domesday Survey of 1086. In the churchyard is the stump of a medieval cross with faint traces of armorial bearings, and near by stands a headstone of 1830 which records the death of two gypsies 'Slain by Lightening'.

Above the church porch a sundial sternly claims to be 'Redeeming the time because the days are evil'.

Inside the church are several memorials to the Dymoke family, the most impressive being a tablet to Captain Edward Dymoke who died in 1739. Above the tablet are arrayed a helmet, breastplate and backplate, fitting symbols for a man who was Hereditary Grand Champion of England.

This title has existed since the time of William the Conqueror, and has been held by the Dymokes since 1377. Until 1821 the champion attended the coronation of the monarch, rode in full armour into Westminster Hall and threw down a gauntlet to challenge anyone defying the monarch's right to succeed. The Dymoke's manor house at Scrivelsby, 7 miles south-west of Tetford, no longer exists, but is marked by a Lion Gateway and a restored gatehouse where Lieutenant-Colonel John Dymoke, the present champion, lives. At the coronation of Elizabeth II his task was to bear the Standard of England.

The Roman highway from Lincoln to Burgh le Marsh skirts the northern fringe of Tetford, and crossing it the road north up Tetford Hill meets one of the loveliest stretches in the county – the Blue Stone Heath Road. It follows a track even older than that of the Romans, along the exposed ridges of the wolds with superb vistas on either side.

MAP 23

WIDE HORIZONS AND THE BEAUTIFUL BROADS

Noël Coward's famous line, 'Very flat, Norfolk', does less than justice to this lovely and often surprising corner of England. Flat it may be, and some low-lying places have long lived under threat from the sea. But flat does not mean dull, and there is variety in both scenery and atmosphere. The beautiful Broads are full of birdlife, breathtaking views and boating enthusiasts. Ashore, tall churches are etched against wide horizons, and country accents delight the ear in busy market towns.

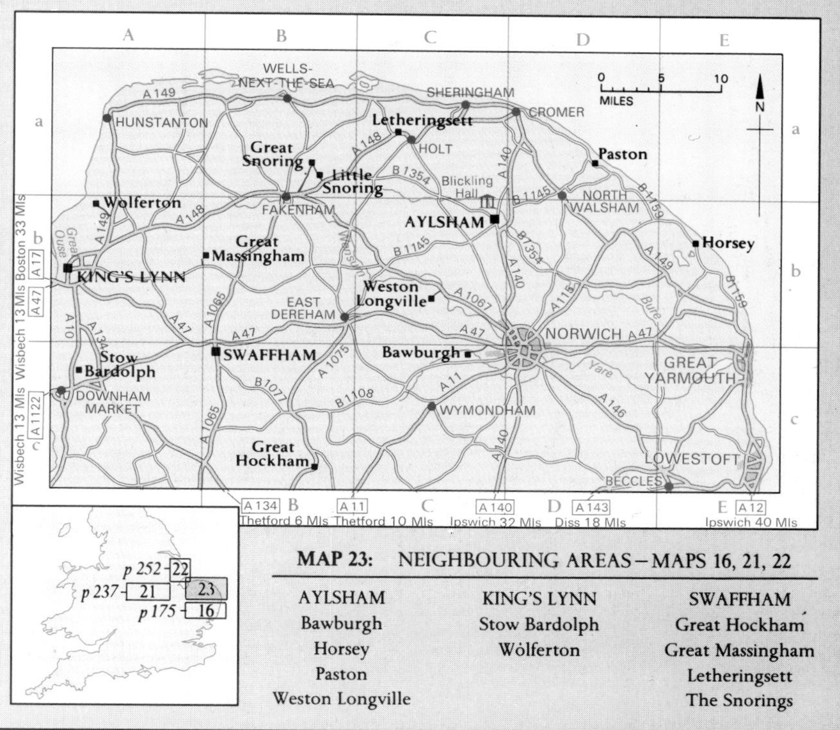

MAP 23: NEIGHBOURING AREAS – MAPS 16, 21, 22

AYLSHAM	KING'S LYNN	SWAFFHAM
Bawburgh	Stow Bardolph	Great Hockham
Horsey	Wolferton	Great Massingham
Paston		Letheringsett
Weston Longville		The Snorings

AYLSHAM

NORFOLK

13 miles north of Norwich (PAGE 257 Cb)

Red brick and flint are the building materials in Aylsham, and a flint facing protects the 14th-century parish church of St Michael, just north of the Market Place. Inside are some good memorial brasses, including two depicting the grinning skeletons of its 15th-century benefactors, Richard and Cecilie Howard. Humphry Repton, the landscape gardener who designed many of the great English parks of the late 18th century, was buried in the churchyard in 1818. One of his favourite flowers was the rose, and rose bushes still cover his grave. The inscription on his memorial reads:

Not like Egyptian tyrants consecrate,
Unmixed with others shall my dust remain;
But mold'ring, blending, melting into Earth,
Mine shall give form and colour to the Rose,
And while its vivid blossoms cheer Mankind,
Its perfumed odours shall ascend to Heaven.

The ample, four-square, red-brick buildings of the Market Place make an apt centrepiece for this solidly prosperous market town. For 500 years, until the Industrial Revolution, it was an important centre for the manufacture first of linen and then of worsted. The Black Boys Hotel, in the square's south-west corner, might not be quite as it was in the 17th century, but its bow front and curious frieze of little black boys still convey a sense of elegant comfort.

The park and gardens of Blickling Hall, 1½ miles north-west of Aylsham, are laid out in Repton's manner, even if he did not actually design them. The present brick and stone mansion – owned by the National Trust – was built between 1616 and 1627, and is a masterpiece of Jacobean architecture.

An earlier house on the same site was the childhood home of Anne Boleyn, Henry VIII's second wife and mother of Elizabeth I. The house had been bought by her great-grandfather from Sir John Fastolf, one of the models for Shakespeare's Falstaff. Anne Boleyn was

HOUSE WITH A LEGEND *Elegant cedars frame the summerhouse of Blickling Hall, near Aylsham. Anne Boleyn lived in an earlier house here, and it is said that her ghost returns – by coach.*

REFLECTING THE PAST *The imposing 18th-century water mill at Aylsham reflects quietly on the past, mirrored in the tranquil River Bure. The mill was still working as recently as 1969.*

beheaded on May 19, 1536, having fallen from the king's favour for failing to produce a male heir. Legend has it that on this day every year her ghost returns to Blickling, severed head in lap, in a ghostly carriage pulled by four headless horses and driven by a headless coachman.

Returning to Aylsham, the Blickling Road passes Aylsham Old Hall, a fine late 17th-century mansion, and the Queen Anne Knoll House. On Norwich Road, Old Bank House is 18th century and the Manor House is early 17th century.

By the River Bure, and forming a distinct community within Aylsham, is Millgate, once busy with flat-bottomed sailing wherries plying the waterways to Norwich and Yarmouth. But the railways and a disastrous flood in 1912 finished Millgate as a trading centre. It is now a peaceful residential area of imposing 18th-century houses, such as Bure House and the former wherry inn, Bridge House, both with fine doorways. A large mill that was built in the 18th century remained in use until 1969.

● **Parking** Burgh Road; Market Place; Buttlands ● **Early closing** Wednesday ● **Market days** Monday, Friday ● **Event** Aylsham Show (agricultural show, Blickling Park, August Bank Holiday) ● **AA 24 hour service** TEL. Norwich 29401.

Bawburgh NORFOLK

16 miles south of Aylsham (PAGE 257 Cc)

The old farmhand was dying, and he knew it. But his last requests were clear. After I die, he told his gathered friends, lay my body on a bullock cart and let the oxen have their head. Bury me where they stop.

So runs the tale of Walstan, a humble labourer who died at the village of Taverham, 5 miles from Bawburgh, on May 30, 1016. According to the legend, the men did as they had been asked, and found to their amazement that a spring began to flow from the ground beside the cart when they laid Walstan's body there. The oxen plodded along the rough road to Costessey (pronounced 'Cossy'), then rested briefly – and a second miraculous spring appeared. Finally the oxen halted for good at Bawburgh – and a third spring gushed forth, the only one of the three still visible.

In time Walstan was canonised by the Church, and the Bawburgh spring became St Walstan's Well: a place of international pilgrimage in the Middle Ages. So many pilgrims came to the miraculous spring, and the shrine that was built over it, that a vicar and six priests were employed full-time to look after them.

The cult came to an abrupt end with the Reformation in the 16th century. Puritan reformers, outraged by what they saw as idolatry, tore down the shrine, burnt the relics of the saint and threw the priests out. The parish church of St Mary and St Walstan, a few hundred yards south of the spring, was also badly damaged by the Puritans. It was restored in 1637, but by then the flood of pilgrims had dwindled to a trickle. Twentieth-century visitors will find that the church is usually locked. The key is available from the nearby Church Farm.

Two other buildings constructed in the 18th century, but associated by local legend with the shrine, now stand in suburban gardens in the village. The Slipper House, probably a local squire's summer house, is said to have been the spot where pilgrims took off their shoes before walking to the church. The Hermit's House, or Dovecote, was apparently once the home of a hermit who sat by the ancient bridge which now carries the main road from Norwich across the River Yare and into the heart of Bawburgh. The hermit is said to have spent his days sprinkling holy water on the pilgrims as they crossed the bridge.

A row of cottages – mostly brick built – lines one side of the village green beside the river. On the other side is a large water mill, once the site of another owned by a miller named Jeremiah Colman, who began his career there in 1802. He moved to Stoke Holy Cross to found in 1823 the mustard company that still bears his name. The present mill, built in 1876, last turned in 1967; it is now a private house.

Horsey NORFOLK

23 miles east of Aylsham (PAGE 257 Eb)

Horsey's story is of an unremitting battle for survival against the sea. Once an island in a bay – its name may mean isle of horses – the village is between 3 ft and 6 ft above sea level and surrounded by flat, wind-scoured

Round-towered church at Bawburgh

SAINT OF THE SOIL

A farmhand named Walstan made Bawburgh a place of pilgrimage. He died in 1016, and a spring is said to have gushed forth where his body was laid to rest in the village. He was canonised, and the village's little church, with its rocket-shaped round tower, is dedicated to him and St Mary. He also appears, handsomely carved, on the village sign.

St Walstan carved on sign

countryside. Nevertheless, it has been occupied since Roman times – elements permitting. In 1938 the North Sea broke through the dunes, and the flood seemed to spell doom for Horsey.

The village was cut off for 4½ months and its inhabitants evacuated. Headlines over successive days in the local newspaper read like war communiqués: 'Horsey defences carried away.' Even when the flood had receded, the land was poisoned by salt, so the locals turned to the Dutch to learn how to cope with their common enemy.

The area was brought slowly back to life, but if you climb the church tower you can still glimpse the menacing sea, barely a stone's throw away, beyond the dunes. Visitors are discouraged from clambering over them for fear of damage to that vital defence.

There are three quite distinctive centres to this scattered village – a pub, a windmill and the church. The mill, a National Trust property, is for drainage, pumping water from ditches into Horsey Mere – one of the remoter and pleasanter Norfolk Broads. These days it is powered by electricity rather than the wind.

The tiny All Saints' Church, tucked among trees, has a thatched roof and a Saxon round tower which was topped in the 15th century with an unusual octagonal belfry. From outside, the church has changed little over the centuries, and the restoration carried out by the Victorians was confined to furnishings inside. There is one outstanding Victorian relic: a stained-glass window showing the artist Catherine Ursula Rising, a member of a wealthy local family, painting a picture.

VILLAGE THAT KEEPS AN EYE ON THE SEA

The handsome little thatched Church of All Saints and an immaculate old mill contribute to an atmosphere of unchanging peace and plenty at Horsey. It was not always so. The village has fought a continuing battle against the North Sea, which in 1938 broke through its defences and villagers were evacuated. Even the windmill is used for drainage – it pumps water from ditches into beautiful Horsey Mere, which lies just to the south-west and links up with Hickling Broad. The octagonal belfry of All Saints was added to its Saxon round tower in the 15th century.

Windmill and thatched church at Horsey

Paston NORFOLK

11 miles north-east of Aylsham (PAGE 257 Da)

Like many of Norfolk's straggling villages, which are often more a collection of farms than centralised communities, Paston has never had a public house or inn and its church is buried in a wood. But there has been a village here for at least a thousand years and from it, in the 15th century, came a remarkable series of letters which tell us much about the turbulent days of the Wars of the Roses. Most of the Paston Letters were written by Margaret Paston, and through them we can trace her career as bride, mother and matriarch.

She went to Paston Hall in 1440 when she married (her mother-in-law asked her father-in-law to buy her a gown of 'a goodly blue or a bright sanguine') and lived there for 44 years until her death. She usually wrote to her husband John, a lawyer in London. His letters mostly dealt with major public events, but hers are more homely.

She tells how the Rector of Great Snoring has been arrested for murder and has been put in the stocks awaiting trial; she pays 4s 6d (22½p) for a cartload of herrings but cannot get any eels; her daughter Margery falls in love with the farm bailiff and is giving trouble.

The Pastons were an autocratic lot, fighting off the Dukes of Norfolk and Suffolk who coveted their lands. The letters record, too, a monumental row in church after Evensong, in which villagers accused Margaret's mother-in-law of diverting a road.

The hall Margaret knew has long since gone, but another was built on its site in the last century and traces of the old one can be seen in the garden. The Church of St Margaret in which she worshipped is still there, with its thatched roof and 14th-century wall paintings, including a large St Christopher. Inside are several monuments to the Pastons, who died out in 1732, ranging from early tomb chests to more ornate and classical ones by Nicholas Stone dating from the early 1600s.

Weston Longville NORFOLK

19 miles south-west of Aylsham (PAGE 257 Cb)

Curiously, Weston is, like Paston, famous for a very personal account of day-to-day life in a bygone age. The village, on a hill above the River Wensum, is a place of pilgrimage for admirers of Parson James Woodforde, whose *Diary of a Country Parson* is a classic. He arrived in Weston in 1776, aged 36, and kept his diary until 2½ months before his death on New Year's Day 1803. He was an amiable, obscure man and recounts no world-shaking happenings – the only amazing ones are his meals:

Jan. 28, 1780: 'We had for dinner a Calf's Head, boiled Fowl and Tongue, a Saddle of Mutton rosted on the Side Table, and a fine Swan rosted with Currant Jelly Sauce for the first Course. The Second Course a couple of Wild Fowl called Dun Fowls, Larks, Blamange, Tarts etc. etc. and a good Desert of Fruit after amongst which was a Damson Cheese. I never eat a bit of a Swan before, and I think it good eating with sweet sauce. The Swan was killed 3 weeks before it was eat and yet not the least bad taste in it.' Then, by way of a change on April 15, 1778: 'My two large Piggs, by drinking some Beer grounds taken out of one of my Barrels today, got so amazingly drunk by it, that they were not able to stand and appeared like dead things almost, and so remained all night from dinner time today. I never saw Piggs so drunk in my life, I slit their ears for them without feeling.'

Dec. 31, 1780: 'This being the last day of the year, we sat up till after 12 o'clock, then drank a Happy New Year to all our Friends and went to bed. We were very merry indeed after Supper till 12. Nancy and Betsie Davie locked me in the great Parlour, and both fell on me and pulled my Wigg almost to Pieces – I paid them for it however.'

So his comfortable, tolerant life went on. He was forgotten after his death until his diaries were published in 1924.

At first sight there seems little relationship between Woodforde's village and today's. His rectory was rebuilt last century, though the pond in the grounds where he hid smuggled gin from the excise men remains. But the Church of All Saints, with a 13th-century tower and a rare 14th-century painting of the Tree of Jesse, is still as it was. So is the great barn where he collected his tithes from local farmers, feasting them in return on roast beef, puddings, rum, wine and strong beer at a 'Frolick'. And some of the best fishing in Norfolk is still to be found at the Lenwade Bridge, where Woodforde caught a 'prodigious pike' which he inevitably served up for dinner.

KING'S LYNN

NORFOLK

44 miles west of Norwich (PAGE 257 Ab)

The Great Ouse river has brought prosperity to this lively port and market town since the Middle Ages, and there are some noteworthy buildings strung along its east bank. Starting at the south end, there is the imposingly named Hampton Court, home of a 17th-century master-baker named John Hampton. Parts of this colour-washed building date back to the 1300s, and the King's Lynn Preservation Trust has converted it into flats.

Near by is the tall, 15th-century Hanseatic Warehouse, brick and timber framed with an overhanging upper storey, which, until 1751, belonged to the Hanseatic League of north European merchants. They formed a protective trading partnership in the 14th century. The town was one of half a dozen English ports welcomed into the league because the Germans had established trading links here.

Downriver the ornate Customs House, built in 1683, has a statue of Charles II over its main doorway. In between these maritime buildings is the Saturday Market Place, the focal point of the town since the early 1100s.

In the Market Place stands St Margaret's Church, built in the 13th century to replace the former St Margaret's, which was begun in 1100 by the first Bishop of Norwich. A severe storm in 1741 wrecked the nave and aisles, which were rebuilt, but the original twin towers are still there. The remains of a Benedictine priory lie on the south side of St Margaret's, and across from the church are two adjacent buildings with a matching design of dark and pale flint squares: the

Guildhall of the Holy Trinity, built in 1421, and the Victorian Town Hall. Among the trophies in the Guildhall's treasury are the King John Sword and a magnificent silver-gilt and enamel cup, called the King John Cup. Both, however, are 14th century and were made at least 100 years after the monarch died.

Between the Guildhall and the river is Thoresby College, founded about 1500 by Thomas Thoresby, a philanthropic merchant and member of the town council, as quarters for the chaplains of the Trinity Guild. It is now made over as flats for retired people, offices, a meeting room and a Youth Hostel. To the north of the college is the elegant 18th-century façade of Clifton House, hiding a much older building, formerly the residence of a rich medieval merchant.

North along the river is the town's second Guildhall, that of St George. It dates from 1407 and is the oldest and largest Guildhall in England. In the 18th century it was turned into a theatre, and today it stages part of the annual King's Lynn Festival. To the side of the Guildhall is Tuesday Market – larger but slightly younger than Saturday Market – with the 15th-century chapel-of-ease, St Nicholas, just above it in St Ann's Street.

The monarch connected with King's Lynn is Henry VIII, who took over the manor during the Dissolution of the Monasteries in 1539. Before that, the town was called Bishop's Lynn, or just plain Lynn, as it is to this day locally.

• **Parking** Baker Lane; St James Street; Blackfriars Street; Ferry Street; Chapel Street; Railway Road; Oldsunway; Albert

Customs House, King's Lynn

TREASURES OF KING'S LYNN

Boats lie moored alongside the 17th-century Customs House at King's Lynn; buoys litter the quayside in this quiet backwater of what has been for centuries a lively, prosperous port with an international flavour. Like other East Coast towns, King's Lynn has always had to battle against the sea and the weather. In 1741 a fierce storm swept the town and almost wrecked St Margaret's Church, but the imposing 13th-century twin towers survived, and the damaged nave and aisles were rebuilt. Another impressive survivor is the Guildhall of the Holy Trinity, built in 1421, in a pattern of dark and pale flint squares. In its crypt are displayed town treasures that include the magnificent King John Cup and King John Sword, both of which were made a century after he died.

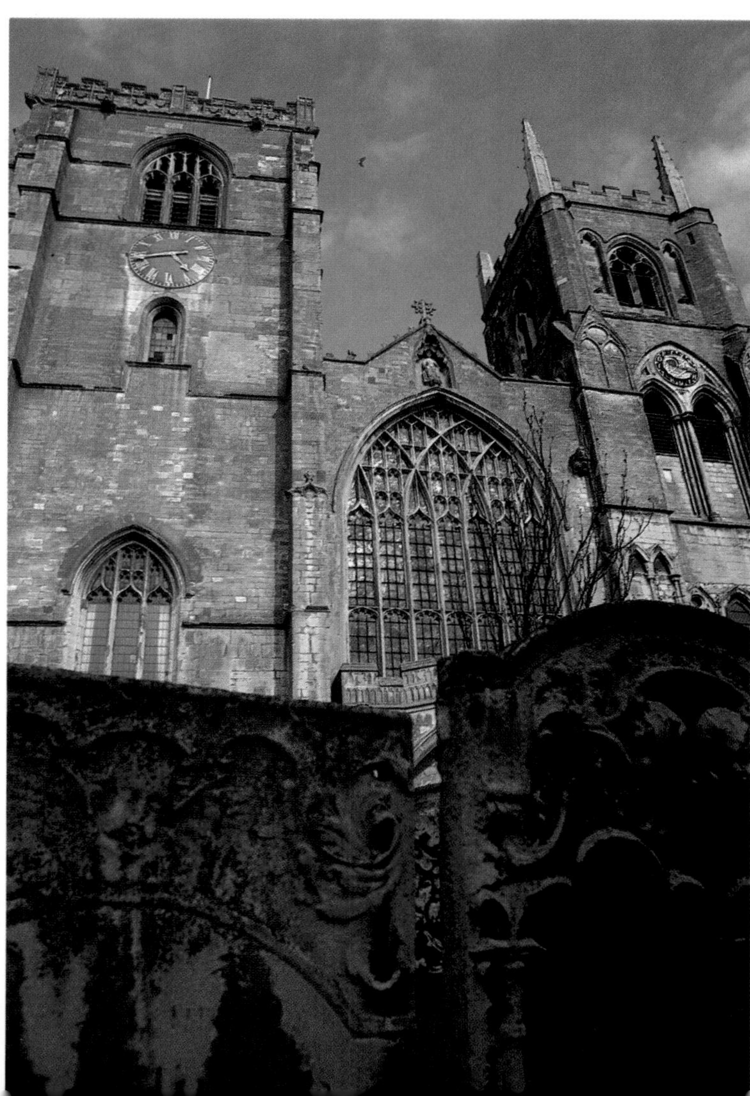

Holy Trinity Guildhall

Twin towers of St Margaret's

Street; Austin Street; Austin Fields; Tuesday Market Place; Saturday Market Place (all car parks) • **Early closing** Wednesday • **Market days** Tuesday, Friday, Saturday • **Theatre** Fermoy Centre, King Street TEL. King's Lynn 3578 • **Cinema** Majestic, Tower Street TEL. King's Lynn 2603 • **Event** King's Lynn International Festival (July) • **Information** TEL. King's Lynn 63044 • **AA 24 hour service** TEL. King's Lynn 3731.

Stow Bardolph NORFOLK

10 miles south of King's Lynn (PAGE 257 Ac)

A flimsy-looking cupboard stands in a corner of a chapel in Holy Trinity Church. It looks like a broom cupboard. Open the door and you come face to face with the upper half of a woman. She is plump and probably in her early forties.

The figure – a wax effigy – is that of Sarah Hare, who pricked her finger while doing needlework in 1744 and died of blood poisoning. She made the arrangements for the strange memorial and left her own ringlets of hair, a white dress and a red cloak to adorn the effigy. It must have been disturbingly lifelike when it was made, but now the wax is deteriorating and may not last many more years.

The Hares have been in Stow since the 14th century. Other monuments to them in the church are more durable than that of Sarah. Her grandfather is carved in marble in the style of a Roman, and the finest statue in the church is of an earlier ancestor, Ralph Hare, knighted at James I's coronation.

The family still live in part of the great Hall. It was rebuilt in 1873 and is hidden behind beech trees, cedars and the crenellated walls surrounding the gardens.

Stow has seen some changes. The vast, grey-brick rectory, almost as big as the church it stands beside, is now the headquarters of a seed firm; and a bypass, busy with traffic, cuts it off from the neighbouring village of Wimbotsham.

But Stow remains essentially an estate village, and most of its inhabitants still work on the land. The cottages are mainly 19th century, built of grey brick and flint. The Hare Arms, a huge inn for so small a village, was probably used to house visitors to the hall in the bygone days of lavish entertaining.

Wolferton NORFOLK

9 miles north of King's Lynn (PAGE 257 Ab)

For about a century, Wolferton was one of Europe's glittering royal centres. Emperors and empresses, kings and queens, leading statesmen and polished courtiers passed through its little station on their way to nearby Sandringham, after the estate was bought by the Prince of Wales – the future Edward VII – in 1862. So heavy was the royal traffic through Wolferton that in 1898 the railway track from King's Lynn had to be doubled and a magnificent set of reception rooms was built at the station.

But as road transport became more popular in the 1960s, fewer people – including royals – used the line. The royal trains halted for good in 1966, so British Rail decided to demolish the unique reception rooms and build a housing estate on the site.

The rooms were saved by an act of courage and vision: Eric Walker, a senior British Rail executive, was sent to take an inventory and was overwhelmed by what he saw. He and his wife decided to buy the station and turn it into a combined house and museum, which now attracts thousands of visitors.

The rooms were filthy and neglected when the Walkers moved in, but beneath the grime everything was intact – even down to the toilet fittings. Painstaking work has created a museum of Edwardian social life and of railway history, for Mr Walker has collected and put on display much long-forgotten equipment.

Near by is another survival from the days of glory, the Gate House. The level-crossing keeper once lived there, and it has been lovingly restored as a private home. In the adjoining churchyard is a last surviving lamp post, exquisitely decorated with a crown on top. The nearby 'gas house' used to supply acetylene gas to all the lamps in the village and to St Peter's Church. The church is late 13th and early 14th century but has been much restored.

SWAFFHAM

NORFOLK

28 miles west of Norwich (PAGE 257 Bc)

One story that many people have heard about Swaffham is the tale of its pedlar. He and his dog feature on the town sign just beyond the Market Place, and anyone in Swaffham can recount the adventures of John Chapman, a poor tinker who lived there in the middle of the 15th century. One night, he dreamt that if he stood on London Bridge he would meet a man who would make him rich. So John and his dog hiked to London, 100 or so miles away, stationed themselves on the bridge and waited for fortune.

After several days, a curious shopkeeper asked what they were doing there, and, on hearing John's story, recounted a recent dream of his own. He said that in his dream, a pedlar from Swaffham had found a pot of gold buried beneath a tree in his garden. John hastened back home, dug beneath the tree, and there, sure enough, he found not one but two pots of gold coins. Much of the money he gave to the parish church of St Peter and St Paul, to rebuild the north aisle. His generosity is recorded in the town's 'Black Book', the parish records, in the church library.

The wedge-shaped Market Place, flanked by graceful 18th-century buildings, is the nucleus of Swaffham. The north end is occupied by the Assembly Rooms of 1817, once the centre of the town's social life. Near by are the 18th-century buildings of the Sixth Form Centre, the Victorian Corn Exchange and Plowright Place, a double row of old workshops that have been converted into a pretty shopping precinct.

In the centre is the Butter Cross or Market Cross, given to the town by the Earl of Orford, nephew of the writer Horace Walpole, in 1783. Butter-sellers once displayed their wares beneath the cross – which is actually a dome held up by eight pillars. The statue on top of the cross is of Ceres, the Roman goddess of agriculture. The spire of Swaffham church, poking over the rooftops to the east of the Market Place, is crowned by a copper ball.

• **Parking** Market Place; Theatre Street • **Early closing** Thursday • **Market day** Saturday • **Event** Carnival (August) • **AA 24 hour service** TEL. King's Lynn 3731.

Wolferton station, with church in background

A station doorway

Gas lamp complete with crown

TIME HALTS HERE

The golden splendour of the past has been preserved or reconstructed at Wolferton station, where once royalty from all over Europe alighted for Sandringham. The luxurious reception rooms they used are now a museum. Queen Alexandra's room, where she entertained train-borne guests, is decorated with panelled walls, paintings, tapestries and elegant glassware — including decanters still containing something to drink. Even one of the old lamp posts, suitably topped by a crown, has been carefully preserved.

Queen Alexandra's room

Great Hockham NORFOLK

15 miles south-east of Swaffham (PAGE 257 Bc)

Had you paused at Great Hockham during an Easter holiday in the last century, you may well have been challenged by a fearsome character holding a huge pair of horns. Fortunately it would have been just a mock attack, averted by a 'gift' of a farthing to the horned man.

This village custom was known as 'dossing', and took place during the Easter Horn Fair. Sadly, it faded out in the 1860s, but there is an attractive reminder on the village green – a carved and painted sign showing a horned man menacing a group of people by a row of medieval houses. And a massive set of dosser's horns hangs in the village hall.

Dossing is one of a number of horn customs once common in parts of England ruled by the Danes. Quite unique, however, is a surviving custom concerned with an immense sarsen stone that lies on the green a few feet from the sign. According to some locals, the stone is turned over on major national occasions. In the village hall, photographs hanging below the horns show the last time the stone ceremony took place, on the jubilee of Queen Elizabeth II.

But there is some disagreement among villagers as to the frequency and significance of the occasion. Some claim its origin was druidic, the stone being turned every century. A local antiquary thinks otherwise: 'The stone is a natural sarsen dug up around 1890 outside the village and dragged in, probably to annoy the lord of the manor,' he says. 'It was spontaneously, and alcoholically, turned at the Relief of Mafeking in 1900, and ever since has been turned during any major village get-together.'

Hockham is the 'Heathly' of Michael Home's books *God and the Rabbit* and *Spring Sowing*, published in the 1930s. They are both evocative descriptions of life in this Breckland village at the turn of the century, with *Spring Sowing* carrying a vivid impression of the Horn Fair. The books ring so true to life that even now there is lively debate among villagers as to which characters are derived from real life.

The village is compact around its triangular green, but the church is a five-minute walk away in the grounds of Hockham Hall. The tower crumbled and fell in the early 18th century (collapsed church towers tend to be a feature of East Anglian villages) and was replaced with a belfry of flint and stone. The church itself is quite old: in 1953 some 14th-century murals were discovered inside, and they have been carefully restored.

Great Massingham NORFOLK

10 miles north of Swaffham (PAGE 257 Bb)

In the bar of the Rose and Crown in Great Massingham is a massive oak post, dark and scarred with age, with an iron ring attached to it.

An old villager, now in his seventies, tells its story: 'That post came from the slaughterhouse where I used to work, and the ring was for holding the bullocks by. Once a bullock tore the ring out – there was a rare old frolic then, I can tell you!'

The pub is the larger of the two in the village. Built in 1668, it incorporates what used to be the saddlery, and, behind it, the slaughterhouse. At the back of the bar is a small treasure trove – a cardboard box full of glass photographic negatives. Prints made from them have been handed down from one landlord to another for at least 80 years. They show the village from about 1900 to the 1950s. Looking at it now, little seems to have changed.

The green is immense and has been divided by roads. To one side is the Church of St Mary where, on entering through the tiny chancel door, your eyes are met by a blaze of gold – the entire front of the high altar is an intricate woodcarving finished in gold leaf, the work of Norwich carver W. G. Cooper, in 1953. He based the central figures on Leonardo da Vinci's *Annunciation*, creating them separately in limewood and placing them upon a block of oak which forms the background.

Sadly that is the only touch of colour in this beautiful, austere church. Cromwell's destroyers of church ornaments must have had a field day here. The only ones left on the walls are two shields so aged that their blue dye has turned black, and the heads of figures on the massive 15th-century pews have been hacked off. For some reason the destruction squads overlooked an extraordinary panel on the back of a pew. Panels on the other pews have purely formal designs, but that on the hindmost left-hand pew shows a woman wearing a horned headdress, and with a rose on her stomach. She holds a dog by the tail, and by her side is a cauldron. Who or what she represents, nobody knows.

The village spreads out on both sides of the church like the wings of a butterfly. It even has a butterfly's spots – three large ponds on the green, probably once the fishponds of the abbey which created Massingham. Nothing remains of the abbey today except the name, adopted by a large farm, Abbey House, which has a few pieces of ancient stonework embedded in it.

The village green is one of the largest in Norfolk. Spreading out from it, the houses are mainly built from split flints, giving a colour-washed appearance in strong sunlight.

Letheringsett NORFOLK

27 miles north-east of Swaffham (PAGE 257 Ca)

'Larnsett', as the village is called by many older folk there, belies claims that Norfolk is a flat, dull county, being situated in the broad and beautiful Glaven valley and set among magnificent trees. The landscape is man-made: William Cobbett noted in his *Rural Rides* in 1821 that it had been 'judiciously planted with trees of various sort' by the local landowner, William Hardy, where before it had been bare. The valley looks its best on a fine winter's day, unfolding behind the branches of the bare trees, with the little river winding through brilliant green meadows or rich brown fields.

The heart of Letheringsett is curiously monumental, with a handful of huge houses or farm complexes set among the oaks, beeches and cypresses. The dominant building is the 18th-century Letheringsett Hall, seat of the Barons Cozens-Hardy (creators of the village with their forebear William Hardy) until a few years ago, but now an old people's home. The massive building, with five great columns in its portico, is adjacent to the church with its round Norman tower.

In the village, flint is a common building material, with brick used to frame doors and windows, making an attractive combination. Seashore pebbles have been used to face some of the houses, creating an unusual surface which, from a distance, resembles lizard skin. The cottages which housed estate workers are a little way from the centre. Built in handsome brick and flint, they carry the ubiquitous Cozens-Hardy crest. New houses built among them are in the same materials and manner and will have blended in with them after a decade or so.

In 1957 Basil Cozens-Hardy published an excellent history of Letheringsett, which included extracts from the diary of a formidable lady named Mary Hardy. She married in 1775 and for 37 years she made an entry every day, except when she was 'poorly'. She tells how they moved into the hall on April 4, 1781 – 'a very cold day' – and almost immediately became involved in a battle for water rights.

Her husband William was a brewer and maltster – his handsome brewery still stands sentinel at the approach to the village – and he and a neighbouring farmer, Richard Rouse, endlessly tried to divert the waters of the Glaven away from each other. Mary not only records the struggle, but also the little incidents that bring history to life: 'Old sow pigged 8 pigs' . . . 'The Clerk of Snoring called and borrowed 20/- of Mr Hardy and went to the fair and lost it at cards among sharpers' . . . 'The town inoculated for smallpox' (June 15, 1807).

The Church of St Andrew was thoroughly – or according to the vicar 'drastically' – restored in the 1870s, but it shelters two remarkable objects: an 18th-century barrel organ and the death mask of an obscure genius. The organ needs two people to work it, one winding the mechanism that moves the barrels, the other pumping the bellows. Skilled operators can produce rich music quite unlike the tinny clatter of street barrel organs.

Tucked away high on a shelf near the door is the other treasure, the mask of Johnson Jex, blacksmith and watchmaker. According to the epitaph on his grave in the churchyard, he passed his days as the village blacksmith but mastered 'some of the greatest difficulties of science, advancing from the forge to the crucible and from the horse-shoe to the chronometer'. The 18th-century writer Arthur Young said of him: 'It is melancholy to see such a genius employed in all the work of a common blacksmith.' But Jex seems to have led a full and happy life – and a prosperous one if his large, comfortable house, still known as Foundry House, is anything to go by. The Castle Museum in Norwich contains a watch made by him, and his lathe.

The Snorings NORFOLK

20 miles north-east of Swaffham (PAGE 257 Ba)

In 1611 when the lord of the manor, Sir Ralph Shelton, sold Great Snoring to Lord Chief Justice Richardson he is reported to have said, 'I can sleep without Snoring'. Apart from being a slur on this charming little village, the remark was the forerunner of many a pun that has plagued Great Snoring and its neighbour Little Snoring over the centuries. As with so many other Norfolk villages the origin of the name is Saxon; in the Domesday Survey it is recorded as Snarringes, the home of the family and descendants of someone named Snear.

Great Snoring is a compact little place with handsome houses of flint and brick running in long terraces on either side of the narrow main street. Its large church, dedicated to St Mary the Virgin, was begun in the 13th century but mainly dates from the 15th. Two panels from that century have survived in the chancel screen. It is a handsome building, and standing beside it is an equally handsome rectory built of brick with octagonal turrets, carved chimneys and terracotta friezes above the ground and upper floors. Yet even this great house is only the remains of an earlier one, probably started about 1500 for the Sheltons. It was reduced to its present size in the 19th century and served as the rectory until 1975. Now it is a guest house whose owners have taken care to maintain its character both inside and out.

Little Snoring, 2 miles to the south-east, grew in size during the Second World War when a bomber airfield was established near by. The village church, St Andrew's, stands on a knoll about half a mile away. It has a flint-built Saxon round tower which stands apart from the nave and chancel and appears to have been part of an earlier church. Round towers built of flint are common to churches of that age, because of the difficulty in shaping corners with the rough stone, but no one knows why it stands apart from the later building. The church doorway is massive and unique, with three Norman arches, each of a different design.

Inside are poignant memories of the wartime years. The Bible on its lectern was a gift by the widow of the last commandant of the airfield who was killed in an air crash in 1946, and there are also 'victory' boards which record the sorties of the RAF bombers over Germany.

CUTTING A DASH WITH PEBBLES

Letheringsett – or 'Larnsett' to many of the older villagers – has houses that are finished in varied and decorative styles. Pebbles gathered from the seashore have been used to face the walls of some of them – including a neat terrace of workers' cottages. On another cottage, they have been used to surround the crest of the Cozens-Hardy family, whose baronial seat, Letheringsett Hall, is now an old folks' home.

Pebble-faced terrace, Letheringsett

Cozens-Hardy crest on a cottage

MAP 24

THE ISLE OF MAN – IT'S A LITTLE DIFFERENT

The flavour of the island is distinctive – from its kippers to its customs and laws. It has the world's oldest continuous parliament, its own money, its own Manx language and its tailless cat. Not to mention fine resorts, medieval castles, romantic glens, scenic waterfalls and the heart-stopping TT motorcycle races. All within a space of only 227 square miles.

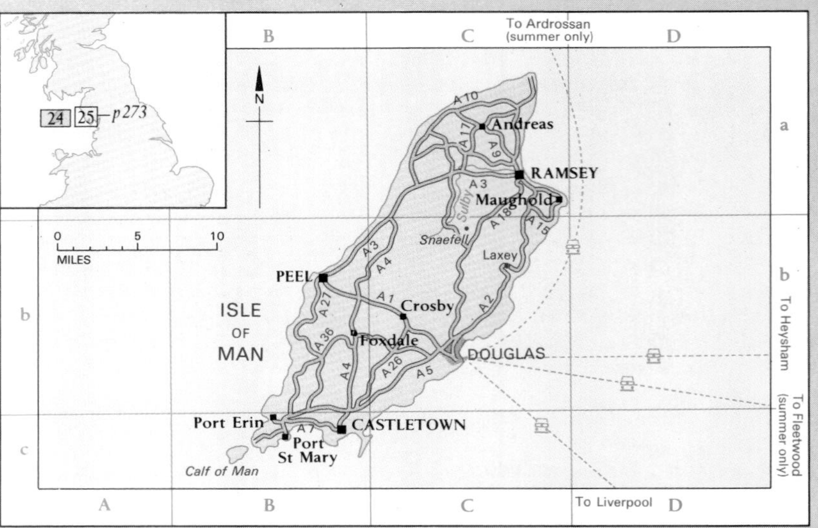

MAP 24: NEIGHBOURING AREA – MAP 25

CASTLETOWN Port Erin Port St Mary
PEEL Crosby Foxdale
RAMSEY Andreas Maughold

CASTLETOWN

ISLE OF MAN

10 miles south-west of Douglas (PAGE 266 Bc)

The little stone town that was once the Manx capital lies at the southern, flatter end of the island – the old racetrack end, where the first Derby was run in 1627, long before the Epsom race acquired the name. The Stanley Earls of Derby were 'kings' and lords of Man for centuries – although in 1764 a descendant sold the title to the British Crown for £70,000. Today the races that attract visitors are the motorcycle Tourist Trophy in June and the Manx Grand Prix in September.

It is also the airport end, so for many people Castletown is their first introduction to this enchanting island. There is no doubt that the visitor from the mainland is 'abroad'; street names given twice – in English and in Manx, a Gaelic language now almost extinct – palm trees mixed with fuchsias and valerian in the gardens, MAN number plates on motor vehicles, different (and handsomely designed) coins, stamps and banknotes, policemen in white helmets.

There are other differences too. There are the houses of rough limestone, with doors and window frames painted in bright pastel colours – primrose, violet, pale green. People stand in their open doorways watching the world go by and chatting with neighbours in the pleasant Manx accent, which is Irish with a dash of North Country, or maybe the other way round. And, perhaps the nicest change of all, the Manx euphoria that seizes the visitor almost at once; a feeling that there is no need to hurry for anything.

Castletown was the island's capital until 1874 when the House of Keys – the Lower House of the Manx parliament, The Tynwald, the oldest continuous parliament in the world – was moved to Douglas. But it still has a Parliament Square that contains the dignified building that was the House meeting place. It is now the Commissioner's Offices, or Town Hall.

Behind it is the deep chasm of the harbour, full of largish, enviable yachts. There, too, is the Nautical Museum, whose star is the schooner-rigged yacht *Peggy*, built in 1791 for the Quayles, a prominent and influential local family. She is housed in a three-storey boathouse built at the same time; in fact, when her sailing days were done, she was bricked up inside it and virtually forgotten until rediscovered in 1935.

The room above the boathouse was designed by the Quayles as a replica of the stern cabin of a warship of Nelson's period – and theirs. Among the other exhibits are models and memorabilia of Manx fishing boats, of the Karran fleet of deep-sea merchantmen whose home port was Castletown, and of the Peel schooner *Vixen* that took emigrants to Australia.

The true heart of the town is Market Square, or Kerrin y Vargee. Here are the banks and some pretty 18th-century houses, one of which was the home of Captain Quilliam RN, Nelson's Flag Lieutenant at Trafalgar. Here, too, is a tall, sandstone column to the memory of Colonel Cornelius Smelt, an early 18th-century Lieutenant-Governor of the island. The column also thriftily commemorates the site of the old Market Crosse – and where Margaret Inequane and her son were burnt at the stake for witchcraft in 1617.

Filling the rear of the square is the battlemented and rather gloomy parish church. Behind it, and the car park, is the low, whitewashed Chapel of St Mary. The chapel dates in part from the 13th century and was for many years the grammar school.

Castletown harbour

Castle Rushen

A GRATEFUL KING'S GIFT TO THE PEOPLE OF MAN

Looking down on the tranquillity of Castletown harbour, flag-hung Castle Rushen was given to the Manx people by George V in 1929 for the part they played in the First World War. The castle is traditionally the island home of the ruling King or Queen of England – who is known as the 'Lord of Man'. However, it can still be hired for private functions and cocktail parties.

The most splendid confirmation of Castletown's capital status is Castle Rushen, which overlooks the square and, indeed, all the rest of the town. Its unblemished limestone walls defy its great age – the earliest parts were built about 1150, although little remains that dates from before 1370. It was the palace of the Norse Kings of Mann and, later, a meeting place of the House of Keys, a prison, lunatic asylum, barracks and court house, which it still is.

Deep beneath its appalling dungeons, giants are said to lie in an enchanted sleep; and among some evocative exhibits is ironmongery employed in hangings, gibbetings and mere imprisonment. There are, too, some fine models depicting Charlotte, widow of James, 7th Earl of Derby and Lord of Man, surrendering the castle to the Commonwealth commander during the Civil War; the preparation of boiling oil; and other lively moments in the building's history. A notice reads: 'When the King of Mann lived here, those who dropped litter had their hands chopped off. Please use the baskets; he may be watching you.'

They take tidiness seriously in the Isle of Man.

• **Parking** Castle Street; Farrants Way; Shore Road (all car parks) • **Early closing** Thursday • **Market day** Thursday mornings in summer • **Events** Castletown Show (July); Southern 100 motorcycle road races (July); World Tin Bath Championships (July); Festival (August); Regattas (various dates) • **Information** TEL. Castletown 823518 • **AA 24 hour service** TEL. Liverpool 709 7252.

Port Erin ISLE OF MAN

5 miles west of Castletown (PAGE 266 Bc)

A pleasant and decorative resort, whose chosen role is to instruct as well as entertain; or so it would seem from the large number of museums here. There is the Railway Museum, for example, crammed with painted steel and wood, gleaming brass and the hushed, reverential train buffs found in all such museums. In fact, this is a very good one, devoted entirely to the island's own railways.

There are gallant little tank engines like *Sutherland*, that first went into service in 1873, brightly painted coaches and a fascinating collection of posters, photographs and other memorabilia. Outside is the station, all red Victorian wrought iron, and bearing large notices saying 'Purt Chiarn' (Port of the Lord) as well as the English name of Port Erin. The station doubles up as a street market, but in summer you can also board a real steam train stopping at all stations as far as Douglas.

There is the Motor Museum, which maintains a large collection of ageing vehicles in full roadworthy condition; a Photography Museum; the Erin Arts Centre; and the Marine Biological Station of the University of Liverpool. This not only instructs students but monitors fish stocks in the Irish Sea, and has a fine aquarium that is open to the public.

Following similar though commercial lines is the Clearwater Sea Farm carved out of the side of the cliff.

SEAFRONT SHELTER *The tall cliffs of Bradda Head stretch a sheltering arm over the seafront at Port Erin – protecting the homes and hotels from the sometimes fierce Atlantic storms.*

It has large seawater tanks in which lobsters, scallops and other marine creatures may be observed.

Yn Shooylaghan, whose splendid name means simply 'The Promenade', leaves the little shopping centre behind and climbs up the steep green cliffs, whose summits are battlemented with tall Victorian and Edwardian hotels. They are magnificently situated, high above the elegant sweep of the bay that culminates in mighty Bradda Head. The curious, key-shaped monument on the summit is in memory of William Milner, of the safe-making firm, who was a generous local benefactor.

There is a little fishing and yachting harbour and, down by the shore, some good, straightforward stone houses with pretty front gardens divided from them by a walkway. Beside them, a little rill of water called St Catherine's Well runs out to the sand. It is fresh water and it was this, centuries ago, that made it possible for fishermen to settle and live in this part of the island.

Port St Mary ISLE OF MAN

4 miles west of Castletown (PAGE 266 Bc)

Purt Le Moirrey (Harbour of St Mary) stands back to back with Port Erin and to some extent mirrors it in its fortunate possession of a grand bay and beach. Here, too, there are some tall and dignified Victorian hotels, but not so many as in Port Erin, and the harbour is bigger and somehow more workmanlike.

There are two harbours really, Chapel Bay, named after the little Celtic chapel that once stood on the cliff, and the Bay of Rocks. Both are crowded with fishing boats and yachts, and between them is a lifeboat station that operates both a deep-sea and an inshore craft; it is worth being there when the station holds its Lifeboat Day, usually in July.

Somewhere close by is a foghorn that rattles the teeth whenever the mist comes in – a not infrequent occurrence. This mist is still known as Mannanan's Cloak; Mannanan is the god, or king, or ancient hero after whom the island is named, and his cloak was traditionally flung over his isle to protect it from enemies. During the last century or so, however, it has been especially all-enveloping when royalty are about to arrive, giving rise to a newer saying that the mist is an indication that someone of royal blood is present. Fairly flattering, since almost every visitor will see the mist at some time during his stay.

Port St Mary is the headquarters of the Isle of Man Yacht Club – an offshore yacht race around the island takes place in May. One of the club's favourite cruises is the 36 mile voyage to the Mull of Galloway. In this, its members are echoing a much earlier connection between the two places, when Port St Mary was the island's chief smuggling outlet.

During the 17th and 18th centuries, customs dues on the island were far lower than those of mainland Britain; therefore, cargoes from all over Europe were landed here, and quietly shipped out again by local entrepreneurs to Galloway.

There are a number of fine old limestone houses and tenements in Port St Mary, some of the best being by The Underway, leading down to Chapel Bay, where bright, flowering shrubs tumble over rough stone walls. Someone, too, has made cunning use of old lifebuoys as flower-basket holders.

PEEL

ISLE OF MAN

11 miles north-west of Douglas (PAGE 266 Bb)

Castle, cathedral and kippers; these are the great landmarks of Peel, but some of its less well-known aspects linger with equal affection in the memory. For example, there are, behind the harbour, steep lanes of little shops and cottages, built from red sandstone boulders of all shapes and sizes, crammed and mortared together. Or there is the beach of red-gold sand running before the wide, old-fashioned promenade where cafes and restaurants sell such nostalgic dishes as cod and chips and pie and chips – as in the days before hamburgers and fried chickens were dreamt of. Finally there are the pleasant, chatty people who will tell you with equal authority about the best way to cook a kipper, about the history of their town, or about the position of the Isle of Man in the Common Market (forget it – it is complicated).

Peel makes its living from the sea. The long harbour shelters all kinds of vessels; yachts and catamarans, big stern-loading trawlers and little drifters bearing the registration letters PL for Peel, RY for Ramsey, and maybe a stocky gunboat of the Fisheries Protection Squadron. Over all drifts a fragrant cloud of woodsmoke to alert the gourmet that he has arrived at the birthplace of the Manx kipper.

The herrings are taken straight from the boats to the smokeries, from which they may be purchased, posted or packed into parcels for the journey home. Behind the smokeries is *Odin's Raven* Boathouse, containing a replica of a Viking longship that was sailed and rowed from Trondheim to Peel by a crew of Norwegians and Manxmen in 1979, to celebrate the millennium of the Manx Parliament.

Drifts of fishing nets lie before the masonry bastions of St Patrick's Isle – truly an island, though it has long been connected to Peel by a causeway. This is the very heart of Manxdom. Stone Age people lived on the islet; St Patrick himself is supposed to have visited it in AD 444 (when he converted the heathen population and banished all snakes); and here, too, so it is said, the Vikings made their first horrendous raid on Man in AD 798. Rather surprisingly, this episode is still commemorated with a re-enactment each July.

Behind the mighty medieval walls is one of the most astonishing ranges of buildings in all of Britain. What lies beneath the steep mound is only now being investigated – a Viking palace is one discovery – but what stands on the surface is remarkable enough. There is the roofless 10th-century Church of St Patrick, and beside it a 50 ft round tower of the same period – rare outside Ireland. It is built of hefty sandstone blocks, and the entrance is 7 ft off the ground. Monks would seek refuge in the tower, drawing a ladder up after them, when Viking raiders landed.

Near by is the partly ruined St German's Cathedral, started by Bishop Simon of Argyll in 1226. The crypt was the prison of the ecclesiastical court. There are monuments to drowned sailors, and to a number of bishops too, for though there is a more complete cathedral church in the town, this is still the official seat of the Bishops of Sodor and Man. Among several other buildings within the curtain wall, the most imposing is the Gatehouse which, despite its name, is the principal fortification of the islet.

Peel and St Patrick's Isle

Peel harbour

St Peter's Church and clock tower

GLORIOUS SPLENDOUR IN THE DUSK

Since it has a cathedral, Peel is the only Manx town which can fairly claim to be a city. Indeed, it is known as the 'Sunset City' because of the splendour of its sunsets. The name Peel, or 'Pile', refers to a stronghold. Near the harbour is the 19th-century clock tower—seen through a gaping window of the ruined Church of St Peter, now in a garden of rest.

The rubble of earlier castles, destroyed in battles long ago, lies beneath the present 14th-century building. This was besieged only once, during the Civil War, when the 7th Earl of Derby was holding the castle for the Royalists. In 1651, discontented members of the local Manx militia rose against the earl and managed to enter the castle; but their success was short-lived and they were soon driven out. In November of that year the Peel garrison was forced to surrender to Parliamentary forces who had sailed from England.

For most of the time, the castle's chief service to the town seems to have been provided by its sundial, a simple affair of whitewash with a black line down the middle, visible all down the harbour. The shadow of a wall opposite fell on the line at noon, and the device, somewhat renovated, is still there.

Sometime in the 1660s, the castle was haunted by a Moddey Dhoo, a creature part demon and part dog more generally encountered along the island's lonelier roads. It seems that this one had a fondness for the guardroom fire and, since it looked just like a shaggy spaniel, the soldiers put up with it, albeit uneasily. However, one man decided to challenge it and followed it down a corridor. There was a fearful banging and crashing, and the soldier reappeared, gibbering and speechless. He died three days later and, according to a witness: 'By the distortion of his limbs and features it might be guessed that he died in agonies more than is common to natural death.'

• **Parking** Market Street; Douglas Street; Albany Road (all car parks) • **Early closing** Thursday • **Events** Viking Boat Race (July or August); Carnival (August) • **Information** TEL. Peel 842341 • **AA 24 hour service** TEL. Liverpool 709 7252.

Crosby ISLE OF MAN

6 miles east of Peel (PAGE 266 Cb)

To savour Crosby's amenities calls for a certain crispness of reaction on the part of the motorist; the village stands astride the Peel to Douglas road and, pushed along by the traffic, it is quite easy to go right through it while making up one's mind to stop. Once off the highway, however, this is a pleasant little place of houses and farms old and newish, climbing up the wooded slopes of Mount Rule to the east, and up again to the parish church of St Runius Marown on its hill to the south.

St Runius was one of the early bishops of the island, and he may well lie beneath the overgrown, wind-bent grass of the churchyard, together with two of his successors. His chapel is a paragon of the early medieval Church of Man – small, simple, but stoutly built (of rough local stones) and meant to last.

Its doorway is like the entrance to a cave, and from it a rope runs up the outside of the wall to the bell in its tiny belfry. The building was restored in the 1950s by volunteers who, with few resources, managed to nurture the spirit of the place. There are some curtains on and about the altar, and some pieces of polished brass and flower vases about the battered box pews. They accord well with the simplicity of the ancient Norse and Celtic monuments in the walls.

A little to the west of Crosby is another chapel, dedicated to the Scottish St Trinian. Four-horned Manx sheep nibble the turf about the building, which is roofless, and always has been, since a local goblin called a buggane will not allow one to be put on. Indeed, whenever anyone tried to, the buggane would rise up through the ground and scatter beams and stones in all directions.

Only one man, a tailor, ever dared challenge it. When the next roof was put on, he volunteered to sit in the chapel 'for as long as it took to sew a pair of breeches', in the hope that this might persuade the creature to desist. And when the buggane arrived, it was disconcerted, but only for a moment. 'Don't you see my big teeth and long claws?' it howled. 'I see 'em,' replied the tailor calmly, and went on stitching.

The buggane stamped until the walls shook, and tore at the roof. The tailor made his last stitch and dived through the window as the rafters crashed behind him. He raced off, pursued by the buggane, and leapt over the wall into St Trinian's churchyard. Seeing its prey escaping, the buggane snatched off its head and hurled it after him. But as the head touched holy ground it turned to stone and broke into a thousand pieces. No one has seen the buggane since. But neither has anyone tried to put a roof on St Trinian's. The tailor's original scissors are displayed in the nearby Highlander Inn.

Foxdale ISLE OF MAN

6 miles south-east of Peel (PAGE 266 Bb)

As any Manx naturalist will confirm, there are no foxes on the Isle of Man, nor have there been in human memory; perhaps St Patrick banished them, together with the snakes. The name of this village is actually derived from the Norse *Fos*, meaning a 'waterfall' or 'rapid'. The fall still exists in Lower Foxdale, close to where the little River Neb runs under a bridge half-buried in flowering plants and creepers, then continues down rocky steps through a wooded glen. The fall is no Niagara in summer, but in winter it has been known to push banks aside and wash cars away.

Close by the bridge is the very attractive Mill House, its walls agleam with white paint and hung with flower baskets filled with petunias. A little uphill is a terrace of hardly less handsome brownstone cottages. There is a gap between Lower Foxdale and Foxdale itself, and this too is pretty, with white and brown houses perched high above the road, and surrounded by walled gardens filled with flowering shrubs. The villages lie in a bowl of towering, wooded hills, whose lower slopes are a smoothly rounded pattern of pastel-coloured fields, neatly divided into rectangles by hedgerows.

This peaceful idyll is by no means ancient. During the 18th and 19th centuries, mines around Foxdale produced large quantities of lead and a fair amount of silver – so much so that a railway was opened in 1886 to carry the minerals to St John's. But the last mine petered out in 1911 and the railway, too, closed – in the 1930s – leaving only the trackway and the fading scars of the mines on the hills to the east above the village. As for the miners, they took their skills – and their Manx names – to Australia, the United States and the goldfields of South Africa.

RAMSEY

ISLE OF MAN

16 miles north-east of Douglas (PAGE 266 Ca)

Ramsey sits by one of the island's loveliest bays, a wide, gentle curve of pale green breakers sweeping in to meet a vast beach of shingle and sand that stretches from the hooked cliff of Gob ny Rona in the south almost to the Point of Ayre in the north.

The town is second only to Douglas in size and, like Douglas, is a resort – though rather more dignified. No casinos or amusement arcades; well, not many, and those that do exist are discreetly disposed. Instead, the backdrop of the promenade consists of towered, deep-bayed Victorian buildings in immaculate cream, white and pale grey. The turn-of-the-century look is enhanced by the half-mile-long Queen's Pier, and the decorous, 40 acre Mooragh Park with its large boating lake and nodding palm trees.

The Sulby, the island's biggest river, sweeps through the town, under a huge iron swing bridge, and out to sea between two massive breakwaters with tall lights at their points. There are quays near the swing bridge with little shops and restaurants, and the harbour is a constant bustle of fishing boats and yachts about the shipwright's yard, where trawlers are pulled ashore and overhauled on slipways.

Almost everyone who invaded the Isle of Man – and there were a fair number – came by way of Ramsey Bay, attracted, no doubt, by its sheltered anchorage. Vikings landed here to plunder, and then settle; Robert Bruce came, to annex the island to the Kingdom of Scotland; and Cromwell's Ironsides arrived, emphasising the benefits of the Commonwealth with cavalry, infantry and artillery.

In 1847, Queen Victoria and Prince Albert also

EARLY BLOOMING *Spring reaches Ramsey two weeks earlier than anywhere else on the island – or so folks say in this dignified sea resort.*

landed inadvertently at Ramsey when the sea was too rough to permit docking at Douglas. This invasion was a welcome one, however, and the gratified inhabitants erected an Albert Tower to commemorate the event.

• **Parking** Station Road; Market Square; St Paul's Square (all car parks) • **Early closing** Wednesday • **Events** Ramsay Motorcycle Sprint (June); Yn Chruinaght Festival (July); Carnival (July); RAFA display (August) • **Information** TEL. Ramsey 812228 • **AA 24 hour service** TEL. Liverpool 709 7252.

Andreas ISLE OF MAN

4 miles north-west of Ramsey (PAGE 266 Ca)

The sizable and strung-out village lies in the midst of what islanders call the Northern Plain – the area of good farmland, and some fen country, north of Ramsey. This was an area seized upon long ago by the land-hungry Vikings, and one of the few places on Man where it is possible to forget that one is on an island. There is no sea in sight; and to the south the majestic hills around Snaefell fill the horizon.

The village has some good modern buildings, including a large school; and some good old ones too, like the big white and red farmhouse, which has solid, outside stairs. There are some pleasant smaller houses in the rough, local stone that shows a subtle range of natural colours – soft, charcoal grey, dark green and biscuit, highlighted here and there with a profusion of pink roses tumbling over the top of a wall or roof.

The church is impressive; very large, with a separate tower that has a curiously jagged top. Apparently it had a spire once, which was removed in the 1940s lest it should endanger low-flying aircraft from the wartime airfields near by. The Andreas airfield has long gone, but the spire was never replaced, though the weathervane still lies, forlorn and broken, in the churchyard. This is surrounded by railings culminating in an unusual piece of cemetery furniture – the cast-iron framework of a lantern, complete with steps for the lamplighter to mount.

Inside, the church is a softly lit cavern, with pulpit, gallery and serried ranks of pews in pale wood. In a corner is an important, and well-displayed, collection of early Christian relics. There are Celtic and Viking crosses and monuments discovered in the parish, some from the recently excavated Keeil – early Celtic chapel – of Knock y Doonee. One stone depicts the legend of the Norse god Odin being devoured by Fenris-wolf at the ending of the world; the other side of the stone shows a figure carrying a cross and trampling a serpent, symbolising the triumph of Christianity over paganism.

Scenes from Scandinavian mythology appear on other stones too; one shows a hero, Sigurd, roasting the heart of the dragon he has slain. This is an incident in the Icelandic *Völsunga Saga*, and emphasises the close connection between the island and the Norse world.

Maughold ISLE OF MAN

3 miles south-east of Ramsey (PAGE 266 Ca)

Fuchsias, roses, foxgloves and valerian glow in the hedgerows and bury the dry-stone walls that divide the country up into a great counterpane that slides into the sea in Port Mooar bay. Above the bay rear the massive cliffs of Maughold (pronounced 'Maccold') Head, with a splendid lighthouse on top.

The headland is named after St Maughold who, so the story goes, landed there at some time in the 5th century, having drifted, possibly from Ireland, in a coracle, allowing the winds of God to blow him where they would. Safe ashore, he gave thanks for his deliverance, and where he did so, a spring gushed forth so pure that he used it later for baptisms. The spring is still there, and people used to say that if a Manx girl gazed into it she would see the man she would wed.

The saint established a monastery on the site now occupied by Maughold churchyard. The remains of three ancient Celtic chapels can be seen here, and the partly 12th-century church itself stands on the foundations of a fourth. Also in the churchyard is the Cross House, sheltering an astonishing collection of Celtic and Norse monuments from the 6th to 13th centuries. All were found within the parish, indicating the importance of the Christian community here during the early Middle Ages. The stones are much worn, but look closely and you can still discern carvings of abbots, a Viking ship and episodes from Norse sagas.

In its way, the churchyard is a monument to Manxdom; the gravestones are a long parade of such Manx names as Kerruish, Quayle, Kermeen and Chris-

Maughold Head lighthouse – foghorn engine-room

In Maughold village

The lighthouse

BURIED IN THE CASTLE OF THE HEIGHTS

A path from Maughold village leads to a tall, white lighthouse, built on Maughold Head in 1914. Rising 212 ft above sea level, its signal is three white flashes every 30 seconds and a foghorn blast every 90 seconds. Just over 2 miles to the south-west is Cashtal yn Ard – Celtic for Castle on the Heights – a Neolithic burial ground more than 4000 years old. Standing stones mark the site of the underground burial gallery, which was entered by crawling through a narrow opening between the two central stones. The bodies of the dead were burnt and their ashes were kept in earthenware urns along the gallery walls. Originally, the gallery had a roof of stone slabs and was covered by a cairn.

Cashtal yn Ard

tian. Among them lies an island novelist famous in his day, Sir Hall Caine (1853 – 1931), whose works include *The Woman thou Gavest Me*.

At the entrance to the village, a notice reads 'Failt erriu dys skyll Maghal – Welcome to Maughold'. The village is tiny indeed, but pretty, consisting of no more than a dozen pink or whitewashed stone houses grouped about a triangular green. Even so, it is large enough for a few minor mysteries. There is the little cottage by the churchyard that has a rose garden, glazed windows, but no roof; and the imposing pedestal on the green that is surmounted by a tiny sundial enclosed by impenetrable mesh.

Most intriguing, however, is the notice on the immaculately mown greensward ordering visitors not to dig it up. A visitor might wonder why anyone would want to. The explanation is that quite recently a chocolate manufacturer buried the ownership certificate of a golden egg worth £10,000 somewhere on the island, and issued clues with its chocolate eggs as to where the document might be. The clues led egg hunters to Man and then to Maughold, and though the company stressed that the casket was neither in private land nor in property belonging to the Manx National Trust, dozens of treasure hunters descended upon the village. The casket was actually buried in a lane behind the churchyard, but before it was discovered, acres had been dug up, including the village green. Hence the notice – in case anyone thinks of looking for another golden egg.

MAP 25

FROM LAKELAND TO THE CUMBRIAN COAST

Hound trailing and Cumberland wrestling are traditional sports in this highly individual corner of Britain. Farming, seafaring and industry have moulded people and places in the fascinatingly varied countryside between Lakeland and Cumbria's lovely coastline. On the lighter side, Egremont has a championship face-pulling competition. And a funny thing happened in Ulverston – the comic genius Stan Laurel, thin half of the immortal Laurel and Hardy, was born there.

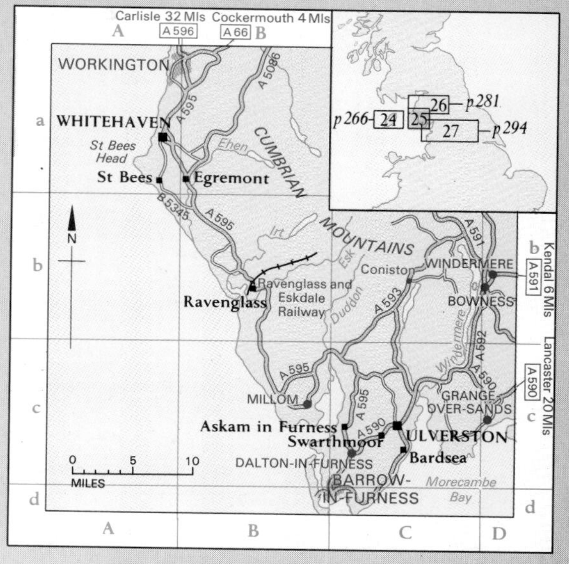

MAP 25: NEIGHBOURING AREAS – MAPS 24, 26, 27

ULVERSTON	WHITEHAVEN
Askam in Furness	Egremont
Bardsea	Ravenglass
Swarthmoor	St Bees

ULVERSTON

CUMBRIA

9 miles north-east of Barrow-in-Furness (PAGE 273 Cc)

Lancashire is famous for comedians and in 1890, when Ulverston was still part of Lancashire, Stan Laurel, the short, skinny half of Laurel and Hardy, was born here. His real name was Arthur Stanley Jefferson, and he spent his first 15 years in a small terraced house at No. 3 Argyle Street. It now has a plaque beside the front door commemorating him, and the local pub has been renamed The Stan Laurel.

Near by in Upper Brook Street is the Laurel and Hardy Museum, open in the summer months and by appointment in the winter. The museum displays photographs and relics of Laurel and of his Hollywood partner Oliver Hardy. It also has a writing case, with the original pens, that belonged to Stan's father, who was a travelling theatre manager.

Part of the museum is a small film theatre, with wooden seats rescued from a 1920s cinema. Laurel and Hardy films are shown all day in the theatre while the museum is open.

The rest of Ulverston is a far cry from Hollywood. Set between Morecambe Bay and the Lake District, it centres around the Market Place. The charter for the market was granted by Edward I in 1280, and on market days the area is packed with stalls selling everything from ducks' eggs to fresh local shrimps and cockles. In summer, gardens at the front of the cottages in the cobbled streets around are bright with a variety of flowers.

Early in the 19th century Ulverston was a thriving commercial centre and port, exporting cotton, iron ore, slate and leather. It was linked with the Leven estuary by a mile-long canal opened in 1796. After the coming of the railway, however, the canal fell into disuse and now – flanked on one side by a towpath – it is a haven for birds and anglers.

The oldest building in Ulverston is the parish church of St Mary, dating partly from 1111. It was restored and rebuilt in the 1860s, and the chancel was added in 1903 – 4. The church is notable for its splendid Norman door and magnificent 19th and early 20th-century stained glass, including one window based on a design by the painter Sir Joshua Reynolds (1723 – 92).

The present tower was built during the reign of Elizabeth I (1558 – 1603). It has an inscription running:

Stan's birthplace

WHERE STAN BEGAN

This is the house in Ulverston where Stan Laurel was born and lived until 1905. He made his first film in America in 1915, and teamed up with Oliver Hardy in 1926. They are shown above in Bonnie Scotland, *made in 1935. Laurel died in 1965, eight years after Hardy.*

Ulverston from Hoad Hill

Lighthouse monument

VOYAGER'S LIGHTHOUSE

The rooftops of Ulverston spread themselves in a pleasing panorama under 435 ft high Hoad Hill, which is topped in turn by a 100 ft tall replica of a lighthouse. This extraordinary monument was built in 1850 in memory of a distinguished traveller, Sir John Barrow (1764–1848), a founder of the Royal Geographical Society and Secretary to the Admiralty for 40 years. He was born in a cottage at Dragley Beck, to the south of the town – the cottage is now a sweetshop. He travelled widely in South Africa, China and the Arctic. The northernmost tip of Alaska, Point Barrow and the nearby settlement of Barrow, are both named after him. Ulverston's oldest building is St Mary's parish church, partly 12th century; but the present tower is Elizabethan, built to replace a steeple destroyed in a storm.

St Mary's Church

'Pray for the sowle of William Dobson, Gen. Ussher to Queen Elizabeth who gave unto this work.' The original steeple was destroyed in a storm in 1540.

• **Parking** The Gill; Daltongate; The Weint; Tank Square (all car parks) • **Early closing** Wednesday • **Market days** Thursday, Saturday • **Cinema** The Roxy, Brogden Street • **Events** Carnival (July); Charter Week (September) • **Information** TEL. Ulverston 52299 • **AA 24 hour service** TEL. Carlisle 24274.

Askam in Furness CUMBRIA

8 miles west of Ulverston (PAGE 273 Cc)

In the 19th century the little settlement of Askam evolved into a thriving, vibrant mining and iron smelting village. The rock beneath is rich in a high quality iron ore called haematite, and in the past the shoreline was red with run-off from the spoil heaps.

Steel Street and Furnace Place are terraced rows of houses whose names recall the past, but the signs of industry have almost gone, and a long hump of slag jutting out into the sea is now grassed over and supports an impressive growth of wild flowers, including centaury and felwort.

To the east, the sleepy hamlet of Ireleth has altered little with the passing of time except for some new housing. The view is magnificent from the parish church of St Peters over the Duddon estuary, which was beloved of the poet Wordsworth (1770–1850). It is seen at its best when the tide is in and the Isle of Man is etched clear against a blood-red sunset.

Clearly visible in the bay is the small Dunnerholme peninsula, where birdwatchers can observe pintail, wigeon, greylag geese and other wildfowl which winter in the area. A mile to the north of Ireleth an isolated group of white-painted cottages, delightfully and aptly named Paradise, overlooks the estuary.

Just beyond Paradise a left turn follows an attractive hedgerow bordering lush green fields and passing through a complex of ruined barns. The road then becomes a track which leads to the shore and passes the 16th-century Marsh Grange. This venerable old house was the birthplace of Margaret Askew, who left home at the tender age of 17 to marry Judge Fell of Swarthmoor (see page 275), and after his death married the founder of the Quaker movement, George Fox.

Three miles south of Askam is Dalton-in-Furness, birthplace of the portrait painter George Romney (1734–1802). He died in Kendal but is buried in St Mary's churchyard near Dalton Castle, a restored 14th-century pele tower built originally as a protection against marauding Scots. The castle is now owned by the National Trust, and contains some interesting pieces of 16th and 17th-century armour. It is not open regularly, but a key may be obtained from No. 18 Market Place, just opposite.

Bardsea CUMBRIA

3 miles south of Ulverston (PAGE 273 Cc)

Standing proudly on a green knoll with the sea lying below it like a silver platter, the pale limestone Church of Holy Trinity dominates the tranquil village of Bardsea. Although the church dates only from the mid-19th century, its lych gate gives an impression of a more historic past.

The Ship Inn near by needs no such disguise. Believed once to have been a barn, the Ship sums up the village, which began as a fishing hamlet surrounded by tiny farms and still retains an unhurried air. There is some modern housing, but many of the cottages are converted barns and their limestone walls reflect each and every golden ray of sunlight, and endow the whole village with a warm, bright appearance. A series of short but attractive well-signposted walks lead from the village centre and make Bardsea an ideal place from which to explore the district.

The path signposted Bardsea Green and Well House is a short stroll through timeless rural scenery. Sheep shelter under stone walls hanging with ferns, and wander through woodlands carpeted in season with primroses and bluebells.

Bardsea Green itself is a little group of houses with flower-rich grassland around it. Some depressions in the grassland speak of ancient quarrying for building stone, but one may well have been a cockpit.

A longer stroll leads from Bardsea to Conishead Priory, just under a mile to the north. Built on the site of an earlier leper colony, the priory was established by the Augustinian canons in the 12th century. They provided a much-needed guide across the treacherous sands of Morecambe Bay to Lancaster.

After the Dissolution, in 1539, a fine private mansion was built here, but the guide service continued – provided by the Duchy of Lancaster, as it still is. In 1821 a Colonel Braddyll demolished the earlier mansion and constructed the present ornate but impressive building. It has served since as a rest home for Durham miners and it is now owned by the Tibetan Buddhist Manjushri Institute as a retreat. It is open on weekday afternoons in summer.

Swarthmoor CUMBRIA

1 mile south-west of Ulverston (PAGE 273 Cc)

At first sight Swarthmoor seems simply a collection of semidetached houses straddling a main road. Those who pause here will, however, be amply rewarded. Take a left turn immediately after the Miners Arms

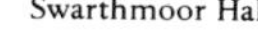

Swarthmoor Hall

WATCH YOUR STEP IN THE QUAKER HOUSE

The gate of Swarthmoor Hall could belong to a modest village house – and the outside of the building is less than awe-inspiring. But inside is an altogether different story – the very stuff of history. The 16th-century hall was the first real home of the Society of Friends – the Quakers. The sect's founder, George Fox (1624–91), was given shelter there, and later married the widow of the owner. One feature of the hall is its newel staircase, built around a framework of four posts. It has a trip-step, built higher than the rest so that a night-time intruder unfamiliar with the place would lose his footing in the dark – and rouse the household from their sleep.

Newel staircase

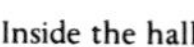

Inside the hall

pub, down Fox Street, and you can go backwards through time.

The cottages of old Swarthmoor sparkle white in the sun, and half a mile along a hedge-bordered lane – splendid in season with blue violet, yellow primrose, white stitchwort and red campion – stands historic Swarthmoor Hall. The hall is seen at its best from the well-kept garden, and although a cement rendering now covers the original stone and disguises its antiquity, the mullioned windows and leaded panes give a clue to its age.

Built around 1586 by George Fell, a wealthy lawyer and landowner, the hall housed some Roundhead soldiers during the Civil War.

The main event in its long history came, however, in 1652 when Margaret, the wife of George's son, the influential Judge Thomas Fell, heard the Quaker George Fox preach. He was getting some rough treatment because of his beliefs, and Margaret persuaded her husband to give him protection.

The hall became the first settled centre of the Quaker sect, where missionary journeys were properly organised and appropriate action taken. But in the mid-18th century it passed out of the Fell family and ceased to have anything to do with the Quakers for about 150 years. Then, in 1912, a descendant of the Fells together with the Society of Friends bought back the old house and restored it. The hall is open four days a week from mid-March to mid-October and at other times by appointment.

Judge Fell died in 1658, and 11 years later Margaret married George Fox. Fox bought a small local property near by and converted it into a meeting house, which is still in use today.

Whitehaven harbour

Inside St James's Church

MORNING ON THE QUAYSIDE

Fishing vessels rest quietly in harbour at Whitehaven, the morning sun gilding hull, mast and rigging. Tall buildings on the quayside are silhouetted sharply against the skyline. In the 18th century, this quiet place was one of Britain's major seaports, and a reflection of its prosperity is the magnificent, Georgian St James's Church. Its interior, in subtle shades of beige, blue, white and gold, seems almost like a delicate piece of Wedgwood pottery.

WHITEHAVEN

CUMBRIA

8 miles south of Workington (PAGE 273 Aa)

The satirist Jonathan Swift (1667 – 1745) is said to have conceived the kingdom of Lilliput in *Gulliver's Travels* after looking down on seemingly tiny figures moving about on the beach below Whitehaven cliffs. He often watched the poor locals, who scoured the sand for sea coal to put on their fires, and he imagined them as a race of very small people, such as the Lilliputians in his book, published in 1726.

Swift – born in Dublin – spent some of the first four years of his life in Bowling Green House, perched high on the clifftop, and he returned there several times as a man. His old home later became an inn – the Red Flag – and today it is a private house.

Farther along the cliffs is a ruined fan house, built in 1747 to drive fresh air into a now disused coalmine, Duke Pit. The building is kept as a memorial to 136 miners, boys among them, who were killed in an underground disaster in the nearby Wellington Pit in 1910. The entrance lodge to Wellington Pit, which closed in 1933, is now a cafe.

Towering behind it is the tall, stone Candlestick Chimney, an air vent to the mine. The man who suggested its unusual shape was Lord Lonsdale (see Lowther, page 292), whose family owned the pit and built Whitehaven Castle (now a hospital) in 1769. Apparently, his lordship was dining when the architect of Duke Pit asked him what type of 'chimney' he should put up – whereupon Lord Lonsdale pointed to the candlestick in front of him and said, 'Like this'.

A steep flight of stone steps leads down from the cliffs to Whitehaven harbour. Originally, warehouses and miners' cottages stood on either side of the steps and some of the buildings remain. The harbour has twice been attacked by enemy vessels. The Scottish-born hero of the American Navy, John Paul Jones, had served his apprenticeship as a seaman in Whitehaven. In 1778, during the American War of Independence, he sailed the privateer *Ranger* into the harbour, landed and set fire to several ships.

The second attack was in 1915, when a German U-boat surfaced close to shore and shelled the area causing some damage, but no deaths. Today the harbour contains Britain's last coal-fired dredger, which works alongside the fishing smacks, cargo ships and pleasure boats which also shelter there.

Whitehaven developed in the 12th century as the port of nearby St Bees Priory. But most of the town was built by the Lowther family in the 17th and 18th centuries. There are many elegant Georgian houses in the town – including some in Lowther Street, the main and most impressive thoroughfare.

Known as 'The Gateway to the Western Lakes', the town used to have two parish churches, St James's and St Nicholas's. The Church of St James stands on a hill at the top of Queen Street. Built in 1752–3, it has – according to experts – the finest Georgian interior in Cumbria.

St Nicholas's Church, in Lowther Street, was built in 1883 on the site of an earlier church. It was mostly destroyed by fire in 1971 and there is now an attractive garden surrounding the ruins, with the tower still rising from their midst. There is a plaque to George Washington's grandmother, Mildred Warner Gale, who died in 1700, and is buried here.

• **Parking** Swingpump Lane; Queen Street; Senhouse Street; West Strand (all car parks). Disc parking in Duke Street; George Street; Lowther Street; Church Street. Free parking discs available from tourist information centre • **Early closing** Wednesday • **Market days** Thursday, Saturday • **Theatres** Civic Hall, Lowther Street; Sir Nicholas Seker Theatre, Rosehill • **Cinema** Gaiety, Tangier Street • **Event** Carnival (August) • **Information** TEL. Whitehaven 5678 • **AA 24 hour service** TEL. Carlisle 24274.

Egremont CUMBRIA

5 miles south of Whitehaven (PAGE 273 Ba)

The mellow ruins of a Norman castle stand high above Egremont, on a grassy hill that overlooks the lovely valley of the River Ehen to the south, and the village's market place and wide, tree-lined main street to the north. There has been a market at Egremont since 1267, and every Friday the street is thronged with shoppers moving among the colourful stalls.

The castle was built between 1130 and 1140 by William de Meschines where a Danish fortification once stood. The most complete part still standing is a Norman arch that once guarded the drawbridge entrance. Near by is the stump of a market cross, which may date from the early 13th century. It stands close to an unusual four-sided sundial. Through the arch lies the grassed centre of the castle, now set with trees, and beyond the ruined walls are views across the village, the valley and the meandering Ehen.

Rising above a screen of trees is the red-sandstone tower of the parish church of St Mary and St Michael, built in the early 1880s and a superb example of Victorian Gothic architecture. Inside, slender pillars support the roof and nave arches, with the capitals at the top carved in foliage designs; there are almost 100 such carvings and no two are alike.

The village is rich in ancient legends, including that of the Horn of Egremont. In the Middle Ages this great horn hung in the castle and could be blown only by the rightful lord.

It is said that in the 13th century Hubert de Lucy arranged to have the rightful lord, his brother Eustace, murdered while on a crusade, so that he could claim the castle for himself. But the plot misfired and Eustace returned to blow the horn and thereby establish his rightful claim. Hearing the horn, Hubert fled and entered a monastery.

In September each year, legend becomes fact when Egremont celebrates its Crab Fair. The fair dates from the 13th century, when crab apples were distributed to bystanders. Now Worcester apples are thrown from a lorry as it drives down the main street and the day proceeds with traditional sports such as wrestling and hound trailing, in which specially bred hounds, similar to foxhounds, follow an arduous trail over hills and across the River Ehen in a kind of fox hunt without a fox. But the highlight of the celebrations is the World Championship Gurning Contest. Each 'gurner' places his head through a horse collar and pulls an ugly face. The ugliest is the winner.

Ravenglass CUMBRIA

18 miles south-east of Whitehaven (PAGE 273 Bb)

Ravenglass lies on an estuary where three rivers – the Esk, the Mite and the Irt – enter the sea, and for long its sheltered position made it an important harbour. The Romans used it and, in the 2nd century, built the large fort of Glannaventa on the cliffs above.

In the 18th century, Ravenglass was much used as a base for smuggling contraband tobacco and French brandy from the Isle of Man. Today, the estuary has silted up. But there are still scores of small boats rocking gently at their moorings at high tide; and the village's main street, edged with a pavement made

OUTPOST OF EMPIRE

Rome liked to make civilised amenities available to her troops when they occupied territories: little wonder, then, that the pink-tinged ruined bathhouse at Ravenglass, known locally as Walls Castle, was once part of a huge Roman fort. The magnificent Muncaster Castle, just to the east, looks ancient but, despite its mellow stonework, most of it was built in Victorian times. However, the core of the house is 14th century and the Pennington family has lived here since the 13th century.

Ruined Roman bathhouse

Muncaster Castle

A Ravenglass and Eskdale train pulls in

ALL ABOARD FOR A RIDE ON RATTY

Immaculate little steam engines, lovingly maintained, pull the miniature passenger coaches of the Ravenglass and Eskdale Railway through glorious Cumbrian scenery on a track that is only 15 in. wide. The original line, more than twice as wide, was opened in 1876 to carry iron ore to Ravenglass from mines near Boot, about 8 miles to the north-east. One of the tiny locomotives dates from 1894, and the railway is known affectionately as 'Ratty' – although just why is not really clear. One theory is that it is short for Ratcliffe, the name of a man who was closely associated with the original line.

Polishing up a loco

from sea-pebbles, still leads up from a shingle beach.

Muncaster Corn Mill, a mile or so up the River Mite, has machinery dating from the late 18th century – a mill has stood there since the 15th century at least – and is still making a variety of stone-ground flours. The mill, which uses different millstones for making different types of flour, can be seen in operation between April and September.

Just east of the village is Muncaster Castle, built in the 1860s round a 14th-century pele tower, and now open to the public. Its owners are the Pennington family, and their greatest treasure is a glass bowl, known as the 'Luck of Muncaster'. It was given to a 15th-century Pennington by Henry VI, who had taken shelter in the castle after the Battle of Hexham in 1464.

Tradition has it that so long as the bowl is unbroken, the family will go on prospering at Muncaster. The Luck itself is kept safe in the castle vault, but a replica can be seen. There are also some fine tapestries, china, 16th and 17th-century furniture and paintings by Van Dyck, Velázquez, Reynolds and Gainsborough.

Outside, the gardens are bright in early summer with rhododendrons and azaleas, and there are outstanding views over the Duddon Valley towards Coniston and the Langdales. There is also a splendid enclosed garden inhabited by a variety of exotic tropical birds, including macaws, zebra finches and rheas, not to mention bears and even wallabies. The Church of St Michael and All Angels, beside the castle, has Norse stones in its spacious churchyard.

The coastline here is particularly rich in animal and plant life. The Ravenglass dunes and beach are both nature reserves. So, too, are the Eskmeals dunes, on the other side of the estuary. They are home to a wide selection of coast-loving flowers, including harebells, the small, creamy, many-spined burnet rose, and the pink-flowered restharrow. Here, too, are ponds where natterjack toads breed – easily identified by the prominent yellow line along their backs.

St Bees CUMBRIA

4 miles south of Whitehaven (PAGE 273 Aa)

St Bees owes its name to the 7th-century St Bega. Legend has it that Bega was the daughter of an Irish king, who, on the day she was supposed to be married to a Norse prince, fled from her father's court and was miraculously transported by an angel to the Cumbrian coast. Here, in a sheltered hollow between towering 300 ft cliffs, she founded a small nunnery that grew

Priory Church, St Bees

WHERE NATURE INSPIRED THE FAITHFUL ONES

Seagulls wheel in the air off St Bees Head, a place of haunting grandeur. In this setting of sea, sky and cliffs, bird life is plentiful: puffins, razorbills, fulmars and the rare black guillemot can be seen and rock pools are alive with crabs, anemones and starfish. Here it is easy to understand why early Christians chose to found communities on remote and beautiful sites—places where it seemed easier to commune with God. Once there was a great priory at St Bees, but only the church remains. Despite the area's religious associations, Archbishop Edmund Grindall, a local man, said in Elizabeth I's time that this was 'the ignorantest part in religion, and the most oppressed of covetous landlords of any one part of this realm'. Not surprisingly, he often found himself at odds with the queen.

over succeeding centuries into the mighty Priory of St Bees. However, after founding the nunnery, she was forced to flee again from her rejected suitor and seek refuge in the court of the king of Northumbria. There, she helped found the Abbey of Whitby, and was loved and revered for the help she gave to the poor and the oppressed.

Of the priory, only the church remains. It dates from the 12th century, when the priory was rebuilt by the Benedictines after the Danes had destroyed St Bega's nunnery in the 10th century. Although the church has been greatly altered since, there is still a magnificent Norman arch, and on a lintel between the church and the vicarage is the carved Beowulf Stone. This shows St Michael killing a dragon, and is thought to date from before the Conquest.

Beside the church are the charming Abbey Cottage and St Bees School—built, like most of the village's old buildings, in red sandstone. The school stands around a courtyard above which rises an elegant clock tower of the 1840s. The north side of the courtyard dates from 1587, four years after the school was founded by Edmund Grindall, the son of a local farmer who became Archbishop of Canterbury under Elizabeth I.

East of the Barrow to Whitehaven railway, which divides the village, the Main Street winds up a steep slope between old farms and cottages. There are magnificent views over a golden sweep of sands, and Seamill Lane leads down to a shingle beach. The recently restored Marsh House, near the end of the lane, looks straight out to sea, and possibly belonged to 18th-century smugglers.

North of the village, red-sandstone cliffs stretch out to St Bees Head, and beyond that is North Head with a lighthouse on its crest.

St Bees Head

MAP 26

VALE OF EDEN AND THE NORTHERN LAKES

The rugged grandeur of the hills, the placid beauty of lake and tarn and the charm of old stone houses combine to endow this northern part of Cumbria with breathtaking vistas. Here is the Vale of Eden, fine country for walkers, and above Borrowdale is tiny Watendlath, Rogue Herries' home in Sir Hugh Walpole's stories. Everywhere too are reminders of times when the border posed a threat.

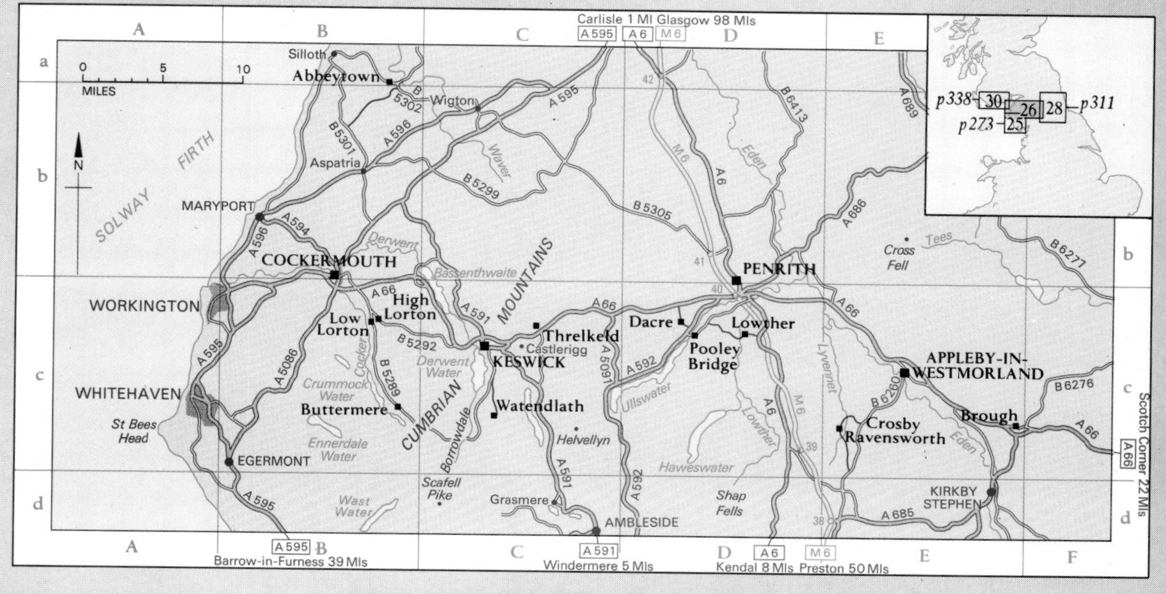

MAP 26: NEIGHBOURING AREAS – MAPS 25, 28, 30

APPLEBY-IN-WESTMORLAND	COCKERMOUTH	KESWICK	PENRITH
Brough	Abbeytown	Buttermere	Dacre
Crosby Ravensworth	The Lortons	Threlkeld	Lowther
		Watendlath	Pooley Bridge

APPLEBY-IN-WESTMORLAND

CUMBRIA

13 miles south-east of Penrith (PAGE 281 Ec)

Appleby lies in the beautiful Eden Valley where it skirts the foot of the Pennines. The town is famous for its lively and colourful horse fair, held every June, and is a popular base for hill-climbing holidays. Boroughgate, its broad main street and market place, has dignified stone buildings of many periods, from Jacobean to Victorian. There are a number of fine Georgian houses, including the Gothic-style White House built in 1756; and on an island in the middle of the road is the late 16th-century Moot – or Town – Hall.

The town is overlooked by a Norman castle, which was restored and much rebuilt in the 17th century. The Norman keep survives and is open to the public from May to September. So are the grounds, which are a Rare Breeds Survival Trust Centre. You can see rare breeds of domestic farm animals and some birds like waterfowl, pheasants, poultry and owls.

One of the castle's 17th-century restorers was the remarkable Lady Anne Clifford (see also Brough, page 283), daughter of George Clifford, 3rd Earl of Cumberland, an Elizabethan courtier and seafarer. Lady Anne married twice, to the Earl of Dorset and to the Earl of Pembroke and Montgomery. She was not happy with either of them and outlived them both. Inheriting the large Clifford estates in 1643, during the Civil War, she retired north where she defied Cromwell's express orders and rebuilt or restored all six of her castles – Appleby, Brough, Brougham, Skipton, Pendragon and Bardon Tower. She lived in each castle in turn, showing great generosity to her friends and dependants, even though she herself lived very simply.

At the Restoration of Charles II, Lady Anne was 70. Nonetheless, she celebrated the event by having 'two stately high scaffolds . . . hung with cloth of arras and gold' put up in Appleby. There, she and the mayor and aldermen 'proclaimed, prayed for, and drank the health of the king upon their knees, the aged countess seeming young again to grace the solemnity'.

Appleby owes much to Anne Clifford. She built St Anne's Hospital in Boroughgate. This stands around a peaceful little courtyard and still provides a home for 13 widows. She also restored the parish church of St Lawrence. On her death in 1676 Lady Anne was

ALL THE FUN AND EXCITEMENT OF THE GREAT APPLEBY HORSE FAIR

Horses in the River Eden at Appleby's New Fair

A balmy June morning . . . and the sun shines on gypsy lads and their horses as they cavort in the sparkling water. The magic of Appleby's ancient horse fair is weaving its spell. Fascinated onlookers line the bridge over the River Eden as animals are watered and groomed, ready for sale. The annual New Fair – which actually got its charter in 1685 – sees the town invaded by hundreds of farmers, gypsy horse-dealers and, in recent years, television cameramen. The gypsies and their brightly painted caravans and motorised caravans start assembling on the Thursday before the fair. New Fair Sunday is when tourists join in, and on Tuesday evening there are trotting races on a nearby meadow. Tuesday and Wednesday bring the real business of the whole event. Prospective buyers watch the gypsy horsemen put their mounts through their paces. Bargaining is often noisy, and usually the deal is sealed with a handslap – followed, perhaps, by a gallop down to the river for a celebratory splash.

Parading for sale

Gypsy caravan at the fair

buried in the church in a suitably impressive black marble tomb decorated with heraldic devices.

A stone wall plaque commemorates Richard Yates, a headmaster of Appleby Grammar School in the 18th century. He taught the two elder half-brothers of George Washington (1732–99), first president of the United States of America. George Washington himself was born and brought up in Westmoreland County, Virginia. In 1743 he was due to follow his half-brothers to school in Appleby – but the untimely death of his father kept him at home in America. The old grammar-school building, dating from the 17th century, has been demolished. The three tallest houses in Chapel Street now stand on the site. In 1887 the school was moved to a new site on the road to Penrith. The present school incorporates the headmaster's porch from the old building, dated 1671.

● **Parking** Chapel Street (2 car parks); The Sands; Boroughgate ● **Early closing** Thursday ● **Market day** Saturday ● **Events**

St Anne's Hospital courtyard, Appleby

COURTESY OF LADY ANNE

This secluded courtyard is part of St Anne's Hospital, in Appleby's main street. The hospital was founded by Lady Anne Clifford in the 17th century and is now home to 13 of the town's widows.

Appleby New Fair (June); Appleby Show (August) • **Information** TEL. Appleby-in-Westmorland 51177 • **AA 24 hour service** TEL. Carlisle 24274.

Brough CUMBRIA

8 miles south-east of Appleby-in-Westmorland
(PAGE 281 Ec)

Brough Castle, frowning over the village from a beetle brow, once belonged to a bloodstained baron fittingly known as The Butcher. He was John, 9th Baron Clifford (1435–61), known also as Bloody Clifford, an unyielding Lancastrian and ruthless persecutor of Yorkists in the Wars of the Roses. He was killed – an arrow through his throat, it is said – just before the Battle of Towton, near Tadcaster, and his castle was taken by the Yorkist Warwick the Kingmaker. But Bloody Clifford lives still, savage as ever, in Shakespeare's *Henry VI*.

His son Henry, 'The Shepherd Lord', eventually got back the castle and large family estates (see Londesborough, page 327), and Brough Castle became his favourite home. Sadly, though, it was burnt down two years before his death in 1523. It remained a ruin for 138 years until his descendant Lady Anne Clifford (see Appleby, page 281) repaired it. But the castle only survived intact for seven years before another fire in 1666. After that it fell once more into decay and has been a ruin since.

Today, visitors with a head for heights can climb the battlements and enjoy glorious views across the Vale of Eden and the Stainmoor Gap to the craggy escarpments of the Northern Pennines.

The ruin – open daily – stands where the Romans built a fort, Verterae, which they garrisoned for 300 years. The Brough Stone, now in the Fitzwilliam Museum, Cambridge, is a sad memorial to a 16-year-old Roman soldier, and practically all that remains of Verterae – the stones of the fort were used by William Rufus to build the castle soon after 1092. The foundations of Rufus's keep and parts of the walled bailey have survived. The fine round tower was built by Anne Clifford.

Brough (pronounced 'Bruff') is in two parts, separated by the main Barnard Castle to Appleby road. Beneath the castle is Church Brough, with medieval St Michael's Church, stone houses and a tree-shaded green that has a maypole where a market cross once

Boroughgate, the main street

stood. Another cross now tops a clock tower built in 1911 in the other part of the village, which is called Market Brough.

Market Brough grew around a 14th-century bridge over Swindale Beck, at the junction with a major road from Kendal. A charter for a weekly market and annual fair was granted in 1331, and a fair is still held on September 30, each year. Great prosperity came in the 18th and 19th centuries, with up to 60 stagecoaches a day halting at the village, on their way from London to Carlisle and on to Glasgow, or from York to Lancaster.

The coaches, passengers, coachmen and horses had their needs attended to by no fewer than 17 inns at Brough and nearby Stainmoor. They employed a small army of stableboys and ostlers, housekeepers and cooks, serving girls and tapsters – not to mention smiths, wheelwrights and harness-repairers.

Only two or three inns remain, among them the Castle Hotel at Market Brough, where the stables and outbuildings have survived. However, many of the others have been put to different uses – the White Swan, built in 1770, is now the post office. The village declined after local landowners opposed the coming of the railway from Barnard Castle: its promoters switched the route to Kirkby Stephen, 5 miles south-west, which in turn became an important rail junction.

Crosby Ravensworth CUMBRIA

7 miles south-west of Appleby-in-Westmorland
(PAGE 281 Ec)

Prehistoric man built burial mounds and settlements on the bare, low fells around this neat village on the delightful Lyvennet Beck. Sheep farming and a consequent absence of the plough have preserved them. Ewe Close, a settlement a mile or so to the south-west, is one of the most important in northern England – a complex system of walls enclosing an area of nearly 18 acres. Among the remains of circular huts within it is one measuring 50 ft across.

The fertile valley has attracted settlers ever since. The Vikings came – Ravensworth derives from the Danish word meaning 'raven-black' – and Saxons built a wooden church here. It was replaced by the Normans with a stone church, destroyed in turn by the Scots in the 12th century. Near the main doorway of the present Church of St Lawrence is the shaft of a medieval cross. The 7th-century missionary and first Bishop of York, St Paulinus, is said to have worshipped here with his followers. The church itself stands like a cathedral in miniature beside the beck, encircled by ancient trees and, though much rebuilt in the 19th century, retaining still a fine 13th-century doorway.

Footbridges span the beck – some narrow and made of wood, others arches of old stone – and standing on its bank amid beautiful grounds is the fine, towered Flass House, with a stepped porch.

Meaburn Hall, just over a mile north and built in the late 16th century, was home to the 1st Earl of Lonsdale, who had the body of his mistress embalmed and placed in a glass-lidded coffin which he kept in a cupboard. The father of the essayist Joseph Addison, creator of Sir Roger de Coverley, was born in Maulds Meadow near by in 1672.

COCKERMOUTH

CUMBRIA

8 miles east of Workington (PAGE 281 Bb)

On April 7, 1770, the poet William Wordsworth was born in a handsome, foursquare Georgian house in Cockermouth's tree-lined Main Street. Dorothy, his sister, was born here the following year, and with their three brothers they grew up in the house until 1783. Wordsworth House, as it is now called, belongs to the National Trust and is open to the public from Easter to October. The family's morning room, dining room and drawing room can be seen, as well as treasures that include Wordsworth's bureau-bookcase and his early 19th-century grandfather clock.

When the Wordsworths lived here, the house was owned by Sir James Lowther of Lowther Castle (see Lowther, page 292). Wordsworth's father, John, was Sir James's agent and lived here rent-free. Not surprisingly, the poet later declared himself 'much favoured' in his birthplace, and the River Derwent, which runs along the bottom of the garden, was for him the 'fairest of all rivers'.

Cockermouth stands where the Derwent and Cocker rivers meet between two hills. On one of the hills stands a castle dating mostly from the 14th century. An earlier castle is believed to have been built in 1134 by a Scottish noble, Waltheof, son of the Earl of Dunbar. At that time much of Cumbria frequently changed hands as England and Scotland disputed for it. The fortress is now mostly in ruins, but Lady Egremont lives in a part of it which is still intact. It is not normally open to the public. The town below is a maze of old streets, alleyways and yards, which come into their own on Mondays, when the weekly market is held.

The sheep and cattle market is held in premises on South Street, where the fast-talking patter of the auctioneer echoes out from the auction sheds. Inside, tiers of brown-painted seats rise from a central ring, with dalesmen simply nodding or moving a hand as they make their bids.

The rest of the market is in the Market Place, on the other side of the Cocker, where there is an old bell which is still rung during the summer months to start the proceedings. In this market, general produce and clothing are bought and sold.

Above the Market Place in Kirkgate is the 19th-century Church of All Saints. Its stained-glass east window is a memorial to Wordsworth, and his father's tomb is in the churchyard. Near the church is a hall which stands on the site of the old grammar school, where for a while the poet was educated. Another famous pupil was Fletcher Christian, ringleader of the mutiny on the *Bounty*, who was born in Moorland Close, a farmhouse 2 miles away, in 1764.

The Derwent is famous for its fine and tasty trout, and among the many who have fished it was the American entertainer Bing Crosby (1904–77). He stayed, appropriately enough, at the Trout Hotel in Main Street, where there is a signed photograph of him displayed in the bar.

• **Parking** Riverside; Fairfield; Market Place; Wakefield Road (all car parks) • **Early closing** Thursday • **Market day** Monday • **Event** Agricultural Show (August) • **Information** TEL. Cockermouth 822634 (summer) • **AA 24 hour service** TEL. Carlisle 24274.

Abbeytown CUMBRIA

15 miles north of Cockermouth (PAGE 281 Ba)

Abbeytown is well named, for not only did it grow up around the 12th-century Hulme Cultram Abbey, but also many of its buildings were constructed of stones taken from the abbey when it fell into ruin after 1536. The village is small, little more than a hamlet, and is surrounded by ancient farms dotting a rolling landscape of green meadows, with an occasional ploughed field exposing its red soil like a bright patch on a well-worn cloak.

From the day of its founding by Cistercian monks in 1150, the abbey and its town often bore the brunt of attacks by the English or the Scots as the borderland continually changed hands. In times of peace the abbey prospered and became the largest supplier of wool in the northern shires.

Edward I stayed there in 1300, and again in 1307 when he made Abbot Robert De Keldsik a member of his council. After Edward's death the Scots returned with a vengeance, and in 1319 Robert Bruce sacked the abbey – even though his father, the Earl of Carrick, had been buried there only 15 years before.

The final blow came in 1536, when Abbot Thomas Carter joined the Pilgrimage of Grace, the ill-fated rebellion against Henry VIII's seizure of Church lands and property. The rebellion was put down with ruthless efficiency, and the red-sandstone Church of St Mary survived only because the locals pointed out that it was the only building that gave them protection against border raids.

It is still the parish church and was restored in 1883 – a strange looking but impressive building with the original nave shorn of its tower, transepts and chancel, and with a low roof. The east and west walls are heavily buttressed and a porch with a new roof protects the original Norman arch of the west door.

A room within the church building, opened by Princess Margaret in 1973, contains the gravestones of Robert Bruce's father, and of Mathias and Juliana De Keldsik who were probably related to Abbot Robert.

Six miles north-west of Abbeytown is Silloth, overlooking the Solway Firth and the coast of Scotland. From Abbeytown itself, short walks lead alongside the River Waver, where there is much to interest naturalists, including butterflies and wading birds.

PASTORAL SYMPHONY *Sheep graze against a background of church, trees and hillside at High Lorton. The 19th-century church serves both High and Low Lorton.*

The Lortons CUMBRIA

4 miles south-east of Cockermouth (PAGE 281 Bc)

The two villages of Low and High Lorton lie in a green valley carved by the River Cocker and known as Lorton Vale. Lorton Hall is partly a 15th-century pele tower, built as a refuge for the villagers against raiding Scots during the Border wars. The rest of the house is part 17th century and part 19th century.

A beech tree in the garden is said to have been planted by Mary Winder, Lady of the Manor at the time of Charles II's Restoration. She had entertained the future king when he was seeking support against Cromwell after the execution of Charles I.

Outside the walled garden the surrounding village consists of trim white cottages, all within a pebble's throw of the babbling Cocker. At Lorton Bridge is Low Mill, now a private house, dating from the late 18th century when the river was diverted to provide a series of weirs and millraces.

Lorton Bridge House was once the hall's working farm and, though largely Georgian, it is still attached to medieval farm buildings and cottages. Next door to the village store are Pack Horse Cottages, once an ale house used by drovers.

High Lorton, just to the east, is an attractive tangle of rambling cottages, some with steps leading up to their doors and with fuel stores beneath. The Horseshoe Inn sells an ale the brewing of which dates back to the 18th century, when the Jennings family at High Swinside Farm had a reputation for a good 'home brew'. This became so popular that the family bought a building in the village and used it as a malt house. The brewery is now based in Cockermouth, and the old malt house has become the village hall.

At the rear stands an ancient yew tree under which the founder of the Quaker movement, George Fox, preached pacifism to a large crowd that included Cromwellian soldiers. William Wordsworth in his poem *Yew Trees* wrote:

There is a yew tree, pride of Lorton Vale
Which to this day stands single, in the midst
Of its own darkness, as it stood of yore.

In the centre of High Lorton is Lorton Park, a Regency mansion now a guesthouse. It was visited by Prince Arthur, Duke of Connaught and son of Queen Victoria, in 1863. In the garden he planted a horse chestnut tree, which is now so large that its massive trunk has split and distorted the plaque and railing surrounding it.

KESWICK

CUMBRIA

18 miles west of Penrith (PAGE 281 Cc)

Derwent Water, its surface dotted with little wooded islands, lies south of Keswick, a greenish-grey stone market town, often known as the Jewel of the Lakeland. In the 19th century the town and its surroundings were loved by poets, artists and writers.

One of the first poets to discover Keswick was Samuel Taylor Coleridge (1772–1834), who came to live in Greta Hall in 1800. The hall, now part of

Keswick and Derwent Water

The Moot Hall

THE JEWEL IN ITS SETTING

The 'Jewel of Lakeland' lies in its superb setting . . . This is Keswick, with Derwent Water stretching behind, a landscape 'almost too beautiful to live in', according to John Ruskin, one of the many literary figures who knew and loved the region. The 19th-century Moot (Town) Hall, with its one-handed clock, now houses the Information Centre.

Keswick School and overlooking the River Greta, later became the home of Coleridge's brother-in-law, the Poet Laureate Robert Southey – who lived there for 40 years until his death in 1843. Among other writers who stayed in the town were Sir Walter Scott (1771 – 1832), Lord Tennyson (1809 – 92), John Ruskin (1819 – 1900) and Robert Louis Stevenson (1850 – 94).

The Keswick Museum and Art Gallery has a rare collection of manuscripts by Southey – as well as some by William Wordsworth and Sir Hugh Walpole (1884 – 1941), whose *Herries Chronicle* series of novels has introduced thousands to Derwent Water and Skiddaw – which looms to 3054 ft north of the town.

Another museum, The Cumberland Pencil Museum, has a display of the lead pencils which are made in Keswick. They have been manufactured since the 16th century, when graphite – from which pencil leads are made – was first mined from the slopes of nearby Borrowdale. The local supply is now exhausted, but pencils are still made with imported graphite.

Overlooking the Market Place is the Moot – or Town – Hall, built in 1813 on the site of an old market building. The bell in the hall's tower is dated 1001.

For a fortnight each July a convention of thousands of Christians from all over the world is held in Keswick. One of their meeting places is the 16th-century Church of St Kentigern, in Crosthwaite, the north-west corner of the town. The church is on a site where the 6th-century Scottish saint set up a cross on a journey south. Indeed, the area owes its name, meaning 'clearing by a cross', to Kentigern's cross.

The present church incorporates fragments from an earlier Norman one. Inside is a marble figure of Robert Southey – who is buried in the churchyard – with an epitaph composed by Wordsworth.

A memorial to John Ruskin stands on Friar's Crag, a short walk to the south of Keswick beside Derwent Water. This is one of the best places from which to see Causey Pike and the slopes of Cat Bells, which rise majestically from the other side of the lake and are reflected, on calm days, in its waters.

Closer at hand in the lake, and often fringed in the early morning with a wisp of mist, is St Herbert's Island. In the Middle Ages there was a shrine here dedicated to Herbert, a 7th-century hermit who lived on the island – and died on March 20, AD 687, the same day as his close friend St Cuthbert of Lindisfarne.

Beatrix Potter modelled Owl Island in *The Tale of Squirrel Nutkin* on St Herbert's Island. Many wildfowl winter here and on the lake's other islands.

• **Parking** Bell Close; Central Car Park; Lakeside; Market Place; Market Square (all car parks) • **Early closing** Wednesday • **Market day** Saturday • **Theatre** Century Theatre, Lakeside (summer) • **Cinema** Alhambra Cinema, St John Street • **Events** Guild of Lakeland Craftsmen Exhibition (July – September); Agricultural Show (August); International Sheepdog Trials (August) • **Information** TEL. Keswick 72645 • **AA 24 hour service** TEL. Carlisle 24274.

Buttermere CUMBRIA

13 miles south-west of Keswick (PAGE 281 Bc)

In 1802 the hamlet of Buttermere found national notoriety with the story of Mary Robinson, 18-year-old daughter of the landlord of the Fish inn and known locally as the Beauty of Buttermere. Her charms attracted a man calling himself the Hon. Augustus Hope, new in the district and impressing local gentry with his extravagant ways. He even franked letters with his own name – in those days a privilege granted only to the high and mighty.

When he asked for her hand in marriage, immediate permission was given, and they were married on October 2, 1802. But after a short honeymoon Hope was arrested. He was a confidence trickster with one other wife and a trail of defrauded victims behind him. But he was not charged with bigamy. His crime was defrauding the Post Office – and franking letters without authority was a capital offence.

At his trial in Carlisle the jury baulked at hanging a man for fiddling the Post Office, but were shocked at the fate of poor Mary and her predecessor. So the Hon. Augustus Hope – born plain John Hatfield – went to the gallows on September 3, 1803.

The case caught the imagination of the Lakeland writers Wordsworth, Coleridge, Southey and De Quincey, and several plays based on the story appeared on the London stage.

And Mary? Far from wringing her hands in anguish, she cashed in by staying on at the inn, where tourists flocked to see the Beauty of Buttermere.

Paths lead from Buttermere to two of Cumbria's most beautiful lakes, mighty tumbling waterfalls, woodlands rich in wildlife, and rolling fields sprinkled with grazing sheep and hedged with hawthorn.

Much of this can be seen from the tiny parish church of St James, reached from the hamlet by a short, steep climb and overlooking farm buildings and Buttermere Lake. For almost 700 years Buttermere hamlet was part of the immense parish of Brigham, and an ordained priest for each was thought too expensive. So Buttermere and similar chapels were served by non-ordained men called readers.

One of these readers, Robert 'Wonderful' Walker, of Seathwaite, who served Buttermere until 1736, lived to be 93 and died in 1803. Despite a low stipend Walker left £2000 in his will, a tribute to his frugality and an iron constitution which enabled him to augment his income by writing letters for the illiterate, ploughing fields, spinning cloth, and availing himself of four ancient customs. These customs were known as clog-shoes, harden-sark, whittle-gate and goose-gate, and gave a reader the right to claim from the parish shoes, clothing, food and board – and grazing for his goose on the common.

Opposite the Bridge Hotel is Ghyll Wood, full of flowers in spring and summer. The Fish Hotel is at the centre of the hamlet and a path to its left leads to Buttermere Lake and the waterfall of Scale Force, while that to the right follows a leafy path to Crummock Water.

Both lakes are overlooked by towering hills, but High Stile, High Crag and Red Pike – down which tumbles the foaming Sour Milk Gill – seem less austere than the towering Mellbreak, brooding over Crummock Water. There are lake walks, and fishing permits for Buttermere can be obtained from Gatesgarth Farm. Fishing and boating permits for Crummock Water can be obtained from Rannerdale Farm.

BEAUTY OF BUTTERMERE *A mountain mist rolls in over the snow-streaked slopes above Buttermere . . . while sheep head smartly in the opposite direction. An innkeeper's daughter at this lovely place found fame as the Beauty of Buttermere after wedding a man who emerged as a notorious trickster and was finally hanged.*

SUN SALUTES STONE *The early morning sunlight gives back a touch of ancient magic to the stone circle of Castlerigg, near Threlkeld.*

Threlkeld CUMBRIA

4 miles east of Keswick (PAGE 281 Cc)

The narrow track which winds its tortuous way between Threlkeld's old stone cottages was once part of the main road from Penrith to Keswick. The village has now been bypassed but in days gone by it must often have rung to the sounds of packhorses, cattle and sheep drives, and regular stagecoaches. The white-walled Horse and Farrier Inn, dating back to 1688, would have done great business servicing the needs of travellers.

Links with the past are maintained in the form of sheepdog trials held during the summer, when the hills resound to the whistles of their handlers, the bleating of driven sheep and the applause of knowledgeable spectators.

The village was once famous for its tough Cumberland and Westmorland wrestlers. It is famous to this day for its teams of fox hunters. These men hunt not upon the backs of well-bred horses, but on foot – and in the old days they used to wear dull grey instead of scarlet. To them, far from being a mere pastime or sport, the fox hunt was, and still is, an essential job to protect their sheep and demands great stamina from man and dog.

In St Mary's churchyard there are some fascinating tombstones and a monument to 45 fox hunters – among them the remarkable John Crozier, master of the hunt for 64 years until his death at the age of 80. Each man is listed and all are remembered by the verse:

The Forest music is to hear the hounds
Rend the thin air, and with lusty cry
Awake the drowsy echoes and confound
Their perfect language is a mingled cry

St Mary's dates from 1777, and replaced a 13th-century church; but a leather-bound Bible and a set of medieval bells survive from the older building, as do many of the parish records going back to the time of Elizabeth I. An unusual wedding vow is still sometimes quoted in the village. Apparently, there was a time when local couples married in Threlkeld used to agree that, if either of them ever broke their promises to each other, they would pay the considerable sum of five shillings (25p) for the benefit of the poor.

A belt of trees screens the church from an extensive granite quarry that until 1982 ate into the hillside. There were also lead mines in the district until about 1910, but Threlkeld bore industry with gentle dignity and remains unspoilt.

Walks lead up to 2847 ft high Blencathra – now usually called Saddleback – and Scales Tarn, set in isolated grandeur like a diamond among dark steep-sided cliffs. Sir Walter Scott in his narrative poem *The Bridal of Triermain* and Sir Hugh Walpole in his tale *A Prayer for my Son* both used this magical setting.

A thousand feet up on these breezy slopes stands the Blencathra Centre, from which holidays in the Lake District are run. Originally the building was a hospital, which opened in 1904 as a tuberculosis sanatorium – the second to be founded in England – and closed in 1975.

About 2 miles along the Keswick road the 4000-year-old stone circle of Castlerigg is signposted. It inspired John Keats (1795–1821) to write his poem *Hyperion* – and small wonder. Even now, the 38 stones making up the 100 ft circle, with a further ten inside forming a second circle, make an inspiring sight in the rising or setting sun, with the looming shadow of Blencathra beyond and the village itself crouched at its foot rather like a contented dog.

Watendlath CUMBRIA

5 miles south of Keswick (PAGE 281 Cc)

When the novelist Sir Hugh Walpole visited and wrote about his beloved Watendlath it was a remote hamlet high above Borrowdale. It remains remote and unspoilt, its whitewashed cottages with their black painted woodwork clustered around a trout-filled tarn from which a chuckling stream spills out and under a stone bridge. Day permits are available to anglers, who can enjoy their sport with the reflection of Watendlath Fells shimmering on the tarn's waters.

Watendlath is reached by turning left off the Keswick to Borrowdale road, along a twisting track lined with high stone walls. By far the best way to approach the hamlet is along one of several footpaths from the spacious tree-fringed car park just over the tiny humpbacked Ashness Bridge.

Well-signposted, these flower-scented paths lead through leafy dells shaded by birch and Scots pine – home to red squirrels and song birds.

Just before the village, a gate leads to the Churn, also called the Devil's Punchbowl. Here the continual splashing and whirling of the stream has eroded a bowl-shaped hollow, and a drink from its crystal waters brings one much nearer to heaven than the Devil's abode.

For the motorist there is a National Trust car park at Watendlath itself, and a cluster of cottages and a couple of farms nestle around it. Foldhead Farm is generally agreed to be the setting for Rogue Herries' farm in Sir Hugh Walpole's tale of *Judith Paris*.

Clearly marked paths follow steep stony tracks to Blea Tarn and Wythburn, the climb often being enlivened by the chattering notes of meadow pipits and the bubbling sound of curlews. Not long ago, hares could be seen scampering over the grassy slopes, but they have now vanished – to the puzzlement of local people. So have starlings and sparrows.

On the opposite side of Watendlath Bridge, tracks lead down to Rosthwaite village and the Lodore falls. From the highest point on the Rosthwaite route there are towering views over Borrowdale towards Lakeland's highest peaks, with ever-changing light patterns on the magnificent slopes of Scafell Pike, Great End and Great Gable.

The gentle walk to Lodore is beautifully serene, even when holiday traffic is roaring through Borrowdale. The waters from Watendlath tarn are followed through the delicate tracery of Lodore woods until they plunge between the high cliffs of Gowder Crag and Shepherd's Crag over the falls. These are especially dramatic and even awe-inspiring after rain.

ROGUISH CHARM OVERLEAF

The tiny, remote hamlet of Watendlath crouches under its surrounding fells, beside a trout-filled tarn . . . a dramatic landscape that inspired the writer Sir Hugh Walpole to set his Rogue Herries *series of stories there.*

PENRITH

CUMBRIA

20 miles south-east of Carlisle (PAGE 281 Db)

Rising 937 ft above Penrith is the tree-covered Beacon Hill, its summit crowned by Beacon Pike, a pointed stone monument built in 1719. It marks the spot where beacons have been lit in times of war and national emergency since about 1296. The last time was during the Napoleonic Wars in 1804, when the beacon was seen by the author Sir Walter Scott (1771–1832), who was visiting Cumberland. The beacon sent him hurrying home to rejoin his volunteer regiment.

The red-sandstone town stands on the slopes beneath Beacon Hill, and was the capital of Cumbria in the 9th and 10th centuries. Later it was attacked frequently by marauding Scots – on the south-western outskirts are the stark ruins of a castle built in the late 1390s to defend the town. In the following century the castle was enlarged and a banqueting hall added by Richard, Duke of Gloucester – later Richard III – when he was Lord Warden of the Western Marches, responsible for keeping order along the western borders with Scotland. The grounds are now a park.

Penrith is a charming mixture of narrow old streets and wide open spaces, such as Great Dockray and Sandgate, where cattle were herded during border raids. Later they became market places and markets are still held each Tuesday and Saturday.

The poet William Wordsworth, his sister Dorothy and Mary Hutchinson, whom he later married, went to Dame Birkett's School in the late 18th century. The building is now part of The Tudor Bar and Restaurant. The poet also has associations with the Town Hall, created in 1905 by joining two 18th-century Adam-style houses – one of which was owned by Wordsworth's cousin John, who died in 1819.

Not far away, in Castlegate, is the Penrith Steam Museum, open daily except Saturdays from April to September. It houses fascinating displays of steam traction engines, vintage farm machinery, a working blacksmith's shop and a furnished Victorian cottage.

In the town centre is the light and airy parish church of St Andrew. Although the tower dates from Norman times, the church was mostly built in 1721–3, and its two magnificent chandeliers – each with 24 candle sockets – were a gift from the 2nd Duke of Portland. He was impressed at the way the townspeople repelled the Scots during the Jacobite rising of 1745. A plaque in the church commemorates 2260 people who died of the plague in 1597.

In the churchyard is an unusual group known as the Giant's Grave. It consists of two ancient crosses – each 11 ft high – and four 10th-century hogs-back tombstones, which have arched tops with sharply sloping sides like hogs' backs. According to legend, the remains of Owen Caesarius, a 10th-century ruler of Cumbria, are buried here. His capital was Penrith.

• **Parking** Southend Road; Princes Street; Blue Bell Lane; Friargate; Market Square; St Andrew's View; Burrowgate; Crown Square; Castle Hill Road (all car parks) • **Early closing** Wednesday • **Market days** Tuesday, Saturday • **Cinema** The Cosy Alhambra, Middlegate • **Events** Agricultural Show (July); Lowther Horse Driving Trials (August) • **Information** TEL. Penrith 67466 (summer) • **AA 24 hour service** TEL. Carlisle 24274.

Dacre CUMBRIA

5 miles south-west of Penrith (PAGE 281 Dc)

A clear stream trickles down the cheek of the hills above Ullswater; its name is Dacre Beck, and Dacre is derived from the Welsh word *daigr*, 'a tear'. But there is nothing sorrowful about the village, which lies in a fold of the hills in unspoilt isolation, though the presence of Dacre Castle shows that it was not always peaceful. The fortress was built in the 14th century, one of a chain of pele towers in and around the Eden Valley, which all too often was attacked by Scots raiding across the border.

Villagers could seek refuge in the towers, and Dacre Castle must have given formidable protection with its 66 ft high walls and impressive battlements. Its present state, little changed from those times, is a testament to its impregnability. It is now a private residence.

Across the beck stands St Andrew's Church, its churchyard overshadowed by splendid old yew trees and, in spring, bright with daffodils. The church has stood on its hillside since before 1296, when its earliest recorded vicar, Nicolas de Appleby, vacated the living.

It is almost certain that an Anglo-Saxon monastery stood on the site, and it was probably here that Athelstan, King of England, Constantine, King of Scotland and Eugenius of Cumberland, met to verify the 'Peace of Dacre' in AD 926. At the meeting Constantine and Eugenius swore allegiance to Athelstan and were baptised into Christianity.

The early medieval historian William of Malmesbury recorded this historic meeting, but no historian or archaeologist has been able to explain the mystery of the four carved stone bears standing at each corner of the churchyard, which appear to tell a story.

About a mile east of Dacre is Dalemain, home of the Hasell family since 1679. It has a Georgian façade but the earliest part of the house is a pele tower which dates from Norman times. It is open to the public daily, except Fridays and Saturdays, during the summer months.

Lowther CUMBRIA

4 miles south of Penrith (PAGE 281 Dc)

When the 1st Earl of Lonsdale decided to rebuild his castle at Lowther, he chose a rising young architect who would do the job in the grand manner. Lowther, which had been in the earl's family since the 13th century, was the first major work of Robert Smirke, who later designed the British Museum. Starting in 1806, Smirke lavished upon it all the splendours and embellishments that a castle worthy of the name should have. The north front was 420 ft long with a battlemented parapet, and a small forest of towers and turrets rose high above the roofline.

Unfortunately such grandeur became a bit too much for the Lonsdales – whose family name is Lowther – in the 1930s, and they abandoned it for Askham Hall on the opposite bank of the River Lowther. In 1957 much of the castle was demolished and now only the shell remains.

North of the castle stands the Church of St

Dalemain House, near Dacre

CONTENTED COWS AND AN IRRITATED BEAR

Cattle rest content before the elegant Georgian façade of Dalemain, a house near Dacre that has been home to one family for more than 300 years. A more enigmatic beast can be seen in the village churchyard – a bear that figures in four mysterious stone carvings. They seem to show a sequence of events during an encounter between the bear and a cat: first the cat wakes up the bear and they start to fight; then the bear grabs and kills the cat, and finally eats it. Nobody is sure of the significance of these medieval carvings standing at each of the four corners of the churchyard.

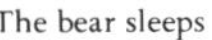

The bear sleeps

Cat rouses bear

Bear grabs at cat

Bear eats cat

Michael, dating from the 12th century but rebuilt by Sir John Lowther in 1686. Inside the porch is a Viking tombstone with a carving showing the souls of great warriors arriving in Valhalla.

At the same time as rebuilding the church, Sir John Lowther pulled down the old village and built a new one, called Lowther New Town. Later, much of this village was, in its turn, pulled down because it blocked the view from the 1st Earl's new castle. Yet another village, called Lowther Village, was started in 1806–7. It was based on a design by Robert Adam, which was adapted by the 1st Earl.

The houses and cottages, around two squares with greens in the middle, are occupied by estate workers. Lowther Park, where once the Lonsdales' deer roamed, is now a wildlife park specialising in British and European species. Among other species, there are red deer, wild boar, badgers, wildcats, otters, Highland cattle and the ancient and rare English longhorns.

Pooley Bridge CUMBRIA

5 miles south-west of Penrith (PAGE 281 Dc)

A large pool in the River Eamont, just before it flows out of Ullswater, gave the name Pooley – a corruption of 'pool by the hill' – to the little farming and fishing community which stood on its banks. Then, in the 18th century, a bridge was built across the river, and the village became Pooley Bridge. Today, the pool has disappeared, but the bridge, commanding superb views of Ullswater, still stands. Beside it, the village is spread out along two principal streets, both of which are lined with many delightful old stone houses and cottages.

South of Pooley Bridge, Ullswater is a shimmering 7 mile stretch of water that mirrors the wooded fells rising from its shores, and is hemmed in by craggy peaks thrusting higher than 2000 ft. The waters of the lake are home to the schelly, a freshwater herring cut off from the sea many thousands of years ago; and living along its banks are two species of fish-eating duck. They are the goosander and the red-breasted merganser, which has a handsome, double-crested green head. Both have bills with serrated edges, which enable them to hold their wriggling, slippery prey.

Leading out along the lakeside from Pooley Bridge are some attractive walks. They pass through woods and copses – where the unusual, tree-hole nests made by the goosander can sometimes be seen – and bring magnificent views at every turn. But perhaps the best way to see Ullswater is from a boat.

The lake is classed as a public highway, and anyone is free to launch a small boat on it, and to explore its creeks and islands. Or you can take a lake boat which calls at Pooley Bridge's little pier, and goes also to Howton and Glenridding.

Back in the centre of the village, St Paul's Church dates only from 1868. Before that time, the nearest church was St Michael's at Barton, 2 miles north-east off the Penrith road. St Michael's was built in about 1150 and was added to over the centuries, especially between 1318 and 1536 when it belonged to the Augustinian canons of Wartre Priory, near York. In the churchyard are buried the poet William Wordsworth's grandfather, Richard, and two of his aunts, as well as his grandson. Near the church stands the fine Church Farm, which probably dates in part from the 17th century.

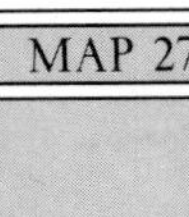

DOWN THE DALES AND INTO THE PENNINES

On either side of the Pennines lie towns and villages that are landmarks of industrial history. But here, too, is some of the most spectacular countryside in the land – between Cumbria's craggy fells and Yorkshire's grey-green dales. Small, busy market towns serve often remote stone villages. And deep in rural Lancashire is the house where 'Sir Loin' was knighted.

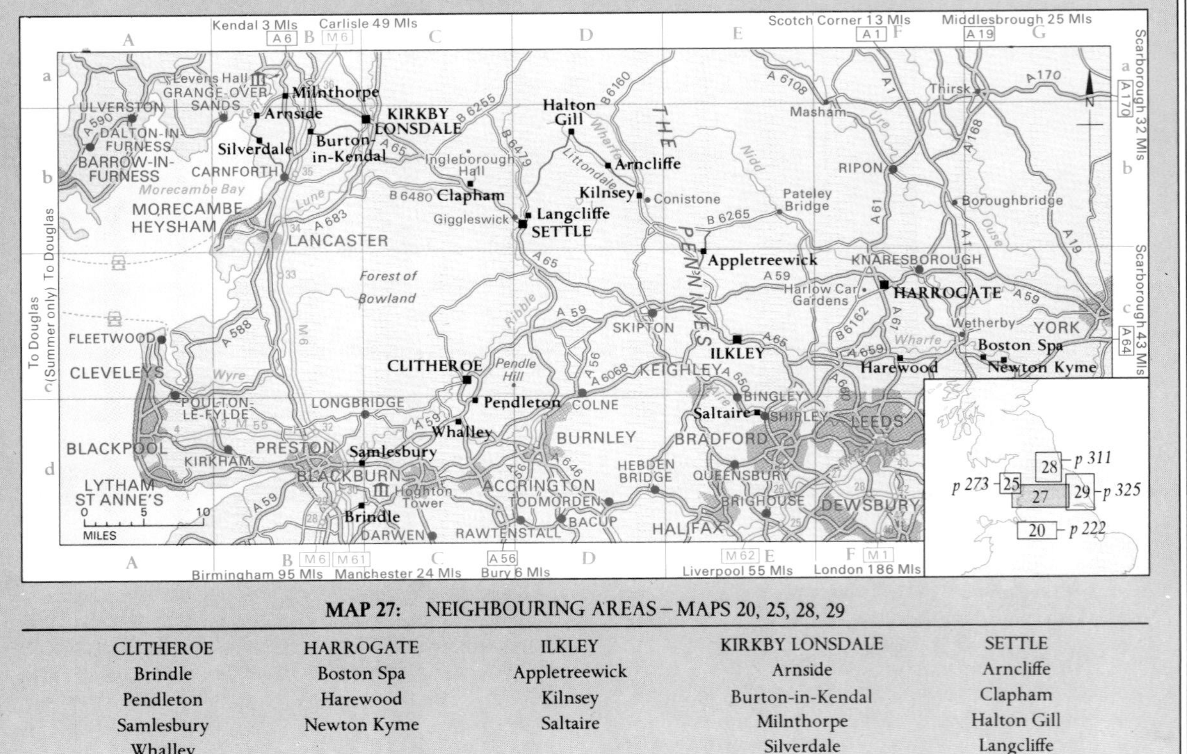

MAP 27: NEIGHBOURING AREAS – MAPS 20, 25, 28, 29

CLITHEROE	HARROGATE	ILKLEY	KIRKBY LONSDALE	SETTLE
Brindle	Boston Spa	Appletreewick	Arnside	Arncliffe
Pendleton	Harewood	Kilnsey	Burton-in-Kendal	Clapham
Samlesbury	Newton Kyme	Saltaire	Milnthorpe	Halton Gill
Whalley			Silverdale	Langcliffe

CLITHEROE

LANCASHIRE

10 miles north-east of Blackburn (PAGE 294 Cc)

This ancient market town lies between two lofty landmarks: the ruins of a small Norman castle on a tall, limestone spur, and a mostly 19th-century church. The town grew around the foot of the castle, started by Roger de Poitou, the first Norman Lord of Clitheroe, but mostly built by the de Lacy family who lived here until 1311. Then the castle went to the Earls and Dukes of Lancaster, passing to the Crown when Henry IV, whose father was Duke of Lancaster, came to the throne in 1399. The keep, measuring less than 36 ft square, is one of the smallest in England, and the entire fortress took up no more than an acre.

During the Civil War, Clitheroe Castle was briefly captured from the Roundhead townsfolk by the Royalists. When the Roundheads eventually won they destroyed it so that 'it might neither be a charge to the Commonwealth to keep it, nor a danger to have it kept against them'. Only the keep survived, and eventually, in 1920, the ruins and their $16\frac{1}{2}$ acres of grounds were taken over by Clitheroe's local authority and opened to the public.

Perched on a hill facing the ruins, the original parish church of St Mary Magdalene was built about the same time as the castle, in the early 12th century. But of that building only part of the east window and the west tower remain. Most of the church dates from the late 1820s and its spire with flying buttresses was added in 1844. In 1981 it was restored after a bad fire.

Inside, two of Clitheroe's most renowned sons are commemorated. There is a brass memorial to the Reverend Dr John Webster (1610–82), headmaster of Clitheroe's Royal Grammar School. He wrote *The Displaying of Supposed Witchcraft*, a celebrated book when it was published in 1677, in which he attacked those who dabbled in the occult. At this time locals believed that the district was overrun with witches. The second memorial is to the Reverend Thomas Wilson, another headmaster of the Royal Grammar School, who compiled a dictionary of archaeology in the 18th century and dedicated it to another dictionary writer, Dr Samuel Johnson. The Alleys Chapel also has two fine 15th-century alabaster effigies of a local landowner, Sir Thomas Radcliffe, and his wife.

Clitheroe's two landmarks are joined by Castle Street and Church Street, with the Market Place in between. Most of the 18th and 19th-century buildings are made of sandstone and limestone. The more modern houses are largely spread out in the surrounding countryside.

Until the 1850s Clitheroe's water came from medieval wells – some have now dried up, but water still flows from Heald Well in Wellgate and Stocks Well in Parson Lane. At the other end of the town, nestling just below the castle, is the Rose Garden. It contains an ornate turret taken from the Palace of Westminster and presented to the town in the 1930s by the local Member of Parliament, Sir William Brass – later Baron Chattisham of Clitheroe.

Clitheroe has long been associated with the occult. As Dr Webster recorded in his book, Pendle Hill was notorious in the 17th century for the impoverished and homeless so-called witches who congregated there. In August 1612, ten of these women – including a half-blind, 80-year-old beggar-woman named Old Chattox – were hanged at Lancaster as witches. The River Ribble is said to be haunted by an evil sprite, named Jennie Greenteeth, who claims a life every seven years. Local children are still warned not to play too near the water, or Jennie will get them.

• **Parking** North Street; Holden Street; Lowergate; Queensway; Whalley Road; Chester Avenue; Railway View; Station Road (all car parks) • **Early closing** Wednesday • **Market days** Tuesday, Saturday • **Cinema** Civic Hall, York Street • **Events** Clitheroe Country Heritage Fayre (June); Fell Race (June); Red Rose Festival (June) • **Information** TEL. Clitheroe 25566 • **AA 24 hour service** TEL. Blackpool 44947.

Brindle LANCASHIRE

16 miles south-west of Clitheroe (PAGE 294 Bd)

Surrounded by a patchwork of rolling farmland, Brindle remains as peaceful today as it has been through many centuries. To the west the land falls away to reveal the vastness of the Lancashire Plain, and to the east the horizon is framed by high Pennine moors.

It is hard to believe that the village, clustered around its old parish church of St James, is but a few miles from several industrial towns. Even a small development of modern homes, hardly in keeping with the rest of the village's sturdy gritstone cottages, scarcely intrudes upon its quiet rural charm.

There has been a church here for at least 800 years, and the present one dates back to the 16th century – a fine stone building enhanced by magnificent stained-glass windows. Two of its six bells are as old as the building itself and, until recently, the locally made tower clock had kept time for the villagers for almost 300 years. Now the original clock is on loan to the Liverpool City Museum and a new clock with a smart white dial looks down from Brindle's church tower. The church is also renowned for its collection of fonts, having no fewer than five.

Next to the church is the whitewashed Cavendish Arms pub – once the manor house. In the 16th century, Sir Thomas Gerard, in whose patronage the church lay, incurred the anger of Elizabeth I for supporting the Roman Catholic Mary, Queen of Scots. To help pay the fine to secure his release from the Tower of London, the manor of Brindle – with suitable exaggeration as to its size and value – was sold to William Cavendish, an ancestor of the Dukes of Devonshire, and the Cavendish family remained associated with the village until the present century.

Farther along the main street an old pound where stray cattle were once held is now marked as a site of interest – evidence of Brindle's agricultural past.

These days, the village has an air of quiet prosperity, but a reminder of harder times can be found at the site of the old workhouse a mile or so along the descriptively named Top o'th Hill Lane. A master of the workhouse and some who were forced to seek its shelter lie buried in the village graveyard.

The ancestral home of the de Hoghton family stands little more than 2 miles to the north-east. Hoghton Tower, high on a hillside at the end of a long and impressive driveway, is mostly 16th century and is the subject of a famous local legend. It is said that during a stay at the house in 1617, James I was so delighted with the beef served to him that he knighted the joint 'Sir Loin' – hence 'sirloin'. The house is open to the public during the summer. It has a collection of antique dolls and dolls' houses, and an old English rose garden.

Pendleton LANCASHIRE

2 miles south-east of Clitheroe (PAGE 294 Cd)

A story persists around Pendleton that a regular customer at the Swan with Two Necks village pub once auctioned his wife to the highest bidder. The pub was built in 1776 and, wife-auctioning stories apart, life in this busy farming community seems little changed over the years.

The pub's unusual name probably has no local connection – there are others similarly named around the country. It may have originated as the Swan with Two Nicks, a reference to the method used by the Vintners' Company of London to mark the bills of its Thames swans.

The Swan stands at the west end of Pendleton, which has four dairy farms in its main street. At milking time the narrow village lanes are crowded with cattle coming in from the fields around. Once these lanes were used by monks travelling between the early 14th-century abbey of Whalley (see page 296) and the 12th-century abbey of Sawley, to the north.

Set low on the western flank of Pendle Hill, the village is built astride a moorland stream, channelled down the middle of the main street and spanned by stone footbridges. Many of the sturdily built stone cottages and farmhouses, some distinguished by mullioned windows, date back 200 or 300 years, and the village itself is mentioned in the Domesday Survey of 1086 as 'Peniltune'. Relics of a far earlier culture have been discovered in a Bronze Age burial site found in one of the village gardens.

The tiny village school at the east end of the village, near the 19th-century parish church of All Saints, was one of the first National Schools in the country, built in 1837. But in 1981 it had only eight pupils and was closed. Beyond the school the pastoral scene gives way to the rugged heights of Pendleton Moor, the road climbing steeply to the high pass known as the Nick of Pendle. From here there are superb views of the Pennines, the Forest of Bowland and the Fylde coast.

Samlesbury LANCASHIRE

13 miles south-west of Clitheroe (PAGE 294 Bd)

Samlesbury sprawls over rolling farmland above the Ribble valley and may go almost unnoticed by travellers between Preston and Blackburn. But it is a district with an interesting history and is noted particularly for Samlesbury Hall.

The hall is a remarkable place, largely because it was built in two totally different styles. Its west side is red brick, with stone mullioned windows and tall chimneys; the other side is wood-framed, the blackened timbers set with panels cut with a quatrefoil (four-leaf) design to show the white plaster beneath.

For 300 years Samlesbury Hall was owned by the Southworth family, but they sold it to pay a debt and it became in turn a tenement house for weavers and labourers, an inn called the Bradyll Arms, a school and then a house in which the author Charles Dickens (1812–70) is said to have stayed. It is now an exhibition hall, antiques market and crafts display centre.

Standing in fields by the River Ribble is the Church of St Leonard, which dates from the 12th century with a stone-built, turreted tower of 1899. A helmet, crest and sword suspended high on a wall inside are believed to be those of Sir Thomas Southworth, who died in 1546 and whose grave is said to be below. A silver penny minted in the reign of Henry III (1216–72) is displayed in the two-decker pulpit.

A Roman Catholic church built in 1818 is dedicated to St Mary and St John Southworth, a relative of Sir Thomas. John was executed at Tyburn in 1654, the last English priest to be martyred for his faith. His body lies in Westminster Cathedral. He was canonised in 1970 by Pope Paul VI.

Whalley LANCASHIRE

4 miles south of Clitheroe (PAGE 294 Cd)

At the foot of a wooded hillside on the northern banks of the River Calder, a jumble of architectural styles – from traditional stone cottages to mock-Tudor fronted shops – blends happily together in the historic village of Whalley, famous for its ruined abbey.

For many centuries Whalley has been a focus of Christian worship, but it is the 13th-century Cistercian abbey that draws most visitors to the village. Nowadays the ruined but majestic walls stand carefully preserved amid lovingly tended lawns and gardens. Happily not all is in ruins, and what was once the abbot's lodging is now a conference centre and retreat run by the diocese of Blackburn.

Another building known locally as the Catholic Hall was originally a dormitory for lay brothers. Now

Timbered front of Samlesbury Hall

Mullioned window of the hall

A SLEEPING BEAUTY AWAKENED

Sold after 300 years in the hands of the same family, Samlesbury Hall became so neglected that it was once described as 'the sleeping beauty of Tudor England'. Then in 1925 it was given the kiss of life, when a trust was formed to restore this splendid building to its former magnificence. Remarkably, one side of the building is timbered and the other brick-built, with mullioned windows. Patterns of quatrefoil shapes are cut into the elaborate, blackened timbering to show white plaster beneath. In the main hall, venerable beams roughly hewn from great oaks support the roof; and a gallery rests upon a beam on which the owner, Sir Thomas Southworth, carved his name in 1532. Other attractions include a handsomely carved stone fountain. Samlesbury Hall is still maintained by the trust, and as well as being open to the public the ancient building is used for exhibitions and antiques markets, and as a craft centre.

Carved fountain

ENDURING FAITH *This Celtic cross, which could be 1000 years old, is one of three in the churchyard of St Mary and All Saints at Whalley. Also in the churchyard are two stone coffins and several 13th-century gravestones. Oddities from comparatively modern times can also be seen. They are tombstones bearing dates that never were — April 31, 1752 and February 30, 1819. Was the stonemason joking or absent-minded?*

it is used for social occasions, including bingo, and the local Catholic priest delights in the thought that he may have the oldest bingo hall in Britain.

The monks who built the abbey started their work in 1296, but it was not until 1380 that a great consecration mass was held, and the whole complex was not completed until the 15th century. By this time, the influence of the abbot was considerable and the abbey lands were extensive, spreading southwards to the very edge of Manchester.

Disaster came after the Pilgrimage of Grace, the northern uprising in 1537 against the seizure of Church lands by Henry VIII. The monks of Whalley did not take part, but an excuse was found to implicate the abbot nonetheless and he was hanged at Lancaster Castle. Later the abbey was confiscated and eventually almost demolished, the stonework being used throughout the district for building.

Fortunately some of the abbey's treasures were saved, among them the richly carved choir stalls now in the nearby parish church of St Mary and All Saints. The church is even older than the abbey, dating from Norman times, and has three Celtic crosses in the churchyard.

A huge, 49-arch brick viaduct spanning the Calder valley at Whalley was opened in 1850. It is said that early railway passengers were so afraid of travelling across it that some would even get off the train and walk to the next station, in the village of Billington.

HARROGATE

NORTH YORKSHIRE

16 miles north of Leeds (PAGE 294 Fc)

Harrogate's imposing Royal Pump Room was opened in the centre of the town in 1842 and six years later the coming of the railway assured the town's popularity and growth as a spa. In its heyday the octagonal Greek-style Pump Room, built on the site of a sulphur well called 'The Stinking Spaw', helped to attract more than 1000 visitors a day to Harrogate.

The sick and the ailing — and those who only imagined they were — drank the pungent sulphur water, which smelt so vile that the merest whiff could bring on what was known as the 'Harrogate headache'. Even so, as late as 1926 the Pump Room served 1500 glasses of sulphur water one morning to those convinced it would cure them of every complaint from neuralgia to 'nervous attacks'.

In 1949 the Harrogate 'water cure' became available under the National Health Scheme, but modern drugs had largely overtaken sulphur. In 1953 the Royal Pump Room became a museum of the town's history — where visitors can sample the waters if they wish. Its companion, the Royal Baths, built in 1897, is now a conference and exhibition centre, and some concerts are held here.

The first well was discovered in 1571 by a local landowner, William Slingsby of Bilton Hall, near Knaresborough, while out riding. A much-travelled man, he preferred the water to 'the tart fountains' he had sampled at continental spas. He built a wall around the well — which he called Tewit Well after the local dialect word for peewit — and encouraged people

Harrogate Conference Centre

House in Promenade Square

Montpellier Gardens

SPA BECOMES BLOOMTOWN

Harrogate made its name as a spa, but in recent years has proudly described itself as Britain's Floral Town. It has, indeed, many attractive public gardens — Montpellier Gardens are a fine example. A sign of changing times is the new role of the former Royal Baths, now a conference centre.

to drink the water for their health. In about 1596 the Tewit Well was described as 'the English Spaw' by a doctor named Timothy Bright, because it was like the wells in the Belgian town of Spa – in this way, the word 'spa' came into the English language. Outsiders began to arrive, but it was not until the mid-19th century that the town was built – mostly of dark, Yorkshire sandstone – around the neighbouring villages of High and Low Harrogate.

The town is flanked to the south and east by a 200 acre common called The Stray – from the stray sheep and cattle that used to roam there. The Tewit Well – now with domed roof and supporting columns – stands amid trees south of The Stray.

Harrogate is, indeed, noted for its parks, its numerous trees and its flower gardens. Among them are the sheltered Valley Gardens with a 600 ft Sun Colonnade, the formal flower beds off Montpellier Terrace, and a mile or so from the centre the Northern Horticultural Society's Harlow Car Gardens, which embrace 60 acres of rock, woodland and ornamental displays.

Each year, Harrogate stages its International Festival of the Arts, in which world-renowned theatre companies, orchestras, chamber groups and soloists take part. Most of the events are staged in the Harrogate Centre, which has an auditorium that seats 2000 people, and the ornate Royal Hall, built in 1903.

● **Parking** Railway Station; Springfield Avenue; East Parade; Montpellier Gardens; Tower Street; Union Street (all car parks). Disc parking in town centre (discs free from Information Centre, banks and shops) ● **Early closing** Wednesday ● **Market days** Monday to Saturday (in Market Hall) ● **Theatres** Harrogate Theatre, Oxford Street; Royal Hall, Ripon Road; Harrogate Centre, Kings Road ● **Cinema** Odeon, East Parade; ● **Events** Spring Flower Show (April); Great Yorkshire Show (July); International Festival of the Arts (July – August); Autumn Flower Show (September) ● **Information** TEL. Harrogate 65912 ● **AA 24 hour service** TEL. Leeds 438161.

Boston Spa WEST YORKSHIRE

10 miles south-east of Harrogate (PAGE 294 Gc)

The source of Boston Spa's wealth was discovered on June 4, 1744. A thatcher, cutting reeds by the River Wharfe near the old village of Thorp Arch, noticed water seeping from a spring into the river. The water was brackish, and left a glutinous, yellow sediment on the riverbed. Aware that fortunes were being made from mineral springs in nearby Harrogate, the thatcher had samples taken to York for testing.

The samples were found to contain salts of iron and sulphur. A small well was dug, and the water was advertised as possessing healing properties, 'effective in the relief of rheumatism and gastric disorders'. Soon up to 300 visitors a day were pouring into Thorp Arch, all eager to take 'the cure'.

A Dr Short of Sheffield, who sampled the waters in 1764, claimed they had a remarkable capacity for whitening the skin – an affectation much in vogue among ladies of fashion in the 18th century. As a result the spring began to enjoy the patronage of the gentry and 'carriage folk'.

In 1753 the first of a number of inns – the Royal Hotel – was begun across the river from Thorp Arch, and a new turnpike road was opened between Otley and Tadcaster, passing through the village.

Wealthy devotees of the waters came to stay, and built elegant town houses on the wooded embankment of the Wharfe. A fine new bridge was thrown across the river in 1770, and between 1810 and 1819 a smart bath house went up near the spring so that enthusiasts could enjoy total immersion. In 1834 this was replaced by a new building where slipper baths could be taken. The community adopted the name of a nearby hamlet, and became Boston Spa.

Spa waters were so popular that Queen Victoria, visiting West Yorkshire, decided to sample their qualities. Unfortunately for Boston Spa she chose to sample those of rival Harrogate and, as the rich and fashionable flocked to emulate her, the village lost its clientele. The handsome buildings remain, however, and a walk down the High Street leaves a lasting impression of crisp Georgian elegance in honey-coloured limestone.

There are also delightful riverside walks in the shallow gorge where the spring was first discovered, and where the spa bath buildings (now an angling centre) still stand. The pump room, too, is still there – converted into Georgian villas.

Across the Wharfe, the village of Thorp Arch remained largely untouched by the development, and its attractive 17th-century cottages grace the tree-shaded green. The church, rebuilt in the 19th century, contains a few Saxon and medieval fragments.

The name of this older village is a curious mixture of Norse and Norman French. Thorp is Norse for village, while Arch recalls the De Arches, medieval lords of the manor.

Harewood WEST YORKSHIRE

7 miles south of Harrogate (PAGE 294 Fc)

In 1738 the Harewood estate, home of the Gascoigne family since the Middle Ages, was bought by Henry Lascelles, a Yorkshire squire who had made his fortune in the West Indies trade. The estate included a ruined castle, a church, a village and an old manor house – Gawthorpe Hall.

The squire was happy to take the estate as he found it, but his son and successor Edwin Lascelles – the future Lord Harewood – had different plans. Inspired by the opening of two new turnpike roads in the mid-18th century, which placed Harewood at the centre of communications between Leeds, Harrogate, Otley and Tadcaster, he set about transforming the whole place – village and all.

In 1755 he commissioned the architect John Carr, of York, to build a replacement for the old hall – a new house to be set in an extensive landscaped park. The scheme involved the removal of the entire village (except the church) to outside the park gates.

Planned to complement the design of the house, Carr's new estate village was built of dark grey stone, in elegantly proportioned terraces ornamented by a pattern of arches. The terraces were faced by several small estate buildings in a similar style, including a pair of lodges flanking a Neoclassical gateway to the park.

Work on Harewood House started in 1759 but, by the time it was ready for occupation in 1771, Carr's original plans had been much modified by the architect Robert Adam (1728 – 92).

Meanwhile, the well-known landscape architect

Harewood House – from the south

Terrace in Harewood village

PLANNED FOR PERFECTION BY ADAM AND CAPABILITY

Elegant 18th-century Harewood House and its surroundings owe much to two of the great names in design – the architect Robert Adam and the great man of gardens, Capability Brown. But the original building and the estate village with its pleasant terraces and arches were designed by a York architect, John Carr. The house is the home of the Earl of Harewood, a cousin of Queen Elizabeth II.

Capability Brown had arrived at Harewood, and he spent nine years totally replanning the grounds. The romantic park he created around an artificial lake is considered one of the finest in England, despite the destruction caused by a gale in 1962, which blew down thousands of trees.

Of the original village in the park, all that remains is the 14th-century church.

Harewood Castle, 12th century but altered two centuries later, had two towers over 100 ft high which overlooked the Wharfe valley. Surrounded by trees, and in a dangerous condition (there is no public access), it is best seen from the Leeds to Harrogate road, or in the view painted by J. M. W. Turner on display at Harewood House. The house and park are open daily from Easter to November.

Newton Kyme WEST YORKSHIRE

12 miles south-east of Harrogate (PAGE 294 Gc)

The origins of Newton Kyme lie half a mile west of the present village, down a rough track which branches north of the main road towards the River Wharfe. This is part of Rudgate, the Roman road from Castleford to Boroughbridge, and the point where it crossed the Wharfe was once defended by a large Roman fort – Long Brough.

The fort was probably occupied for several centuries after the Romans left, but then a new village – Newton – was founded on higher ground to avoid the danger of flooding. The name was enlarged to Newton Kyme by the Kyme family, who owned the manor in the 13th century.

Little remains of the Roman fort, although a small well immediately across the river is still known as St Helen's Well, honouring the mother of Constantine the Great – first Christian emperor of Rome. The well would have been a holy spring in those days, and love tokens and magic charms were left there up until the First World War.

Probably most of the good building stone from the fort was plundered by villagers. Some may have been used for the church, built in a variety of 12th and 13th-century styles and having a 12th-century font and some medieval stained glass.

Among the monuments inside is a carving of a sailing ship, a memorial to Rear-Admiral Robert Fairfax who took part in the capture of Gibraltar in 1704. He lived in nearby Newton Kyme Hall, later rebuilt, mainly in the 1730s, as a splendid colonnaded house which looks out over magnificent parkland. The garden is protected by a fine example of a ha-ha – a walled ditch to keep out cattle without spoiling the view.

The Fairfax family acquired Newton Kyme in 1602, and owned it until the 1880s. The great Civil War general, Sir Thomas Fairfax, lived at Nun Appleton House, some 8 miles downriver, and was probably a frequent visitor to the estate in the 1650s. His ghost is said to haunt the well.

The hall, church and two fine Georgian houses are at the eastern end of the village. The western end has a more modest appeal. Cottages and farm buildings, some with red pantile roofs, line a quiet lane which leads to fields near the river.

ILKLEY

WEST YORKSHIRE

13 miles north of Bradford (PAGE 294 Ec)

A whitewashed cottage called White Wells stands on the edge of Ilkley Moor, overlooking this elegant and spacious spa town. The cottage contains a deep circular plunge bath, supplied with pure cold spring water. The bath was built in 1756 by a local benefactor named Squire Middleton, who believed that plunge-bath treatment was curative. For those without funds, he constructed a 'charity' bathhouse. Sufferers from arthritis, rheumatism and other ailments could take cold-water cures at White Wells.

But it was not until the 1840s that 'taking the cure' became fashionable at Ilkley and the town established its reputation as the 'Malvern of the North'. In 1844 a special hydropathic establishment or 'hydro' – a sort of health farm – was opened east of the town to take full advantage of the medicinal springs. People from all over Britain stayed there to take cold showers, to be swathed in chilly, wet sheets, and to undergo rigorous bouts of dieting.

The spa's popularity grew, and so did the town. Rows of Victorian stone houses were built around and beyond the railway station, above the old town. Its decline as a spa coincided with the First World War, and by the early 1970s White Wells was falling into ruin. It was saved in 1972, when a retired Bradford businessman restored the cottage. It is now open to the public at weekends and on Bank Holidays – and although the spring is no longer there, the famous plunge bath can be seen as it was in the 18th century.

The town's broad, tree-lined shopping streets still reflect its heyday as a spa, and a number of shops in The Grove retain their original Victorian iron-and-glass canopies.

Ilkley lies in the heart of Wharfedale and rising to the south is the moor, made famous by the Yorkshire 'national anthem', *On Ilkla Moor baht'at.* The words of the song were supposedly written early this century by members of a Wesleyan church choir.

One of the older houses in Ilkley is the Elizabethan Manor House, complete with gables and mullioned windows and overlooking the Wharfe valley. It is now a museum and art gallery. Heathcote, a three-storey building in Kings Road, was designed by the architect Sir Edwin Lutyens in 1906.

All Saints' Church stands on part of the site of the Roman fort of Olicana. The oldest part of the church is its 13th-century south doorway, decorated with fine mouldings and dog-tooth carving.

Inside the church stand three oddly carved Anglo-Saxon crosses, dating from about AD 770 to AD 850. The shortest has the figure of a saint on one side and some grotesque animals on the other. The second has a scroll pattern and animals. And the tallest has Christ on one side and, on the opposite side, symbolic representations of the four evangelists – a human head for St Matthew, a lion's head for St Mark, an ox's head for St Luke and an eagle's head for St John.

• **Parking** Brook Street; Station Road; Railway Road; Wharfe View Road (all car parks) • **Early closing** Wednesday • **Theatres** King's Hall, Station Road; The Playhouse, Weston Road • **Event** Wharfedale Music Festival (May) • **Information** TEL. Ilkley 602319 • **AA 24 hour service** TEL. Bradford 724703.

Appletreewick NORTH YORKSHIRE

12 miles north-west of Ilkley (PAGE 294 Ec)

A Dick Whittington of the dales came from Appletreewick. William Craven was born about 1548 in one of the cottages now forming the Chapel of St John, at the top of the village. He was apprenticed to a London merchant tailor and by 1601 was wealthy and well-established enough to become sheriff of the city and, in 1610, lord mayor. His son did even better, becoming Earl of Craven in 1665. He was famous in his day for his devotion to Charles I's beautiful but tragic sister, Elizabeth (1596 – 1662) the 'Winter Queen' of Bohemia, and lent her his house in Drury Lane, London when she returned to England a year before her death.

William Craven the elder never lost sight of his humble beginnings. In 1602 he endowed the grammar school that still stands in the neighbouring village of Burnsall, also repairing the church there and restoring the bridge after a disastrous flood.

Appletreewick, as pretty as its name, lies along a hillside on a narrow, switchback road. It was once an important grange – farming complex – owned by the canons of Bolton Priory, who mined lead, raised sheep and, under a charter of 1310, held a weekly market and four-day annual fair. This died out only in the last century, but is still commemorated in the names of Sheep Fair Hill and Onion Lane, a walled green track leading to the river, where onion-sellers once set up their stalls.

After the Dissolution of the Monasteries in 1539 the manor passed through many hands. Mock Beggar Hall is on the site of the old grange but was rebuilt in 1697. It still retains some original decorative features and ornate pigeonholes on the outside. There are several other fine mansions: High Hall, at the top of the village, was built in 1665 in what was then old-fashioned Elizabethan style. It has a banqueting chamber, minstrels' gallery and 720 leaded window panes.

In those times, Appletreewick was the centre of a prolonged feud between the Earl of Cumberland and Sir John Yorke, whose grandfather had bought the manor. The dispute was over who had the right to hunt deer in the surrounding country. Armed bands of the quarrelling landowners' retainers would range the dales, killing deer on principle and frequently coming to blows with each other. The feud resolved itself, inevitably, when no deer remained to be killed.

Near Appletreewick is Parcevall Hall, a Jacobean yeoman-farmer's house, which was restored and rebuilt in the 1930s. It is now a diocesan centre, and has beautiful terrace gardens open to the public. Also close by is Trollers' Gill, a steep limestone gorge of dramatic appearance, associated in Wharfedale legend with the Barguest, a large dog-like beast which set upon unwary (and usually inebriated) travellers. It could only be deterred by its fear of water – the traveller usually escaping by leaping across a stream.

Kilnsey NORTH YORKSHIRE

18 miles north-west of Ilkley (PAGE 294 Db)

Kilnsey faces its neighbouring village of Conistone across the River Wharfe and its flat, green meadows. In both villages, grey houses huddle under limestone knolls. Kilnsey itself is dwarfed by the overhanging Kilnsey Crag, whose base was undercut by an ancient glacier. The crag and the wild moorland surrounding it are not the village's only dramatic features – it was once the focal point of a sensational murder back in the 18th century.

An old inn, the Anglers' Arms – now a private house – was the haunt of Tom Lee, a blacksmith from Grassington, 2 miles south. He was heard boasting at the inn of his exploits as a robber by Dr Petty, the local physician, who threatened to expose him. Lee murdered Dr Petty as he was returning home, but was caught, hanged at York and his gibbeted bones hung near the scene of the crime in nearby woods.

Just behind the village, where a lane rises steeply to Malham, there is a small, stone outbuilding with some carved corner stones and cornices. This is a gatehouse of the now demolished Kilnsey Grange, once owned by the monks of Fountains Abbey, to the north-east. They ran flourishing industries in the area, growing corn, owning mills and driving sheep down from the dales along Mastiles Lane, a medieval 'green road' which crosses Malham Moor into Kilnsey. Behind the old gatehouse are the remains of the old hall, built in 1648, but now serving as a barn.

The village's surviving inn, the Tennant Arms, is

a centre for visitors to Upper Wharfedale, as is Kilnsey Park, to the south of the village, which has a trout farm selling fresh fish, and contains an information centre exhibiting displays and video film of local history and wildlife.

On the Tuesday after August Bank Holiday, Kilnsey Show takes place. The biggest and most popular agricultural show of the dales – and frequently televised – it includes a famous fell running race to the top of Kilnsey Crag, riding and farming displays, a dry-stone wall building competition, exhibitions of produce and an atmosphere of dales life second to none.

In evening sunshine or light snow, ancient, grassy terraces called lynchets are still visible on the hillsides above Conistone. They are the remains of fields cultivated originally by Anglo-Saxons where the staple crop of oats was grown until the 18th century. There is, too, another Anglo-Saxon feature – farmhouses clustering close to the village centre, contrasting with the much more scattered pattern of farm holdings adopted by Viking settlers in the higher and western dales in the 10th century.

The cottages and farmhouses scattered around the green date from 200 to 300 years ago, a period of prosperity when yeoman farmers replaced their homes of timber and thatch with fine stone houses.

The little Church of St Mary is reputedly on the site of one of the dales' most ancient chapels, Anglo-Saxon in origin. The present church was entirely rebuilt in 1846 but some medieval features remain, including two massive Norman arches in the north side of the nave. John Crowther (1858 – 1930), a Grassington botanist and antiquarian who wrote a now much-sought-after minor classic on local and national history, called *Sylva Gars*, is buried in Conistone. Many of his archaeological discoveries made in the area are in the Craven Museum at Skipton, 12 miles south and open daily except Tuesdays and Sundays.

Saltaire WEST YORKSHIRE

11 miles south of Ilkley (PAGE 294 Ed)

This remarkable village is the creation of one man – Sir Titus Salt (1803 – 76) who combined business acumen with a concern for his fellow beings while becoming a millionaire. The son of a Bradford wool merchant, he

THE LINGERING TASTE OF TITUS SALT

Enlightened industrialist Titus Salt created Saltaire as an alternative to 'dark satanic mills' – and his presence persists; not only in his name and statue, but in such elegant monuments to his good taste as the Almshouses and the stunning Nonconformist church.

Saltaire Hospital entrance

Sir Titus's statue

The Almshouses

Nonconformist church by the canal

made a fortune from manufacturing worsted and developing the use of alpaca (llama) wool. He soon operated four Bradford mills and showed his products at London's Great Exhibition of 1851.

Horrified at the filth, overcrowding and pollution of Bradford in the 1840s, and by the conditions endured by the working people, Salt built a great new mill on what was then a green field outside the city. With it he built an entire new 'factory' village embodying the latest ideas of economy, planning and hygiene. He chose a site close to glorious countryside, where links by road, rail and canal were excellent. His name, added to that of the adjoining River Aire, gave his creation its title.

A practising Congregationalist, Salt believed that a happy workforce reflected both Christian principles and good economic sense. He also believed that industry and beauty could go together, and had his village built in Italian style, but embodying the latest advances in engineering. The mill, which had a chimney disguised as a slender Venetian-style bell-tower, was opened on September 20, 1853. It was centrally heated and air conditioned at a time when such advanced features in a factory were unheard of. Part of the mill is still working, and its products can be bought in a shop there.

Opposite is the exquisite Congregational Church, now the United Reformed Church, completed in 1859 in Roman classical style and nominated by some experts as the most beautiful Nonconformist church in the North of England. Sir Titus is buried in the mausoleum in the south side. Victoria Hall, near by in Victoria Road, is the village institute and library. Built like a small chateau, it has great lions outside, which were originally intended to be set in Trafalgar Square, London.

Directly opposite was the Factory School, built for 750 boys and girls. Later it became Salt's Grammar School, which still thrives as the local comprehensive, but on a new site across the river. The Almshouses, near the top of Victoria Road, were modelled on Italian villas, to house elderly and infirm villagers in some style. They were rent-free and, 36 years before government pension schemes, single residents got a pension of 7s 6d (37½p) per week and married couples 10s (50p), equivalent to many times that value today.

Just beyond the station, which was restored and reopened for regular trains from Leeds and Bradford in 1984, is the Works Dining Room. Decades before such ideas became accepted, it provided mill workers with a bowl of breakfast milk and porridge for 1d (less than ½p), a choice of beef or meat-and-potato pie for lunch for 2d and a cup of tea for 1d.

The residential area contained about 750 well-built and well-designed homes, originally rented to employees, now privately owned. The streets are named after Queen Victoria, her consort Albert, Salt and his wife – Titus and Caroline – and their children.

Nor did Sir Titus neglect his workers' leisure. Immediately across the river is the Victorian boat-house, where boats were first hired out in 1871. You can still take a trip or have tea in a perfectly restored Victorian dining room.

Two minutes' walk beyond the park is Shipley Glen Tramway, a cable railway built in 1895 and restored in 1982. It passes through a beautiful wooded glen to the Victoria pleasure gardens. Worth exploring, too, is the historic Leeds to Liverpool Canal, running through the village; a waterbus service operates in summer, to Bingley and Shipley.

KIRKBY LONSDALE

CUMBRIA

16 miles north-east of Lancaster (PAGE 294 Cb)

St Mary's churchyard has an unusual feature – an elegant eight-sided gazebo, or pavilion. It was probably built in the 18th century to provide a sheltered point from which to enjoy magnificent views of the Lune valley, which the 19th-century art critic John Ruskin called 'one of the loveliest scenes in England – therefore in the world'. Another admirer of the views was the artist J. M. W. Turner (1775 – 1851), who painted the valley as seen from near the churchyard. A wall plaque marks the spot where Turner worked.

The Norman church is noted for the distinctive diamond patterns on some of its columns on the north side of the nave. St Mary's was extensively restored in the mid-1880s, when workmen uncovered burn marks in the tower. The marks were probably made in 1314, when the church was set on fire by roving Scots celebrating their victory at the Battle of Bannockburn.

Kirkby Lonsdale is on high ground overlooking a bend in the River Lune. It is a town of dignified, stone buildings, which spread out from the Market Square. Market day is on Thursday, when the small square is crammed with produce stalls.

Dotted among the more modest buildings are some on a grander scale. They include the mid-Victorian Market House, built on the corner of Market Street, and the early 18th-century Old Manor House in Mill Brow. There are several interesting inns – including the 17th-century Sun Hotel, with three pillars at the front, and the Royal Hotel, named in honour of William IV's widow, Queen Adelaide, who convalesced here in 1840.

Leading off Market Square is a street with the appealing name of Jingling Lane. According to local tradition, the lane 'jingles' if someone treads heavily along it. This may be an echoing effect from an old tunnel said to exist beneath the surface.

The town has two bridges over the Lune – an ancient one called Devil's Bridge, supposedly built by Satan; and a new one, definitely built by man in 1932. It is said that when Satan put up his bridge, he claimed the first living thing to cross it – which turned out to be an old dog. More prosaically, local historians say that the bridge dates from before 1368 – there are records to show that repairs were carried out then – and that the vicar of St Mary's raised the money to pay for its construction.

● **Parking** New Road (car park); Market Square ● **Early closing** Wednesday ● **Market day** Thursday ● **Event** Victorian Fair (September) ● **Information** TEL. Kirkby Lonsdale 71603 ● **AA 24 hour service** TEL. Blackpool 44947.

Arnside CUMBRIA

13 miles west of Kirkby Lonsdale (PAGE 294 Bb)

Arnside was once a busy port until more accessible places took its trade and left it to yachtsmen; now the village is an unspoilt little resort on the sandy estuary where the River Kent enters Morecambe Bay. It was created by the coming of the railways in the last century. A spectacular viaduct, one-third of a mile long, connecting it to the north bank of the Kent was built by the Furness Railway Company to complete the railway links between Lancashire and the large district of Furness.

Local limestone was used to build the houses that now rise steeply from the riverside promenade. Small hotels and guesthouses cater for nature lovers exploring the surrounding countryside's rich variety of plants and wildlife, including deer, red squirrels, foxes and badgers. Anglers fish the estuary for eels and flounders in fast currents that can create a strong tidal bore.

A hill called Arnside Knott, a mile south of the village and owned by the National Trust, gives walkers magnificent views although it is only just over 500 ft high. To the north are many of the rugged, broken peaks of Cumbria's highest mountains, with Shap Fell farther round to the north-east. The panorama is completed by the great chain of the Yorkshire Pennines sweeping south towards the Bowland fells, the far-off Lancashire Plain and, just below, Morecambe Bay, noted for the speed with which its tide comes in.

Around Arnside Knott wooded hills, heathland and salt marshes give the district the justifiable distinction of being an official Area of Outstanding Natural Beauty – some of it given over to nature reserves.

Burton-in-Kendal CUMBRIA

7 miles west of Kirkby Lonsdale (PAGE 294 Bb)

This old village lies quiet and unseen to the east of the busy M6 motorway. A jumble of cottages and fine old houses – some whitewashed, others pebbledashed and many rough-dressed in the silver-grey local limestone – blends with the rolling sheep-farming country around. Sheltering the village from east winds are the wooded slopes of Dalton Crags, while to the north, Farleton Fell raises a high shoulder of bare rocky scree, indicating that this is the beginning of the southern Lake District.

Maybe it was this feeling of being about to leave gentle countryside for the rugged mountains ahead that made Burton the important staging post it used to be – a tradition echoed by its small motorway service station. Both remaining pubs, the Royal Hotel and the King's Arms, almost opposite each other near the market square, were coaching inns, and stone mounting steps still stand outside the King's Arms.

Another relic of an earlier form of transport is a disused section of the Lancaster Canal. A lane beyond Deerslet Farm, south of the village, leads to a flight of

A HAVEN OF PEACE IN THE OLD PORT

Fields, woods, water and white-fronted houses create an enchanting vista on the approach to Arnside – which was once a port but is now a resort. The whole area has been declared one of outstanding beauty – and small wonder. But there are reminders still of the unquiet times when this was anything but a peaceful region. Ruined Arnside Tower, on the Shilla Slopes, was only one of a whole chain of forts built in the 14th century as a defence against raids across the Scottish border – though in fact stealthy raiders could arrive with very little notice by sea, sailing quietly along the lonely coastline. Fire all but destroyed the tower in 1602, and now sheep graze contentedly in the shadow of the ruin.

Arnside Tower

Arnside from the south

locks, now gateless and abandoned, that have become cascades of clear water – a delight to angler and walker alike. Sea-going ships also figure in Burton's history: a long-since silted-up inlet provided a safe anchorage only two miles or so away. Beams and joists used in many of the village's old cottages were fashioned from the timbers of laid-up ships, and display tell-tale wooden dowelling and other unmistakable signs of the shipwright's craft.

Trading in corn was the village's principal occupation, and the tall Georgian houses around the market square underline the importance of its market, established in 1661. Recesses in the base of the 18th-century market cross show where leg irons were once fitted to hold law-breakers. Despite the imposing buildings here and on Main Street, it is the nooks and crannies, like the old stabling yards, that give Burton its atmosphere. So, too, do the quaint street names – Boon Walk, Cocking Yard, Neddy Hill, Tanpits Lane. Several houses have projecting upper floors supported by columns.

Worshippers have attended the parish church of St James since at least 1180, and parts of a Saxon cross found in the churchyard suggest an even earlier date. The church was restored in the last century.

Milnthorpe CUMBRIA

10 miles west of Kirkby Lonsdale (PAGE 294 Ba)

Milnthorpe was a notorious traffic bottleneck on the A6 road into Lakeland, until it was bypassed by the M6 motorway. Unknown to most of the motorists suffering delays, there was – and is – a delightful detour round the village through an avenue of massive old beech trees, alongside a well-stocked deer park by the foreshore of the River Kent.

Ironically, the road that tried the tempers of motorist and villager alike helped in the 18th century to bring the prosperity which created the village much as we now see it. Several turnpikes were installed, and it captured the coach traffic from an older Kendal to Burton route. Nine inns catered for the coaches, their crews and passengers, and also for the thriving local industries along the smaller River Bela. These industries and the village's seaport – the Bela was then navigable for small vessels – were the other source of its prosperity.

Nowadays, although the estuary sands have silted up the port, and the canals, railways and other roads have bypassed the village, Milnthorpe still earns its keep as a working community. Local industries include quarrying and comb-making.

Although many of the stone cottages either side of the market square date from the 18th and early 19th centuries, the village is truly ancient. Earthworks in parkland surrounding Dallam Tower, a Queen Anne-style manor house on the south-west edge of the village, were probably built by Iron Age settlers.

Colonised successively by Celts, Romans, Angles and Norsemen, the village owes its name to the Norse-Irish, who arrived 1000 years ago and called it the 'village by the mill'. Despite this long history, Milnthorpe took on an independent identity only in the 1830s, when St Thomas's parish church was built in the market square. Previously it had been part of the nearby parish of Heversham. Milnthorpe's Friday market maintains a tradition going back to 1280. So does the annual funfair on May 12, which preserves an ancient right which was originally granted in the same year for holding cattle fairs.

A gentle stroll will reveal how the old builders, working in local limestone and without too many rules and regulations, managed to create a village that has both human scale – odd nooks and crannies and narrow twisting lanes – and a feel of spaciousness.

Two miles north is Levens Hall. It was originally a 13th-century pele tower built as a protection against Scots and other marauders. But in the time of Elizabeth I, James Bellingham, whose father had bought the hall from his cousins the de Redmans, rebuilt it as a sumptuous home. It was further adorned in the late 17th century by Colonel James Grahme, a cousin of the last of the Bellinghams. The panelling is richly carved, the plasterwork intricately beautiful and the walls bear paintings by Rubens, among others.

The house and gardens are open to the public on Sundays to Thursdays inclusive from Easter Sunday until the end of October. There is also a notable collection of steam engines and models. Weather permitting, the engines get steam up on Sundays and Bank Holiday Mondays.

Silverdale LANCASHIRE

16 miles west of Kirkby Lonsdale (PAGE 294 Bb)

'I think that one is never disappointed in coming back to Silverdale', novelist Elizabeth Gaskell wrote in 1858. She gave as her reasons 'the expanse of view . . . such wide plains of golden sands with purple hill shadows, or fainter wandering filmy cloud shadows, and the great dome of the sky'.

Twisting, leafy lanes flanked by old limestone walls meander around Silverdale, and a labyrinth of footpaths crisscross the surrounding woods and craggy broken ground which, from springtime, are carpeted

Milnthorpe deer park

Topiary Gardens at Levens Hall

Market day in the square

MONSIEUR BEAUMONT'S GARDEN OF DELIGHTS

Deer grazing in an idyllic riverside setting; an extraordinary garden of trees, shrubs and hedges clipped and pruned into strange shapes; and a road charmingly named Harmony Hill . . . Milnthorpe is full of delights and surprises. The deer park is by the bank of the broad River Kent; the leafy fantasies can be seen in the Topiary Gardens of Levens Hall, just north of the village. The garden is the creation of a Monsieur Beaumont, who arrived at Levens in 1689, after serving as royal gardener to James II. There have been only eight head gardeners since M. Beaumont, and his original layout has remained virtually unchanged. Back in the village, the little square becomes packed every Friday, when the thriving market maintains a tradition going back 700 years.

Doorway on Harmony Hill

in a profusion of wild flowers. This is a naturalist's paradise, especially for birdwatchers. Along the shoreline the salt marshes are internationally renowned for several species of ducks and waders, including the colourful shelduck and the black-and-white oystercatcher. Inland, a reserve run by the Royal Society for the Protection of Birds provides a reed-bed habitat for species such as the bittern and bearded reedling.

Signposted walks lead from the railway station to beauty spots such as Jack Scout, a headland overlooking Morecambe Bay and owned by the National Trust, and to the Pepper Pot, a monument on Castlebarrow built for Queen Victoria's Diamond Jubilee. Visitors can also enjoy golf on a nine-hole course, or fish along the shore or in the many dykes.

The village was a fishing port until the 1850s, and craft would tie up alongside the harbour just below the Silverdale Hotel. Here, too, cattle drovers would come ashore at low tide after crossing the north-east corner of Morecambe Bay from Kent's Bank, 3 miles west on the other side. They preferred to risk navigating the treacherous paths across the shifting sands rather than face the often more arduous and longer route that led through Kendal.

Silverdale's earlier inhabitants also included wildfowlers, quarrymen and miners. A splendidly preserved old copper-smelting furnace stands on an isolated spot named Jenny Brown's Point. Known locally as 'the chimney on the shore', it is a survivor of a business established in the late 18th century to smelt ore mined at nearby Crag Foot.

The village's scattered buildings include none of great age, but St John's parish church, built in 1885–6, has some exuberant carvings and the Trinity Methodist Church, a little older, has among its features an imposing rose window.

Settle – a view from the west

The Folly, Settle

THE NAKED MAN AND A HOUSE CALLED FOLLY

Hidden among the pleasant prospects of Settle are some notable eccentricities – the Naked Man Café, a shopping precinct (The Shambles) and The Folly, a house whose builder ran out of cash, it is said.

SETTLE

NORTH YORKSHIRE

16 miles north-west of Skipton (PAGE 294 Db)

A fascinating three-storey building called The Shambles stands in Settle's Market Place. It has a street-level arcade of shops and, perched on top, a row of cottages. Originally, the arcade housed butchers' shops or shambles – hence the name – which were built around 1680. At the same time, one-storey cottages were built above them for the butchers and their families. A top storey was added in the 19th century.

The Shambles is now a smart shopping precinct. On the south side of the Market Place is the gabled, brown-stone Town Hall, which was built in 1832 in Elizabethan style. Settle was granted a market charter by Henry III in 1249, and each Tuesday the area is packed with brightly coloured stalls, and lively with traders and shoppers. Opposite the Market Place is the Naked Man Café, so called because of a stone carving dated 1663 and set into the wall. It depicts a naked man, who is preserving his modesty with a carpenter's plane, and is framed by a coffin and a chair.

The town shelters under high limestone crags in the green pastures of Upper Ribblesdale, and will eventually benefit from a bypass road in the process of being built. It has many fine Georgian and 17th-century cottages and houses – some accessible only along narrow, cobbled alleyways. In Chapel Square is the Museum of North Craven Life – open every afternoon except Monday in the summer and on Saturday afternoons in the winter – which charts the history of that region.

Settle's largest and most spectacular house is The Folly, a three-storey confection built in 1679 by Richard Preston. It is composed of an elaborate mixture of Italianate columns, Gothic decorations, corner windows, an off-centre main doorway, and a hall that occupies most of the ground floor. Preston reputedly ran out of money before the house was finished and today The Folly is used as an antiques showroom.

Two other notable men born in Settle were Dr George Birkbeck (1776 – 1841) and Benjamin Waugh

WHERE ELGAR STAYED WITH A MUSICAL GP

Divided from Settle by a bridge over the Ribble, the village of Giggleswick has a manor of its own, and near by is a cottage called Cravendale, where the composer Sir Edward Elgar (1857 – 1934) liked to stay. It was the home of his friend, Dr Charles Buck, a local GP who was a keen violinist and cellist. They met when Dr Buck played in an orchestra conducted by the composer.

Manor house, Giggleswick

Cravendale, where Elgar stayed

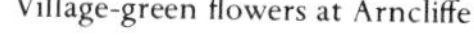

Village-green flowers at Arncliffe

View of the village

GOLDEN SPLASH IN A DALE OF DELIGHT

High-growing buttercups weave a deep carpet of gold on the village green at Arncliffe – in happy contrast to the sober grey houses. This pretty village lies deep in Littondale – fine farming country where, in medieval times, the monks of Fountains Abbey kept large flocks of sheep. Charles Kingsley visited Littondale, naming it Vendale in his book The Water Babies.

(1839 – 1908). Birkbeck, son of a local banker and merchant, was a pioneer of adult education. He founded the Mechanics' Institutions in Glasgow and London, which were soon imitated throughout the country. He was also a founder of University College, London, and Birkbeck College – part of London University – is named after him. Waugh was born in a saddler's shop – now a bank – behind the Market Place. He was a passionate social reformer and philanthropist, and founded the London Society for the Prevention of Cruelty to Children in 1884 – it became the National Society in 1895.

Castleberg Crag rises 200 ft above the town and from the summit there are magnificent views of the town and the Ribble valley. High up on the moors near by is the Victoria Cave. In prehistoric times the cave was a hyena den and later a refuge for Stone Age hunters who left behind their flint tools.

• **Parking** Church Street; Station Road; Chapel Square (all car parks) • **Early closing** Wednesday • **Market day** Tuesday • **Event** Carnival (July) • **Information** TEL. Settle 3617 (summer) • **AA 24 hour service** TEL. Bradford 724703.

Arncliffe NORTH YORKSHIRE

11 miles north-east of Settle (PAGE 294 Db)

Buried deep in the heart of the lovely Littondale, Arncliffe stands four square around its large village green – a cluster of greystone houses and cottages, the totally unspoilt Falcon inn and the village shop and post office.

It is an idyllic scene, with the wild fells rising to the north before dropping down to Wharfedale. But in medieval times it was across these fells that marauding Scots came to pillage and plunder – and then the village green became a stockaded pen where sheep and cattle were herded while the raiders were repulsed.

Small wonder, therefore, that in 1513 the men of Littondale accompanied Lord Henry Clifford of Barden in Wharfedale to the Battle of Flodden, the crushing defeat inflicted on the Scots by the English, in which more than 10,000 Scottish soldiers and their king, James IV, were killed. The dalesmen's names are recorded on parchment in St Oswald's Church.

The church stands by a bridge over the River Skirfare, just after it mingles with the Cowside Beck, and beyond the bridge is a house called Bridge End. Here the Victorian writer Charles Kingsley came to visit while staying at Malham Tarn House, across the hills to the south in Airedale, and turned his thoughts to his story of *The Water Babies*.

Bridge End and the church make a charming group, with a few 17th-century cottages and the millhouse, which once spun yarn that was then woven into material by cottage weavers. The mill closed in 1875 and now farming is the mainstay of the valley.

Clapham NORTH YORKSHIRE

6 miles north-west of Settle (PAGE 294 Cb)

A turbulent Pennine stream, the Clapham Beck, runs off the shoulders of Ingleborough mountain and through the centre of Clapham. Tree-lined and spanned by four attractive bridges, the rippling waters

LEFT IN THE SHADE OVERLEAF

A sycamore leans low to shade an ancient bridge and a clear, blue stream . . . out in the sunlight, greystone cottages are framed by its leafy boughs. Quiet Clapham, once noisy with the din of a main road, is bypassed and at peace again.

divide the village and its three main streets, each bordered with greystone houses standing in gardens bright with flowers in season.

Until the 1970s, when a bypass was built, the main Kendal to Leeds road ran through Clapham, crossing the beck near the New Inn. It was a road that brought in turn merchants and clothiers carrying their wares to the Leeds market, stagecoaches clattering up to the three coaching inns and motorists streaming pleasure-bent towards the Lake District.

Now the rattle of coaches and the roar of traffic are distant memories, but evidence of Clapham's busy past remain in the shape of the New Inn (the others have gone) and the market cross about half a mile from the main road bridge.

Much of the northern end of the village was remodelled in the 19th century by the Farrer family, who built Ingleborough Hall and dammed the beck to create an artificial lake. Its waters cascade over a waterfall and into a wooded ravine before subsiding to a murmur as they flow through the village.

The hall, built about 1830, is in the classical style with giant columns gracing the entrance. It is now used as an Outdoor Education Centre for Yorkshire schools. There is a walk through the grounds called the Reginald Farrer Trail, in recognition of that member of the Farrer family who was a famous botanist.

He travelled extensively in the Far East, bringing back new species of rhododendron and many other shrubs and plants which are now common in gardens throughout the world. The mile-long walk passes through woodland planted by Reginald Farrer himself, and leads to Ingleborough Cave, where there is a spectacular display of stalactites and stalagmites.

Information about the trail, along with other guides, is available at the National Park Information Centre, housed in Clapham's Old Manor House of 1705. Near by, overlooking the Clapham Beck, is the Church of St James, largely rebuilt in classical style in 1814, but keeping a fine medieval tower.

Halton Gill NORTH YORKSHIRE

11 miles north-east of Settle (PAGE 294 Db)

Littondale is one of the loveliest of the dales, although it is the smallest, thrusting a mere 8 miles into the fells and with only four villages and hamlets along its enchanting length. Halton Gill is one, a cluster of limestone cottages and farmhouses at the head of the dale, below the crumpled face of Horse Head Moor.

The hamlet has no church – the little 19th-century church of St John's and its adjacent 17th-century school is now a private house, and worshippers and scholars alike have to make their way down the valley to Arncliffe.

But in the early years of the 19th century Halton Gill had a parson-schoolmaster who also held the living at Hubberholme, in Upper Wharfedale. His name was Thomas Lindley, and the only way he could travel between his two churches was on horseback, across the wild Horse Head Pass, a medieval packhorse trail that climbs to 1900 ft.

It is said that Parson Lindley made the 6 mile round trip every Sunday, regardless of weather, for 40 years until his 80th birthday. Asked why he did it on wild and stormy days he replied: 'Duty must be attended to.'

CALL FROM THE WILD *Lonely, boulder-strewn moors rise around remote Halton Gill – a prospect of subdued greens and greys enlivened by a sudden spark of red – the essential phone box.*

Langcliffe NORTH YORKSHIRE

1 mile north of Settle (PAGE 294 Db)

In the 14th century, Langcliffe was one of many dale villages that suffered the unwelcome attention of Scottish raiders. Indeed, in one raid in 1318 it was completely destroyed. When the village was rebuilt a more defendable position was found for it, some half a mile south-east of the craggy limestone headland of Langcliffe Scar.

Built around a large green – where originally cattle had been guarded during raids – are the village church, 17th, 18th and 19th-century stone cottages, and the school, all looking across a peaceful scene where today the only rivalry is between cricketers. One area has been cobbled, around a mature sycamore tree and a fountain which is also the war memorial.

Until recently Langcliffe was a mill and quarry village, the River Ribble supplying the power for a mill built first to grind corn, and then converted in the 19th century to spin cotton. Workers were brought in from as far afield as Devon and East Anglia and, just after the Second World War, even from Italy. Many of the girls later married and settled locally.

Langcliffe Hall, built in the 17th century, belongs to the Dawson family and was the home of Geoffrey Dawson, editor of *The Times* from 1912 to 1919 and from 1922 to 1941. An earlier Dawson, Major William, was a friend of Sir Isaac Newton, a frequent visitor to the hall. Two gnarled apple trees in the garden are said to be from cuttings of a tree planted by Major Dawson to commemorate Newton's theory of gravity.

Langcliffe once had an inn, The Naked Woman, so called from a figurine carved into a stone tablet which can still be seen built into the wall of a house opposite the telephone box. The stone bears the date 1660 and the initials ISMS.

MAP 28

HERRIOT COUNTRY AND HADRIAN'S WALL

Many people who have never set foot in North Yorkshire feel they know the wild, dramatic landscape from the books and TV series of James Herriot. Here he practised as a vet and came to love the moors, the dales and, perhaps even more, their inhabitants – both human and animal. From this love, he created the fictional town of Darrowby – an amalgam of four real towns. The Romans, and later the Norsemen and Normans have left their marks – and their names – in this once turbulent region where miles of Hadrian's Wall still guard against ghostly border raiders.

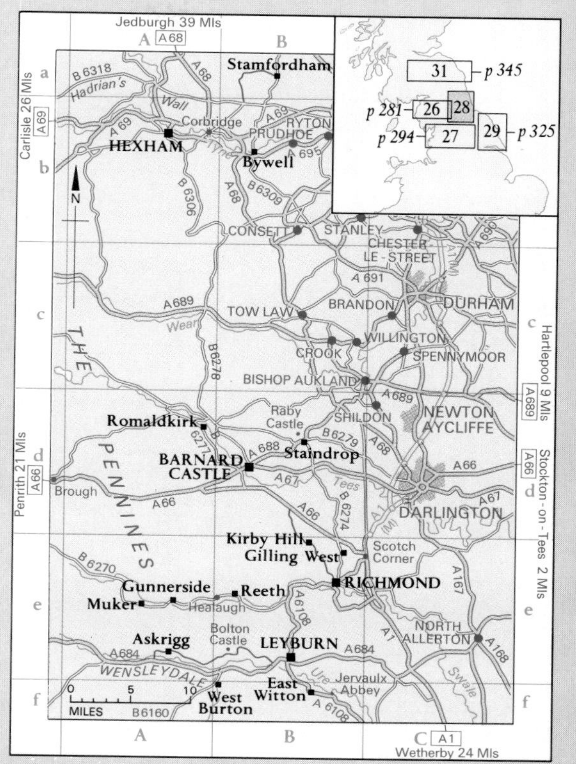

MAP 28: NEIGHBOURING AREAS – MAPS 26, 27, 29, 31

BARNARD CASTLE	HEXHAM
Gilling West	Bywell
Kirby Hill	Stamfordham
Romaldkirk	
Staindrop	

LEYBURN	RICHMOND
Askrigg	Gunnerside
East Witton	Muker
West Burton	Reeth

BARNARD CASTLE

DURHAM

16 miles west of Darlington (PAGE 311 Bd)

Barnard Castle is named after the castle whose rugged ruins, rising from a rocky cliff above the River Tees, still make an impressive spectacle. The castle was started at the beginning of the 12th century by Bernard de Baliol, son of a Norman baron who fought alongside William the Conqueror at Hastings. Over the next two centuries Bernard's descendants enlarged it to cover 7 acres, with room for some 800 troops.

The grand scale is hardly surprising, because the Baliols were an important family in both England and Scotland. One of them founded Balliol College, Oxford, in the 13th century, and two became kings of Scotland, albeit of little distinction. John de Baliol, probably born at Barnard Castle, was king for only four years before abdicating after a defeat by the English in 1296. At the same time he lost the family estates around Barnard Castle – they were seized by Edward I (1272 – 1307). John de Baliol's son, Edward, ignominiously ceded most of southern Scotland to Edward III of England.

The castle returned to royal hands when it was acquired by Richard III (1483 – 5) and remained a royal possession until the Civil War in the mid-17th century. In 1569, during the Rising of the North against Elizabeth I (see Staindrop, page 314), it was besieged by the rebel Earls of Northumberland and Westmorland. Sir George Bowes of nearby Streatlam Castle, who was steward of Barnard Castle for the queen, held out for 11 days. But the townsfolk were not with him and fear of treachery forced him to surrender. By 1630, the castle had fallen into ruin, much of its stone being carted off by local people as building material.

In their years of power the Baliols had established a market in Barnard Castle and the town still radiates from Market Place, at the centre of which is the Market Cross. This is a large, eight-sided stone pavilion built in 1747. The verandah around its base was used as a market for butter and other dairy produce, while its upper floor served as a lock-up and, in the early 19th century, as a courtroom.

Two bullet holes in the Market Cross's weather-vane are the result of a shooting match in 1804 between a volunteer soldier and a local gamekeeper. The two men stood outside the Turk's Head 100 yds away and each took a shot at the vane. They both scored hits and the match was declared a draw.

A short way down from Market Place, in the street called The Bank, stands the bay-windowed Blagraves House – named after the Blagrave family who lived here until the mid-17th century. After that it was an inn – it is now a restaurant – and was probably visited by Oliver Cromwell on October 24, 1648. According to a diary kept by one of the townsmen, the people rode out to meet Cromwell and 'conducted him into his lodgings and presented him with burnt (mulled) wine and shortcakes'. On the outside of the house are three carved figures of musicians, probably

Market Cross at Barnard Castle

Blagraves House, with carved musicians

Bowes Museum

A room in the museum, furnished Paris style

THE 'CHATEAU' THAT IS REALLY A MUSEUM

Apart from Barnard Castle itself, there are some fascinating buildings in the town: the fine Market Cross; Blagraves House, with carved musicians on its front; and the chateau-like Bowes Museum, crammed with 15th to 19th-century furniture, pottery and paintings by such masters as Goya, El Greco and Boucher. Local archaeological finds are also displayed in several rooms.

added in the 19th century. The town's most unusual building is the Bowes Museum, created in 1869–92 by John Bowes and his French actress wife Josephine. He was a descendant of Sir George Bowes. The Queen Mother, born Lady Elizabeth Bowes-Lyon, is a member of the same family.

Two famous authors have associations with Barnard Castle. Sir Walter Scott (1771–1832) was inspired by the view from the castle ruins when he wrote his narrative poem *Rokeby*, set in the district. In 1838 Charles Dickens stayed at The King's Head Hotel in Market Place, while researching his novel *Nicholas Nickleby*, and recommended the hotel in the novel.

• **Parking** Galgate (car park); Galgate; Horse Market; Market Place • **Early closing** Thursday • **Market day** Wednesday • **Event** Carnival (Spring Bank Holiday Weekend) • **Information** TEL. Teesdale 38481 • **AA 24 hour service** TEL. Stockton-on-Tees 607215.

Gilling West NORTH YORKSHIRE

12 miles south-east of Barnard Castle (PAGE 311 Be)

Gilling West was an important town in pre-Norman England. In the 7th century it lay within the tiny Anglo-Saxon kingdom of Deira, whose capital was York, and here in AD 651 Deira's last king, the holy Oswin–later made a saint–was murdered on the orders of his enemy Oswy, king of neighbouring Bernicia. Oswy then united the two kingdoms to form Northumbria.

Later, Gilling West was the capital of an extensive 'wapentake'–one of the North's administrative districts. It also had an important monastery, founded by Oswy at his wife's insistence, where prayers were offered for Oswin and also for his murderer.

But the Norman Conquest spelt doom for Gilling West. It may have been one of the many Anglo-Saxon towns and villages that were ruthlessly devastated, during the terrible 'Harrowing of the North', for their part in the rebellions against the Normans of 1069. In any case, Gilling West rapidly declined into a quiet agricultural community, and nearby Richmond, with its great castle, became the administrative centre for the region.

Today, Gilling West – Gilling East lies a full 35 miles away over the Cleveland Hills – stretches out along the Richmond to Barnard Castle road, and its pantiled cottages, mingled with a handful of larger stone houses and two old coaching inns, give little clue to its great antiquity.

Set back from the road is the mostly 14th-century Church of St Agatha. Some fragments of Anglo-Saxon crosses in its porch show that although no traces of Oswy's monastery remain, Gilling West was still a seat of Christianity in the 9th and 10th centuries. Outside, the graveyard has a memorial stone to Ann and William Waller, a brother and sister who both died – for reasons unexplained – on the same day: July 12, 1764. Ann was 21 and William six. The inscription reads:

'Adieu vain world I've had enough of thee
But now I'm careless what thou say'st of me.
Thy smiles I court not, nor thy frowns I fear
My Days are past, my head lies quiet here.
What Faults in me you've seen take care to shun
Look but at home – enough there's to be done.'

Running from north to south for several miles near Gilling West is a long earthwork called Scots Dike. It may have been built before the Roman occupation to mark the boundary between the territories of different clans.

Relics of a later period were found in the 1970s by Gilling Beck, which runs through the north of the village. One was a magnificent Viking sword made of iron. It is about $2\frac{1}{2}$ ft long and has a hilt and pommel beautifully inlaid with silver. This ancient weapon can be seen in the Yorkshire Museum at York.

Kirby Hill NORTH YORKSHIRE

10 miles south-east of Barnard Castle (PAGE 311 Be)

Every other year in the late summer, Kirby Hill is the scene of an ancient ceremony known as the Kirby Hill Races. The purpose of this ceremony – which has nothing to do with racing – is to elect the two wardens who administer the valuable Dakyn Trust, which owns extensive farmland in the area and still provides charity for the aged and educational grants for local children.

The procedure, which dates from 1556, is intriguing. First, six local people considered suitable for the task are chosen, and their names written on slips of paper. The slips are then wrapped in wax to make little waterproof balls, which are thrown into an earthenware pitcher filled with water. Finally, in a public ceremony, the vicar stirs the wax balls with a shepherd's crook and takes out 'two balls as chance shall offer them'. The two people whose names are chosen in this way 'shall be wardens for the two years following and no longer'.

The man who laid down this remarkable procedure was John Dakyn, a 16th-century vicar of Kirby Hill. Dakyn was a zealous Catholic who took an important part in the religious persecutions of the reign of Mary I, and had one Protestant burnt for 'heresy' at Richmond. But he also founded the Trust and a Free Grammar School, which would include among its pupils an 18th-century scholar and Archbishop of Canterbury, Matthew Hutton. The grammar-school building, with its fine mullioned windows, stands beside Kirby Hill's pleasantly proportioned village green. Near by, among some 18th-century houses and cottages, is Dakyn House, built by the Trust in the 20th century to house old people. But holding pride of place on the hilltop upon which the village stands is the greystone 14th-century Church of St Peter and St Felix. Its magnificent buttressed tower is a prominent landmark for miles around, and the churchyard commands superb views to neighbouring Ravensworth and across the Stainmore Gap to the northern Pennines.

A direct footpath leads from Kirby Hill to Ravensworth, which surrounds an enormous village green, three quarters of a mile north. Some of the village's brown sandstone houses have pantiled roofs and date from the 18th century, but 20th-century development blends in well using the same materials. The Bay Horse Inn, which overlooks the green, has a fine sign and there is a tiny but delightful sandstone Methodist church with Gothic-style windows.

Just outside the village are the ruins of Ravensworth Castle, which has been derelict since the 16th century. The castle had been the seat of the FitzHugh family (see also Romaldkirk). In the Middle Ages they were one of the great baronial families of the wild north. In the 14th century, Henry FitzHugh enlarged the castle, made a deep moat and created a 400 acre walled park around it.

Romaldkirk DURHAM

5 miles north-west of Barnard Castle (PAGE 311 Ad)

Saint Romald, to whom Romaldkirk's fine parish church is dedicated, was the son of a Northumbrian prince. He was born, around AD 800, as his mother was fleeing south to escape a war between the kingdoms of Northumbria and Mercia. Legend has it that at the moment of his birth, the infant Romald cried out: 'I am a Christian', and proceeded to make a 'noble sermon with marvellous good eloquence'. Sadly, the miraculous baby lived for only three days and was buried where he was born, in Buckingham.

The village named after his church stands on a terrace where the River Tees flows through a green and fertile valley below wild fells and moorland. Its cottages and houses lie around a series of attractive village greens, which still have stocks and two pumps, one dated 1866.

Of the five pubs the village once supported, only two – the Kirk Inn and the Rose and Crown – have survived. North of the village, the handsome Collingwood House, which was a working corn mill until 1870, has now been converted into flats. Beside it, the 17th-century Egglestone Bridge crosses the Tees and a beautiful wooded ravine.

The church dates from the 12th and 13th centuries, but incorporates some Saxon fragments. Its splendour reflects the prosperity of the medieval wool and cloth trades. There is a fine font and a pulpit, which

Romaldkirk – Middle Green and the church

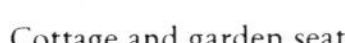

Cottage and garden seat

Church font

Parish pump of 1866

A VILLAGE THAT IS GREEN, GREEN, GREEN

Until 1930 two annual fairs were held in Romaldkirk, when traders sold everything from sheep to 'Cure All' toffee. Local industries once included lead mining, quarrying and pencil manufacture – now gone, like the fairs. The village remains attractive: its three interlinked greens are a delight; the church has a 13th-century font patterned with a charming leaf design and there are two parish pumps.

once had three tiers. Most interesting of all, however, is the tomb of Hugh Fitz Henry, Lord of Bedale, Ravensworth and Cotherstone.

He was one of Edward I's knights and was gravely wounded in the king's Scottish wars at the beginning of the 14th century. He died as a result of his wounds at Barwick-on-Tees, near Darlington, and is buried in Romaldkirk. His effigy shows him in the rare straight-legged position – figures on medieval tombs normally have their legs crossed in a more relaxed posture – and the details of his armour are more than usually precise, giving a fascinating insight into its design. The arms on his shield are, for some reason, those of the FitzHugh family, who owned much of the land around Ravensworth.

Staindrop DURHAM

6 miles north-east of Barnard Castle (PAGE 311 Bd)

An armed rebellion that shook the peace of Elizabethan England in 1569 was planned in the great Baron's Hall of Raby Castle, just north of Staindrop. The plan was to replace the Protestant Elizabeth with her Catholic cousin Mary, Queen of Scots.

Leading the rebellion were the great Catholic families of the North of England, including the Nevills of Raby Castle, who resented the rule of the Protestant queen. But they failed – the support they expected from the powerful Percy family never came. Finally they had to flee for their lives, and their estates were seized by the crown.

Until then, the fortunes of the Nevill family and Staindrop had been closely bound together; and Staindrop owed its importance to the weekly market established here by John Nevill of Raby in the 14th century – and which ended at the beginning of the present century. Today, the village's many imposing houses – most of them dating from the 18th century – are evidence of the wealth and prosperity brought by the market.

Oldest among them is the late 16th-century Manor House in Office Square. Next door is the fine mainly 18th-century Raby Estates Office. Also dating from the 18th century are Westfield House and Raby House at the western end of the village; the impressive Malvern House, in the centre; and a fine row of shops with their original doorways. Lining the large, tree-shaded green are more 17th and 18th-century houses. Two of them still have heavy stone posts in front. These once held chains to protect the houses from sheep and cattle straying on their way to market.

Not far away, the Church of St Mary shows traces of an original Saxon building, but has been considerably enlarged over the centuries. On its south side there is an intriguing little vestry which for many years doubled as the village lock-up. Inside the church are some superb alabaster effigies, one showing a 13th-century lady in court dress; and another the recumbent figure of Ralph Nevill of Raby. Beside him are his two wives; Margaret, daughter of the Earl of Stafford, and Joan, daughter of John of Gaunt and sister of Henry IV. Ralph Nevill had helped Henry win the throne of England.

Raby Castle still looms impressively by the Bishop Auckland road. The spectacular fortress dates from the reign of Canute, the 11th-century Danish king of England, but the Nevills enlarged it in the 14th century. It was transformed in the 18th century into a country house and enlarged in the mid-19th century.

The castle, now open to the public, has a beautifully restored medieval chapel and fine collections of furniture, sculpture, ceramics and paintings. There are portraits by the 17th-century court painter Sir Peter Lely and the great 18th-century English painter Sir Joshua Reynolds. In addition, there are portraits by other painters of two Sir Henry Vanes who owned the castle in the 17th century. Sir Henry Vane the younger was a brilliant republican statesman, executed at the Restoration by Charles II because the king considered him 'too dangerous to let live'. The present owner of the castle, the 11th Lord Barnard, is a descendant of both the Vanes and the Nevills.

HEXHAM

NORTHUMBERLAND

21 miles west of Newcastle upon Tyne (PAGE 311 Ab)

Hexham owes its existence to a controversial 7th-century bishop and saint. He was Wilfrid (about AD 634 – 709), the urbane son of an important local nobleman. Educated at Lindisfarne, Canterbury and Rome, Wilfrid rose by the time he was 35 to become bishop of a vast diocese centred on York and stretching from The Wash in the south to the Firth of Forth in the north. He was immensely wealthy and ran his household on a princely scale. He was also a close friend of Northumbria's powerful King Egfrith and his queen, Etheldreda.

However, Wilfrid somewhat overreached himself a few years later when he encouraged Queen – later Saint – Etheldreda to leave her husband and become a nun. Having earned the resentment of the king, Wilfrid was demoted and eventually imprisoned, despite an appeal to the pope in Rome. He was released on condition that he left Northumbria – and spent many years in exile before returning in AD 686 with reduced powers. Five years later he was again exiled, but he finally returned four years before he died.

Wilfrid spent these last years as Bishop of Hexham, which was fitting because of the many monasteries he had founded in his years of power, the most magnificent was at Hexham. Indeed, the church he built here was said at the time to be the finest and largest church north of the Alps. Sadly, the Danes destroyed most of it little more than 150 years after his death – by which time Hexham had ceased to have a bishop.

Wilfrid's crypt, however, survives. Its fabric dates back even farther than the saint's time, because his church was built with stone taken from the former Roman camp at Corstopitum (Corbridge), 4 miles east. In the south transept of the abbey is the gravestone of Flavinus, a 25-year-old Roman standard bearer. It has a carving showing an ancient Briton in combat with a mounted Roman soldier – a reminder that this was a frontier of the empire and that Hadrian's Wall strides across the countryside only 3½ miles north of Hexham.

The present abbey was built above the crypt by Augustinian canons – mostly in the 12th and 13th centuries. But in 1296 it was attacked yet again – this time by Scots. They slaughtered many novices, some of whom were cruelly burnt alive, and destroyed the nave, which was not rebuilt until 1908.

Inside the abbey is the well-worn Midnight Stair, which the canons descended at midnight for Matins. A stone seat in the choir is called St Wilfrid's Chair, or the Frith stool, and may have been the seat on which the kings of Northumbria were crowned. In medieval times it was a seat of sanctuary, where a fugitive from justice was deemed to be absolutely safe from pursuers: nobody could seize him from the chair, and anyone who tried would be condemned as 'bootless, incapable of pardon' by the church authorities.

Hexham lies in a rich green valley, just south of the River Tyne, and grew up around the monastery and abbey. Beneath the abbey's east front – which was added in the late 1800s – is Market Place. Sheep and cattle sales are held at the market, which attracts farmers from all over Northumberland.

Outstanding buildings near by are the recently restored Moot Hall, a fortress-like place built in the late 14th century and used today for exhibitions, meetings and social functions; and the early 14th-century Manor Office. This was built as a prison and, as in the abbey's crypt, stones from Roman remains were used. It now houses a Border History Museum and the tourist information centre.

Leading north-west off Market Place is Market Street, which turns into Gilesgate and Fore Street. The streets' mellow stone buildings include two late 17th-century houses with bay windows, and also some attractive Georgian ones. At the far end, in the little street called Holy Island, a 17th-century town house with fine gables and mullioned windows has survived the centuries completely unaltered outside.

Spanning the Tyne just north of the town is the

AT EIGHT BELLS *The tall tower of Hexham Abbey overlooks a row of 18th-century buildings – now public offices – and a stone cross commemorating local people killed in the two World Wars. From the inside, the tower is climbed by a Midnight Stair – which leads to the ringing chamber, housing the clock and bell ropes. Eight mighty bells hang in the chamber above.*

nine-arched, 18th-century Hexham Bridge, from which there is a matchless view of the town and its surroundings. The Battle of Hexham was fought near by in 1464, during the Wars of the Roses. The Lancastrians of the deposed Henry VI were heavily defeated by Edward IV's Yorkists and, after the battle the Duke of Somerset, the Lancastrian general, was summarily beheaded – probably in Hexham's Market Place.

• **Parking** Town Centre; Loosing Hill; Tyne Green (all car parks) • **Early closing** Thursday • **Market day** Tuesday • **Theatre** Queens Hall, Beaumont Street • **Cinema** Forum, Market Place • **Events** Fair (August); Abbey Festival (September) • **Information** TEL. Hexham 605225 • **AA 24 hour service** TEL. Newcastle upon Tyne 610111.

Bywell NORTHUMBERLAND

9 miles east of Hexham (PAGE 311 Bb)

Bywell today is a tiny, peaceful village set in leafy parkland where the River Tyne makes a broad and majestic curve. But it was once a busy little community which resounded to the roar of furnaces and the clash of hammers from 15 workshops. Four centuries ago Bywell was an important centre for making harness equipment, and the horsemen of the unruly Borders could buy their stirrups, bits and bridles here.

Now all trace of the workshops has gone – the last of them were cleared away in the early 19th century. The 13th-century market cross was moved to the edge of a field where it now stands.

Bywell Castle, probably built in 1430 by Ralph Nevill, 2nd Earl of Westmorland, has survived the centuries. In its courtyard, guarded by a fortified tower and gatehouse, the villagers of Bywell and their livestock could shelter from the frequent raids of borderland marauders. Here, too, the Lancastrian Henry VI found refuge after his forces were defeated in the Battle of Hexham (see above). It is said, though, that his crown, helmet and sword were later captured by his enemies, the Yorkists, when the castle surrendered. Today the castle is strictly private.

Across the fields from the castle, and in sharp contrast to its grim aspect, is elegant Bywell Hall, in a splendid setting on a bend of the River Tyne. This superbly proportioned house was built in 1760 from designs by the Georgian architect James Paine (1716–89). It was then enlarged in 1820. The public can view the house, which now belongs to Viscount Allendale, on occasional open days.

Bywell has two churches, one known as the White Church, and the other as the Black Church. The White Church of St Andrew – now managed by the Redundant Churches Commission – has one service a year, in July. It belonged to the 'White Canons' of Blanchland, and has a fine Saxon tower whose lower stages date from before AD 950. The Black Church of St Peter, less than 200 yds away, belonged to the black-clad Benedictine monks of Durham.

Fragments of the north wall of St Peter's date back to an 8th-century church destroyed by the Danes in AD 793–4. Its 13th-century tower could provide shelter from raiders, and the 14th-century St Peter's Chapel was later used as a village school. There is also a rare medieval scratch clock on the south wall. This is a primitive form of sundial which has a small hole at its centre; a stick is inserted into the hole and the shadow thrown by the stick marks the hours as it crosses scratched marks on the dial.

In November 1771 the village suffered from a devastating flood, when the Tyne burst its banks. Houses were demolished, and water stood 8 ft deep in Bywell Hall. Six people died, and coffins were washed out of the graveyard, with the living and the dead tossed together amid the swirling torrent. The squire's horses, led into St Peter's Church for safety, saved themselves by holding onto the tops of the high pews by their teeth. Another horse belonging to a visitor to the village survived by climbing onto the altar.

Stamfordham NORTHUMBERLAND

13 miles north-east of Hexham (PAGE 311 Ba)

A frequent visitor to Stamfordham in the first years of the 18th century was the ill-fated 3rd Earl of Derwentwater. This outstandingly good-natured and gifted young man – a grandson of Charles II and one of his mistresses, the actress Mary Davis – was largely brought up in France at the court of the exiled James II. But in 1709 he returned to England, where he had estates in Cumberland and Northumberland. While staying at Dilston Hall, near Corbridge, he liked to ride over to Stamfordham to play bowls in the garden of Cross House, which still stands, next to the post office, on the village green.

But tradition has it that Cross House was also a meeting-place for Jacobite conspirators before the 1715 rising in favour of Lord Derwentwater's childhood companion, James II's son James Edward Stuart, the Old Pretender. Lord Derwentwater was deeply involved in this rising. Indeed, before it broke out, George I's government, suspecting his Jacobite sympathies, tried to arrest him. However, such was the young earl's popularity with his tenants that they warned him in good time and enabled him to go safely into hiding.

Sadly, the government caught up with him after the Jacobites' disastrous defeat at Preston. He was taken prisoner and, with other leaders of the rising, held in the Tower of London. His devoted wife made desperate attempts to have him freed. She and other ladies were even introduced into George I's bedchamber, where they begged the king for mercy. But it was to no avail. The 26-year-old earl was executed at Tower Hill on February 24, 1716.

Stamfordham centres on a huge village green, which has long rows of well-proportioned 18th and early 19th-century houses. As in many other northern villages, the green once had a defensive role: it could be stockaded against Border raiders who were a constant threat in these parts. As late as 1522, a nightly vigil was maintained at the village, by order of the Watch upon the Middle Marches – the Middle Marches being this section of the border with Scotland.

Later, in more peaceful times, the threat to order came from drovers, who, having sold their animals, enjoyed too much of the local hospitality. The village jail and lock-up, where they would be held, still stands in the middle of the green. Near by is the market cross – in fact, an arched shelter – built in 1735 by Sir Edward Swinburne of Capheaton Hall. Sir Edward was the ancestor of the 19th-century poet Algernon Charles Swinburne, who frequently visited Capheaton and knew the area well. Stamfordham has a neat, whitewashed pub called the Swinburne Arms.

On the edge of the village, St Mary's churchyard commands a beautiful view up the Tyne valley, across green rolling countryside which is dominated by the line of Hadrian's Wall. The porch has a memorial to Arthur Bigge, Lord Stamfordham. He was the son of one of Stamfordham's vicars and served as private secretary to both Queen Victoria and her grandson George V.

LEYBURN

NORTH YORKSHIRE

10 miles south-west of Richmond (PAGE 311 Be)

In the late 1930s an up-and-coming vet named James Alfred Wight came to work in North Yorkshire. One of his partners lived in Leyburn, and Wight often visited him here, learning from him to love the bleak but magical countryside of Wensleydale and the North Yorkshire moors.

Some 30 years later, when, as James Herriot, he came to write his best-selling semi-autobiographical sketches, Leyburn was one of the four places on which he based his fictional market town of Darrowby. The other three were Richmond, Thirsk and Middleham. Herriot has spoken warmly of the town: 'Leyburn has a thousand happy associations for me. Architecturally, it is not a glamorous place but its situation is exciting . . . That windswept little town on the hillside can fix you up with everything you want from groceries, home-baked pastries and butcher meat to wearing apparel for both sexes.'

Leyburn lies at the foot of Wensleydale, and its spacious Market Place really comes alive on Fridays, when farmers and their wives and other shoppers from all around the dale and its side valleys come by bus or car to buy and sell all manner of goods. In one corner stands the former Town Hall, a sober, mid-Victorian building, now an ironmonger's shop.

The town has two churches. One is the Anglican Church of St Matthew, which has a battlemented tower built in 1868, in St Matthew's Terrace, off Market Place. The other is the Catholic Church of St Peter and St Paul, on the road to Richmond. Dating from 1835, it has an imposing west gallery and fine stained glass in the east window.

Just off Market Place is the bay-windowed Thornborough Hall, built in Georgian times but considerably altered in 1863. It stands on the site of a house in which lived Father John Huddleston, the priest who is generally believed to have admitted Charles II to the Catholic Church shortly before his death in 1685. The hall now houses the district council offices, the magistrate's court and the public library. Its pleasant, well-tended gardens are open to the public.

Mary, Queen of Scots, imprisoned in Bolton Castle, 5½ miles to the north-west, escaped through a window in the summer of 1568. But her freedom was short-lived. According to a local story she was recaptured on Leyburn Shawl, a steep limestone ridge above the top of the town, and the place was so named because she dropped her shawl while trying to escape.

A tree-lined footpath runs from Leyburn's Market Place along the Shawl, from which there are superb views of Wensleydale and the flat-topped uplands of Wether Fell, Addleborough and Pen Hill.

• **Parking** Market Place (car park); Market Place • **Early closing** Wednesday • **Market day** Friday • **Event** Wensleydale Show (August) • **Information** TEL. Wensleydale 23069 (summer) • **AA 24 hour service** TEL. Stockton-on-Tees 607215.

Askrigg NORTH YORKSHIRE

12 miles west of Leyburn (PAGE 311 Ae)

Lovers of the James Herriot stories will already know Askrigg, which was the setting for the TV series based on his books about vets working in the Dales. Here, opposite 'Darrowby' market cross, is the solid, early 19th-century 'Skeldale House', home and surgery of Siegfried Farnon, MRCVS. In real life, it is a home for the elderly, but the village is still much as it would have been when young Herriot learnt his profession among the dour Dalesfolk. Its tightly packed houses wind up the main street in unbroken lines, with the wild moors forming a backdrop.

Askrigg's 17th and 18th-century houses reflect its days of glory as the chief town in Upper Wensleydale. The work of its three clockmakers – Mark Metcalfe, James Ogden and Christopher Caygill – was famed throughout the north. At one time all parts of an Askrigg clock – weights, chimes, face, works and case – were made in and around the village. Examples can be seen in the Upper Dales Folk Museum at Hawes, 5 miles to the west.

The village was also a bustling market, with two annual fairs for which Queen Elizabeth granted a charter in 1587. Cattle, horses, sheep and pigs filled the streets, while packhorses brought in the products of the Dales hand-knitting industry. The King's Arms coaching inn dates from 1767, built by John Pratt, a local man who made a fortune as a Newmarket jockey.

St Oswald's Church, overlooking the market square, is the 'Cathedral of Wensleydale', dating from the late 15th and early 16th centuries. Many of its gravestones proudly bear the occupation as well as the names of former village residents – clockmaker, hosier and even 'honest attorney'.

A once-popular event in Askrigg, which died out within living memory, was an annual fell race over a stiff local course. The winner received a large garland of flowers, bought from the income derived from the rent of a field on the Swaledale road still known as Garland Hill. The race was said to have been founded by a jilted local woman for the perpetual punishment of the men of Wensleydale.

A short walk from Askrigg (signposted from the market square) leads to Mill Gill Force, a beautiful, slender waterfall tumbling over bare rocks in a leafy glade. It became a popular beauty spot in Victorian times, and ladies in crinolines would walk there from Askrigg station, no doubt negotiating the narrow stiles with great difficulty.

Mill Gill's waters once powered the wheels of three mills; the top one, passed on the way to the waterfall, was a corn mill; the middle one was first a cotton and then a flax mill; and the lower one was a woollen mill. This one is now a hostel for disabled youngsters and those from deprived backgrounds, who can experience the delights of the Dales. The other two mills are now houses.

East Witton NORTH YORKSHIRE

4 miles south-east of Leyburn (PAGE 311 Bf)

East Witton casts a spell which could mean your staying in the village forever. According to an old local saying:

> *'Whoever eats Hammer nuts and drinks Diana's water*
> *Will never leave Witton town while he has a rag or tatter.'*

Hammer nuts are the hazelnuts which grew in profusion in Hammer Woods, part of the forests which once surrounded the area. Diana's water used to come from a spring called Diana's Well – named, it is said, by the Romans who hunted boar and deer near by.

Nowadays, Diana's water comes from a fountain set in a great boulder on the village green. The boulder was dragged here in 1859 by a team of 16 horses from a field a quarter of a mile away, where it had been deposited by an ancient glacier. Water from a well above the village was piped to it to form what was once the village's main supply.

Reluctance to leave East Witton is understandable. Its original heather-thatched cottages were built around a large green as a defence against raiding Scots. Livestock would be herded here in times of danger, while the houses formed a defensive stockade. The green was the site of a fair and market for 250 years until 1563, when a plague struck Wensleydale and put an end to the custom.

The historic pattern of the village was retained when Thomas, Earl of Ailesbury, rebuilt it totally at the start of the 19th century as what we see now: plain but elegant cottages in local sandstone, harmonising perfectly and free from through-traffic, which uses the main road to the east. The combined grocer's, butcher's and post office is a fine example of an old-style village shop, little changed since Georgian times and retaining its old butcher's sign.

East Witton's Church of St John the Evangelist was also built by the Earl of Ailesbury, in elegant Gothic style in 1809. An extensive inscription on the tower rejoices in the long reign of George III (1760 – 1820). From the churchyard there are fine views across Lower Wensleydale.

About 1½ miles east of the village are the ruins of Jervaulx Abbey. This Cistercian house was probably originally founded in Fors in Upper Wensleydale, in the mid-1140s; but an inhospitable climate and the ravages of wolves forced the brothers to seek a more favourable place. So in 1156 they came to Jervaulx – Norman-French for Urevale, the valley of the River Ure.

The abbey ruins, in fine parkland surrounding Jervaulx Hall, are in private hands but open daily. They date from the 12th to 15th centuries and are notable for fine arches and walls, windows, remnants of cloisters and tombstones. They are particularly beautiful in spring when many of the walls are hung with purple aubrietia and the wild flowers which are allowed to flourish are coming into bloom.

West Burton NORTH YORKSHIRE

7 miles south-west of Leyburn (PAGE 311 Bf)

When a Quaker preacher named Samuel Watson tried to address a meeting at West Burton in 1660, 'one wicked fellow with a great staff and pistol threatened to lodge a brace of bullets in his belly . . . and knocked him down so that he was thought to be killed, but afterwards he was put in the stocks and thrown in the river'. Or so a local story goes.

The stocks stand on a great, elongated green that bisects the village, deep in Dale country. Greystone houses and cottages line both sides of the huge green, which slopes upwards a good quarter of a mile from east to west.

The growth of the wool trade in medieval times was such that by 1301 there were wool-combers, dyers and hand-knitters busily at work in West Burton, and the green became the setting for regular market fairs that flourished until the start of this century. It was also a source of the famous Wensleydale cheese, made originally by the monks of Jervaulx Abbey, about 12 miles to the east.

At the heart of the village green is a spire cross, built in 1820 and restored in 1898. An inn on the green served its last pint in the 1930s and is now a substantial house – a stone mounting block for customers arriving on horseback can be seen near the door. However, the Fox and Hounds, just across the road, is still thriving. The smith also worked on the green: the back of his stone smithy now shelters waiting bus passengers.

The clear waters of Walden Beck, tumbling past wooded banks to the pretty Cauldron Falls, once powered a woollen mill at the bottom end of the village. At the beginning of the century the mill was converted into an electricity generator – and in the 1930s it became a factory for making Wensleydale cheese. Now it is a private house, and just behind it a narrow packhorse bridge crosses the beck, leading the way to Flanders Hall, an imposing gabled stone house that was the local manor.

The village was mentioned in Domesday Book as Borton ('owner at the time of St Edward the Confessor, Turchill . . . owner in 1083, Gosfrid . . . acres liable to taxes, 360 . . .'). Among several large houses and

Looking into West Burton

The Grange

HEADING FOR THE FALLS

Stocks stand beside an elegant spire cross midway down West Burton's long, sloping green; the house near by was once an inn. The pretty Cauldron Falls, a local attraction, are at the east end of the village, as is a fine Georgian house, The Grange.

The green – with spire cross and stocks

Cauldron Falls

buildings is Galloway House, originally seven cottages but converted about 1900, when its battlemented mini-tower was added. Near by are the Victorian Wesleyan Methodist chapel and village school, facing each other across the green, and a house that started life as a stable block in the middle of the 19th century. It has some stones dated 1702 which were taken from another building, and the weathercock on its windowless gable end was rescued from an earlier market cross that stood on the green.

Sheep and cattle are still raised around West Burton, which lies near where the valley of Walden Beck joins Wensleydale. Dry-stone walls pattern the hills which rise protectively around the village.

Richmond Castle above the River Swale

Market Place

THE FORTRESS OF ALUN THE RED

The once mighty walls of Richmond Castle were built in 1071 to protect the fortress's owner, the Norman warrior Alun the Red, from attack by the English or the Danes. But his proud new castle was not put to the test—the attacks never came and warfare passed the stronghold by. The town's Market Place is busy and full of colour. Shoppers throng the stalls, while in the background a cricket match runs its quiet course. Off the Market Place is the Georgian Theatre Royal, where such famous players as Edmund Kean, Roger Kemble and Mrs Siddons once trod the boards.

RICHMOND

NORTH YORKSHIRE

12 miles south-west of Darlington (PAGE 311 Be)

Set on the banks of the River Swale and at the eastern entrance to Swaledale, Richmond is a fascinating mixture of gracious main streets, narrow twisting lanes, handsome town houses and pretty cottages. It grew around a castle and a market. The castle was started by the Normans and took some 200 years to complete. By the 16th century it had fallen into ruins, but its massive keep and substantial parts of the curtain-walls and towers survive, on a bend in the Swale, looking out splendidly over the town and surrounding countryside.

The market was established in the 12th century, and a cobbled Market Place, just below the castle, is still the town's centre. It is flanked by attractive Georgian and Victorian buildings. On the south side is the Town Hall, built in 1756, and on the north side is the early 18th-century King's Head Hotel. A 65 ft high pillar called The Obelisk was put up in 1771 to replace a 15th-century stone market cross.

Rising in the centre of Market Place near The Obelisk is one of the oddest church buildings in England. Holy Trinity Church was founded in the 12th century by the Normans, and, as well as being a church, it has served a number of other purposes. On occasion it has been an assize court, prison, school, warehouse and granary. Until it finally ceased to be a church in 1971, it also had a shop in a lower floor beneath the north aisle. The building now houses the headquarters and museum of the Green Howards regiment. The museum is open to the public, except in December and January and certain days in February, March and November.

The Green Howards also have a memorial chapel in the parish church of St Mary, which was built outside the old town walls in the 12th century. This church was restored in 1859–60 by the Victorian architect Sir Gilbert Scott. In Queens Road is a tall, elegant 15th-century tower called Greyfriars – all that remains of a church founded by the Franciscan friars in the 13th century.

In Ryder's Wynd is the Richmondshire Museum, open from the end of May to October. As well as being a museum of local history, it has the surgery sets from the BBC TV series *All Creatures Great and Small*, based on the James Herriot stories (see Askrigg, page 317).

Standing out against a background of trees, on the west side of the town, is the Gothic-style Culloden Tower, which can be seen from the castle. The tower was built by the local Yorke family shortly after the Battle of Culloden in 1746. One of the Yorkes helped to defeat Prince Charles Edward Stuart on Culloden Moor, and the family built the tower to mark his safe return home.

The jewel of Richmond is the delightful little Georgian Theatre Royal, built in 1788 and restored in 1962. The auditorium is small, ornate and intimate. The original staircases, boxes, gallery, pit and ticket office are still in use – and the audience is seated close to the little stage. As well as plays and musicals, audiences can also hear recitals by prominent musicians. A small theatrical museum in the same building includes among its exhibits a complete set of painted stage scenery dating from 1836 – believed to be

Inside the Georgian Theatre Royal

the oldest and largest set still to be found in Britain.

Above the Darlington road is Hill House. This was the home of Frances I'Anson, heroine of the song *The Lass of Richmond Hill*. In 1785 she was wooed and won by Leonard MacNally, who wrote the words of the song and took her to the other Richmond, in Surrey.

Charles Lutwidge Dodgson (1832–98), better known as Lewis Carroll, the author of *Alice's Adventures in Wonderland*, spent part of his childhood in Richmond. His father was its archdeacon, and the young Dodgson attended the grammar school from 1844 to 1846. The school's headmaster sent the archdeacon a perceptive report on the boy who was to become an Oxford maths don and author: 'You must not entrust your son with a full knowledge of his superiority over other boys. Let him discover this as he proceeds. The love of excellence is far beyond the love of excelling.'

• **Parking** Hurgill Road; Victoria Road; The Green (car parks). Disc parking in town centre (discs free from tourist information centre) • **Early closing** Wednesday • **Market day** Saturday • **Theatre** Georgian Theatre Royal, Victoria Road • **Event** Richmond Meet (Spring Bank Holiday Weekend) • **Information** TEL. Richmond 3525 (summer) • **AA 24 hour service** TEL. Stockton-on-Tees 607215.

Gunnerside NORTH YORKSHIRE

17 miles west of Richmond (PAGE 311 Ae)

The Norsemen gave Gunnerside its name – it means gunnar's, or warrior's, pasture – well illustrated by the imposing sign outside the Old King's Head pub, showing a fearsome horn-helmeted axeman. Some of the local farmhouses are built in the style of Norse longhouses – reminders of the first inhabitants who arrived in the early 10th century.

But mining and Methodism formed the character of the village as it is now. Lead has been mined from Roman times, and at the beginning of the last century as many as 2000 men and boys worked in the industry centred around Gunnerside. Conditions were hard, with a life expectancy for a miner of only 46 years.

The industry collapsed with the import of cheap Spanish and South American lead in the 19th century, but the scars remain. Follow the path which runs from the village centre along the right-hand side of Gunnerside Beck to Gunnerside Gill. All around this steep ravine is dramatic evidence of centuries of labour – the remains of crushing floors, storage areas, entrances to old workings, spoil tips and, at the top of the valley, a great peat store and a smelt mill near by. All bear witness to the scale of activity, as do the deep grooves or 'hushes' cut into the hillsides by the action of artificially formed watercourses. These washed away the earth to reveal the veins of lead.

Several smaller, scattered buildings and farmhouses above Gunnerside were originally miners' cottages, their owners combining farming with partnership in small independent groups which would bid for mining rights. Many of the cottages around the sloping village green also belonged to miners. There is a prosaic reason behind their picturesque siting – a need to cling to natural shelves well above the unpredictable waters of the Swale, Britain's fastest-flowing river.

Swaledale people were great self-improvers and Methodism flourished in the valley, which was left to its own devices by the established Church. John Wesley was an occasional and welcome visitor. Gunnerside's fine Methodist chapel, built in 1789 at a cost of £600, was rebuilt in 1866 in plain, simple style in keeping with its users' characters. About a mile west of Gunnerside, at Ivelet, stands a small hump-backed bridge across the Swale, which is regarded as the most beautiful of the Dale's packhorse bridges.

Muker NORTH YORKSHIRE

20 miles west of Richmond (PAGE 311 Ae)

A plaque on the wall of Muker's 300-year-old schoolhouse commemorates a true story as fascinating as any Swaledale legend. It records that the distinguished naturalists Richard and Cherry Kearton were pupils here in the 1870s. Richard (1862–1928) was crippled as a result of a childhood accident. But he took what work he could, and as a young man managed to act as a beater for grouse shoots on the local moors.

A London publisher, up for a shoot, was amazed by the youth's knowledge and love of natural history, and offered him a job in his company. Richard accepted and before long was writing natural history books, illustrating them with his own and Cherry's photographs, which were unique in their close-up detail. The brothers became world renowned as writers, photographers and later as broadcasters, and Richard became a friend of the American President Theodore 'Teddy' Roosevelt.

Odd names as well as famous ones are Muker's speciality. Once, so many people shared the same surnames in this remote area that they had to be

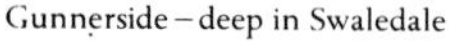

Gunnerside – deep in Swaledale

Packhorse bridge at Ivelet

Stone cottages in Gunnerside

THE HAUNT OF THE HEADLESS DOG

Until the 19th century, ponies carried lead from local mines across a packhorse bridge over the River Swale, where it flows through a little wooded ravine at Ivelet. The bridge has a corpse stone on which coffins were rested while being taken to consecrated ground, and according to legend is haunted by a headless dog. Gunnerside lies amid a patchwork of green fields, deep in Swaledale.

identified by bizarre nicknames – Tripy Tom, Moor Close Jamie, Bill Up T'Steps and Rough and Strong Metcalfe.

Muker – pronounced 'Mewker' and meaning 'narrow field' – has one of Britain's few parish churches built during the reign of Elizabeth I, in 1580. Originally thatched with heather, it was welcomed by the poor Dalesfolk who, to bury their dead in consecrated ground, previously had to carry bodies in wicker coffins to Grinton, 10 miles east. The path the mourners took still exists as a bridleway over Kisdon Hill (1636 ft) which looms above the village.

The church, dedicated to St Mary the Virgin, was largely restored in 1890, and combines with a scatter of cottages, the 'Literary Institute' public hall, post office and Farmer's Arms pub, to form one of the most harmonious-looking of Swaledale villages.

The Keartons' school, founded in 1679 and now a crafts centre, has curious Gothic-arched windows. A sundial on an adjoining cottage which was once the schoolmaster's house grimly warns in Latin: '*mox nox*' – 'it will soon be night'. A stone bridge crosses the Muker Beck, which flows through the village on its way to the Swale.

Every autumn, Muker holds a famous show of Swaledale sheep, the hardy, black-faced animal that is the symbol of the Yorkshire Dales National Park. Prize specimens change hands for thousands of pounds. Their wool is tough and wiry to withstand the harsh Pennine winter, and has traditionally been used for carpets because of its hard-wearing qualities. Recently it has become fashionable for sweaters, and a Swaledale woollens shop has opened in Muker – a happy echo of the days when the area was a hand-knitting centre.

Reeth NORTH YORKSHIRE

11 miles west of Richmond (PAGE 311 Be)

The road from Richmond to Reeth has been called the most beautiful in England, and Reeth itself is an imposing place, set at the junction of Swaledale and Arkengarthdale, with a large, sloping village green and solid Georgian houses, as befits the 'capital' of the area.

A line of 18th-century shops, cafes and inns, including the King's Arms and Black Bull, form High Row, which overlooks the green. To the north is the handsomely proportioned Burgoyne Hotel. The view from the green, looking down the valley towards Grinton and Fremington Edge, is magnificent.

The green once had a strictly functional purpose. Phillip, Lord Wharton, was granted a charter to hold fairs in 1695, and no fewer than seven fairs a year – two for cattle sales – together with a weekly market, were

High Row, Reeth

Wee Cottage, Reeth

NO FRILLS – JUST REETH

The forthright stone buildings of Reeth reflect the tastes of a simple and hardy people with little time for unnecessary decoration. Even so, flowers provide a splash of colour outside the Kings Arms in High Row and homes such as Wee Cottage. The neighbouring village of Healaugh lies on a hillside, a mile away.

Healaugh, on its hillside

held on it over the next two centuries. The founder, one of a Nonconformist family of land and mine owners, is remembered for presenting 'Wharton Bibles' to children who had learnt parts of the Psalms.

The fairs declined with the collapse of lead mining in the area by the mid-1860s, and the population fell by two-thirds. Most of the houses around the green or in the quiet back courts and lanes hark back to the great days of the mines.

The old miller's house in the north-east corner of the village uses millstones as lintels, and the former Methodist Sunday School now contains the Swaledale Folk Museum – open daily in the summer – which displays relics of the lead industry.

Quaker Lane leads from the south-west corner to a beautiful little iron suspension bridge over the Swale. In the lane is the site of a school built in 1787 by three Quaker brothers, George, Leonard and John Raw. And the county primary school, on the Gunnerside road, is known as The Friends' School. Fine 18th-century Wesleyan and Congregational chapels confirm the strong Nonconformist tradition of the area.

The village of Healaugh, a mile west on a hillside above the Swale, is a compact cluster of stone cottages around quiet back lanes and gardens overlooking the river and the fells beyond. In the 13th and 14th centuries there was a hunting lodge here, for the region was famous for its red deer, wild boar and wolves. Lord Wharton gave his deer-hunting lodge at Smarber, to the west of the village, for the Dissenters to worship in. Each August a pilgrimage celebrates the start of Nonconformism in the Dale.

MAP 29

MONASTIC SPLENDOURS AND THE CRUMBLING COAST

In winter, North Sea gales lash this exposed coast, tearing great slabs of rock from the soft, red-grey cliffs. But summer visitors rarely feel the sea's full fury, and ancient fishing ports are restful holiday havens. Vikings pillaged here, then settled – forebears of the men who braved the northern oceans in pursuit of the whale. And here Captain Cook learnt seacraft. Inland, countless sheep grazed the rich pastures in medieval times. They brought wealth to their owners, who have left a legacy of magnificent churches and the inspiring ruins of Whitby and Rievaulx abbeys.

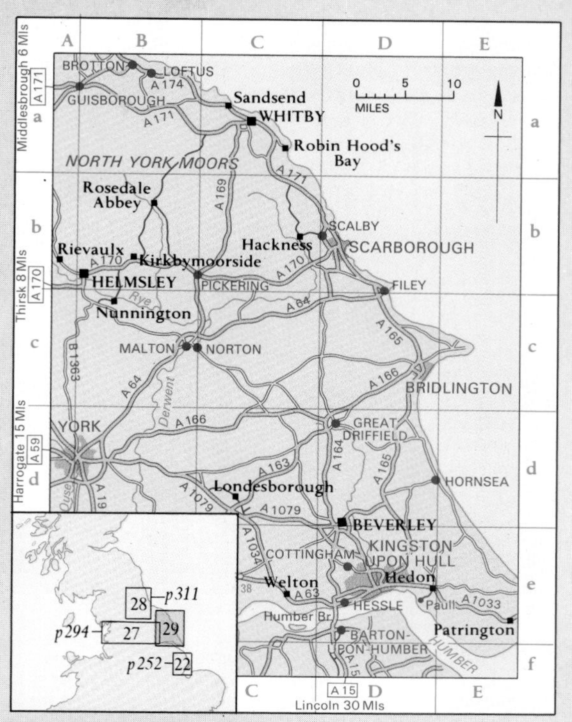

MAP 29: NEIGHBOURING AREAS – MAPS 22, 27, 28

BEVERLEY	HELMSLEY	WHITBY
Hedon	Kirkbymoorside	Hackness
Londesborough	Nunnington	Robin Hood's Bay
Patrington	Rievaulx	Rosedale Abbey
Welton		Sandsend

BEVERLEY

HUMBERSIDE

8 miles north of Hull (PAGE 325 Dd/e)

Two magnificent churches – the twin-towered Minster and the parish church of St Mary – stand one at either end of this pretty market town. Beverley Minster was founded in the early 10th century, partly as a shrine to St John of Beverley, who some 250 years before had built the Church of St John the Evangelist. This church was destroyed, as were others that replaced it – probably by the Danes. The present Minster – the fourth to be built on the site – was begun about 1220 and completed some 200 years later.

A stone slab in the middle of the Minster marks John of Beverley's tomb. Another monument to the saint is the 7 ton Great John bell, hung in the south tower in 1902. A Saxon stone seat, named The Fridstol, stands to the north of the altar. Chief among the Minster's monuments is one at the east end dating from about 1365 with an elaborately carved canopy. It is to Lady Idonea, wife of the 2nd Lord Percy – a member of the family which almost ruled northern England in the Middle Ages. The Minster is at the southern end of Beverley, and north of its superbly carved west door is the old part of the town, with its profusion of red-tiled roofs.

To the north of these is St Mary's Church, built in the 12th to 16th centuries with the backing of the town's rich medieval guilds. The chancel ceiling has panels showing the kings of England up to Henry VI (1422 – 71). The central pinnacled tower and nave were restored in the 16th century after the original tower had collapsed, killing a number of worshippers.

St Mary's stands below the North Bar. This is the sole survivor of five ancient gateways to the town, and was built in 1409 of local brick. Attached to it is Bar House, dating from the 17th century, where Charles I and his sons – the future Charles II and James II – stayed when besieging nearby Hull in 1642. The house was altered in the 18th and 19th centuries.

Above the gate is North Bar Without, cobbled on one side. It has many handsome town houses of the 18th and early 19th centuries. Leading farther north again is New Walk, with an attractive row of chestnut trees. Here stands the 19th-century Sessions House – a law court – crowned by a figure of Justice.

Below the gate is North Bar Within, lined by elegant Georgian houses. It also has the Beverley Arms hotel, which was rebuilt in 1794 on the site of an earlier inn. It appears as the Percy Standard in Anthony Trollope's novel *Ralph the Heir*, published in 1871.

The commercial centre of Beverley lies between its two medieval markets: Saturday Market in the north of the town and Wednesday Market in the south. They are linked by two winding pedestrian streets – Toll Gavel and Butcher Row. Just off Toll Gavel is the old Guildhall, largely built in 1762.

Saturday Market is where townsfolk used to exchange and sell their wares. It has an early 18th-century Market Cross decorated with shields bearing the arms of Queen Anne, Beverley Borough and two local families, the Whartons and Hothams, who helped to pay for the cross. Wednesday Market was where merchants from London sold their wares. Near by, in

FROM PILGRIMS TO PUNTERS

In the Middle Ages, the market town of Beverley was a place of pilgrimage, to the tomb of St John of Beverley. In the 8th century, he founded a forerunner of the present magnificent Minster. The church is a Gothic masterpiece inside and out. It soars above ancient streets lined with many attractive houses. Today's successors to the pilgrims are the followers of horse racing, who flock to Beverley Racecourse, known throughout the North as 'the friendly course'.

Lairgate

Inside the Minster

Beverley Minster from St Mary's

Lairgate, is The Hall, built as a mansion house in about 1760. Its drawing room has a ceiling decorated with musical motifs, and the hand-painted wallpaper came from China in the late 18th century. The building is now council offices and the Chinese Room can be viewed by appointment. Altogether Beverley has some 350 buildings of historical or architectural interest, including Ann Routh's Almshouses, in Keldgate, built in 1749 'for 12 . . . poor old women' – although they now house more people.

Beverley has its own green belt – Beverley Pastures – which surrounds three sides of the town and covers 2 square miles. The largest pasture is Westwood, on which is the local golf course. Set high above the town is Beverley Racecourse, where there has been horse racing since 1762.

• **Parking** Butcher Row; Morton Lane; Saturday Market; Grayburn Lane; School Lane; Princes Gardens; Minster Moorgate; Flemingate (all car parks) • **Early closing** Thursday • **Market days** Wednesday, Saturday • **Cinema** The Picture Playhouse, Saturday Market • **Events** Folk Festival (June); Walkington Victorian Hayride (June); Carnival (July) • **Information** TEL. Hull 867430, 882255 • **AA 24 hour service** TEL. Hull 28580.

Hedon HUMBERSIDE

14 miles south-east of Beverley (PAGE 325 De)

Though now 2 miles from the sea, Hedon was once a flourishing port on the Humber estuary. But when the port silted up, and the rich and influential de la Pole family, along with traders and bankers, decided in the 14th century to take their trade to the new port of Hull, Hedon declined.

However, traces of its former glory can still be seen. The late 17th-century stone-built Town Hall, on St Augustine's Gate, has a Neoclassical façade and a coat of arms over its elegant front door. The long main street, with its Market Place and large number of inns, also suggests headier days.

The vast parish church of St Augustine boasts cathedral-like dimensions. It is 165 ft long and has a massive 128 ft tower built using funds raised from town burgesses in 1428. Much of the church is older, built in the 13th and 14th centuries when Hedon's prosperity was at its height. Cruciform in plan, with fine traceried windows and a wealth of decorative detail, St Augustine's is a landmark for miles.

In the garden of Holyrood House (now a home for the elderly) in Baxtergate stands the Kilnsea Cross – tall, weather-worn and medieval, with what was once an elaborately carved head, now unfortunately rubbed almost smooth by the ages. The cross was originally erected near by at Ravenser on Spurn Head, where Henry Bolingbroke, the exiled son of John of Gaunt, landed in 1399 to oust his cousin Richard II and become Henry IV. Ravenser was later washed away by the sea and the cross disappeared with it – only to be washed up again in 1818 on the beach near Kilnsea, 16 miles south-east of Hedon, and re-erected.

To the north of the church, only a few yards away from the main street, is Hedon's quiet green, overlooked by the magnificent north front of St Augustine's, and surrounded by comfortable houses and large, walled gardens. Many of the streets in Hedon have names recalling its medieval origin – Baxtergate, Distaff Lane and Fletcher Gate, once Flecherman's (meaning Butcher's) Gate.

By the grey-brown choppy Humber, 2 miles south-west of Hedon, lies Paull, an unpretentious former fishing community. At the end of the village, a 19th-century lighthouse building has been converted into a row of unusual cottages. The beautiful 15th-century church lies somewhat apart from the village, in open fields.

Londesborough HUMBERSIDE

13 miles west of Beverley (PAGE 325 Cd)

The quiet village of Londesborough, on the edge of Yorkshire's rolling chalk wolds, has no through road and only one bus service a week, but it has close links with some of the most illustrious names in English history. Among these were the Cliffords, who owned Londesborough for nearly two centuries.

During the Wars of the Roses, the notorious Lord 'Butcher' Clifford was killed by a stray arrow (see Brough, page 283) and his widow, Margaret, who is buried in Londesborough church, secretly brought their seven-year-old son to the village. According to local stories, he was brought up here as a shepherd's son to keep his identity hidden from his father's enemies; when young Henry Clifford came of age and inherited the family estates, following the accession of Henry VII in 1485, he was still known as 'The Shepherd Lord'.

The estate eventually passed to the Boyle family, Earls of Burlington. Richard, the 1st Earl, was a friend of Charles I, and his great-grandson, Richard Boyle, the 3rd Earl, was an influential figure in 18th-century England. A distinguished architect, he designed the Assembly Rooms at York and improved Burlington House in Piccadilly, London, which now houses the Royal Academy of Arts. Among his friends were the poet Alexander Pope and the actor David Garrick, who was a frequent visitor to Londesborough. Burlington may have laid an avenue of elms in the park to Garrick's memory; he certainly landscaped and laid out all the gardens and parkland. He also rebuilt the Elizabethan Hall, but it fell into decay and was demolished by a later owner, the 6th Duke of Devonshire, in the early 19th century.

In 1845 Londesborough was bought by George Hudson, who was known as 'The Railway King'. He wanted the estate just to block a rival railway scheme. He built his own private railway station on the now-vanished line from York to Hull via Market Weighton, with a tree-lined drive, which can still be traced, direct from Londesborough Hall.

Londesborough Park, as the hall is now known, was originally a hunting lodge built for the Dukes of Devonshire in 1839 and extended in the Victorian 'baronial' style in 1874. A public right of way goes through the park, and a prominent planting of trees on nearby hilltops, known as Londesborough Clumps, is visible across the Humber.

Most of the cottages in the village belong to the 5000 acre estate and date from the 18th and 19th centuries. The Burlington stable block survives, as does a group of almshouses built between 1677 and 1678 by the 1st Earl of Burlington for six men and six women. One of the most unusual village buildings is the

Concert Hall, originally the estate laundry, which is now used for village events. Two German prisoners billeted here during the Second World War painted the walls with murals, on historic themes, using brushes made out of their hair.

Hanging in the Church of All Saints are three frail, faded banners and two gauntlets carried at the funerals of the Earls of Burlington, many of whom lie in the family vault below. It is said that in 1809 when workmen broke into the 3rd Earl's tomb and opened the coffin, his features were perfectly preserved, but vanished in moments after contact with the air.

Patrington HUMBERSIDE

23 miles south-east of Beverley (PAGE 325 Ee)

'It sails like a galleon of stone over the wide, flat expanse of Holderness.' So wrote the late Sir John Betjeman, Poet Laureate from 1972 to 1984, about St Patrick's Church, Patrington. Known as 'The Queen of Holderness', the church is generally acknowledged to be one of the finest in England. A building of pale stone, and in perfect proportion, its graceful spire is visible for miles across the arable countryside around.

But how did such an architectural masterpiece, built in the 13th to 14th centuries, come to be in this quiet, Humberside village? One reason is that, from Saxon times until the Reformation, the lords of the manor at Patrington were the powerful Archbishops of York.

Another reason for the church's size and splendour is that Patrington used to be an important market town, with a weekly market and an annual two-day fair. It stood on the road from the once-flourishing medieval port of Ravenspurn and the coastal towns of Frismarck and Therlesthorp. All three towns, however, were swept away by the ever-encroaching North Sea long before Hull became Humberside's major port, and Patrington declined in importance as a result.

St Patrick's stands on the site of earlier churches but work on the present one began in 1310. Then progress was halted in 1349 because of the terrible effects of the Black Death, and it was another 50 years or so before men and money were available for work to continue. Fortunately, the later builders carried on in the same style, creating a marvellous sense of unity. The moment you step inside, the feeling of space is overwhelming. Unusually for a parish church, there are double aisles in both the nave and the twin

A MASTER'S TOUCH

Robert of Patrington, master mason at York Minster in 1369, may have had a hand in building Patrington's splendid Church of St Patrick, with the help of his sons Ralph and Robert. Carvings here and at York have many similar features. The east window behind the altar is a masterpiece of delicate stone tracery, while carved human heads between the arches add a lighter air.

The east window

Human touch

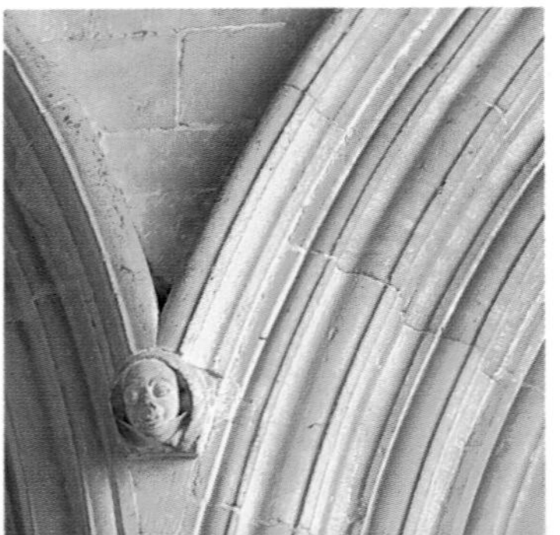

St Patrick's Church

transepts, and the window tracery is particularly elegant. There is a beautifully carved 14th-century font and a Jacobean pulpit.

If the village has little to match the glory of its church, the cheerful, locally made red brick gives a pleasing appearance to many of the roadside cottages, and the 18th-century Holderness Inn recalls the village's former importance. Just over a mile away, in the tiny village of Winestead, there is a pleasant house of Tudor origin standing near the main road. This is the birthplace of one of the greatest 17th-century English poets—Andrew Marvell, who was born here, son of the local parson, in 1621.

Welton HUMBERSIDE

11 miles south-west of Beverley (PAGE 325 Ce)

The highwayman Dick Turpin was held under arrest at the Green Dragon inn here, in 1736. He was tried at York Assizes and later hanged. The legendary villain was arrested, however, not for highway robbery but after a drunken evening in which he had shot a game cock and threatened a labourer.

The village is one of the prettiest to be found on the edge of the wolds, with a stream that flows under bridges, past the church and the village green, and then widens to a pond where ducks dabble. The green is graced by scattered trees and a pump dating from the early 19th century. All around the stream and green are attractive houses. Some are particularly fine—such as the imposing Welton Grange, built in 1741 for a Hull merchant, complete with a Venetian window of the latest fashion of the day.

Welton was no rural backwater but a country retreat, where men of taste and fashion could build fine houses and cottages—close enough even in the days of horse and carriage to reach Hull for business.

Welton House, home of a prominent local family, the Raikes, has been demolished, but the lovely 18th-century Welton Lodge remains in Dale Road, as well as the Manor House, Welton Hall, and what is now the brick Memorial Hall, all dating from the late 18th century. A number of pleasant red-brick cottages and a shop give Welton a period flavour which recent additions to the village have not destroyed.

Welton church, dedicated to St Helen, dates from Norman times, but was practically rebuilt in 1862–3 by Sir Giles Gilbert Scott, the Victorian architect who designed London's St Pancras Station. Some earlier work remains, however, and there are some remarkable Pre-Raphaelite windows made by the company set up by the artist-craftsman William Morris and designed by, among others, Morris himself and his associate, the artist Sir Edward Burne-Jones. In the churchyard is the gravestone of Jeremiah Simpson who outlived eight wives and 'died in 1719 in the 84th year of his age'.

Welton High Mill, in Dale Road, is a five-storey building of brick and tiles; the top two storeys were added in 1871 and the lower three are almost certainly Georgian. The mill was driven by a water wheel until 1949 and went on working under electricity until 1966.

A track forming part of the Wolds Way Long Distance Footpath leads from Dales Road into Welton Dale, a beautiful, partially wooded valley. Higher up Welton Dale, just visible from the path but without public access, is the Raikes family mausoleum, a circular, colonnaded building built in 1818.

COUNTRY RETREAT *Brown stone, cut into brick-size blocks, gives a warm appearance to Welton Grange, built in the 18th century as a country retreat for a well-to-do Hull merchant.*

HELMSLEY

NORTH YORKSHIRE

24 miles north of York (PAGE 325 Bb)

Approached from the south or west, across the rolling green plateau of the Hambleton Hills, Helmsley's beautiful position on the edge of the North York Moors is immediately appreciated. It lies on a crook of the River Rye, protected from northerly gales by the wild expanse of the high moors, and yet catching the sun on the orange-scarlet pantiled roofs of its creamy stone buildings. It was a vantage point not lost on the builders of Helmsley Castle.

Much of this imposing semi-ruin dates from the 12th and 13th centuries, including the 13th-century barbican (fortified gate). But the massive keep was added to in the 14th century, and there are fine Tudor domestic buildings which were in use until the early 18th century.

Helmsley itself has a sense of dignity and purpose, and in the spacious market square shops, inns and a sober town hall reflect centuries of peace and prosperity. In the centre of the square stands a monument built in 1867 in memory of the 2nd Lord Feversham, whose family, the Duncombes, bought the Helmsley estate from the heirs of the 2nd Duke of Buckingham in 1708 (see Kirkbymoorside, page 330).

There is a mixture of several styles. Part of the Black Swan Hotel is Georgian, but another part is 16th century and timber-framed in the diagonally braced style more commonly found in Cheshire and Shropshire. The town hall was built in 1901 in 17th-century style. All Saints' Church, behind the square, dates from 1866 but has traces of Norman work taken from an earlier church.

Along Castlegate runs a stream overlooked by quiet cottages and houses, and beyond the church there is another street of attractive houses. Duncombe

DOUBLE DEFENCE *A double ring of ditches encircles the massive raised earthworks on which Helmsley Castle was built. The castle has a fine Tudor Hall with impressive oak panelling.*

Park, just south of the town, is a splendid 18th-century house built for the Duncombes in the style of the Restoration playwright-architect Sir John Vanbrugh (1664 – 1726) and added to in 1843 by the Victorian architect Charles Barry. The magnificent grounds were mostly laid out in the mid-18th century, and a Doric Temple was probably designed by Vanbrugh himself.

• **Parking** Bowling Green Lane (car park) • **Early closing** Wednesday • **Market day** Friday • **Event** Festival (July-August) • **Information** TEL. Helmsley 70401 • **AA 24 hour service** TEL. York 27698.

Kirkbymoorside

NORTH YORKSHIRE

6 miles east of Helmsley (PAGE 325 Bb)

In 1687 George Villiers, 2nd Duke of Buckingham, caught a chill while hunting, and shortly afterwards he died, penniless and alone, in a house in Kirkbymoorside's main street. His name is recorded in the church register: 'Gorges Viluas, Lord Dooke of bockingham.' Thus was the passing of a dazzling author, wit, courtier and politician recorded by the pen of a semi-literate country cleric. Buckingham, a favourite of Charles II, had squandered a fortune inherited from his father, the 1st Duke, and ended up living in poverty at Helmsley Castle (see Helmsley, page 329).

Another name of ill-fortune associated with Kirkbymoorside was that of the Nevills, Earls of Westmorland, who supported the abortive Rising of the North by the Catholic followers of Mary, Queen of Scots in 1569. As a result, their estates were forfeit to the Crown, including Kirkbymoorside Castle, little of which remains. Its stones were probably used as building material, particularly for the Tollbooth, a hall opposite the house where George Villiers died. The Tollbooth dates from the early 18th century, but was rebuilt in 1871 after being destroyed by fire.

The most impressive building in the broad, main street is the Black Swan Inn, dated 1634, with an overhanging, decorative porch. There are a number of fine Georgian and Victorian houses and shops in the street, in Crown Square and in nearby side roads. One of the shops is an unusual chemist's, which was once a pub and still sells wines and spirits and can dispense drinks in a back room.

The wooded valley of Kirkdale (valley of the church), 1½ miles west of the village, takes its name from the little St Gregory's Minster, a late Saxon church with many details unaltered. In the porch is a Saxon sundial with an inscription which, roughly translated, reads: 'Orm, Gamel's son, bought St Gregory's Minster when it was all ruined and fallen down, and he caused it to be built new from the ground in the days of Edward and in the days of Tosti the Earl. This is the day's sun marker at each hour. Haworth made me and Brand, priests.'

A short distance from St Gregory's Minster, across Hodge Beck, is Kirkdale Cave, in a quarry. Discovered in 1821, it contained the bones of many Ice Age animals including hyenas, rhinoceroses, bison and hippopotamuses. The cave can be seen between the limestone beds high up in the quarry face.

Nunnington NORTH YORKSHIRE

6 miles south-east of Helmsley (PAGE 325 Bc)

The quiet village of Nunnington slopes down between the low ridge of Caukley's Bank and the River Rye. Its narrow streets of pantile-roofed stone cottages are contained almost entirely in a rectangle. Above the village stands the church, dating from the 13th and 17th centuries, and below it, by the river, the handsome Nunnington Hall.

The hall dates from both Elizabethan and Stuart times and is remarkable for some of its previous occupants. In the 16th century it was the home of Dr Robert Huicke, doctor to Henry VIII, Edward VI and Elizabeth I. To him fell the unpleasant task of telling Elizabeth I that she would never bear children. Another occupant was Sir Thomas Norcliffe who, at the outbreak of the Civil War, swore loyalty to Charles I in Nunnington Church, and then promptly joined the Parliamentary cause.

The hall was eventually bought by the Graham family in the 17th century. One of them, Richard, was ambassador to France and created Viscount Preston.

ELEGANT RESTRAINT *Outside, Nunnington Hall is a model of 17th-century restraint. Inside, the rooms are hung with fine tapestries.*

After William III's bloodless seizure of the throne, Preston was caught plotting the restoration of James II and was taken to the Tower of London for execution. He was later reprieved after his young daughter had pleaded with Queen Mary for his life.

Preston returned to Nunnington, restored the house and built the charming almshouses that stand close to the hall. He died in 1695 and is buried in the Church of All Saints and St James.

The hall is now owned by the National Trust and open to the public five days a week from April to October. It has a fine south front whose centre is a doorway, and over it a window leading onto a small balcony. Both door and window have elegant classical frames and are crowned by Lord Preston's coat of arms. At the side, gate piers and archways lead to what was once a formal garden. Inside is a panelled hall with an elaborate carved chimneypiece, and there are some 17th-century tapestries from designs by Rubens.

A 17th-century bridge crosses the Rye opposite the hall and 2 miles away is Muscoates Grange, which was the birthplace of the poet and art critic Sir Herbert Read (1893 – 1968), much of whose writing was inspired by the beautiful scenery of Ryedale.

Rievaulx NORTH YORKSHIRE

3 miles north-west of Helmsley (PAGE 325 Ab)

Without its magnificent ruined abbey, Rievaulx would be no more than a pretty but unremarkable village beside the River Rye. The abbey makes it very special; the majestic, roofless shell that remains is a striking testimony to the enterprise and skills of the Cistercian monks who founded it eight centuries ago. They came from France in 1131, to land granted to them by Walter Espec, Lord of Helmsley. The name they gave their foundation, Rievaulx (pronounced 'rivers'), means 'Valley of the Rye'. And they flourished mightily, developing an important farming and industrial community and building a major abbey church.

The abbey was an enormous task for the brother-

CATTLE COUNTRY *Cattle ruminate beneath the gaunt ruins of Rievaulx Abbey, on land where the abbey's huge flocks of sheep grazed between the 12th and 16th centuries.*

SHADES OF THE PAST *From Viking longboats to wooden whalers, in its time Whitby has seen them all. But now the fishing fleet that finds*

hood's stonemasons. To avoid rapids on the River Rye they even built a short canal along which they ferried stone from a quarry near by. The main building was completed in the 12th century, and enlarged in the 13th – at one time the abbey had about 140 monks and 600 lay brothers.

Sheep farming on a grand scale was the community's main commercial enterprise – by the 15th century Rievaulx owned about 12,000 sheep. The monks were also pioneers in iron-making technology. Iron ore mined locally in Ryedale and Bilsdale and brought also from Wakefield was smelted in four furnaces, and there was a forge and a water-powered trip-hammer on the site of the present mill.

Even after the Dissolution of the Monasteries in 1539, iron-making continued in Ryedale and the first blast furnace in Yorkshire was built there in 1576. The furnace was working until 1647, turning out more than 200 tons of iron yearly.

The finest view of the abbey ruin is across landscaped woodland from Rievaulx Terrace, built in 1758 on a hilltop to the east by Thomas Duncombe, of nearby Duncombe Park. The terrace, owned now by the National Trust and open to the public, has a very

shelter among the friendly harbour lights is outnumbered by cheerful yachts and pleasure craft, and the port has become a busy holiday centre.

long lawn and two Neoclassical 'folly' temples.

The village itself is a scatter of handsome stone cottages, one of them thatched – a fairly rare sight in North Yorkshire. They shelter behind dry-stone walls below wooded hills in the lovely Ryedale Valley. The Church of St Mary is the abbey's former gatehouse chapel; though restored, some 13th-century work remains. A three-arched, 18th-century bridge crosses the river about a mile south of Rievaulx.

Harold Wilson, Prime Minister in 1964 – 70 and 1974 – 6 took the title of Lord Wilson of Rievaulx when he became a life peer in 1983.

WHITBY

NORTH YORKSHIRE

20 miles north-west of Scarborough (PAGE 325 Ca)

The 13th-century sandstone ruins of Whitby Abbey loom eerily from a clifftop above this historic fishing port. The abbey was founded in AD 657 by St Hilda for both monks and nuns, but was destroyed by the Danes some 200 years later. After the Norman invasion it was

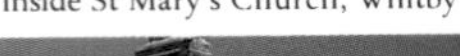

Inside St Mary's Church, Whitby

rebuilt by Benedictines for monks only and then abandoned when Henry VIII dissolved the monasteries in 1539.

The ruins provided one of the sinister settings for Bram Stoker's classic horror novel, *Dracula*, published in 1897. In the book, a schooner carrying Count Dracula and his collection of coffins is driven ashore at Whitby during a fierce storm – and the vampire prepares to start his evil activities in England.

Whitby consists of two towns, the 'old' and the 'new': the River Esk separates them and each has its own lighthouse and pier. The old town sprawls beneath the abbey on the East Cliff. Around its Market Place is a maze of red-roofed houses, narrow winding streets and steep alleyways.

An iron swing bridge, built in 1909, links old Whitby with the new town below the West Cliff. Although built mostly in the 19th century, the area has its share of ancient streets – notably the shopping precinct called Flowergate, which appears in the Domesday Survey of 1086 under its original name, Flore. The scene is overlooked by a life-size statue of the navigator Captain James Cook (1728 – 79), who was born in Marton, Yorkshire (now Cleveland). Cook came to Whitby as an apprentice to a local shipowner named John Walker and for three years he lodged in Walker's house, which stands in Grape Lane in the old town. The three ships which took Cook on his voyages of discovery in the Pacific – *Endeavour*, *Resolution* and *Discovery* – were built in the town. And Whitby Museum, in nearby Pannett Park, has an impressive display devoted to Captain Cook and his exploits.

The museum also commemorates the deeds of another prominent mariner, the whaling captain, William Scoresby (1760 – 1829). In the late 17th and 18th centuries, Whitby was a prosperous whaling port – and Captain Scoresby's haul topped the 500 mark. He also invented the crow's-nest lookout platform, and kept a colourful journal, which can now be seen in the museum.

ALL SHIPSHAPE FOR THE PREACHER

There is a distinct nautical air about the wooden interior of the Church of St Mary, Whitby. Little wonder – it was constructed by local shipbuilders in the 18th century. And they made it as they would have made the 'tween-decks space of the whaling vessels they used to build – with simple elegance enlivened by some artistic touches of decoration. The church is reached by a flight of 199 steps, and has room for 2000 worshippers in box pews and galleries. Appropriately, the pulpit is a three-decker, reached by a sort of companionway.

Steps and cottages, Whitby

An archway made from a whale's jawbone stands near Captain Cook's monument as an added reminder of the town's maritime role. The whaling fleet no longer exists, but Whitby fishermen still put out to sea in their flat-bottom cobles and keel boats.

Whitby's other time-honoured business is producing jewellery made from the ebony-coloured jet – fossilised wood – gathered along the shore or mined locally. Ornaments have been fashioned from local jet since the Bronze Age, but the jewellery reached the peak of its popularity when Queen Victoria wore it during her mourning for Prince Albert. Visitors to the town can also sample another local speciality – herrings smoked over an oak fire to make specially tasty and sharp-smelling kippers.

• **Parking** Church Street (2); New Quay Road (2); Abbey Plain; Cliff Street; Royal Crescent; North Terrace; St Hilda's Terrace Back (all car parks) • **Early closing** Wednesday • **Market day** Saturday • **Theatre** Spa Theatre and Pavilion, off North Terrace • **Events** The Horngarth (eve of Ascension Day); Regatta (August); Folk Week (August) • **Information** TEL. Whitby 602674 • **AA 24 hour service** TEL. Middlesbrough 246832.

Hackness NORTH YORKSHIRE

17 miles south-east of Whitby (PAGE 325 Cb)

Narrow, twisting valleys, some romantically named Deepdale, Troutsdale and Whisper Dale, cut through moor and forest before joining the River Derwent. At their meeting point lies Hackness.

In AD 680 St Hilda, Abbess of Whitby, sent a number of monks and nuns to the village to establish a small monastery. It flourished until AD 867 when it was destroyed by pillaging Danes. The Church of St Peter – one of the oldest on the North York Moors, dating from Anglo-Danish times – contains a Saxon cross with inscriptions in Latin, Anglo-Saxon and Ogam (an ancient Irish alphabet). One reads: 'Blessed Aethelberga, may they always remember thee, dutifully loving thee; may they ask for thee the verdant everlasting rest of the saints, O loving mother apostolic.'

Lady Margaret Hoby, a noted 17th-century diarist, is buried in the church. She was a member of the Hoby family, owners of Hackness Hall in Elizabethan times, and she died in 1633 – her husband was the somewhat morbidly named Sir Thomas Posthumus Hoby. The original house stood near a lake. Both house and estate were bought by a Dutch merchant, John Bempde, and the present hall was built by his grandson, Sir Robert Vanden Bempde Johnstone, in 1795. John Carr of York (1723 – 1807), architect of Harewood House, was responsible for the fine Neoclassical design. In 1910 part of the building burnt down, including the only bathroom – later more than replaced by 12 new ones. Sir Harcourt Johnstone, the 3rd Baronet, was created Baron Derwent and the house remains the seat of the present Lord Derwent.

Hackness is essentially an estate village, with a delightful canalised stream running through under an ornamental bridge, and a pleasant complex of church, school and post office. Near the T-junction are a number of attractive cottages, many of them having aubrietia in their neat gardens giving a bright splash of purple to the valley in spring.

The village is the focal point for a number of walks and forest drives, such as the four through the 3300 acres of Wykeham Moor Forest immediately to the south-west. Forge Valley, 3 miles south of Hackness on the Great Ayton road, is a narrow, thickly wooded gorge, created by melting glaciers in the last Ice Age cutting through the soft boulder clays to what was then Lake Pickering. Until the early 19th century, this proved a major flood hazard in the Vale of Pickering as fast-flowing streams overflowed and burst their way through the gorge. But between 1800 and 1810 a channel 5 miles long – and known as a 'Sea-cut' – was dug by hand to regulate the river and carry overflows straight to the coast north of Scarborough. Taking its name from a forge that once stood at its head, the valley is an attractive area of semi-natural woodland and wildlife. There are numerous parking places and lay-bys, and pleasant walks that follow the pretty banks of the river.

Robin Hood's Bay

NORTH YORKSHIRE

6 miles south-east of Whitby (PAGE 325 Ca)

Smuggling thrived for centuries in Robin Hood's Bay, whose steep, narrow streets and alleyways crowd into a deep ravine in the cliffs. This East Coast fishing village, only accessible by sea or wild moorland road, was the perfect place to land contraband – such as silks, tea and brandy – which was brought over from Holland in small boats under cover of darkness. The goods were then carried south by pack-pony over moorland roads and tracks to the markets in Pickering, Malton and York. It has even been said that in 1800 every resident of the village was involved.

So narrow are the streets and courts of Robin Hood's Bay – or Bay Town as it is known locally – that apparently a roll of silk could be carried from house to house, window to window, right across the village without the smugglers once having to touch the ground. If perchance the excisemen could not be bribed to keep away, and if lookouts proved to be ineffective, running battles would rage with the customs men, both on land and at sea, with local people often helping the smugglers to gain the upper hand and afterwards enjoying a generous share in the booty. No doubt it was this reputation for lawlessness that led to the village being called Robin Hood's Bay rather than any direct connection with the legendary medieval outlaw of Sherwood Forest.

The sea, crashing against the relatively soft cliffs, has played a dramatic part in Bay Town's history. In the early years of the 19th century the village had more than 120 fishermen, mostly operating the traditional cobles – small fishing boats unique to the North Yorkshire, Durham and Northumberland coasts whose design is related to the Viking longship. Many of these fishermen prospered to become shipmasters, and some of the more elegant 18th-century terraced houses in Bay Town bear witness to the wealth created from the sea.

But the sea also took a heavy toll of lives. The bay has frequently been the setting of dramatic shipwrecks, none more spectacular than the loss of the brig *Visitor* in terrible blizzard conditions in 1881. Ferocious gales prevented the launching of a lifeboat, which horses and villagers had dragged through deep snow from Whitby, but the locals managed to save the crew nonetheless. A plaque at the top of the village recalls the lives that have been saved by local lifeboats.

Storms have constantly eroded the cliffs, causing sensational landslips, occasionally taking whole streets of cottages with them. To prevent this from happening again, a new sea wall 500 ft long and 40 ft high was built in 1975.

With its jumble of red pantiled roofs and honey-coloured stone walls, Bay Town lures visitors into its winding streets and passageways. But access by road is severely limited, cars being parked at the top of the

Robin Hood's Bay from the west

Near Way Foot

Narrow houses in narrow King Street

CLINGING TO THE CLIFFS

Crammed into a cleft in the cliff, Robin Hood's Bay is a maze of twisting alleys and small courtyards. They are marvellous to explore, giving unexpected glimpses of the sea. The town's two main streets meet at Way Foot, where fishing boats were brought ashore on the Landing Scar, a rock shelf. Like the streets, many of the town's houses are narrow, because of the lack of space to build outwards.

hill, to leave the village traffic-free. A complicated labyrinth of steps, courts and little alleyways leads off the two main streets – the broader New Road and the narrower King Street, which run down either side of King's Beck.

In a little cottage in King Street, author Leo Walmsley lived as a boy between 1894 and 1913. He captured the atmosphere of the East Coast and depicted Robin Hood's Bay as Bramblewick in novels such as *Three Fevers*.

Rosedale Abbey NORTH YORKSHIRE

17 miles south-west of Whitby (PAGE 325 Bb)

Few villages in the north of England have a more magnificent setting than Rosedale Abbey, in the heart of the North York Moors National Park. In a splendid green basin between the wild ridges of the moors, the village lies at a crossroads of moorland tracks and roads, some of them still marked with medieval wayside crosses.

Despite its name, the village does not have an abbey. Close to the little Victorian Church of St Mary and St Lawrence are a few fragments of a stone buttress – all that remains of a Cistercian nunnery established in the mid-12th century. The church served as a chapel for the nunnery and its interior has recently been restored.

Iron was the reason why this tiny settlement grew. In the 13th century, rich iron finds in the surrounding hills attracted the attention of the monks of Byland Abbey, near Helmsley. They worked the ores in small furnaces, or bloomeries, until the Dissolution of the Monasteries in 1539.

Interest in local iron was not revived until the mid-19th century when Cleveland had developed into one of the world's major iron-producing centres. The Rosedale iron ores were found to be particularly rich, and new mining techniques were developed to work them. A furnace where the ores were treated before transport to Teesside was built on the hill above Rosedale; its chimney, the Rosedale Chimney, was a prominent landmark until 1972. Eight stone arches, once part of the furnace complex, still survive at Bank Top, immediately above the village and reached by a road with a 1 in 3 gradient. From the top there is a superb view back across Rosedale and Rosedale Abbey.

From Bank Top, the old railway line runs along the moors to Battersby where trains carrying ore used to join the railway along the Esk Valley to its Teesside destination. However, despite the intense activities of the late 19th century, few signs of the industry remain. Waste tips and ruined buildings have been absorbed into the moorland, though the faint line of the railway can be discerned curving away across the wild countryside.

Around the attractive village green, the cottages and little shops which largely make up Rosedale Abbey today were once industrial workers' homes. Lined with bluish furnace brick, they are pleasant straightforward terraces typical of any Victorian town, but in Rosedale part of a rural scene. The old Methodist Chapel, in similar style, is being restored and may be used for craft shops and accommodation.

Sandsend NORTH YORKSHIRE

3 miles west of Whitby (PAGE 325 Ca)

Here the western part of Whitby's golden sands comes to an end – an ancient village recorded as far back as 1254, when there was a 'sea-fishery', and 53 cottages were among the lord of the manor's assets.

Sandsend is really two villages, developed around the mouths of two becks (streams) running into the sea at Dunsley Bay. The first of these is East Row, an attractive group of cottages hugging a tight hairpin bend on the road from Whitby and continuing along East Row Beck. From here, paths lead into Mulgrave Woods. These are private, but open on certain days. They encompass some fine landscaped parkland and a mixture of broadleaved and coniferous woods, as well as plantations.

Footpaths lead to the top of Lythe Bank – a 1 in 4 hill giving superb views back across the bay to Whitby. Within the woods and parkland are two castles: the remains of a 13th-century fortress built high on a ridge by Peter de Mauley (one of King John's favourites); and the Gothic-style Mulgrave Castle (closed to the public) dating from the 18th and 19th centuries. The landscape gardener Humphry Repton (1752 – 1818) laid out the grounds.

In the second village, Sandsend proper, cottages are scattered up the little valley of Sandsend Beck which runs parallel to East Row Beck. From the 17th until the late 19th century, the village owed much of its prosperity to alum, used in tanning and dyeing. Former alum quarries and waste tips still make a dramatic impact on the landscape at Sandsend Ness.

A car park occupies part of old Sandsend, destroyed in a great East Coast flood in 1953. Immediately above, and reached by steps, what was once the track of the Whitby to Saltburn railway now forms a fine high-level walkway ending at the old tunnel entrance beyond Sandsend Ness.

Sandsend is part of the ancient parish of Lythe, and a mile from the village, up Lythe Bank, is St Oswald's Church, Lythe. It stands on a high vantage point which is the site of a Viking burial ground, and there is much that recalls the Viking past. Anglo-Danish 'hogback' graves, incised slabs and cross-heads are all relics of Viking settlers in Whitby.

A former rector of the church, John Fisher, became Bishop of Rochester and a cardinal. But he ended his life – with his friend, the statesman and scholar Sir Thomas More – at the Tower of London in 1535. Like More he was accused of High Treason for refusing to accept Henry VIII as head of the English Church. Both Fisher and More were made saints in 1935. Two years after their deaths another rector of Lythe church, James Cockerell, and his curate, John Pickering, were hanged, drawn and quartered for their part in the abortive Pilgrimage of Grace – a rising of northern Catholics discontented at Henry VIII's changes to the English Church.

St Oswald's was largely rebuilt and restored in 1910 – 11 by the Edwardian architect Sir Walter Tapper. It has a fine Edwardian screen, a beautiful Lady Chapel, and is considered one of Tapper's masterpieces. Even so it must have been a great relief to the people of Sandsend when their chapel of ease, dedicated to St Mary, was built in the village, saving them from the steep ascent of Lythe Brow.

BY THE BECK *Quarrymen's cottages straggle along the bank of the Sandsend Beck, one of the two attractive little streams that reach the sea near the village of Sandsend.*

MAP 30

GLORIES OF GALLOWAY AND SMUGGLERS' HIDEOUTS

Saints and smugglers people the legends of the Galloway coast, an area of sweeping sandy bays and rocky coves. The first Christian missionary to Scotland, St Ninian, preached here 1500 years ago. In the 17th century, the area was racked by religious conflict. All is quiet now, and artists flock to capture the scenery on canvas.

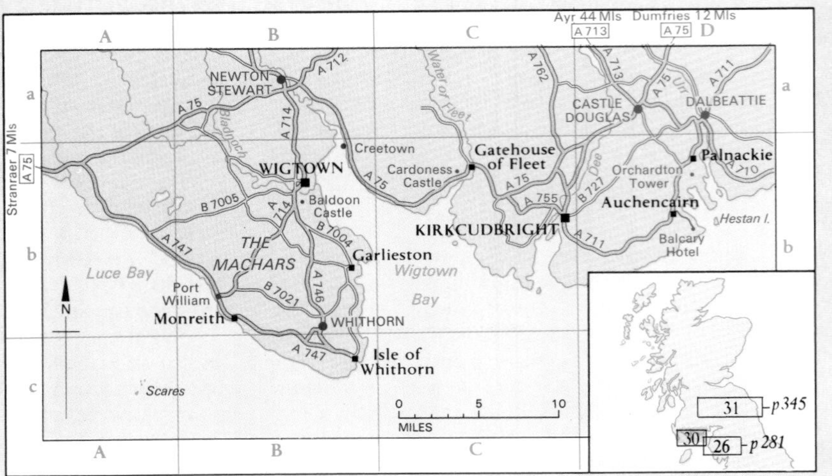

MAP 30: NEIGHBOURING AREAS – MAPS 26 AND 31

KIRKCUDBRIGHT Auchencairn Gatehouse of Fleet Palnackie
WIGTOWN Garlieston Isle of Whithorn Monreith

KIRKCUDBRIGHT

DUMFRIES AND GALLOWAY

28 miles south-west of Dumfries (PAGE 338 Cb)

In 1773 John Paul, the captain of a small merchant ship, was held prisoner in Kirkcudbright's Tolbooth (town hall), charged with murdering a mutinous sailor on board his ship. The charge was later dismissed for lack of evidence, but the experience seems to have been a turning point in the young captain's life.

When the American War of Independence broke out two years later, he assumed the name Jones and enlisted in the newly formed US Navy. As John Paul Jones (1747 – 92) he became one of America's greatest naval heroes, harrying Britain's coasts and winning an outstanding victory against superior forces off Flamborough Head, Humberside, in 1779.

John Paul Jones was born in Kirkbean – 20 miles east – near where his father worked as a gardener. The Tolbooth, where he was imprisoned, stands in the broad High Street. It was built around 1600 and is topped by a weathervane shaped like a ship.

In the century after the Tolbooth was built a number of witch trials were staged here, and many of the women were condemned to death. The last to be executed was Elspeth McEwen, in 1698. The jougs (neck rings) worn by prisoners can still be seen.

Until 1975 Kirkcudbright (pronounced K'coobri) was the county town of the Stewartry of Kirkcudbright – so called because in the 14th and 15th centuries the county was ruled by a steward directly appointed by the king of Scotland. The Stewartry Museum in St Mary Street charts the county's long history, and includes among its exhibits John Paul Jones's tobacco box, and a gun given to the town by James VI of Scotland (1567 – 1625).

Standing in a spacious square on the eastern edge of the town are the gaunt ruins of McLellan's Castle, built in the 1580s by Sir Thomas McLellan, a one-time provost, or mayor, of Kirkcudbright. He is buried in the small Old Greyfriars Church near by.

The town, whose neat, often colour-washed houses rise gently from the Dee estuary, has long attracted artists. One of them was the Scottish painter E. A. Hornel (1864 – 1933), who lived at Broughton House, an early 18th-century mansion in the High Street. On his death he left the house to the town, and it is now a library and art gallery, which displays several of his works.

The poet Robert Burns (1759 – 96) stayed in another fine building in the High Street, the Selkirk Arms Hotel. Here he wrote the celebrated *Selkirk Grace*, still widely used in Scotland:

'Some hae meat and canna eat,
And some wad eat that want it;
But we hae meat and we can eat,
Sae let the Lord be thankit.'

Kirkcudbright's patron saint is Cuthbert, who converted many of the southern Scots to Christianity in the 7th century, and the town probably owes its name to the Church of St Cuthbert, which is known to have existed here since AD 878. The present St Cuthbert's dates from 1838.

A short distance east of the town is the Old Churchyard, containing the foundations of an ancient church and the graves of three Covenanters, who were among many Scottish Presbyterians executed in the mid-1680s for refusing to use the Book of Common Prayer. There is also the tomb of a tinker named Billy Marshall, who died in 1792 supposedly aged 120. He claimed to have been married seven times and boasted that he fathered his last four children when he was over 100 years old.

Stretching south of Kirkcudbright is St Mary's

Isle – now a peninsula – which ends in Paul Jones's Point. In 1778 John Paul Jones made a daring raid on the island hoping to kidnap the Earl of Selkirk who had a house here (later burnt down). But the earl was not at home and Jones could not prevent his disappointed men from plundering the earl's silver plate. Later, however, Jones bought the silver back from his men and returned it with a note of apology.

• **Parking** St Cuthbert Street • **Early closing** Thursday • **Information** TEL. Newton Stewart 2549/3401 • **AA 24 hour service** TEL. Dumfries 69257.

Auchencairn

DUMFRIES AND GALLOWAY

11 miles east of Kirkcudbright (PAGE 338 Db)

The Old Smugglers' Inn recalls in its name the most lucrative of Auchencairn's one-time trades. Easy access to the Isle of Man – which then as now had its own tax laws – a series of deep inlets and tidal bays made the place a smugglers' paradise.

Two miles or so to the south-east, where the public road ends, stands the white-painted Balcary Hotel, possessed of peaceful gardens and a dubious history. It was built in the 18th century by three men named Clark, Crain and Quirk, who were shareholders in a company shipping contraband from the Isle of Man. Its cellars – now a bar – were laid out as a hiding place for brandy, rum, wine, lace, tobacco and many other valuable but illicit cargoes.

The hotel looks out to Hestan Island and Balcary Point. Two of Balcary Point's natural features are a rock pillar called Lot's Wife and a recess known as Adam's Chair. The first is a Biblical reference; the second is said to have been a lookout point for a smuggler named Adam, who would signal to ships out to sea when the coast was clear for a clandestine landing.

Smuggling being more profitable than farming or industry may well account for the late development of much of Galloway. However, 'the trade' declined towards the end of the 18th century, when new tax laws made it less profitable. Only then did Auchencairn turn to industry, a cotton mill blossoming briefly in the village, then turning for a while into a paper mill.

Many of the whitewashed houses climbing the steep Main Street date from this time. An easier gradient sweeps left onto Church Street, past the high-roofed church of the 1840s. Between the two streets is Spout Row, where beside a garden wall the old communal water pipe and trough which gave the street its name are still maintained.

A small square contains a neat lamp commemorating Queen Victoria's diamond jubilee, the village hall and a noticeably untypical guesthouse, built of two-coloured brick rather than the usual Galloway stone. The house was built around 1870 by a Lancashire businessman who decided to impose his home county's architectural ideas on an improbable location. The bricks were made locally, but bricklaying was so rare

ARTISTS' HAVEN ON THE DEE

Colourful Kirkcudbright's mild climate and soft light make the town a painter's paradise and the home of an internationally famous summer art school. Seen from above, the prevailing grey of the town's buildings is attractively broken by fine trees; and the remains of the 16th-century McLellan's Castle look over the tranquil estuary of the River Dee to gently rising slopes on the western shore. More trees line the quays of Kirkcudbright harbour, where brightly coloured fishing boats and an occasional coaster continue the town's long seafaring tradition. At low tide, the water drops dramatically in the harbour and below the arched road bridge.

McLellan's Castle and Kirkcudbright town

Low tide at the road bridge

Fishing boats still use the harbour

a craft in the area that men had to be brought in to do the building.

Auchencairn Bay dries out at low tide, and this led to the establishment of stake-net fishing where salmon are drawn in on the flood tide and caught in nets stretched between stakes. The Balcary Fishery has been worked for more than 150 years. Its old buildings and net-drying frames stand on a rocky point in Balcary Bay.

Beyond the bay is one of the finest footpaths of the Solway coast, leading through woods and farmland, along a rocky shore and on, eventually, to spectacular cliffs where rock stacks plunge dizzily down to the sea.

Gatehouse of Fleet

DUMFRIES AND GALLOWAY

9 miles north-west of Kirkcudbright (PAGE 338 Cb)

There was a time when Gatehouse was no more than a single house on the 'gait', or road, to the bridge over the Water of Fleet. Then, in 1763 the landowner, James Murray, moved into his new home, Cally House, the first granite-built mansion in Galloway, set in 1000 acres of woodland, gardens, orchards and a deer park. After that, he set about establishing a village beyond the estate's boundary walls. Gatehouse soon took on the shape it has today – a broad High Street lined with handsome two-storey buildings and, branching off it, smaller streets of colour-washed cottages.

Robert Burns visited Gatehouse in 1793 and remarked on 'roaring Birtwhistle' – referring to the noisy cotton mills set up in the village by a Yorkshire family named Birtwhistle. While walking on the moors near by, he composed the stirring, patriotic song, *Scots wha hae wi' Wallace bled . . .* setting down the words at the Murray Arms Hotel in High Street.

By 1795 Gatehouse had become a fully fledged burgh, or town. Cotton was the source of its fortune. There were four cotton mills – one later becoming a bobbin mill – a soap works and two tanneries, a brass foundry and even a shipyard on a canalised stretch of the Fleet. But the industries faded away early in the last century, overtaken by those of larger neighbours. In 1975 Gatehouse lost its status as a burgh, and now only two ruined mills, together with the water wheel of the old bobbin mill, survive.

The (then) town was called 'Kippletringan' in Sir Walter Scott's novel *Guy Mannering*, published in 1815. In more recent times the crime novelist Dorothy L. Sayers (1893 – 1957) stayed at the Anwoth Hotel while writing *The Five Red Herrings*, her mystery story about the Kirkcudbright artists' colony. The village and the area around were for many years a favoured haunt of the Glasgow School of Scottish artists, who included E. A. Hornel (see Kirkcudbright, page 338), George Henry, James Guthrie and John Faed. The coastal road running west and north to Creetown is magnificent, with Wigtown Bay and the distant Isle of Man on one side, and hills and moorland on the other.

Back in the village there are prominent reminders of its time as a burgh – including the red-sandstone façade of the old town hall in High Street. The Tourist Information Office near by – open in summer – shows a video on 'Rural Galloway'; and from the clock tower, the graceful Georgian buildings of Ann Street and Neilson Square lead to the grounds of the former Cally House – now a hotel.

The more usual approach to the hotel is along a driveway off the Castle Douglas Road. Much of the hotel grounds are surrounded by the Forestry Commission's Fleet Forest Park. Walks lead past tumbling burns through woodland where deer roam. One path

WHERE MILLS ONCE ROARED

Graceful Georgian houses straddle the Water of Fleet at Gatehouse. Impressive public buildings such as the granite clock tower of 1871 survive from the time when the village was a booming cotton town. Rutherford's Kirk, now an antiques shop, is named after Samuel Rutherford (1608 – 61), a founder of the Presbyterian church. The Temple, a Gothic folly, lies in Fleet Forest Park.

The peaceful heart of Gatehouse of Fleet

The clock tower

skirts a mound on which a Norman castle once stood. The path continues past an 18th-century Gothic folly and into the forest nursery.

A mile south-west of Gatehouse there is a complete change of view at Cardoness Castle, reached by a short climb between steeply sloping lawns. Surrounded by a few ash trees, the partly restored 15th-century castle is maintained as an ancient monument. A grim vaulted room on the ground floor was the castle's prison and has a 'murder hole' – a steel grill in the roof – through which boiling pitch could be poured onto enemies. Cardoness was a McCulloch stronghold. In the 17th century Godfrey McCulloch murdered a neighbouring laird, fled the country then came back, only to be recognised at a church service in St Giles in Edinburgh and arrested. He was one of the last men to be executed by the 'maiden', an old Scots version of the guillotine.

A bypass to funnel heavy traffic away from the centre of Gatehouse was begun in 1984.

Palnackie DUMFRIES AND GALLOWAY

14 miles north-east of Kirkcudbright (PAGE 338 Db)

Motorists on the beautiful road from Dalbeattie to Palnackie were frequently startled by the sight of a ship moving slowly through the farmlands to the east. For there used to be sea-going traffic on the adjacent tidal stretch of the River Urr. Granite was carried on the river from the nearby Craignair quarries until the 1930s, and fertiliser until the 1950s. Indeed, Palnackie once succeeded in cornering the lion's share of the granite business.

The village came into existence around 200 years ago, beside a handy harbour called Boglescreek long well known to Solway smugglers. The new village soon became a significant inland port, shipping out building blocks, setts and cobbles, with something like 40 trading schooners owned by local families.

The granite went to build Liverpool Docks, the Thames Embankment, Manchester Town Hall – and the infamously rough pavé of many old Belgian roads. Shipping declined after 1863 when the railway reached Dalbeattie, about 5 miles to the north-east, though the schooners continued in business until just after the First World War. The granite is still quarried, but only in the form of crushed stone for road building, and is now carried by heavy lorries.

The centre of the village remains as the schooner sailors knew it, although the tiny harbour is now heavily silted up. Colour-washed houses hug a curve of the old main road; two streets on either side of a burn head down towards the river. In the old days sailors from other ports would find lodgings in the upstairs rooms of the two-storey houses set around the harbour. Locals still remember when what is now a private house was the Gordon Arms, a favourite sailors' inn.

A minor road south of the village leads to the 15th-century round tower of Orchardton, once part of a fortified house and now designated an ancient monument. Hidden within its double walls is a 35-step spiral staircase leading to a parapet walk unsuspected from ground level.

Another minor road climbs south-east of the village to the former farmhouse of North Glen, now a crafts gallery with a reputation for glassware. From here there is a fine view up the valley of the Urr.

Near the mouth of the Urr is the Glen Isle peninsula where the receding tide leaves wide mudbanks. This is the site of a 'barefoot flounder-tramping' competition started in the 1970s, which Palnackie folk have jocularly nominated a world championship. At the end of July or beginning of August – depending on the tide – competitors walk through the mud, feeling for flounders with their feet. The heaviest and lightest catches earn a prize and a unique title.

Rutherford's Kirk

The Temple

WIGTOWN

DUMFRIES AND GALLOWAY

7 miles south of Newton Stewart (PAGE 338 Bb)

A memorial stone on Wigtown salt marshes marks the spot where two women Covenanters (Scottish Presbyterians who refused to use the Book of Common Prayer) were drowned at the stake in 1685. The women – Margaret McLachlan, aged 18, and Margaret Wilson, 65 – were tied to stakes and then, refusing to the last to renounce their religious beliefs, left to drown as the tide came in. They were buried in the yard of the parish church not far away by the seashore, and their tombstones tell their story.

The two women were not alone in their stand. Near by in the churchyard are buried three local men, George Walker, John Milroy and William Johnstone, who were hanged as Covenanters in the same years of persecution, and a monument on Windy Hill behind the town commemorates scores of other martyred Covenanters from Wigtown and the country around.

The town centre is a spacious square on a windswept north-facing slope. Until 1975 Wigtown was a county town and the Wigtownshire County Buildings of 1862 still rise confidently on one side of the square, with the coats of arms of all the county's former burghs carved on the front. On the ground floor there is a small museum of town history and relics.

The square also has two crosses; one dates from 1748 and has a sundial on its top; the other was put up in 1816 to celebrate the defeat of Napoleon at Waterloo the previous year. A bowling green and well-tended flower garden fill the centre of the square.

The town lies on the edge of a rich agricultural region called The Machars, and was once a prosperous seaport. The harbour is a short way outside the town, at the mouth of the River Bladnoch, but at the beginning of the century it silted up and was not used for many years. Recently, however, it has been dredged and restored for use by small pleasure craft.

A picnic place above the river channel and harbour has good views out over the sands and salt marshes of Wigtown Bay, where each year thousands of greylag and pink-footed geese spend the winter – sharing the marshes with resident waders and sea ducks such as the eider. Higher up the river on the opposite bank stand the ruins of the 17th-century Baldoon Castle, setting of part of Sir Walter Scott's melodramatic novel *The Bride of Lammermoor*.

• **Parking** North Main Street; South Main Street (both car parks) • **Early closing** Wednesday • **Event** Agricultural Show (August) • **Information** TEL. Newton Stewart 2549/3401 • **AA 24 hour service** TEL. Dumfries 69257.

Garlieston DUMFRIES AND GALLOWAY

8 miles south of Wigtown (PAGE 338 Bb)

Protected by a sea wall beside a bay with a remarkable rise and fall of tide – up to 30 ft on occasions – Garlieston takes its name from the wealthy landowner who created it. He was Lord Garlies, then heir to the Earl of Galloway, and this planned village of the 1760s was built on the edge of the wooded grounds of his large estate.

The original layout of the sea front – a pair of curving crescents – has survived unaltered, their two-storey, colour-washed houses overlooking the bay. Those in North Crescent are fronted by gardens, while in the corresponding space in South Crescent hiring fairs used to be held. These were a kind of labour exchange where employers could come to find and take on labourers for the coming year. For more than 100 years, however, the space has been a bowling green.

For a long time Garlieston was in the curious position of being a port without a harbour. Rivers flowing into the sea here silted up the coast, so boats had to anchor in the nearest stretch of deep water; smaller boats were then used to take passengers and cargo ashore. But eventually in the 19th century a proper harbour was built. Ships importing coal and lime in particular called in on runs from London, Liverpool, Dublin, the Isle of Man, Whitehaven and Greenock. Several shipowners lived in the village, as well as many fishermen. A rope walk and sail factory – which still stands – were established, and boat-building was a full-time industry. Coasters still come to the harbour, which is now dredged regularly.

Monreith DUMFRIES AND GALLOWAY

12 miles south-west of Wigtown (PAGE 338 Bb)

A life-size bronze otter, poised alertly on a rock atop a hill south-east of Monreith, pays tribute to the author Gavin Maxwell (1914 – 69), whose book *Ring of Bright Water* – later made into a film – chronicled his adventures with an otter he 'adopted'.

He was one of the Maxwells of Monreith, major local landowners for generations who still own Monreith House, north of the village. Gavin learnt to love otters while travelling far away in the marshes of the River Tigris in Iraq, and is more commonly associated with the far north-west of Scotland where he lived and wrote about the animals. But it was his Galloway boyhood and family background which, as he tells, bred his love of nature. For all the Maxwells had an enduring interest in wildlife, gardening and history. Indeed, Gavin's grandfather, Sir Herbert Maxwell (1845 – 1937), was a world-respected naturalist.

The family burial ground is at the ruined church

BIRD'S EYE VIEW FOR AN OTTER

The ruins of Kirkmaiden church and the memorial to the author Gavin Maxwell, who spent much of his childhood at Monreith, look down from the cliffs to Front Bay and the Point of Lag. Monreith is near two safe, sandy beaches. But much of the coast is craggy and scarred, with layers of rock twisted into spectacular patterns and trees shaped weirdly by south-westerly winds.

Kirkmaiden

The Maxwell memorial

Front Bay

The sea pink, or thrift, blooms on the craggy cliff faces near Monreith

of Kirkmaiden, farther to the south-east – although Gavin was cremated in Inverness and is not buried here. Among the memorials in the church is a plaque to François Thurot, a French naval captain killed in action and buried at sea 200 years ago. His body drifted ashore and was reburied with full honours by the Maxwell laird.

Monreith village is laid out on both sides of the Stranraer to Whithorn road, where a double bend takes it away from the bayside cliffs. Old maps call it Milltown of Monreith, and the site of an old water mill can still be made out where the Monreith Burn, after wandering across a field, tumbles sharply to the rocky shore. The single-storey cottages along the main road were built for farm labourers and workers in a long-disused tile and brickworks.

Gorse-covered cliffs mark the curve of Monreith Bay, a little indentation off Luce Bay. The rocky westward side, pleasant for picnics, is reached from a car park on the main road at the start of the Kelton Steps – all 152 of them. There is a fine view from the top across to the Mull of Galloway, and the little rock-stack islands known as the Scares – and even, on a clear day, to the coast of Ireland. The Scares are a bird sanctuary and a famous nesting ground for gannets. Lobster fishermen at Port William – 2 miles or so along the coast to the north-west – take visitors on day trips to the Scares.

Isle of Whithorn

DUMFRIES AND GALLOWAY

14 miles south of Wigtown (PAGE 338 Bc)

One of the Solway area's most rollicking smuggling stories concerns a shingle bar that once ran between Isle of Whithorn and the mainland.

A smuggling skipper named Joughkin, hard-pressed by a revenue cutter faster than his own ship, made for Isle of Whithorn harbour. The revenue men slackened sail, assuming that Joughkin would not be able to come out again except past them, as the bar blocked the only alternative exit. But when they entered, the harbour was empty. Knowing the tide was at its highest, and cramming on all sail, Joughkin had steered directly for the bar. He struck it at such speed that the momentum carried his ship across the bar and into the neighbouring bay, where he quickly set course for the Cumberland coast, to the east.

As the tide receded and the bar broke water, astonished locals found Joughkin had cut things so fine that his keel had left a furrow stretching for 100 yds across the shingle.

In the harbour is a church that juts out into the water – the subject of another good tale. In the 1840s, when the Free Church broke from the Church of Scotland, the local landowner refused to provide ground on which the new congregation could put their church. So they raised up a base from below the high-water mark – the limit of his land – and built the church on it.

Isle of Whithorn was the place where Irish pilgrims landed on their way to St Ninian's shrine at the town of Whithorn, 6 miles inland to the north-west. The preserved ruin of a chapel named after the saint and built for the pilgrims' use stands amid parkland near where they landed. A stroll here shows how the village is set between its two deeply indented bays. Behind the village, farms stretch to the skyline; tall cliffs and craggy rock stacks extend along the coast to the north.

Highest point on the isle is a white tower, formerly used to signal the state of the tide to approaching sailing ships. Fishing boats, sea anglers and .holiday craft still use the waters, under the eye of a coastguard station. Wigtown Bay Sailing Club is located in the village and The Steam Packet Inn recalls the days of regular sailings.

ISLE NO MORE *A shingle bar between Isle of Whithorn and the mainland is no longer covered at high tide, and now has houses built on it.*

MAP 31

EMBATTLED BORDER AND THE TUMBLING TWEED

Listen hard and it seems you can still hear the war-cries of the Scots and English as they raided, plundered and massacred each other relentlessly among the hills and heather. This is a land of ruined abbeys and battle-scarred castles, celebrated in the romantic and stirring books and ballads of Sir Walter Scott.

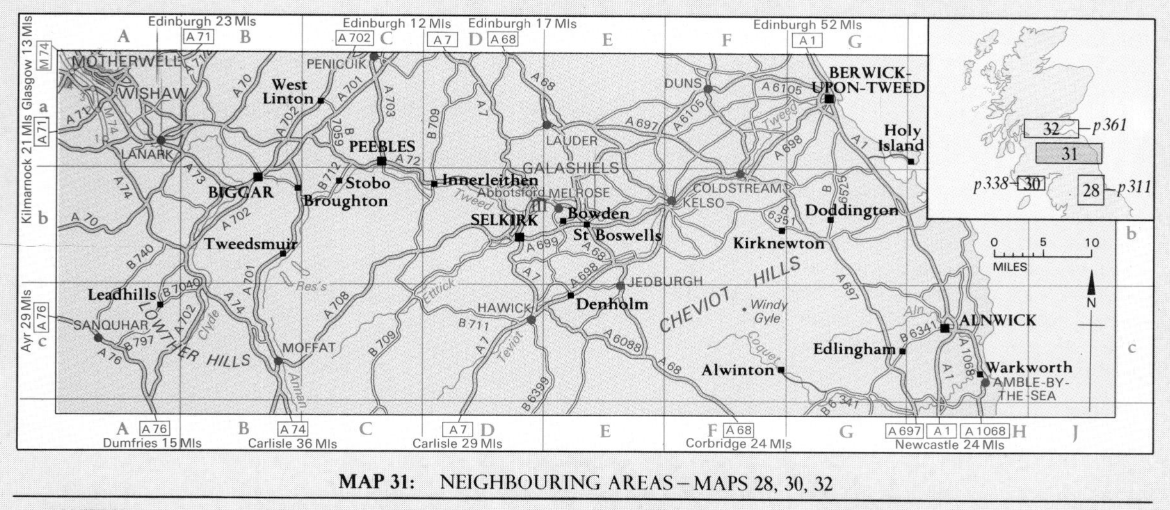

MAP 31: NEIGHBOURING AREAS – MAPS 28, 30, 32

ALNWICK	BERWICK-UPON-TWEED	BIGGAR	PEEBLES	SELKIRK
Alwinton	Doddington	Broughton	Innerleithen	Bowden
Edlingham	Holy Island	Leadhills	Stobo	Denholm
Warkworth	Kirknewton	Tweedsmuir	West Linton	St Boswells

ALNWICK

NORTHUMBERLAND

19 miles north of Morpeth (PAGE 345 Hc)

Since the Middle Ages Alnwick has been the seat of the powerful Percy family, Earls and Dukes of Northumberland who for centuries ruled most of northern England – and their stamp is still on this noble market town.

It is first seen in a stone pillar, the Percy Tenantry Column, which stands 83 ft high near the southern entrance to the town. It was erected in 1816 by tenant farmers in honour of the 2nd Duke of Northumberland, who lowered their rents during an economic and agricultural slump. The column is surmounted by a proud Percy lion, its tail rigidly outstretched, while four more stone lions crouch around the base. Set in the foundation stone is a glass tube containing the names of more than 1500 members of the Percy Volunteer Artillery, Cavalry and Infantry Riflemen raised to combat a possible invasion during the Napoleonic Wars.

Near by is another reminder of the Percys – the 15th-century Hotspur Tower, last remaining medieval gateway in the walls that once ringed the town. The tower was built by Henry, the 2nd Earl of Northumberland in about 1450.

The Percys employed a large number of 'bonded' servants – people owing service to their local lord – who lived mainly in Bondgate. This is one of a number of streets ending in 'gate' – the Anglo-Saxon term for 'passage'.

Each passage recalls its character in former days. Canongate, for instance, is named after the White Canons who walked along it to and from the abbey on the far side of the River Aln. Bailiffgate once led to the bailey, or outer walls, of the Percy stronghold, Alnwick Castle. At the end of Bailiffgate is the castle's massive, 14th-century barbican – which defends the castle gateway – its battlements manned by life-sized stone statues of armed soldiers.

Alnwick Castle seems still to be on guard against Scottish marauders. Built in the 11th century, the castle was restored in the mid-18th century for the 1st Duke of Northumberland by the Scottish architect Robert Adam (1728 – 92). Further restoration was done a century later for the 4th Duke, who employed the Victorian architect Anthony Salvin. And the castle owes most of its present outside appearance to Salvin.

Outwardly, it still appears a stern and forbidding fortress, but inside are marble-lined staircases and ornate apartments and state rooms. It is also a treasure-house of books, antiques and paintings – among them pictures by Canaletto, Titian and Van Dyck. The castle is still the home of the present duke, but is open to the public usually from the middle of May until the end of September.

Until the 18th century, a market was held on a broad area of manorial wasteland, but now the weekly

Bondgate Within

Percy Tenantry Column

ON THE SHADY SIDE OF THE STREET

Shaded by trees and lined with shops which have a comfortable, old-fashioned look, Bondgate Within is a street for strolling along at leisure, just as Alnwick people have done since Anglo-Saxon times. They still speak of 'ganging your own gait' – walking at your own pace. In the south of the town stands the Percy Tenantry Column, designed by David Stephenson, an architect from Newcastle upon Tyne. Built in 1816, the cost of the column was raised by local tenant farmers whose rents had just been reduced by the 2nd Duke of Northumberland. He received a gold medal struck to commemorate the building of the column – but died before it was completed – and used to live in Alnwick Castle.

Alnwick and Alnwick Castle from the south-west

market is held in the Market Place on Saturdays. From the last Sunday in June a week-long 'ancient fair' is staged, during which townsfolk assume medieval costume and the spirit of the age is vividly recaptured.

• **Parking** Bondgate Without; Pottergate; Dispensary Street; Lagny Street (all car parks); Market Square; The Cobbles; Bondgate Within • **Early closing** Wednesday • **Market day** Saturday • **Events** Fair (June); International Music Festival (August) • **Information** TEL. Alnwick 603120, 603129 (summer) • **AA 24 hour service** TEL. Newcastle upon Tyne 610111.

Alwinton NORTHUMBERLAND

22 miles west of Alnwick (PAGE 345 Fc)

The remains of illicit whisky stills symbolise the remoteness and frontier-post feeling of Alwinton; they were hidden where the distillers felt safe from excisemen – in the deep bowl of bare hills around the village. All the fresh water needed was available from tumbling burns, and Rory's Still, beside the Usway Burn to the west, was in use until the last century.

The stone and slate cottages and farms of Alwinton lie at the confluence of the Coquet and Alwin. Face north-west and there is nothing between you and the Scottish border – and very little habitation immediately beyond it. The name of the Rose and Thistle Inn reveals the village's status between the two countries – the rose for England and the thistle for Scotland. Sir Walter Scott was once a guest at the inn, and nowadays it is a meeting place for Upper Coquetdale farmers. On the second Saturday in October a show for sheep breeders is held in the village.

Alwinton's Church of St Michael and All Angels, at Low Alwinton, is built on two levels on a superb hillside site close to the river. The original mainly 12th-century church was greatly altered in 1851.

Old drovers' roads wind their way up into the Cheviot Hills and one of them, Clennel Street, follows a spectacular route by way of 2034 ft Windy Gyle, 6 miles or so to the north-west. Oats and barley were grown on terraces still easily seen among the hills, which are rich in earthworks, hill-forts and prehistoric hut circles. Close to the border is Russell Cairn, commemorating Lord Francis Russell, who was killed by Scots in 1585, on a day when a truce had been declared so that local disputes could be settled.

Edlingham NORTHUMBERLAND

7 miles south-west of Alnwick (PAGE 345 Gc)

This hillside hamlet in a moorland setting has three remarkable monuments for so tiny and remote a place – a ruined castle, a church designed to combat earthly and spiritual enemies, and a railway line which curved down to and across Edlingham Burn. The five-arched bridge that carried it remains a landmark long after the passing of the last train.

Close by the burn is the ruin of Edlingham Castle, in an extremely dangerous state but in process of repair by the English Heritage, which looks after ancient buildings and monuments for the Department of the Environment. Originally, it was a 'hall house' having one great room – probably built in the 13th century by the de Edlingham family – but in the next century a defensive courtyard was built to shelter people and livestock during Border raids, and a massive tower was added in the early 15th century. The castle lost its purpose after England and Scotland were united in 1603, and has gradually deteriorated.

The little Church of St John the Baptist, which stands close by, dates mainly from the 12th century and its squat, square tower, pyramid roof and narrow slit windows were also designed with defence in mind.

Inside, nevertheless, is a beautiful round chancel arch and three 12th-century pillars in the nave. The porch has fine barrel vaulting, giving the impression of a tunnel. Sheep and cattle graze the green fields around castle and church. There are farms which extend into the valley, a vicarage and some low traditional stone cottages along the village street.

About 1200 years ago a chieftain named Eadwulf arrived from Bamburgh to settle here, and a wooden church serving the farming community was founded. The manor passed to the Gospatrics, a celebrated local family, and then to the de Felton family. One of the de Feltons, Sir John, fought alongside Harry Percy – Shakespeare's Hotspur – when they were beaten by the Scots at Otterburn in 1388. A cairn on a hillside above Edlingham, known as Nanny Felton's Cairn, recalls the family name.

Warkworth NORTHUMBERLAND

7 miles south of Alnwick (PAGE 345 Hc)

Here is another great Percy castle, its tower jabbing the air like a clenched-fist salute – a fitting symbol for a building renowned in history and literature. Best known of the Percys who lived here was the hot-headed Henry – the 'all praised knight' Harry Hotspur of Shakespeare's *Henry IV*. Or as Prince Hal (later Henry V) puts it in the play:

'. . . the Hotspur of the north, he that kills me some six or seven dozen of Scots at a breakfast, washes his hands and says to his wife, "Fie upon this quiet life! I want work." '

The castle itself, where a number of scenes in *Henry IV* take place, is described as: 'this worm-eaten hold of ragged stone.'

There were Percys in Warkworth for 600 years (see also Alnwick, page 345), but today the castle is in the care of the Department of the Environment. It stands on a promontory whose rocky slopes provide a natural defence on three sides, while on the fourth is a deep ditch crossed by a bridge to the gatehouse. Inside is the great keep, with elegant turrets and towers. Dating mainly from the 12th to 15th centuries it is complex yet remarkably intact, with splendid chambers giving the feel of life in a medieval fortress.

The more ruinous parts of the castle date from the 12th century, and the whole building owes much of its beauty to the variety of styles and types of stone used in its construction. Above the entrance to the Lion Tower is a shattered statue of the Percys' lion emblem, with the family motto *Esperance* – meaning 'hope'. The castle is open daily.

Follow the path beside the River Coquet for about half a mile and, from a little landing stage, a steward will row you across to Warkworth Hermitage. This is a cave retreat, common in the Middle Ages, established by the Percys for a priest who would pray for their souls and those of their friends. Warkworth's dates from the 14th to early 15th centuries and is made up of a series of chambers hewn from the rock, including a small chapel and sacristy with remarkable carved windows, shelves and figures. Extra living quarters, including a simple kitchen and fireplace, were provided later. The last resident hermit was Sir George Lancaster, whose annual stipend in 1531 was 20 marks (about £13.30), pasture for cattle, two loads of wood and a 'draught of fish every Sunday'. The hermitage is open daily from Easter until October. The village matches

GATEWAY TO THE VILLAGE

Set on a horseshoe bend of the River Coquet, Warkworth is overlooked by its castle – remarkably intact, with splendid chambers giving a real impression of what life was like in a medieval fortress. The nearby stone bridge has a rare, fortified gatehouse.

Warkworth from the castle

Bridge and gatehouse

the glories of its castle. As you approach from Alnwick, the road dips to a wooded gorge of the Coquet. The river is crossed by a new road bridge, but immediately to the right is the original fortified stone one built in 1379, although much altered in the centuries since. A massive gateway at one end was designed to repel intruders from over the Border.

Over the bridge, the main street leads to the junction with the Market Place and Cross, while the heavily restored Norman Church of St Laurence lies to the right. From here the street climbs past rows of 18th and 19th-century houses and shops, some with red pantiled roofs and all of mellow stone.

BERWICK-UPON-TWEED

NORTHUMBERLAND

62 miles north of Newcastle upon Tyne (PAGE 345 Ga)

Three historic bridges link England's most northerly town with the south – Berwick Bridge, the Royal Border Bridge, and the Royal Tweed Bridge.

Berwick stands on the north bank of the River Tweed, which for part of its length – until 3½ miles upstream from the town – marks the border between England and Scotland. Until 1624 the river here was spanned only by a crude wooden bridge. Then, 21 years after James VI of Scotland complained about the lack of a 'proper' bridge on his way to London to be crowned James I of England, a stone bridge was at last built. Resting on 15 low and sturdy arches, Berwick Bridge is still in use.

The Royal Border Bridge was built in 1850 by the Northumberland engineer Robert Stephenson, son of George Stephenson who built the steam locomotive *Rocket*. Soaring 126 ft above the river bed on 28 elegant arches, it was opened by Queen Victoria and carries the railway line between Edinburgh and London. The last bridge built here, the concrete Royal Tweed Bridge, was opened in 1928 by the Prince of Wales (later Edward VIII) and was designed to take most of the ever-increasing flow of heavy road traffic.

Because of its position on the border, Berwick changed hands between the Scots and English no less than 13 times before 1482. Since then it has been firmly English but continued to be heavily fortified until the crowns of England and Scotland were united. Its first defensive wall was built in the Middle Ages and restored in the late 18th century. A walk along the top of the wall gives magnificent views of the river, the harbour and the town's cobbled streets.

A second and much stronger wall was put up in the reign of Elizabeth I (1558 – 1603). It was based on a new Italian design and included massive stone bastions for mounting guns and a wide ditch in front. It still stands on the east and north sides of the town.

Soldiers have been part of the scene in Berwick since the 12th century, when the town was first fought over. By the start of the 18th century, however, the townsfolk had tired of having often rowdy troops billeted upon them, so, in 1717, a stone barracks was built to accommodate 600. It was the first barracks in Britain and was in use until 1965. Today it houses the museum of the King's Own Scottish Borderers.

Facing the barracks is the parish church of Holy Trinity, one of very few churches built in England during the rule of Oliver Cromwell. Holy Trinity was built in 1648 – 52, work being supervised by the town governor, Colonel George Fenwick, who made sure that Cromwell's order forbidding bells in the church was carried out. Cromwell is said to have loathed the very idea of church bells, which for him conjured up images of hated Roman Catholic rites.

Holy Trinity has one bell today and there are also bells in the 150 ft spire of the nearby Town Hall which are still rung on festive occasions. The Town Hall was built in the 1750s of stone taken from the ruins of Berwick Castle, which also provided the stone for the church and barracks. Remains of a castle wall can be seen on a steep hill near the river, but most of what was left now lies beneath Berwick railway station.

• **Parking** Parade; Castlegate; Bridge Street; Pier Road; Sandgate; Railway Street (all car parks); Marygate • **Early closing** Thursday • **Market days** Wednesday, Saturday • **Cinema** Playhouse, Sandgate • **Events** Riding of the Bounds (May); Berwick and Tweedmouth Festival (July-August); Running of the Walls Race (September) • **Information** TEL. Berwick-upon-Tweed 307187 (summer) • **AA 24 hour service** TEL. Newcastle upon Tyne 610111.

Doddington NORTHUMBERLAND

14 miles south of Berwick (PAGE 345 Gb)

A terrible fate overtook a raiding army of 3000 Scots on the road just south of Doddington in 1513. They were returning, loaded with loot and flushed with victory, from a foray into England under Lord Home, when out of the tall broom which lined each side of the road there materialised 500 archers and men-at-arms led by Sir William Bulmer. Their revenge was ruthless and complete – 1000 Scots were killed or captured for the loss of 60 English.

For years afterwards the Scots called the road through Doddington the Ill Road – though the ambush was only the start of their woes. In September that same year their army suffered its shattering defeat at Flodden, some 8 miles to the west.

With such a bloody history, it is little wonder that Doddington is the place where the last of the fortified pele towers was built. It was put up in 1584, less than 20 years before England and Scotland were unified. The massive ruins of the tower stand in a farmyard with trees growing through the masonry fragments, close to where a lane branches off the main road to the church. In the churchyard is a guardhouse of a different sort, the Watch House, put there in 1826 so that a guard could be maintained on the churchyard against the body-snatchers – or 'Resurrection men' – who stole corpses for dissection in Edinburgh's medical schools. The Church of St Mary and St Michael is 13th century, restored in 1838. The original Norman bowl of the font survives.

East of the village is the massive flank of Dod Law, an open hillside of rough grazing. It is rich in prehistoric remains, notably Celtic hut circles and encampments, including an Iron Age fort. Several rock outcrops have mysterious 'cup and ring' markings – so called from their appearance – carved in the Bronze Age. These mysterious markings are found all over Western Europe, always in high places.

There are also mysterious vertical grooves on a 20 ft high natural crag on the south of Dod Law. Their origin is not known either, though local legend has it that they are rope marks caused when the Devil hanged his grandmother. Near the stone is a small cave, Cuddy's Cove, where St Cuthbert (see Holy Island, below) reputedly sheltered from the elements while a shepherd lad.

Holy Island NORTHUMBERLAND

13 miles south-east of Berwick (PAGE 345 Ha)

Holy Island, or Lindisfarne, is only approachable by boat or by a long causeway that is regularly submerged by the tide – not truly an island village, but having all the romantic appeal associated with small communities beset by the sea. Salt breezes wash over cottages and houses in narrow streets and tiny squares. The working boats of a few lobster and crab fishermen bob in a small natural harbour. Herring boats, sawn in half amidships and upended, serve as storage sheds ashore. The dramatic ruin of a priory nearly nine centuries old stands to one side of the harbour; and overlooking all, a magic castle rears on a pinnacle to the south.

But it is to the priory that the real romance of the island attaches, linked as it is to the very founders of Christianity in England. In AD 635, King Oswald of Northumbria invited the monks from Iona, off the west coast of Scotland, to found a monastery within his kingdom. Aidan later chose to build on Holy Island, and he made it a centre for learning and missionary work in the north of England.

On the night Aidan died, 16 years after coming to Northumbria, a shepherd lad on a chill hillside, not far away on the mainland, saw a flurry of shooting stars as he tended his flock. Later he heard that Aidan had died at that same moment and he believed that what he had seen was Aidan's soul being transported to heaven by angels. He took this as a sign that he himself should become a monk.

The shepherd, whose name was Cuthbert, joined a community at Melrose in Scotland and, by the time he was 30, became prior of Lindisfarne. Here he carried on Aidan's work for many years, but his missionary activities and extraordinary healing powers attracted such crowds that he had to seek greater quiet. He went first to an islet off Holy Island and then to the even more remote Farne Islands, off Bamburgh. He later returned to Lindisfarne to become its bishop, but died in the peace and quiet of the Farne Islands in AD 687.

Both Aidan and Cuthbert were made saints. When Cuthbert was canonised a few years after his death a Lindisfarne monk named Eadfrith, a skilled scribe, marked the event by making a series of superb illuminated manuscripts, now known as the Lindisfarne Gospels. These masterpieces of Saxon artistry, their pages aglow with colour and intricate decoration, are now in the British Museum, but the little 12th-century Church of St Mary has copies.

The present priory ruins, however, do not date from Cuthbert's time. In the 9th century the island was sacked by Viking raiders and the monks fled to Durham with Cuthbert's remains and Eadfrith's Gospels. In 1093 a new Benedictine priory was established on Lindisfarne. It was built with the lovely deep-red sandstone of Cheswick on the mainland, and it is recorded that local people carried the stone across the treacherous sands in ox carts and wagons, giving their labour free because of their love for Cuthbert.

Some of the Benedictine priory's fine stonework survives, including a delicate rainbow arch that forms a fragile curve between two columns. But when Henry VIII dissolved the monasteries in 1539 much of the priory's stone was used in the castle which was built on the island's south-east corner – as part of a chain of defences against the Scots.

The castle had a fairly uneventful history. A story is told that in 1715 some Jacobite rebels invited its garrison on board a ship, got them drunk and captured the stronghold. But it seems that the Jacobites' victory was short-lived. They received no reinforcements and had to flee – only to be captured among the rocks.

In 1903 the architect Sir Edwin Lutyens converted the castle into an unusual country house, now owned by the National Trust and open in summer.

Holy Island now lives mostly by tourism, fishing and the production of a traditional mead. Its northern side is a National Nature Reserve, which has footpaths allowing visitors to observe a rich variety of birdlife – and sometimes seals along the shore. One of the island's most magical spots, reached at low tide by scrambling over rocks and seaweed from St Mary's Church, is St Cuthbert's Islet. Here a wooden cross marks a medieval chapel; farther south are the foundations of what may have been Cuthbert's cell.

Visitors should consult local information centres to find out the safe times for crossing to the island.

St Aidan's statue

Fishermen's cottages

A BLESSING ON COTTAGE AND CASTLE ALIKE

Hand raised in blessing, St Aidan stands in the grounds of Holy Island's ruined priory. Beyond him are fishermen's cottages and Lutyens' reconstructed Tudor castle.

Kirknewton NORTHUMBERLAND

12 miles south of Berwick (PAGE 345 F/Gb)

A farm, a row of cottages, a little school, a church and a Women's Institute lie under the north flank of the Cheviot Hills where the College Burn and Bowmont Water come together. Such is peaceful Kirknewton, but being a Border hamlet it inevitably has its mementoes of 'old, unhappy, far-off things and battles long ago', as Wordsworth – who knew these hills – put it.

Near the churchyard gate are the graves of young pilot officers from RAF Milfield near by, who died in the Second World War. In the opposite corner are graves of four German airmen killed in the same conflict, in 1943. About 1½ miles east, on the roadside beyond Old Yeavering, is a huge single stone in a field – a monument to the victory of Robert Umfraville in 1415, when he put to flight 4000 Scotsmen with only 600 stout-hearted Northumbrians. Three miles to the east, at Homildon Hill, the Percys of Northumberland and George Dunbar, Earl of March, defeated the Earl of Douglas in 1402 and took him prisoner after he lost an eye and was wounded five times.

English longbowmen decimated the Scots from a vantage point on the hill, the survivors fleeing across the Tweed. A Scottish bard lamented: 'Some fled, some died, some mained there forever, that to Scotlande agayne came they never'.

But Kirknewton has more civilised claims to fame. A famous Victorian social reformer is buried in the churchyard. She was Josephine Butler, who retired, after her husband's death, to Woolmer, 5½ miles east of Kirknewton, where she died in 1906. The church itself, dedicated to St Gregory, dates from the 13th century and was restored in the 19th.

Only half a mile east of Kirknewton is the site of the capital of Edwin, the first Christian king of Northumbria. A great complex of timber buildings once stood between the road and the River Glen, including halls 100 ft long and a great amphitheatre. This was the royal township of Gefrin, or Ad-Gefrin, referred to by the historian Bede (about AD 673 – 735) who recorded how the missionary Paulinus spent 36 days there in AD 627, instructing the people and baptising them in the Glen. No traces of the palace or amphitheatre are visible, but a stone monument now stands where Gefrin stood.

Several of the dome-like hills behind the village bear the marks of ancient camps and settlements, including the remains of a huge Iron Age hill-fort on Yeavering Bell, a mile to the south-east. A wall encloses an area of about 13 acres in which at least 130 hut sites have been discovered.

BIGGAR

STRATHCLYDE

17 miles west of Peebles (PAGE 345 Bb)

Mary, Queen of Scots had four ladies-in-waiting named Mary, and one of them, Mary Fleming, lived in Biggar in the 16th century. Her home, Boghall Castle, in marshland just south of the town, now lies in ruins, but each June she is commemorated in a ceremony in which a girl from the area is chosen and crowned Fleming Queen. This recalls an occasion at the royal palace of Holyroodhouse in Edinburgh when, in a game with the queen and her fellow ladies-in-waiting, Mary Fleming was made queen for a day.

The Fleming family, who owed their name to their Flemish origin, came to Biggar in the mid-12th century when Baldwin Fleming built a castle on the bank of Biggar Burn which flows down the western edge of the town. A ruined tower and two small walls are all that now remains of his castle.

Baldwin's descendants built another much finer stronghold, Boghall Castle, Mary Fleming's home. Dating mostly from the 15th century, Boghall was once one of the largest castles in southern Scotland, protected by three walls and a deep moat crossed by a stone bridge. But in the 18th century it was badly neglected by the Elphinstone family, who had inherited it from the Fleming Earls of Wigtown, and it became a ruin.

About 300 years after the Flemings arrived, Biggar was made a burgh by James II of Scotland, in token of his 'great respect' for Robert, Lord Fleming. Around the broad High Street a maze of wynds (narrow alleys) and courtyards developed.

In 1545 St Mary's Church was built on the site of an earlier church – it was one of the last built in Scotland before the Reformation. Inside is the burial place of Lady Clementine, the last of the Flemings, who died in 1799; outside in the churchyard are the tombs of the Gladstone family, ancestors of the Liberal prime minister, William Ewart Gladstone (1809 – 98).

The Gladstone Court Museum, in Gladstone Court, parallel to High Street, shows the town as it was in Victorian times. Its exhibits include full-scale replicas of mid-19th-century shops, a telephone room and a bank.

Offering another fascinating glimpse into the past is the Greenhill Covenanters' House, on a bank of the Biggar Burn in the north of the town. This is an ancient farmhouse which in the 1970s was moved stone by stone to its present position from Wiston, some 10 miles south-west. In the 17th century it

belonged to a lady named Marie Dick, who gave shelter here to many outlawed covenanting ministers. They were Presbyterian ministers who were excluded from their churches for refusing to accept the Book of Common Prayer, preferring instead to risk severe government persecution by holding illegal services on the open moors.

The house is open to the public from Easter to October in the afternoons. Inside there are relics of the Covenanters, including the sword of one who was executed after the Battle of Rullion Green in 1666. There is also a good collection of 17th-century farmhouse furniture.

At the foot of the High Street is the old Cadger's Brig (or 'Bridge' in English), a memorial to the Scottish victory at the Battle of Biggar. Tradition has it that in 1297 the Scottish patriotic leader William Wallace (about 1272 – 1305) disguised himself as a cadger (or pedlar) and crossed the bridge on the eve of the battle to spy on the forces of the English king, Edward I. Cadger's Brig has been much repaired since.

Not far from the bridge, in the old town, is the Victorian gasworks where coal gas was manufactured from 1839 until the coming of North Sea gas in 1973. The building is now protected by the Ancient Monuments division of the Department of the Environment.

• **Parking** High Street • **Early closing** Wednesday • **Market day** Saturday (most) • **Events** Crowning of the Fleming Queen (June); Blackwood Murray Rally (August); Agricultural show (August); Horticultural show (September) • **Information** TEL. Biggar 21066 • **AA 24 hour service** TEL. Edinburgh 225 8464.

IN THE HEART OF BUCHAN COUNTRY

The writer John Buchan (1875 – 1940) spent many boyhood holidays in Broughton, and he used the village as a setting for several of his novels. Now Broughton has a centre devoted to his life and works. Other attractions are delightful cottages, a modern carved blacksmith's sign on a house in Dreva Road and a fine garden at Beechgrove.

Broughton – in Buchan country

Broughton BORDERS

5 miles east of Biggar (PAGE 345 B/Cb)

This is the very heart of John Buchan country. Here, the novelist, historian, politician and, as Lord Tweedsmuir, Governor General of Canada, had his roots. His mother's family home, the two-storey white house called Broughton Green, stands beside a crafts shop in the main street and still belongs to the family. The former Free Church, where his father was minister for a while, has become the John Buchan Centre, open in the afternoon from Easter to October.

Apart from exhibits relating to his political career and writings, it also has a memorial window to a local man named Hannay – a name Buchan may well have taken for his fictional hero Richard Hannay, who fought his way through *Greenmantle*, *The Thirty-Nine Steps* and other adventure stories. Now the local hotel – and even the ale made in the village brewery – is called Greenmantle.

There are two separate parts to Broughton. The core of the older part, known locally as The Village, is a double line of cottages, mostly in local stone, on either side of the main Moffat to Edinburgh road. They were built by James Dickson, laird in the 1750s.

In the 1920s, however, many of The Village's cottages were remodelled and extended by a local architect named James Grieve. He also reconstructed St Llolan's Cell on a hill above Broughton. Llolan was a Pictish hermit who lived here in the 7th century.

Blacksmith's carved sign

Cottages in The Village

Beechgrove

Beside the cell are the ruins of a church of which only an end wall and the belfry are still intact.

Below the ruined church, by the turning to Biggar, is Beechgrove. In the 1960s its owner transformed $1\frac{1}{4}$ acres that surrounded the house into a beautiful formal garden which is now open to the public on weekdays in the summer.

The newer part of Broughton lies nearly half a mile south of Beechgrove, near where the Broughton Burn joins Biggar Water, before they flow into the Tweed. Just beside the main road is the parish church built in 1804 and near by is Gala Lodge, home of John Buchan's sister Anna, also a novelist, who wrote under the name O. Douglas.

North of the village an avenue of trees leads from the main road to Broughton Place, which looks like an old Border castle but was designed in 1938 by the architect Sir Basil Spence. There are art and crafts exhibitions in the house throughout the year.

A previous mansion on the site, which had been derelict since a fire in 1775, was the home of the infamous John Murray of Broughton. In the Jacobite rising of 1745, Murray was one of Prince Charles Edward Stuart's closest followers, serving as his private secretary. But after the rising ended in defeat, Murray turned king's evidence and denounced many of his former companions in arms, who were executed.

Leadhills STRATHCLYDE

19 miles south-west of Biggar (PAGE 345 Ac)

It comes as a surprise, up on the heathery, sheep-grazing and grouse-moor slopes of the Lowther Hills, to find a village as big as Leadhills, and so obviously industrial in origin. Rows of single-storey stone and slate cottages, many of them colour-washed, climb to a church set high among woodland. Beyond it, a pass leads over the hills to Wanlockhead, a similar place, which vies with Leadhills for the title of highest village in Scotland – both are at nearly 1500 ft.

Silver was mined in the Lowthers in Roman times and after, and gold has been panned from its burns, but it is to lead that Leadhills owes its name and existence. In the 17th century the Hope family of Hopetoun (see Abercorn, page 367) began to exploit veins of lead in the hills round about, and their mines went on working until 1928.

The village grew up where miners built their own homes, also farming rent-free on the settlement's fringes. The poet Allan Ramsey (1686 – 1758) was born here, the son of the lead-mine manager. However, the poet moved to Edinburgh, where he prospered first as a wig-maker and then as a bookseller. Ramsey fathered a revival in Scottish literature in the 18th century, and using a Scots dialect in his poetry, he preserved it from extinction as a written form of the language.

In 1726 Ramsey also founded Britain's first circulating library, in Edinburgh. Fifteen years later he set up another in his birthplace, and the Allan Ramsey Library still stands opposite the post office. Most of the original 18th and 19th-century volumes can be seen still on its shelves.

Also born in Leadhills was William Symington (1763 – 1831). He designed the engine for a steam paddleboat which sailed on Dalswinton Loch, near Dumfries, in 1788 (the engine is now in the Science Museum, in London). Later he designed another engine which was used to power the *Charlotte Dundas*, a steam paddle-wheeler launched by the Forth and Clyde Canal Company in 1802 – and the world's first commercially successful canal steamer.

Symington is commemorated in Leadhills by an obelisk high on a hillside. Just above it is the village cemetery, in which is the grave of Robert Taylor, an 18th-century mine overseer. Almost as an afterthought, the inscription on his tombstone points out that he is buried beside his father John, 'who died at the remarkable age of 137 years'.

Back in the village, an old curfew bell beside Ramsey Road used to be rung at funerals and also to raise search parties when someone was lost in the hills.

In winter there is skiing, and the village has Britain's highest golf course – it lies at over 1300 ft. Industrial archaeologists are drawn by the remains of the old lead mines; and the Lowthers Railway Society has been formed to rebuild a narrow-gauge track on part of the old Leadhills and Wanlockhead Light Railway. The society hopes to reopen the $1\frac{1}{4}$ mile stretch which winds up from Leadhills to Wanlock Dod, a hill about 1800 ft high, and then to Wanlockhead.

Tweedsmuir BORDERS

13 miles south-east of Biggar (PAGE 345 Bb)

The name Tweedsmuir became more widely known in 1935 when the writer John Buchan, who had spent much of his childhood in the region (see Broughton, page 351), took the title Baron Tweedsmuir.

The village is a scattering of white farmhouses and cottages in the narrow valley of the River Tweed. Above and to the west, the bare, sheep-raising slopes of Weird Law and Upper and Nether Oliver Dod rise to around 1600 ft. Forestry plantations climb the lower, rounded Cockiland and Quarter hills to the east.

Winding through the valley is the main Moffat to Edinburgh road, and a smaller road turns off it at Tweedsmuir, crossing a stone bridge, below which the Tweed dashes down tiny falls into rocky pools.

Turning left at a crossroads beyond the bridge, the road comes to an unexpectedly fine parish church built in 1874. Set on a knoll where Talla Water joins the Tweed, the church has a strong square tower topped by an elegant tapering spire. Inside the porch is Tweedsmuir's war memorial, made from the wood of an oak which was planted more than 100 years earlier by the writer Sir Walter Scott (1771 – 1832) at his home Abbotsford (see Selkirk, page 358).

There was a church here long before the present one, and several moss-covered tombstones in the churchyard recall the 17th-century Covenanters (see Biggar, page 350). One was 'John Hunter martyr' who in 1685 'was cruelly murdered for his adherence to the word of God and Scotland's Covenanted Work of Reformation'. There is also a memorial to over 30 men who died between 1895 and 1905 during the building of the Talla Reservoir, which supplies Edinburgh with water, and the railway that once served it.

Back at the crossroads by the bridge, a pleasant road leads south-east down the tiny valley of Talla Water to the reservoir. Forest plantations rise on either side and, near the dam, rhododendrons mingle with some older pines. The road sweeps down the north bank of the reservoir to the hamlet of Talla Linnfoots, before rising to Fans Law, which is 1500 ft high.

Peebles parish church and bridge over the Tweed

Mercat (market) cross

Lamp with town motto

BARONIAL STYLE IN THE HIGH STREET

A stone bridge over the Tweed leads to a Gothic-spired parish church in Peebles High Street – built for £10,000 in the 1880s. The mercat (market) cross was moved from the older part of town to High Street in 1895. It overlooks an elegant hotel, turreted in Scottish baronial style. Near by are street lamps bearing the town's Latin motto, Contra nando incrementum, *which means 'multiplying against the stream' when translated.*

The more recent Fruid Reservoir lies south-west of Tweedsmuir, beyond the hamlet of Menzion, near which are three small standing stones – believed to be the remains of an ancient Druid circle.

There is good fishing in both reservoirs, and the Crook Inn, which was established in 1604 and stands 1½ miles north-east of Tweedsmuir along the Tweed valley, caters for anglers. The inn can also offer guests 30 miles of trout fishing in the rivers and streams around, and 7 miles of salmon fishing on the Tweed.

PEEBLES

BORDERS

23 miles south of Edinburgh (PAGE 345 Ca)

Two famous families – the Chambers and the Douglases – have close ties with this pleasant town on the banks of the River Tweed. Peebles was the birthplace of William and Robert Chambers who, in the 19th century, founded a publishing house which still produces a whole range of dictionaries, encyclopaedias and educational books. The brothers were inspired to start their business by reading an encyclopaedia found by Robert (1802 – 71) in the attic of their home when he was a boy of 11.

The Chambers family lived in a narrow street called Biggiesknowe, in the old part of the town. The house is marked by a plaque and the brothers are also commemorated by the Chambers Institution in the High Street. William (1800 – 83) gave it to the town in 1859 as an art gallery, museum and library. The turreted 16th-century building is still open throughout the year. It was once called the Queensberry Lodging and William Douglas, the notorious 4th Duke of Queensberry, was born here in 1724. The millionaire nobleman, known in later years as 'Old Q', was renowned as an eccentric gambler, dandy and rake.

The Douglas family home was 14th-century Neidpath Castle, a mile west of Peebles. Set dramatically on a bluff above the Tweed, it has 12 ft thick walls, a pit prison and a well sunk through solid rock. The castle now belongs to the family of the Earl of Wemyss and March, and is open to the public from the Thursday before Easter until the second week in October.

Peebles grew around a long-vanished medieval wooden castle, and was created a royal burgh in 1367 by David II of Scotland. Its centre is a 13th-century market cross, in the High Street. Near by is the Old Town House, built in 1753, and used during the Napoleonic Wars to house French officer-prisoners on parole. A room on the upper floor was turned into a theatre in which the prisoners put on French plays.

Set back from the High Street, in a cobbled square, is the early 19th-century Tontine Hotel – partly built by French prisoners. It was financed and first run on the tontine system, under which a group of people invest in a project. When one member of the group dies the share of each of the other investors becomes greater, until the last to survive becomes sole owner. In this case it was Sir John Hay of Haystoun.

Near by is Parliament Square, where the Scottish Parliament met in 1346, after King David II had been captured by the English. In the square is a small part of the defensive wall built around the town in the 16th century. Leading down from it is a flight of steps called the Stinkin' Stair, probably because of the tannery and brewery that stood at the bottom. To the north of the

A PROSPECT OF PEEBLES OVERLEAF

A meadow newly mown and, beyond, another grazed by contented sheep . . . then a peaceful prospect of Peebles against a backdrop of rolling, wooded hills . . . This is the splendid setting for a town named from the Celtic word pebyll, *meaning simply 'a tent'.*

High Street, behind Biggiesknowe, are the ruins of the 13th-century Cross Kirk, founded by Alexander III (1241–86). It became the parish church in the 16th century and was in use until 1784. An occasional outdoor service is still held here; the present Gothic-style parish church – at the bottom of the High Street – was built in 1887.

Near Cross Kirk are the ruins of an even older church – St Andrew's, built in the late 12th century. It was repeatedly damaged and finally burnt by English raiders in the 15th and 16th centuries. But its tower was restored in 1876 by William Chambers.

• **Parking** Greenside; Kingsmeadows Road; Edinburgh Road; Eastgate; School Brae (all car parks) • **Early closing** Wednesday • **Market day** Thursday • **Events** Beltane Festival (June); Arts Festival (September) • **Information** TEL. Peebles 20138 (summer) • **AA 24 hour service** TEL. Edinburgh 225 8464.

Innerleithen BORDERS

6 miles south-east of Peebles (PAGE 345 Db)

The pen of Sir Walter Scott and a saint who, according to legend, attacked the Devil and grabbed one of his legs with his crook, put this spa village on the map. The saint was St Ronan, patron of the town, who favoured the local mineral spring in the 7th century. It is said that during his diabolical encounter he tripped the Devil, and the place where the Devil fell is now a sulphur well.

Sir Walter's contribution was the novel, *St Ronan's Well*, published in 1823. Readers immediately identified Innerleithen as the spa mentioned in the book, and visitors arrived in their hundreds. The local landowner, the Earl of Traquair, had a pavilion-like pump room built beside the well and the blue-and-white building is now the home of the caretaker. Mineral water from the well can be bought at the pump room.

For many years, Innerleithen men were known for being 'much addicted to athletic exercises and games'. As the popularity of the spa brought in more visitors, so outside enthusiasm for these competitions grew. A parish minister explained: 'The gay loungers at the watering place came habitually to take an interest in the games; and in 1827 forty-two noblemen, knights and gentlemen joined in instituting an annual competition for prizes in all gymnastic exercises.'

That was the start of St Ronan's Games, which continue and are held over a full week every July. They now include parades recalling the saint's story, and at dusk on the closing day a procession climbs the footpath to the site of an ancient fort on the summit of Caerlee Hill. Fireworks are set off, and a bonfire topped by an effigy of the Devil is lit.

The village has a thriving knitwear industry – much of it in cashmere wool – and its High Street is a busy shopping centre. Some of the shops, hotels and houses retain their stone frontages; others are colour-washed, but no two look alike. Many minor streets have surprisingly metropolitan names – Bond Street, Piccadilly, Princes Street – named thus by one of the Earls of Traquair.

Near the start of Leithen Road, a Memorial Hall is open on certain weekdays in summer as a local museum. The heather and rock garden in front of it is a miniature representation of the site of Innerleithen itself, among the forested Tweed valley hills. One of the miniature paths leads over a tiny stone bridge. In full scale, this is the Cuddy Bridge across the Leithen beyond the ornate parish church of 1870. It was originally a packhorse bridge, and leads to a riverside picnic place and a network of footpaths through pinewoods on the slopes of a hill called Pirn Craig.

There is a golf course and the village is also an angling centre, located as it is beside the salmon and trout waters of the Tweed – but permission is required to fish them. In the neighbouring village of Walkerburn, 2 miles east, there is a museum devoted to the woollen industry, open from Easter to October.

Stobo BORDERS

6 miles south-west of Peebles (PAGE 345 Cb)

Weary travellers toiling up Tweeddale in the 18th century would sigh with relief when they came along by 'Stobo hedges'. That was the name given to the road through the village because of its neatly trimmed hedge boundaries – unusual at that time. Stobo has been a well-kept place ever since. The modern village is along the same road, the hedges still flourish and Stobo is now backed by forest plantations and shelter-belts of trees which sweep up the hills from riverside fields.

Some of the most famous woodlands in Scotland lie 2 miles south of the village, on the Dawyck estate across the Tweed. Generations of lairds from the Veitch, Naesmyth and Balfour families planted hundreds of thousands of trees on the hillsides, not only for commercial benefit and simple ornamentation, but also from a real love of tree cultivation.

Carolus Linnaeus, the 18th-century Swede renowned as the man who classified plants in the universal system used today, visited Dawyck House to see his pupil Sir James Naesmyth, who was one of the first people to plant silver firs and birch in Scotland. Dawyck lairds helped finance many tree and plant-collecting expeditions to North America and Asia in this and the previous century.

The present Dawyck House, built in 1830 with later additions, stands among lawns and terraces. It is not open to the public, but the Arboretum – tree garden – now in the care of the Royal Botanic Garden of Edinburgh, welcomes visitors from April to September. It is laid out in a glen down which the Scrape Burn tumbles in a series of cascades, seen at their best when framed by a high-arched humped bridge. There are many fine specimen trees and a splendid display of rhododendrons in late spring and early summer.

Among the many grass and gravel pathways, one leads to a red-roofed private chapel which can be visited and is still sometimes used for services. Memorial plaques to past lairds are set round the walls.

The village stretches for 1½ miles and its houses were almost all built by the Stobo lairds, using locally quarried stone and slate. There are cottages, gate lodges and some more substantial houses, with farms set back from the road. Running alongside the road for part of the way through the village, before veering off to follow the Tweed, is the old railway line to Peebles. It has long since gone back to grass and makes an attractive walk.

Stobo's church is at the north end of the village, above the bridge over the Easton Burn. There has been a church here since the 6th century, and Stobo Kirk was once a deanery of Glasgow Cathedral, dedicated to St Kentigern, the city's patron saint.

Much of the present building, which has a plain, rough-cast exterior, is Norman in design, and its porch was renovated in 1513. Inside the porch are the local jougs – the iron collar in which miscreants were once held. Two of the original Norman windows now have narrow panels of Victorian stained glass.

The towers of Stobo Castle, to the south-west, which was completed in 1811, can be seen above its sheltering woodland. It is now a health farm, the private driveway guarded by eagle-topped pillars.

West Linton BORDERS

14 miles north-west of Peebles (PAGE 345 Ca)

West Linton men once had a wide reputation as stonemasons and carvers, and traces of their work can still be found in the village: the odd statue, a carving on a gable end and among the 17th-century gravestones of the churchyard. The churchyard is also the centre of a gruesome story.

In 1839, a Linton medical student at Edinburgh recognised the body of a recently dead neighbour on the dissecting table. This was the era of the infamous Burke and Hare body-snatchers, who supplied Edinburgh's Medical School with corpses. As a result, an armed guard was stationed in Linton churchyard to prevent any further horrors. Kindly villagers kept the fate of the dead man, Robert Farquharson, from his widow to the end of her days.

Another memento of the masons is the village's centrepiece, the clock tower in Main Street. It was built originally as a market cross in the 17th century by self-taught sculptor and 'architector' James Gifford. The tower took its present form when the old parish-school clock was added to it, but it still incorporates a statue that Gifford carved of his wife.

The village as a whole – built where the Lyne Water comes down from the Pentland Hills into a sweep of level farmland – has a rambling charm. Main Street winds between low-set cottages, two-storey terraces and villas in many different styles. The street used to follow the twists of a burn, long since diverted, called Rumbling Tam, which is still commemorated in a shop name.

The lanes which turn off Main Street conceal many well-restored homes, like the Old Meeting House of 1784, later Trinity Church and which is now a private house.

There are two handsome village greens, Upper and Lower. Upper Green lies next to the Biggar to Edinburgh road. Lower Green follows the Lyne as it curves past the parish church of St Andrew, a pleasant building with white-rendered walls, a stone tower, spire and some fine ornamental woodwork carved by two local ladies. The church was built in 1782 on what had been the garden of the old manse, and enlarged to its present form in 1871. Part of the manse garden wall still has two recesses in which the minister once kept his beehives.

In the 18th century, Linton (before having West added to distinguish it from East Linton, in Lothian) was a hive of activity itself. As well as regular markets, the biggest sheep sales in Scotland were held four times a year. Weavers, thatchers, bootmakers and many carriers and carters thrived. In 1803 the ploughmen's society started a festival, with one of the members being voted Whipman for the year. The 'Whipman Play', a week-long gala in June, was restarted in 1931 and is now the major event of the village year.

In the days of the Linton markets, sheep and cattle were taken south to England across the Pentlands by the drove road over the pass of the Cauld Stane Slap, now a popular walkers' right of way. Another walk along the edge of the Pentlands follows part of the old Edinburgh to Biggar coach road, which was in use until 1833. Earlier, on a similar route, Roman legions marched to and from their major fort at Inveresk, on the Forth.

West Linton golf course is on the hillside beyond the Roman road. More hill-walking tracks lead from it towards the western edge of the Pentlands.

An alleyway off Main Street, West Linton

MONUMENTS TO STONEMASONS

The skill and artistry of West Linton's stonemasons and sculptors is evident in carvings such as that on an 18th-century tombstone in St Andrew's churchyard. In about 1660 James Gifford, one of the most renowned craftsmen, carved portraits of himself and his wife in a wall opposite Raemartin Square. Mellow stone houses can be seen in the alleys off Main Street.

Carved tombstone

Wall carving of the Giffords

SELKIRK

BORDERS

12 miles north of Hawick (PAGE 345 Db)

For almost 33 years the author Sir Walter Scott presided over Selkirk's sheriff court. He was a lawyer as well as an author, and was appointed sheriff (judge) in 1799. At first his court sat in the Tolbooth (town hall) which stood in the triangular Market Place. Then the Tolbooth was demolished and in 1803 he moved into a new Sheriff Court House.

Today a statue of Scott (1771 – 1832) stands in the middle of the Market Place on the site of the old Tolbooth. Behind it rises his Court House – now the Town Hall – its front suitably imposing with clock tower and steeple. Inside are Scott's bench and chair, a collection of his letters and his robing room.

At the other end of the spacious High Street is a statue to another distinguished Selkirk man, the explorer Mungo Park (1771 – 1806) who was the first European to trace the course of the River Niger in north-west Africa. He was born in the village of Foulshiels, 4 miles west of Selkirk, and was apprenticed to a Selkirk doctor whose daughter he married.

A third statue, at the junction of Scott's Place and Dovecot Park, was put up in 1913 to commemorate a man named Fletcher. He was the only one of 80 Selkirk fighting men to return alive from the Battle of Flodden in 1513. Although the Scots were heavily defeated, Fletcher brought back a captured English banner, which he waved over his head in the Market Place – and then cast sorrowfully down.

His gesture is repeated each year during the Selkirk Common Riding, in June. After hundreds of riders and followers on foot have traced the boundaries of the town's common land, they converge on the Market Place for the 'casting of the colours'. On a raised platform in the middle of the square, representatives of local guilds cast down large embroidered banners one by one. Then the town band breaks into the moving lament, originating from Selkirk, called *The Flo'ers o' the Forest*. The ceremony honours all Selkirk people killed at Flodden and in wars since.

The town rises in tiers to more than 600 ft above the River Ettrick – along whose banks 19th-century tweed mills are still working. Selkirk was once also famous for shoemaking, and to this day its natives are known as 'souters', or shoemakers.

Viewed from a distance, the town is a charming mixture of towers, spires and trees. Its clean, bright streets are studded with handsome town houses and pretty cottages – mainly 18th century or earlier, some with mid-Victorian frontages – and there is a profusion of ancient alleys, courts and closes. In Halliwell's Close, just off the Market Place, stands a museum devoted to old ironmongery and household utensils. Near by is the former shop of Robbie Douglas, a Victorian baker who created the round, yeasty fruit-loaf called the Selkirk bannock.

Douglas used only the purest local butter and specially imported sultanas from Turkey. If the right ingredients were not available, Douglas would not bake. His fruit-loaf received royal approval in 1867 when Queen Victoria, on a visit to the district, spurned a rich display of delicacies and selected some slices of Selkirk bannock.

Four miles north-east of the town, overlooking the River Tweed, is Sir Walter Scott's home, Abbotsford. He transformed it from a simple farmhouse into a Gothic-style mansion of turrets and battlemented towers, and the house did much to start the 19th-century fashion for mock-medieval castles in Scotland.

Abbotsford still belongs to Scott's family and is open from April to October. Its treasures include Napoleon's pencase and blotting book, Prince Charles Edward Stuart's drinking cup, and a pocket book made by Flora Macdonald, who ferried Prince Charles Edward 'over the sea to Skye'. All were acquired by Sir Walter himself – he was an avid collector of mementoes of the famous.

• **Parking** Scott's Place; Chapel Street; Market Square; Market place (all car parks) • **Early closing** Thursday • **Event** Common Riding (June) • **Information** TEL. Selkirk 20054 (summer) • **AA 24 hour service** TEL. Edinburgh 225 8464.

Bowden BORDERS

7 miles east of Selkirk (PAGE 345 Eb)

The great abbeys – Kelso, Melrose, Jedburgh – whose ruins brood over the Scottish border country, first brought civilisation to this once savage region. Bowden, a neat, peaceful place, can claim to have played its part in the transformation. The church was one of Scotland's earliest of this era, founded in 1128 by the Benedictines of Kelso, who were also pioneer farmers in the region.

Set among ash and beech trees, and a little apart from the village, the present building is mostly of the 17th century and later. But it occupies the site and follows the general plan of the 12th-century church. Notable features include the 17th-century 'laird's loft' – the black oak pew of the Riddell Carre family – which was moved to its present position during a restoration of the building in Edwardian times.

The village flourished under the abbots and there were 36 cottages, a mill and four brewhouses in the original settlement. After the Scottish Reformation in the mid-16th century, when the great religious houses lost their lands, Bowden continued as a place of consequence. In 1571, it was the first village in Scotland (rather than a town) to be granted the right to hold a regular market.

The oldest house here dates from the following century – one of a row of cottages at the west end in which linen was once woven. Until the 18th century, flax was grown, spun and woven into cloth locally. The trade later became industrialised and moved to the mills of Galashiels in the 19th century. Bowden became a residential village, as it remains today, with handsomely restored whitewashed cottages sheltered to the north by the treble peaks of the Eildon Hills.

The main street climbs gently alongside the well-kept triangular village green, crossed by driveways and planted with trees. The upkeep of the green and public rights of way is the responsibility of the District Council of the Borders Region. The Village Committee, formed in 1972, ensures that Bowden remains worthy of its status as a Conservation Village, the first in the former county of Roxburgh.

By the road at the top of the hill, the war memorial stands on the base of the old market cross. Opposite, on the far side of a little square, is the post office – originally a school, as is shown by a plaque high on the front wall commemorating an early teacher. Near by is a recently restored octagonal building which contains a well.

The houses south of the road stand on rising ground above the Bowden Burn, which flows eastwards to the River Tweed. They enjoy a splendid view over farmland, woods and moorland to the faraway summits of the Cheviot Hills.

Footpaths lead northwards over the village common to link up with the Eildon Walk. The three rounded Eildon summits are easy to reach, on heathery moorland which is fine territory for birdwatchers.

Denholm BORDERS

17 miles south-east of Selkirk (PAGE 345 Ec)

Denholm has one of Scotland's most imposing and attractive village greens, complete with a miniature Albert Memorial-style monument to a local hero. All pillars, Gothic arches, gables and carving, it was put up by Victorian admirers of John Leyden, who demonstrated the virtues and self-reliance that they held in such esteem.

Born the son of a shepherd in 1775, in a thatched cottage which still stands near by, he was a doctor and minister, friend of the novelist Sir Walter Scott and a poet who became a master of Oriental languages. Most of his working life was spent in India, where he served as a surgeon in Madras and as a judge in Calcutta, before dying of fever on an official mission to Java. He was then only 36 years old.

His memory is still revered – the monument was restored in 1982 with funds raised from a sponsored walk by local young people. They followed the route taken by Leyden himself when he set off for his studies at the University of Edinburgh.

In Leyden's day, Denholm was famous for stocking weaving, and one of the stocking mills, at the north-west corner of the green, still has its original large, many-paned windows. Large windows were needed to let in enough light, but in the days before sheet glass they had to be divided into several smaller panes. The mill building has been restored for use as a private house.

For a time in the 19th century, the village seemed set for greater things as a manufacturing centre, but the landowner, the Earl of Minto, refused to allow the railway in and business faded.

On the east of the green, the parish church was built in 1844 for the newly formed Free Church congregation. Lacking funds, they did a great deal of the building themselves. Now the church is linked with others at Minto, 2 miles north, and Bedrule, 2 miles east. They combine on Easter Day and Advent Sunday to hold daybreak services on the summit of Ruberslaw, a hill which rises sharply to the south. This revives an old tradition, as Ruberslaw was the site of many a preaching when dissenting freechurchmen were outlawed and hunted down by the troops of Charles II.

On the south of the green, completing the picture, is a line of mostly two-storey houses of stone and slate, including two old coaching inns. There is just one three-storey building, the curious Text House, built in 1910 to the design of a local doctor, John Haddon. It is named after the pairs of plaques sunk in its walls which bear proverbs in Border Scots and whose wording has puzzled many a visitor. One pair says: 'Tak Tent in time, ere time be tint', which translates roughly as 'Take care of time before it takes care of you'.

Denholm stands on high ground above the River Teviot, and the nearby three-arched bridge over the river was built in 1864. This replaced a suspension bridge built in 1820, whose sandstone piers still stand – the southern one well inland from the water's edge, showing how the course of the Teviot has shifted northwards.

Before the bridges, there were three ways to cross the river – by ferry, by a ford north-east of the village, or by stilts. Every household is reputed once to have had stilts for just that purpose.

The Teviot is a salmon and trout water, and here it runs through horse country. There is a riding centre at Hazeldean, and the 1979 Grand National winner, Rubstic, was trained at Bedrule.

St Boswells BORDERS

9 miles east of Selkirk (PAGE 345 Eb)

A stately avenue of lime trees, planted in 1898 by the 6th Duke of Buccleuch and leading from the 18th-century Buccleuch Arms hotel across the village green, forms a noble approach to St Boswells. A Conservation Village, much of it is built of warm red sandstone, including a row of villas known as The Croft, angled along the north of the green; the late Victorian village hall; and the two-storey houses lining the main street, which curves through the village to Mertoun Bridge across the Tweed.

Until two centuries ago, both village and parish were known as Lessudden. The present name commemorates St Boisil, a 7th-century prior buried in Durham Cathedral, who founded an earlier village about a mile south of the modern site. Why the change was made is uncertain, but for decades the village used both names.

St Boisil's Day is July 18, and that is the date of St Boswells Fair, started at about the same time as the change of name. 'If the day is fine,' reads an account published in 1834, 'St Boswells Green presents a very gay and animated scene. The whole place being planted with tents, covered with a profusion of goods, consisting of Scotch and Irish linen, hardware, toys, crockery, shoes, bowls, etcetera, or crowded with sheep, lambs, horses and horned cattle.'

Nowadays the fair is smaller, but still held annually on the part of the green south of the avenue. The village cricket team plays in the Border League on a pitch beside the Buccleuch Arms.

St Boswells is at the centre of a network of public footpaths. One leads to a suspension bridge over the River Tweed and on to Bemersyde on the east bank about a mile north of St Boswells. From here it is a short road walk to the beautifully kept grounds of Dryburgh Abbey, founded in 1150 and the most complete of the great ruined religious houses of the Borders.

The 15th-century west doorway, the north and south transepts, the cloister, the chapter house and the refectory with its fine rose window all survive. Dryburgh is famous as the burial place of Sir Walter Scott and of Earl Haig of Bemersyde, British commander in chief on the Western Front during most of the

St Boswells – The Croft

Dryburgh Abbey

The Tweed at St Boswells

HERE LIE MEN OF WORDS AND DEEDS

A shattered rose window casts its shadow amid the impressive ruins of Dryburgh Abbey, near St Boswells, where Sir Walter Scott and First World War commander Earl Haig are buried. The abbey was bought for the nation by Lord Glenconnor in 1919. The village lies on a lovely stretch of the Tweed and has a riverside golf course. Many of its houses are, like the abbey, of local stone.

First World War. The graves of both men are in the north transept chapels.

The well-trimmed abbey lawns are planted with trees varying in size and shape from box to cedar, sycamore, lime and sequoia. Rooks and wood pigeons nest near by; the old water channel used by the monks, now a grassy ditch, is planted with daffodils. Another pleasant walk goes from the riverside golf course along the curving south bank of the Tweed to the five broad arches of the Mertoun Bridge, and on to the neighbouring village of Maxton, which lies a mile or so south-east. A short cut back to St Boswells is up a flight of steps called Jacob's Ladder, following the carefully angled brickwork of an estate boundary wall.

MAP 32

THE GOLF COAST AND ROB ROY COUNTRY

To the east lies St Andrews, spiritual and temporal cradle of golf, home of the Royal and Ancient on a coast full of fairways, greens and bunkers. To the west is 'Bonnie Strathyre', bandit country when Rob Roy Macgregor roamed there. In between are palaces and ports on both sides of the Forth – made accessible by fine bridges and handy motorways.

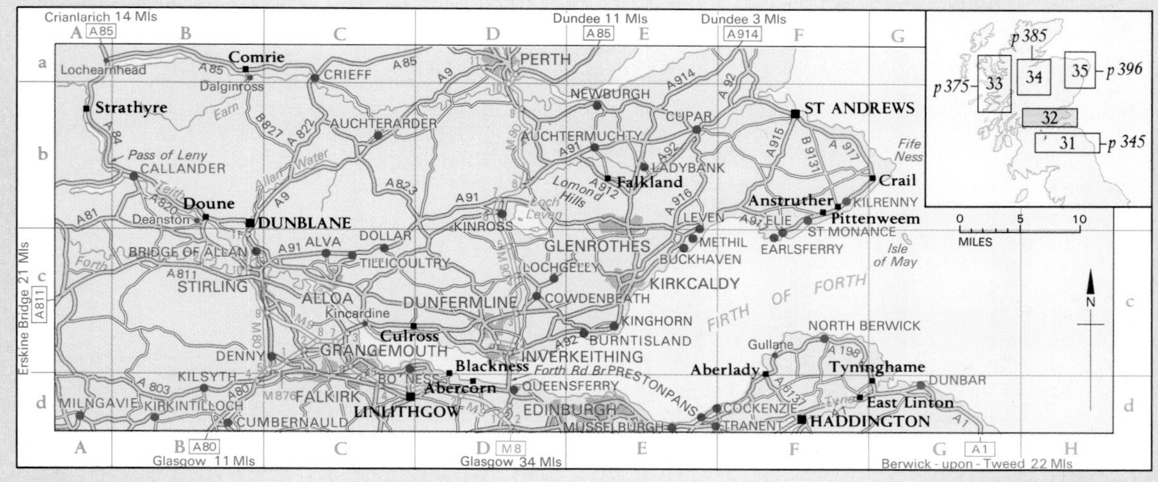

MAP 32: NEIGHBOURING AREAS – MAPS 31, 33, 34, 35

DUNBLANE Comrie Doune Strathyre
HADDINGTON Aberlady East Linton Tyninghame
LINLITHGOW Abercorn Blackness Culross
ST ANDREWS Anstruther Crail Falkland Pittenweem

DUNBLANE

CENTRAL

5 miles north of Stirling (PAGE 361 Bb)

Set on a rise above the Allan Water, Dunblane Cathedral is the centre and focal point of this small and ancient country town. The English critic and architectural writer John Ruskin (1819 – 1900) visited the building and wrote: 'He was no common man who designed that Cathedral of Dunblane. I know not anything so perfect in its simplicity, and so beautiful . . . in all the Gothic with which I am acquainted.'

The man whom Ruskin praised was Bishop Clement, a Dominican friar, who masterminded most of the cathedral in the 13th century. He dedicated it to St Blane – the late 6th-century Scottish missionary who founded a church on the site – and St Lawrence.

Dunblane Cathedral is noted for the magnificent oak carvings on the screen in the choir; the six stained-glass south windows in the choir, depicting *The Benedicite* and the archangels; and its elaborately carved, late 15th-century stalls put up by Bishop James Chisholm and bearing his coat of arms. Set on one side of the main building is the square tower which has a parapet dating from about 1500. The rest of the tower is Norman, and the lower storeys were in existence when the cathedral was built. They probably formed a defence tower for an earlier church here.

In the late 1500s the roof of the nave fell in, and for the next 300 years – while the nave remained roofless – services were held in the choir. The roof was finally restored in 1893 and the congregation moved back into the nave.

Opposite the cathedral is the Cathedral Museum, the former home of James Pearson of Kippenross, who became the Dean of Dunblane in 1624. The museum has a large and varied collection of historical documents and a number of interesting relics of the cathedral and the district. It is open to the public from late May to early October.

Almost opposite is the Leighton Library, built in 1687 by Edward Lightmaker, nephew of Bishop Robert Leighton, who governed the cathedral for nearly ten years in the late 17th century. The library contains all the bishop's religious books, which he left to the local clergy. The cost of new books, and the maintenance of the building, came from an endowment of £300. By the river is the tree-shaded Bishop's Walk where Bishop Leighton liked to stroll.

Dunblane is named after St Blane (its name means 'the fort of Blane') and it was burnt to the ground twice: by the Britons in AD 857 and by the Danes in AD 912. It was created a city in 1500 by James IV but became a town again in the late 17th century.

Allan Water was – and still is – one of the town's main attractions, and in the 19th century Dunblane was noted as a spa. Its narrow streets, lined with old greystone buildings, spread out on both sides of the Allan Water, which splits the town in two.

Spanning the river are two road bridges: the Old Bridge and a wide, modern, main road bridge. The Old Bridge has a single arch and was built by Bishop Finlay Dermoch in the early 15th century. It was added to and widened in 1842 and 1927. The other bridge was built during the Second World War.

• **Parking** The Haining; Mill Row (both car parks) • **Early closing** Wednesday • **Event** Highland Games (September) • **Information** TEL. Dunblane 824428 (summer) • **AA 24 hour service** TEL. Glasgow 812 0101.

Comrie TAYSIDE

18 miles north of Dunblane (PAGE 361 Ba)

The Victorians used to visit Comrie in search of a most unusual diversion – the chance of being involved in an earthquake. The village is built on the Highland Boundary Fault, a great cleft in the Earth's crust whose visible expression is the contrast between the rich plains of Strathearn and the hills of Glen Lednock.

The first recorded earth tremor was in 1789, when local people, puzzled by sudden loud noises, put them down to guns being fired on the nearby Dunira estate. It was not for some years that the tremors were correctly identified. The most substantial shudder was in 1839, after which Comrie began to gain fame as the earthquake capital of Scotland.

The layout of the now almost tremor-free village is dictated by three rivers. Flowing from west to east, the River Earn takes in two tributaries – the River Lednock, which tumbles down a steep-sided glen from the north, and the Water of Ruchill, whose source is to the south among the forest peaks of Glenartney.

Present-day Comrie is an amalgam of three villages. Comrie proper is built along the main road from Crieff to Lochearnhead, and, apart from earthquakes, it offers visitors the Museum of Scottish Tartans which is housed in an 18th-century building in the main street. The present parish church, a striking Victorian building in French Gothic style, is much admired. It replaces the former parish church of 1804, which is now used as a youth and community centre.

The main bridge over the Earn leads to the adjoining parish of Dalginross, where the wide central thoroughfare, with regularly spaced side streets, is quite different from the more cramped arrangement in Comrie itself. Possibly there is some far-off influence of the grid plan of Roman towns. Dalginross was very nearly the northern limit of the Roman Empire, and the outlines of three legionary camps have been traced upon its plain.

Dalginross is bounded on the west by the Water of Ruchill. Farther west again is Ross, the third section of modern Comrie and joined to it by a well-preserved stone bridge of 1792.

Set on a little hilltop you will find the Earthquake House, built in 1869 to house records of earth tremors.

Comrie enjoys sport. The Earn is a good autumn trout river, and there is a well-kept if hilly golf course. Unusually for Scotland, it also has a cricket club, which was founded in 1909 and down the years has entertained many famous cricketers as guest-players, including the Yorkshire and England batsman Wilfred Rhodes (1877 – 1973).

Among several fine walks in the neighbourhood is the path up the Lednock glen to the Deil's Caldron, where the River Lednock rushes down a narrow channel and through a hole in the rock. A tougher path leads to the Melville Monument, a spectacular viewpoint on the summit of Dunmore. It commemorates Henry Dundas, 1st Viscount Melville (1742 – 1811), the laird of Dunira and chief minister in Scotland under William Pitt the Younger. He was also Treasurer of the Navy in Nelson's time, but fell from grace in 1806. He was impeached for misapplying public funds, but was later exonerated.

Comrie Fortnight, usually held in the last week of July and the first week of August, presents the village to the world in a festival of sport, music and drama, guided walks, gardens and a wild raft race down the Earn to Crieff. But those who wish to enter the true spirit of the village must visit it on New Year's Eve, or Hogmanay, the time of the Flambeaux Procession. Torches are lit at midnight and paraded round the village.

Doune CENTRAL

4 miles west of Dunblane (PAGE 361 Bb)

The village sign depicts the 17th-century Mercat (market) Cross flanked by pairs of pistols – a salute to the days when Doune pistols were famed throughout Scotland and far beyond. A gunsmith named Caddell began making them here in 1645 – the old workshops, now modernised, can still be seen in an alley off Main Street – and local tradition insists that it was a Doune pistol that fired the first shot in the War of American Independence.

Doune's principal attraction is its castle, which stands on a narrow hillock close to the joining of the Ardoch Burn and the River Teith. It has a chequered history not untypical of Scottish castles. It was built by the Duke of Albany in the late 14th and early 15th

LIFE IN THE OLD CAR YET . . .

Well-polished brass gleams on the lamps and radiator of a Citroën 5CV which first took to the road in 1923. Now it takes life easy – in the Earl of Moray's fascinating Doune Motor Museum. His splendid collection includes such treasures as the second-oldest Rolls Royce in the world, made in 1905, and a 1913 Sunbeam rescued from a field where it had lain for half a century. Some of the old cars are even wheeled out to compete in the timed hill-climbs that are held in Doune Park in April, June and September every year.

BONNIE EARL'S CASTLE *Doune Castle is home of the Earls of Moray, one of whom was murdered and became the subject of a ballad.*

centuries, then it was confiscated by James I and used as a royal residence for many years, and finally it was presented to the Stuart Earls of Moray who own it to this day.

One of the earls was murdered at Donibristle, in Fife, in 1592, in the course of one of the dark conspiracies that surrounded James VI – later James I of England. The earl was a vain young man and historically unimportant, and the incident might have been long forgotten, had it not become the subject of one of the most famous and poignant of Scottish ballads, *The Bonnie Earl o' Moray*:

O lang, lang will his lady
Look ower the Castle Doune
Ere she sees the Earl o' Moray
Come sounding through the toun.

Much later, the castle was used by Prince Charles Edward Stuart to house prisoners of war taken at the Battle of Falkirk in 1746.

Doune is an attractive old place with a fine stone bridge over the River Teith. The bridge was built – so the story goes – in 1535 by Robert Spittal, the king's tailor. Apparently he did it to spite the local ferryman who had refused to carry him over the river one day when he had forgotten his purse. A little upstream is a village now called Deanston, though its original name was Newtown of Doune. It grew up about Deanston Mill, a cotton-spinning works established in 1785. Textiles went on being made in the old building until 1965, when it was converted into a whisky distillery. Where the mules and throstles used to clatter and rattle, there is now only a gentle hiss from the copper stills. Rows of cottages lie along the bank of the millstream.

About a mile along the Callander road from Doune is Doune Park, 60 acres of woodland walks, rhododendrons, azaleas and other shrubs laid out by 19th-century Earls of Moray. In more recent times different tastes have prevailed, as is apparent from the splendid collection of motor cars in the Motor Museum, established close by and open to the public from April to October.

Strathyre CENTRAL

20 miles north-west of Dunblane (PAGE 361 Ab)

'Bonnie Strathyre', the old song calls it, but it was probably meant more as a compliment to the valley than the village which, though pleasant, is no architectural gem. It consists mostly of Victorian houses and hotels strung along the Lochearnhead road and the bank of the River Balvaig at the head of Loch Lubnaig. But there are some fine old stone cottages and a handsome, high-arched stone bridge, and the setting of high, forested hills is bonnie indeed.

This is the Highlands in picturesque rather than savage mood, just the thing to attract Victorians brought up on a diet of Sir Walter Scott who, in fact, describes the country round about in both *The Lady of the Lake* and *A Legend of Montrose*. To the north is Balquhidder, where that unjustly celebrated brigand Rob Roy MacGregor and his family are buried, and to the south, the Pass of Leny, which has spectacular rapids and falls. All these delights helped to bring the Callander and Oban Railway in 1865 and, once it had its own station, Strathyre's future was assured.

A landslide to the north blocked the railway exactly 100 years later, and a decision was taken to dismantle the line. But by that time, those in search of not too strenuous outdoor holidays – walkers, anglers, pony-trekkers, photographers, canoeists – had found their own way there by road.

Some grand walks in the vicinity include an easy one south-east of Strathyre where there are labelled specimen trees, and the chance to see roe deer feeding in the plantations. There is a forest information centre, open in summer, at the southern edge of the village. This is also the starting place for some more energetic walks, including one that crosses the Balvaig by footbridge, then runs up through the forest to open ground on the 1800 ft summit of Ben Shian – Hill of the Fairies. Like all the hilltops hereabouts, it gives splendid views of lochs and mountains, given emphasis by the varying greens of spruce, larch and pine trees.

The plantations about Strathyre make ideal country for the capercaillie, Britain's largest game bird. Its name means 'the great cock of the wood'. It became extinct in Scotland in the 18th century due to the dwindling of the native Scots pine forests and because it was an easy target. However, it was reintroduced from Sweden in the 1830s, and has settled very well again in the Highlands. The males can reach a weight of 17 lb and look, in flight, like airborne turkeys. In the spring they establish a territory from which they challenge other males in a mixture of clicks, rattles, gargles and popping noises. They will even attack dogs or humans venturing on their territory.

HADDINGTON

LOTHIAN

17 miles east of Edinburgh (PAGE 361 Fd)

To drive into Haddington is to step back in time – in fact to take several distinct steps back – yet all seems so pristine perfect it might be newly built. There are 284 buildings of outstanding historical interest in the town, some of which are marked with a small bronze plaque. Whether large or small, grand or humble, nearly every one of them has been lovingly and enthusiastically restored by local authorities, private owners and an independent registered charity called the Lamp of Lothian Trust. In 1975 Haddington received a Council of Europe Architectural Heritage Year award.

The town was made a royal burgh in the 12th century, and through medieval times and beyond did a thriving trade in corn, oats and barley (for whisky distilling) grown in the rich farming country around. Corn is still one of the most important crops grown here today, along with potatoes.

By the late 18th and 19th centuries Haddington's thoroughfares were lined with elegant stone and colour-washed buildings that reflected its continuing prosperity. The three main streets – Court Street, High Street and Market Street – were laid out to form a long and slender triangle. At the centre of it is the dignified 18th-century Town House. Its tapering 170 ft spire was added in the early 1830s. Several other fine buildings of the period – including the graceful Bank of Scotland in Court Street – have attracted visitors from all over Britain.

A Scottish king, Alexander II (1198 – 1249), was born in Haddington, as was the social reformer Samuel Smiles (1812 – 1904), author of the 'improving' book, *Self-Help*. It is also believed to be the birthplace of the

HADDINGTON SPEAKS UP FOR ITSELF

The buildings of Haddington speak up for themselves. Many old shops and workplaces bear signs indicating their trade – like the boot over the cobbler's door and the horse at the saddler's – and the many buildings of historical interest carry little plaques. The Town House has a particularly elegant spire added by Gillespie Gordon, who also designed the steeple of St John's Tolbooth in Edinburgh.

Town House

Cobbler's shop

Antiques shop

St Ann's Place

Saddler's sign

great Presbyterian leader John Knox (about 1505–72).

The town's most famous woman was a surgeon's daughter, Jane Welsh, who in 1826 married the historian and writer Thomas Carlyle, author of the *Parliamentary History of the French Revolution.* When she died 40 years later her grief-stricken husband penned a memorable and touching epitaph, which is carved on her grave inside the parish church of St Mary. The epitaph reads, in part:

'. . . In her bright existence she had more sorrows than are common, but also a soft invincibility, a clearness of discernment and a noble loyalty of heart, which are rare . . . she was the true and ever loving helpmate of her husband . . .'

The house in Lodge Street where Jane was born has recently been restored and is open to the public. Two rooms have been furnished in Regency style and contain portraits of literary figures of the time.

There are local history museums at Newton Port and in Lady Kitty's Doo'cot (dovecote) off Sidegate. The doo'cot is a miniature 18th-century castellated tower that still houses some pigeons. Its key is available from the Peter Potter Gallery and Bookshop which stands close by.

The 14th-century parish church of St Mary was badly damaged in 1548, when the English were besieged in the town by a force of Scots and French, and it was not fully repaired until the 1970s.

• **Parking** Newton Port; Hardgate; Tynebank Road; Sidegate (all car parks) • **Early closing** Thursday • **Event** Festival Week (May–June) • **Information** TEL. Haddington 4161 • **AA 24 hour service** TEL. Edinburgh 225 8464.

Aberlady LOTHIAN

5 miles north of Haddington (PAGE 361 Fc/d)

Along the High Street of this village, which turns its back to the Firth of Forth, there are neatly restored rubblestone and red-pantiled buildings of the 17th to 19th centuries – such as Hunter Cottage, Shell Cottage, the Wagon Inn and Cross Cottage, beside the Mercat (market) Cross. Then, at the east end of the village, the main road turns down The Wynd, and there you reach salt water.

It was the sea which made Aberlady's early fortune, even if it recedes at low tide far across the rocks, mud flats and salt marshes of Aberlady Bay. Through the 2 mile long sand flats north of the village the Peffer Burn cuts a winding course. It was a chancy landfall for sailing vessels in an unsuitable wind, but from 1149 it gave Aberlady the status of a port on a coast which had few anchorages. In 1633 Aberlady was confirmed as the port for Haddington.

There are still clues that this residential village had a mercantile past; a house at the foot of The Wynd has a wall plaque of a sailing ship, and out near Aberlady Point, beside the entrance to Kilspindie golf course, stands the one-time Customs House.

The view eastwards from the point is across the nature reserve of Aberlady Bay, a famous winter roost of waders and ducks, towards the old volcanic peak of North Berwick Law. On the east side of the bay, Gullane Hill was once a training ground for racehorses, but it has now been given over to golf – Gullane has so many golf courses round about it that some are known only by numbers.

Aberlady parish church is at the west end of the village, its gate guarded by wych elms. On the pavement outside is the old 'loupin' on stane' – five steps up to a platform which allowed farmers' wives to mount gracefully onto their horses for the homeward ride. The square tower, which has a pyramid spire, is almost all that remains of a 15th-century church, having survived a demolition and rebuilding in 1773 and another in 1886. A replica of the 8th-century Aberlady Stone – part of a beautifully carved Celtic cross – is kept in the church.

A notable private house is Gosford, home of the Earl of Wemyss and March. It is screened by banks of trees angled curiously by the wind, and is largely the work of the architect Robert Adam (1728–92). The house is open to visitors on certain days in summer, and so are the grounds of Luffness, a 16th-century tower house on the site of a large 12th-century castle. It has a fruit garden planted by French prisoners during the Napoleonic Wars, and near by is the ruined chapel of an early Carmelite monastery.

Myreton Motor Museum is along a side road beyond Luffness, and is open all year. The collection includes cars, motorcycles and military vehicles.

East Linton LOTHIAN

6 miles east of Haddington (PAGE 361 Fd)

The historic centre of this one-time burgh is The Square – actually a narrow triangle at the junction of High Street and Bridge Street, with tall colour-washed 18th-century houses looking onto a tiny garden which has an illuminated cast-iron fountain. On the south side of The Square, on a rather cramped site, stands St Andrew's Church. Its well-proportioned spire was added in 1880, and seven years later, at the Jubilee of Queen Victoria, the East Linton clock was installed in it. The clock is still affectionately called 'Jessie', after the local butcher's attractive daughter, who was said to be in the habit of meeting her boyfriend here before the clock was put up.

East Linton takes its name from a rocky linn or waterfall on the Scottish River Tyne. Bridge Street leads to the often-repaired 16th-century sandstone bridge, which still carries traffic, although a bypass was opened in 1929. Downstream are the rapids of the linn. Blasting was once carried out here in an unsuccessful bid to make it safe for salmon to go up river to spawn.

Set into a wall at the east end of the village, there is a memorial to the great civil engineer John Rennie, who was responsible for three bridges over the Thames, as well as many commercial and naval dockyards. He was born at East Linton in 1761, at the manor house called Phantassie. The memorial features one of the balusters from his original Waterloo Bridge.

Inside the Phantassie grounds is a dovecote, or doo'cot, built probably in the 16th century to house no fewer than 500 birds. Owned by the National Trust for Scotland, it remains in excellent condition.

North-east of the village, on the Preston road, stands the parish church of Prestonkirk, which now shares duties with St Andrew's. There are records, which date back to the 8th century, of a church standing on this pleasant hilltop site overlooking a magnificent, sweeping bend on the Tyne. Part of the present building is more than 700 years old.

East Linton is in an area with a long tradition of

GOOSE MILL *Snow white geese are part of the scene at Preston Mill, East Linton. Much of its stonework dates from the 17th century, but the millstream was created by medieval monks.*

milling and market gardening. The old walled garden of Smeaton House, north of the church, is now a nursery. However, all but one of the water mills powered by the Tyne have disappeared. The sole survivor is Preston Mill, a little way beyond the church. It closed for commercial milling as recently as 1957, but it has been completely restored and is in the care of the National Trust for Scotland.

The mill, which can also be reached by a footpath from Phantassie, has its 18th-century machinery in full working order. The conical roof of the oat-drying kiln is topped by a wind vane. All the roofs are clad in red Lothian pantiles.

Tyninghame LOTHIAN

8 miles east of Haddington (PAGE 361 Gd)

Tyninghame is an estate village which has scarcely altered in layout and extent since it was built in the early 19th century. Its cottages, many with characteristic red-pantiled roofs, lie along an east-west street near the entrance to Tyninghame House, home of the Earl of Haddington.

At the west end of the street is the Widows Row, a group of single-storey cottages built in the early 1840s round a small green. Other attractive buildings include the post office, set back from the village pump, the dormer-windowed village hall, which was once the bakehouse, and Green Corner with an espalier pear tree trained up its west gable wall.

Although several houses are now in private hands, the life of the village revolved for generations around work on the farms and extensive woodlands of the Tyninghame estate. Indeed, until 1761, the village stood within what is now the park of Tyninghame House. It was demolished during improvements to the grounds in the time of the 7th Earl of Haddington.

His grandfather, the 6th Earl (1680 – 1735), was one of the great pioneering tree planters in Scotland, although the idea was put into his head by his wife, whom he allowed to plant the 300 acre Binning Wood on what had previously been rough common moorland north of the village. Binning Wood's great beeches were felled in the Second World War, but the wood has been replanted.

Tyninghame House was remodelled into its present form in 1829 by William Burn, the distinguished Scottish architect. The warm red-sandstone mansion, with its turrets and gables, stands in the heart of beautifully wooded gardens which are open to the public, except at weekends, during the summer. The 17th-century Walled Garden has a yew alley inside and an apple walk outside.

In the parkland south of the house there are the archways of a 12th-century Norman church, dedicated to the local saint, Baldred, who died about AD 756. The church was largely dismantled when the old village of Tyninghame was demolished, and is now the burial chapel of the Earls of Haddington.

The John Muir Country Park opened in 1976 adjacent to the grounds of Tyninghame House. John Muir, born in 1838 in nearby Dunbar, was a pioneer of the National Park movement in the United States and a keen conservationist.

Old Ale and Porter House, Tyninghame

NO ROOM AT THE INN

Tyninghame has acquired a lasting character, though life here has changed over the years. The Old Ale and Porter House is no longer an inn and the smithy is now silent. But it is business as usual at the post office.

Post office (left) and the old smithy

LINLITHGOW

LOTHIAN

18 miles west of Edinburgh (PAGE 361 Cd)

The romantic ruin of one of Scotland's royal palaces stands on a hillock overlooking the tranquil waters of Linlithgow Loch. Work on the palace started in 1425 for James I of Scotland. But the building, its tall battlemented blocks forming a square around a spacious central courtyard, was not completed until 100 years later, when James IV was on the throne. James V, born here in 1512, built a new, imposing south entrance and added the elaborate fountain, whose waterspouts are shaped like grotesque human and animal heads, in the centre of the courtyard.

In 1542 Mary, Queen of Scots was born in the palace, but after her son James united the crowns of Scotland and England in 1603, it fell out of royal favour. The last monarch to spend the night here was Charles I in the summer of 1633, and final indignity came just over 100 years later in 1746. The Duke of Cumberland's troops stayed here overnight on their way back from defeating Prince Charles Edward Stuart at the Battle of Culloden. In the morning they burnt the straw on which they had slept – and the flames spread, gutting the inside of the building.

Adjoining the palace ruin is The Peel, the former royal grounds, now a public park. The name comes from 'pale', meaning an area enclosed by a fence or boundary. Backing onto The Peel is the parish church of St Michael, dedicated in 1242 but largely rebuilt after a fire in 1424. In 1964 its squat tower was capped with an abstract construction in aluminium and timber – representing Triumph arising from Christ's Crown of Thorns.

Spread along the south shore of Linlithgow Loch, the town, which had its own port at nearby Blackness (see page 368), reached the peak of its prosperity in the 15th and 16th centuries. Then it had an official monopoly of all trade on a 14 mile stretch of shore along the Firth of Forth. It lost the monopoly after 1603, but when the railway arrived in the 19th century the town enjoyed a second, though shorter, boom period. Many of its old houses were replaced, giving the streets a Victorian look which they still have.

Linlithgow centres around the old market square called The Cross, in which is Cross Well. The first well was built in about 1535. It was rebuilt in 1628 and 1807, and it is topped by an elaborate stone structure crowned with a unicorn supporting the Scottish National Arms. The work carried out in 1807 was by a one-handed stonemason named Robert Gray, who used a mallet strapped to the stump of his right arm.

Towering over The Cross is the stately Town House, dating from the late 17th century. After being badly damaged by fire in 1847, it was largely rebuilt – and its imposing double staircase at the front was added in 1907. Beside it, in the north-west corner of the square, is the attractive 18th-century Cross House, once home of James Glen, governor of South Carolina in America between 1738 and 1757. In 1745 his sister, an ardent Jacobite, set the Linlithgow Palace fountains flowing with wine in honour of Prince Charles Edward Stuart, who was entertained there.

Running east-west through The Cross is High Street, one section of which is named The Vennel. The street contains imposing stone tenement blocks dating from the late 16th or early 17th centuries. The tenements, which were restored in 1958, are separated by a roofed staircase.

At the other end of High Street, the large stone West Port House rises high and grandly imposing above the road. It was completed in 1600 but the side facing the street may be much older than that. The house belonged to the local Hamilton family and was altered in the 18th century.

Two other Hamiltons were involved in an event recalled on a bronze tablet in the wall of the Court House near The Cross. On January 23, 1570, Mary, Queen of Scots' half-brother, the Protestant Earl of Moray, who had become regent of Scotland after her abdication, was assassinated near here in High Street. He was shot by James Hamilton of Bothwellhaugh from a position inside the house – long since gone – of Archbishop Hamilton of St Andrews. Unfortunately, both the date of the assassination and the spelling of the regent's name on the tablet are incorrect.

Climbing steeply south from High Street are three attractive little alleys called Well Wynds; beyond them to the south runs the Edinburgh and Glasgow Union Canal. The canal was opened in 1822 and officially closed in 1965, but a section between Linlithgow and Winchburgh, 6 miles east, was re-opened for pleasure boats in 1978.

Every June, Linlithgow holds a Riding of the Marches which recalls the days when the town was on guard against raids.

● **Parking** The Vennel; Lochside; High Street (west); Blackness Road (all car parks) ● **Early closing** Wednesday ● **Events** The Riding of the Marches (June); Gala (July) ● **Information** TEL. Linlithgow 84 4600 ● **AA 24 hour service** TEL. Edinburgh 225 8464.

Abercorn LOTHIAN

6 miles east of Linlithgow (PAGE 361 Dd)

Abercorn is tiny, tucked away on the southern shore of the Forth. Its few stone and slate houses are grouped around a parish church that was completely restored in 1893, but has a 12th-century south wall. Treasures inside the church include a finely carved wooden cabinet, a 17th-century lectern, and – most fascinating of all – several cross shafts that were intricately carved in the 8th century. There are also special pews for two prominent local families: the Dalyells of the Binns (see Blackness, page 368), and the Hopes of Hopetoun. On display is the flag of the Marquis of Linlithgow, head of the Hope family.

The first church in Abercorn is believed to have been founded by St Serf, a disciple of the great missionary to southern Scotland St Ninian, who was working in Lothian in the first years of the 5th century. Later, in the 7th century, when the Forth was the northern boundary of Northumbria, there was a monastery here. Its site has been located in the present churchyard.

To the east of the village, the road runs alongside the high stone walls that surround the park of the Marquis of Linlithgow's seat, Hopetoun House – open from May to mid-September. The oldest part of this immense, elegant mansion is the west block, which was completed in 1703 for the marquis's ancestor, the 1st Earl of Hopetoun. But it was considerably enlarged between 1721 and 1767 by the architect William Adam, who regarded Hopetoun as his masterpiece. His sons Robert and John added the Neoclassical front, with its grand outer staircase, curving colonnades and symmetrical wings.

Robert and John also decorated many of the main rooms, including the magnificent red and yellow drawing rooms and the state dining room. The house has fine plaster ceilings, some early 18th-century tapestries, furniture made specially for it by the 18th-century cabinet-maker James Cullen, and a collection of paintings. There is also a museum in the north wing; and the stables house an exhibition called 'Horse and Man in Lowland Scotland'.

In the grounds there is a flock of the rare black St Kilda sheep, whose rams have four magnificent horns. Two deer parks are reserved for red and fallow deer, and a nature trail leads past yew hedges to the Bastion Walk high above the Forth. It also passes the site of the original Abercorn Castle, which belonged to the Douglases and was destroyed by James II in 1455 when the family was involved in a rebellion.

Blackness LOTHIAN

4 miles north-east of Linlithgow (PAGE 361 Dd)

Every year, at about 7 a.m. on the first Tuesday after the second Thursday in June, villagers here are awakened by the music of two flute players and a drummer. The musicians, having already roused the townsfolk of Linlithgow, are heralding the annual Riding of Linlithgow Marches – a procession which has included Blackness villagers for nearly six centuries.

A royal charter made Blackness Linlithgow's official seaport in 1389. At the same time, the office of Baron Baillie of Blackness was created to deal with the village's civil and criminal court cases. There is still a Baron Baillie, and although he no longer holds trials he has an important role in the celebrations, which originated as a march around Linlithgow's boundaries. When the procession has reached Blackness and wreaths have been laid at the war memorials, the Baron Baillie entertains marchers with Blackness milk – a mixture of milk and whisky.

Later, the procession heads along the shoreline road, passing some 19th-century houses, the Boat Club and a curving sandy beach before halting on Castle Hill. Here the Baron Court is held, when either a new Baron is installed or the old one re-installed.

Blackness Castle, which is open to the public, occupies an imposing position on a neck of land jutting into the Forth. It dates in part from the 15th century, and viewed from some angles looks rather like a ship. Indeed, the towers at either end are known as the stem and the stern, and the central tower is called the mainmast. It is said that when permission was asked to build a castle here, the English king, who then dominated much of Scotland, refused and suggested that a ship instead should be built to defend the coastline. So the castle was built . . . like a ship.

South of Blackness is another, quite different castle – The House of the Binns, now owned by the National Trust for Scotland. This delightful little place was built in the 17th century and added to in 1820 by the Dalyell family. The family's most remarkable member was General Sir Tam Dalyell, who in 1681 raised the Royal Scots Greys – now merged into the Royal Scots Dragoon Guards. During the Civil War, Dalyell was an important Royalist commander; but, after the king's defeat, he entered the service of the Tsar of Russia.

Returning home after the Restoration, Dalyell served Charles II as the scourge of the rebellious Covenanters – Scottish Presbyterians who refused to give up their own form of worship. His wild appearance and often brutal methods led to stories of special powers conferred on him by the Devil – like being bulletproof.

Most of his later years, however, were spent peacefully at the Binns, adorning it with 'avenues, large parks, and fine gardens'. The parkland is still fine, and is open to the public all year. The castle is open from Easter to September.

Culross FIFE

22 miles north of Linlithgow (via Forth Road Bridge) (PAGE 361 Cc)

Culross – pronounced 'Coo-ross' – was once a busy port that reached a peak of prosperity in the late 16th and early 17th centuries. This it owed largely to the merchant and engineer Sir George Bruce, who built up an immense fortune from local coal and salt. He had large salt pans (in which salt was extracted from sea water by evaporation) along the shoreline. And by inventing new systems of ventilation and drainage, he was able to mine coal at almost unheard of depths. He exported his coal and salt to Scandinavia, the Baltic ports and the Low Countries.

The magnificent Culross Palace is no royal residence – it was Sir George's home and office combined, built between 1597 and 1611 around a fine courtyard with a terraced garden to the north. Walls and ceilings in its main rooms are decorated with superbly luminous paintings in tempera – a technique in which raw egg or animal glue is used when mixing pigments.

In one room Sir George entertained business partners; and another, which has a ceiling 9 ft thick, was his strongroom. The palace is open all the year.

A bedroom was specially decorated for James VI (James I of England), who visited Culross in 1617. Sir George proudly showed the king his Moat Pit, one of the wonders of 17th-century coal-mining. They finished their underground walk by climbing up a stairway to an artificial island in the Forth, which acted both as a ventilation shaft and mooring place for colliers. The king was notoriously suspicious, and when he emerged to find himself surrounded by water he immediately suspected – until reassured – that he was being kidnapped.

Culross is now a quiet place, much of it – including the palace – owned by the National Trust for Scotland. Low Countries connections are evident in the Dutch-style gables of 17th-century houses in the cobbled streets; and Culross ships brought the red pantiles home from Dutch and Flemish ports.

At the top of Culross is the abbey, founded by Cistercian monks in 1217. Much of it is a ruin, but its choir was preserved and is now the parish church. Inside is the tomb of Sir George and Lady Bruce, with their effigies recumbent on top and statues of their children in front. In another tomb lie Sir Robert and Lady Preston of Valleyfield, $1\frac{1}{2}$ miles east. Sir Robert was involved in coal-mining in the early 19th century; the

Mercat Cross and cobbled square, Culross

Culross rooftops and the Forth

The Study

The Gate House

COBBLES THAT MAY BE FAMILIAR

The little cobbled square at Culross, with its fine Mercat (market) Cross, makes a picture pretty enough to be used as a film setting. And it has been. Notable buildings in Culross include The Study, once a bishop's retreat, and the Gate House.

ruins of his workings can be seen on Preston Island – now part of the mainland.

In the churchyard are several gravestones with the device of a hammer topped by a crown. This was the royal warrant mark of the Hammermen of Culross, who had a lucrative monopoly throughout Scotland in the manufacture of iron baking girdles – or griddles.

ST ANDREWS

FIFE

13 miles south-east of Dundee (PAGE 361 Fb)

The world's most revered golf course, dating from the 15th century, overlooks the golden sands and blue-grey water of St Andrews Bay. This is the Old Course used by the Royal and Ancient Golf Club, a venue for the British Open and other major events, and famous for its difficult natural hazards.

St Andrews rightly regards itself as the headquarters of golf, which evolved in Scotland in the Middle Ages. The game was introduced to England by James I in the early 17th century, and in 1754 the Society of St Andrews Golfers was formed by a group of 22 men. In 1834 the society became the Royal and Ancient, which is now the game's governing body.

The Old Course is one of four courses in the town – the others are the New, the Eden and the Jubilee. Visitors do not have to be members, nor is an introduction needed, to play on any of them.

The dignified, stone-built town takes its name from Scotland's patron saint, and was one of the country's main places of pilgrimage in the early days of Christianity. A medieval community grew up around the vast Cathedral Church of St Andrew, founded in 1160 and consecrated in 1318 in the presence of King Robert Bruce. The building was later damaged by followers of John Knox, the Scottish Presbyterian leader, who preached in St Andrews in 1559.

In the cathedral's burial ground is a life-size effigy of a young Scot about to tee off. He was Tom Morris, who won the Open Championship four times in the 1870s. He died in 1876 at the age of only 24.

On the coast south of the Old Course are the gaunt ruins of St Andrews Castle, founded in 1200 as the bishop's main residence. Buffeted by man and sea,

NEXT TO GODLINESS, GOLF

OVERLEAF

The massive pinnacled ruin of a 12th-century cathedral rises in splendour above St Andrews – a reminder that the town, named after Scotland's patron saint, was once a great religious centre. It is also the capital of the game that is almost a religion in Scotland – golf, as played at the Royal and Ancient.

it was destroyed by the English in the early 14th century but was rebuilt about 1380. Three hundred years later it was all but demolished to provide stone to repair the nearby harbour. Now its grassy ramparts and jagged walls rise above the fortress's 24 ft deep Bottle Dungeon.

In 1546 the Scottish Reformation leader George Wishart was burnt at the stake for heresy outside the castle, while the Catholic Cardinal David Beaton watched from a window. But Wishart was avenged three months later, when his friends entered the castle dressed as workmen and stabbed Beaton to death in his quarters. The cardinal's body was then hung by an arm and a leg from the castle wall.

Three main streets – North, South and Market – split the town from east to west. North Street is overlooked by the imposing tower of St Salvator's College, the centre of St Andrews University. This is the oldest of Scotland's universities, dating from the early 15th century. Each April there is a pageant recalling the university's past. This is named after Kate Kennedy, a niece of Bishop James Kennedy, St Salvator's founder. Kate is said to have given food to impoverished students.

At the foot of South Street is the West Port, or burgh gate. Its original date is not known, but it was rebuilt in 1589 at a cost of £140 and renovated once more in the 1840s.

• **Parking** Argyle Street; Murray Place; City Road; Doubledykes Road; Old Station Road; Bruce Embankment; West Sands; East Sands (all car parks) • **Early closing** Thursday • **Theatre** Byre Theatre, South Street • **Cinema** New Picture House, North Street • **Events** International Festival of Food and Wine (March); Kate Kennedy Procession (April); St Andrews Golf Week (April); Craigtown Country Fair (June); Lammas Market (August); St Andrew's Day Celebrations (November) • **Information** TEL. St Andrews 72021 • **AA 24 hour service** TEL. Dundee 25585.

Anstruther FIFE

9 miles south-east of St Andrews (PAGE 361 Fb)

Anstruther's most curious building is the Buckie Hoose. Buckie is the local word for shell, and the end wall of the house is partly covered by elaborate designs made of seashells. They were put here by the owner, Alexander Batchelor, in the 19th century – and he did not stop at the outside of the house. The ceiling of what he called the grotto room was also covered with shells, and so too was a coffin he built for himself. For a charge of three pence (about $1\frac{1}{2}$p) Batchelor would show visitors the inside of his house, and for an extra penny (about $\frac{1}{2}$p) he would, as an added attraction, climb into the coffin.

The Buckie Hoose – no longer open to the public – is on the corner of High Street in Wester Anstruther – the most westerly of the three one-time royal fishing burghs that make up Anstruther (pronounced locally 'Ainster'). The other two are Easter Anstruther and Cellardyke. Together they stretch out along the coast of the East Neuk – east corner – of Fife, and their fine quayside houses, roofed with local slate or red pantiles, press close to the sea.

The most easterly of the three is Cellardyke, which has a well-maintained harbour and once supported some 50 fishing boats. Behind a house in East Forth Street is an archway made from the vast jawbone of an Arctic whale – a reminder of the whalers that also worked from here in the 19th century. Easter Anstruther, in the middle, has the largest harbour – nowadays used mostly by shellfish boats, holiday yachts and dinghies. The bright red North Carr light vessel – now retired – is moored here permanently and is open to the public in summer. Once it kept station off the dangerous reefs of Fife Ness. The village also houses the Scottish Fisheries Museum, which has a reconstructed turn-of-the-century fisherman's home. Old fishing vessels can be seen in the museum courtyard and the harbour.

Two outstanding clipper-ship captains of the 19th century lived in Anstruther – Captain Keay of the *Ariel*, who lived opposite the Buckie Hoose, and Captain Rodger, who owned the *Taeping* and lived in Cellardyke. The *Ariel* and the *Taeping* were crack tea-clippers in the days when there was an annual race between ships to arrive first in London with the new season's cargo of China tea – and so command the highest prices. In 1866, the two ships cast off at the same time from Foochow (Fuzhou) in south-eastern China, raced halfway round the world, and arrived in the Thames within 20 minutes of each other. The race was declared a draw and the prize money was split.

Weather permitting, boat trips run from Easter Anstruther to the offshore Isle of May, where there is a ruined priory. It was built around the grave of St Adrian, an Irish missionary to Scotland who was killed here in AD 875 by the Danes. Now there is a lighthouse on the island, which is a nature reserve, notable as a nesting ground for sea birds.

Crail FIFE

10 miles south-east of St Andrews (PAGE 361 Gb)

Crail has a most attractive little harbour, tucked snugly into the East Neuk coastline, with two red leading lights on tall whitewashed towers high above a sandy beach. They mark a safe channel through dangerous rocks that stretch well out to sea.

Centuries ago, Crail was an international trading port, earning royal burgh status as early as 1310. It exported salt and animal hides, salt herrings and Crail capons – cured haddock – to the Low Countries. A certain Dutch influence remains, notably in the red pantiles on many houses, brought back from the Netherlands as ballast. Nowadays, fishing is mostly for lobsters and crabs, and the harbour is also popular with holiday sailors, few of whom see it when the storm gates – large wooden booms – are closed against winter gales.

Many of the houses, white roughcast and built of local sandstone, have been carefully restored – among them the old harbour Customs House. From the harbour, the cottages of Shoregate lead into the upper part of Crail, where the most notable street is Marketgate, flanked by elegant 17th and 18th-century houses set well back from a roadway with two lines of trees. Here is where Crail's regular markets were held – most unusually, on Sundays. The Tolbooth (town hall) has a Dutch-cast bell of 1520, and its weathervane is a gilded model of a Crail capon. Not far away is a reconstructed market cross, topped by a unicorn. On the other side of the Tolbooth, two old houses have been converted into the Crail Heritage Centre. Displays

Falkland Palace

Antiques shop

Marriage lintels on Falkland homes

House in Horse Market

PALACES, GREAT AND SMALL

Falkland has its royal palace—handsome, turreted and possibly Scotland's finest Renaissance building. However, the people, too, have their palaces—modest houses proudly proclaimed as home by couples who inscribed their initials on 'marriage lintels' above the doorways, along with the date they moved in. Cobbled streets and small cosy shops complete the picture.

recall Crail's long history—its European commerce, old craft guilds and lifeboat service.

Farther along Marketgate is the Kirk of Crail, the earliest parts of which are 12th century. But inside there is a Pictish stone slab with a cross carved on it, which is four centuries older. North of the church is the site of the Bow Butts, where marks on the wall of the church tower are said to have been made by archers pausing to sharpen their arrows.

Beyond Marketgate, a dead-end road towards Fife Ness goes through farmlands and past the derelict buildings of a wartime Royal Naval Air Station. Much of the area has been landscaped, and access to the shore provided. There is also a fine golf course.

The North-East Fife Coastal Walk runs along the shoreline, coming to Crail at the sands, rocks and swimming pool of Roome Bay, below a dovecote beside Denburn Park. Finally, it continues to the harbour.

The view extends across the Forth estuary as far as St Abb's Head, 30 miles away on the Berwickshire coast, except when a haar (sea mist) rolls in.

Falkland FIFE

20 miles west of St Andrews (PAGE 361 Eb)

The gentle countryside at the foot of the Lomond Hills was a favourite royal hunting ground of the Scottish monarchs, and in the 1450s James II began rebuilding Falkland Castle here as a hunting lodge. By 1603, when James VI went to London to become James I of England, the lodge had become a magnificent palace.

Falkland Palace is still a royal possession, but has been occupied for generations by the Crichton Stuart family, its Hereditary Keepers, who restored the building after it had fallen into ruin. Since 1952, the National Trust for Scotland has been officially Deputy Keeper, responsible for the upkeep of the building and gardens, both of which are open to the public.

The most outstanding feature of the palace is the courtyard front of the south range. It was built early in the 16th century by James V, who admired the great chateaux of the Loire valley. The front, which has fluted columns and circular panels, is probably the finest piece of Renaissance architecture in Scotland.

Inside the palace, visitors may inspect the humble bakehouse, as well as the splendid staterooms which include the fine oak-timbered Chapel Royal and the King's Bed Chamber.

Along the north side of the gardens is the royal (or real) tennis court. The game, from which lawn tennis was developed, is played on a special court with high stone walls on all sides, and partly covered by roofs, known as penthouses, off which the ball may be bounced. The Falkland court is the oldest in Britain, dating from 1539, and is still used for tournaments. It is unique among surviving royal tennis courts in having four window-like holes in one wall through which the ball may be hit for an extra point, and two, as opposed to three, penthouses.

The rest of Falkland clusters around the palace, with charming cobbled streets and a tiny Parliament Square. It centres on a group of houses built for royal courtiers, among them, facing the palace gatehouse, the thatched Moncrief House, dating from 1610. Carved in stone on its wall is an extravagantly phrased blessing on James VI of Scotland and I of England. It gives 'al praise to God and thankis to the most excellent monarche'.

Near by on the other side of High Street are St Andrew's House, another courtier's home, and the 18th-century Saddler's House, both with harled (roughcast) walls and red-pantiled roofs. Also noteworthy are a little harled building in the cobbled Rotten Row that now ingeniously houses an electricity sub-station, and the Bruce Fountain, ornamented with magnificent red-painted lions, in the centre of the main square. In the south-western corner of the square is the house where, in about 1648, Richard Cameron was born.

Cameron was a leading Covenanter – one of the Scottish Presbyterians persecuted by the government for refusing to use the Book of Common Prayer. He was killed in 1680 defending his religious beliefs in a skirmish against government troops at Airds Moss, not far from Ayr. His name lives on, however, for only nine years after his death, a regiment made up of his followers was used in suppressing 'Bonnie' Viscount Dundee's Jacobite rising. The modern Cameronians (Scottish Rifles) are descended from this regiment.

Falkland is the northern gateway to the beautiful Lomond Hills, rolling open moors reached by a winding road running through a pass at Craigmead.

Pittenweem FIFE

10 miles south of St Andrews (PAGE 361 Fb)

Pittenweem means 'place of the cave' – the cave in this case being in the sandstone cliff behind the harbour. Here, in the 7th century, St Fillan made his home, using a stone shelf for a bed and drinking from the cave's spring, from which clear, running water still flows. Later, his cave became a shrine, reverently tended by the monks of Pittenweem Priory, on top of the cliff.

But after the monks were scattered at the Reformation, St Fillan's cave was, for many centuries, the scene of less saintly activities. It became a hideout for smugglers, and later a fisherman's store. But in the 1930s the shrine was restored.

Below the shrine and in contrast to its meditative silence, Pittenweem harbour with its fish market is a scene of hectic activity on weekday mornings.

The village has been busy since 1542 at least: in that year, it was thought important enough to be made a royal burgh. For long afterwards it was not only a fishing port, but also carried on a flourishing trade with the Baltic ports and the Low Countries.

Dutch influence can still be discerned in many of the fine buildings around the harbour, in the streets called Mid Shore and East Shore. In East Shore, the 17th-century Barracks – which is now a block of private houses – would, with its elegantly curved gable, fit neatly into a Dutch harbour scene. Near by stand The Gyles, which have been restored by the National Trust for Scotland.

Pittenweem is not all on the seafront, however. Uphill, Market Square and the narrow High Street are lined with fine 16th to 18th-century houses and have quite a different and more dignified air. Protruding into the pavement of High Street is the stone tower of Kellie Lodging. The Lodging, which still has its tiny windows, crow-stepped gables and high-set roof, was built by the Oliphant family around 1590. They also built Kellie Castle, a few miles inland. Both buildings were bought by the Earl of Kellie.

The attractive North-East Fife Coastal Walk crosses Pittenweem. Coming from the east, it passes the harbour, continues along Mid Shore and so to the Well, a semi-natural harbour set among rock pools. After that, it leads to West Shore, where 18th-century fishermen's houses look out to sea. Beyond, it follows the curve of a bay and climbs up the West Braes.

PRAWN PATROL *It is early morning on the quayside at Pittenweem, and the catch is being unloaded . . . A single perfect cloudlet in a blue sky, crates of coral-red prawns, glistening oilskins . . . the colourful scene is almost Mediterranean. There is a fish market here every weekday; the cries of the auctioneers ring out, and the busy little harbour is strewn with nets, floats, crates and other gear. Sometimes, indeed, the port is so busy that boats with catches to land have to form a queue that stretches out into the open sea.*

MAP 33

THE ROAD TO THE ISLES AND OVER TO SKYE

On Skye, the darkly impressive Cuillin Hills rise from a cold northern sea; while on gentler Mull, inland lochs gleam between grandly rounded peaks. The neighbouring mainland has the vast stretch of Loch Awe and the busy port of Oban. The harbours of Portree and Tobermory, the tiny island capitals, are quieter, giving shelter and a friendly welcome to visiting yachts. There are echoes of history and romance all around – lonely houses and castles that provided safe refuge for Bonnie Prince Charlie and Flora Macdonald; or where, later, Dr Johnson – that most English of travellers to Scotland – and James Boswell were entertained. Centuries before, tranquil Iona, St Columba's isle, was one of the earliest seats of Christianity in Britain.

MAP 33: NEIGHBOURING AREAS – MAPS 32, 34, 36

OBAN	PORTREE	TOBERMORY
Barcaldine	Broadford	Bunessan
Dalmally	Dunvegan	Dervaig
Port Appin	Kilmuir	Lochbuie

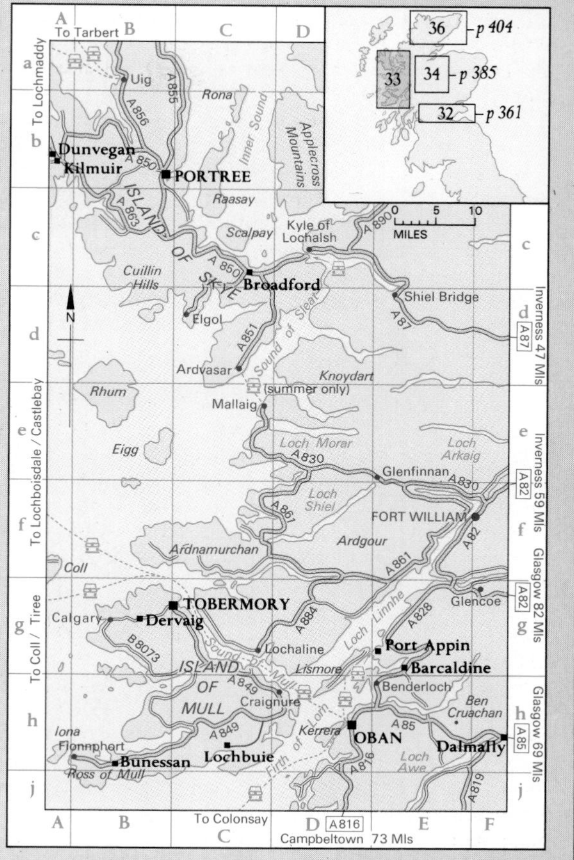

OBAN

STRATHCLYDE

93 miles north-west of Glasgow (PAGE 375 Dh)

Perched like a vast amphitheatre on top of Battery Hill, the unfinished granite folly called McCaig's Tower has overlooked Oban since the late 1890s. Standing 228 ft above sea level, the 'tower' was built by a wealthy local banker named John Stuart McCaig. His circular folly has a circumference of 630 ft and is in two tiers, with almost 100 pointed windows. It was built for two quite different reasons.

First of all, Mr McCaig wanted to provide work for the town's stonemasons, as they seemed to suffer long periods of unemployment. He stipulated that they should only work on his project when they were in between jobs. Secondly, he wished to erect a large-scale monument to his family. He planned to put huge stone or bronze statues of himself, his father and mother, and his brothers and sisters around the parapet. His intention was that each would cost at least £1000 and would be created by Scotland's most brilliant young sculptors.

When his 'new Colosseum' was completed, he apparently wanted it to be a museum and art gallery, as well as an observation tower. But McCaig died in 1902, after spending some £5000 on the building. Work on it had been abandoned two years before. However, it is still an impressive sight – especially at night when it is floodlit and can be seen from miles away. From the windows there are stunning views of Oban Bay and the hilly, wooded countryside behind the town.

Oban began to grow in the late 18th century, when the first stone cottages were built around an inn near the harbour. In 1773 Dr Johnson (1709 – 84) and his biographer James Boswell (1740 – 95) stayed at the 'tolerable inn' during their famous tour of the Highlands. Boswell House in Argyll Square now stands on the site of the hostelry. But the town did not reach maturity until the 1860s, when grand hotels went up along the Esplanade. In 1880 the railway arrived and the pretty, blue-and-white station is still in use.

Today it retains the look of a prosperous Victorian town, with rows of gabled houses lining the lower slopes of Battery Hill. But on the other side of the harbour, on the island of Kerrera, are the ruins of Gylen Castle, built in the 16th century by the local MacDougall family.

The MacDougalls also own Dunollie Castle, whose ruins rise from a rocky promontory at the mouth of the bay. This was the family's main fortress, and its existence was first recorded in the 7th century. In 1831 the poet William Wordsworth (1770 – 1850) visited the remains and was outraged to see an eagle chained to a rock. He later wrote a bitter sonnet about the bird's fate.

A much newer building is the Catholic Cathedral of St Columba, which was begun in 1932 but not completed until after the war. Built of pinkish granite,

GATEWAY TO THE ISLES

Oban's wide harbour is sheltered by the island of Kerrera, while on the far side of Loch Linnhe rise the beautiful Morvern hills. With the coming of the railway, Oban established itself as an important port from which ferries left – and still leave – for the Western Isles. Brightly coloured fishing vessels use the harbour too; and on a hill is what looks like Rome's Colosseum – in fact, the tower was built by John Stuart McCaig, a local Victorian banker who was a passionate admirer of Roman art.

Oban harbour and Loch Linnhe

The harbour front and McCaig's Tower

it was designed by the English architect Sir Giles Gilbert Scott (1880 – 1960), the creator of the Anglican cathedral in Liverpool. Standing at a corner of the Esplanade, St Columba's used to attract Gaelic-speaking residents, who form about one-eighth of the population, but services are no longer held in Gaelic.

Each year the town stages a major sporting event – the Argyllshire Gathering, which is held on the last Thursday in August. Pipers welcome top athletes to the Gathering Ground near the golf course. Tossing the caber, putting the shot and a hill race are among the events.

People visiting Oban for the first time sometimes feel that they have seen the place before – and they may well have done. For, under the name of 'Glendoran', the town was the setting of the popular BBC television series *Sutherland's Law*, starring Iain Cuthbertson as the redoubtable fiscal, or public prosecutor.

• **Parking** Albany Street; Corran Halls; Tweeddale Street; Longsdale Road; Lochavullin Road; North Pier (all car parks); Glencruitten Road; Pulpit Hill • **Early closing** Thursday • **Market days** Tuesday, Friday • **Cinema** Phoenix, George Street • **Events** Oban Raft Race (May); West Highland Yachting Week (July – August); Argyllshire Gathering (August) • **Information** TEL. Oban 63122, 63551 • **AA 24 hour service** TEL. Glasgow 812 0101.

Barcaldine STRATHCLYDE

12 miles north-east of Oban (PAGE 375 Eg)

The name is that of a forest, a castle and a scattered village set back from the shore of Loch Creran, one of the most beautiful sea lochs in Argyll. The village is so scattered that it scarcely looks like a village at all; the main Oban to Fort William road, flanked by clumps of yellow-green gorse, runs between crofters' fields, among which there is a vague collection of cottages and bungalows. There is, too, a clutch of Forestry Commission houses set on the hillside among sheltering trees.

But it is by no means a dull place. Work on the spruce plantations is organised from a busy office on the Gleann Salach road, and there is a marina offering boats for hire, sea angling, trips, sailing for children and facilities for visiting yachtsmen. Tucked inside an old walled garden is a neat and attractive caravan site. There are also one or two industries. The grey buildings by the shore of the loch are those of the 'seaweed factory', which refines alginates from seaweed for use as emulsifiers and food thickeners; and a craftsman in the village makes wood-burning stoves.

Footpaths are laid out in three different areas of Barcaldine Forest. On the northern edge of the village there is a picnic site among 120-year-old Douglas firs, from which a pine-scented footpath climbs up Gleann Dubh – the Black Glen – where there are waterfalls, rock pools, and a timber footbridge over a sheer-sided ravine. Farther north, a circular path goes to Eas na Circe – the Waterfall of the Grouse – while by the neighbouring village of Benderloch there are more forest walks to the summit of Beinn Lora (1010 ft).

Above Gleann Dubh there is a reservoir beneath whose surface is a 'drowned' croft house. The reservoir was created to provide a head of water for the alginate factory. It is stocked with rainbow trout, and is a fine place even on a day when no fish are biting. The view includes a jigsaw of islands and inlets; the peaks of Mull, Kingairloch and Morvern; and closer at hand the red deer country of the inland hills, the upper plantations and lonely corries inhabited by eagles.

Closer to the shore, at St Columba's Bay, the former Oban to Ballachulish railway track has been turned into a series of Forestry Commission picnic sites, each with a splendid seaward view. But for most people, the greatest attraction is the Sea Life Centre, whose show-stealers are the orphaned seals playing in their outdoor pool, showing off outrageously to visitors. They can also be seen through a glass wall inside the centre itself, tumbling aquatic cartwheels and pressing their noses to the glass to observe the curious antics of the human race.

There are open tanks where thornback rays half-spin out of the water, and a circular tank round which silver herring urgently swim, apparently under the impression that they are crossing the Atlantic. Moray eels gaze glacially out from rocky hideaways, and there are displays showing the techniques of fish farming. For younger visitors, so disposed, there is a 'touch tank' where they are encouraged to discover for themselves the feel of harmless sea creatures like starfish.

Dalmally STRATHCLYDE

25 miles east of Oban (PAGE 375 Fh)

Ben Cruachan, to the west of the village, tops 3600 ft, and to complete the classic Highland scene there are steep forests on one side and a sparkling river on the other. Despite this romantic and seemingly remote setting, Dalmally is easily reached by either road or rail from the great city of Glasgow.

The heart of the village, mostly made up of Victorian stone-built cottages and villas, is on a hill beside the station. Many of the houses are of stone quarried from the slopes of Ben Cruachan by convicts.

Opposite the station is a craft shop that also sells books and fishing tackle, for Dalmally is a fine angling centre. There are brown trout, sea trout, rainbow trout and salmon in the broad waters of Loch Awe; just over 8 miles west of Dalmally, where the waters of the loch flow out towards the sea, a hydroelectric barrage in the River Awe has an automatic counter to tick off the salmon as they fight their way upstream.

Running past Dalmally is the River Orchy, which has many famous angling beats all the way from its source in Loch Tulla on the Glencoe road to its outflow into Loch Awe just west of the village. Other anglers in search of solitude make for the lonelier hill lochs, well away from the roads.

A stone bridge over the railway cutting beside the station leads to a winding road that climbs up between forestry plantations to Monument Hill, whose summit is crowned by a rotunda of Appin granite. This commemorates the life of Duncan MacIntyre, a famous Gaelic bard who died in 1812. He could not read or write, but could recite up to 6000 lines of his poems, mostly tender celebrations of the Highland scene.

The short walk from the roadside to the monument on the crown of the hill reveals one of the finest views in the Highlands. To the west, the mighty ramparts of Ben Cruachan stand guard over lovely Loch Awe, with its scattering of wooded islands.

Back on the main road there are the livestock sales that on market days are attended by farmers and drovers from all over Scotland. The markets take place

A WILD WESTERN RAILWAY VILLAGE

Dalmally grew in the 1880s about a branch of the West Highland Railway. But scattered in the awesome countryside around are reminders of an older and sterner way of life. Lonely crofting houses are dwarfed by vast mountains and, on a narrow peninsula jutting out into Loch Awe, are the ruins of Kilchurn Castle.

Dalmally and the railway station

A cottage near Dalmally

Kilchurn Castle

at a number of times in the year, but the most important are the series of autumn sales in which as many as 20,000 sheep may be auctioned in one day. By the riverside is Dalmally's other claim to fame – its shinty pitch. The village fields two teams in this vigorous Highland form of hockey.

Two stone bridges cross the twin channels of the Orchy, which make an island setting for the early 19th-century church and manse. The church has an octagonal tower and is seen at its best from the east, standing out against the great corrie on the east face of Cruachan.

A side road follows the course of the Orchy upstream. Most visitors pass it by, but it offers any number of ideal picnic sites with rock pools, rapids and miniature waterfalls for company.

Near the shore of Loch Awe, along the Oban road, a small car park has been laid out. From there, a gravel track leads to the 15th-century ruin of Kilchurn Castle. Kilchurn, which is open to the public, was built by the Campbells of Lochawe, later the Earls and then the Marquises of Breadalbane. The Breadalbane estates once amounted to some 400,000 acres, stretching from the heart of Scotland to the Atlantic coast. Not one of those acres now remains in the family's possession.

West along the Oban road, past Lochawe village, there is another car park and a visitor centre, from which a minibus may be taken down a tunnel nearly a mile long into the heart of Ben Cruachan. It concludes at a vast chamber, cut out of the solid granite. Here a viewing gallery overlooks a scene like a James Bond film set, whose stars are the four mighty reversible turbines of the hydroelectric station. The force of falling water on the turbine's blades makes them rotate the generators to which they are coupled, so producing electricity. They are switched on about 12,000 times a year to compensate for surges in the nation's electrical demands.

Port Appin STRATHCLYDE

25 miles north of Oban (PAGE 375 Eg)

This is one of those places where mainland Scotland comes dreamily to an end at a little harbour and a ferry pier serving some faraway island that most people have never heard of. The island in this case is long and hilly Lismore, whose rugged coastline protects an interior of farmlands and narrow freshwater lochs. Beyond Lismore is the open water of Loch Linnhe, and beyond that again are the jumbled silhouetted peaks of Mull, Kingairloch and Ardgour.

Nowadays, apart from the regular passenger ferry to the north end of Lismore, Port Appin is used mainly by holiday yachts. But the massive timber piling beside the modern concrete jetty tells of a grander past, when this was an important calling place on the steamer route to Fort William. In 1820 it was the final port of call for the world's first sea-going passenger steamship, the *Comet*. She was wrecked on the rocks of Craignish Point a few hours after leaving Port Appin, having been launched on the Clyde eight years before.

The Lismore ferry is still the most important feature in Port Appin life, even if some of its trade has been captured by the car ferry from Oban. Nevertheless, the most substantial building in the village remains the whitewashed Airds Hotel, whose dining room, together with the floor above, formed the original ferry inn that was established in about 1700.

Almost every building in Port Appin looks towards the sea. On the northern approach road, the houses have fields in front sloping down to the water's edge, though the shoreline by the road to the ferry is rocky. Yachts and dinghies are moored here, and the boats may be hired for fishing or exploring. A favourite one-hour summer sail is to the seal colonies on the lighthouse island close inshore, while farther off are the islets on the far side of Lismore.

The long ridge of Clach Thoull – pronounced 'Clach-towl' – gives Port Appin a dramatically craggy backdrop. The ridge, which forms a headland, is easily climbed by narrow footpaths that start beside the hotel. Near one end there is a great buttress of rock with a deep recess weathered out of it. This gives the ridge its name – Clach Thoull means 'hole in the rock'. Offshore, there are islets where more seals can be seen basking in the summer sun, and patient watchers will occasionally glimpse otters at play. Above and about the crags, dark and ragged ravens wheel and squabble. The favourite walk at Port Appin is along the right of way which starts near the silversmith's workshop behind the jetty. It follows the shoreline south-west to the tip of Clach Thoull, then comes back through farmland above Airds Bay to finish near the hotel.

South-east of the village a narrow and winding road offers magnificent views across the narrow and many-bayed inlet of Loch Creran, while north-east of the village at the mouth of Loch Laich there is the brooding tower of Castle Stalker. It was built on the instructions of James V for the Stewarts of Appin in the 16th century and was used by the king as a hunting lodge. The name comes from the islet it is built on, Eilean an Stalcaire, which means 'hunter's island' in Gaelic. The castle fell into disrepair after the Jacobite risings, but was later restored as a private house.

Above the main Oban to Fort William road, the whitewashed mansion of Kinlochlaich stands among lawns that in spring are sprightly with daffodils. Its walled garden and garden centre are open to the public, adding a sparkle of cultivated colour to an area of already outstanding natural beauty.

PORTREE

ISLAND OF SKYE

34 miles north-west of Kyle of Lochalsh (ferry)

(PAGE 345 Bb)

Long ago, the perfect natural harbour, sheltered behind the 12 mile long shield of Raasay, was known as Loch Columcille – Columcille meaning the 'old chapel of Columba'. It had been named after St Columba, the remains of whose chapel may lie under a green mound on the islet in the loch. Though if that wandering saint built every chapel ascribed to him, he would have had little time for missionary work.

The present name is an anglicising of *Port an Righ*, meaning 'port of the king'. The monarch concerned is James V of Scotland, who certainly came here in 1540 with a fleet of 12 ships in an effort to settle the endless bickering between the MacLeods and the Macdonalds. He set up court where Somerled Square is now, gave judgment in some venerable disputes, bade what chiefs could be found to swear allegiance to him, and then sailed away.

Portree harbour

Houses on the waterfront

HARBOUR OF TRANQUILLITY

*The wooded, protective arm of Vriskaig Point guards Portree's little harbour, where on a calm summer's day dinghies rock gently at their moorings. More sailing dinghies are drawn up on the shingle in front of the attractive slate-roofed guesthouses and cottages that line the waterfront, while the pier is a terminal for a ferry to the mainland. In the background, the Cuillins stand out clearly, making a jagged silhouette on the skyline. Often, though, the mountains are obscured by mist rolling down their screes in everlasting affirmation of the old Norse name for Skye—*Skuyo, *'the Isle of Clouds'.*

The little port that became Skye's capital was a long time a-growing, but somehow the memory of James's visit stuck, and became enshrined in its name. Portree had to wait a little more than two centuries for its next royal visitor and he came, not with a fleet, but as a fugitive with a price on his head. It was in MacNab's Inn, on a site now occupied by the Royal Hotel, that Bonnie Prince Charlie parted from Flora Macdonald on July 1, 1746.

She had brought him 'over the sea to Skye' from Benbecula a few days earlier and, after hair's-breadth escapes, conveyed him to Portree, whence he would depart for the mainland, more adventures and final exile. Whatever his faults, the prince lacked neither personal charm nor a sense of occasion. He gave Miss Macdonald a locket with his portrait, saying that despite everything, he hoped that one day he would greet her at the Court of St James in London. But she never saw him again.

Portree is a fine setting for such tales of romance. Its buildings climb steeply up the hill from the harbour. A large number of churches of different denominations, and an almost equally large number of banks, suggest a population that is spiritual, thrifty and highly individualistic. And learned too; the High School is famous throughout western Scotland, though not for its architecture, whose concrete and glass strike something of a jarring note. Big Somerled Square and the streets running down to the harbour wall are much more sympathetic. The square was named after a 12th-century Lord of the Isles.

Portree's festivals, the annual Highland Games, the Agricultural Show and an occasional National Mod—the Gaelic Eisteddfod—attract people with Highland names from all over the world. Most of them will call in at the tourist information centre, which is one of the more unusual of its kind. It was built in the early part of the 18th century, and apart from being the oldest building in Portree it was also the jail, and the Information Officer's room was the condemned cell. A prisoner named Buchanan was hanged outside the back door in 1742 for the murder of a pack-man. He was sentenced by 'Old Kingsburgh', Flora Macdonald's future father-in-law.

● **Parking** The Green; Bayfield (both car parks) ● **Early closing** Wednesday ● **Events** Agricultural Show (July); The Skye Games (August); Folk Festival (August) ● **Information** TEL. Portree 2137 ● **AA 24 hour service** TEL. Aberdeen 639231.

Broadford ISLAND OF SKYE

26 miles south-east of Portree (PAGE 345 Cc)

The island seems to spread in all directions. But in the southern part of the sprawl every road, including those from the ferries, runs through Broadford, so most visitors are bound to arrive here sooner or later. Rather like the island, Broadford too has no particular shape; but it is the largest crofting community on Skye, a scattering of small farmhouses among flat pastures and, vaguely at their centre, a few shops, hotels and a bank.

All about the village is some tremendous scenery. Before it is Broadford Bay, with the tiny flat-topped island of Pabay, then a collection of jewel-like islets, and finally the operatic backdrop of the Applecross Mountains on the mainland that change shape and colour hourly, according to light and weather.

Inland are the granite screes of the Red Hills and the 2403 ft Beinn na Caillich—Mountain of the Old Woman—on whose summit, so it is said, a 13th-century Norwegian princess is buried, where the winds from Norway can blow over her for ever.

In Broadford's shops, local people speak Gaelic among themselves, but when a stranger enters they switch to softly accented English—a courtesy that has long impressed visitors to the village. In 1773, a Mrs

MacKinnon welcomed Dr Johnson to her home with a smacking kiss and the unanswerable query: 'What is it to live and not to love?' The house of Coire-Chatachan, where the incident took place, is only a tumble of stones now, but the memory of that delightful moment – recorded by Boswell – remains fresh. So does the memory of Skye's even more famous visitor, Prince Charles Edward Stuart, who spent several days as a fugitive on the island in 1746. Many islanders helped and sheltered him at risk of their lives, but he must have been especially grateful to the landlord of the Broadford Hotel, to whom the prince presented a secret recipe from which the liqueur Drambuie was first made in Scotland.

Dunvegan ISLAND OF SKYE

22 miles west of Portree (PAGE 345 Ab)

In contrast with the stern grandeur of most of Skye, the country about Dunvegan might actually be called pretty. The bay is patterned with islets, there is white coral sand by the shore, and there are woodlands of venerable trees – a rare sight indeed in the near-naked Hebrides. The moors are a dark shadow in the background, and about the village the fields of the crofts are bright and green, punctuated by white houses and farm cottages looking snug and permanent. As well they might, for this is MacLeod country.

MacLeod chieftains would have none of the 19th-century Clearances, when so many people of the Highlands were thrown off the land to make way for sheep. Neither did they commit their clansmen to the Jacobite Risings, so sparing them from the bloody Battle of Culloden and subsequent reprisals – although 700 MacLeods had died for an earlier Stuart, Charles II, at the Battle of Worcester in 1651.

The great symbol and repository of MacLeod permanence lies about a mile to the north of the village – Dunvegan Castle where, true to their motto of 'Hold Fast', MacLeod chiefs have lived for 600 years, since the days when the clan evolved from the descendants of the Norse king, Harold Hardraade, and Olav the Black, King of the Isle of Man. Looking from the outside like the epitome of a Highland stronghold, the interior has been considerably altered to suit the needs of succeeding generations.

The hall, for example, where a number of Campbells were served with goblets of blood then dirked to death in 1557, is now a delightful drawing room. Beneath its floor is a dungeon reached by trapdoor and ventilated by a slit in the kitchen stair, so that starving prisoners could be entertained by the scents of cooking wafting down to them.

There are all kinds of treasures in the castle; among them family portraits, a lock of Prince Charles Edward's hair, and the silver-chased drinking horn of Rory Mor – Big Rory – a 17th-century chieftain. The horn holds about 2 litres, preferably of claret, and is supposed to be drained at a draught by each new chieftain on his succession.

The castle's most famous possession, however, is the Bratach Sith, the Fairy Flag of the MacLeods. It is now only a tattered wisp of yellow silk, faintly spotted with red; but once it was a bright banner, said to have been given to a long-ago chief by his fairy mistress.

Other stories of its origin are hardly less marvellous; that it was the shirt of a saint, a Saracen banner captured during the Crusades, or that once it was 'Land Ravager', the standard of Harold Hardraade, who was defeated by Harold of England at Stamford Bridge in 1066. Whatever the truth, it is the clan's luck and protector, which, according to tradition, is destined to save the clan three times from dire necessity. Twice, apparently, it saved the clan from massacre in battle. The third occasion is yet to come.

Strong ties still bind MacLeods together, wherever they may be. Fostering this spirit was the life work of the best-loved of recent chiefs, Dame Flora MacLeod who died, aged 98, in 1976. She founded a Clan Parliament in Dunvegan composed of MacLeods from all over the world. Its theme is Dame Flora's own declaration that the clan family is 'beyond and outside divisions between nations, countries and continents . . . it takes no note of age or rank or wealth, success or failure . . . Clanship embraces them all'.

HEART'S HOME OF ALL MACLEODS *Standing high on a crag by the loch that shares its name is the forbidding mass of Dunvegan Castle – home of the Macleod chiefs for over 600 years.*

Kilmuir ISLAND OF SKYE

22 miles west of Portree (PAGE 345 Ab)

Skye has a wonderful knack of putting colour into the sketch of legend. At the old house of Monkstadt, the colour is fading now, and there is scarcely more than a roofless shell with what remains of its paint flaking

WINDSWEPT *In the wind-blown Western Isles, the thatched roofs of many crofting cottages – like this one at Kilmuir – are held in place by nets or ropes weighted down with boulders.*

off the walls. But battered though it is, it is still remarkably evocative of great romantic moments in the island's history.

In 1746, Monkstadt, in the crofting community of Kilmuir, was the home of Macdonald of Sleat and of his wife, Lady Margaret Macdonald. It was to them, in June of that year, that their kinswoman, the 24-year-old Flora Macdonald, brought the fugitive Prince Charles Edward Stuart, arrayed in the unlikely guise of her maid. They had landed at what is now Prince Charles's Point, after the 16 hour row and sail from Benbecula, which was to be the inspiration for the Jacobite song *Over the Sea to Skye*.

The prince sheltered in a cave while Flora walked to Monkstadt to tell her aunt of their arrival. To her horror, there was already another visitor, the commanding officer of the redcoat garrison, whom she coolly engaged in conversation while Lady Macdonald made arrangements for Charles's safety. From Monkstadt he walked to Kingsburgh and then on to Portree where he bade Flora farewell. From Portree he sailed to Raasay and finally to the mainland, whence a ship took him to France.

Flora was arrested and taken prisoner to the Tower of London. After being released, to her astonishment she was fêted as a heroine. On her return to Skye, she married a clansman, Allan Macdonald, bore him a large number of children, and later emigrated to America with her family. During the American Revolution, her husband fought on the Loyalist side and was taken prisoner; on his advice, she went back once more to her island, was wounded during an attack by a privateer on the voyage, and died on Skye, 11 years later, in 1790.

Dr Johnson, who met her in the 1770s while on his tour of the Hebrides, wrote a tribute to her: 'A name that will be mentioned in history, and if courage and fidelity be virtues, mentioned with honour.' These are the words carved on a stone Celtic cross which marks her resting place in the cemetery at Kilmuir, which overlooks roofless Monkstadt and the miles of sea to her birthplace on the island of South Uist.

Close by the cemetery is a scene that Flora would have been totally familiar with – a cluster of old, thatched houses crouched low beneath the wind. These have been restored and refurbished as the Skye Cottage Museum, to present a picture of a crofting community a century or so ago. It was a hard life, but one of great ingenuity and self-reliance, in which everything – food, cloth, dyes, furniture, whisky and even musical instruments – was grown or contrived by the community; the only exceptions were books and inherited china. The museum also has relics of Prince Charles Edward Stuart and Flora Macdonald.

TOBERMORY

ISLAND OF MULL

21 miles north-west of Craignure (PAGE 345 B/Cg)

The lure of gold – and the love of beautiful scenery – have attracted people to Tobermory since the early 17th century. The gold-seekers came in search of a Spanish galleon which sank in Tobermory Bay in 1588, after the defeat of the Armada. The galleon lies 300 yds off the pier and is buried beneath 30 ft of silt and stones. So far, she has resisted a number of professional attempts to raise her. The last one, in 1982, cost about £6000 a day in men and machinery, and lasted for more than a month.

At first, the galleon was thought to be a treasure ship, the *San Francisco* or *Florencia*, driven from the Channel up the west coast by English warships. She was trying to escape around the north of Scotland, but blew up while sheltering off Tobermory. One of the first recorded salvage attempts was made by a diver named Archibald Millar in the early 1680s. He worked for the Duke of Argyll, whose family still holds the salvage rights. In 1740 a salvage operation yielded a bronze gun and a couple of fine brass cannons and plates.

This seemed modest enough, but stories grew about the gold, doubloons, silver plate and chests of jewels supposedly on board the galleon. To say nothing of the pay chests of the defeated Armada. However, historians later learnt that the *San Francisco* had returned safely to Spain, and that the sunken vessel was an 800 ton merchantman carrying troops, and contained little or nothing in the way of treasure.

Research showed that she was built in Ragusa, now Dubrovnik, in Yugoslavia, and the troops aboard were commanded by one of Spain's better captains, Don Diego Tellez Enriquez. But despite the sober historical evidence, rumours of treasure circulated again when a coin was found near the wreck in 1873.

Tobermory is the capital of Mull, built in the 1780s by the British Fisheries Society – who also created Ullapool (see page 406). The town takes its name from *Tobar Mhoire*, Gaelic for 'The Well of St Mary'. The sparse remains of the Christian community that centred around the well are in the ancient graveyard. Near by is the church, long since abandoned by the ministry and now an arts and crafts centre.

Tourism is the mainstay of Tobermory these days, and one particular shop – in business since 1830 – says it all. It sells everything for the visitor from locally brewed malt whisky to fishing tackle; from camping gear to rubber boots; from fine wines to protective clothing. As well as all that, you can also buy permits to fish the nearby Mishnish Lochs, and tickets to play on the local Western Isles' golf course.

• **Parking** Main Street (car park) • **Early closing** Wednesday • **Events** Music Festival (April); Mull Highland Games (July); Clyde Cruising Race (July); West Highland Yachting Week (July or August); Car Rally (October) • **Information** TEL. Tobermory 2182 (summer) • **AA 24 hour service** TEL. Aberdeen 639231.

Bunessan ISLAND OF MULL

43 miles south-west of Tobermory (PAGE 345 Bh)

Down the long road that runs from Craignure, the ferry port on the east coast of the island, to the top of the Ross of Mull in the far south-west, signs of current human habitation are few and far between. Delightful Mull may be, but its loneliness can induce a stir of unease that is not dispelled by the melancholy little crofting houses left roofless and overgrown since the infamous Clearances of a century and a half ago.

However, Bunessan, some 6 miles from the end of the Ross of Mull, is just the place to dispel it. By Mull standards, it is positively bustling – a pleasant collection of stone houses, smallish hotels and shops that look onto a deep rocky inlet of Loch na Lathaich, that is draped with dark gold seaweed at low tide. Sometimes a puffer – one of the ubiquitous little tramp steamers that service the Highlands and Islands – is tied up by the pier, loading and unloading; or some yachts or a visiting fishing boat.

Bunessan has had its ups and downs, but has always managed to keep going. Traditionally, its role was that of a port serving the little crofting communities of the southern part of the island. To some extent, it continued to do so even after the Clearances, since they did not affect the south-western peninsula quite so badly as other parts of Mull. Even now, minor roads and tracks radiate from Bunessan to connect with tiny crofting 'townships' buried deep in the Ross.

Bunessan began to realise its potential as a tourist centre in the years after the Second World War. Its chief attraction is that of a pause on the road from the Craignure mainland ferry to Fionnphort (pronounced 'Finnafort') and the ferry to Iona; an overnight stopping place too, since accommodation on Iona is fairly limited. But before pressing on to St Columba's island, it is well worth exploring some of the other things that Bunessan has to offer.

There is a minor road to the south, for example, that leads to the crofts and sandy bays around Uisken on the southern shore of the Ross; basalt columns and layers of rock containing fossil leaves and petals to the north about Ardtun; and prehistoric monuments everywhere. To the west there is the curiously named Loch Poit na h-I (pronounced 'p'tee'), which is where Iona's monks used to fish, and which is haunted by a kelpie or water-horse; and, also to the west, are some now disused quarries whose vivid pink granite was taken up by Victorian architects for major works all over Britain. Opposite the quarries is Eilean nam Ban, the tiny Isle of the Women to which St Columba banished the nuns of Iona (he did not like women); and farther down the coast is the tidal island of Erraid, on which David Balfour was shipwrecked in Robert Louis Stevenson's *Kidnapped*.

WELCOMING ANCHORAGE *The bright colour-washed houses of Tobermory's main street curve around the harbour, overlooked by the imposing 19th-century Western Isles Hotel. Here, at Mull's capital, yachtsmen can take advantage of a sheltered anchorage; and ferries go to the even remoter islands of Coll and Tiree.*

Sooner or later, though, all visitors to Mull will cross to Iona. It is a magical place, and Fionnphort, the ferry point, with its red-pink rocks, white sand and crystal sea, hardly less so. Iona was the Rome of the Celtic Church. Forty-eight Scottish kings are said to be buried here – Shakespeare's Macbeth and Duncan among them – and a number of Irish, Norse and French monarchs beside them, whose wish it was to be buried in the holy precincts of the monastery established by St Columba in the 6th century.

His building has long gone – destroyed by the Vikings who also massacred 68 monks at nearby Martyr's Bay. But the 15th-century cathedral is still in use, and close by are the remains of a 13th-century nunnery. Here, too, is the restored 11th-century St Oran's Chapel, in whose cemetery lie the kings.

Dervaig ISLAND OF MULL

6 miles west of Tobermory (PAGE 345 Bg)

Old-time Mull landowners were more generally famed for evictions than for acts of generosity towards their tenants. But Dervaig, perhaps the prettiest village on the island, was built by Maclean of Coll to house some of his people in the Loch Cuan area in 1799. Then it consisted of 26 houses, each with a vegetable garden and common grazing rights on the hillsides behind.

There are perhaps a dozen more houses now, which, like the others, are stone and mostly single-storeyed, though clever use of dormer windows has induced a second storey under the roofs of many. Only a few of the more recent ones look as though they were actually meant to have second floors. The little houses sparkle with brightly painted window frames and doors giving each one individuality.

Beside the bridge there is a handsome little church with a 'pencil' steeple of a type common in Ireland but rare in Scotland. It was built at the beginning of this century on the site of a much older church. A little farther to the east, down the steep, writhing road to Tobermory, is the cemetery of Kilmore. It contains a number of ancient tombs and the graves of nameless seamen, washed up upon Mull's western coast.

Despite its size, Dervaig is a lively, bright place, not least because it has the Mull Little Theatre, which lays claim to being the smallest professional theatre in Britain. It is very popular and, since it has only 40 seats, booking is essential. It also possesses the Old Byre, a folk museum based upon brilliantly conceived exhibitions and tableaux of crofting life at the time of the Clearances. By modern standards, crofting was a far from idyllic existence, in which people and livestock shared the same building, and almost everything, furniture and clothing included, had to be made by hand. But it had a cosiness, and music and laughter too, as is apparent from the sound tracks made by local people to accompany the tableaux. And it was better than the destitution that followed eviction.

Dervaig and the country round about suffered cruelly. In mid-century, the Quinish estate, including

Dervaig, came into the possession of James Forsyth, who persuaded the villagers to sign new tenancies. They also unwittingly signed away their grazing rights, leaving them nothing but their vegetable plots. Elsewhere, he forcibly threw his tenants out and put their cottages to the torch; Glen Gorm – the blue glen – on the estate, is so called from the memory of the smoke of burning thatch.

The population of Mull is now about one-fifth of what it was in the 1820s, and evicted men and women of Mull took their names, and those of the places they had left behind, to Australia, the United States and Canada. Perhaps the best known of these transported names is Calgary in Alberta, whose origin is a coastal hamlet to the west of Dervaig. The Calgary in Canada was not named by an emigrant from Mull but by a Colonel MacLeod, of the North-West Mounted Police (later the Royal Canadian Mounted Police), who established a barracks and township in Alberta in 1876. He was a native of Skye, and named his creation in memory of happy boyhood holidays on Mull.

Lochbuie ISLAND OF MULL

33 miles south of Tobermory (PAGE 345 Ch)

Only a mile or so from the ferry port at Craignure, the magic of Mull begins to assert itself. Its seas are sapphire, its seaweed gold, its sea-moss emerald and its sheep have fleece truly as white as snow. Perhaps these things are not really so, but on the road that runs beside the Sound of Mull, then bends along the head of Loch Spelve, they seem to be.

From the loch head, a road minor even by Mull standards shoots steeply away along the waterside, then flattens out at Kinlochspelve before striking out along the north shore of the freshwater Loch Uisg. Another surprise, this, for with its piled up woods and rhododendrons it is momentarily reminiscent of a lake in an English estate. But the Hebrides soon reassert themselves, as the road runs out on the windy, rocky shores of Loch Buie and the Atlantic.

Behind the shore is a little grassy plain with the first slopes of Ben Buie rising at its back. Here is the scattering of stone cottages that is the village of Lochbuie with, before it, the wooded grounds of the mansion that was once the seat of the MacLaines of Lochbuie. Most of it is 19th century, but part is older.

Earlier MacLaines lived in their stronghold by the shore – the grim Moy Castle, that still stands four-square, draped in ivy like a tattered, dark green plaid. It was built in the 15th century with every convenience demanded by the day, including a well that never dries out and an awful dungeon in which the prisoner was forced to sit upon a boulder surrounded by 9 ft of water. On the beach below the castle, there is a channel cleared of rocks; here, the war galleys of Moy were drawn up on their return from sackings and plunderings around the Highlands and Islands.

Naturally, the place has a ghost – a decapitated phantom that gallops round and round the castle whenever the death of a MacLaine is imminent. In life, he was Ewen a'Chinn Bhig – Ewen of the Little Head – the son of a chieftain killed in battle long ago. Apparently he was warned by a wise woman that if his wife did not give him butter for breakfast, he would certainly die that day. She did not, and he did.

The castle is in a fairly dangerous state of decay, and is not generally open to the public; those wishing to see it should enquire at the estate lodge.

Long before even MacLaines were thought of, perhaps about the time that Stonehenge and Avebury Ring were being built in Wiltshire, other people lived on the plain at Loch Buie's head. Who they were is an enigma, but their monuments are a standing stone and a stone circle, 22 ft across.

Lochbuie and Lochbuie House

IN WHICH DR JOHNSON IS RENDERED SPEECHLESS

Dr Johnson and his biographer Mr Boswell stayed at Lochbuie House, the MacLaine family seat, during their famous Hebridean tour of 1773. Here the great lexicographer was treated to a superb piece of Highland snobbery. 'Are you,' the old MacLaine chief demanded, 'of the Johnstons of Glencro, or of Ardnamurchan?' The doctor did not reply, but Boswell reported that he gave the old chief 'a significant look'.

354 JOURNAL OF A TOUR

both in ſize and manners; but we found that they had ſwelled him up to a fictitious ſize, and clothed him with imaginary qualities.—Col's idea of him was equally extravagant, though very different: he told us, he was quite a Don Quixote; and ſaid, he would give a great deal to ſee him and Dr. Johnſon together. The truth is, that Lochbuy proved to be only a bluff, comely, noiſy old gentleman, proud of his hereditary conſequence, and a very hearty and hoſpitable landlord. Lady Lochbuy was ſiſter to Sir Allan M'Lean, but much older. He ſaid to me, "They are quite *Antediluvians.*" Being told that Dr. Johnſon did not hear well, Lochbuy bawled out to him, "Are you of the Johnſtons of Glencro, or of Ardnamurchan?"—Dr. Johnſon gave him a ſignificant look, but made no anſwer; and I told Lochbuy that he was not Johnſ*ton*, but John*ſon*, and that he was an Engliſhman.

Lochbuy ſome years ago tried to prove himſelf a

From Boswell's story of the Hebridean tour

MAP 34

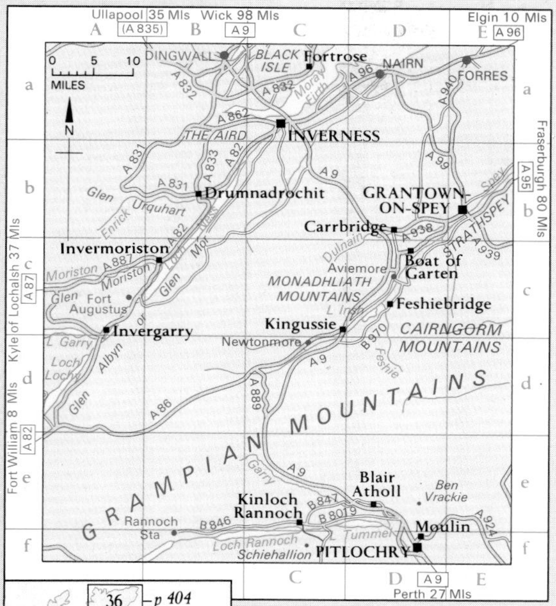

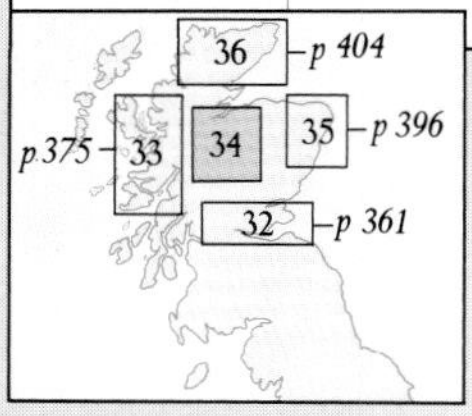

THE MONSTER'S DEEP AND SKIERS' PARADISE

High peaks, heathery moors and serene lochs are spread in a broad, summer landscape. In winter, skiers swoop down the steep, snow-clad slopes of the mighty Cairngorms. Loch Ness seems to stretch endlessly between the wild mountains – and there is always the hope that you might catch a glimpse of the elusive monster. Near the loch's head is Inverness, 'capital' of the Highlands. And Britain's only private army guards the splendid Blair Castle. Also guarded jealously are the magnificent ospreys, mysteriously returned to their nesting places near Boat of Garten after being either exterminated or driven away.

MAP 34: NEIGHBOURING AREAS – MAPS 32, 33, 35, 36

GRANTOWN-ON-SPEY	INVERNESS	PITLOCHRY
Boat of Garten	Drumnadrochit	Blair Atholl
Carrbridge	Fortrose	Kinloch Rannoch
Feshiebridge	Invergarry	Moulin
Kingussie	Invermoriston	

GRANTOWN-ON-SPEY

HIGHLAND

31 miles south-east of Inverness (PAGE 385 Eb)

A little over 200 years ago, in 1765, Sir James Grant, of an ancient local family of lairds, founded this pretty little town near the tree-clad banks of the River Spey. He meant his new town to be a market centre which would encourage both agricultural improvements in the area and the local linen and wool industries. At about the same time, he also established some small textile mills, mostly in partnership with others.

But the mills had a working life of only about 50 years, before the developments of the Industrial Revolution put them out of business. Instead, a new source of prosperity opened for Grantown – tourists, who started coming from all over Britain. In 1860, Queen Victoria stayed at the stately Grant Arms Hotel in The Square. In her *Highland Journal* she said that her visit had been 'very amusing and never to be forgotten'. This royal approval put Grantown firmly on the map and the town's popularity boomed.

Some visitors came for the beauties of the surrounding countryside, to walk through the pine forests, clamber up the Cairngorms and fish for salmon and trout in the swift-running Spey and its tributary, the Dulnain. Others, heeding their doctors' advice, came here for the fresh, pure and invigorating air.

In the late 19th century, the town largely took its present shape – gracious granite houses, grand hotels and respectable guesthouses lining clean broad streets

GRACIOUS LIVING

Elegant, gracious Grantown, with its tree-shaded main square and turreted granite buildings, is a fitting memorial to 'Good' Sir James Grant, of nearby Castle Grant, the town's founder and one of the most benevolent and well-loved lairds of the 18th-century Highlands. One story goes that he founded the town for fellow clansmen who had sought his protection after a brawl at a local fair.

Grantown turrets

The main square in Grantown

and a tree-lined square. Then, in the 1960s, some £300,000 was spent in turning it into a ski resort. Scotland's main skiing mountains – the Cairngorms – are within easy driving distance, and their slopes are busy from before Christmas until Easter.

The town now has its own ski schools and ski shop – and when the hotels are full, and the guest-houses bulging, the 2000 or so inhabitants are almost outnumbered by visitors.

• **Parking** High Street; The Square (both car parks) • **Early closing** Thursday • **Events** Square Fair (August); Agricultural Show (August) • **Information** TEL. Grantown-on-Spey 2773 • **AA 24 hour service** TEL. Aberdeen 639231.

Boat of Garten HIGHLAND

9 miles south-west of Grantown-on-Spey (PAGE 385 Dc)

The village lies in the midst of a wilderness of pine and heather, bitterly cold in winter and hot in high summer, when forest fire is an uneasy thought at the back of every resident's mind.

Boat of Garten usually figures in the memory for two things – the oddness of its name, and its ospreys. The name recalls a ferry across the Spey that was long ago ousted by a bridge, while the ospreys actually live a couple of miles away by Loch Garten – a dark, pine-framed patch of water that could be in Labrador, were it not for the notices that warn in several languages of the ever-present risk of fire.

The warnings are doubly necessary here, for this is where the ospreys – large fish hawks – decided to give the United Kingdom one last chance. Once common in Scotland, they were exterminated or driven away at the beginning of the century, partly because they competed with anglers for trout. Not until about 25 years ago did one or two pairs make a tentative return to their ancestral breeding place from their wintering grounds in Africa.

Now, about 20 pairs come back to nest in Scotland each spring, and one pair, closely guarded by the Royal Society for the Protection of Birds, comes to Loch Garten, arriving in April and staying on until October. The society has provided a hide from which you can see – through binoculars set on fixed lines – a large and untidy nest with perhaps an uncombed white head bobbing about on top. This is the female that through April and May hatches the chicks and attends them. She is fed by the male, which brings her a trout or pike from the loch once a day. Delays obviously vex her and bring forth shrill whistles of impatience.

In Boat of Garten, as elsewhere in Strathspey, architectural charm takes a modest second place to the tourist attractions the village provides, though among the small hotels and guesthouses, there are some pretty, square-cut, granite villas with fretwork frames about the doors and windows.

As well as birdwatching, the village offers one of the most stylish and picturesque of Scotland's smaller golf courses, and excellent fly-fishing in the Spey. For steam enthusiasts, there is the Strathspey Railway that runs a train service over 5 miles of old Highland Line track between Boat of Garten and Aviemore. The railway's steam engines, carriages and station buildings are kept clean and gleaming in the way they always used to be on the bigger railways. Altogether a fine essay in nostalgia.

Carrbridge HIGHLAND

9 miles west of Grantown-on-Spey (PAGE 385 Db)

At one end of the village, a modern bridge crosses the turbulent River Dulnain. But beside it there is a more ancient structure, a dizzying, rail-less, half-moon of a bridge. This was apparently built by the 1st Earl of Seafield in 1717 for the benefit of funeral parties travelling to Duthill, traditional burial-place of the chieftains of Clan Grant, some 2½ miles away. Possibly Lord Seafield had a quirky sense of humour, for even though the bridge is wider than it looks in most photographs, it would take but a breeze to send coffin, bearers and all into the cataract below. A more logical explanation, perhaps, is that, once upon a time the bridge had a rail.

Carrbridge was one of the first villages to promote the Cairngorms as a winter sports area, and itself as an après-ski resort. Its sturdy granite villas, hotel and guesthouses may lack a little of the sophistication of, say, Switzerland's Gstaad, but among them is the Austrian Ski School, decorated with murals of gentians, skiers, and with mounds of skis for hire. The building is also the Struan Hotel.

But Carrbridge's most splendid creation is the Landmark Visitor Centre, a unique complex of cinema, folk-life exhibition of crofting in the Spey Valley, nature trails, sculpture park, restaurant and craft shop. The cinema presents, each half hour, *The Highlander*, a 'multi-vision' account of Europe's last tribal society – the clans of the Scottish Highlands.

Feshiebridge HIGHLAND

18 miles south-west of Grantown-on-Spey (PAGE 385 Dc)

The buildings of Feshiebridge would not delay most people for long. They consist of four houses; and there is also a postbox and a telephone box. But the bridge that leaps over the gorge of the Feshie river is well worth seeing and lingering by; not only is it a fine, soaring piece of Highland bridge building but, in a way, it offers two rivers for the price of one.

From the southern railing, on the side where the Feshie comes down from the Cairngorms, it is a swirling, boiling, roaring rapid that shapes itself over crags whose placing might have been arranged by some Victorian landscape painter.

Once having shot the bridge, however, the waters rapidly compose themselves, and run decorously down towards the Spey in a succession of glassy pools that writhe about reefs of pale green birches rising from the banks of the gorge. The dark mountains peep over their tops, seeming much more remote than they really are.

Below is pretty, little – by local standards – Loch Insh, also framed in tall woods and busy with dinghies and canoes. From here, the mountain background of the Cairngorms is much more in evidence.

On a knoll above the loch stands Insh church, surrounded by Caledonian pines populated by vociferous rooks. The present building dates from the 18th century, but the site is believed to be the only place in Scotland that has been a place of Christian worship since the 7th century. It still owns a hand-bell that was used to call people to prayer in Celtic times. By the churchyard gate, a memorial stone to a woman who died in 1937, 'lost in the hills she loved', is a poignant reminder of the mountains' dangers.

No one should come to Feshiebridge without visiting the splendid wildlife parks in the neighbourhood. The Insh Marshes are an odd stretch of country between Loch Insh and Kingussie (see below). They are liable to flooding at any time of year, and consequently harbour a wide range of waterfowl that, since 1973, have come under the wing of the Royal Society for the Protection of Birds.

Then, too, there is the Highland Wildlife Park that has restored to the area all the creatures that used to live in it – brown bears, wolves, lynxes, beavers – to accompany those that managed to hang on, such as wild cats, red deer, pine martens and badgers. Pets must be left in the free kennels at the entrance.

Kingussie HIGHLAND

24 miles south-west of Grantown-on-Spey (PAGE 385 Cc)

It is not quite certain whether Kingussie would care to be classified as a village. Despite its size, it thinks of itself – with some justice – as the capital of Badenoch, catering with Aviemore, about 12 miles north-east along the Spey Valley, for the energetic folk who hasten to the Cairngorms in all seasons to ski, skate, curl, canoe, ride, fish, glide, sail, walk or mountaineer.

Kingussie lies beside the already majestic River Spey, and consists mostly of a long, straight street of chunky granite buildings, among which are hotels, guesthouses, ski schools, souvenir and craft shops. There are, too, notice boards that advertise such traditional pursuits as ceilidh folk song and dancing sessions, and shinty – a fairly savage type of hockey at which Kingussie men excel.

Nevertheless, tradition is best served and remembered at the splendid Highland Folk Museum, founded by Dr I. F. Grant in 1935 to preserve recollections of a way of life that was, even then, disappearing. The main building houses a collection of Highland crafts, textiles, furniture and musical instruments, all made within small communities; and there is also an open-air museum. The picture that emerges is harsh, implying a life of subsistence farming, yet one not without a richness of laughter, music and story-telling about the hearth on winter nights.

Another powerhouse of Highland memories is the forlorn ruin of Ruthven Barracks, standing high on a knoll just outside Kingussie. The barracks were built in 1719 – 21 as part of the Government scheme to pacify the Highlands. They stand on the site of a castle belonging to a late 14th-century Earl of Mar.

The barracks were captured by the Jacobites during the '45 Rising, and here the clans rallied for the last time, still prepared to go on fighting, even after the disaster of Culloden. But all they received was a message from Prince Charles Edward Stuart ordering them to disband, and bidding each man to seek what succour he could. No thanks were mentioned.

Some 4 miles to the south is Newtonmore, in many ways a mirror to Kingussie. Its equivalent of the Highland Folk Museum is the Clan MacPherson Centre, which presents an altogether more warlike portrait of the Highlands than that suggested by the gentle crafts at Kingussie.

Each exhibit has a story, gladly recounted by the warden; a particular favourite is a broken fiddle that belonged to a freebooter named James MacPherson. Sentenced to death for numerous robberies, he was hanged in Banff (see page 396) in 1700. Also in the museum are the remains of a clock, said to have been

Kingussie and the Monadhliath Mountains

GRANITE STRENGTH

The pointed dormers and slate roofs of Kingussie crouch below the boulder-strewn flanks of the Monadhliath Mountains, which rise to the north. The village shops cater mostly for visitors, but there is a butcher's famed for its home-made haggis. And along the main street there is a fine door in the style of the turn-of-the-century Scottish architect, designer and painter, Charles Rennie Mackintosh.

Rennie Mackintosh-style door

Kingussie's famous family butcher

The 'clack mill'

'Black house' from Lewis

BACK TO THE 'BLACK HOUSE' DAYS

A small grain mill from the Isle of Lewis in the Outer Hebrides shows Viking influence. This 'clack mill' – so-called because of the noise made by the mill as it turns – is a direct descendant of Norse mills introduced to Scotland in the Middle Ages and is one of the exhibits at the Highland Folk Museum in Kingussie. The museum, which brings together relics of the old Highlands and their culture, has some of its most evocative showpieces in the open-air section, where reconstructed buildings give a feeling of long-vanished ways of life. Among them, also from Lewis, is a 'black house', a low, windowless cottage ideally suited to the bitter, windswept winters of the outer isles. Its walls are double rows of massive boulders with sand between to aid drainage. There is no chimney – instead smoke from the peat fire on the hearth was allowed to filter out through the thatch. The thatch was replaced each year and the old one used to fertilise potato beds. At the entrance to the house are two whale vertebrae. Wood was scarce in the almost treeless islands, and the vertebrae of whales, caught by local whalers or washed up on the beaches, were used in the home for anything from seats to chopping blocks.

deliberately advanced at the rumour that a last-minute reprieve for MacPherson was on its way.

This is still MacPherson country, and local people recall with pride how their ancestors maintained their chief, Cluny MacPherson, in a cave in the heights of nearby Craig Dhu for several years after Culloden. Each August, coinciding with the Highland Games, there is a Clan Gathering in the village, attended by MacPhersons from all over the world.

INVERNESS

HIGHLAND

113 miles north of Perth (PAGE 385 Ca)

The first Cabinet meeting ever to be held outside London took place in Inverness under Prime Minister David Lloyd George in September 1921. The premier was on holiday in northern Scotland when he received an urgent letter from the Irish revolutionary leader Eamon De Valera.

Lloyd George hurried to the 'Capital of the Highlands', and was joined by senior ministers – including Stanley Baldwin and Winston Churchill. The Cabinet made their deliberations about the Irish troubles in the august atmosphere of the Town House, a Gothic-style building, which contains superb crystal chandeliers and portraits of Bonnie Prince Charlie and Flora Macdonald. The historic meeting in the council chamber is marked by a document bearing the signatures of those present. The Town House, built in 1878–82, now serves as the town hall and offices of the Provost (chief magistrate) and Council.

Outside the Town House, in High Street, is the mercat (market) cross, which incorporates the *Clach-na-cuddain*, Gaelic for 'Stone of the tubs'. Townswomen used the stone as a resting place for their tubs of water when returning from the River Ness, which splits the town from north to south. Locals say that the stone was once the seat of a visionary, who stated that as long as it remained intact no harm would come to the town or its people.

Near by looms Inverness Castle, whose massive bulk looks much older than it is. It was built on the site of two former fortresses in 1834–46, not for defence but to provide a new sheriff court house. It still houses the sheriff court, as well as a district court and administrative offices. A statue of Scotland's greatest heroine, Flora Macdonald, stands on the castle esplanade. In 1746 she helped Bonnie Prince Charlie to flee to the Isle of Skye after his defeat at the Battle of Culloden, 6 miles east of the town. She is shown gazing anxiously south-westwards, in the general direction of the island.

Inverness's oldest building is the superb Abertarff House in Church Street. It dates from 1594 and contains a turnpike stair – a form of spiral staircase which graced many homes of the wealthy. Abertarff House now belongs to the National Trust for Scotland. Also in Church Street are the headquarters of the An Comunn Gaidhealach, a society devoted to preserving the Gaelic culture and language. The town's museum is in Castle Wynd, a narrow street that twists below the castle. The exhibits depict, among other things, the history of the town, and a gallery has pictures of old Inverness and some modern art.

In Gaelic, Inverness means 'the mouth of the River Ness' – which is just where it stands. One of the oldest towns in Scotland, it was first mentioned in the 6th century in a biography of St Columba, who in AD 565 visited the Pictish King Brude at his fort, thought to have been at nearby Craig Phadrig. The ruins of a fort are still there – and even older remains have been found in the area, including prehistoric carved stones, a number of burial mounds and some memorial cairns.

In the 1650s Inverness was occupied by Cromwell's troops, who built an imposing, five-sided stronghold. Ten years later, when Charles II came to the throne, this was destroyed – although its clock tower still stands. Some of the citadel's stones were used in 1668 to build Dunbar's Hospital in Church Street. Originally an almshouse, the building became a grammar school and now belongs to the National Trust for Scotland.

At the other end of Church Street rises the 150 ft high Steeple, once part of the old town prison. Particularly violent criminals were kept in a small cell beneath the bells. And across the river to the west is St Andrew's Cathedral. Built in the 1860s, the cathedral has elegantly carved pillars, exquisite stained glass and a font copied from the one in Copenhagen Cathedral, in Denmark.

• **Parking** Eastgate; Rose Street; Bishop's Road; Riverside Street; Castle Street; Station Yard; Station Square (all car parks) • **Early closing** Wednesday • **Theatre** Eden Court, Bishop's Road • **Cinema** La Scala, Strothers Lane • **Events** Music Festival (March); Folk Festival (April); Highland Games (July); Highland Field Sports Fair (August); Northern Piping Competitions (September) • **Information** TEL. Inverness 234353 • **AA 24 hour service** TEL. Aberdeen 639231.

Drumnadrochit HIGHLAND

14 miles south-west of Inverness (PAGE 385 Bb)

Whatever it is that draws the underwater cameras, the midget submarines, the helicopters and the sonar systems to the depths of Loch Ness, is no recent arrival. A note on a 14th-century chart of the loch comments upon 'waves without wind, fish without fins, islands that float', and from long before that, there is a record of a notable encounter between a great water-beast and St Columba, who brought Christianity to the Picts of Glen Mor.

According to Adamnan, Columba's biographer, he bade a monk swim across the Ness river to fetch a boat, but the unfortunate man was no more than halfway across when the monster surfaced close by, jaws agape, intent upon devouring him. Then, from the bank, there rang Columba's stentorian command: 'Go no farther, nor touch the man! Go back!' Considerably abashed, the creature submerged, and has never harmed anyone since.

In fact the monster, or presumably its descendants, have done the area a great deal of good, particularly since 1933 when the road down the north-western shore of Loch Ness was built. From this, and other points about the loch's 24 mile length, more than 1000 witnesses have testified to seeing mysterious humps and bumps on the surface of the water, all of which corroborate or enhance the remarks of the 14th-century chart. Each reported sighting brings hundreds of eager visitors, and if their vigil is unrewarded, no one minds very much. The countryside is grand and beautiful, and there is always a chance of seeing the monster tomorrow.

Drumnadrochit, the little stone village about halfway down the loch at the mouth of lovely Glen Urquhart, has made 'Nessie' – as the monster is irreverently called – particularly its own. And with some justice. There have been more sightings in the vicinity of the village than anywhere else; the water before it is about 800 ft deep, reaching down to a silt bed where anything could hide; and by the shore there is the shell of Urquhart Castle, romantic enough to give credence to any tale.

Drumnadrochit does a roaring trade in Monster toys, Monster ice creams and Monster postcards depicting the animal in a tam o' shanter. But there is also the Official Monster Exhibition that takes the visitor through various attempts to explain away the monster as a fake – otters swimming in line astern, mats of floating vegetation and a First World War Zeppelin occasionally bobbing to the surface – before introducing more serious possibilities. Certainly, the photographs of humps, fins and slim necks and heads protruding from the water, taken down the years, are startling, and sonar trackings made by scientific expeditions immensely intriguing. But the conclusions are all rather fuzzy and uncertain, and perhaps that is the way they should remain. Any mystery in these small islands that refuses to be confirmed, denied or categorised is worth cherishing.

Urquhart Castle stands on a point overlooking Urquhart Bay, commanding almost the entire length of the loch. It played an important role in the Wars of Scottish Independence in the 13th and 14th centuries, and also in the ages-long squabbles between the Lords of the Isles and the Kings of Scotland as to whether the north-western seaboard should, or should not, be part of the Scottish realm. During this time, the castle was destroyed, rebuilt, sacked, harried, captured and recaptured.

The 16th-century tower was the last part of the castle to be built and, even in its present shattered state, it is apparent that the occupants lived in some style. Not for long, however. In 1689, a Government garrison successfully withstood a Jacobite siege, then blew the castle up, so as to deny it to any future Highland rebels. The remains were used as a quarry by the people of Glen Urquhart for some time; all in all, it is remarkable that the ruins reflected in the peat-dark water are as dignified and evocative as they are.

One last point: however hot the day, do not be tempted to swim in Loch Ness. The water is nearly freezing, never more than 43°F (6°C), winter or summer, and who knows what might be rising out of the depths to meet you?

Fortrose HIGHLAND

16 miles north-east of Inverness (PAGE 385 Ca)

The Black Isle is neither black nor an island, and the reason why it should be called so has given rise to a number of ingenious explanations. Perhaps the most reasonable is that it was once called, in Gaelic, *Tir an Dubh Ghoill*, 'the land of the black Danes', to distinguish it from the country round about that was held by the relatively more pleasant Norwegians. Gaelic and English became mixed, leading to 'black Ghoill', and thence to 'Black Isle' – or so it is said.

At any rate, the Black Isle is a surprisingly fertile piece of northern Britain, lying between the Moray and Cromarty firths, and its jewel is Fortrose, though it must be admitted that neighbouring Rosemarkie runs it a close second. Fortrose is perhaps the more 'douce', a neat Scots word implying a gentle graciousness, sedateness and a few shades of meaning between.

In its centre is the cathedral, whose ruined south

Fortrose harbour

Dormers and painted railings

A TOUCH OF ENGLAND IN SCOTLAND

It is hard to believe that the green and gently rolling country of the deceptively named Black Isle belongs to the Highlands. Here it slopes down to Fortrose's pebbly harbour, which these days is used mostly by enthusiastic members of a thriving local sailing club. In the centre of Fortrose, the sedate spirit of the region is translated into decorous houses of pink sandstone with fine gables and smartly painted railings. The ruins of a medieval cathedral are, however, a reminder of much grander times.

Cathedral ruins

aisle and Chapter House still stand among the trees in Cathedral Square. Most of the cathedral was built in the 13th century, but it began to crumble at the Reformation and local people used some of the stones for their own houses. The south aisle was built after the rest of the cathedral on land donated in 1379 by Euphamia, Countess of Ross, whose somewhat battered tomb may be seen there. This unfortunate lady was a grand-niece of Robert Bruce, and was forcibly married to Sir Walter Lesley. When he died she was again forced to marry – this time to Alexander Stewart, Earl of Buchan, the notorious 'Wolf of Badennoch'. She herself conceived a passion for one Alexander Mackenzie, but when he failed to return her love, she threw him into a dungeon in Dingwall.

For much of its history, Fortrose and the country round about was the domain of the Mackenzie Earls of Seaforth, one of whom in the 17th century was the patron of Coinneach Odhar Mackenzie, the Brahan Seer, whose prophecies and 'second sight' were famous throughout Scotland. They were somewhat double-edged gifts, however.

Lady Seaforth pestered him to tell her what her absent husband was doing. The seer accurately, if rashly, informed her that her husband was in Paris in the arms of another woman, whereupon she had the poor seer burnt to death in a spiked barrel of tar for his impudence. But before he expired, he told the crowd that the last Seaforth would be a deaf mute, and his four sons would die before him. The line did indeed come to an end in this manner during the lifetime of Sir Walter Scott, who recorded it in 1815.

On a more cheerful note, Fortrose is also famed for its Academy which was founded in the 16th century on the sturdy Scots principle that the laird's son and the crofter's son should learn side by side. The place is likewise celebrated for its gardens, which are bright all summer long – thanks to good soil, a gentle climate and the considerable skill of the people.

Invergarry HIGHLAND

40 miles south-west of Inverness (PAGE 385 Ac)

The cottages scattered along the wooded glen of the River Garry wear an attractive uniform of rough, grey stone, outlined in pink ashlar – smoothed and squared stone. Such conformity suggests that Invergarry is a Victorian estate village, and indeed it is – most of the houses were built by the Ellice family in the 1860s and 1870s. Their crest, a mailed fist clutching a serpent, can be seen above the door of the Inn on the Garry.

Near by, the church, in the same pink and grey dress, stands on a steep slope where springtime's daffodils give way to the rhododendrons of early summer. The whitewashed post office bears a sign declaring that this is the last store for 42 miles – which is not actually true, as there is a store at Sheilbridge, 30 miles away. From Invergarry, the road runs through some of the wildest and most beautiful country in Britain, past Lochs Garry, Loyne, Cluanie and Duich to the Kyle of Lochalsh and the ferry for Skye.

Glen Garry was not always so demure, and there is a memory of older, wilder days in the gaunt, ivy-patched ruin of Invergarry Castle, which stands above Loch Oich, the highest stretch of water on the Caledonian Canal. The castle was the seat of the Macdonnells of Glengarry, a warrior tribe whose exploits ring through Highland history and legend.

Prince Charles Edward Stuart stayed here before and after the Battle of Culloden – a hospitable gesture that cost the Macdonnells dear, since it led to the castle's destruction by the victorious Duke of Cumberland shortly afterwards. A notice announces that it was 'burnt by Butcher Cumberland in 1746'. This ruin is unsafe and visitors enter at their own risk.

The old spirit of adventure never quite died, however. In 1785 a number of Macdonnells emigrated to Canada, where they founded the town of Glengarry, while Alastair Macdonnell, the last chieftain who owned and lived upon the ancestral estates, introduced the Glengarry bonnet to the world by wearing one during George IV's visit to Edinburgh in 1822. Alastair was a colourful character by all accounts. He founded his own regiment of Glengarry Fencibles in 1794, is said to have killed a man in a duel in 1798, and was probably the model for Fergus MacIvor, the Jacobite hero of Sir Walter Scott's *Waverley*.

He was also responsible for the extraordinary piece of ancestor worship that can be seen by the road along Loch Oich. It is a tall monument put up in 1812 and surmounted by a carving of seven severed heads tied by their hair to a dirk – a dagger Highlanders used to wear. It commemorates in four languages 'the ample and summary vengeance which in the swift course of feudal justice' overtook the murderers of a Macdonnell and his two sons in the mid-1660s.

The executioners were a party sent out by a kinsman of the murdered men, and before presenting the heads 'at the feet of the Noble Chief at Glengarry Castle', the avengers washed them in the spring beside the monument. Another version says that the heads were still gnashing their teeth in rage, and were dipped into the spring to cool off. Whatever the truth of the matter, the spring has been known as Tobar nan Ceann – the Well of the Heads – ever since.

Invermoriston HIGHLAND

27 miles south-west of Inverness (PAGE 385 Bc)

Most Highland settlements are more renowned for their beauty of setting than for attractiveness of architecture. But Invermoriston has a very reasonable share of both. Before it, the Moriston river opens out onto the wide, dark waters of Loch Ness; behind and all around, steep forests climb to the wild, bare hills.

Most of the buildings are turn of the century, owing their charm to good, strong lines and the contrast of whitewashed stone and slate. There is, too, the odd cheerful addition – as in the post office especially – of scarlet doors and window frames. In more recent times a number of craftsmen have made their home in Invermoriston, including a potter whose workshop is the old stone smithy by the bridge.

The little church, with its low, battlemented tower, dates from the late 19th century, but the burial ground off the Inverness road is far older and may have been the site of St Columba's first church, and so the first Christian settlement on the Scottish mainland. Its headstones are a reminder that since time immemorial this was and is the country of Clan Grant. The Grants of Glenmoriston offered shelter to Prince Charles Edward Stuart on his flight from Culloden in 1746, and the family still lives on the Glenmoriston estate, as have 15 generations before them.

The chief glory of the village is undoubtedly its river, which flows brisk and peaty-brown through a steep, wooded glen, then turns abruptly white as it drops over a fall whose boulders and cascades are so handsomely arranged that they might have been deliberately planted. The landscaping effect is enhanced by an elegant arched bridge, cunningly dovetailed into the rock. It is one of many Highland bridges built by the engineer Thomas Telford at the beginning of the 19th century. This one took eight years to complete – due, it is said, to 'idle workers' and a 'languid and inattentive' contractor.

With the battlefield of Culloden only 20 or so miles up the road to the north-east, it is not surprising that memories of that unhappy April day in 1746 – and its bitter aftermath – still linger in the district. Some 13 miles to the west of Invermoriston, the Moriston is joined by the River Doe, up whose glen runs a track which becomes a path, which in turn fades out among rock and heather. There is a cave here that sheltered the fugitive Prince Charles Edward during his wanderings in the hills. He was guarded by seven kinsmen, who could have become rich by betraying him; yet they did not. They remained poor – but they entered

Jacobite legend as the Seven Men of Glenmoriston.

Close by, where the rivers meet, stands a cairn that is yet another reminder of the personal devotion the 'Bonnie Prince' seems to have inspired among his followers. It marks the place where one of his officers died – a young man who bore a more than passing resemblance to the prince. He allowed himself to be pursued by Government troops who mistook him for Charles. When they finally caught and shot him down, he cried with his dying breath, 'You have murdered your prince!', so delaying the hunt for Charles.

Near by, another cairn commemorates the English powerboat racer John Cobb, who died on Loch Ness in 1952 while attempting to establish a world water speed record. His jet-powered boat broke up at more than 200 miles per hour.

Back down the road to Invermoriston, a little to the east of Torgyle Bridge, yet another cairn points the way to a pair of mysterious footprints. The story is that the prints were made by a wandering preacher named Finlay Munro in 1827. On being barracked by onlookers, he swore that grass would never grow on the ground on which he stood, thus bearing witness to the truth of his teaching. It does not, to this day.

PITLOCHRY

TAYSIDE

28 miles north-west of Perth (PAGE 385 Df)

It is hard to imagine a beauty spot not being spoilt by a dam and power station. But this is so at Pitlochry, where the North of Scotland Hydro-Electric Board built a generating station across the salmon-teeming River Tummel in the late 1940s.

The station's concrete dam – 54 ft high and 475 ft long – helped to create the artificial but beautiful Loch Faskally. A fish pass by the dam continues for 1000 ft, allowing the salmon to fight their way upstream to spawn in the upper reaches of the river. From the observation room you can see fish 'on the run', mainly in the spring and early summer, but sometimes into September. A special exhibition is devoted to their life cycle, and efforts made to protect and preserve them.

Pitlochry stands back from the wooded shores of the river and the loch. Geographically, it is in the very heart of Scotland and it originally consisted of three primitive hamlets – of which nothing remains. The town today dates mainly from the 1860s to 1890s, when it was developed as a major Highland health resort.

The waters of the Moulin burn, which winds through the town, were said to cure all kinds of physical aches and pains, as well as being a tonic for the nerves. As visitors eager to taste the water arrived by the trainload, so hotels and guesthouses sprang up until eventually they outnumbered the private homes. A large and imposing 'hydropathic' – a cross between a hotel and a clinic – was built for the richer invalids. These days it is the Pitlochry Hydro Hotel.

The town's ornate Victorian appearance still has great appeal. Today more people than ever flock to the area. But the age of hypochondria is over, and visitors are now drawn by the trout and salmon fishing, the golf, the mountain climbing, the pony-trekking, the theatre and the Highland Games.

The Pitlochry Festival Theatre, which has a wide stage and intimate, fan-shaped auditorium, is idyllically set on a tree-clustered slope above the River Tummel. The theatre season lasts from April or May to early October, and attracts some 70,000 theatregoers each year from many nations. As you arrive at the 'Theatre in the Hills' you are greeted by the kilted manager. The annual Highland Games take place on the second Saturday in September. They include tossing the caber,

Bonnethill Road, Pitlochry

Tower of West Church, Pitlochry

RED ROSES AND GREY GRANITE

Pitlochry lies where the Lowlands meet the Highlands, and fertile green meadows mingled with starker wooded slopes make a fine backdrop to a steep little shopping street. Here stern grey granite is offset by ornate gables and dormers, some painted rich red; red roses add a softening touch to a porch that is supported by painted rustic poles.

Houses in Pitlochry

Blair Castle – a general view

Inside the Kirk of St Bride

wrestling and Highland Dancing competitions. The gathering ends with a march past of up to 14 pipe bands in mass formation. If you cannot get to the games, there are twice-weekly Summer Highland Nights in the town, with country dancing, music by pipes and drums, and traditional Scottish songs.

● **Parking** Atholl Road; Ferry Road; West End (all car parks) ● **Early closing** Thursday (winter only) ● **Theatre** Pitlochry Festival Theatre, Port-na-Craig ● **Cinema** Regal, West Moulin Road ● **Event** Highland Games (September) ● **Information** TEL. Pitlochry 2215, 2751 ● **AA 24 hour service** TEL. Dundee 25585.

Blair Atholl TAYSIDE

6 miles north-west of Pitlochry (PAGE 385 De)

The village lies in a great bowl of landscape, in which steep woods of tall trees give way to upland meadows and moors. They yield in turn to the hills and, beyond, to the vast outer ring of the mountains. The bowl is threaded through by the River Garry, flowing swift and clear over its bed of big, pale boulders.

A bridge is the southern entrance to the village, whose wide street and granite buildings look as though they are freshly scrubbed each morning before visitors arrive. It is a toytown of a place. There is a miniature

Turrets and gables of Blair Castle

SYMPHONY IN GREEN

The landscape around the Duke of Atholl's Blair Castle seems clothed in all possible shades of green, from the dark green of the conifers to the pale green of the meadows, and the green verging on blue of the distant mountains. The sparkling white castle itself has turrets and tall stepped gables, and is roofed in sober black. A memorial in the now roofless Kirk of St Bride shows a Highlander mourning the 6th Duke. And in nearby Blair Atholl, corn was being ground by a water mill in the 17th century and still is – providing the flour for locally baked wholemeal scones.

Water mill, Blair Atholl

bank, a water mill, a church, country museum, post office, shops, houses, the Atholl Arms Hotel, and a large building that may once have been a school.

Almost all were built towards the end of the last century, squarely, with stepped gables and, here and there, a sprinkling of the pepper-pot turrets so essential to the Victorian notion of the Highlands. The exception is the mill, which was working in the 17th century. Behind the hotel is a neat railway station on the Highland line, all of a piece with the village, and a railway bridge with castellated towers.

The reason for this uniformity is the commanding presence of Blair Castle, which lies at the end of a magnificent avenue of limes off the village street. The castle, too, was given its present fortified face in the 19th century; before that, it wore the look of a Georgian mansion and before that again, it was a real castle, which it always has been at heart. Whatever the mask, it is only a dressing upon the massive medieval fortifications.

For centuries Blair Castle has been the seat of the Dukes of Atholl, and almost every player in the romantic version of Scottish history has put in an appearance here. Mary, Queen of Scots attended a hunt of Homeric proportions at the castle; it was garrisoned by Montrose, and again by John Graham of Claverhouse, Viscount Dundee – 'Bonnie' Dundee or 'Bluidy Clavers', depending on whether sympathies lay with the Jacobite cause or with William III. In 1689 the Jacobite viscount was mortally wounded at the moment of victory in the Battle of Killiecrankie, a little way along the river. He was carried back to Blair Castle by his men, and died that night.

Prince Charles Edward Stuart stayed at the castle in 1745; the Duke of Atholl's brother, Lord George Murray, was perhaps the most professional of the prince's officers. In the following year, Murray was forced into the painful duty of besieging his old family home when it was occupied by Hanoverian troops, so giving Blair the distinction of being the last castle in Britain to have been besieged.

A last, and very suitable, touch of romance is provided by the Duke's Athole Highlanders. The only private army authorised in Britain, it still performs ceremonial duties about the castle.

The castle's treasures suit its history. Family, Stuart and Jacobite portraits and relics are on view, along with the cuirass and helmet worn by Dundee at the time of his death. The collections of furniture, china, tapestries and arms are truly magnificent.

Something over a mile from the village is Old Blair. Here, guarded by immensely tall Scots pines, is the ruined Kirk of St Bride, where lie the Dukes of Atholl, their duchesses and children, and neighbours, great and humble. In the vault, too, sleeps John Graham of Claverhouse; thus, as Sir Walter Scott put it, 'died away the wild war-notes of Bonnie Dundee'.

Kinloch Rannoch TAYSIDE

18 miles west of Pitlochry (PAGE 385 Ce)

In 1861, Queen Victoria came along the narrow, twisting road from Pitlochry and graciously assented to clamber up the rocky spur that overlooks the River Tummel. The royal breath was taken away, as many other breaths have been since, by the glorious panorama of moor and rock, of water and forest, leading the eye south and east to the bulk of Schiehallion and west to the mountains of Glencoe, wearing snow in their high corries well into May.

To everyone's satisfaction, Her Majesty agreed that the spot should thenceforward be known as Queen's View; it has been further benefited in recent years by a visitors' centre and viewing platform supplied by the Forestry Commission.

The panorama, however, is not quite that enjoyed by Queen Victoria, since the Tummel, far below, has been dammed as part of the great Tummel-Garry hydroelectric scheme. What you see now is an awesome sheet of water, out of which old patches of high ground emerge as romantic-looking, wooded islands. However, between Tummel Bridge – built by General Wade in 1730 as part of his scheme to civilise the Highlands with a system of military roads – and Kinloch Rannoch, the river has been allowed to retain its old size and speed, tumbling in spates of white water over rocky steps.

At the village itself, where the river emerges from Loch Rannoch, it is spanned by a graceful, arched stone bridge, about which are gathered some low stone and slate cottages, a Scots-baronial hotel with elaborate turrets, a few post-war houses, a couple of shops and a blacksmith's forge. That is about all there is of Kinloch Rannoch, but the fishing is grand, and the place looks rather gallant and frontierish, leant over as it is by the majestic ramparts of the great mountains.

Loveliest and mightiest of these is Schiehallion (3554 ft) with a topmost peak of white quartz. Despite its formidable appearance, it is not too difficult to climb, and the views from the top seem to take in half of Scotland. On its foothills, along a moorland road running south-east from the village, are the tumbled and evocative ruins of an ancient chapel dedicated to the Celtic St Blane.

Along the southern shore of Loch Rannoch is the Black Wood, where the native Scots pine – once eaten by deer – is now protected by fencing and is re-establishing itself. Beyond the end of the loch, 15 miles from Kinloch Rannoch and seemingly a million miles from anywhere, is the lonely Rannoch Station. The road to it 'by Tummel and Loch Rannoch', is the famous Road to the Isles of the song, but nowadays it finishes at the station.

Moulin TAYSIDE

1 mile north of Pitlochry (PAGE 385 Df)

The greeting 'It seems to be clearing very nicely from the west' is the local equivalent of the Irish assurance, 'It's a fine soft day'. In other words, the rain is bucketing down. But even when the sky weeps and the wind blows, and the clouds sweep in skeins and tatters among the high forests behind Loch Faskally, there is no denying the grandeur of the scene.

Moulin was once an important place on the road to the north, when Pitlochry was hardly thought of; and it still commands a great sweep of country. Pitlochry lies below, and Ben Vrackie (2760 ft) rears its noble head above, sometimes swathed in cloud. Near by is Baledmund Hill, to which the village probably owes its name; Moulin derives from the Gaelic *Maoil-inn*, meaning 'a bare, rounded hill'.

Robert Louis Stevenson stayed in Kinnaird Cottage at the top end of the village during the summer

The village green, Moulin

The Moulin Inn

A BEECH'S SHADE

A magnificent copper beech tree shelters and graces the village green of tiny Moulin. Its glory is matched by that of the fine open countryside all around, glimpsed here over low stone cottages. Staying one summer at Kinnaird Cottage, where roses now climb up the front wall, Robert Louis Stevenson wrote his eerie tale, Thrawn Janet. *Near by is the Moulin Inn, where blackened tree trunks form the pillars of a balconied porch.*

Kinnaird Cottage

of 1881, and wrote to a friend 'We have a lovely spot here: a little green glen with a burn . . . Behind, great purple moorlands reaching to Ben Vrackie . . . Sweet spot, sweet spot'. All the same, he managed to distil sufficient malevolence out of the atmosphere to write *Thrawn Janet*, a story of Satanic possession.

Possibly he drew some inspiration from An Caisteal Dubh, 'the Black Castle'. Not much more than a ramshackle group of stones now, it was for many years a key fortress of the area. It was built in the 1320s by Sir John Campbell of Lochow, and inhabited until 1500, when plague broke out among the castle's garrison. The soldiers all died, and so fearful were the local people of infection that the walls were cannonaded down on top of the victims as the safest way of burying them. Or so it is said.

Whatever the cause of their destruction, the ruins are tranquil enough now, and stand on a rocky knoll among meadows where cattle graze. In the castle's heyday, apparently, the knoll was an island in the middle of a shallow lake. The village is tiny. The centre is a small, mown green, about which is a grouping of cottages, an inn, a post office and the kirk.

The present church dates mostly from 1875, but it stands on the site of several earlier ones, the oldest of which was probably founded by St Colman about AD 670. This is not so clear-cut as it sounds, since it seems that there were 230 saints called Colman in the calendar of the Celtic Church. There are ancient tombstones in the churchyard, some of which bear carvings of medieval swords.

The single street swings down and around, following the course of a clear, busy stream running among mossy stones, until both touch upon the outskirts of Pitlochry. All about are green meadows and cornland, giving way to moors and high, forested hills climbing above. This grand, rich and romantic setting is what the Victorians meant by the Highlands, rather than the deserts of dark, wet rock to the far north-west.

MAP 35

FISHERMEN'S COAST – AND SCOTLAND'S HIDDEN CROWN

Fishing ports past and present lie all along this ruggedly beautiful coast. Nets, floats and lobster pots litter quaysides in colourful confusion, their vessels sharing the harbour, often as not these days, with pleasure craft. Inland lie rolling cornlands and the Grampians' eastern slopes, set with many a mansion and historic castle. But none is more historic than battered Dunnottar, on its sea-girt crag. Here the Honours of Scotland – the crown jewels – were spirited past Cromwell's besiegers and safely hidden beneath the floor of the tiny village church at Kinneff, near by.

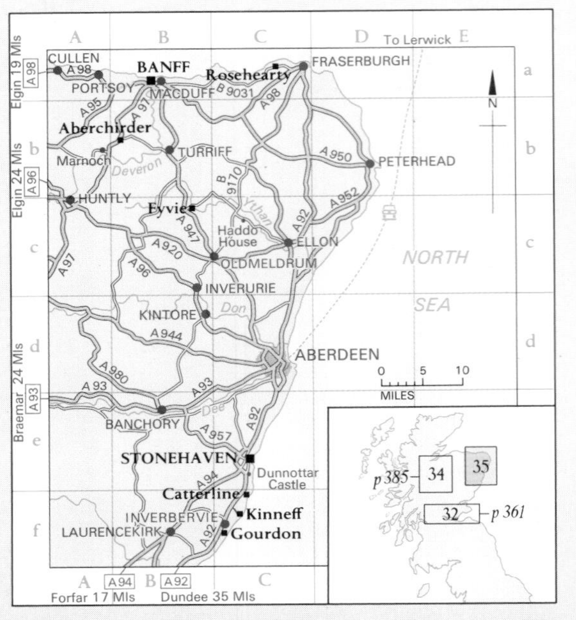

MAP 35: NEIGHBOURING AREAS – MAPS 32 AND 34

BANFF	STONEHAVEN
Aberchirder	Catterline
Fyvie	Gourdon
Rosehearty	Kinneff

BANFF

GRAMPIAN

47 miles north-west of Aberdeen (PAGE 396 Ba)

In November 1700 a half-gypsy bandit and fiddler named James MacPherson was hanged in the centre of Banff. MacPherson had been a kind of Scottish Robin Hood who robbed rich farmers in the district and gave to the poor. His last defiant act in this world was to play on his fiddle (see Kingussie, page 387) the wild *MacPherson's Rant*, which he is said to have composed while awaiting execution. He then broke the instrument over the hangman's head and, with the rope around his neck, jumped into space to his death.

Standing at the mouth of the River Deveron, Banff was already a busy port in the 12th century, and was made a royal burgh by Robert II in 1372. But it was in the 18th century, when the harbour was cleared of rocks, that it began to reach its prime. Further harbour improvements were made by John Smeaton (who also built the fine, seven-arched bridge over the Deveron)

Bridge over the Deveron at Banff

Duff House, Banff

GENTLE GRACE

Gentle countryside lies to the landward side of Banff, where the clear waters of the River Deveron are spanned by a graceful bridge built in the 18th century by the engineer John Smeaton. No less graceful is Duff House, designed by William Adam for the Duff family.

in 1770–5, and in 1818–19 by the engineer Thomas Telford. By the 1830s there was safe berthing for large schooners and merchant brigs, and some 30,000 barrels of herrings caught by the fishing fleet were being cured each year and shipped for sale in both Britain and on the Continent.

In the early 20th century, however, the harbour silted up and Banff declined as a commercial port. Nonetheless, the town's imposing municipal buildings and many gracious mansions and houses still testify to the wealth of its merchants and gentry in earlier centuries.

The town centre is an area of raised paving called Plainstones, on the corner of Low Street and Carmelite Street. Here is the Biggar Fountain and the rugged 16th-century mercat (market) cross, which has a carving of the Virgin and Child on one side and the Crucifixion on the other. Overlooking Plainstones is the Town House (town hall), a dignified building of 1796, which has a slender, tapering steeple probably designed by the architect James Adam (1730–94).

In Low Street is Carmelite House, built on the site of part of a Carmelite monastery in the 1750s. A short flight of stone steps leads up to a prominent central doorway – giving the place the appearance of a grand country mansion. This elegant note is maintained by St Mary's Church, built in 1789–90 in the High Street and, just below it, the imposing Collie Lodge which has a fine colonnaded front.

Collie Lodge used to be one of the lodges of Duff House, Banff's grandest mansion, built in 1725–40 for William Duff, Lord Braco, and later 1st Earl Fife. Standing on a slope south of the town and modelled on an Italian Baroque villa, it was designed and constructed by the great architect William Adam – father of James and Robert – at a cost of more than £70,000. But Lord Braco had to quit his elegant brand-new home when cracks appeared in the main block. Happily the problem was later solved and Duff House stayed in his family until 1906, when the 1st Duke of Fife gave it to the town. In the Second World War it housed German prisoners of war. The house and its handsome grounds are now open to the public.

North of a small wooded hill on which stands Banff Castle – another fine, but simpler 18th-century mansion built for Lord Deskford – is the part of the town known as Seatown of Banff. This lies nearest to the harbour and has much smaller houses and cottages where fishermen and sailors lived. The harbour itself, which was partially dredged in 1974, now shelters brightly coloured sailing yachts and dinghies, instead of the trading vessels of its prime.

• **Parking** St Mary's, Low Street; Carmelite Street (both car parks) • **Early closing** Wednesday • **Events** Daffodil Show (April); Gala (July); Flower Show (August); Golf Week (September) • **Information** TEL. Banff 2789, 2419 (summer) • **AA 24 hour service** TEL. Aberdeen 639231.

Aberchirder GRAMPIAN

9 miles south of Banff (PAGE 396 Bb)

There is a very English-looking road to Aberchirder, a gravelly road overhung by beeches, sycamores and limes linked by neatly trimmed beech hedges. The country round about, too, is strongly reminiscent of downland – great, rolling waves of green patterned on the lower slopes with milk-chocolate coloured ploughland, and hedged pastures where cattle graze. It seems odd to think the mighty Grampians and Cairngorms are only a few miles away.

No one, however, could mistake Aberchirder for an English village. Historically, it is not a village at all, but was the smallest burgh in what used to be Banffshire. It was laid out all of a piece in 1764 by Alexander Gordon of Auchintoul, and Auchintoul is still the great house of the district. Aberchirder consists of three parallel streets of two-storey granite houses, in the midst of which is a rather bare little square containing half a dozen small shops.

There is no nonsense about the place: the main street is called Main Street and the square is The Square, and perhaps the overall effect would be somewhat bleak, were it not for the outlook onto the smiling countryside all about. That the burgh spirit is still maintained is apparent from the very fine woodland walk that Aberchirder has recently laid out for the benefit of residents and visitors alike.

A couple of miles down the road to Huntly, the handsome greystone Bridge of Marnoch crosses the stately River Deveron, a delightful scene given grace and point by Kinnairdy Castle standing high above the stream. This is one of those tall, charming, pointed-roofed Scottish castles that do not look as if they were ever intended for serious warfare. But though it was considerably remodelled earlier this century, it was at one time a stronghold of the Gregorys.

Near by is the Kirk of Marnoch that played a key role in the great Disruption of 1843. Briefly, this amounted to a number of Scottish parishes, Marnoch among them, refusing to have unpopular ministers forced upon them by the Established Church and local landowners who held the livings. This led to the founding of the Free Church, which was joined by many ministers who surrendered 'tied' parishes and endured considerable hardship to ensure the movement's success.

It may all seem long ago and far away now, but to many Scots the Disruption was the last successful and significant battle in the long struggle for Scottish Nationalism.

Fyvie GRAMPIAN

20 miles south-east of Banff (PAGE 396 Bc)

Rich, rolling pasture and cornland is Fyvie's countryside, with some not too alpine hills covered with dark conifers in the background, to remind the visitor that he is still in northern Britain. The village is a pleasant mixture of 19th-century granite and 20th-century pebbledash, and is chiefly memorable for having within its boundaries one of the most remarkable castles in the country, built in the theatrical-baronial style so admired by Sir Walter Scott.

Fyvie Castle was begun by Sir Harry Preston, who distinguished himself at the Battle of Otterburn in 1388. His castle has been added to, and gloriously improved, by two or three other families since. Set in a wooded park going down to the River Ythan, it has been bought by the National Trust for Scotland and will be open to the public in May 1986. Several monuments to the Forbes-Leith family – until recently the owners of the castle – may be seen in front of the church. In the centre of the village, a pink granite

NOBLE STANDARDS *Flying proudly over Haddo House is the standard of the Marquis of Aberdeen. In 1731 the 2nd Earl of Aberdeen commissioned William Adam to build this fine Palladian-style mansion, and the family live there still – although it now belongs to the National Trust for Scotland.*

column and a white quartz boulder called The Buchan Stone mark the medieval frontier between the territories of the Earls of Buchan and the Thanes of Formartine.

This is a land of castles and great houses, whose positions are marked on the map of the area in a rash of Gothic lettering. Not far from Fyvie is Haddo House, the home for centuries of the Gordons of Haddo, later Earls and Marquises of Aberdeen. For many years, the present 18th-century mansion failed to charm the 4th Earl, one of Queen Victoria's prime ministers. He warmed to it later, though, planting, he reckoned, 14 million trees in the park and around his estates, and covering the walls of the house with dark panelling – a setting that suited the dour, upright man who never recovered from the death of his beloved first wife. The present interior, gay with late-Victorian chintzes, watered silk and bright, soft colours, is the work of Ishbel, wife of the 7th Earl, who continued to love Haddo until she died in 1939, at the age of 82.

Deep in the woods between Haddo and Fyvie is the ruined Castle of Gight – pronounced 'Gecht'. It was built by Gordon of Gight in about 1560, and almost from then on, the story of its family was a tale of death in battle, or by murder, treachery or suicide. The 13th Laird, Lady Catharine Gordon, an awkward, gawky girl, was dispatched to Bath to gain polish and a husband. There, she met and married Captain 'Mad Jack' Byron, who rapidly drank and gambled away her entire inheritance, including the Castle of Gight. Their son was the poet Lord Byron.

Long before, the 13th-century poet Thomas the Rhymer of Ercildoun prophesied:

When the heron leaves the tree
The lairds o' Gight shall landless be.

Sure enough, in Lady Catharine's time the herons that used to nest at Gight decided on a change of scene and flew off to take up residence instead at Haddo. Who can blame them?

Rosehearty GRAMPIAN

18 miles east of Banff (PAGE 396 Ca)

Fishermen's cottages, low and square, rise abruptly from a coastline of shattered rock, or from about the inner harbour where a very few inshore fishing boats still lie on the sand at low tide. The outer harbour wall has a great gap hammered through it, and it is apparent that Rosehearty has ceased to signify as a fishing port.

The cottages remain, however, with brightly painted doors and window frames of massive stone slabs set into rough-cut granite walls. Between each large, pale block a vertical row of small, dark blocks has been inserted, a most attractive local fashion that is repeated in the walls of the relatively new church that shares a churchyard with the old, roofless kirk on a hill above the sea.

This is a fine vantage point from which to look out over the wide, curving vista of the windswept coast and the little port. It is no great beauty even from this distance, but it is tough and uncompromising, and fits in well with the dark, uneasy sea and the boulder-strewn shore. A little to the east is the melancholy ruin of Pitullie Castle, built by the Frasers towards the end of the 16th century and later allowed to crumble undramatically into decay.

Ahead, there is a wood whose trees are bent and coiffed into a kind of crew-cut by the winter gales. Among them is the ruin of another castle, Pitsligo, whose massive, 15th-century keep now houses hay bales and sacks of fertiliser. It was the home of the Forbes of Pitsligo. The last of them was involved in the Rising of 1715, and when Prince Charles Edward landed

30 years later, he once more rallied to the standard, though by then he was 67 years of age and had the gravest misgivings about the outcome of the campaign.

However, his sense of honour left him no alternative, and he cheerfully led his troop of horses into the debacle of Culloden. Possibly to his own surprise, he survived, and spent the rest of his life as a fugitive, hiding in the attics of friends and relatives, or under bridges or in caves such as the one now called Lord Pitsligo's Cave, in the cliffs a little to the west of Rosehearty.

On one occasion, in his son's house, he was hidden behind a guest's bed when Government troops searched the room – while the lady occupying the room coughed and chattered loudly to drown the old man's asthmatic breathing. When the men left the room, the old fugitive ordered a servant to get breakfast and a hot drink for the soldiers, for it was a cold morning and they were only doing their duty. The gallant Lord Pitsligo died in 1762, aged 84, and is buried in the old kirk.

STONEHAVEN

GRAMPIAN

15 miles south of Aberdeen (PAGE 396 Ce)

Stonehaven's 16th-century Old Tolbooth (town hall) stands on a little spit of land jutting out into Stonehaven Bay. Its front faces a semicircular harbour and the red-sandstone cliffs of Downie Point beyond. At the back a small barred window looks over jagged shoreline rocks and out to sea. For a while in 1748 this window served as an extraordinary form of baptistery. At this time the Episcopalian or Anglican Church of Scotland was suffering for its involvement in the Jacobite Rising three years before. Three local Episcopalian ministers fell foul of a law forbidding them to hold services for more than five people, and were imprisoned for six months in the Tolbooth.

But the women of their congregations were determined to have their babies properly baptised. Carrying the infants on their backs in wicker baskets, they scrambled along the rocky shore, sometimes up to their knees in water, until they came to the back of the Tolbooth. Here the baskets with the babies inside were held up to the window, where the ministers performed the baptismal rites.

The Tolbooth – which now houses a tea shop and a museum of local history – stands in the part of Stonehaven called the Old Town. This is the part which grew around a fishing harbour. The other part, north-west of the harbour, is the New Town, founded in the late 18th century by Captain Robert Barclay, a

SHELTER SHARED *Yachts and other pleasure craft share the harbour at Stonehaven with a few fishing vessels . . . a peaceful scene far removed from the hectic days of the 1880s when the local herring fleet was 100 boats strong. Nowadays the fishermen's catch is mainly cod, haddock and whiting, with crab and sometimes an occasional lobster. Nets lie draped over the harbour wall to dry in the heat of the noonday sun; a woman saunters hand in hand with a child along the quay. A pleasant place to be.*

member of an ancient local family, who lived at Ury House, a mile to the north-west. The New Town's trim terraces are laid out on a gridiron pattern and its centre is a spacious Market Square. The imposing Market Buildings, rising on one side of The Square, have a 130 ft high spire with a clock.

In 1824 Captain Barclay's son, Captain Robert Barclay-Allardice, established the Glenury Royal Distillery, north of the town. He opened the whisky distillery with the encouragement of his friend George IV – to bring much-needed work and prosperity to the area. But the captain also had other claims to fame. In 1809 he performed the considerable feat of walking 1000 miles round and round Newmarket, Suffolk, in as many successive hours . . . his portly figure wearing a tailcoat, narrow trousers and a gleaming top hat.

Possibly he inherited this prodigious stamina and strength from his ancestors. His grandfather was known as 'the strong' and a 17th-century ancestor was David Barclay of Ury, who served in the army of the warlike King of Sweden, Gustavus Adolphus. David Barclay was one of the strongest men in Scotland, and his sword was too heavy for ordinary men to use.

Another local man was Robert William Thomson, born in 1822 in a house in the New Town's Market Square and inventor of the world's first pneumatic tyre. His tyre had an air-filled inner tube protected by an outer canvas, with leather treads. But it was expensive to make and difficult both to fit and remove. He did not develop the invention, and it was left to another Scotsman – John Dunlop, a vet practising in Belfast – to exploit the pneumatic tyre commercially. However, Thomson is not forgotten in his home town – his birthplace is marked with a plaque, and each June a vintage car rally is held in his honour.

Two other annual events are the Feeing Market, on the first Saturday in June, and the unique and spectacular Fireball Ceremony, which begins the moment the Old Town clock chimes midnight on December 31. Specially chosen local men and women march along the High Street in the Old Town skilfully swinging blazing fireballs over their heads. The fireballs are made of wire netting stuffed with rags which are set alight. The ceremony dates from pagan times, when it was supposed to keep the town from evil spirits during the coming year.

The Feeing Market is held in the Market Square in the New Town, and is a reminder of days when farm servants were annually 'fee'd' or hired. Today the only selling is done from stalls, where the stallholders are encouraged to wear colourful period costumes and hats. For entertainment there is traditional country music and Highland dancing.

• **Parking** Market Square (car park) • **Early closing** Wednesday • **Events** Feeing Market (June); R. W. Thomson Vintage Car Rally (June); Fireball Ceremony (New Year's Eve) • **Information** TEL. Stonehaven 62806 (summer) • **AA 24 hour service** TEL. Aberdeen 639231.

Catterline GRAMPIAN

5 miles south of Stonehaven (PAGE 396 Cf)

Out to sea the scene is a contrast in greys, as often as not; pale grey sky, blue-grey horizon, battleship grey in the mid-distance. But within the tiny horseshoe of the harbour, the water is green – olive in the depths and pale green marbled white where the wavelets hiss among the gravel on the shoreline. Behind, grassy cliffs, with ribs of red rock showing through, climb up to a row of white, single-storey cottages with black slate roofs. At one with them in architectural style is the Creel Inn, long famed for its seafood.

Within its natural defences of seaweed-draped reefs, the harbour possesses a single rough-stone quay, furnished with fish crates, lobster pots and a couple of small, freshly painted inshore fishing boats. Most of the time, the quay's population consists of a group of remarkably arrogant herring gulls.

How could any marine artist resist such a scene? As a matter of fact, several have not, most notable among them being Joan Eardley, a distinguished painter of landscapes and townscapes, who had a studio in Catterline until her tragically early death aged 42 in 1963. Her work, and that of fellow artists, brought a degree of fame to the village, which must have aided it in its successful appeal to be made a conservation area. True, there are some modern buildings, but mostly on the landward side of the inn, and from the harbour at least, the place is still the personification of an old Kincardineshire fishing village.

Actually, Catterline is a good deal older even than it looks. There was a prehistoric settlement on the easily defended headland, and by the 12th century there was a kirk dedicated to St Katerin, to which the village probably owes its name. Together with a mill, the kirk was gifted to the Abbey of Arbroath by William the Lion in 1178. The kirk stood at the site of the present churchyard, and fragments of it can still be seen, near the churchyard entrance.

Catterline is a private little place. Indeed, it is almost moated, since its only means of access from the land is a stone bridge over a deep 'den', or miniature gorge. On the sides of the den, golden gorse divides near-vertical allotments where vegetables manage to grow in perfect alignment.

Gourdon GRAMPIAN

11 miles south of Stonehaven (PAGE 396 Cf)

Set deep in a gorse-dusted, green bowl of cliff, Gourdon is one of the few ports on this part of the Scottish coast that still makes a living from fishing, though only about a dozen boats put out now, compared with 100 or so at the beginning of the century.

Nevertheless, Gourdon still has a busy fish market, at which boats from other harbours along the coast – as well as those of the home fleet – deposit their catches. There are fish sales at the pier each weekday at 11.30 and 3.30, and visitors can sometimes buy fish straight from the filleting sheds.

But on Saturday the place goes into a kind of trance, and about the quayside there is scarcely a human being to be seen until the mobile butcher's shop arrives from Inverbervie and causes a brief flurry. Then, it seems, there is little to do but lean against the wall near the barometer given in memory of Lieutenant Farquhar RN, who was lost in the China Sea in 1864, and watch the fishing boats – *Quest III*, *Concord*, *White Wing* and the rest – gently grounding themselves on the falling tide. The only real activity is on the part of the gulls that busy themselves among the lobster pots and orange piles of fishing-nets and floats, stabbing viciously at an overlooked crab.

HIDDEN GLORY *Kinneff Old Kirk, where the Honours of Scotland — Crown, Sword and Sceptre — were hidden under the floor for nine years.*

Kinneff GRAMPIAN

8 miles south of Stonehaven (PAGE 396 Cf)

There is a string of houses along the Stonehaven to Montrose road that, with sound Scots logic, is called Roadside of Kinneff; it is a village perhaps more notable for its gorgeous farmland setting than for its architecture. The Kinneff that had a brief hour of glory in the Scottish historical firmament — and because of it is known to Scots all over the world — is situated about a mile off, down a deep lane through cornfields that sweep to the edge of the cliffs and the sea.

It consists of a small group of farm buildings, the Manse, and the angular, white pebbledashed Kinneff Old Kirk — an attractive collection in a charming countryside. But it is the kirk itself that beckons the seekers after legend.

In 1651, a year after Cromwell's army crossed the border, the Honours of Scotland — the Crown, Sceptre and Sword that comprise the Scottish Crown Jewels — were sent to Dunnottar Castle, between Kinneff and Stonehaven, for safe keeping. It would have seemed a sensible choice, for even in its present battered state, Dunnottar, high on a crag with the sea snarling round the rocks at the base, looks fairly impregnable.

But Cromwell had no intention of storming the place. He established his batteries on Black Hill (where Stonehaven's war memorial is now) and began to cannonade the castle into submission. When it was apparent that surrender could not be long delayed, the Governor, Sir George Ogilvy, had the Honours smuggled out of Dunnottar. The usual story is that they were carried out in a basket of flax, with the Sceptre disguised as a distaff, by Mrs Grainger, the wife of the minister of Kinneff; but there are other accounts, too. At any event, the regalia was brought reverently to the kirk, wrapped in linen by Mrs Grainger, and buried, according to one version of the story, somewhere beneath the stone flags of the floor or, according to another, beneath the pulpit.

The exact whereabouts were communicated to Lady Ogilvy by the minister, 'for if it shall please God to call me by death before they be called for, your Ladyship will find them in that place'. The Honours remained beneath the floor for nine years, having their cloths replaced now and then by the Graingers to ward off damp. Then, at the Restoration, they were returned in triumph to Edinburgh Castle, where they can be seen to this day.

The kirk has been much restored, and probably only the west wall remains as it was in the days of the great adventure. But the Ogilvys are buried here, as is Mr Grainger: 'He who his country's honour saved below, Now wields a sceptre in the realms of bliss.' The visitors' book reveals the constancy of expatriate Scots in coming to the place; coupled with a visit to Dunnottar, this is exploring the stuff that ballads and all the best yarns are made of.

JEWEL CASTLE OVERLEAF

Dunnottar Castle, on a rocky promontory almost severed from the mainland, was knocked about a bit by Cromwell's men in a vain search for the Scottish crown jewels. But even the ruin is vastly impressive: it dates mostly from the 14th century, but this seemingly impregnable crag has been fortified for 1500 years.

MAP 36

ROARING WRATH AND THE SUTHERLAND WILDERNESS

This is as far north as you can get on mainland Britain. There is light at midnight in the long days of high summer at Wick and Thurso – once Viking ports. Winter is something else, when roaring combers crash around Cape Wrath and mighty winds scour the mountains, moorlands and lonely lochs of the Sutherland wilderness. Yet palms grow at Scourie, where the Gulf Stream spreads its warmth.

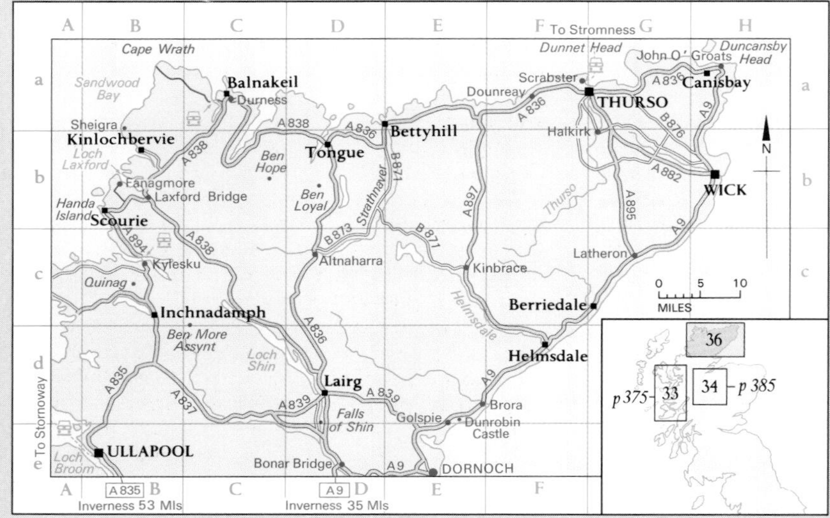

MAP 36:
NEIGHBOURING AREAS – MAPS 33 AND 34

THURSO
Balnakeil
Bettyhill
Tongue

ULLAPOOL
Inchnadamph
Kinlochbervie
Lairg
Scourie

WICK
Berriedale
Canisbay
Helmsdale

THURSO

HIGHLAND

20 miles west of John o' Groats (PAGE 404 F/Ga)

Though the most northerly town in mainland Britain – so far north that it is able to celebrate its Midsummer Week with midnight games of golf, tennis and bowls – Thurso has little to do with Highland Gaeldom. Far-off, its roots are Norse; many of its people have names with Scandinavian echoes, and the name of the town itself is thought to be derived from *Thors-a*, 'the river of Thor the God'.

Thurso, most handsomely situated by the river and bay of the same name, probably began as a beach-head and base for the Viking invaders of Scotland, and later became an important settlement. It is frequently mentioned in the Norse Sagas, but nothing now remains to be seen of the Viking years, unless you count Harald's Tower, which is said to stand on the spot where Earl Harald Ungi, who ruled half of Caithness, the Orkneys and the Shetlands, was slain in the midst of battle in 1196.

From the Middle Ages onwards, Thurso was an important fishing and trading port that shipped grain, fish, meat and hides to Scandinavia and the Baltic. The name of Rotterdam Street recalls the town's dealings with the Continent, while the old streets of beautifully restored fishermen's houses down by the harbour reflect the long vitality of its fisheries. In the 1820s, Thurso added flagstone cutting to its repertoire; the large Caithness flags were quarried, cut and polished locally, then exported all over the world to pave city streets. And in this windy part of Scotland they are used in place of hedges to divide the land into fields.

It was in the latter part of the 18th century that Thurso acquired its wide streets of Georgian houses, laid out in the manner of Edinburgh's New Town, so creating, on the shores of the wild Pentland Firth, what must be the most northerly Georgian townscape in the world. The begetter was Sir John Sinclair (1754 – 1835), local MP for more than 30 years. His statue stands in Sir John Square, arrayed in the uniform of the Rothesay and Caithness Fencibles, a militia regiment he founded during the Napoleonic Wars. He was the author of many other innovations, within and without his constituency, including the introduction of the Cheviot sheep – a breed well suited to the rigours of the north – to Caithness. Though innocently done, this act was to cause great hardship when thousands of Highland families were evicted from their crofts to make way for flocks of Cheviots.

Since 1954, when a nuclear power research station was built at Dounreay, 10 miles west, Thurso has undergone yet another metamorphosis. The population has trebled and new housing estates have arisen, though thoughtfully constructed to blend with the old town.

Dounreay has an observation room and exhibition open to the public in summer, and there are daily tours of parts of the station. But once sated with the wonders of modern technology, there is still much of the older Caithness to admire in Thurso. To the east of the harbour, near Harald's Tower, is the ruin of a Victorian castle built on the site of the 17th-century castle of the Sinclairs, while on the opposite side are the scanty remains of The Bishop's Castle. During the 13th century, this was the home of Gilbert Murray, Bishop of Caithness, who founded the Old Kirk of St Peter, now a substantial ruin in the town. A committee, under the patronage of Queen Elizabeth the Queen Mother, is making strenuous efforts to preserve the old building. There is also a fine museum including an exhibition devoted to the work of Robert Dick, a baker and self-taught botanist and geologist who lived in Wilson Street from 1830 to 1866. He did some remarkable work in the area, such as identifying the northern holy grass *Hierochloë odorata*. Though common in Norway, until 1930 at least, it grew nowhere else in Britain save on the banks of the River Thurso, and in very few other places since. Perhaps long ago, some Viking planted the ancestral seeds there, to remind him of home.

• **Parking** Riverside Road (2); Ormlie Road; Grove Lane; Manson's Lane; High Street; Janet Street; Princes Street; Harbour (all car parks) • **Early closing** Thursday • **Market day** Tuesday (cattle) • **Events** Gala Week (July); Caithness Highland Gathering (July); Caithness County Show (July, alternating annually between Thurso and Wick) • **Information** TEL. Thurso 62371 (summer) • **AA 24 hour service** TEL. Aberdeen 639231.

Balnakeil HIGHLAND

74 miles west of Thurso (PAGE 404 Ca)

Durness parish encompasses 140,779 acres, about one and a half times the size of the old English county of Rutland. The parishioners are spread very thinly indeed over this vast area of moor and rock, and Balnakeil, though quite a busy hamlet almost at the end of the parish – and of Britain, too – is unlikely to cause any new problems of overcrowding. There is not much of it; a little huddle of stone and concrete by a great sweep of white shell sand backed by marram-clad dunes reaching up to Faraid Head, one of the fang-like capes of Britain's dramatic north-west corner.

Neither is there easy access to it, which makes its relatively large number of visitors all the more remarkable. Its chief attraction, hard to credit at first glance, is one of those glum collections of concrete buildings that is HM Forces' contribution to architecture. This one was intended to be a radar station, but it was obsolete before it was completed, and abandoned in 1954. In 1963, an imaginative Development Officer of Sutherland County Council suggested its conversion into a craft village. He advertised it, offering a close-knit community of craftsmen, the outstanding natural beauty of the area and a local population density of one person per 96 acres. The response was encouragingly enthusiastic, and the place is now a thriving cooperative of weavers, potters, metal, wood and leather workers, bookbinders and other craftsmen and women. The village's cosy Visitor Centre has a coffee shop – which must be the most northerly in mainland Britain – offering, among other things, home-made cakes and an exhibition of Balnakeil's history.

The name means 'Place of the Church', an acknowledgment of the chapel built here by St Maelrubha some 1300 years ago. Its site is now occupied by a picturesquely ruinous kirk of 1619, in whose graveyard lies Robert MacKay, a much venerated Gaelic poet who died in 1778. He is often called the Burns of the North; his lifestyle at least was not unlike that of the Ayrshire bard, for he was a herdsman – and poacher – on the estates of Lord Reay, whose fortress-like house is one of the few other buildings in the village. Inside the church, a skull and crossbones on the south wall marks the grave of Donald MacLeod, a local villain responsible for the deaths of at least 18 people. He chose to be buried within the wall to prevent anyone wreaking vengeance on his corpse.

Having made the fairly adventurous journey to Balnakeil, it would be a pity not to extend it for a few miles to see something of the last great wilderness in Britain. Inland is difficult – 100 square miles of moor and peat bog – but the coast is possible, given good boots and reasonable determination. One of the great sites is the Smoo Cave, a mighty cavern in the sea cliffs off the Durness road. The main chamber – the only one accessible to anyone not a potholer – is 200 ft long and 110 ft wide with the Allt Smoo burn running through it and out to the sea. There are two more chambers, the first of which has a hole in its roof, said to have been burst through by the Devil in his efforts to escape from a Lord Reay who was a famous wizard. But more likely it was the work of the burn, which drops through it from the moor above to the cave floor below in an 80 ft waterfall.

A little to the south of Durness, a ferry may be taken across the translucent waters of the Kyle of Durness and, with luck, meet up with a minibus that takes passengers to Cape Wrath, Britain's extreme north-westerly point. The name seems particularly appropriate, especially when wind and waves howl about its majestic 360 ft cliffs, but, in fact, it is simply an Anglicising of *Hvarf*, the Norse for 'turning point', since it was here that the longships used to turn south and west for the Hebrides. Cape Wrath's uninhabited hinterland of rock and bog is called the Parbh, a less happy adaptation of the same word into Gaelic.

Among the wild flowers and the short-cropped grass at the top of the cliff there is a lighthouse which may be visited, and not much else, apart from a few coastguard cottages. These were abandoned long ago, and it is difficult to imagine their purpose in the first place. Yet Cape Wrath is well worth coming to, since nowhere else in Britain is it possible to experience such a feeling of geographical finality. True, there is Lewis 50 miles to the west, and Orkney about the same to the east. Somewhere to the north-west is Iceland, but due north there is nothing at all but the polar ice.

Bettyhill HIGHLAND

31 miles west of Thurso (PAGE 404 D/Ea)

The casual scattering of stone houses above the white-gold sands of Torrisdale Bay is known chiefly nowadays for the excellence of the trout and salmon fishing in the area, and for the rare plants that flourish in the nearby Invernaver Nature Reserve. The name of the village, cosy and surprisingly southern, is said to be derived from that of Elizabeth, Countess of Sutherland, who owned some 1700 square miles of northern Scotland, stretching from Cape Wrath to the Dornoch Firth. In 1785 she married George, Marquis of Stafford, perhaps the richest landowner in England.

The fortunate pair were also imbued with boundless energy and a full share of the progressive notions of the day, to which the wild – and unprofitable – state of their Sutherland possessions was totally contrary. They built nearly 150 bridges and more than 400 miles of roads. But this did not strike at the heart of the problem, which was the feckless subsistence farming methods of their peasantry. This, they felt, was the worst possible use to be made of the poor, thin soil; much better to turn it into grazing for the newly introduced Cheviot sheep.

Clearly, the two kinds of farming could not co-exist, and so the people had to go. When offers of inferior parcels of land or employment failed to persuade the peasants to leave their homes, the Staffords lost patience, and ordered their agents to begin evictions. No time could be allowed for harvesting the meagre crops, and, in case any of the evicted should try to steal back to their houses for want of anywhere else to go, this would be prevented by firing the roofs. Altogether, some 15,000 people were expelled.

Strathnaver, the long and lovely glen that runs south from Torrisdale Bay, was one of the areas worst hit. The local minister later recalled: 'They were all – man, woman and child – from the heights of Farr to the mouth of Naver, on one day, to quit their tenements and go. For a few, some miserable patches of ground along the shores were dealt out . . . Upon these lots it was intended that they should build houses at their own expense, and cultivate the ground, at the same time occupying themselves as fishermen, though the great majority had never set foot in a boat in their lives.'

The place by the shore came to be called Bettyhill, whether in honour of Lady Stafford or not would be hard to say. Despite the near satanic reputation they left behind, neither she nor her husband had any doubts about the rightness of their course. In the fullness of time, they were further ennobled as the Duke and Duchess of Sutherland, and he at least has a memorial statue standing high on the hill beside one of their old homes, Dunrobin Castle.

Many of the people who were driven to the shore went to Australia, Canada and the Lowland cities. Only a few remained, and it is their descendants who live in Bettyhill now. The story of the Clearances is most poignantly told in the Strath Naver Museum, housed in an old whitewashed church to the east of Bettyhill post office. And a wander up the glen by the pretty River Naver will reveal roofless cottages, testimony to a later depopulation which still goes on. But these are not the most conspicuous remains along the valley. There are in addition much older hut circles, standing stones and cairns left behind by a people even more thoroughly removed than the victims of the Clearances.

Tongue HIGHLAND

44 miles west of Thurso (PAGE 404 Db)

After the monochromes of the wild and near-deserted hinterland, it is something of a relief to reach the white-gold sands and pale green seas of the Kyle of Tongue. The moors surrender reluctantly, however, and grassy tussocks push through the sand. Inland rise a pair of mountains of the kind that the Victorians called 'noble' – the 3042 ft Ben Hope, and the slightly lower, multi-peaked Ben Loyal.

Scattered among all this picturesqueness, the village of Tongue – sometimes called Kirkiboll – is large by Highland standards, and possesses a bank and two hotels. The majority of the houses are of stone, with dormer windows, and there is a pretty white-washed church with a tiny bell tower. This, the Church of St Andrew, which dates from 1680, contains a boxed wooden pew that was formerly used by the Earls of Reay and their families; it was Donald Mackay, the 1st Lord Reay, who brought the Protestant faith to this part of Scotland in the early 17th century.

All the land for miles about is, or rather was, Mackay country. The chiefs, the Earls of Reay, lived in the House of Tongue, which was burnt by Parliamentarian troops in 1658, and most attractively rebuilt 20 years later. It still stands, in the midst of wooded gardens that are very occasionally open to the public. But in 1829, the house and all the estate passed to the 1st Duke of Sutherland in payment of a debt. No sooner had he acquired the land, than he included the Mackay tenants in his sweeping programme of Clearances, and they too joined the dolorous exodus to the New World and the Lowlands; the House of Tongue is still part of the Sutherland estate.

In the 17th century one of the Mackay chiefs raised a clan regiment to fight in Germany on the Protestant side during the Thirty Years' War, and another was a notable soldier under William of Orange. A curiosity about the chiefs is that, for some time, they were Dutch. In the late 17th century one of them became a naturalised Dutchman through marriage. An early 19th-century descendant married a Dutch heiress and became a baron in the Dutch peerage. A member of this branch was even appointed Prime Minister of the Netherlands, but since the late 19th century, when a Dutch Mackay inherited the Barony of Reay and became a British subject, the Mackay chiefs have been Scots.

A fine causeway carries the main Thurso road across the Kyle of Tongue. To the south there is a highly dramatic ruin, just right for this setting. This is Castle Varrich, traditionally said to be a Viking watch-tower, or the home of a Norse king, though more recent research suggests that it was a 14th-century stronghold of the Mackays. To the north, just off the mouth of the Kyle, are the Rabbit Islands, where a French sloop, the *Hazard*, was wrecked in March 1746. She was driven into the shallows by a frigate of the Royal Navy, whose captain probably had no idea that his victim was carrying a considerable amount of gold. It had been sent by the French to aid the campaign of Prince Charles Edward Stuart, but he was never to see it. His army was already falling back in the retreat that was to end at Culloden three weeks later. As for the gold, it simply vanished. No one knows what happened to it, but it is not difficult to guess. It was probably rescued from the wreck by Mackay clansmen who were both anti-Jacobite and poor. As so often with French aid to the Stuart cause, it was too little and too late.

ULLAPOOL

HIGHLAND

60 miles north-west of Inverness (PAGE 404 Be)

Ullapool was born in 1788 when the British Fisheries Society decided to build an impressive fishing station near the mouth of Loch Broom, which runs out into the open sea. The loch had been famed for its herring

LIGHT AND SHADE *A white cottage, wild, green pastures and little copses catch the sun at Tongue, with Ben Loyal silhouetted behind.*

since the 16th century, but its waters had not been fished on a large scale. To remedy this, the society spent £10,000 – a huge sum in those days – on building warehouses, a pier and laying out the streets in an orderly grid pattern.

Next came the planning of the houses – rows of neat, mostly whitewashed cottages, which run down to the banks of the loch. To ensure that the town was planned as perfectly as possible, the society showed its designs to the renowned engineer Thomas Telford (1757 – 1834).

Telford, who built about a thousand miles of roadway in Scotland, gave the scheme his full approval. He liked the idea of the broad, straight streets; the trim cottages in Shore Street for the fishermen and their families; and the cheerful Arch Inn, which is still there.

CALM WATERS Brighter Morn, Kittiwake, Albion . . . *trim little fishing vessels lie moored alongside a quiet quay in the harbour at Ullapool. Fishermen's cottages stand opposite and behind them rise the moors. But this tranquillity is deceptive – Ullapool is a busy place. There is a regular ferry to Lewis; in summer a smaller ferry crosses to the other side of Loch Broom and there are boat trips to the charmingly named Summer Isles. The fishing fleet puts out in search of whiting and skate, although the town once prospered from herring.*

Looming in the distance are some of the most majestic mountains in the north-west Highlands. Their Gaelic names, Beinn Ghobhlach, Sgurr Mor and Beinn Dearg, conjure up visions of the past. And the Gaelic language is kept up in Ullapool itself, where the street signs are in both Gaelic and English.

The fact that the town was built especially for fishing almost caused its downfall. By the middle of the 19th century, too many herrings had been taken from the loch and the shoals had disappeared for good. But during the Second World War, the eastern coastal waters were mined against the Germans and it was too hazardous for the fishing boats to put out there. So commercial fishing was revived in the North Minch between the mainland and the Western Isles. Today Ullapool's harbour is used by trawlers from Scotland and eastern Europe.

Ullapool's short but unusual history is depicted in a small museum, housed, appropriately enough, in the Fisheries Society's old herring-curing store.

• **Parking** Quay Street (car park) • **Early closing** Tuesday • **Event** Regatta (July) • **Information** TEL. Ullapool 2135 (summer) • **AA 24 hour service** TEL. Aberdeen 639231.

Inchnadamph, Loch Assynt and the Quinag ridge

Inchnadamph HIGHLAND

24 miles north of Ullapool (PAGE 404 Bc)

Presided over by the mighty many-peaked Quinag ridge, the land of Assynt is a tremendous, sterile place of dark hillside, white rushing water and little slaty lochs. It has been so always, for much of the landscape is Archaen gneiss, one of the oldest-known rock formations. Against this larger-than-life backdrop, the scattered white buildings of the little crofting community of Inchnadamph look particularly gallant.

There is not much of it really; a hotel, some crofters' cottages, and a more or less cottage-sized kirk, whose miniature spire stands guard over lichen-encrusted graves and a monument to the crew of an RAF aircraft that crashed on 3273 ft Ben More Assynt in 1941. In the churchyard there are also the remains of an earlier church built in the 15th century by a MacLeod chief. It is said that after burning churches in other districts he had to go to Rome to seek the pope's forgiveness. The pope granted it on the condition that

WHERE THE MARQUIS WAS DELIVERED TO HIS ENEMIES

The sparkling white gables and walls of Inchnadamph contrast vividly with its setting. A river winds its way through pastures to join the brisk waves of Loch Assynt; clouds boil and spill over the rugged peaks of the Quinag ridge beyond. The scene seems ready made for drama — and there has been plenty here. Rising starkly above a shingle beach is the ruin of Ardvrech Castle, an old MacLeod stronghold that was the scene of one particularly dark deed. Here, in 1650, that most loyal of Stuart supporters, the Marquis of Montrose, was delivered into the hands of Parliamentarian troops.

Ardvrech Castle, by Loch Assynt

the chief repented and built two new churches.

Close by, a cairn pays 'international tribute' to Ben Peach and John Horne who 'played the foremost part in unravelling the geological structure' of this part of the Highlands towards the end of the last century. Among their unravellings was the history of a pair of caves that lie between the burns of Traligill and Allt nan Uamh. Excavations revealed the bones of reindeer, bears, lemmings and lynxes, as well as prehistoric human remains.

Geological curiosities of the neighbourhood include caves hung with stalactites and the 'disappearing river'. A mile or so uphill from Inchnadamph, the Traligill suddenly plunges into a natural drain, and reappears again some 400 yds farther down.

The road from Inchnadamph to Kylesku passes the tattered remains of Ardvrech Castle, growing from a headland that juts into the dark waters of Loch Assynt. Here was played out the last act but one in the career of that most chivalrous of Stuart partisans, James Graham, 1st Marquis of Montrose.

By 1650, the forces of Parliament were everywhere victorious, but in April of that year, Montrose made one last attempt to raise the Highlands for Charles II. He landed at Duncansby Head with several hundred half-trained Orkney levies. Two weeks later, this pitiful army was cut to pieces by Lowland dragoons in a skirmish at Carbisdale (see Lairg, page 410), and Montrose was a fugitive with £20,000 on his head.

He was discovered, starving and fevered, by MacLeod clansmen, who brought him to their chief at Ardvrech. What happened next is unclear. One story has it that Neil MacLeod fed and entertained the wanderer, then committed the only crime unforgivable in the Highlands, that of betraying a guest. Another says that MacLeod, as a loyal Presbyterian, simply clapped the marquis in a dungeon and informed the authorities. For Montrose, both stories had the same ending, on a 30 ft gallows in Edinburgh's Grassmarket.

MacLeod was paid the reward, or part of it at least, in bags of oatmeal. But it did him little good. The Royalist MacKenzies, incensed at his supposed perfidy, sacked Assynt from end to end and, at the Restoration, seized the land itself. They built a house by the lochside—Calda House—and its ruins are still there, close by the ruins of the MacLeod castle.

Kinlochbervie HIGHLAND

60 miles north of Ullapool (PAGE 404 Bb)

Since it lies a mere 12 miles from Cape Wrath in a countryside of dour and unremitting grandeur, Kinlochbervie might well be described as remote. But its communications and dealings with the rest of the world are excellent and efficient; its older children, for example, attend school in Golspie, 64 miles away on the other side of Scotland, boarding during the week and coming home at weekends. From Golspie, too, the travelling butcher's shop comes to call, once a week. Bread and milk are delivered from Lairg, 46 miles off down a single-track road.

It certainly does not feel remote. In fact, after a long drive through the awe-inspiring landscape, it seems positively bustling and cheerful, and you look upon the low stone cottages and fish curing sheds with warm approval. The village is magnificently sited on a narrow isthmus between two sea lochs, Clash and Inchard, with snug harbours on both of them. Although the old harbour in Loch Clash is no longer used, Kinlochbervie is the busiest fishing port in north-west Scotland.

Sometimes more than 40 boats sail from here, though as can be seen from their registration letters—UL for Ullapool, BF for Banff, INS for Inverness and so on—many of their home ports are elsewhere. Long before the fish are loaded onto lorries for the long journeys to Aberdeen, Hull, Grimsby and London, the crews, smart in their shore-going clothes, are into their cars and on their way home.

The catch safely disposed of, peace descends upon the little port, broken only by the incessant crying of gulls and the gentle slap of wavelets on the hulls of the moored boats. These hulls used to be the only note of colour in the sombre scene, but recently the local Free Church minister has taken to painting abstract, two-storey murals upon his end wall. He amends one of the murals each year, and the subjects are said to be religious.

Kinlochbervie is not quite where the tarmac ends in Britain, but it is not far from it. Actually, a road of a kind goes on to Oldshoremore, where a little cemetery balances on the edge of a pale gold beach, and proceeds still farther to Blairmore and Sheigra; here, the road fades without fuss into the peat moss. Booted adventurers may care to take the track from Blairmore that runs for 4 miles through rock, bog and water to Sandwood Bay.

About halfway along, there is a ruin where a number of hikers have reported seeing the phantom of a bearded man. Sandwood Bay also has its uncanny side. For one thing, here is true remoteness, the most northerly beach on the west coast of mainland Britain and, when the weather is fine, utter stillness over the 2 miles of shining white sand, the pale green sea and the freshwater loch behind.

In 1900 a shepherd reported that he had seen a mermaid in the bay. She had reddish-yellow hair and green eyes and looked just like a bonny human lass, he said. Except, of course, for her fishy tail. Sightings of her have been reported on a number of occasions since then. Sometimes she has been seen swimming on the surface, but more often she appears as a wash of golden hair in the turning of a wave.

Lairg HIGHLAND

49 miles east of Ullapool (PAGE 404 Dd)

In August, the roads stretching north and west, south and east bring the shepherds to Lairg, for the biggest one-day sheep and lamb sale in Britain. Then the little streets are filled with a crescendo of whistles and barking and bleating; and, when the sales are over, drovers and farmers from distant places gather to take up conversations they had abandoned in the previous August auctions.

But for most of the year, the village is quiet enough. It is a pleasant little place of neat stone houses, some whitewashed, some warmly weathered. Some have crow-stepped gables and others dormer windows with brightly painted surrounds; together, they make a harmonious picture standing by the waters of Little Loch Shin. To the north-east lies the upper loch, a grand, almost 20 mile long sheet of water that is the power source for a massive hydroelectricity scheme.

The local salmon and trout have always brought anglers to Lairg – the Gaelic word for 'meeting-place'. But in recent years a number of discerning tourists have also appeared here, realising, like the shepherds, what a splendid centre this is for exploring the Highlands in general, and for enjoying the scenery of Sutherland in particular.

What scenery it is! There have been suggestions that the Highlands were invented by a consortium of Queen Victoria, Prince Albert and Sir Walter Scott, and some of the country in Sutherland would have been the consortium's ideal. It is not like the wild deserts of Torridon and Assynt, but grand, majestic and romantic, and exactly the kind of scenery that appealed to the Victorian landscape painters.

A good way to come to Lairg is from the south, by way of Bonar Bridge, driving inland by the sharply narrowing waters of the Kyle of Sutherland. Here, high on a wooded crag, sits Carbisdale Castle, a modern Camelot with dozens of sparkling windows and ornate turrets sprouting from every angle. The Highlands affect architects that way; if large houses are built at all, they more or less have to be castles. This castle was completed in 1914, having been started for the widow of the 3rd Duke of Sutherland. The duke's family, it seems, did not get on with his widow and bribed her to leave what was then the county of Sutherland. Accepting the bribe the dowager used it to start building the castle, which was not finished, however, until two years after she died. It stands just on the south-west side of the Kyle of Sutherland, which used to mark the border between Sutherland and Ross and Cromarty, and is now a Youth Hostel.

A little to the north, the turbulent River Shin joins the Kyle, and it was here, or very close by, in 1650, that the great Royalist soldier, the 1st Marquis of Montrose, fought his final battle. His last, scratched-together army was pinned against the water by Parliamentarian dragoons and annihilated. Montrose escaped, but after desperate weeks as fugitive and captive, he was hanged before a vast crowd in Edinburgh (see Inchnadamph, page 410).

The River Shin flows through a ravine that grows steadily upstream towards Lairg. Rowan, oak and birch grow from cracks in the rock, then, all at once, there are the Falls of Shin – a series of great steps over which the peaty-brown water foams and tumbles. Salmon leap the falls in season, and there is a platform from which it is possible to watch them. Rock, water and trees combine to make as glorious a picture as Landseer himself could have wished; in autumn especially, when the green of bracken and trees gives way to clear gold, yellow and crimson.

Scourie HIGHLAND

44 miles north of Ullapool (PAGE 404 Bb)

This small crofting village, spread out along a lane skirted by the main road from Ullapool to Durness, lies between the sheltered sands of Scourie Bay and a vast, breathtaking wilderness of craggy mountains, rocky outcrops, peat bogs and countless tiny lakes where brown trout breed. It attracts anglers, walkers, climbers, birdwatchers and others who just enjoy the rugged beauty of a region where the 20th century has made remarkably little impact.

The Scourie Hotel stands on the site of a house fortified by the Clan Mackay, and the village was the birthplace of General Hugh Mackay, who commanded William III's army at Killiecrankie in 1689. He was defeated there, but fought many successful campaigns before falling at the Battle of Steinkirk in 1692. King William, speaking at Mackay's funeral, said that 'an honester man the world cannot produce'.

Ice Age glaciers, Atlantic waves and complex geology have combined to create a spectacular coast of cliffs, sandy bays, sea lochs and islands. It is the haunt of such birds as puffins, great and Arctic skuas, oystercatchers, herons, eider ducks, cormorants, razorbills and herring gulls. Porpoises, dolphins and whales may sometimes be seen swimming in waters warmed by the Gulf Stream. The current's benevolent influence also accounts for Scourie's claim to be the northernmost point in the world where palm trees grow out in the open air.

Handa Island, 2 miles from the village, where cliffs rise more than 400 ft from the sea, is a reserve of the Royal Society for the Protection of Birds. During the holiday season, boats run to the island from Tarbet, about 3 miles north of Scourie. North of Tarbet is Loch Laxford, which, with its many small islands, reveals its beauty during cruises starting from the hamlet of Fanagmore. Tarbet and Fanagmore are reached by a hilly, single-track road which leads westwards off the road between Scourie and Laxford Bridge.

Scourie Bay, where water from a reedy stream filters through a bank of shingle, has a slipway and a small jetty. Sands sweep round to a low headland with a burial ground where primroses grow between old gravestones mottled with lichens.

The village's other attractions include a small, friendly art and craft shop with paintings and drawings of local views and wildlife.

WICK

HIGHLAND

17 miles south of John o' Groats (PAGE 404 Hb)

Brightly painted fishing boats, and fishermen's huts with red and blue nets piled outside, bring gay splashes of colour to Wick's greystone harbour. The main catch is white fish, such as haddock, whiting and cod – and the fish are sold in the nearby market, where the fast-talking auctioneers raise the bids at a speed which almost defeats the ear.

Wick's fishing port, originally a separate community called Pultneytown, was built in the early 19th century by the British Fisheries Society. Its straight, wide streets were designed by the engineer Thomas Telford, who also advised on the building of Ullapool (see page 406). In 1902 Wick and Pultneytown joined under the single name of Wick.

Sheltering between two headlands, Wick is the nearest sizable town to John o' Groats. The town began as a Viking settlement and anchorage, and its name comes from the Old Norse word *vik*, meaning 'bay'. The Viking influence has lasted, and although Gaelic is common throughout the Highlands, not a word of it is spoken in the town – which was made a royal burgh in 1589 by James VI of Scotland.

Until 1975 Wick was the main town of the former county of Caithness, and its auction market in Victoria Place was the county's centre for buying and selling sheep and cattle. The town's history is recorded in the

Wick harbour

HAVEN OF PEACE BY THE WILD NORTH SEA

'The bleakest of God's towns on the bleakest of God's bays,' wrote Robert Louis Stevenson, commenting on Wick. But this fishing port, spread along the southern shore of the estuary of the River Wick, has an austere magic of its own. Sturdy fishing vessels, built to withstand the wild Atlantic and North Sea storms, line its quays. One boat is proudly named after Ben Loyal, the great mountain south of Tongue which soars alongside Loch Loyal. Farther along the quayside, a festive touch is added by a boat 'dressed' with bunting and balloons for a local celebration. The port was designed by the Scottish engineer Thomas Telford in the early 19th century, with later work done by Robert Louis Stevenson's father, Thomas.

Fishing vessels moored alongside

Wick Heritage Centre in Bunk Row – open all summer. Near by is the Carnegie Library, which was largely paid for by the Dunfermline-born steel magnate and philanthropist Andrew Carnegie (1835–1919), who emigrated to America at the age of 13.

Among the library's chief treasures is a 16th-century effigy of St Fergus, the town's patron saint. The effigy, one of the oldest and best preserved in Scotland, originally stood in the parish church on the north of the river. The present church dates from 1830, but its surrounding churchyard goes back to the 1570s. The church roof – said to be the widest in Scotland – is not supported by pillars. Instead, its rafters are tied to the side walls. In 1960 a new industry was born in the town – that of glass-making. Today hand-blown Caithness Glass is successfully sold both at home and overseas. The glassworks is in Harrowhill in the south-east of the town. Tours – showing the whole glass-making process, from its simple raw materials to the elegant finished product – take place throughout the year on weekdays.

• **Parking** Louisburgh Street; Scalesburn Road; Whitechapel Road (all car parks) • **Early closing** Wednesday • **Market day** Thursday (cattle) • **Events** Gala Week (July); Caithness County Show (July, alternating annually between Wick and Thurso) • **Information** TEL. Wick 2596 • **AA 24 hour service** TEL. Aberdeen 639231.

Berriedale HIGHLAND

26 miles south-west of Wick (PAGE 404 Gc)

There is not much of Berriedale, but the curtain-raiser is unforgettable. From the north, the road drops 540 ft in a mile into a wide, steep-sided valley, then rises 300 ft to the south, allowing tantalising glimpses of Langwell House, a shooting lodge belonging to the Dukes of Portland. Closer glimpses of the lodge are obtainable in summer, when the gardens are occasionally open to the public.

Altogether, Berriedale's situation is most attractive. The tiny hamlet is squeezed between steep slopes at the wooded confluence of the Berriedale Water and the Langwell Water. Both rivers were born in the vast, uninhabited and virtually trackless wilderness that sprawls westwards to the remote road between Helmsdale and Thurso. The country was not always so deserted, however; brochs and souterrains (Pictish forts and grain storage pits), along with other ancient remains down the river valleys, are evidence of a fairly sizable prehistoric population.

At Berriedale the combined rivers race past an old, water-powered sawmill and a gathering of estate cottages before coming to a suspension footbridge that bounces like a trampoline when foot is set upon it. The river then sweeps past a tiny quay, and curls round a rocky headland about which fulmars, herring gulls and guillemots crowd in perpetual argument.

A few tumbled, overgrown stones on the headland are all that remain of a 12th-century castle; or more likely a fort where the fisherfolk used to take shelter when the Norse pirates came a-calling. At the top of a steep, zigzag path there is a lookout post, from which there are magnificent views of the rugged coast. Out to sea are the giant rigs of a North Sea oilfield, dwarfed by distance.

Below the cliffs, white baby seals haul out on shingle beaches to bask in the pale sunlight of the north's late autumn. A row of low cottages, which were originally occupied by fishermen, stands behind the beach, but the post office, the war memorial and the remainder of the village all lie a few hundred yards inland. Along the main road to the south, two of the cottages are hung with the antlers of deer which were shot by stalkers in the surrounding forests. The forests are privately owned by the family of the Duke of Portland.

Canisbay HIGHLAND

20 miles north of Wick (PAGE 404 Ha)

Dunnet Head and Duncansby Head are the most northern and north-eastern points of mainland Britain. When it blows in this part of the world, great breakers snarl in, their tops whipped off in streamers by the wind, to explode against the cliffs and hurl spray hundreds of feet into the air. Inland, on fields as

LIVING ON THE BEACH *Cottages stand almost on the beach in the tiny, sheltered cove where Berriedale Water flows into the North Sea.*

flat and green as those of Lincolnshire, cows stand like soldiers, shoulder to shoulder. Their sterns point resolutely into the wind; their eyes gaze mournfully over the upright stone flags that take the place of hedges and divide the rectangular fields one from another. Even in good weather, the Pentland Firth, which divides the mainland from the Orkneys, is uneasy, heaving and foaming like yeasty ginger beer between the fangs of the stacks and the red cliffs.

Canisbay lies between the two mighty points and, very sensibly, a little inland. It is made up mostly of snug, single-storey stone houses of indeterminate age, but its whitewashed church, topped by a handsome, saddlebacked tower, almost certainly dates from the 15th century. It is the northernmost of mainland churches, and among its parishioners is Queen Elizabeth the Queen Mother, whose summer home is the nearby Castle of Mey.

In the south transept there is a monument to the de Groot or Groat family, one of whom, Jan de Groot, or John o' Groats, started a ferry service between the mainland and Orkney in the early 1500s. Passengers were charged a fourpenny piece which, it is said, became known as a groat in the ferryman's honour. Certainly, he bequeathed his name to the hamlet in which he lived, a couple of miles east of Canisbay, though his house is long gone. Apparently it had an octagonal room with eight doors, and an eight-sided table in order to avoid any squabbles about precedence among his eight descendants who had inherited the business equally.

The hamlet, which contains a number of Last Houses, Shops, Inns and so forth, is perhaps a little worn by visitors who have come to see the most northerly mainland community in Britain, or who have traversed the 876 miles from Land's End on foot or by bicycle, roller skates, pram, wheelbarrow, or any other improbable mode of travel. But it is fun to have your photograph taken beside an amazing signpost whose arms can be altered to give the name of, and the distance to, your home town, wherever in the world it may happen to be.

Helmsdale HIGHLAND

37 miles south-west of Wick (PAGE 404 Fd)

The houses, hotel and cottages are mostly white, but there are sufficient walls and roofs of powder-blue, buff, pink, and of natural stone colour among them to make a very pretty picture – in early summer especially, when the gorse comes into full bloom and drapes the hills behind in swathes of gold. Rows of orange lobster pots along the harbour wall, nets hung up to dry and a gaggle of smartly painted inshore fishing boats show that Helmsdale is still making a living from the sea, which is more than may be said of some other small ports along this coast. A scattering of cottages on the hillside, surrounded by rectangular fields neatly walled in stone, indicate that crofting, too, is prospering.

This is quite a large village by Highland standards. Most of it dates from the early 19th century when the Duke of Sutherland evicted thousands of unprofitable tenants from his land to make way for sheep. Some of the people drifted to the coast, where – with not entirely disinterested generosity – the duke founded Helmsdale and a fishing industry to help them. Others of the Sutherland tenantry arrived penniless in the New World.

The village streets are laid out in grid pattern; those running north and south were named after the duke's English estates, such as Stafford and Trentham, while the east and west thoroughfares, like Sutherland Street, bore the names of his Scottish possessions. The fisheries were forward-looking from the beginning. As early as the 1840s, salmon from the Helmsdale river – still one of the best salmon rivers of the north – were being shipped, packed in ice, to London. In the winter, the ice was taken from an artificial pond by the church and stored in a nearby ice house which still survives, dug deep into the hillside. The house's thick walls, and the insulating turf above, kept the ice from melting.

The ice house stands below an enormous war-memorial clock tower that would be conspicuous in a city square. However, it has only the wild hills as a backdrop, while before it is a graceful Telford bridge that carried traffic over the river from 1812 until the 1970s. It was usurped by a less graceful high-span bridge a few hundred yards downstream. Close by is the Tourist Information Bureau, a picnic site and a viewing point.

This was the site of Helmsdale Castle, whose ruins were cleared to make way for the bridge, and here was enacted one of those bizarre murder cases that figure so frequently in Scottish history. In 1567 Isobel Sinclair poisoned the Earl and Countess of Sutherland at the castle, hoping that her son, the Earl of Caithness, would inherit the title. But the boy partook of the same meal, and he died, too.

Knowledgeable strollers along the shingle beach may spot jasper, jet, amethyst, fossil coral and other semiprecious stones. But this is gentle prospecting indeed when compared with what happened in 1868. Then, a local man named Robert Gilchrist, just home from the Australian goldfields, was given permission by the Duke of Sutherland to pan for gold in the lovely Strath of Kildonan, through which the Helmsdale river runs. Once gold was found, the duke allocated plots of land, 40 ft square, to prospectors and issued them with licences to prospect, charging them a fee of £1 a month. He also took 10 per cent of all the gold they discovered.

Eventually, the area was overrun by hundreds of hopeful prospectors, who ruined things for the wealthy sportsmen – and took over land where the local sheep farmers normally brought their ewes at lambing time. There were so many protests about this that after a while the duke was forced to put an end to the prospecting. The prospectors' short-lived shanty town was built where the Kildonan Burn meets the Helmsdale river – and to this day the site is known as *Baile an Or*, the 'Town of Gold'. Young men still sometimes pan the river in the hope of finding at least enough gold to make a wedding ring.

Two miles or so north-east of Helmsdale is the Ord of Caithness, a 700 ft granite headland. It divided the former counties of Caithness and Sutherland, and is a wonderful place from which to view this wild and noble coast. On a Monday morning in 1513, the Earl of Caithness came over the Ord leading 300 green-clad Sinclair clansmen on the march south to support James IV at the Battle of Flodden. Like thousands of James's troops – and including the king himself – they never returned, and even now it is said to be unlucky for a Sinclair to walk over the Ord on a Monday. Especially if he is wearing green.

ASPECTS *of* COUNTRY LIFE

The Country Pub

It has a style, an atmosphere – and sometimes a local brew – that is all its own. Its origins lie in lodging houses built by monks offering shelter to medieval travellers. Some of those houses still do so.

Crafts that live on

They live on in astonishing variety . . . boatbuilding, woodcarving, saddlemaking, basket-weaving, woodturning – just a few of the dozens thriving in town and village workshops.

Fairs, Feasts and Games

Horse fairs, mop fairs and plain old funfairs; point-to-points and ploughing matches; customs kept and devils defied . . . the rural calendar is rich and varied.

The Great House

Moated castle, in fact . . . one family's home for over 500 years, where local workers by the dozen tended the house, the garden, the large estate – and the family. A surprising number still work there.

The Old Mill

Windmills, water mills, tide mills . . . hundreds survive and many still grind flour for crusty country loaves. The tough, adaptable and multi-skilled millwright keeps their wheels turning.

The Living Past

Looking back down the years in a small town and one of its neighbouring villages . . . images and recollections lovingly preserved, and much else, as present-day photographs reveal.

The Country Pub

A COOL PINT IN SUMMER OR A GLOWING FIRE WHEN FROST NIPS • A HEARTY MEAL OR A SIMPLE SNACK • WHATEVER A TRAVELLER'S TASTE, A COUNTRY PUB STILL OFFERS A TRADITION OF HOSPITALITY THAT BEGAN IN MEDIEVAL TIMES

For most people the image of the country pub is one of low-beamed ceilings, a flagstoned floor, and walls bedecked with gleaming brass and copper. Then, to delight the nose, there is the sweet smell of woodsmoke from a warm, open fire, mingling with the pungent odour of the wines, beers and spirits which – as the sign above the door proclaims – the landlord is licensed to sell. For once, the popular image may turn out to be correct, for most country landlords know very well what attracts townsfolk tired of plastic-topped tables, neon lighting, space invaders, jukeboxes and other signs of modern times that make many customers prefer to drink at home.

Behind the cosy country image lie centuries of tradition, going back to medieval days, when the inn was a place offering travellers shelter for the night and something to eat and drink. Perhaps surprisingly, such inns were established by hospitable monks.

In a sparsely populated, predominantly rural Britain monasteries provided the only safe and certain shelter for travellers. Whether they were pilgrims or ordinary wayfarers, monks deemed it a Christian duty to welcome them.

Rather than bring strangers into the monastery itself, they set up hospices outside. There travellers were entitled to a 'dole' of food and drink. Some of these buildings still survive, and one of them, the Hospice of St Cross, just outside Winchester, Hampshire, continues the ancient custom of doling out bread and ale to those who ask for it.

In due course, particularly after the Dissolution of the Monasteries in 1539, the hospices became inns run by lay brothers who were, in effect, the first innkeepers. The George and Pilgrims at Glastonbury, the Angel at Guildford, another Angel at Walsingham and the King's Head at Aylesbury are all inns which began in this way. In addition to those of monastic origin there are the inns on great estates, where guests could stay when there was no room at the manor house. Many of these still bear the name and arms of the local family – the Davenport Arms at Marton, in Cheshire, for example.

As villages grew in size, so the function of the village inn changed. It became a social centre for the community as well as a lodging house for travellers. This led to the public house having separate sections – the public, saloon and private bars, where people who worked together during the day could avoid each other in the evening if they wished. In the public bar, with its sawdusted floor, solid wooden benches and a dartboard, the farm workers relaxed away from their employers. They in turn would entertain their friends in the more comfortable saloon or private bar – but they had to pay a little

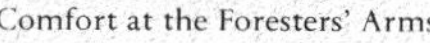

Comfort at the Foresters' Arms

Homely hearth at the Victoria

BEAMS, BRASSES AND A FRIENDLY BLAZE

A customer takes his ease in the Foresters' Arms at Carlton, in Coverdale, North Yorkshire; brass gleams on the mantelpiece and flames flicker in the hearth. There is a glowing welcome, too, in another snug Dales pub, the Victoria at Worton.

ABBOT'S ALE *The George and Pilgrims at Glastonbury, once an abbey guesthouse, became an inn run by lay brothers.*

The King's Head, Hethersett

GOOD EVENING AND WELCOME . . .

Sunset, and across a field the pink-washed walls of the King's Head beckon like an oasis at Hethersett, in Norfolk. Country pubs come in all shapes and sizes – away in Somerset the deep thatch, white walls and friendly neighbourhood geese of the Royal Oak at Winsford make a delightful contrast. But in one aspect they are all the same: their tradition of hospitality seldom varies. For local regular customers the pub is a home from home – not just a place to drink but a meeting point for a quiet chat and perhaps a game of darts or shove-ha'penny. And for a traveller, there will always be a welcome.

The Royal Oak, Winsford

more for their drinks as a price for the privilege.

Thus the country inn provided variety under one roof, catering for all types. For those who wanted a drink at home there was the 'jug and bottle', still found in some older communities, where customers could buy draught beer to take away – usually in a jug or bottle. Larger villages often had several pubs or inns, giving people a choice.

Country inns range from timber-framed and thatched buildings, dating from the 16th century or earlier, to red-brick Victorian 'drinking parlours'. But all have one thing in common – the inn sign which announces not only what the place is but often tells something of its history, too. The inn sign is one of the few surviving examples of how symbols were once used to advertise the trade or profession of a building's occupant – the pestle and mortar of the chemist or the bloodstained wrappings of the barber-surgeon were just two.

One of the earliest types of inn sign was a bush or branches of greenery attached to the outside of the building, symbolising Bacchus, the Greek god of wine. It is from this early sign that pubs called The Bush take their name.

The origin of conventional inn signs makes a fascinating study. Often they are straightforward

Morris dancers at Snettisham

Blue Anchor skittle alley

IT'S ALL BEER AND SKITTLES AT THE OLD BLUE ANCHOR

Alongside the little brewery where Helston's Blue Anchor makes its own beer there is a 300-year-old skittle alley. It had just been reopened when this picture was taken in 1957, after being closed for 19 years. Skittle alleys are fairly rare nowadays – darts, dominoes and shove-ha'penny take less room. But morris dancing is popular, with teams often based at a pub.

enough, simply names associated with trades or professions: the Carpenters' Arms, the Jolly Farmer and – for carriers – the Wagon and Horses. And national heroes are frequently commemorated – Lord Nelson and the Duke of Wellington are two favourites who gaze down from hundreds of pub signs.

But the meanings of some pub names are more obscure. The unlikely combination of Pig and Whistle probably derives from the Saxon *piggen* (a milking pail) and *wassail* (good health), because in early days beer was served in pails into which the customers dipped their mugs. The unusual Goat and Compasses may date from when inns were run by monks, for it is thought to be a muzzy-headed drinker's attempt to say 'God encompasseth us'.

Alehouses, as distinct from inns, go back to the Middle Ages when a good housewife could brew beer as well as bake. If she brewed more than her family could drink, she could sell it to thirsty travellers passing by. There are still a few alehouses in country districts, usually small establishments run by the woman of the household as a part-time occupation.

Two means of transportation, the stagecoach and the canal, brought changes in the role of country inns from the late 18th century onwards. Coaching inns are usually found in towns or villages that were on, or near, major stage routes. They can generally be recognised by a large archway leading to a courtyard. Here the passengers would alight, either to stay overnight or to enjoy a good meal while fresh horses were harnessed up. Such inns have changed little in character, offering the same low-ceilinged, cosy bedrooms while the courtyard is often a car park.

The oldest waterside inns were established where a ferry crossed a river or waterway of some kind. Two that still thrive are The Ferry at Horning, on the Norfolk Broads, and the Ferryboat Inn at Holywell, on the River Ouse in Cambridgeshire. On the canals the bargees' pubs were usually near lock gates. Their names – the Navigation, the Black Horse and the Boat and Horses, for example – often had links with the canal way of life.

The modern innkeeper may stock everything from American wines to Japanese whisky, but beer is still his main stock-in-trade. Until the 16th century, ale was the universal English drink – dark, mild and fairly sweet. But in Germany a brewer discovered a pungent-smelling plant with greenish flowers which gave a sharp flavour to the drink. This was the hop, and it apparently came to England in the 16th century.

Most inns brewed their own beer, until the 19th century. Water is the basic component, and some areas have better beer-making water than others – which is why Burton upon Trent has been famous for its beers for a thousand years. Naturally, brewers with a good beer-making water supply sought ways of getting their products to a wider market, and so the large brewing companies evolved. They in turn set up chains of pubs in which their beers were the only ones sold.

The key figure in all breweries is the master brewer, who decides the proportions of the ingredients that he hopes will make his beer better than others. However, the process is the same for all. Crushed malted barley is steeped in hot water, and the extract is boiled with hops and fermented with yeast.

There are still a few country inns that brew their own beer – the Blue Anchor at Helston, Cornwall, is one; the Three Tuns at Bishop's Castle, Shropshire, is another. Furthermore, not all local breweries have been absorbed into the giant companies. Several remain independent and are now enjoying wide popularity with the renewed demand for traditionally brewed beers – a reaction to the pressurised beers introduced in the 1950s.

Traditional pub games are also enjoying a revival – though in a few remote places they never went away. Darts, which probably grew out of archery contests, has always been a popular game; and in many public bars, regulars still meet for a game of dominoes. Some pubs even boast a skittle alley which, in its earliest form, had flat wooden 'cheeses', instead of a ball, to pitch at the skittles. Bar billiards, shove-

A SNUG BERTH UNDERNEATH THE ARCHES

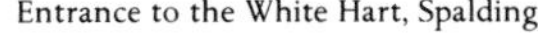
Entrance to the White Hart, Spalding

Galleried courtyard of the George Inn, Huntingdon

The arrival of the stagecoach had a tremendous influence on the pub map of Britain. It was responsible for giving the country some of its most attractive inns and hotels, usually recognisable by arched entries to inner courtyards – once stable yards. Here horses could be fed and watered, or fresh animals harnessed up; passengers would alight and others join the coach; welcomes and farewells were exchanged. Small armies of ostlers, farriers and harness repairers saw to the coach and horses; tapsters, kitchen hands and serving girls saw that thirst and appetite were satisfied; simple but snug rooms provided a bed for the night if needed. Cars or tables may occupy the courtyard now; coaches are seldom seen. Two splendid survivors from bygone days are the White Hart at Spalding, Lincolnshire, with a porticoed entrance, and the George Inn at Huntingdon, Cambridgeshire.

ha'penny and a version of table skittles known as Devil among the Tailors are also making a comeback, to take up the challenge of the current space-invader games and the pool tables.

From the late 19th century onwards many inns were 'modernised', and in the process lost their identity and character. But in recent years the trend has been reversed. Plasterboard and plastic coverings have been ripped away to reveal once more old beamed ceilings, and walls of mellow stone and warm brick.

In truth, the country inn today is as vital and real a part of the rural heritage as the stately home.

Three Willows, Birchanger, Essex

Two Brewers, Thornborough, Buckinghamshire

Lord Nelson, Burnham Market, Norfolk

SIGNS OF THE TIMES

Some pub names seem destined to remain a riddle. Did the Elephant and Castle start out as the Infanta of Castile? The point will be argued so long as there is still a pub of that name. But there can be no doubt about the popularity of national heroes: Nelson appears on signs all around the country. More unusual is the elaborate Three Willows pub sign at Birchanger, in Essex, showing batsmen of 1780, 1900 and 1946 in action. Among numerous signs celebrating crafts and trades, brewing itself is not too well represented – although the Two Brewers is quite popular. So are such ancient rustic landmarks as the Plough or Harrow.

Crafts that live on

WORKING WOOD AND LEATHER • WEAVING WILLOW AND MAKING FINE CHEESES • THESE ANCIENT ARTS LIVE ON IN THE HANDS OF DEDICATED CRAFTSMEN, INHERITORS OF THE SKILLS OF BYGONE DAYS

THE BASKET MAKER

Whatever the shape, size or purpose of a basket, the skilled craftsman is able to fashion hazel, rushes, reeds and even grass into a useful work of art. But the traditional material is the supple willow.

The colour of willow wands, or 'withies', depends on how they are prepared. Brown willow is dried naturally, buff willow is boiled, and white willow is left in water until young leaves appear. The bark on both white and buff willow rods is stripped before use.

Most baskets are made from the base upwards and develop from what is called a slath. This is made by laying four or more sturdy willows, or 'sticks', across each other. These are often 'slyped' (have a small groove cut in them lengthways) so that they lie flat, but sometimes they are slit and threaded through each other. The craftsman binds the sticks in the centre and opens them out to form an asterisk shape. A withy is woven around these sticks until the base is large enough, then trimmed and the sticks cut to size.

The basket maker mostly works on a board on his lap. He inserts side stakes into the edge of the base, using a bodkin lubricated with grease or tallow kept in a horn. Then the stakes are bent upwards and gathered into a cane hoop.

Now the 'upsetting' begins – weaving the sides of the basket. Different weaving methods may be used, but the craftsman always works round and round from the bottom upwards. When the sides are complete, each stake is tucked away to form the border edge and untidy ends are trimmed off.

Forming the border edge

Bodkin Makes holes and opens weave

Shop knife Slypes and cuts

Commander and dog Straightens rods

Grease horn Lubricates bodkin

Secateurs Cuts the sticks

Beating iron Packs down the weave

THE BOATBUILDER

Wooden boats are now a luxury, but they are still built in a few boatyards for those who appreciate their beauty – and can afford it.

A boatbuilder first draws the hull shape, in side view and cross-section. He copies the drawings full scale on a floor, and from them makes wooden patterns for bulkheads and frames – vertical partitions and ribs across the hull which support and shape it. These are fixed to the keel, once a solid length of wood, now usually laminated.

The frames are held in place by ribbands, strips of wood running fore and aft. Then planking begins from the keel upwards, ribbands being removed as it progresses.

There are three planking methods: clinker-built boats have overlapping planks; carvel-built have edge-to-edge planks; and diagonal-built have planks laid diagonally from keel to deck, with a second layer at right angles to them. Copper nails or oak pegs fix planks to frames and bulkheads. Carvel boats are made watertight by caulking – oakum (unravelled rope) is packed between the planks with a mallet and broad chisel.

The stem (bow post) and transom (stern) are fitted, then deck beams, decking, interior fixtures, and finally fittings for mast, rigging and rudder.

Fixing a rib to a clinker-built boat

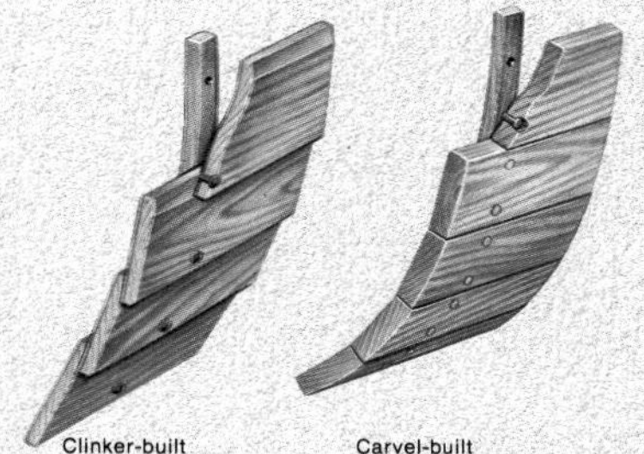

Clinker-built

Carvel-built

THE CHEESEWRIGHT

Most cheeses are made on a massive scale today, but some cheesewrights still make Cheddar, Derby, Caerphilly and other favourites by hand.

First the milk is heated and a bacterial culture, called a starter, is added to produce lactic acid. The milk is reheated and rennet, an enzyme from cows' stomachs, is now also added so that the milk separates into curds and whey. This mixture is cut repeatedly with long multi-bladed curd knives.

The cheesewright drains off the whey, and then the curd is crumbled, sprinkled with salt and put in moulds lined with coarse muslin.

Most cheeses are pressed and wrapped again in finer muslin (some are also dipped in wax so a rind forms). Each cheese is turned while it matures – for nine months, in the case of good Cheddar.

Blue cheeses, like Stilton, are not pressed at all. The veins in the cheese are caused by airborne bacterial spores while it matures.

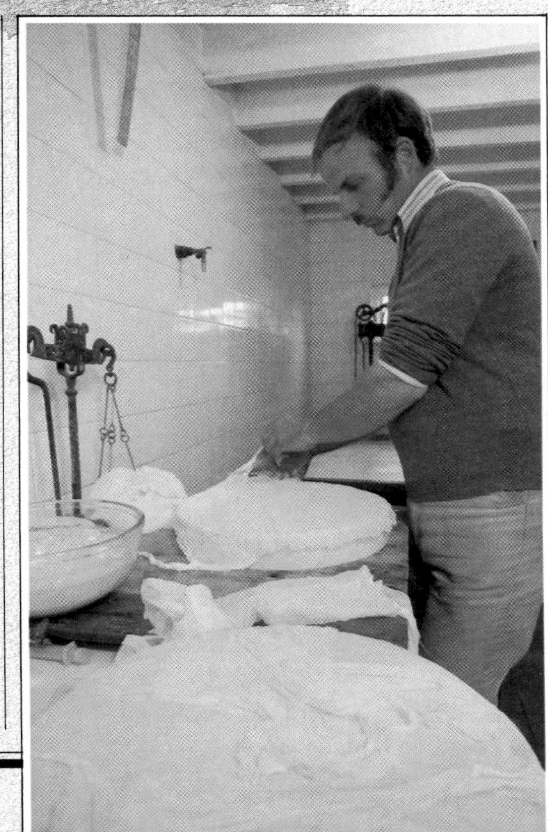

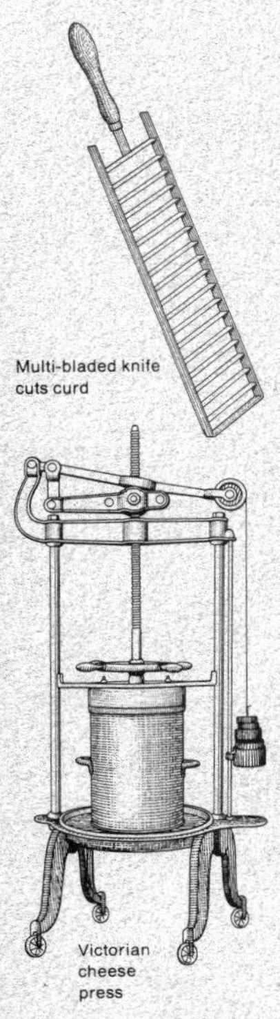

Multi-bladed knife cuts curd

Victorian cheese press

Wrapping a cheese in muslin

THE SADDLER

Saddles cannot be made by machine, so the skills of a master saddler are always in demand. It takes over four years' apprenticeship to learn the craft and up to 35 hours to make an everyday riding saddle.

All saddles are built around a 'tree', a frame usually made of laminated beechwood strengthened with steel. Webbing and saddle linen are tacked across the length and breadth of the tree. Then the saddler attaches shaped leather or felt pads on either side of the cantle and covers the whole seat with a layer of saddle serge.

The space between the linen and serge is stuffed through a narrow slit with woollen or nylon flocking to give the seat padding. The saddler reaches awkward places with a curved stuffing stick and the stuffing is shaped with a masher. Next comes the 'blocking'. A taut, wet pigskin, cut to pattern, is stretched over the seat, tacked underneath the tree, then left to dry into shape.

The saddler handles a dozen tools or more but the one used most is a wooden 'clam', which looks like a huge pair of tweezers. Held between the knees, this grips components firmly while they are being stitched. Also invaluable is a half-moon knife, with a crescent blade that cuts leather easily.

The stitching requires great skill because each stitch must be at just the right tension. The skirts are sewn to the seat, and the flaps, girth straps and finishing touches are added. Finally, the saddler makes a panel of hide, lined with felt or soft leather, which sits on the horse's back under the saddle.

Stitching a saddle

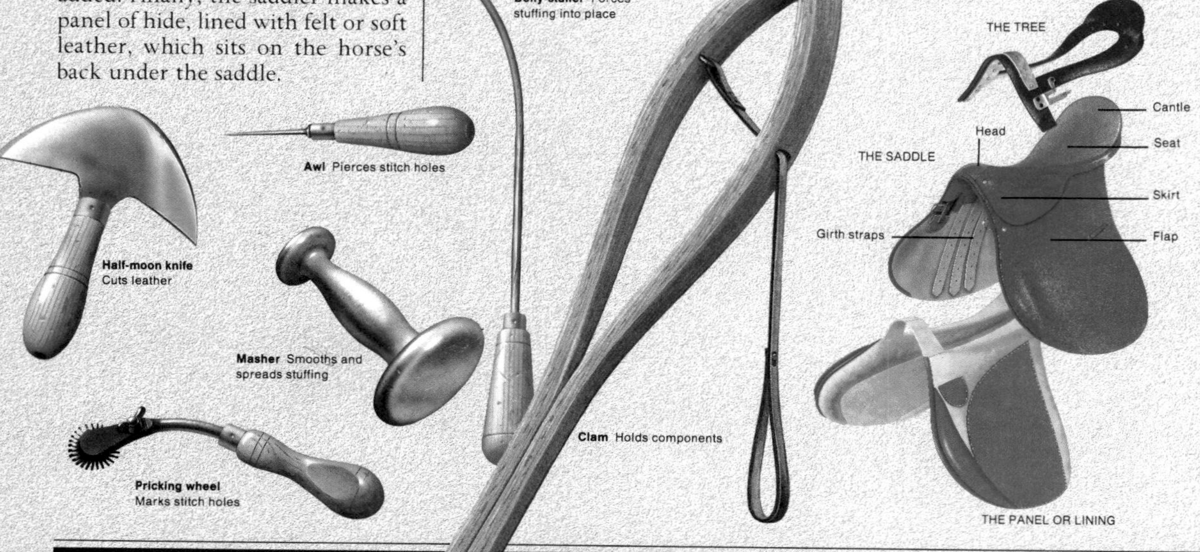

THE WOODCARVER

A woodcarver's very special feeling for his material means that he knows exactly how to use the grain and colour of different woods to enhance a carving. It is as if the block of wood already has a shape hidden inside, and the carver's skill coaxes it out.

First the carver usually makes detailed drawings of his subject, and perhaps a clay model to give a three-dimensional view. Then, by scaling up the model, if necessary, he calculates how much wood he requires and if joints are needed.

Small carvings can be made from a single block; but large carvings made from one block can split or warp, so the carver often makes up a laminated block, using thick, carefully matched planks. The enlarged drawings serve as a guide, the carver cutting each plank roughly to shape, perhaps with a mechanical band saw. The planks are glued, pegged together with wooden dowels, then clamped and left to bond. Then, using great care and precision, the craftsman chips away, using a mallet and broad chisels for coarse work. At least 30 smaller chisels and gouges may be needed to complete it.

Carving a lectern

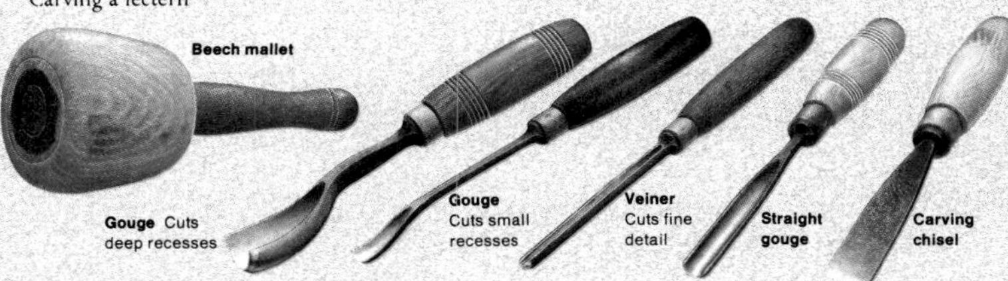

THE WOODTURNER

Plates and bowls have been made by the woodturner since prehistoric times, and the craft is practised now in much the same way as it was then. The woodturner, like the woodcarver, understands the properties of each piece of wood he uses, watchful for knots or hairline cracks which might flaw his creation.

Most varieties of wood can be turned. Sycamore is particularly popular because it can be worked while still green and does not crack when put in water.

Bowls are turned on the faceplate of the lathe, using specially shaped bowl-cutting gouges. They have long handles to help the craftsman hold them steady against the wood while the lathe is turning. The turner hollows out the inside first, cuts away the central core and smoothes the rest by hand.

Articles like chair legs and balusters are made by spindle turning. A long piece of wood, shaped roughly with a plane and spokeshave, is clamped in the lathe. As the wood revolves, the turner eases strong-bladed gouges and chisels against it, using rubbing or scraping movements. Then he separates the work from the rest of the wood with a parting tool before sanding and polishing.

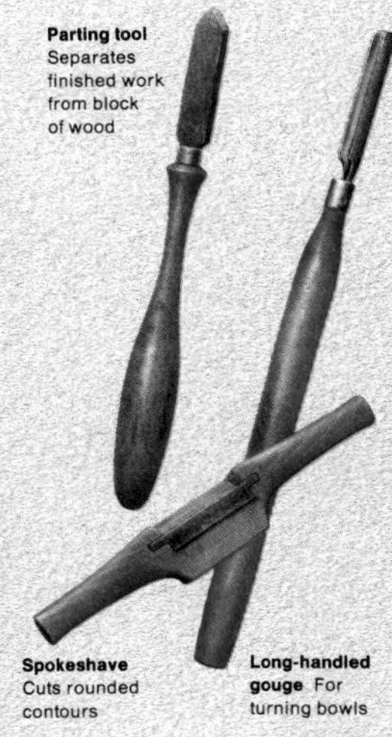

Turning a bowl

Fairs, Feasts and Games

SEASONS ARE CELEBRATED, RURAL RITUALS OBSERVED • MEN AND ANIMALS VIE IN FEATS OF STRENGTH, SPEED AND SKILL • FUN AND FANTASY PLAY THEIR PART IN THE CYCLE OF THE COUNTRY YEAR

The sports, merrymaking and colourful customs of rural Britain are as much a part of the calendar as the seasons of ploughing, sowing and harvest. In past days, a fair or festival was perhaps all that a farm worker could look forward to as a relief from his heavy toil.

Now working hours are shorter, towns more accessible and few households are without TV. Yet enthusiasm remains as strong as ever for the wrestling and maypole dances, the ploughing matches and sheepdog trials, the horse trading and racing which are just a few features of the countryside in festive mood. Many of the old fairs have become a complex of helter-skelters, merry-go-rounds and dodgem cars. Yet even these funfairs tend to be held on dates and in places which have been unchanged for centuries.

An example is Nottingham's Goose Fair, now a vast annual three-day general festivity starting on October 2. It began more than 700 years ago and was probably a fair where geese were bought and sold in time for Michaelmas – roast goose being a traditional Michaelmas dish. The geese walked all the way from Lincolnshire and Norfolk and, before making the long journey, their feet were protected with a mixture of tar and sand.

Most fairs originated in this way, as gatherings for buying and selling livestock – and sometimes even people were on offer. Thomas Hardy fictionalised one such transaction in his novel *The Mayor of Casterbridge*, when the drunken Michael Henchard sells his wife and child for five guineas at a sheep fair. A more generally accepted form of trading in people took place at the mop fairs, some of which survive in name at least – such as the one at Stratford-upon-Avon. They originated as occasions for hiring domestic and farm staff. For example, a girl seeking work as a maidservant would hold a mop – hence the name for such fairs.

For spectacle and atmosphere, horse fairs have always been popular. Up to the end of the 19th century they flourished all over

OPEN TO BIDS – SHEEP, HORSES AND EVEN MEN

Buying and selling has always been the serious business of fairs and market days. Even so, there is still time for a chat by the sheep pens at Andoversford, Gloucestershire; and at Stow-on-the-Wold's hectic horse fair, which dates back to 1476, the auctioneer feels free to have a refreshing glass on hand in case his throat dries up. At mop fairs, people were for hire and job seekers wore a token of their trade. Three men at Stratford-upon-Avon all sport pieces of whipcord – emblem of the carter.

By the sheep pens, Andoversford

Horse auction at Stow

Carters at Stratford-upon-Avon mop fair in 1899

Padstow's 'Obby 'Oss

Preparing for the dance, Kibworth

Children on Garland Day, Charlton-on-Otmoor

MAYPOLE AND 'OBBY 'OSS WELCOME SUMMER

A photograph, taken in 1908, of May Day festivities in Kibworth, Leicestershire, captures a rural idyll. White-frocked girls, with ribbons in their hair, and their serious-looking partners prepare to dance around the village maypole. Supervising them is a formidable lady in the centre, while the adults look on from the side. May Day is still the most widely celebrated of Britain's festivals, its origins going back to pre-Christian fertility rites marking the beginning of summer. In Charlton-on-Otmoor, Oxfordshire, it is called Garland Day, and the celebrations include a procession of children bearing bunches of flowers. Padstow in Cornwall has its bizarre 'Obby 'Oss, which proceeds through the streets with morris dancers leaping round it. The dancers' name comes from 'Moorish' (or foreign) dances introduced to medieval Britain.

Britain, and plenty still do – such as the one held on Barley Saturday (the last Saturday in April) at Cardigan, Dyfed. Its programme opens with a grand parade of stallions of many traditional breeds, from shire horses to highly bred hunters, which proceeds through the town.

Mechanisation has all but ended the horse's role in farming, but the horse itself remains as popular as ever. One of the best-supported rural sports is point-to-point racing, which started around 1870. Most British hunts hold annual point-to-points, originally on courses running straight across country – hence the name. The point-to-point season runs from February to late May or early June.

What is claimed to be the world's oldest horse race is the Kiplingcotes Derby, held on the first Thursday of March at South Dalton, North Humberside. It was first run in 1519, and nearly 100 years later Lord Burlington and another Yorkshire squire invested a sum to ensure that it would be held annually. The race starts at 11 a.m. and the course passes through several parishes.

Many British festivals and customs are inextricably bound up with rites dating from pre-Christian times. The maypole, centre of most May Day festivities, is a pagan fertility symbol. At one time it was the custom for a tree to be cut down and brought in from the woods in the early morning. After some branches had been lopped, it would be hung with garlands and put up as the centrepiece of the dancing and celebrations that welcomed summer. Some villages, such as Iron Acton, in Avon, keep permanent maypoles.

Morris dancers also play an important part in May Day ceremonies and are often accompanied by a man dressed as a hobby horse. In the West Country, in particular, special giant horses are seen. The body of the horse is formed by a frame over which material is spread in a sort of skirt, with gaily coloured streamers attached. A fierce looking painted mask serves as a face. Padstow in Cornwall has its famous 'Obby 'Oss; and there is one at Minehead, Somerset, called the Sailor's Horse.

The Sailor's Horse – which is based on the quayside – was once a fearsome beast, accompanied by two masked men called Gullivers who were supposed to bring summer luck to the townsfolk. However, they also carried tongs and whips to encourage 'donations'.

In churches, the gathering of the harvest in autumn is a time of

Sheepdog in action at a trial in Ormsary, Strathclyde

Matching the ploughs in a contest at Stannington, Northumberland

SHEEPDOG TRIALS AND PLOUGHING CONTESTS

In a sheepdog trial, the dog should move in perfect obedience to its handler's whistles and calls. It has six distinct actions to perform: the outrun – getting behind the sheep; the lift – starting them moving; the fetch – bringing them to the handler; the drive – shepherding them through gates; the shed – separating some from the rest; and the pen – putting them into a pen. All must be accomplished within a time limit, and judgments are made on the dog's skill in performing the different actions. Contrasting with the dog's nimble manoeuvres is the steady gait of handsome draught horses, their decorated harnesses bright in the sun, as they show their paces in a ploughing contest. The ploughman is required to work on both grass and stubble. The furrows should be straight, consistent and cleanly finished, with the soil's top surface fully buried.

festival, with special services where seasonal fruits and vegetables are displayed before being given to hospitals or other charitable causes. Many harvest customs, however, survive from pagan times.

A belief once widely held was that the last sheaf of the harvest held the Corn Spirit. The reaper who cut it was thought to have killed the spirit and was expected to attract bad luck.

The Corn Spirit had to be restored, so that it could return next year. To ensure this, a tiny figure known as a corn dolly was woven from straw and brought in from the fields amid suitable festivities. It was carefully preserved until early the following year, when it would be put back into the earth.

ALL DRESSED UP FOR FIREWORKS

Giant fireworks are borne aloft through the streets of Lewes in Sussex on Guy Fawkes Night, escorted by fancy dress processions which include mock bishops, Mr Punch, a dragon and other colourful characters in an uninhibited extravaganza. Nearly four centuries have passed since Parliament escaped being blown up by Guy Fawkes and his plotters on November 5, 1605, but the anniversary is still a time for rejoicing and general gaiety. Nowhere more so than in Lewes, where six bonfire societies stage magnificent processions to the town's war memorial. There, hymns are sung and then fireworks, bonfire ceremonies and more processions go on until nearly midnight. Finally a blazing tar barrel is flung into the River Ouse, which flows through the town.

Guy Fawkes Night at Lewes

A Corn Spirit custom at St Keverne, Cornwall, is called Crying the Neck. As the final swath of wheat is cut – and the spirit supposedly perishes – the workers divide into groups and a dialogue ensues:

'We have it!'
'What have 'ee?'
'A neck!'

The 'neck' or wheatsheaf is then taken to the farmhouse and hung up above the fireplace until the time comes for it to be buried.

Bonfire nights are celebrated throughout Britain – and not just on November 5, Guy Fawkes Night. A great bonfire, on which an effigy of the Devil himself is burnt, is the culmination of Cleikum Week, in July, at Innerleithen, Borders. St Ronan is said to have done battle with the evil one here and Cleikum Week commemorates the encounter. A local schoolboy is appointed to impersonate the saint, and is given a crozier with which to 'cleik' (smite) the Devil.

The beautiful scenery of the Lakes is the setting for some of the finest country sports meetings in Britain. Outstanding are the Grasmere Sports, the Keswick Show, the Cockermouth Show and the Ambleside Sports – all in August. Here there are events traditional in the area and rarely seen outside – like Cumberland and Westmorland wrestling, hound trailing and fell running.

Hound trailing grew out of fox hunting. A rag is soaked in a mixture of aniseed – which has a strong smell that is attractive to dogs – and paraffin, which keeps the scent lingering. This is dragged along the ground over the course by two men called trailers.

The hounds have to negotiate stone walls, fences, hedges and fells as they follow the scent. It is an exciting spectacle with a noisy finish – as handlers get their dogs to the finishing line by shouting, whistling and shaking rattles.

Trail hounds are specially bred for speed and toughness to deal with the rugged mountain courses they have to traverse.

Athletes who go in for the tough sport of fell running must climb, run and scramble up to a flag marking the top of the chosen fell, then make a hair-raising dash down again, often leaping walls and streams. It all ends in an arena, perhaps with the winner acclaimed by a band playing 'See the conquering hero comes'.

Champions at Highland Games have to be truly mighty men – tossing tree-trunks around is not for those of just average physique. These games, which uphold a tradition going back more than a thousand years, have a world-wide appeal because of Royal interest in them – especially the Braemar Gathering, at which the Queen takes the salute.

It was the kings and clan chiefs of Scotland who started the games in far-off times, and those who took part often came from the households of rival chiefs. In the beginning the contests were built around the tools the men used and the jobs they did. They threw hammers, hurled rounded stones, ran up hillsides and tossed huge tree-trunks stripped of their branches – 'cabers'.

The cabers tossed in modern games each have their own particular characteristics. The most famous of them, the great Braemar Caber, measures 19 ft 9 in. and weighs 132 lb.

Most Highland Games are held in July and August. But the Braemar Gathering is in September.

Caber tossing at Crieff, Tayside

Cumberland wrestling at Grasmere

TESTS OF SKILL AND STRENGTH

Tossing the caber demands skill as well as sheer strength. The caber must turn over cleanly and fall in a '12 o'clock' position to the thrower. In Cumberland wrestling the trick is to get an opponent where he can be thrown off balance to achieve a 'fall'.

Fine feathers . . .

. . . Punch and the dragon

The Great House

IN SOME WAYS THE ROLE OF THE GREAT HOUSE IN RURAL LIFE HAS HARDLY CHANGED IN 500 YEARS, WHICH IS HOW LONG ONE FAMILY HAS LIVED AT BROUGHTON CASTLE • NOW, AS ALWAYS, LOCAL SKILLS SERVE ITS NEEDS

The castle, the mansion and the manor have probably kept their influence in rural England longer than anywhere else in Europe. The part played by the family at the great house – as employers, lawgivers, mentors and general controllers of local people's destinies – was inherited from the Roman villa in Britain and remained largely unchanged until the end of the First World War.

Soaring taxation and agricultural depression in the wake of the war made an immediate impact on life in such houses. By the time of the Second World War, many had become schools, offices or institutions. Since then many more have been divided into flats.

Those that have changed least are the greatest of all – ducal palaces and the like, much of whose wealth is derived not only from the land but also from coal, iron and other resources on their estates. But a surprising number of the less great have also survived, still with a leading part to play in their communities. One of these is Broughton Castle, near Banbury in Oxfordshire, where the Fiennes family banner can still be seen flying as proudly as it did when Broughton's own troops of cavalry clattered through the arch on their way to fight for Oliver Cromwell.

But in this century changes have been swift. In 1910 there were 14 outdoor servants at Broughton – coachman, grooms and gardeners – and about 20 indoor staff: butler, housekeeper, cook, valet, lady's maid, footmen, housemaids and the rest. Their quarters were, for the most part, the cavernous attics beneath the mighty Tudor rafters. The attics have been empty now for several decades, and the endless cleaning and polishing of the great house is accomplished by three daily ladies. Outdoors there is a single regular gardener, Bert Dancer, but there is occasionally a second one if you count the 21st Baron Saye and Sele, whose family have owned Broughton throughout most of its existence.

It was not the Fiennes family who built Broughton, but one of Edward I's knights, Sir John de Broughton, who raised a fortified manor house on an already moated

REFLECTING ON THE PAST

Broughton Castle, mirrored to perfection in its glassy moat, is set in a green and gold Oxfordshire landscape of cornfields and pasture. The building itself seems hardly less permanent than its surroundings. Its not-too-serious medieval fortifications and fine Tudor front sit on a velvety lawn, approached over a bridge and through a battlemented gatehouse.

Broughton Castle gatehouse

The castle, reflected in its moat

site in about 1300. The property passed to William of Wykeham, Bishop of Winchester, who founded Winchester public school and New College, Oxford. He settled Broughton on his sister's grandson, whose grand-daughter and heiress, Margaret Wykeham, married William Fiennes, 2nd Lord Saye and Sele, in the mid-1400s.

The first part of the unusual double title, like the family name, was acquired in Artois, where the Fiennes lived before one arrived in England in the 13th century with Edward I's bride, Eleanor of Castile.

In the 1550s, Richard, Lord Saye and Sele, decided to bring his medieval dwelling into line with the new age of the Renaissance. The result, in which his son's work is also seen, is a high-gabled, tall-windowed Elizabethan mansion. Richard accomplished this by adding two storeys to the old building, and encasing it all in a new shell. So the Great Hall, apart from its windows and plastered ceiling, is much the same as it was in 1300.

After that the Fiennes family never took up building again on anything like the same scale. In the 17th century their main interests, in common with most of their countrymen, were religion and politics. William, the 8th Baron, was a Puritan and a Parliamentarian, bitterly opposed to the doctrines and policies of Charles I. He had meetings in a secret room at Broughton with men of like mind.

When the Civil War broke out, William showed his mettle. With his sons and his locally raised regiment, he rode out in October 1642 to fight Charles I's forces at nearby Edgehill. The battle was inconclusive, but the Parliamentary army withdrew towards Warwick, leaving the Royalists free to besiege first Banbury, then Broughton. The garrison, watching the placing of the enemy's guns on an overlooking hill, prudently surrendered.

THE 21ST BARON *Lord Saye and Sele – gone are the butler, footman and valet, along with the coachman and grooms.*

The king ordered that Broughton should be demolished stone by stone. But somehow the instruction was disregarded and the castle survived the war unscathed – and so did William. He was deeply shocked by the execution of Charles I, and because of it refused to serve in Cromwell's government. Instead he took himself off to the island of Lundy in the Bristol Channel. There he stayed until the Restoration, when he was granted a full pardon and later appointed Privy Councillor.

Above the porch in the Oak Room at Broughton there is a cartouche, said to have been placed there by William, together with a Latin inscription that might be translated as 'Brooding on the past does not help' – a philosophical touch by no means at odds with William's pleasant bearded face in his portraits. With Lord Brooke, he founded a Puritan colony in North America – Saybrook, on the Connecticut river. Its citizens still visit the castle.

In one room at the castle there is a photograph of the present Lord Saye and Sele, with a Mohican chief in full war bonnet and regalia. It

The Great Hall and pendant ceiling

Carved oak panelling in the Dining Room

Interior porch in the Oak Room

WORKS OF ART IN OAK AND PLASTER

The Great Hall at Broughton incorporates the original hall, built around 1300. But its superb plastered ceiling – known as a pendant ceiling – dates from the 1760s. The Oak Room, with its unusual, delicately carved interior porch, was built on the foundations of the 14th-century kitchens. The Dining Room has 16th-century carved panelling in a double linenfold pattern – like folded cloth.

was the chief's direct ancestor who opposed the landing of the first Connecticut river colonists.

Family portrait paintings are among the great pleasures of Broughton. One is of a Regency buck who temporarily devastated the family fortunes by gambling. He is famed for telling his valet: 'Place two bottles of sherry by my bed and call me the day after tomorrow.'

The sense of closeness with the past is maintained in the Church of St Mary in the park beside the castle. Here are all Broughton's people of the past, or their monuments – among them Sir John de Broughton, who built the place, and William, the Parliamentarian warrior who became a Privy Councillor. A sergeant-pilot killed in 1941 is commemorated. He was brother of the present baron.

The 21st Baron Saye and Sele's circumstances do not permit him to recruit a private army or employ a large full-time staff. Some 20 local people act as part-time guides and custodians when Broughton is open to the public. Days to visit are Wednesdays, Thursdays and Sundays in July and August, and also on Bank Holidays (but parties can go by appointment at any time).

About 17,000 visitors turn up in

William's secret chamber

THE SECRET CHAMBER

William, 8th Baron Saye and Sele, was a committed Parliamentarian who led his own army out to fight the Royalists in the Civil War. Nicknamed 'Old Subtlety', William conferred with fellow anti-Royalists in a secret chamber at Broughton known as 'the room that hath no ears'.

Portrait of 'Old Subtlety'

UPSTAIRS, DOWNSTAIRS AND OUTSIDE – A LOT OF CHANGES HAVE BEEN MADE

In terms of numbers, the staff at the great house may not be what it was at the turn of the century. But the people who keep Broughton Castle running today retain a strong loyalty, and a sense that they are helping to preserve something that is both a part of history and yet, at the same time, remains very much alive. The men posing for their picture in 1864 were just nine of the many servants considered necessary to run Broughton in those days. Mr Joy, the butler, and Mrs Collins, posed with equal dignity, were of the same era: they appear with others in one of the family's Victorian photograph albums. In those days, a row of large jangling bells on a wall summoned members of the staff to clear a table, or perhaps a maid to see to her ladyship's hair. Today the bells can be seen by visitors in the castle's tearoom. Now, of course, the atmosphere is a good deal more relaxed, but that does not mean that standards have slipped – both house and garden are kept as immaculate as ever. Bert Dancer, the present gardener, was a railwayman, but his prize-winning allotment prompted Lord Saye and Sele to lure him to Broughton. Bert's wife Muriel also works at the castle, where Joyce Taylor is cook. Stonemason Peter Hillman is employed by a local firm, but has worked for 40 years at Broughton. Repairing the battlements was Mr Hillman's most recent monumental task.

Servants photographed in 1864

Mrs Collins

Mr Joy, the butler

Bells that once called servants

Peter Hillman at work

Joyce Taylor dishing up

Muriel Dancer dusting

Bert Dancer, the gardener

a year. According to Lady Saye and Sele, who supervises the presentation of the house, this is about as many as the old building can take. They are essential to Broughton's survival, not only for the entrance fee but for the tax relief and grants the castle gains by being open.

An estimated £1½ million will have to be spent on repairs in the next 20 years. The visitors will help. So will the rents from the 750 acres let to tenant farmers, and profits from the home farm that Lord Saye and Sele helps to run – when he is not working as a chartered surveyor and manager of other people's estates with his firm of land agents.

He does not want any sideshows or gimmicks at Broughton, preferring people to see it as it really is, a family home. In fact the family – there are four children – use the public rooms very little, and live mainly in fairly modest quarters at one end of the castle. There they can keep reasonably warm in cold weather, for most of the building cannot be adequately heated. Lady Saye and Sele says with feeling: 'You have no idea what cold is like until you have sat in the Great Hall in winter.'

But Broughton carries on weathering the seasons, an estate drawing its strength from the country round about – and giving much in return.

The Old Mill

A WATER MILL DREAMS BY A STREAM • A STATELY WINDMILL CROWNS A HILL • AND MANY SKILLS MUST BE MASTERED BY THE MILLWRIGHT WHO KEEPS THEIR MASSIVE MACHINERY TURNING

The romantic image of the old mill, beloved of artists, writers and composers, does rather less than justice to a highly sophisticated machine – and one that could also be a harsh taskmaster. But the beauty of its massive simplicity cannot be denied; nor can the romance of what it was: an example of man's earliest ventures in harnessing the forces of nature to work for him. Its success is apparent from the huge number of mills built and the fact that the water mill and windmill designs were unchanged for centuries. Until the coming of steam, the mill was the perfect machine.

Fine examples are the 18th-century flint mills at Cheddleton, near the ancient little textile town of Leek, in Staffordshire, where the River Churnet has driven a water wheel since 1253. The North Mill here was evidently constructed to grind flint for the nearby Potteries. Its output was eventually combined with that of the South Mill, which was originally a corn mill but was rebuilt for flint-grinding. The ground flint was used at the famous Minton works in Stoke-on-Trent.

The flints, from Kent and Sussex, arrived by canal and were unloaded straight into kilns, where they were heated for three days until they became brittle. They were then immersed in water and crushed in the mill – this at least saved the workers' lungs from the lethal dust of the early years when the flints were dry-crushed. The creamy slurry in the grinding pan was diluted, mixed and put in a settling ark, where the flint powder sank to form a thick sediment. When dried it was cut into blocks and dispatched to the potteries, where it was used to strengthen certain clays and for glazing.

Both mills have been preserved, together with a collection of millwrights' tools, and are open to the public. They illustrate perfectly how mills could be adapted to heavier and more sophisticated tasks than the simple grinding of corn. They show, too, how sites continued to be used for the same purpose over hundreds of years, though the mills themselves might be rebuilt several times because they shook themselves to pieces with constant punishing work.

An astonishing 5642 mills were listed in the Domesday Survey of 1086, and many of the sites mentioned still have mills on them. Among them is Houghton in Cambridgeshire, which now has a handsome 18th-century brick and timber mill on the ancient site by the River Ouse.

Water mills were probably introduced by the Romans, continuing to develop through the so-called Dark Ages that followed the departure of the legions in the 5th century. There are records of mills in the 8th and 10th centuries. What is now Hampshire seems to have had a number of them in AD 983, some being operated by draught animals. The first reference to windmills does not appear until 1191; they may well have been introduced to Europe by Crusaders returning from the Middle East, where their development had been forced by water scarcity.

In Britain the windmill was especially welcome in waterless areas such as the Downs, and in parts of East Anglia where the rivers were too sluggish to drive water mills. Three main types of windmill gradually evolved – the post mill, the smock mill and the tower mill. The post mill is the most primitive and is mounted on a heavy, swivelling post so that the whole structure can be swung into the wind. On the tower mill and the smock mill – with its triangular shape reminiscent of an old-time farm worker's smock – only the cap bearing the sails revolves.

Most British mills have their sails kept to the wind by a fantail, a brilliant 18th-century invention consisting of a small windmill set behind and at right angles to the main sails. As the wind veers, it catches the fantail and turns the cap, and the main sails, into the wind. The same idea was applied to many post mills, enabling the whole structure to be turned by the wind rather than by a team of horses or oxen.

Building the complex turning mechanism was part of the old millwright's job. The millwright of

BEAUTY AT WORK *The chuckling waters of the River Churnet have been turning a mill at Cheddleton since 1253. This mill, one of two which used to grind flint for the famous Minton pottery, worked until 1963. Both are open to the public.*

TOWER MILL *The sails are set on a revolving cap on top of a tower. The building is often brick, with a timber cap.*

SMOCK MILL *The name comes from the shape of the tower, resembling that of a farmhand's traditional smock. The swivelling cap is kept facing the wind by a fantail — a smaller windmill which is set behind and at right angles to the main sails.*

POST MILL *The earliest type of mill — the whole tower revolves around a centre post and is swivelled to face the wind by moving the large beam fitted at the rear.*

DRESSING THE MILLSTONES

A bearded millwright bends to his task of dressing a stone – getting it in shape again after heavy work on the harvest. This picture, taken around 1890 in Herefordshire, shows the furrows being recut. Dressing the stones is still one of the most exacting tasks a millwright faces. His principal tool for this job is a mill-bill. In the old days a millwright could be recognised by the blue scars on his hands and face, caused by steel splinters flying off the bill. The modern bill is manufactured with a tough tungsten tip and does not splinter.

HARPS, BUTTERFLIES AND JOURNEYMEN

The millstone, 4 ft across and weighing about a ton, has its working surface divided into segments called harps. This 14-harp stone shows how the furrows, which have names like 'butterfly' and 'journeyman', are arranged.

today, who must repair and replace parts both great and small, must be as ingenious – and as strong – as his predecessor.

Of all country craftsmen, the millwright is the most versatile, combining the skills of builder, engineer, carpenter, blacksmith, sailmaker and stonemason. It is no coincidence that from the ranks of millwrights sprang the talented civil engineers who helped create the Industrial Revolution.

In the old days, the millwright also had to have something like the country doctor's readiness to be called out for an emergency by day or by night. After the harvest, for example, mills working round the clock were liable to break down at any time.

But the modern millwright seldom has to undertake emergency work – or build a mill from scratch. Most of them are conservationists, restoring or rebuilding old mills. Even so, the traditional skills are still needed. The great wheels of the mill's gearing system may have to be replaced – including the mighty 'wallower' connected to the millstones.

In some mills the wallower is made of cast iron, and the millwright must make a wooden facsimile which is then sent to a foundry for casting. Other mills have wooden gear-wheels, which the millwright has always fashioned from elm, hornbeam or apple wood, with cogs or teeth of oak.

The focal point of the mill, whether powered by wind or water, is its stones. Generally these are of Derbyshire grit or French burr – a very hard stone from the Paris basin – though some modern ones are manufactured, using a composite of quartz and emery. In all cases the stones are 4 ft across and weigh about a ton, so it is not easy to manoeuvre them into position for fine adjustments.

The stones are set in pairs. The lower one, the bedstone, is stationary, while the runner stone turns above it, powered by the drive shaft from the sails or water wheel. They are set only a fraction of a distance apart, close enough to grind the grain but never touching. If they touch it means severe damage to the stones, and the friction may start a fire.

In bygone days, many of the millwrights would keep themselves going through the winter by travelling from mill to mill to dress the stones – removing wear and tear caused by heavy harvest work, and recutting the furrows in the faces of the stones, which throw the flour out to the chute. The job is now done at any time, generally in the millwright's workshop.

With a small tool called a mill-bill – a small, double-bladed pick – the millwright first cuts the master furrows that run at a tangent from the eye or centre of the stone, and divide its surface up into segments called harps. Within each harp are shorter furrows of varied length known by such names as 'journeyman' and 'butterfly'. Between these is the 'land', whose surface is pocked with tiny chips, cut at 16 to the inch to hold the grain, and becoming gradually shallower towards the rim of the stone.

To complicate the business further, the faces of runner and bedstones must be exact images of each other, calling for a remarkable accuracy of eye and hand.

Like the giants of their creation, millwrights are fewer than they used to be. In practical terms, windmills and water mills have had their day. Yet it seems there is still a sufficient number of would-be apprentices to keep the craft going – attracted not only by the joy of perpetuating old skills, but by the satisfaction of ensuring that the handsome monuments to their predecessors' ingenuity remain part of the landscape.

The Living Past

TRAINS AND CARS BROUGHT DRAMATIC CHANGES TO COUNTRY PEOPLE AND PLACES • BUT THE CAMERA ALSO CAME, TO CAPTURE THE SCENE AS IT WAS . . . AND OFTEN STILL IS

People living in today's world of easy travel and instant communication find it difficult to envisage a restricted rural life geared to the slow rhythm of the changing seasons. Yet even as the century turned, many country folk remained bound, by lack of means and transport, to the farms, villages and small towns where they lived. Cranbrook and its neighbouring village of Hawkhurst, in the Weald of Kent, are just two of many such places that look much today as they did then. And here it is still possible to take an imaginary leap backwards in time.

Though life has changed dramatically since the first motor cars and buses chugged down local lanes, many landmarks in both town and village survive almost untouched by the passing years. Inevitably, people have changed and there are more these days who work in larger neighbouring towns and cities. Yet they choose to live in the area because of the character moulded by its past.

Standing in the very centre of Cranbrook, one building that seems almost a symbol of that past is the George Inn. The George has been thriving for 700 years. Its existence is mentioned in records as early as 1290, and in its cellars there is stonework from the 14th and 15th centuries. Over the years, the old inn has been part of almost every important local event, from sombre witch trials to meetings of rich local wool merchants and the pomp of royal visits.

Edward I may have been a guest here in 1299. Nearly three centuries later Good Queen Bess stayed at the George when she visited Cranbrook in 1579. All work stopped in the town that day and the celebratory peal of bells was heard for miles around. Elizabeth responded by granting a royal charter.

It was the local cloth looms that drew the queen to the area, for the Weald was then a great centre of the weaving industry. It had started in the early 14th century when Flemish weavers began to settle here, encouraged by Edward I.

By the late Middle Ages practically everyone in Cranbrook was involved in the cloth trade. Great warehouses and halls were built to store the finished material, and every day processions of packhorses loaded with it took the narrow, bumpy roads for London and the Channel ports.

Goddards Green in Cranbrook still bears witness to the prosperity of those medieval weavers. The large, timber-framed house was built by the Courthope family of weavers, whose descendants went on living here until 1919. Another wealthy clothier family were the Henleys, who owned the George Inn at the time of Elizabeth I's visit. No doubt a Henley was one of the delegation of townspeople who

Hawkhurst green, from the church tower

HANDSOME IS AS HANDSOME WAS . . .

Stately trees still shade The Moor, Hawkhurst's large green; the same old houses look onto it and even the stores survive. Little seems to have altered since the Second World War. Yet signs of change are there: white lines speak of busier roads, and neat posts and chains demonstrate a more conscious care for the handsome village scene.

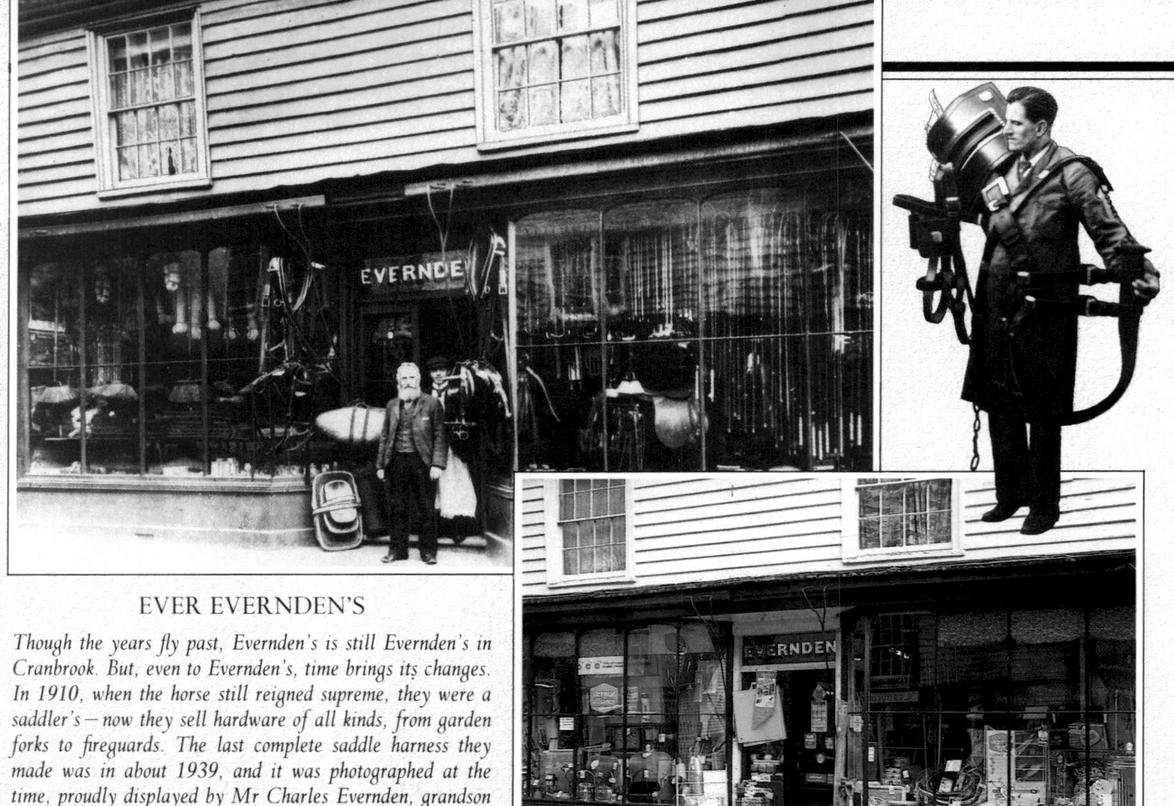

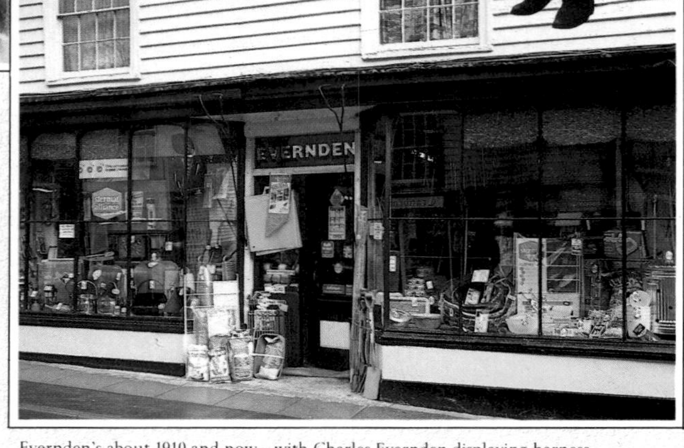

EVER EVERNDEN'S

Though the years fly past, Evernden's is still Evernden's in Cranbrook. But, even to Evernden's, time brings its changes. In 1910, when the horse still reigned supreme, they were a saddler's – now they sell hardware of all kinds, from garden forks to fireguards. The last complete saddle harness they made was in about 1939, and it was photographed at the time, proudly displayed by Mr Charles Evernden, grandson of the white-bearded gentleman in the earlier picture. Other shops may have changed hands, but their fronts are much as they were. The magnificent old Union Mill, built in 1814 and restored to working order, still looms down Stone Street, where brick buildings alternate with clapperboard.

Evernden's about 1910 and now – with Charles Evernden displaying harness

Stone Street – at the turn of the century and now

met the queen in a large room on the inn's first floor.

But the George was also the scene of some less attractive occasions. During the wave of witch-hunting that swept the land in the 17th century, many witchcraft hearings were conducted here. In those times folk lived in dread of the evil eye, and the law itself dealt severely with so-called witches. In a climate of superstitious fear, generated largely by ignorance, innocent folk were condemned to death simply because they had a deformity or a speech defect that singled them out as different.

In July 1652, five Cranbrook women were hanged for 'evil practices' and for 'bewitching unto death Elizabeth Wilding, aged $3\frac{1}{2}$ years, and Elizabeth Osbourne, wife of Alexander Osbourne'. Two of the five were said to be 'poor idiots' who could not give a sensible answer to a simple question.

Further grisly memories are associated with a large house which once stood at Seacox Heath, near Hawkhurst. The present house is Victorian, but the earlier mansion was built in 1745 by a villain named Arthur Grey, leader of the Hawkhurst Gang of smugglers.

Smuggling was rife in this part of the country in the 18th and 19th

ALL WORK AND A LITTLE PLAY IN THE COUNTRY

Farm workers, 1899

Puppet show, 1906

Scurry Weddall, Bowley Marchant, Cheesman, Huggins, Willard . . . and the rest of the workforce at Cowden Farm, Hawkhurst, pose dutifully for the camera in 1899. Men like these, each holding the tool of his trade – spade, scythe, shepherd's crook and so on – might spend all their working lives on one farm. Some workers never travelled beyond their village, but on occasion, the world outside came to them, when travelling entertainers arrived. One such show which used to call in at Hawkhurst regularly at the beginning of this century, was Clowes Excelsior Marionettes. They presented puppet shows, and the start of each programme was heralded by Mr Ted Clowes himself blowing a cornet. He and his like were not, however, too popular with local shopkeepers. Instead of settling outstanding bills, villagers would often spend as much as 1s 3d (about 6p) to see the show.

centuries. Cargoes of contraband were shipped from the Continent to deserted stretches around Romney Marsh, and at dead of night the smugglers brought tea, coffee and silk inland to be hidden.

But these smugglers were far from being the romantic figures of popular legend. Instead they were ruthless and often brutal criminals, and the Hawkhurst Gang were particularly nasty. One of their more savage acts occurred as a member of the gang was leaving an inn and found an old woman in his way. He asked her how old she was and, when she told him, replied: 'You have lived too long' – and clubbed her to death.

However, a time came when local people would stand no further outrages by the Hawkhurst Gang. A group of them banded together under the leadership of a former soldier named Sturt, calling themselves the Goudhurst Militia. A bloody battle took place in the churchyard at Goudhurst, another village near Cranbrook; and although a third of the militia was killed, they still managed to rout the smugglers. The Hawkhurst Gang's death blow came when most of its leaders were captured and hanged in 1749.

But the Weald did not live by smuggling and weaving alone. For many centuries it had a number of other industries, generated by the abundance of water to drive machinery and of wood to turn into charcoal. A great forest, known to the Saxons as Andredsweald, still covered most of the Weald, and it provided the fuel needed for glass-making, lead-extracting and iron-founding.

Iron had first been discovered in the Weald in the 2nd century, and the industry thrived here until the late 18th century. Many of today's imposing houses stand on the sites of mansions originally built by rich ironmasters, such as the Dunks of Tongswood, in Hawkhurst.

Such then were the sources of the Weald's wealth in centuries gone by. But while these industries and businesses came and went, the ordinary people stayed, likely to spend all their lives in the place where they were born. For them, regardless of change, old customs and ways of life went steadily on from generation to generation. Many of the old ways survived into the 20th century. A few survive today.

A century ago the streets of Cranbrook and Hawkhurst were lined with shops and businesses where craftsmen might be practising skills learnt from their fathers, grandfathers and beyond. Even today many of the buildings remain, although in most cases the shops as they then were can be seen only in old photographs. A pleasant exception is Evernden's, the saddler's in Cranbrook, which now sells hardware.

Gone completely, though, are the fairs and markets which were once big occasions for both town and village. In 1289 Edward I granted Cranbrook the right to hold a weekly market and fairs in May and September.

For centuries, people coming on market day would be able to get practically all they needed – from pottery, cloth and farm implements to freshly baked bread.

All that began to change as roads improved, diverting trade to other places; then the railway, bus and finally the car diverted people too.

The railways reached both places in the 1890s. Suddenly, town and village were no longer islands in the Weald; London could be reached in 90 minutes. Cars came to Hawkhurst as early as 1901, when the local bicycle dealer, William Rootes, started selling and servicing them. His sons, William and Reginald, later founded the Rootes Group, which made Hillman, Humber and Singer vehicles.

In the years since, change has been rapid – and in many ways for the better. Life for many families in the old days was hard. The weekly wage of a farm labourer around the turn of this century might be 15 shillings (75p), with a cottage and the right to free firewood.

But he considered himself lucky

ARTISTIC END FOR A DONKEY

A delightfully eccentric old artist named Thomas Webster sits in his donkey-drawn bath chair – photographed in 1898. He was one of a number of Victorian painters attracted by Cranbrook's country-town charm. He disapproved of his donkey's sparse little tail and insisted on giving it a neatly combed artificial one, which he could remove for grooming.

CHANGING TIMES IN THE OLD WORKHOUSE . . . AND

Many of the handsome old buildings in both Cranbrook and Hawkhurst were clearly meant to last – and a good few have – whatever the changes going on around. The Paper Mill at Hawkhurst was probably built in the 15th century as a home for the miller and his family. A private house now, it seems little changed since the turn of the century. Although Russell and Son no longer grind corn at the village's Slip Mill, this building, too, survives as a private home, as does the Old Studio in Cranbrook. In Victorian times it was the home of two local artists, F. D. Hardy and Thomas Webster (see also picture above). Hawkhurst's Old Workhouse – now well-kept cottages – was once a pesthouse, where those suffering from plague or other infectious diseases were confined. Timber was plentiful in this well-wooded region and many old houses are timber-framed. The timber used in them was cut in the woods near by, and the framework was made and assembled there. Each beam or rafter was marked, then the whole frame was dismantled and the pieces were taken by wagon to be put up again on the chosen site.

Paper Mill, Hawkhurst – early 1900s and now

Slip Mill – about 1880 and now

to have a steady job, for those out of work could expect little or no charity. At most there might be a few shillings from their local slate club – a primitive form of insurance scheme to which contributions were paid while the men were in work. For the totally destitute, there was the dreaded workhouse, where through the 19th century, paupers, orphans, lunatics and criminals were thrown together. Hawkhurst's Old Workhouse still stands by the church.

Yet the country year was not without its carefree interludes, and in the memories of old folk it is mostly the pleasant things that survive. Some can recall that until the turn of the century, a newlywed couple in Cranbrook would leave the church to find their path strewn with emblems of the bridegroom's trade. Carpenters walked on wood shavings, shoemakers on leather cuttings and blacksmiths on scraps of rusty iron.

Or there might be a visit from some great personage. On a hot summer's day in 1886, Princess Mary Adelaide, Duchess of Teck, and her daughter, the future Queen Mary, visited Hawkhurst.

Three elaborate triumphal arches were put up on the royal route, decorated with masses of greenery. By the roadside enterprising local tradesmen set up stalls to sell biscuits, brandy snaps, lemonade and ginger beer.

In those days professional theatres were an unthinkable distance away – but sometimes the theatre travelled to the country. Strolling players would appear as if from nowhere, and pitch their tent. Taylor's Pavilion, a highly flammable structure of wood and canvas, used to come regularly to Hawkhurst. Plank seats were placed on the wagons and more expensive, red-draped stalls were set up in front of the stage. Each night there was a different play or melodrama, and on Fridays and Saturdays there were special sensations, with titles such as *Sweeney Todd, the Demon Barber of Fleet Street* and *Maria Marten; or The Murder in the Red Barn*. Another travelling show visiting Hawkhurst was Clowes Excelsior Marionettes.

The show has moved on, never to return. But in this corner of rural Kent, as in others around the country, the past may still be glimpsed in those age-old buildings and customs that have survived.

VILLAGE HERO

Hawkhurst's own First World War hero was Clarence Marchant, of the Royal Flying Corps, who shot down two enemy planes and won the French *Croix de Guerre*. He died in a mid-air collision in 1918.

OTHER LOCAL LANDMARKS THAT WERE BUILT TO LAST

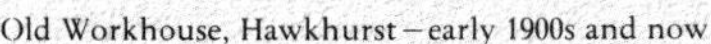

Old Workhouse, Hawkhurst – early 1900s and now

Old Studio, Cranbrook – about 1865 and now

INDEX OF TOWNS AND VILLAGES

Page numbers in bold type indicate a major entry on a town or village. Photographs and illustrations are identified by numbers in italic.

GENERAL INDEX

Page numbers in *italic* refer to illustrations.

B

C

D

E

F

L

M

N

O

P

Q

R

S